EARLY BLACK BRITISH WRITING

SELECTED NEW RIVERSIDE EDITIONS

Series Editor for the British Volumes
Alan Richardson

For a complete listing of our American and British New Riverside
Editions, visit our web site at **http://college.hmco.com**

NEW RIVERSIDE EDITIONS
Series Editor for the British Volumes
Alan Richardson, Boston College

OLAUDAH EQUIANO, MARY PRINCE,
AND OTHERS

Early Black British Writing

Selected Texts with Introduction · *Critical Essays*

Edited by

Alan Richardson

BOSTON COLLEGE

Debbie Lee

WASHINGTON STATE UNIVERSITY

Houghton Mifflin Company
BOSTON · NEW YORK

Sponsoring Editor: Michael Gillespie
Associate Editor: Bruce Cantley
Editorial Assistant: Lisa Minter
Project Editor: Jane Lee
Editorial Assistant: Talia Kingsbury/ Melissa Mednicov
Production/Design Assistant: Bethany Schlegel
Manufacturing Manager: Florence Cadran
Marketing Manager: Cindy Graff Cohen
Marketing Assistant: Sarah Donelson

Cover image: © Comstock IMAGES

Printed in the U.S.A.

Library of Congress Control Number: 2003107916
ISBN: 0-618-31765-1

1   2   3   4   5   6   7   8   9-MP-07   06   05   04   03

CONTENTS

ABOUT THIS SERIES
Alan Richardson

The Riverside imprint, stamped on a book's spine or printed on its title page, carries a special aura for anyone who loves and values books. As well it might: by the middle of the nineteenth century, Houghton Mifflin had already established the Riverside Edition as an important presence in American publishing. The Riverside series of British poets brought trustworthy editions of Milton and Wordsworth, Spenser and Pope, and (then) lesser-known writers like Herbert, Vaughan, and Keats to a growing nation of readers. There was both a Riverside Shakespeare and a Riverside Chaucer by the century's end, titles that would be revived and recreated as the authoritative editions of the late twentieth century. Riverside Editions of writers like Emerson, Hawthorne, Longfellow, and Thoreau helped establish the first canon of American literature. Early in the twentieth century, the Cambridge editions published by Houghton Mifflin at the Riverside Press made the complete works of dozens of British and American poets widely available in single-volume editions that can still be found in libraries and homes throughout the United States and beyond.

The Riverside Editions of the 1950s and 1960s brought attractive, affordable, and carefully edited versions of a range of British and American titles into the thriving new market for serious paperback literature. Prepared by leading scholars and critics of the time, the Riversides rapidly became known for their lively introductions, reliable texts, and lucid annotation. Though aimed primarily at the college market, the series was also created (as one editor put it) with the "general reader's private library" in mind. These were paperbacks to hold onto and read again, and many a "private" library was seeded with the colorful spines of Riverside Editions kept long after graduation.

Houghton Mifflin's New Riverside Editions now bring the combination of high editorial values and wide popular appeal long associated with the Riverside imprint into line with the changing needs and desires of twenty-first-century students and general readers. Inaugurated in 2000 with the first set of American titles under the general editorship of Paul Lauter, the New Riversides reflect both the changing canons of literature in English and the greater emphases on historical and cultural context that have helped a new generation of critics to extend and reenliven literary studies. The series not only is concerned with keeping the classic works of British and American literature alive, but also grows out of the excitement that a broader range of literary texts and cultural reference points has brought to the classroom. Works by formerly marginalized authors, including women writers and writers of color, will find a place in the series along with titles from the traditional canons that a succession of Riverside imprints helped establish beginning a century and a half ago. New Riverside titles will reflect the recent surge of interest in the connections among literary activity, historical change, and social and political issues, including slavery, abolition, and the construction of "race"; gender relations and the history of sexuality; the rise of the British Empire and of nationalism on both sides of the Atlantic; and changing conceptions of nature and of human beings.

The New Riverside Editions respond to recent changes in literary studies not only in the range of titles but also in the design of individual volumes. Issues and debates crucial to a book's author and original audience find voice in selections from contemporary writings of many kinds as well as in early reactions and reviews. Some volumes will place contemporary writers into dialogue, as with the pairing of Irish national tales by Maria Edgeworth and Sydney Owenson or of vampire stories by Bram Stoker and Sheridan Le Fanu. Other volumes provide alternative ways of constructing literary tradition, juxtaposing Mary Shelley's *Frankenstein* with H. G. Wells's *Island of Dr. Moreau,* or Byron's *The Giaour,* an "Eastern Tale" in verse, with Frances Sheridan's *Nourjahad* and William Beckford's *Vathek,* its most important predecessors in Orientalist prose fiction. Chronologies, selections from major criticism, notes on textual history, and bibliographies will allow readers to go beyond the text and explore a given writer or issue in greater depth. Seasoned critics will find fresh new contexts and juxtapositions, and general readers will find intriguing new material to read alongside familiar titles in an attractive format.

Houghton Mifflin's New Riverside Editions maintain the values of reliability and readability that have marked the Riverside name for well over a century. Each volume also provides something new—often unexpected— and each in a distinctive way. Freed from the predictable monotony and rigidity of a set template, editors can build their volumes around the special opportunities presented by a given title or set of related works. We hope that the resulting blend of innovative scholarship, creative format, and high production values will help the Riverside imprint continue to thrive well into the new century.

INTRODUCTION
Alan Richardson and Debbie Lee

Imperial expansion and crisis cast a heavy shadow over the history of the eighteenth and early nineteenth centuries—a period of colonial ventures and revolts, global wars and migrations, and systematic exploration and exploitation of the "new" or "dark" lands to the west and south of Eurasia. The rise of empire profoundly transformed British culture (Said 1994); more dramatically, it created a newly globalized economy such as the world had never known, including a massive and controversial traffic in human beings. The ideologies and anxieties of empire and colonization played themselves out in literary and other artistic forms, helping to shape not only many individual works of British literature, but also the modern senses of both "British" and "literature" themselves (Colley 1992b; Viswanathan 1989). Few literary scholars would now deny that issues of empire, colonialism, and slavery crucially affected the literary culture, both canonical and "minor," official and underground, of the fraught period from 1760, the year of the "Tacky" slave rebellion in Jamaica, to 1838, when slavery was finally abolished in the British West Indies. Only quite recently, however, have British writers of African descent garnered much acknowledgment for their significant role in creating and contesting images and ideologies of empire, colonialism, slavery, and "race." Not content with being represented (and misrepresented) by others, with passively assenting to antislavery arguments or mutely protesting the rise of racialist thinking, the writers featured in this volume actively intervened in the literary culture and political debates of their time. In the process, they created a body of written texts—slave narratives, public and private letters, poems, journals, and polemics—that constitute not just a compelling documentary record but a set of lively, affecting, and complexly layered literary works.

Our volume begins with a generous selection of slave narratives and related examples of self-representation and antislavery polemic, from the pioneering works of Ignatius Sancho and Ukawsaw Gronniosaw in the 1770s and 1780s to the wrenching and withering accounts of Mary Prince and James Wedderburn in the 1830s. By providing generous selections from the key texts of Sancho, Ottobah Cugoano, and Olaudah Equiano, a representative sampling of the little-known John Jea, and the complete narratives of Gronniosaw, Wedderburn, and Prince, this volume displays an extensive range of early Black British writing. The selection of poetry by Equiano, Jea, Phillis Wheatley (an African American writer published and promoted in England), and Juan Francisco Manzano (an Afro-Cuban poet first widely known through a London translation) demonstrates how the issues of self-expression and ideological contestation raised in the prose works carry over into a variety of lyrical forms, from the neoclassical epistle to the proto-"Gospel" hymn. These published works are supplemented by a selection of "voices" captured in unpublished letters and colonial documents, broaching a range of experiences, from informal labor negotiations to threats of rebellion, that might otherwise have gone unheard.

In introducing a volume of "Black British writing," we want to stress at the outset that all three terms in our title could be — and have been — contested. *Black* here is used to describe persons of sub-Saharan African descent, as it was in the eighteenth and early nineteenth centuries, yet the term had then a vaguer definition and larger compass than it does now, especially outside of Britain (Myers 1996). At a time when significant numbers of non-Europeans were first coming into regular and sustained contact with native Britons, *Black* described persons of Asian, Amerindian, and Pacific origin or ancestry as well as Africans and their descendants. This extended use of *Black* and like terms can be found in the works of Black British writers themselves, as when Equiano (1789), living among the Amerindians of the Mosquito Coast, describes customs held by the South American aborigines in common with "any other sable people" (2:189).[1] Such usages imply that, from a British perspective, the peoples encountered in the course of imperial expansion and global trade could seem more alike (in their very "otherness") than not, although contemporary naturalists and philosophers spilled no small amount of ink on various racial taxonomies. The instability of terms like *Black* also, of course, reflects the now well-established fact that, in the absence of any biologically meaningful notion of human "races," racial categories are always culturally constructed and thus constantly subject to revision (Appiah 1992, 28–46). Nevertheless, the claim to an "African" identity proved rhetorically useful

---

[1] All citations of works included in this volume refer to this edition unless otherwise noted; citations of an earlier, complete edition of the same work are preceded, as here, by the date of the edition.

to virtually all of the writers represented in this volume, from Gronniosaw, the "African Prince," to Wedderburn, the son of a creole Jamaican slave and her White owner. Against the backdrop of the slave trade, colonial slavery, and growing racial discrimination in Britain, to write as an African meant implicitly to write on behalf of all those of African descent, whether free (though generally oppressed) in England or enslaved in the Americas.

Precisely because their histories are scored through by the transatlantic movements of the African slave trade, writers of slave narratives can be termed "British" only provisionally. Other critics and editors have preferred adjectives like "Transatlantic" and "Black Atlantic," while still others have claimed Equiano as an early American, Prince as an early Caribbean, writer. Rather than insist on any one of these identifying labels — including our own — we would stress instead that each has its advantages and all, therefore, need to be kept in view. Placing Equiano as an early American writer, for example, has elicited significant links between his prototypical slave narrative and the earlier "Indian captivity" narratives that had found wide audiences both in colonial North America and in England (Sayre 2000). The "Black Atlantic" perspective has proved indispensable for delineating the experiences of dislocation, trauma, and cosmopolitanism that mark a great deal of Black British writing from the eighteenth century to the present (Gilroy 1993; Carretta and Gould 2001). "Transatlantic" and analogous terms underscore the shared history — not least the history of the triangular slave trade — that kept Africa, the Americas, and Britain intertwined throughout this period and gave rise to any number of culturally hybrid artifacts, forms, and motifs (Thomas 2000). In proffering the term "Black British," we intend only to claim that no history — or collection — of eighteenth- and early nineteenth-century British literature can be considered complete without taking this notable body of work into account. If the term *British* gets unsettled as a result, so much the better. The provisionality of the term "Black British" underscores how the idea of a "British" identity itself was largely a construct of this period, intended to help stabilize and unify Britain's "three kingdoms" in the face of imperial expansion, global warfare, and the influx of foreign goods, ideas, and people (Colley 1992a). Whether born in Africa (like Cugoano), in the Americas (like Prince), or on the voyage in between (like Sancho), the writers represented here found themselves enmeshed in questions of national identity upon settling in England, and their histories make no insignificant part of modern "British" culture.

Any overview of early Black British writers must qualify the term *writing* as well. The attainment of literacy skills played a significant part in defenses of "African genius" at a time when the educability of sub-Saharan

Africans was hotly contested (Lyons 1975), and the subtitle "Written by Himself" introducing the narratives of Equiano and Jea constitutes an implicit antiracist (and antislavery) argument in itself. Yet "Related by"—the rival formulation featured in titles by Gronniosaw and Prince—would have been more accurate in the case of Jea, who could read Scripture but never learned to write. Given the lack of educational opportunities for non-Whites (and, in the colonies, outright hostility toward educating slaves), fluent literacy came only by good fortune, as in Sancho's case, or by the tireless exploitation of chance opportunities, as in Equiano's. Even the exceptional group of Black Britons represented here, then—those who managed to narrate and publish their lives and thoughts—relied for the most part on an amanuensis, editor, or other collaborator. Slave narratives and related texts tended to reach their audiences only after significant revision—corrections and omissions, additions and explications—provided (often silently) by White mediators. That does not, of course, render the texts in question inauthentic, but readers would do well to attend closely to "what is *not* articulated" in them explicitly, signified instead by systematic "blindspots, silences, and erasures" and other strategies of indirection (Thomas 2000, 178).

Although Africans and their descendants have been continuously present in Britain at least since the 1600s, the late eighteenth century saw the first significant rise in England's Black population (Fryer 1984; Myers 1996). Those unprecedented numbers (estimates range as high as 20,000, although most fall closer to 10,000) were due almost entirely to Britain's increasing domination of what Cugoano calls the "commerce of the human species." The transatlantic slave trade had begun in 1518, when Charles V of Spain granted the first licenses to Europeans to take African people from their homes and bring them to the Spanish American colonies to be used as slave labor (Postma 1990, 3). Shortly thereafter, during the 1520s, the slave trade developed into a full-blown operation managed by the Portuguese, who controlled the slave forts and "factories" on the west coast of Africa. Within a hundred years, by the 1640s, the trade had mushroomed into an international business as sugar plantations continued to proliferate from Brazil to the Caribbean. By this time, European proprietors had decided that sugar cultivation could turn a profit only if fueled by cheap labor in the form of slaves. The Portuguese, who had controlled the transatlantic trade (with continued Spanish involvement) for a hundred years, now faced competition from the Dutch, French, Danish, and finally the British, who would dominate the trade from 1713 to 1807.

By the late eighteenth century, the African slave trade represented the largest migration of people in history up to that point (Manning 1990, 104). Millions of human beings were torn from their homeland and deposited on foreign shores. Just how many remains a matter of historical debate. The number seems to range from between 10 and 50 million. Toni Morrison (1987) dedicates her Pulitzer Prize–winning novel *Beloved* to "Sixty Million and more," a number that may include the generations of Blacks born into American slavery as well as those transported from Africa (iii). Most recent research suggests that around 12 million Africans fell victim to the transatlantic slave trade between 1500 and 1867, with British ships alone carrying nearly 3.5 million slaves from Africa between 1662 and 1807 (Curtin 1969, 3–13; Lovejoy 1982, 496–497). Historians estimate that 10 to 15 percent of those transported from Africa to the Caribbean and the Americas died on shipboard during the Middle Passage, one of the most horrific and resonant memories of slavery. Those who survived to reach the New World had then to undergo a year or so of "seasoning," a period of acclimatization to a new disease environment and the physical and psychological rigors of colonial slavery. Seasoning took off another 30 percent of the African captives. The vast majority of the survivors could look forward only to bleak and uncertain lives as field slaves on colonial plantations. Yet however pressed down, colonial slaves nevertheless managed to find ways of forming strong social bonds and exercising personal autonomy and political power.

From the very beginning of plantation slavery, owners had to deal with slave resistance on a daily basis. Slaves used both subtle strategies (such lying in a sickbed for weeks or practicing "obeah," an Afro-Caribbean religion often used to resist slavery) and blatant rebellions throughout the history of the trade. The pattern of resistance and revolt intensified in the mid-1700s, when White—and later, Black—abolitionists began campaigning in England and America against the use of slave labor. One of the first and most influential early abolitionists was the American Quaker John Woolman, whose essay *Some Considerations on the Keeping of Negroes* appeared in 1754. Woolman traveled around America as an itinerant minister speaking against slaveholding. Along with those of his fellow abolitionist Anthony Benezet (also an American Quaker), Woolman's writings soon found their way to Britain, serving as the initial inspiration behind Britain's antislavery movement. The leading British abolitionist Thomas Clarkson gave Woolman credit for his own conversion to the antislavery cause.

The combination of slave resistance in the colonies and antislavery agitation in Britain brought about a change in the attitudes of British lawmakers by 1771, when the slave James Somerset was ordered to appear before Judge Mansfield at the Court of King's Bench in London. Somerset, who had been brought from America to Britain by his owner, Charles Stewart, ran away and was immediately returned to Stewart, who then put him on a Westindiaman bound for the slave market of Jamaica (Shyllon

1974, 77). Mansfield proceeded reluctantly, knowing that his decision would represent a major precedent: if Somerset could be forced to return to colonial slavery, it meant that he was effectively Stewart's slave in Britain, a nation that prided itself on "English" liberty. Mansfield ruled that slavery had no legal status in England and that Stewart could therefore not force Somerset to return to Jamaica.

The Somerset decision was not, however, all it might have seemed. Mansfield remained intent on upholding the property basis of British slavery, and his carefully worded ruling did not result in the liberation of all slaves in England, where Blacks continued to be privately bought and sold into the nineteenth century (Walvin 1993, 17–19; Shyllon 1974, 125–140). Nevertheless, the case reverberated in the popular imagination to mean that slavery was abolished on British soil. It had been widely followed, and its settlement took on an almost mythical status. Long, rambling opinion pieces, filled with an eighteenth-century spirit of debate, crowded out lesser news in the *Morning Chronicle, London Chronicle, Gazetteer,* and *Gentleman's Magazine* in 1772. Some proclaimed it a judgment in "universal liberty," reasserting an older legal tradition that "*England* was too pure an air for slaves to breathe in" (Fryer 1984, 113). Even so fervent an abolitionist as Granville Sharp took Mansfield's decision to mean that "the exercise of the power of a Master over his Slave must be supported by the Law of the particular Countries; but no foreigner can *in England claim a right over a Man:* such a Claim *is not known to the Laws of England"* (Davis 1975, 476).

Ten years later, the British people would hear another case, one that forcibly reminded them how brutal the business of slavery had become, even in a land that supposedly had banished slavery from its shores. This was the case of the slave ship *Zong.* In 1781, the *Zong* sailed on a common trade route, from Liverpool to the west coast of Africa and on to the Americas, with a cargo of 470 Africans bound for Jamaica. Disease and death tore through the ship, and in less than three months over 60 Africans and 7 crew members had died. Although shipboard epidemics counted as one of the stock hazards of the trade, the reaction of Luke Collingwood, the *Zong's* captain, made for an unprecedented exercise in sheer callousness. Calculating that loss through "natural causes" (which insurers would not cover) would decimate his and his backers' profits, Collingwood proposed that the crew throw the remaining sick slaves overboard. The crew did not argue and duly proceeded on November 29 to throw 54 Africans into the sea, 42 the next day, and 26 the next. Ten of the slaves, in a show of resistance against the mass murder, committed suicide by throwing themselves overboard in despair (Walvin 1993, 17; Shyllon 1974, 185).

As with the Somerset case, so it was with the *Zong*. Letters to the daily and weekly newspapers brought the case before the public. And just as the Somerset case had won national praise for British liberty, the *Zong* affair registered profound revulsion at British tyranny. A letter published in the *Morning Chronicle* of March 18, 1783, from a correspondent who attended the case stated, *"The narrative seemed to make every one present shudder"* (Shyllon 1974, 188). The *Zong* scandal has been seen as precipitating the full unleashing of antislavery sentiment in Britain (Walvin 1993, 18–21). Not only did it help catalyze the abolitionist movement, but the agitation the scandal inspired also epitomized the kind of integrated teamwork that would eventually bring slavery to an end. The day after the March 18 article, the Nigerian-born Londoner Olaudah Equiano personally called on the White abolitionist Granville Sharp to discuss the incident, setting in motion the process that would bring the *Zong* to the forefront of the national consciousness (Shyllon 1974, 189).

Both the Africa trade and the antislavery movement coincided with the rise of print culture. Although the British public massively consumed slave products—tobacco, rum, steel, cotton, indigo, mahogany, coffee, and most important, sugar—the vast majority knew about Africans and slaves only through written accounts. From the 1780s onward, the British presses issued millions of pages in the form of parliamentary debates and newspaper columns, sermons and speeches, poems, novels and plays, medical tracts and anatomical inquiries, African travelogues, and West Indian histories. Antislavery propaganda spread prolifically during the height of abolitionist activity in 1788–1789, a period when thousands of tracts, pamphlets, broadsheets, and poems were disseminated throughout Great Britain (Sypher 1942; Dykes 1942). Ballads by William Cowper and other prominent poets were set to well-known tunes and sung in taverns, at antislavery meetings, and in the streets. Josiah Wedgewood designed antislavery medallions, jewelry, and even tea services. Yet the abolitionist culture of the time inadvertently played its own part in spreading, or at least codifying, racial prejudice. However well meaning, the literature of the antislavery movement helped to popularize stereotyped, simplified, patronizing, and (often) degrading images of Africa, its peoples, and their descendants in the Americas and Britain. Black British writing represented a prominent intervention in this implicitly colonialist discourse.

Despite popular opposition to the slave trade, abolition legislation failed to pass both houses of Parliament in 1791, 1793, and a number of years thereafter. The powerful West India lobby, a nervous and increasingly reactionary political climate inspired by the French Revolution (which had erupted in 1789), and crude economic self-interest all kept abolition at bay. The slave trade, widely acknowledged as the worst single feature of the slave system, if not of the empire itself, was finally abolished in 1807, but out-lawing slavery as an institution and emancipating the West Indian slaves entirely would take another thirty years. Yet, just as Black British writing would help bring about emancipation, slaves in the colonies would also play a crucial role. In fact, the first heated debates over the emancipation of slaves took their impetus from a major slave revolt in Barbados, one of Britain's most lucrative colonies. It was here, on Easter Sunday of 1816, that slaves laid waste to seventy plantations and set a third of the island on fire. They burned cane fields and houses as the Whites fled to the nearby cities of Bridgetown and Oistins. The White plantocracy immediately estab-lished martial law, and in addition to the 100 slaves who were killed in the uprising, 144 more were executed, 170 were deported, and hundreds of oth-ers were sentenced to death or excessive punishments (Craton 1982, 262–264). At every juncture in the British parliamentary debates over the eman-cipation of slaves, a major slave rebellion occurred.

The slaves and children of slaves who managed to get to England repre-sented only a small percentage of the Black colonial population and a frac-tion (if a highly visible one) of the British population as a whole. Some, like Sancho and Cugoano, were sent to England to serve as personal slaves; some, like Gronniosaw, Equiano, Jea, and Wedderburn, came as seamen, whether indentured or free; still others, like Somerset and Prince, accom-panied their owners to England and then refused to return to slavery in the Americas. Freedom, effectively provisional both before and after the Mansfield decision, made for a chancy and often desperate life. Slave own-ers (like Sancho's three mistresses) might threaten to sell their servants into plantation slavery; former slaves could be surreptitiously recaptured and forcibly returned to colonial bondage; freedom might be held out as a reward and then (as in Equiano's case) abruptly retracted. Neither resi-dence in England, Christian baptism, nor marriage to an Englishwoman (Black Britons were disproportionately male) could safely guarantee free-dom, though each had a reputation for doing so and all held advantages as pragmatic moves.

Those who managed to remain free and in Britain lacked civil rights and decent employment opportunities, with little in the way of a social welfare system and next to nothing reserved for "aliens" and "strangers." The ma-jority of Blacks in Britain worked as servants, although as the Revolution-ary and Napoleonic Wars (1793–1815) dragged on, a growing number found employment on naval and merchant ships. A smaller group found better situations as upper servants (Sancho helped run a ducal household as butler before becoming England's first Black shopkeeper) or musicians in military bands. A handful grew famous (though not rich) for successful prizefighting careers. Julius Soubise, Sancho's friend, made an enviable reputation as a celebrated dandy and man about town (and notoriously successful womanizer). But as the narratives of Gronniosaw and Prince starkly attest, many Black Britons had to struggle merely to survive, with homelessness a constant threat and outright starvation an urgent possibility. A Black urban population of transients and petty thieves, prostitutes, and beggars—London's "blackbirds"—provoked such anxiety among civic authorities that a number were brusquely packed off for "repatriation" to Sierra Leone, Britain's West African colony intended for freed slaves (Fryer 1984, 195–202). Blacks regularly suffered jeering and other forms of casual harassment in the streets. Yet many formed real and satisfying connections with Whites, from the fashionable employers who provided Sancho and Cugoano with situations that left them time to write, to the religious communities that welcomed Gronniosaw and Jea, to the abolitionist reformers and political radicals who made common cause with Equiano and Wedderburn. Not to mention the many lower-class women widely held to show a "strong partiality for Black mates" (Sandiford 1988, 25).

If the disproportionate number of Black males made intermarriage with White Englishwomen the default option—so much so that a distinctively Black British population had largely dwindled from sight by the mid-nineteenth century—expressions of community and solidarity were by no means unknown. Contemporary periodicals describe (in lively if smirking prose) festive Black weddings, christenings, and musical evenings in taverns reserved for Blacks only. Some of Sancho's letters display an informal network of "African" friends, acquaintances, and supporters in action, dispensing advice, leads, and recommendations for employment. As abolitionist agitation gained steam in the late 1780s, the "Sons of Africa"— Equiano, Cugoano, and some dozen others—began promulgating denunciations of the slave trade, in addresses to influential statesmen and in public letters to the press. In addition to exposing the *Zong* incident, Equiano publicly attacked the Sierra Leone scheme once its flaws and mismanagement became evident, again seconded by his friend Cugoano.

Most notably, Black Britons attacked the slave system, combated racial prejudice, and asserted their title to full humanity through narratives, polemics, and poems such as those included in this volume. Not all of the works in question include direct critiques of slavery: pioneering essays in Black self-representation such as Sancho's or Gronniosaw's tend to attack slavery obliquely, leaving sustained antislavery arguments to Benezet and other White abolitionists. But a number of themes, images, and motifs running throughout the early Black British tradition convey a shared antislavery and antiracist agenda, at times implicit and at others overt. Writers who recount their kidnapping in Africa—as do Gronniosaw, Cugoano, and Equiano—portray their motherland in terms of warm domestic ties, robust traditions and social institutions, and self-sustaining (if small-scale) agricultural and crafts economies. This is far from the pristine, primitive "southern wild" of hunters and gatherers presumed by one European fantasy of Africa after another (Hammond and Jablow 1970). In contrast to the vague, undifferentiated Africa evoked throughout the mainstream British tradition, Black narrators encounter a variety of cultures, languages, and nations on their way to slave-trading forts, with African societies tending to become more corrupt as they approach the Atlantic coast—and the rapacious Europeans that frequent it. They acknowledge the existence of indigenous African slavery but contrast its comparatively benign character with the dehumanizing barbarities of colonial slavery in the Americas. In a common reversal of Eurocentric notions of superiority, the Europeans, not the Africans, are depicted as savages and barbarians: more than one African captive expects to be eaten by them. The African slaves, though systematically and extensively brutalized by their masters, heroically resist becoming brutish themselves.

The horrors of the Middle Passage—well known to the British reading public from abolitionist propaganda—gain disturbing new facets from a first-person perspective, eliciting the trauma, cultural dislocation, and suicidal despair that add psychological torture to the shipboard beatings and rapes. The tyrannical cruelty of slave-ship captains—to their crews as well as to their human cargo—adds a lurid, demonic glow. The "seasoning" period—which deprived Sancho of both his parents—gets less attention, perhaps because it lost much of its terror for those who managed to survive it. But the rigors, hazards, and uncertainties of colonial slavery again gain sharper definition and powerful emotional tonalities from the accounts of those who endured it. Field slavery, whether in the farms of colonial New York or the salt marshes of Turks Island, seems nearly *un*endurable, and the deaths by beatings and sheer overwork of fellow slaves are described with a poignant overlay of empathy and solidarity. House slavery can make for a longer but not necessarily better life, as readers encounter cooks wearing iron muzzles, servants working days and nights in despite of illness or injury, maids of all work summoned to perform sexual services, and brutal punishments given on the slightest of pretexts. The dehumanizing effects of slavery on White masters becomes painfully clear, as the effectively unlimited power of owners and overseers, coupled with the sadistic mentality endemic to plantation culture, provokes one moral outrage after another. Even slaves who attain a certain measure of free agency (both Equiano and Prince manage to accumulate savings through working and dealing on the side) face the prospect of being cheated without redress or sold off at a moment's notice. And the determined and fortunate slave who, like Equiano or Jea, manages to negotiate for manumission (or purchase it outright) can always be kidnapped and sold by unscrupulous slave-catchers and traders.

England provides a desirable alternative to the colonies, though by no means an earthly paradise. For Sancho, England represents a cultural center, a locus for patronage and self-advancement, an engaging and infinitely amusing social environment. Yet for all his patriotism (especially evident in his scorn for the rebellious American colonists), Sancho continues to identify himself as an "African" and acknowledges that he can never be fully integrated into English society. Equiano, too, becomes "almost"—but never quite—"an Englishman" (page 148). Nevertheless, he keeps gravitating back to England throughout a life of voyaging, feeling a greater sense of freedom there than in the colonies and eventually finding in London, the imperial metropolis, the best position from which to assail the worst features of the imperial system. For Gronniosaw and Jea, England connotes the heart of Dissenting Protestant culture, the homeland of Bunyan and Fox, Wesley and Whitefield, a land of racially mixed religious communities and marriageable churchwomen. Yet Gronniosaw also conveys the cheating, duplicity, and outright thievery characteristic of naval towns like Portsmouth and soon enough discovers (as Prince and Wedderburn will later) that one can go hungry in England as well as in the Americas. Both Equiano and Cugoano note the double edge of English efforts to relieve the "Black poor," tacitly exposing the xenophobia fueling African resettlement schemes in their cool assessments of the Sierra Leone colony. Prince and Wedderburn, writing after the abolition of the slave trade in 1807, attempt in their different ways to bring colonial slavery home to the metropolitan center. Prince presents her own dilemma—technically free in England, but doomed to reenslavement if she returns to her home and husband in Antigua—as a study in imperial contradiction and British hypocrisy. Wedderburn, issuing pamphlets, journals, and fiery speeches during a time of postwar depression and radical agitation, links the cause of Jamaican slaves to that of the dispossessed laborers of England, calling for a joint strategy of protest and work stoppages and raising the specter of transatlantic rebellion.

At the same time that a "British" identity began to develop as a support and counterweight to imperial expansion, "Englishness" was being redefined in terms of bloodlines and "race" (Hudson 1996; Doyle 1996). The Black presence in England inspired a good deal of racial prejudice and miscegenationist anxiety, even among many White abolitionists. The growth of empire provoked fears concerning the dilution or degeneration of an allegedly pure English race as British men formed sexual attachments with slaves and indigenous women in the colonies, and colonial "others" found their way to England. Such anxieties could readily reach hysterical proportions, as in the novelist Clara Reeve's fear that, thanks to the meddling of abolitionists, West Indian slaves would revolt, descend upon England, and "spoil the breed of the common people" (1974, 91). Simultaneously, justifications of slavery took on a more blatantly racist character, as pseudoscientific racialist theories began proliferating (Kitson 1999). Black British writers had no choice but to remain intensely aware of this "new racism" (Blackburn 1988, 154–156), encountering its effects on a daily basis and comprehending its role in maintaining the slave system. Their works seek to challenge and counter racism in a number of ways, from Cugoano's trenchant critique of popular racialist thinking to Wedderburn's scathing exposure of his slave-owning father's racist denial of his mulatto progeny. Both Gronniosaw and Equiano describe fair-skinned (albino) Africans in an effort to unsettle racial dichotomies; Equiano adds that, in his region of Africa, white skin is considered a deformity (page 123). Throughout these texts, exhibitions of intelligence and wit, domestic feeling, religious aspiration, and the unquenchable desire for liberty cogently and repeatedly testify to the writer's or teller's humanity and equality. As Prince states with characteristic directness, English readers will find slavery intolerable if they can be made to acknowledge the human feelings of the enslaved. "I have felt what a slave feels, and I know what a slave knows; and I would have all the good people in England to know it too, that they may break our chains, and set us free" (page 251).

Black writers also asserted their title to equality by the act of writing itself. The struggle for abolition and emancipation had made the intelligence and educability of sub-Saharan Africans a hotly contested issue: racist allegations of mental inferiority buttressed arguments that slavery suited Africans, who were perhaps even better off under the guidance of European owners. Abolitionists tended to reply, patronizingly enough, that Africans and their descendants might indeed appear inferior but lacked the advantages of schooling and "civilization"; educational and missionary efforts would gradually but surely render the slave populations of the New World fit for emancipation. (The French intellectual Henri Grégoire devoted an entire book to this defense, *De la littérature des nègres* [1808], soon translated into English as *An Enquiry Concerning the Intellectual and Moral Faculties and Literature of Negroes,* which features sympathetic vignettes of Wheatley, Sancho, Cugoano, and Equiano.) The very literacy of a given Black writer thus became an important piece of evidence within the debates on slavery and "race," and testimonials to a work's authenticity were often featured, along with subtitles like "Written by Himself." Both Sancho and Wheatley owed a good deal of their early notoriety to their exemplary status in such debates. The high stakes associated with literacy were quickly recognized by Black writers and narrators, who embodied the issue in a symbolic motif known as the "talking book" (Gates 1988, 127–169). Gronniosaw, Cugoano, and Equiano all discuss their early encounters with printed writing, a foreign and seemingly magical technology. Gronniosaw and Equiano each recalls placing a book to his ear and despairing of its ever speaking to him, a graphic image of cultural alienation. Jea describes miraculously learning to read the Bible through divine intervention, an angel appearing to instruct him in a vision after weeks of fervent prayer. Jea's sudden ability to read leads directly to his manumission, one of the more overt of many instances in which literacy and freedom come together in Black British writing.

Learning to tell one's story in written English also meant working with the available genres and plot types, accommodating and transforming them in the process. A number of critics, from Angelo Costanzo to Helen Thomas, have emphasized the importance of the Protestant conversion narrative for early Black autobiographers. (Bunyan's *Grace Abounding to the Chief of Sinners*, the best known today, was only one of countless examples in circulation throughout the eighteenth-century English-speaking world.) Spiritual autobiographies such as Bunyan's featured a common narrative arc—from worldly despair, through the quickening and painful cultivation of religious hopes, to rebirth in Christ—that readily lent itself to a story of slavery, struggle, and manumission. Literacy (especially Bible reading) played a salient part in accounts of Protestant salvation, and their Calvinistic emphasis on spiritual crisis—the dark night of the soul—spoke to the experiences of severe trauma and "social death" inflicted upon slaves (Patterson 1982). The Bible itself, in the story of the Jews' enslavement in Egypt and their arduous but triumphant exodus, offered a ready link between the spiritual quest and the journey to freedom. Most early Black British writers, moreover, belonged to Dissenting or Evangelical religious sects that placed a high value on both written and oral stories of Christian redemption. Professing a sincere conversion to Christianity could in addition help bridge the cultural divide between the "African" narrator and English reader. Finally, Christian teachings presented ready ammunition in the struggles against the more virulent, polygenetic forms of racism (since Genesis taught that all people were descended from Adam and Eve) and against slavery, particularly in the New Testament emphasis on brotherly love and doing as one would be done by.

The template of the conversion narrative was not, however, followed blindly but could be refashioned, disrupted, or even inverted as need be. (Wedderburn goes so far as to invent a doctrine of "Christian Diabolism.") Although Equiano describes his Christian conversion experience in familiar Protestant terms, he makes a point of repeatedly mentioning his alternate desire to move to Turkey, where he had been earlier welcomed, and become a Muslim instead (pages 165, 167). Little remarked on by Equiano's modern critics, the flirtation with Islam lends an aura of autonomy and spiritual independence to his narrative, implying that Christianity was not the sole option and that a British Protestant identity was chosen only after weighing the alternatives. More generally, one Black writer after another exposes the hypocrisy of a nation of Christian slaveholders with varying measures of irony and invective. Enfranchisement and Christian conversion may typically converge in a slave narrative, but Christian culture nevertheless appears all too amenable to the institution of slavery.

The picaresque novel, following its errant hero through a series of misfortunes, reversals, and chance rescues to a (typically) happy conclusion, served as another key generic exemplar. Critics have pointed to Daniel Defoe's *Robinson Crusoe* in particular (Potkay and Burr 1995, 2), but Jonathan Swift's *Gulliver's Travels,* an anticolonialist rather than colonialist fiction, was no less readily available and seems still more apt. Like the African captive, Gulliver finds himself in profoundly alien cultures, unable to speak the local language, puzzled by foreign customs and traditions, and for the most part treated as an outsider, inferior, and slave. His alienation, however, brings with it a distanced and relentlessly ironic perspective revealing the contradictions and underscoring the abuses of his various adoptive cultures. *Gulliver's Travels* fuses the picaresque novel with the pseudorealistic traveler's tale, one of Swift's satirical objects and another important resource for Black autobiographers. They frequently drew as well, of course, on abolitionist treatises, with their host of antislavery arguments backed by historical accounts and statistical tables. In addition, writers like Sancho and Equiano show a cagey awareness of the stock stage Africans of the time, the most popular by far being Shakespeare's Othello and Southerne's Oroonoko. Equiano's flitting desire to settle in Smyrna and convert to Islam, in fact, recalls Othello's more violent threat to "turn Turk" and subvert the Venetian imperial order he serves. *Oroonoko,* adapted by Southerne from Aphra Behn's 1688 novella, made the "Black Prince" or "royal slave" a familiar icon for British audiences, and Gronniosaw, Cugoano, and Equiano all stress their high-born status in Africa as one means of forestalling the racial and cultural chauvinism of their White readership.

In addition to importing and manipulating the generic and plot conventions of the time, early Black British writers deployed a diverse set of literary and oral styles. Sancho, a keen admirer of Laurence Sterne's *Sermons* and *Tristram Shandy,* developed his own version of Sterne's "Shandean" technique, with its dashes and digressions, ironic self-awareness, and knowing sentimentality. Readily lending itself to the familiar letter-writing that Sancho excelled at, the Shandean style also proved ideal for conveying a magnanimous, affectionate, arch sensibility, thoroughly versed in English ways but finely detached from them. Cugoano enlivens the Enlightenment rationalism of antislavery rhetoric with personal anecdotes and pointedly direct appeals to the reader. Equiano skillfully and exuberantly mingles a host of genres and styles, by turns coolly descriptive, warmly affective, harshly satirical, credibly self-justifying, and comically amusing. Jea, Prince, and Wedderburn display (through the filtering layers of transcription and editing) a transatlantic repertoire of oral styles, from the spontaneous exhortations of American field preaching, to the distinctive cadences of West Indian speech, to the rhetorical blasts and irreverent asides of radical London oratory. Unexpected stylistic blends and hybridized genres predominate — what Sancho calls, showing his stylistic hand under cover of self-mockery, "a true Negroe calibash" (page 39), a transatlantic gumbo mingling African, European, and American motifs and traditions.

Poetry, then regarded as the highest literary form, held a special status of its own in the debates on African genius. Francis Williams, a free Jamaican Black allegedly brought by the Duke of Montagu (Sancho's patron) to study at Cambridge University, became famous for his ability to write verses in Latin, joining Sancho and Wheatley as a prime example in the literature on African slavery and educability (Fryer 1984, 421). Ironically, his best-known poem, the "Ode" to George Haldane, governor of Jamaica, found its way into English through the proslavery apologist and virulent racist Edward Long, who included a translation in his *History of Jamaica* only to proclaim its inferiority (1773, 2:478–485). Despite the disparagement of detractors like Long, however, poetry remained one of the strongest proofs Black writers (or their White promoters) could give of Afro-Caribbean intelligence at a time when the "new," pseudoscientific racism persisted in placing sub-Saharan Africans at the bottom of racial hierarchies (Stepan 1981). Phillis Wheatley's handlers operated under this assumption as they paraded her around America and Britain in the 1770s. Her verse has sometimes been criticized as too conventional in its stylistic allegiances and not outspoken enough on the issue of slavery, but the very conventionality of her poetry made a crucial part of her claim to be taken seriously by White audiences. Equiano's use of poetry, both his own and that of other British writers, manifests a cagey ability to deliver a narrative embroidered with cues calculated to appeal to an educated British readership. In Cuba, Juan Francisco Manzano earned his contemporaries' respect — and his freedom — by mastering the intricacies of Spanish verse. Not all early Black poetry, however, sought to emulate the conventional literary styles of the day. A rich improvisational tradition also developed, from work chants collectively invented and orally circulated among the slave-gangs to the religious hymns represented here by Jea. Such work songs, ritual chants, lullabies, and hymns frequently included subversive and self-affirming messages, coded or not, intended to build solidarity and endurance among slave populations while mocking, berating, or cursing their colonial masters.

The unvarnished complaints and rebukes of British slaves and former slaves have also been preserved in unedited letters and other archival sources. In the section entitled "Voices," we present a revealing slice of such documents, which can read as powerfully as the published texts. Although most Blacks living in the Caribbean and in England lacked literacy skills and could neither write their accounts of slavery nor (with rare exceptions) have them published, historical records show that their voices were never completely silenced. In many cases, in fact, quite the opposite was true. Take the example of the slave "Princess," in the judicial proceedings reprinted here (pages 364–65). A colonial house slave, Princess complains to the magistrate of the British colony of Berbice about the very subject of a Black woman speaking. According to Princess, one morning she saw another slave, by the name of Cuba, sitting down asleep in the middle of the day. Princess asked Cuba, "What was you doing last night that you did not sleep?" At that moment, the master vaulted out of his bedroom and asked Princess what she said. Princess boldly answered, "I don't speak with you, I speak with Cuba." Though brief, the exchange is highly suggestive. Why did her master not want Princess to know what the other Black slave woman had been doing all night? Whatever the reason, the White master takes offense at Princess's sharp reply and then reprimands her for speaking: "You always have something to say; better you shut your mouth." But instead of silence, Princess once again articulates her right to speak. She tells the magistrate:

> I answered him again, "Master, I don't speak with you, I speak with Cuba"; and then I came down stairs and went into the kitchen. Master followed me into the kitchen, and told me I had better go to my work than meddle my tongue; I answered him, "I am doing my work, and you come to trouble me; I was not speaking to you." Then he went to the store and took a horse-whip, and began to flog me. I asked him for what he flogged me? He said, "For badness." I told him, "So long as you flog me for nothing, I shall go to the Fiscal," and I came away.

Princess speaks about speaking itself. She defiantly points out how the slave's voice is deeply contested because undeniably powerful, even in the most practical and routine activities of domestic life. Ultimately Princess is doubly punished for speaking—both by her master and by the magistrate—but she nonetheless grants herself agency to voice her opinion and to thus define herself. Even though her master insists he punishes her "for badness," she counters that he punishes her "for nothing."

Of the 10,000 or so Blacks living in Britain, only a few can be traced through records in the historical archives, and those mentions that survive can be tantalizingly brief or fragmentary. Madge Dresser (2001), for example, records the instance of a ten-year-old boy who had survived smallpox and was to be sold in Bristol in the early 1800s. The well-meaning gentleman who went to preach Christianity to the young boy on a cold November day records the Black boy's equally chilling response:

> I went to see the poor sick Negro but he was got down by the Kitchen Fire and there being a Heap of Servants about he told Br[other] Walters the less said about our Saviour there the better . . . therefore we soon walked home again. Yet I really liked the young Man. (81)

The letter by James Harris reprinted here (also discovered by Dresser) stands out as an uncommonly and memorably direct expression of the plight of London's "blackbirds." The selection of letters to John Clarkson from the freed slaves resettled in the Sierra Leone colony reveal the hardships, negotiations, and struggles for Black agency demanded even by an allegedly benign and quasi-democratic colonial regime. As all of these records make clear, in the Americas or in Sierra Leone, colonial Blacks had specific individuals—plantation owners, overseers, even medical doctors—and clear-cut institutions—the monarchy, British Parliament, former governors—to single out for complaint. Once in England, the offending parties were no longer owners and managers, governors or Parliament, but poverty, unemployment, filth, cramped housing, racial profiling, begging, petty crime, homelessness, and fatal disease (often the same problems faced by poor and laboring-class Whites). Such living conditions made the terms *freedom* and *liberty*, central to Britain's self-image and rhetorical posturing, all the more hollow in relation to its Black subjects.

Adding their distinctive voices to the British literary tradition, Black writers transformed it, although specific trains of influence can prove difficult to trace. Blake's "The Little Black Boy," probably the best-known work of antislavery literature, may well owe a debt to Gronniosaw's *Narrative* for its portrayal of African religious teachings (Echeruo 1992; Henry 1998). (Blake would have known Cugoano, who cites Gronniosaw, through the Cosways, fellow artists who employed Cugoano as a servant [Edwards 1990].) Sancho first became widely known for his request that Sterne address the subject of West Indian slavery in a forthcoming work. Sterne (1983a) responded that he had already sketched a sympathetic vignette of a "poor negro girl" for his novel *Tristram Shandy,* then in progress, as is well known (493). In a later work, however, the *Sentimental Journey,* Sterne

(1983b) included a second denunciation of slavery, this one triggered by the spectacle of a caged starling who repeats, parrotlike, "I can't get out—I can't get out" (197–199). (European starlings are black birds, and Starling was used as a slave name in Britain [Fryer 1984, 62]). Whether or not the inspiration for this second vignette can be traced solely to Sterne's friendship with Sancho, it became one of the best-known passages of the work, quoted, for example, by Maria Bertram in Jane Austen's novel *Mansfield Park:* "I cannot get out, as the starling said" (Austen 1966, 127). Though most obviously relevant to the constraint of Maria's unfortunate engagement, the quotation, resonant with Sterne's antislavery stance and the famous correspondence with Sancho attached to it in the British public mind, also broaches the issue of colonial slavery simmering just under the surface of Austen's novel. (Mansfield Park, the Bertrams' paradigmatic English estate, runs on the proceeds from their slave plantations in Antigua.) Though long invisible to her critics, Austen's critique of Britain's dependence on the slave system would have been more obvious to contemporary readers who knew their Sterne—and their Sancho.

Early Black writers, of course, were less concerned with reshaping the British literary canon than with effecting urgently needed political change. Their published works undeniably played a part in ending the slave trade and bringing down the colonial slave system, as did slave resistance and rebellion in the colonies. They presented English-speaking readers with model Black subjects, militating against the stereotypes emanating from proslavery and antislavery writings alike and claiming kinship, empathy, and recognition. They provided first-person accounts of slavery and oppression that retain a gut-wrenching power over a hundred and fifty years after British emancipation. They countered an increasingly entrenched racism with arguments, with their own examples, with outrage, and with sly humor. These works demand attention today as indispensable cultural-historical documents: they repay it with indomitable eloquence.

A NOTE ON THE TEXTS
Alan Richardson and Debbie Lee

The primary texts included in this edition are based on first editions, with a minimum of modern editorial intervention. We have preferred to present the texts as they appeared to their contemporary readers, including (when possible) the sometimes quite elaborate framing devices—prefaces, letters of attestation, editorial annotations, interventions, and "supplements"—through which they were mediated by editors, publishers, and patrons. Older spellings (and misspellings) and original punctuation have been retained except in a very few cases in which they would be prove misleading. Some obvious misprints, however, have been silently corrected, and archaic printing conventions like the eighteenth-century "long s" have not been retained.

A few of the texts reprinted in full or in part below exist in single editions only, while others had much more complicated early publication histories. Gronniosaw's *Narrative,* sometimes dated 1770 but more likely first appearing in 1772, went through a confusing number of imprints, not always easy to differentiate though representing as many as twelve separate editions. The version presented here follows the presumed first edition, Bath [1772]. Sancho's *Letters* was first published (posthumously) in 1782 (the edition followed here), with four more early editions appearing by 1803. (The fifth edition, published by Sancho's son, forms the basis for Paul Edwards's and Polly Rewt's scholarly edition of 1994.) Cugoano's *Thoughts and Sentiments* was first published in London in 1787 (the edition excerpted here), with a second imprint (by T. Becket) following in the same year and a shorter version published under a similar title in 1791. (Both versions are reprinted by Vincent Carretta's 1999 edition.) Equiano's *Interesting Narrative,* first published in London in 1789, proved remarkably popular and went through nine British editions in Equiano's lifetime. Our excerpts follow the first edition (the ninth edition, the last Equiano himself seems to have personally supervised, can be consulted in Carretta's scholarly edition of 1995). Jea's *Life, History, and Unparalleled Sufferings,* in contrast, was rarely reprinted, and the 1815 date of the first edition (followed here) remains uncertain. Wedderburn's texts follow the early editions published by Wedderburn himself, *The Axe Laid to the Root* being the first number of his radical magazine of that title (1817), and *The Horrors of Slavery* appearing in pamphlet form in 1824. Mary Prince's *History* was first published in London in 1831 (the text reprinted here in full) and went into two more editions the same year. The second and third editions added a short postscript and appendix that Moira Ferguson reprints in her scholarly edition of 1997.

We owe a significant debt to the pioneering scholarship represented in the modern editions by Edwards, Rewt, Carretta, and Ferguson cited above, not to mention their related editions and critical writings. We have also drawn on the editions of Jea by Graham Russell Hodges and Wedderburn by Iain McCalman, and the collections (listed under Works Cited) edited by Edwards and David Dabydeen, Carretta, Adam Potkay and Sandra Burr, and Sukhdev Sandhu and Dabydeen, our fellow editors in the Slavery, Abolition, and Emancipation series (1999). We are especially grateful to the John J. Burns rare books library at Boston College (and senior librarian John Atteberry) for generously supplying copy texts for Cugoano and Prince. We also are grateful to Christopher Fyfe, who located the original Sierra Leone Settlers' letters held in various specialized archives. We have made our own transcriptions of the letters, which differ in some ways from Fyfe's transcriptions, and thus we wish to thank the British Library, the London Public Record Office in Kew, and the University of Illinois at Chicago for allowing us to reproduce the letters here. Debbie Lee thanks her research assistant, Dometa Wiegand, for her help on the Sierra Leone letters and Phillis Wheatley's poetry and Washington State University for the Buchanan Distinguished Scholar Award, which helped fund her work on this project.

Part One

NARRATIVE

From Letters of the Late Ignatius Sancho, An African

Ignatius Sancho

Ignatius Sancho (c. 1729–1780), the best-known Black British writer of his time, was also the first to come to widespread public attention. Although Ukawsaw Gronniosaw's *Narrative* preceded Sancho's *Letters* into print by a decade, Sancho had already begun to emerge as a notable public character when he sent his well-known letter to Laurence Sterne in 1766, urging the famous writer to pen a denunciation of slavery in a future work. (Sterne included one in *Tristram Shandy* [1759–1767], his novel in progress, and he and Sancho remained in touch throughout Sterne's life.) Published with a posthumous edition of Sterne's letters in 1775, Sancho's eloquent plea—written in a sophisticated style obviously modeled on Sterne's own—quickly became a celebrated document in its own right, and was reprinted the next year in the *Gentleman's Magazine* for January 1776. By 1782, when one of Sancho's correspondents (Frances Crewe) edited a large selection of Sancho's letters for publication in two volumes, Sancho's fame had grown considerably enough that some twelve hundred subscribers agreed to buy the work in advance, and a second edition was called for by the end of the next year. Along with Phillis Wheatley, Sancho became an icon of "African genius" in the debates on slavery, "race," and the educability of dark-skinned peoples that proliferated during the late eighteenth and early nineteenth centuries.

Sancho's life was summarized by Joseph Jekyll (1754–1837) in a brief memoir written for the 1782 edition of Sancho's letters. Sancho was born around 1729 on a slave ship on its way from the West African coast to the Spanish American settlements in the Caribbean. The bishop at Cartagena (on the Caribbean coast of present-day Colombia) baptized the child in the name of Ignatius Loyola (the sixteenth-century founder of the Jesuit order). Neither of his parents survived the brutal two-year "seasoning" period endured by African captives in the Americas. His mother died of an unspecified colonial disease, and his father committed suicide rather than live in chains. Their two-year-old child was taken to England, where he became the slave of three unmarried sisters in Greenwich. They named him Sancho (after the earthy, comical squire in *Don Quixote*) and determined to keep him ignorant, despite his obvious intelligence. His keen qualities did not escape the attention of a neighboring aristocrat, however. John Montagu, the second Duke of Montagu (c. 1688–1749), had already befriended a free-born Jamaican of African descent, Francis Williams (c. 1700–c. 1770), bringing him to England to have him educated in a well-known attempt to vindicate African intelligence. [Montagu's part in this famous experiment, however, has not been historically substantiated.] Montagu provided Sancho with books and encouragement, although Sancho's mistresses remained inexorable and threatened to sell him into American slavery after the duke's death in 1749. Like many other slaves in England forced to renegotiate the terms of their servitude by simply absconding, Sancho ran away and eventually found a protector in Montagu's widow. Sancho became the Duchess of Montagu's butler, helping to run her large household until her death in 1751, which brought him an annuity of £30 on top of £70 he had amassed through savings and gifts.

Sancho made the predictable next move for a young servant in his position: relocation to London for a life of gambling and womanizing, partying and playgoing, until his savings ran out. (He allegedly spent his last shilling to see David Garrick, the great Shakespearean actor, perform *Richard III.*) Sancho thought of becoming an actor himself, with an eye to African roles like Othello and Oroonoko, but his speaking style was not clear enough for the stage. Perhaps around this time he wrote the two plays that are now lost and the *Theory of Music* (lost as well, though a few of Sancho's musical compositions have survived). He returned to a life of service in the Montagu household and became attached to the new duke, Montagu's son-in-law George, who assumed the title in 1766. Two years later Sancho had his portrait painted by Thomas Gainsborough, one of the era's preeminent artists, perhaps as a compliment to his patron, the duke, but perhaps as well in testament to Sancho's own growing notoriety as a musician, connoisseur, and correspondent of Sterne.

Attacked by the gout (a painful disease of the joints and feet for which there was then no cure) and increasingly corpulent, Sancho needed a more sedentary occupation and in 1774 opened a grocery on Charles Street in Westminster, a few blocks from St. James's Park. He ran the shop with his wife, Anne, an Afro-Caribbean woman he had married in 1758 and who bore him at least seven children. His published letters, many written at this time, portray him as a fond husband, doting father, close observer of politics, avid reader—and critic—of literary works, correspondent, adviser, and confidant to a large circle of friends. They also reveal a close study of contemporary literary style and a studied decision to emulate Sterne's ironic, playful, self-conscious, and sentimental mode. Sancho's stylistic debt to Sterne has provoked criticism from his own time to the present, but it evidently served him well. His "Shandean" style established Sancho at once not simply as a literate African, but as one who recognized, understood, and could manipulate the literary innovations of his day. Its self-referential and indirect qualities also lent themselves well to a writer whose position remained, as Sancho (1782) himself put it, "only a lodger—and hardly that" in his adoptive culture (2:92). Sancho's ironies are frequently (and winningly) directed at himself, but they take in as well the burgeoning racism of the time, British imperial arrogance, and the "Christians' abominable traffic for slaves" (page 35). Sancho died on December 14, 1780, after a period of acute suffering from gout and related ailments.

VOLUME 1, LETTER XIII.
To Mr. S——E.[1]

Richmond, Oct. 11, 1772.

YOUR letter gave me more pleasure than in truth I ever expected from your hands—but thou art a flatterer;—why dost thou demand advice of me? Young man, thou canst not discern wood from trees;—with awe and reverence look up to thy more than parents—look up to thy almost divine benefactors—search into the motive of every glorious action—retrace thine own history—and when you are convinced that they (like the All-gracious Power they serve) go about in mercy doing good—

From Ignatius Sancho, *Letters of the Late Ignatius Sancho, An African, To Which Are Prefixed Memoirs of His Life* (London: J. Nichols, 1782).

[1] Julius Soubise (1754–1798), brought to England as a slave from the British West Indies in his childhood, became a protégé of the Duchess of Queensbury, who had him instructed in such gentlemanly arts as fencing and horse riding. He gained considerable notoriety as a dandy, womanizer, and dilettante but left England in 1777 for virtual exile in Calcutta after raping one of the duchess's maids. He taught fencing and horsemanship in India until his death from a riding accident in 1798.

retire abashed at the number of their virtues—and humbly beg the Almighty to inspire and give you strength to imitate them.—Happy, happy lad! what a fortune is thine!—Look round upon the miserable fate of almost all of our unfortunate colour—superadded to ignorance,—see slavery, and the contempt of those very wretches who roll in affluence from our labours superadded to this woeful catalogue—hear the ill-bred and heart-racking abuse of the foolish vulgar.—You, S——e, tread as cautiously as the strictest rectitude can guide ye—yet must you suffer from this—but armed with truth—honesty—and conscious integrity—you will be sure of the plaudit and countenance of the good; --- if, therefore, thy repentance is sincere --- I congratulate thee as sincerely upon it --- it is thy birth-day to real happiness. ---- Providence has been very lavish of her bounty to you --- and you are deeply in arrears to her --- your parts are as quick as most mens; urge but your speed in the race of virtue with the same ardency of zeal as you have exhibited in error --- and you will recover, to the satisfaction of your noble patrons --- and to the glory of yourself. --- Some philosopher --- I forget who --- wished for a window in his breast --- that the world might see his heart; --- he could only be a great fool, or a very good man: --- I will believe the latter, and recommend him to your imitation. --- Vice is a coward; --- to be truly brave, a man must be truly good; --- you hate the name of cowardice—then, S ------ e, avoid it --- detest a lye --- and shun lyars --- be above revenge; --- if any have taken advantage either of your guilt or distress, punish them with forgiveness --- and not only so --- but, if you can serve them any future time, do it --- you have experienced mercy and long-sufferance in your own person --- therefore gratefully remember it, and shew mercy likewise.

I am pleased with the subject of your last --- and if your conversion is real, I shall ever be happy in your correspondence --- but at the same time I cannot afford to pay five pence for the honour of your letters; --- five pence is the twelfth part of five shillings—the forty-eighth part of a pound --- it would keep my girls in potatoes two days. --- The time may come, when it may be necessary for you to study calculations; --- in the mean while, if you cannot get a frank, direct to me under cover to his Grace the Duke of ———. You have the best wishes of your sincere friend (as long as you are your own friend)

Ignatius Sancho.

You must excuse blots and blunders --- for I am under the dominion of a cruel head-ach --- and a cough, which seems too fond of me.

———————

frank: signature, mark, or stamp covering the cost of postage otherwise paid by a letter's recipient.

LETTER XXIV.
To Mr. B——.[2]

August 12, 1775.

Dear Sir,

I F I knew a better man than yourself—you wou'd not have had this application—which is in behalf of a merry—chirping—white tooth'd—clean—tight—and light little fellow;—with a woolly pate—and face as dark as your humble;—Guiney-born, and French-bred—the sulky gloom of Africa dispelled by Gallic vivacity—and that softened again with English sedateness—a rare fellow!—rides well—and can look upon a couple of horses—dresses hair in the present taste—shaves light—and understands something of the arrangement of a table and side-board;—his present master will authenticate him a decent character—he leaves him at his own (Blacky's) request:—he has served him three years—and; like Teague, would be glad of a good master[3]—if any good master would be glad of him.—As I believe you associate chiefly with good-hearted folks—it is possible your interest may be of service to him.—I like the rogue's looks, or a similarity of colour should not have induced me to recommend him.—Excuse this little scrawl from your friend, &c.

Ign. Sancho.

For conscience like a fiery horse,
Will stumble if you check his course;
But ride him with an easy rein,
And rub him down with worldly gain,
5   He'll carry you through thick and thin,
Safe, although dirty, to your Inn.

Guiney-born: born in West Africa.
Gallic: French.
[2]Charles Browne, steward to Sir Charles Bunbury (1740–1821).
[3]Teague was a stock name in stage plays for a comically loyal Irish servant, a type first introduced in Sir Robert Howard's *The Committee* (1662).

LETTER XXXV.
To Mr. Sterne.[4]

July, 1776.

Reverend Sir,

I T would be an insult on your humanity (or perhaps look like it) to apologize for the liberty I am taking. —I am one of those people whom the vulgar and illiberal call *"Negurs."*—The first part of my life was rather unlucky, as I was placed in a family who judged ignorance the best and only security for obedience. —A little reading and writing I got by unwearied application. —The latter part of my life has been—thro' God's blessing, truly fortunate, having spent it in the service of one of the best families in the kingdom. —My chief pleasure has been books. —Philanthropy I adore. —How very much, good Sir, am I (amongst millions) indebted to you for the character of your amiable uncle Toby![5]—I declare, I would walk ten miles in the dog-days, to shake hands with the honest corporal. —Your Sermons have touch'd me to the heart, and I hope have amended it, which brings me to the point. —In your tenth discourse, page seventy-eight, in the second volume—is this very affecting passage— "Consider how great a part of our species—in all ages down to this—have been trod under the feet of cruel and capricious tyrants, who would neither hear their cries, nor pity their distresses. —Consider slavery—what it is— how bitter a draught—and how many millions are made to drink it!" —Of all my favorite authors, not one has drawn a tear in favour of my miserable black brethren—excepting yourself, and the humane author of Sir George Ellison.[6]—I think you will forgive me;—I am sure you will applaud me for beseeching you to give one half hour's attention to slavery, as it is at this day practised in our West Indies. —That subject, handled in your striking manner, would ease the yoke (perhaps) of many—but if only of one—Gracious God! —what a feast to a benevolent heart! —and, sure I am, you are an epicurean in acts of charity. —You, who are universally read, and as universally admired—you could not fail—Dear Sir, think in me you behold the uplifted hands of thousands of my brother Moors. —Grief (you pathetically

---

Moors: dark-skinned Africans (in eighteenth-century usage).

[4]Laurence Sterne (1713–1768), Anglican clergyman and acclaimed (and somewhat controversial) writer, whose works include *The Sermons of Mr Yorick* (1760) and the novel *The Life and Opinions of Tristram Shandy, Gentleman* (1759–1767).

[5]Memorable, warm-hearted uncle of the hero in *Tristram Shandy.*

[6] *The History of Sir George Ellison* (1766), a sentimental novel by Sarah Scott (1723–1795), addressed the abuses of plantation slavery.

observe) is eloquent;—figure to yourself their attitudes;—hear their sup-
plicating addresses!—alas!—you cannot refuse.—Humanity must comply—in which hope I beg permission to subscribe myself,

Reverend, Sir, &c.

I. Sancho.

LETTER XLIX.
To Mr. M——.[7]

September 3, 1772.

I FEEL it long since I heard from you—very long since I saw you—and
three or four days back had some notion—I should never, in this paltry world, see thee again—but (thanks to the Father of Mercies!) I am
better, and have a higher relish of health and ease, from contrasting the
blessings with the pains I have endured.—Would to God you could say that
your dizzy dismal head-achs were flown to the moon, or embarked for
Lapland—there to be tied up in a witch's bag—and sold to Beelzebub[8] with
a cargo of bad winds—religious quarrels—politics—my gout—and our
American grievances.[9]—But what are you about in your last (where you
dropt the candid friend and assumed the flatterer).—You hinted as if there
was a chance of seeing you in Charles Street: I wish it much.—My friend, I
have had a week's gout in my hand, which was by much too hard for my
philosophy.—I am convinced, let the Stoics say what they list—that pain is
an evil;—in short I was wishing for death—and little removed from madness—but (thank heaven) I am much better—my spirits will be mended if
I hear from you—better still to see you.—I find it painful to write much,
and learn that two hands are as necessary in writing as eating.—You see I
write, like a lady, from one corner of the paper to the other.—My respects—and love—and admiration – and compliments—to Mrs. ——,
and Mrs. and Miss——, tell M——l, he kept his word in calling to see us
before he left town!—I hope ● confound the ink! what a blot! Now
don't you dare suppose I was in fault—no, Sir, the pen was diabled—the
paper worse, there was concatenation of ill-sorted chances—all—all—

---

diabled: bedeviled, cursed.

[7] John Meheux, an official (First Clerk in the Board of Control) and amateur artist.

[8] A name for the devil.

[9] Mounting tensions between England and the thirteen North American colonies would
lead to the outbreak of the American Revolutionary War by 1775.

coincided to contribute to that fatal blot—which has so disarranged my ideas—that I must perforce finish before I had half disburthened my head and heart:—but is N—— a good girl?—And how does my honest George do? Tell Mrs. H—— what you please in the handsome way of me.—Farewell, I will write no more nonsense this night—that's flat.

Ign. Sancho.

How do you like the print?—Mr. D——[10] says and his wife says the same—that you are exceedingly clever—and they shall be happy to do any thing, which is produced by the same hand—which did the original—and if Mr. D—— can be of any service to you in the etching—you may command him when you please.

LETTER LVII.
To Mr. F——.

Charles Street, January 27, 1778.

FULL heartily and most cordially do I thank thee—good Mr. F——, for your kindness in sending the books[11]—that upon the unchristian and most diabolical usage of my brother Negroes—the illegality—the horrid wickedness of the traffic—the cruel carnage and depopulation of the human species—is painted in such strong colours—that I should think would (if duly attended to) flash conviction—and produce remorse in every enlightened and candid reader.—The perusal affected me more than I can express;—indeed I felt a double or mixt sensation—for while my heart was torn for the sufferings—which, for aught I know—some of my nearest kin might have undergone—my bosom, at the same time, glowed with gratitude—and praise toward the humane—the Christian—the friendly and learned Author of that most valuable book.—Blest be your sect!—and Heaven's peace be ever upon them!—I, who, thank God! am no bigot—but honour virtue—and the practice of the great moral duties—equally in the turban—or the lawn-sleeves[12]—who think

---

[10] Matthew Darley, engraver and seller of prints.

[11] Jabez Fisher, a Quaker living in Philadelphia, Pennsylvania. The "books" sent by him to Sancho include an antislavery work that may well be *A Short Account of That Part of Africa, Inhabited by the Negroes . . . and the Manner by Which the Slave Trade Is Carried On* (1762) by Fisher's fellow Quaker Anthony Benezet (1713–1784).

[12] In this context, the turban signifies Islam, lawn-sleeves (worn by Anglican bishops) the Established Church of England.

Heaven big enough for all the race of man—and hope to see and mix amongst the whole family of Adam in bliss hereafter—I with these notions (which, perhaps, some may style absurd) look upon the friendly Author— as a being far superior to any great name upon your continent.—I could wish that every member of each house of parliament had one of these books.—And if his Majesty perused one through before breakfast— though it might spoil his appetite—yet the consciousness of having it in his power to facilitate the great work—would give an additional sweetness to his tea.—Phyllis's poems do credit to nature[13]—and put art—merely as art—to the blush.—It reflects nothing either to the glory or generosity of her master—if she is still his slave—except he glories in the *low vanity* of having in his wanton power a mind animated by Heaven—a genius superior to himself—the list of splendid—titled—learned names, in confirmation of her being the real authoress[14]—alas! shews how very poor the acquisition of wealth and knowledge are—without generosity—feeling—and humanity.—These good great folks—all know—and perhaps admired—nay, praised Genius in bondage—and then, like the Priests and the Levites in sacred writ, passed by—not one good Samaritan amongst them.[15]—I shall be ever glad to see you—and am, with many thanks,

Your most humble
servant,

Ignatius Sancho.

LETTER LXV.
To Mr. M——.[16]

June 10, 1778.

"'Tis with our judgements as our watches—none
"Go just alike—yet each believes his own."

—*POPE.*[17]

---

[13] Phillis Wheatley, *Poems on Various Subjects* (1773), discussed and excerpted below, on pages 289–299.

[14] Wheatley's *Poems* included a list of eighteen dignitaries and sponsors attesting to her authorship, including Thomas Hutchinson, then governor of Massachusetts, and "*Mr.* John Wheatley, *her Master.*"

[15] For the biblical story of the "good Samaritan," see Luke 10:30–37.

[16] John Meheux (see note 7, above).

[17] Alexander Pope (1688–1744), *An Essay on Criticism* (1711), Part I, lines 9–10.

So, my wise critic—blessings on thee—and thanks for thy sagacious discovery!—Sterne, it seems, stole his grand outline of character from Fielding—and who did Fielding plunder? thou criticizing jack ape!—As to S——, perhaps you may be right—not absolutely right—nor quite so very *altogether* wrong—but that's not my affair.—[18] Fielding and Sterne both copied Nature—their pallettes stored with proper colours of the brightest dye—these masters were both great originals—their outline correct—bold—and free—Human Nature was their subject—and though their colouring was widely different, yet *here* and there some features in each might bear a little resemblance—some faint likeness to each other— as for example—in your own words—Toby and Allworthy[19]—the external drapery of the two are as wide as the pole—their hearts—perhaps—twins of the same blessed form and principles;—but for the rest of the Dramatis Personæ, you must strain hard, my friend, before you can twist them into likeness sufficient to warrant the censure of copying.—Parson Adams[20] is yet more distant—his chief feature is absence of thought—the world affords me many such instances—but in the course of my reading, I have not met with his likeness, except in mere goodness of heart—in that perhaps Jack M——may equal him—but then he is so confounded jingle-headed!—Read boy, read—give Tom Jones a second *fair* reading!—Fielding's wit is obvious—his humour poignant—dialogue just—and truly dramatic—colouring quite nature—and keeping chaste.—Sterne equals him in every thing, and in one thing excels him and all mankind—which is the distribution of his lights, which he has so artfully varied throughout his work, that the oftener they are examined, the more beautiful they appear.— They were two great masters, who painted for posterity—and, I prophesy, will charm to the end of the English speech.—If Sterne has had any one great master in his eye—it was Swift, his countryman—the first wit of this or any other nation;—but there is this grand difference between them— Swift excels in grave-faced irony—whilst Sterne lashes his whips with jolly

---

[18] Sancho is evidently responding to Meheux's criticisms regarding the literary merits of Laurence Sterne (see note 4, above), Henry Fielding (1707–1754), and Jonathan Swift (1667–1745).

[19] Uncle Toby, character in Sterne's *Tristram Shandy* (1759–1767) and Mr. Allworthy, character in Fielding's *History of Tom Jones* (1749).

[20] Parson Adams features in Fielding's *History and Adventures of Joseph Andrews* (1742).

laughter.—I could wish you to compare (after due attentive reading) Swift and Sterne—Milton and Young—Thomson and Akenside[21]—and then give your free opinion to yours ever,

I. Sancho.

I want a handful or two of good fresh peach leaves—contrive to send me them when opportunity serves—and word, at the first leisure period, how Miss *Anne Sister-like—George Grateful-look*—Mrs. &c. &c.—and how your worship's hip does.—You had set up my bristles in such guise—in attacking poor Sterne—that I had quite forgot to give you a flogging for your punning grocery epistle—but omittance is no quittance.—Swift and Sterne were different in this—Sterne was truly a noble philanthropist—Swift was rather cynical;—what Swift would fret and fume at—such as the petty accidental *sourings* and *bitters* in life's cup—you plainly may see, Sterne would laugh at—and parry off by a larger humanity, and regular good will to man. I know you will laugh at me—do—I am content;—if I am an enthusiast in any thing, it is in favor of my Sterne.

END OF THE FIRST VOLUME.

VOLUME 2, LETTER I.
To Mr. J—— W——E.[22]

1778.

YOUR good father insists on my scribbling a sheet of absurdities, and gives me a notable reason for it, that is, 'Jack will be pleased with it.'—Now be it known to you—I have a respect both for father and son—yea for the whole family, who are every soul (that I have the honour or pleasure to know any thing of) tinctured—and leavened with all the obsolete goodness of old times—so that a man runs some hazard in being seen in the W——e's society of being biassed to Christianity.—I never see your poor Father—but his eyes betray his feelings—for the hopeful youth in India—a tear of joy dancing upon the lids --- is a plaudit not to be equalled this side death!—See the effects of right-doing, my worthy

---

[21] John Milton (1608–1674), Edward Young (1683–1765), James Thomson (1700–1748), and Mark Akenside (1721–1770) figured at the top of most eighteenth-century lists of serious poets.

[22] Jack Wingrave, son to the bookseller John Wingrave (1729–1807), another of Sancho's correspondents.

friend --- continue in the tract of rectitude --- and despise poor paltry Europeans --- titled --- Nabobs. --- Read your Bible --- as day follows night, God's blessing follows virtue --- honour --- and riches bring up the rear --- and the end is peace. --- Courage, my boy --- I have done preaching. --- Old folks love to seem wise --- and if you are silly enough to correspond with grey hairs --- take the consequence. --- I have had the pleasure of reading most of your letters, through the kindness of your father. --- Youth is naturally prone to vanity --- such is the weakness of Human Nature, that pride has a fortress in the best of hearts --- I know no person that possesses a better than Johnny W——e --- but although flattery is poison to youth, yet truth obliges me to confess that your correspondence betrays no symptom of vanity—but teems with truths of an honest affection --- which merits praise --- and commands esteem.

In some one of your letters which I do not recollect --- you speak (with honest indignation) of the treachery and chicanery of the Natives*. --- My good friend, you should remember from whom they learnt those vices: --- the first christian visitors found them a simple, harmless people --- but the cursed avidity for wealth urged these first visitors (and all the succeeding ones) to such acts of deception --- and even wanton cruelty --- that the poor ignorant Natives soon learnt to turn the knavish --- and diabolical arts which they too soon imbibed --- upon their teachers.

I am sorry to observe that the practice of your country (which as a resident I love --- and for its freedom --- and for the many blessings I enjoy in it --- shall ever have my warmest wishes --- prayers --- and blessings); I say it is with reluctance, that I must observe your country's conduct has been uniformly wicked in the East—West-Indies—and even on the coast of Guinea.—The grand object of English navigators—indeed of all christian navigators—is money—money—money—for which I do not pretend to blame them—Commerce was meant by the goodness of the Deity to diffuse the various goods of the earth into every part—to unite mankind in

---

Nabobs: Europeans returned home with a large fortune made in India or elsewhere in the East.

Blacks: In eighteenth-century Britain, this term could refer to any dark-skinned people.

*Extracts of two letters from Mr. W——e to his Father, dated Bombay, 1776 and 1777.

"1776. I have introduced myself to Mr. G——, who behaved very friendly in giving me some advice, which was very necessary, as the inhabitants, who are chiefly Blacks, are a set of canting, deceitful people, and of whom one must have great caution."

"1777. I am now thoroughly convinced, that the account which Mr. G—— gave me of the natives of this country is just and true, that they are a set of deceitful people, and have not such a word as Gratitude in their language, neither do they know what it is—and as to their dealings in trade, they are like unto Jews." [Sancho's notes.]

the blessed chains of brotherly love—society—and mutual dependence:—the enlightened Christian should diffuse the riches of the Gospel of peace—with the commodities of his respective land—Commerce attended with strict honesty—and with Religion for its companion—would be a blessing to every shore it touched at.—In Africa, the poor wretched natives—blessed with the most fertile and luxuriant soil—are rendered so much the more miserable for what Providence meant as a blessing:—the Christians' abominable traffic for slaves—and the horrid cruelty and treachery of the petty Kings—encouraged by their Christian customers—who carry them strong liquors—to enflame their national madness—and powder—and bad fire-arms—to furnish them with the hellish means of killing and kidnapping.—But enough—it is a subject that sours my blood—and I am sure will not please the friendly bent of your social affections.—I mentioned these only to guard my friend against being too hasty in condemning the knavery of a people who bad as they may be—possibly—were made worse—by their Christian visitors.—Make human nature thy study—wherever thou residest—whatever the religion—or the complexion—study their hearts.—Simplicity, kindness, and charity be thy guide—with these even Savages will respect you—and God will bless you!

Your father—who sees every improvement of his boy with delight—observes that your hand-writing is much for the better—in truth, I think it as well as any modest man can wish:—if my long epistles do not frighten you—and I live till the return of next spring—perhaps I shall be enabled to judge how much you are improved since your last favour:—write me a deal about the natives—the soil and produce—the domestic and interior manners of the people—customs—prejudices—fashions—and follies.—Alas! we have plenty of the two last here—and what is worse, we have politics—and a detestable Brother's war[23]—where the right hand is hacking and hewing the left—whilst Angels weep at our madness—and Devils rejoice at the ruinous prospect.

Mr. R—— and the ladies are well.—Johnny R—— has favoured me with a long letter—he is now grown familiar with danger—and can bear the whistling of bullets—the cries and groans of the human species—the roll of drums—clangor of trumpets—shouts of combatants—and thunder of cannon—all these he can bear with soldier-like fortitude—with now and then a secret wish for the society of his London friends—in the sweet blessed security—of peace—and friendship.

---

[23] The United States War of Independence (1775–1783), viewed by Sancho (and others in Britain) as a civil war between the English colonists in North America and their fellow English at home.

This, young man, is my second letter—I have wrote till I am stupid, I perceive—I ought to have found it out two pages back.—Mrs. Sancho joins me in good wishes—I join her in the same—in which double sense believe me,

Yours, &c. &c.

I. Sancho.

VERY SHORT POSTSCRIPT.

It is with sincere pleasure I hear you have a lucrative establishment—which will enable you to appear and act with decency—your good sense will naturally lead you to proper œconomy—as distant from frigid parsimony, as from a heedless extravagancy—but as you may possibly have some time to spare upon your hands for necessary recreation—give me leave to obtrude my poor advice.—I have heard it more than once observed of fortunate adventurers—they have come home enriched in purse —but wretchedly barren in intellects—the mind, my dear Jack, wants food—as well as the stomach—why then should not one wish to increase in knowledge as well as money?—Young says—"Books are fair Virtue's advocates, and friends"[24]—now my advice is—to preserve about 20*l.* a year for two or three seasons—by which means you may gradually form a useful, elegant, little library—suppose now the first year you send the order—and the money to your father—for the following books—which I recommend from my own superficial knowledge as useful.—A man should know a little of Geography—History, nothing more useful, or pleasant.

Robertson's Charles the 5th, 4 vols.
Goldsmith's History of Greece, 2 vols.
Ditto, of Rome, 2 vols.
Ditto, of England, 4 vols.[25]

Two small volumes of Sermons useful—and very sensible—by one Mr. Williams,[26] a dissenting minister—which are as well as fifty—for I love not a multiplicity of doctrines—a few plain tenets—easy—simple—

---

[24]Edward Young, *Night Thoughts on Life, Death, and Immortality* (1742–1745), *Night VIII*, line 275, "books (fair Virtue's advocates)."

[25]William Robertson (1721–1793), *History of the Reign of Charles V* (1769), Oliver Goldsmith (c. 1730–1774), *Grecian History* (1774), *Roman History* (1769), and *History of England* (1764).

[26]Perhaps David Williams (1738–1816), *Sermons, Chiefly upon Religious Hypocrisy . . . in Two Volumes* (1774).

and directed to the heart—are better than volumes of controversial non-sense.—Spectators—Guardians—and Tatlers[27]—you have of course.— Young's Night-Thoughts—Milton—and Thomson's Seasons[28] were my summer companions—for near twenty years—they mended my heart— they improved my veneration to the Deity—and increased my love to my neighbours.

You have to thank God for strong natural parts—a feeling humane heart—you write with sense and judicious discernment—improve yourself, my dear Jack, that if it should please God to return you to your friends with the fortune of a man in upper rank, the embellishments of your mind may be ever considered as greatly superior to your riches—and only inferior to the goodness of your heart. I give you the above as a sketch— your father and other of your friends will improve upon it in the course of time—I do indeed judge that the above is enough at first—in conformity with the old adage——"A few Books and a few Friends, and those well chosen."

Adieu, Yours,
I. Sancho.

LETTER XLI.
To Mr. M———.[29]

October 5, 1779.

YOU mistake—I am neither sick—idle—nor forgetful—nor hurried—nor flurried—nor—lame—nor am I of a fickle mutable disposition.—No! I feel the life-sweetening affections—the swell of heart-animating ardor—the zeal of honest friendship—and what's more— I feel it for thee.—Now, Sir, what have you to say in humble vindication of your hasty conclusions? What, because I did not write to you on Monday last? but let a week pass without saying (what in truth I know not how to say, though I am now seriously set about it); in short, such hearts and minds (if there be many such, so much the better), such beings I say—as

---

flurried: fluttered.

[27] The *Tatler* (1709–1711), *Spectator* (1711–1712, 1714), and *Guardian* (1713) were all popular eighteenth-century periodicals associated with Joseph Addison (1672–1719) and Sir Richard Steele (1672–1729) and considered models for prose style.

[28] See notes 21 and 24, above; Thomson's *The Seasons* was published in parts from 1726 to 1730.

[29] John Meheux (see note 7, above).

the one I am now scribbling to—should make elections of wide different beings—than Blackamoors for their friends:—the reason is obvious—from Othello[30] to Sancho the big—we are either foolish—or mulish—all—all without a single exception.—Tell me, I pray you—and tell me truly—was there any Blackamoors in the Ark.—Pooh! why there now—I see you puzzled—well—well—be that as the learned shall hereafter decide.—I will defend and maintain my opinion—simply—I will do more—wager a crown upon it—nay, double that—and if my simple testimony faileth—Mrs. Sancho and the children five-deep will back me—that Noah,[31] during his pilgrimage in the blessed Ark—never with wife and six children set down to a feast upon a bit of finer—goodlier—fatter—sweeter—salter—well-fed pork; we eat like hogs.

When do your nobles intend coming home?—the evenings get long, and the damps of the park after sun-set—but a word to the wise.

Oh! I had like to have almost forgot—I owe you a dressing for your last letter—there were some saucy strokes of pride in it—the ebullitions of a high heart—and tenderly over-nice feelings—go to—what have I found you? My mind is not rightly at ease—or you should have it—and so you would not give me a line all the week—because—but what? I am to blame—a man in liquor—a man deprived of reason—and a man in love—should ever meet with pity and indulgence:—in the last class art thou!—nay, never blush—plain as the nose in thy face are the marks—refute it if you are able—dispute if you dare—for I have proofs—yea, proofs as undeniable as is the sincerity of the affection and zeal, with which thou art ever regarded by thy

Ignatius Sancho.

How doth the ladies—and Mr. M——? Mind, I care not about——so tell her, and lye.—You may tell George the same story—but I should like to hear something about you all.

Blackamoors: then a term for dark-skinned Africans.

[30] The title character of William Shakespeare's (1564–1616) *Othello, the Moor of Venice* (c. 1603) was one of the best-known African characters on the eighteenth-century stage.

[31] Sancho alludes here in a bantering way to theories that tried to account for the dark skin of sub-Saharan Africans through various interpretations of the story of Noah in Genesis.

LETTER LIX.
To —— Mr. S——.[32]

1780, January the 4th day.

My Dear Friend,

Y O U have here a kind of medley, a heterogeneous, ill-spelt, hetero-clite, (worse) excentric sort of a—a—; in short, it is a true Negroe calibash—of ill-sorted, undigested chaotic matter. What an excellent proem! what a delightful sample of the grand absurd!—Sir—dear Sir—as I have a soul to be saved (and why I should not—would puzzle a Dr. Price),[33] as I have a soul to be saved—I only meant to say about fifteen words to you—and the substance just this—to wish you a happy New-year—with the usual appendages—and a long et cætera of cardinal and heavenly blessings:—à propos, blessings—never more scanty—all beggars by Jove—not a shilling to be got in London;—if you are better off in the country, and can afford to remit me your little bill, I inclose it for that good end.—H—— is—but he can better tell you himself what he is; for in truth I do think he is in love, which puts the pretty G--- into my head—and she brings her father in view.—My love and respects to each.—Mrs. Sancho joins me; and the girls, her—and God keep you!

Yours sincerely,
I. Sancho.

LETTER LXVII.
To J—— S——, Esq.[34]

Charles Street, June 6, 1780.

Dear and Most Respected Sir,

I N the midst of the most cruel and ridiculous confusion—I am now set down to give you a very imperfect sketch of the maddest people—that the maddest times were ever plagued with.—The public prints have

---

calibash: calabash, a tropical gourd (or similar fruit) that can be hollowed out and used as a cooking vessel or container.

[32] William Stevenson (1741–1821), a bookseller and printer.

[33] Richard Price (1723–1791), well-known Dissenting minister and controversialist on religious and political issues.

[34] This letter and the two following are addressed to the banker John Spink (1729–1794). They recount Sancho's horrified observation of and disgusted reaction to the Gordon

informed you (without doubt) of last Friday's transactions; —the insanity of Ld G. G. and the worse than Negro barbarity of the populace;—the burnings and devastations of each night—you will also see in the prints:—this day, by consent, was set apart for the farther consideration of the wished-for repeal;—the people (who had their proper cue from his lordship) assembled by ten o'clock in the morning.—Lord N ——,[35] who had been up in council at home till four in the morning, got to the house before eleven, just a quarter of an hour before the associators reached Palace-yard:—but, I should tell you, in council there was a deputation from all parties;—the S —— party[36] were for prosecuting Ld G ——, and leaving him at large;—the At ——y G ——l laughed at the idea, and declared it was doing just nothing;—the M ——y were for his expulsion, and so dropping him gently into insignificancy;—that was thought wrong, as he would still be industrious in mischief;—the R ——m party,[37] I should suppose, you will think counselled best, which is, this day to expel him [from] the house—commit him to the Tower[38]—and then prosecute him at leisure—by which means he will lose the opportunity of getting a seat in the next parliament—and have decent leisure to repent him of the heavy evils he has occasioned.—There is at this present moment at least a hundred thousand poor, miserable, ragged rabble, from twelve to sixty years of age, with blue cockades in their hats—besides half as many women and children—

Riots, mob actions that swept through London and Westminster (then as now the location of Parliament) in early June 1780. Ignited by the politician Lord George Gordon (1751–1793), president of the Protestant Association to repeal the Catholic Relief Act of 1778, the turbulence began on June 2 as a mass demonstration to protest the minor concessions the act granted to Roman Catholics, then excluded from most civil rights. Gordon lost control of the mob, and the rioters began burning down Catholic chapels and residences and assaulting known or suspected Catholics (especially London's many Irish laborers) and Catholic sympathizers. By June 8, the rioters had been put down by thousands of armed troops, and the overall loss of life and property was unprecedented.

At ——y G ——l: Attorney General.

M ——y: Ministry.

cockade: ornament worn on one's hat, here to signify Protestant opposition to Catholic relief.

[35] Frederick, Lord North, prime minister from 1770 to 1782.

[36] The Shelburne party, reformist party led by William Petty, Lord Shelburne (1737–1805).

[37] The Rockingham party, opposition party led by Charles Watson-Wentworth, Lord Rockingham (1730–82).

[38] The Tower of London, long used as a prison (and place of execution) for political crimes.

all parading the streets—the bridge—the park—ready for any and every mischief.—Gracious God! what's the matter now? I was obliged to leave off—the shouts of the mob—the horrid clashing of swords—and the clutter of a multitude in swiftest motion—drew me to the door—when every one in the street was employed in shutting up shop.—It is now just five o'clock—the ballad-singers are exhausting their musical talents—with the downfall of Popery, S——h, and N——h.—Lord S——h[39] narrowly escaped with life about an hour since;—the mob seized his chariot going to the house, broke his glasses, and, in struggling to get his lordship out, they somehow have cut his face;—the guards flew to his assistance—the light-horse scowered the road, got his chariot, escorted him from the coffee-house, where he had fled for protection, to his carriage, and guarded him bleeding very fast home. This—this—is liberty! genuine British liberty!—This instant about two thousand liberty boys are swearing and swaggering by with large sticks—thus armed in hopes of meeting with the Irish chairmen and labourers—all the guards are out—and all the horse;—the poor fellows are just worn out for want of rest—having been on duty ever since Friday.—Thank heaven, it rains; may it increase, so as to send these deluded wretches safe to their homes, their families, and wives! About two this afternoon, a large party took it into their heads to visit the King and Queen, and entered the Park[40] for that purpose—but found the guard too numerous to be forced, and after some useless attempts gave it up.—It is reported, the house will either be prorogued, or parliament dissolved, this evening—as it is in vain to think of attending any business while this anarchy lasts.

I cannot but felicitate you, my good friend, upon the happy distance you are placed from our scene of confusion.—May foul Discord and her cursed train never nearer approach your blessed abode! Tell Mrs. S——, her good heart would ach, did she see the anxiety, the woe, in the faces of mothers, wives, and sweethearts, each equally anxious for the object of their wishes, the beloved of their hearts. Mrs. Sancho and self both cordially join in love

---

Popery: hostile term for Roman Catholicism.

glasses: carriage windows.

light-horse: mounted dragoon guards.

chairmen: carriers of sedan chairs.

[39] John Montagu, Earl of Sandwich (1718–1792), first lord of the Admiralty in Lord North's administration.

[40] St. James's Park, the promenade leading to the Queen's Palace (now called Buckingham Palace) and located only a few blocks from Sancho's grocery in Westminster.

and gratitude, and every good wish—crowned with the peace of God, which passeth all understanding, &c.

I am, dear Sir,

Yours ever by inclination,

Ign. Sancho.

POSTSCRIPT.

The Sardinian ambassador offered 500 guineas to the rabble, to save a painting of our Saviour from the flames, and 1000 guineas not to destroy an exceeding fine organ: the gentry told him, they would burn him if they could get at him, and destroyed the picture and organ directly.—I am not sorry I was born in Afric.—I shall tire you, I fear—and, if I cannot get a frank, make you pay dear for bad news.—There is about a thousand mad men, armed with clubs, bludgeons; and crows, just how set off for New-gate,[41] to liberate, they say, their honest comrades.—I wish they do not some of them lose their lives of liberty before morning. It is thought by many who discern deeply, that there is more at the bottom of this business than merely the repeal of an act—which has as yet produced no bad consequences, and perhaps never might.—I am forced to own, that I am for an universal toleration.[42] Let us convert by our example, and conquer by our meekness and brotherly love!

Eight o'clock. Lord G —— G —— has this moment announced to my Lords the mob—that the act shall be repealed this evening:—upon this, they gave a hundred cheers—took the horses from his hackney-coach—and rolled him full jollily away:—they are huzzaing now ready to crack their throats

Huzzah.

I am forced to conclude for want of room—the remainder in our next.

---

crows: crowbars.

[41] The rioters succeeded in destroying Newgate prison and freeing the prisoners there.

[42] That is, toleration of all religious groups; at this time, Dissenting (nonconformist) Protestants as well as Catholics and Jews were denied many civil rights.

LETTER LXVIII.
To J.—— S——, Esq.

Charles Street, June 9, 1780.

My Dear Sir,

GOVERNMENT is sunk in lethargic stupor—anarchy reigns—when I look back to the glorious time of a George II. and a Pitt's administration—[43] my heart sinks at the bitter contrast. We may now say of England, as was heretofore said of Great Babylon—"the beauty of the excellency of the Chaldees—is no more;"[44]—the Fleet Prison, the Marshalsea, King's-Bench, both Compters, Clerkenwell, and Tothill Fields, with Newgate, are all flung open;[45]—Newgate partly burned, and 300 felons from thence only let loose upon the world.—Lord M——'s house in town suffered martyrdom;[46] and his sweet box at Caen Wood escaped almost miraculously, for the mob had just arrived, and were beginning with it—when a strong detachment from the guards and light-horse came most critically to its rescue—the library, and, what is of more consequence, papers and deeds of vast value, were all cruelly consumed in the flames.—Ld. N——'s house was attacked; but they had previous notice, and were ready for them. The Bank, the Treasury, and thirty of the chief noblemen's houses, are doomed to suffer by the insurgents.—There were six of the rioters killed at Ld M——'s; and, what is remarkable, a daring chap escaped from Newgate, condemned to die this day, was the most active in mischief at Ld. M——'s, and was the first person shot by the soldier; so he found death a few hours sooner than if he had not been released.—The ministry have tried lenity, and have experienced its inutility; and martial law is this night to be declared.—If any body of people above ten in number are seen together, and refuse to disperse, they are to be fired at without any further ceremony—so we expect terrible work before morning;—the insurgents visited the Tower, but it would not do—they had better luck in the Artillery-ground, where they found and took to their use 500 stand of arms;

---

box: small country house.

[43] William Pitt "the elder" (1708–1778), prime minister under George II from 1756 to 1761 and from 1766 to 1768, a period of British imperial expansion.

[44] Isaiah 13:19.

[45] All prisons attacked by the Gordon rioters.

[46] William Murray, Lord Mansfield (1705–1793), who had supported the Catholic Relief Act.

a great error in city politics, not to have secured them first. —It is wonder-ful to hear the execrable nonsense that is industriously circulated amongst the credulous mob—who are told his M ——y regularly goes to mass at Ld. P ——re's[47] chaple—and they believe it, and that he pays out of his privy purse Peter-pence to Rome. Such is the temper of the times—from too re-laxed a government;—and a King and Queen on the throne who possess every virtue. May God in his mercy grant that the present scourge may op-erate to our repentance and amendment! that it may produce the fruits of better thinking, better doing, and in the end make us a wise, virtuous, and happy people!—I am, dear Sir, truly Mrs. S ——'s and your most grateful and obliged friend and servant,

I. Sancho.

The remainder in our next.

Half past nine o'clock.

King's-Bench prison is now in flames, and the prisoners at large; two fires in Holborn now burning.

LETTER LXIX.

June 9, 1780

Dear Sir,

HAPPILY for us the tumult begins to subside—last night much was threatened, but nothing done—except in the early part of the eve-ning, when about fourscore or an hundred of the reformers got decently knocked on the head;—they were half killed by Mr. Langdale's spirits[48]—so fell an easy conquest to the bayonet and but-end.—There is about fifty taken prisoners—and not a blue cockade to be seen:—the streets once more wear the face of peace—and men seem once more to resume their accustomed employments;—the greatest losses have fallen

---

his M ——y: his Majesty (the King).

privy purse: discretionary funds from public revenue.

Peter-pence: or Peter's pence, an annual tribute of a penny formerly paid by English householders (in pre-Reformation days) to the pope at Rome.

[47] Robert Petre, Baron Petre (1742–1801), a prominent Catholic aristocrat.

[48] The large distillery owned by the Catholic gin merchant Thomas Langdale was pil-laged and destroyed by the rioters.

upon the great distiller near Holborn-bridge, and Lord M——; the former, alas! has lost his whole fortune;—the latter, the greatest and best collection of manuscript writings, with one of the finest libraries in the kingdom.—Shall we call it a judgement?—or what shall we call it? The thunder of their vengeance has fallen upon gin and law—the two most inflammatory things in the Christian world.—We have a Coxheath and Warley of our own[49]; Hyde Park has a grand encampment, with artillery, Park, &c. &c. St. James's Park has ditto—upon a smaller scale. The Parks, and our West end of the town, exhibit the features of French government.[50] This minute, thank God! this moment Lord G. G. is taken. Sir F. Molineux[51] has him safe at the horse-guards. Bravo! he is now going in state in an old hackney-coach, escorted by a regiment of militia and troop of light horse to his apartments in the Tower.

"Off with his head—so much—for Buckingham."[52]

We have taken this day numbers of the poor wretches, in so much we know not where to place them. Blessed be the Lord! we trust this affair is pretty well concluded.—If any thing transpires worth your notice—you shall hear from

Your much obliged, &c. &c.

I. Sancho.

Best regards attend Mrs. S——; his lordship was taken at five o'clock this evening—betts run fifteen to five Lord G—— G——is hanged in eight days:—he wished much to speak to his Majesty on Wednesday, but was of course refused.

---

[49] Military camps established in 1778 after France allied itself with the rebellious American colonies during the War of Independence.

[50] France was associated with political tyranny and absolutist rule in the mind of the British public at the time.

[51] Sir Francis Molyneux (c. 1736–1812).

[52] A line from Shakespeare's *Richard III* (c. 1591) as modified in the 1700 adaptation by Colley Cibber (1671–1757).

LETTER XCII.
To J——— S——— Esq.[53]

Dec. 7, 1780.

Dear Sir,

I am doubly and trebly happy, that I can in some measure remove the anxiety of the best couple in the universe. I set aside all thanks—for were I to enter into the feelings of my heart for the past and present, I should fill the sheet: but you would not be pleased.—In good truth, I have been exceeding ill—my breath grew worse—and the dropsy made large strides.[54]—I left off medicine by consent for four or five days, swelled immoderately:—the good Dr. N———f———d eighty miles distant—and Dr. J———bb heartily puzzled through the darkness of his patient.[55]—I began to feel alarm—when, looking into your letter, I found a Dr. S———th recommended by yourself. I enquired—his character is great—but for lungs and dropsy, Sir John E———t, physician extraordinary, and ordinary to his Majesty, is reckoned the first.[56] I applied to him on Sunday morning—he received me like Dr. N———f———d;—I have faith in him.—My poor belly is so distended, that I write with pain—I hope next week to write with more ease. My dutiful respects await Mrs. S——— and self, to which Mrs. Sancho begs to be joined by her loving husband, and

Your most grateful friend,
Sancho.

Mr. Sancho died December 14.

FINIS.

---

[53] John Spink.

[54] Dropsy (edema) is a morbid condition marked by abnormal swelling from the accumulation of watery fluid in the bodily tissues and cavities, symptomatic of kidney and heart diseases and probably related (like his gout) to Sancho's obesity.

[55] Sancho's physicians included a Dr. William Norford and Sir Richard Jebb, formerly attached to Westminster Hospital and, in 1780, physician to the Prince of Wales.

[56] The identity of Dr. S———th (Smith?) is uncertain; Sir John Elliot was (like Dr. Jebb) a physician to the Prince of Wales at this time.

A Narrative of the Most Remarkable Particulars in the Life of James Albert Ukawsaw Gronniosaw, An African Prince, As Related by Himself

Ukawsaw Gronniosaw

Our knowledge of the life of Ukawsaw Gronniosaw (born c. 1710), also called James Albert, comes almost entirely from his own narrative, which inaugurates the autobiographical tradition in Black British writing. The precise dating of the narrative has eluded scholars, but 1772 has been suggested as the best approximation so far (Carretta 1996, 52–53). Although he could read Dutch, Gronniosaw apparently could neither read nor write English and dictated his story to the "young LADY" of Leominster mentioned in the preface. The lady in question has recently been identified as Hannah More (1745–1833), the prolific writer, abolitionist, conservative social reformer, and Evangelical philanthropist. The connection to More, however, rests on a single footnote ("Supposed to be Miss HANNAH MORE") included in the 1809 edition, published in Salem, New York, under the title *The Black Prince* (Potkay and Burr 1995, 53). This may well be a mistaken supposition on the part of the 1809 American editor, however, prompted by the coincidence that More had published an unrelated pamphlet under the same title (*The Black Prince*, c. 1799) in her Cheap Repository Tracts series. All that remains certain is that Gronniosaw's narrative shows up in advertisements by 1772; for the rest, we must rely on the narrative that follows and the brief preface by the clergyman Walter Shirley.

According to his own account, then, Gronniosaw was born sometime around 1710 in Borno (Bornu), a region in the northeast corner of present-day Nigeria. The grandson of the region's king, Gronniosaw recalls feeling a strong mutual bond with his mother and an urgent desire to know more about the world's creator. This early religious sense provides the foundation, at least in retrospect, for Gronniosaw's eventual Christian conversion. As an adolescent, he was tricked by an African merchant (and, it turns out, slave dealer) into making a long voyage on foot to the Gold Coast (present-day Ghana), where he was sold to the captain of a Dutch slaving ship, who sold him in turn upon reaching Barbados to a North American of Dutch descent. His new master, Vanhorn, brought Gronniosaw to New York City, where he eventually met the Reformed Dutch minister Theodorus Jacobus Frelinghuysen. Frelinghuysen bought Gronniosaw and took him to New Jersey, where he undertook Gronniosaw's Christian conversion and freed him at about the time of his own death (c. 1747). Gronniosaw worked for a time for various members of Frelinghuysen's family before setting out as a privateer in the Seven Years' War (1756–1763), enlisting in a British infantry regiment, assisting at the sieges of Martinique and Havana (1762), and finally realizing his hope of sailing to England. He lived in the rough naval town of Portsmouth before going to London, where he came under the protection of the celebrated Methodist preacher George Whitefield. After a visit to Holland, Gronniosaw returned to London to marry Betty, a weaver he met through their common religious community. With Betty, he began a family and a life of sometimes abject poverty that took them from place to place in England seeking work and food. Gronniosaw is last glimpsed, according to Shirley's preface, at about sixty years of age, established in the English midlands town of Kidderminster, and having his narrative published in hopes that the profits from its sale might help his "distressed Family" (page 51).

Gronniosaw's slender volume, cited by Cugoano and certainly known to Cugoano's friend Equiano as well, inaugurates a number of themes that will run throughout the British and early American slave narratives to come. As will both Cugoano and Equiano after him, Gronniosaw lays claim to aristocratic birth, placing himself in the "royal slave" tradition that had already been well established by fictional works such as Aphra Behn's *Oroonoko* (1688). His captivity and travels lead him through elaborate variations on the triangular movement of the transatlantic slave trade, from West Africa to various locations in the Americas—ranging from New York City to St. Domingue—to England and the Netherlands (via Spain). Gronniosaw demonstrates how the structure of the Protestant conversion narrative can lend itself to a story of enslavement and manumission—and how the religious dimensions of that story, whether entirely sincere, exaggerated to please a patron or publisher, or even augmented by an amanuensis or editor, can sometimes take over. Perhaps the most celebrated motif established by Gronniosaw's *Narrative* is the "talking book," underscoring not only the trauma of cultural dislocation but the importance of literacy within the Black British tradition (Gates 1988, 127–169). No less striking, however, is Gronniosaw's stark portrayal of the grinding poverty that he would have shared with many other freed slaves in the cities and towns of eighteenth-century Britain.

A
NARRATIVE
OF THE
Most Remarkable Particulars
In the LIFE of
James Albert Ukawsaw Gronniosaw,
An AFRICAN PRINCE,
As related by HIMSELF.

I will bring the Blind by a Way that they know not,
I will lead them in Paths that they have not known: I
will make Darkness Light before them and crooked Things
straight. These Things will I do unto them and not
forsake them. Isa. xlii. 16.

BATH:
Printed by W. GYE in Westgate-Street: and
sold by T. MILLS, Bookseller, in King's-Mead
Square. Price Six-PENCE.

TO THE
RIGHT HONOURABLE
The *Countess* of HUNTINGDON,[1]
THIS
NARRATIVE
Of my *LIFE,*
And of GOD's wonderful Dealings
with me, is,
(Through Her LADYSHIP's Permission)
Most Humbly Dedicated,
By her LADYSHIP'S
Most obliged
And obedient Servant,
JAMES ALBERT.

---

[1] Selina Hastings, the Countess of Huntingdon (1707–1791), a prominent patron of the early Methodist movement, took a special interest in assisting black slaves and former slaves, including Phillis Wheatley and Olaudah Equiano.

THE PREFACE
To the Reader.

THIS *Account of the Life and spiritual Experience of JAMES ALBERT was taken from his own Mouth and committed to Paper by the elegant Pen of a young LADY of the Town of LEOMINSTER, for her own private Satisfaction, and without any Intention at first that it should be made public.[2] But she has now been prevail'd on to commit it to the Press, both with a view to serve ALBERT and his distressed Family, who have the sole Profits arising from the Sale of it; and likewise as it is apprehended, this little History contains Matter well worthy the Notice and Attention of every Christian Reader.*

Perhaps we have here in some Degree a Solution of that Question that has perplex'd the Minds of so many serious Persons, viz. In what Manner will God deal with those benighted Parts of the World where the Gospel of Jesus Christ hath never reach'd? Now it appears from the Experience of this remarkable Person, that God does not save without the Knowledge of the Truth; but, with Respect to those whom he hath fore-known, though born under every outward Disadvantage, and in Regions of the grossest Darkness and Ignorance, he most amazingly acts upon and influences their Minds, and in the Course of wisely and most wonderfully appointed Providences, he brings them to the Means of spiritual Information, gradually opens to their View the Light of his Truth, and gives them full Possession and Enjoyment of the inestimable Blessings of his Gospel. Who can doubt but that the Suggestion so forcibly press'd upon the Mind of ALBERT (when a Boy) that there was a Being superior to the Sun, Moon, and Stars (the Objects of African Idolatry) came from the Father of Lights, and was, with Respect to him, the First-Fruit of the Display of Gospel-Glory? His long and perilous Journey to the Coast of Guinea,[3] where he was sold for a Slave, and so brought into a Christian Land; shall we consider this as the alone Effect of a curious and inquisitive Disposition? Shall we in accounting for it refer to nothing higher than mere Chance and accidental Circumstances? Whatever Infidels and Deists may think; I trust the Christian Reader will easily discern an All-wise and Omnipotent Appointment and

---

From Ukawsaw Gronniosaw, *A Narrative of the Most Remarkable Particulars in the Life of James Albert Ukawsaw Gronniosaw, An African Prince, As Related by Himself* (Bath: Gye and Mills, [1772]).

viz.: namely.

[2] The "young lady" has sometimes been identified, on slight evidence, with Hannah More (1745–1833), who spent her youth in Bristol, not Leominster (see page 148).

[3] Guinea then referred to a large tract of the West African coastal region, from present-day Senegal to as far south as Angola.

Direction in these Movements. He belong'd to the Redeemer of lost Sinners; he was the Purchase of his Cross; and therefore the Lord undertook to bring him by a Way that he knew not, out of Darkness into his marvellous Light, that he might lead him to a saving Heart-Acquaintance and Union with the triune God in Christ reconciling the World unto himself; and not imputing their Trespasses. As his Call was very extraordinary, so there are certain Particulars exceedingly remarkable in his Experience. God has put singular Honour upon him in the Exercise of his Faith and Patience, which in the most distressing and pitiable Trials and Calamities have been found to the Praise and Glory of God. How deeply must it affect a tender Heart, not only to be reduc'd to the last Extremity himself, but to have his Wife and Children perishing for Want before his Eyes! Yet his Faith did not fail him; he put his Trust in the Lord, and he was delivered. And at this Instant, though born in an exalted Station of Life, and now under the Pressure of various afflicting Providences, I am persuaded (for I know the Man) he would rather embrace the Dung-hill, having Christ in his Heart, than give up his spiritual Possessions and Enjoyment, to fill the Throne of Princes. It perhaps may not be amiss to observe that JAMES ALBERT *left his native Country, (as near as I can guess from certain Circumstances) when he was about 15 Years old. He now appears to be turn'd of Sixty; has a good natural Understanding; is well acquainted with the Scriptures, and the Things of God, has an amiable and tender Disposition, and his Character can be well attested not only at Kidderminster, the Place of his Residence but likewise by many creditable Persons in London and other Places. Reader, recommending this Narrative to your perusal, and him who is the Subject of it to your charitable Regard,*

I am your faithful and obedient Servant,
For Christ's Sake,

W. Shirley.[4]

---

triune God in Christ: the Christian Trinity.

[4]Walter Shirley (1725–1786), clergyman and cousin to the Countess of Huntingdon.

An Account of James Albert, &c.

I was born in the City BOURNOU;[5] my mother was the eldest daughter of the reigning King of ZAARA,[6] of which BOURNOU is the chief City. I was the youngest of six children, and particularly loved by my mother, and my grand-father almost doated on me. I had, from my infancy, a curious turn of mind; was more grave and reserved in my disposition than either of my brothers and sisters. I often teazed them with questions they could not answer: for which reason they disliked me, as they supposed that I was either foolish, or insane. 'Twas certain that I was, at times, very unhappy in myself: it being strongly impressed on my mind that there was some GREAT MAN of power which resided above the sun, moon and stars, the objects of our worship. My dear indulgent mother would bear more with me than any of my friends beside.—I often raised my hand to heaven, and asked her who lived there? was much dissatisfied when she told me the sun, moon and stars, being persuaded, in my own mind, that there must be some SUPERIOR POWER.— I was frequently lost in wonder at the works of the Creation: was afraid and uneasy and restless, but could not tell for what. I wanted to be informed of things that no person could tell me; and was always dissatisfied.—These wonderful impressions begun in my childhood, and followed me continually 'till I left my parents, which affords me matter of admiration and thankfulness.

To this moment I grew more and more uneasy every day, in so much that one saturday, (which is the day on which we keep our sabbath) I laboured under anxieties and fears that cannot be expressed; and, what is more extraordinary, I could not give a reason for it.—I rose, as our custom is, about three o'clock, (as we are oblig'd to be at our place of worship an hour before the sun rise) we say nothing in our worship, but continue on our knees with our hands held up, observing a strict silence 'till the sun is at a certain height, which I suppose to be about 10 or 11 o'clock in England: when, at a certain sign made by the priest, we get up (our duty being over) and disperse to our different houses.—Our place of meeting is under a

---

sabbath: day of rest.

[5] Bornu (or Borno), a region bordering on Lake Chad in the northeast corner of modern Nigeria and site of an African empire that reached its height of power in the fifteenth century.

[6] Zaara would usually connote Sahara, that is, the Saharan desert region in northern Africa; perhaps, here, it is meant to indicate a large expanse of northwest Africa.

large palm tree; we divide ourselves into many congregations; as it is impossible for the same tree to cover the inhabitants of the whole City, though they are extreamly large, high and majestic; the beauty and usefulness of them are not to be described; they supply the inhabitants of the country with meat, drink and clothes;* the body of the palm tree is very large; at a certain season of the year they tap it, and bring vessels to receive the wine, of which they draw great quantities, the quality of which is very delicious: the leaves of this tree are of a silky nature; they are large and soft; when they are dried and pulled to pieces it has much the same appearance as the English flax, and the inhabitants of BOURNOU manufacture it for cloathing &c. This tree likewise produces a plant or substance which has the appearance of a cabbage, and very like it, in taste almost the same: it grows between the branches. Also the palm tree produces a nut, something like a cocoa, which contains a kernel, in which is a large quantity of milk, very pleasant to the taste: the shell is of a hard substance, and of a very beautiful appearance, and serves for basons, bowls, &c.

I hope this digression will be forgiven. — I was going to observe that after the duty of our sabbath was over (on the day in which I was more distressed and afflicted than ever) we were all on our way home as usual, when a remarkable black cloud arose and covered the sun; then followed very heavy rain and thunder more dreadful than ever I had heard; the heav'ns roared, and the earth trembled at it: I was highly affected and cast down; in so much that I wept sadly, and could not follow my relations and friends home. — I was obliged to stop and felt as if my legs were tied, they seemed to shake under me: so I stood still, being in great fear of the MAN of POWER that I was persuaded in myself, lived above. One of my young companions (who entertained a particular friendship for me and I for him) came back to see for me: he asked me why I stood still in such very hard rain? I only said to him that my legs were weak, and I could not come faster: he was much affected to see me cry, and took me by the hand, and said he would lead me home, which he did. My mother was greatly alarmed at my tarrying out in such terrible weather; she asked me many questions, such as, what I did so for, and if I was well? My dear mother says I, pray tell me who is the GREAT MAN of POWER that makes the thunder? She said, there was no power but the sun, moon and stars; that they made all our country. — I then enquired how all our people came? She answered me, from one another; and so carried me to many generations back. — Then says I, who

---

cast down: downcast, depressed.

*It is generally received opinion, in *England,* that the natives of *Africa* go entirely unclothed; but this supposition is very unjust: they have a kind of dress so as to appear decent, though it is very slight and thin. [Gronniosaw's note.]

made the *First Man?* and who made the first Cow, and the first Lyon, and where does the fly come from, as no one can make him? My mother seemed in great trouble; she was apprehensive that my senses were impaired, or that I was foolish. My father came in, and seeing her in grief asked the cause, but when she related our conversation to him, he was exceedingly angry with me, and told me he would punish me severely if ever I was so troublesome again; so that I resolved never to say any thing more to him. But I grew very unhappy in myself; my relations and acquaintance endeavoured by all the means they could think on, to divert me, by taking me to ride upon goats, (which is much the custom of our country) and to shoot with a bow and arrow; but I experienced no satisfaction at all in any of these things; nor could I be easy by any means whatever: my parents were very unhappy to see me so dejected and melancholy.

About this time there came a merchant from the *Gold Coast* (the third city in GUINEA) he traded with the inhabitants of our country in ivory &c.[7] he took great notice of my unhappy situation, and enquired into the cause; he expressed vast concern for me, and said, if my parents would part with me for a little while, and let him take me home with him, it would be of more service to me than any thing they could do for me. —He told me that if I would go with him I should see houses with wings to them walk upon the water, and should also see the white folks; and that he had many sons of my age, which should be my companions; and he added to all this that he would bring me safe back again soon. —I was highly pleased with the account of this strange place, and was very desirous of going. —I seemed sensible of a secret impulse upon my mind which I could not resist that seemed to tell me I must go. When my dear mother saw that I was willing to leave them, she spoke to my father and grandfather and the rest of my relations, who all agreed that I should accompany the merchant to the Gold-Coast. I was the more willing as my brothers and sisters despised me, and looked on me with contempt on the account of my unhappy disposition; and even my servants slighted me, and disregarded all I said to them. I had one sister who was always exceeding fond of me, and I loved her entirely; her name was LOGWY, she was quite white, and fair, with fine light hair though my father and mother were black.[8] —I was truly concerned to leave my beloved sister, and she cry'd most sadly to part with me, wringing her hands, and discovered every sign of grief that can be imagined. Indeed if I could have known when I left my friends and country that I should

---

[7] The Gold Coast region on the coast of West Africa (present-day Ghana) was a major center for trade between Africa and Europe, including the trade in slaves.

[8] Gronniosaw's sister seems to have been an albino.

never return to them again my misery on that occasion would have been inexpressible. All my relations were sorry to part with me; my dear mother came with me upon a camel more than three hundred miles, the first of our journey lay chiefly through woods: at night we secured ourselves from the wild beasts by making fires all around us; we and our camels kept within the circle, or we must have been torn to pieces by the Lyons, and other wild creatures, that roared terribly as soon as night came on, and continued to do so 'till morning.—There can be little said in favour of the country through which we passed; only a valley of marble that we came through which is unspeakably beautiful.—On each side of this valley are exceedingly high and almost inaccessible mountains—Some of these pieces of marble are of prodigious length and breadth but of different sizes and colour, and shaped in a variety of forms, in a wonderful manner.—It is most of it veined with gold mixed with striking and beautiful colours; so that when the sun darts upon it, it is as pleasing a sight as can be imagined.—The merchant that brought me from BOURNOU, was in partnership with another gentleman who accompanied us; he was very unwilling that he should take me from home, as, he said, he foresaw many difficulties that would attend my going with them.—He endeavoured to prevail on the merchant to throw me into a very deep pit that was in the valley, but he refused to listen to him, and said, he was resolved to take care of me: but the other was greatly dissatisfied; and when we came to a river, which we were obliged to pass through, he purpos'd throwing me in and drowning me; but the Merchant would not consent to it, so that I was preserv'd.

We travel'd 'till about four o'clock every day, and then began to make preparations for night, by cutting down large quantities of wood, to make fires to preserve us from the wild beasts.—I had a very unhappy and discontented journey, being in continual fear that the people I was with would murder me. I often reflected with extreme regret on the kind friends I had left, and the idea of my dear mother frequently drew tears from my eyes.— I cannot recollect how long we were in going from BOURNOU to the GOLD COAST; but as there is no shipping nearer to BOURNOU than that City, it was tedious in travelling so far by land, being upwards of a thousand miles.—I was heartily rejoic'd when we arriv'd at the end of our journey: I now vainly imagin'd that all my troubles and inquietudes would terminate here; but could I have looked into futurity, I should have perceiv'd that I had much more to suffer than I had before experienc'd, and that they had as yet but barely commenc'd.

I was now more than a thousand miles from home, without a friend or any means to procure one. Soon after I came to the merchant's house I heard the drums beat remarkably loud, and the trumpets blow—the persons accustom'd to this employ, are oblig'd to go upon a very high structure appointed for that purpose, that the sound might be heard at a great distance: They are higher than the steeples are in England. I was mightily pleas'd with sounds so entirely new to me, and was very inquisitive to know the cause of this rejoicing, and ask'd many questions concerning it: I was answer'd that it was meant as a compliment to me, because I was Grandson to the King of BOURNOU.

This account gave me a secret pleasure; but I was not suffer'd long to enjoy this satisfaction, for in the evening of the same day two of the merchant's sons (boys about my own age) came running to me, and told me, that the next day I was to die, for the King intended to behead me. —I reply'd that I was sure it could not be true, for that I came there to play with them, and to see houses walk upon the water with wings to them, and the white folks; but I was soon inform'd that their King imagined that I was sent by my father as a spy, and would make such discoveries at my return home that would enable them to make war with the greater advantage to ourselves; and for these reasons he had resolved I should never return to my native country. —When I heard this I suffered misery that cannot be described. —I wished a thousand times that I had never left my friends and country. —But still the ALMIGHTY was pleased to work miracles for me.

The morning I was to die, I was washed and all my gold ornaments made bright and shining, and then carried to the palace, where the King was to behead me himself (as is the custom of the place). —He was seated upon a throne at the top of an exceeding large yard, or court, which you must go through to enter the palace, it is as wide and spacious as a large field in England. —I had a lane of life-guards to go through. —I guessed it to be about three hundred paces.

I was conducted by my friend, the merchant, about half way up; then he durst proceed no further: I went up to the KING alone —I went with an undaunted courage, and it pleased GOD to melt the heart of the King, who sat with his scymitar in his hand ready to behead me; yet, being himself so affected, he dropped it out of his hand, and took me upon his knee and wept over me. I put my right hand round his neck, and prest him to my heart. — He sat me down and blest me; and added that he would not kill me, and that I should not go home, but be sold for a slave, so then I was conducted back again to the merchant's house.

The next day he took me on board a French brig; but the Captain did not chuse to buy me: he said I was too small; so the merchant took me home with him again.

---

scymitar: scimitar, curved saber.
brig: brigantine, a two-masted ship.

The partner, whom I have spoken of as my enemy, was very angry to see me return, and again purposed putting an end to my life; for he represented to the other, that I should bring them into troubles and difficulties, and that I was so little that no person would buy me.

The merchant's resolution began to waver, and I was indeed afraid that I should be put to death: but however he said he would try me once more.

A few days after a Dutch ship came into the harbour, and they carried me on board, in hopes that the Captain would purchase me.—As they went, I heard them agree, that, if they could not sell me *then*, they would throw me overboard.—I was in extreme agonies when I heard this; and as soon as ever I saw the Dutch Captain, I ran to him, and put my arms round him, and said, "father, save me." (For I knew that if he did not buy me, I should be treated very ill, or, possibly, murdered.) And though he did not understand my language, yet it pleased the ALMIGHTY to influence him in my behalf, and he bought me *for two yards of check* which is of more value *there*, than in England.

When I left my dear mother I had a large quantity of gold about me, as is the custom of our country, it was made into rings, and they were linked into one another, and formed into a kind of chain, and so put round my neck, and arms and legs, and a large piece hanging at one ear almost in the shape of a pear. I found all this troublesome, and was glad when my new Master took it from me—I was now washed, and clothed in the Dutch or English manner.—My master grew very fond of me, and I loved him exceedingly. I watched every look, was always ready when he wanted me, and endeavoured to convince him, by every action, that my only pleasure was to serve him well.—I have since thought that he must have been a serious man. His actions corresponded very well with such a character.—He used to read prayers in public to the ship's crew every Sabbath day; and when first I saw him read, I was never so surprised in my whole life as when I saw the book talk to my master; for I thought it did, as I observed him to look upon it, and move his lips.—I wished it would do so to me.—As soon as my master had done reading I follow'd him to the place where he put the book, being mightily delighted with it, and when nobody saw me, I open'd it and put my ear down close upon it, in great hope that it wou'd say something to me; but was very sorry and greatly disappointed when I found it would not speak, this thought immediately presented itself to me, that every body and every thing despis'd me because I was black.

---

check: cloth woven with a checkerboard pattern.

I was exceedingly sea-sick at first; but when I became more accustom'd to the sea, it wore off. — My master's ship was bound for Barbadoes.[9] When we came there, he thought fit to speak of me to several gentlemen of his acquaintance, and one of them exprest a particular desire to see me. — He had a great mind to buy me; but the Captain could not immediately be prevail'd on to part with me; but however, as the gentleman seem'd very solicitous, he at length let me go, and I was sold for fifty dollars (*four and sixpenny-pieces in English*). My new master's name was Vanhorn, a young Gentleman; his home was in New-England in the City of New-York;[10] to which place he took me with him. He dress'd me in his livery, and was very good to me. My chief business was to wait at table, and tea, and clean knives, and I had a very easy place; but the servants us'd to curse and swear surprizingly; which I learnt faster than any thing, 'twas almost the first English I could speak. If any of them affronted me, I was sure to call upon God to damn them immediately; but I was broke of it all at once, occasioned by the correction of an old black servant that liv'd in the family — One day I had just clean'd the knives for dinner, when one of the maids took one to cut bread and butter with; I was very angry with her, and called upon God to damn her; when this old black man told me I must not say so. I ask'd him why? He replied there was a wicked man call'd the Devil, that liv'd in hell, and would take all that said these words, and put them in the fire and burn them. — This terrified me greatly, and I was entirely broke of swearing. — Soon after this, as I was placing the china for tea, my mistress came into the room just as the maid had been cleaning it; the girl had unfortunately sprinkled the wainscot with the mop; at which my mistress was angry; the girl very foolishly answer'd her again, which made her worse, and she call'd upon God to damn her. — I was vastly concern'd to hear this, as she was a fine young lady, and very good to me, insomuch that I could not help speaking to her, "Madam, says I, you must not say so," Why, says she? Because there is a black man call'd the Devil that lives in hell, and he will put you in the fire and burn you, and I shall be very sorry for that. Who told you this replied my lady. Old Ned, says I. Very well was all her answer; but she told my master of it, and he order'd that old Ned should be tyed up and whipp'd, and was never suffer'd to come into the kitchen with the rest of the servants afterwards. — My mistress was not angry with me, but rather diverted with my simplicity and, by way of talk, she repeated what I had

---

[9] Barbados, an island in the Caribbean and then part of the British West Indies.

[10] New York City, formerly a Dutch possession but at this time a trading center in Britain's North American colony of New York, maintaining a good deal of its Dutch heritage.

said, to many of her acquaintance that visited her; among the rest, Mr. Freelandhouse,[11] a very gracious, good Minister, heard it, and he took a great deal of notice of me, and desired my master to part with me to him. He would not hear of it at first, but, being greatly persuaded, he let me go, and Mr. Freelandhouse gave £50. for me. —He took me home with him, and made me kneel down, and put my two hands together, and pray'd for me, and every night and morning he did the same. —I could not make out what it was for, nor the meaning of it, nor what they spoke to when they talk'd —I thought it comical, but I lik'd it very well. —After I had been a little while with my new master I grew more familiar, and ask'd him the meaning of prayer. (I could hardly speak english to be understood). He took great pains with me, and made me understand that he pray'd to God, who liv'd in Heaven; that He was my Father and BEST Friend. —I told him that this must be a mistake; that *my* father liv'd at BOURNOU, and I wanted very much to see him, and likewise my dear mother, and sister, and I wish'd he would be so good as to send me home to them; and I added, all I could think of to induce him to convey me back. I appeared in great trouble, and my good master was so much affected that the tears ran down his face. He told me that God was a GREAT and GOOD SPIRIT, that He created all the world, and every person and thing in it, in Ethiopia, Africa, and America, and every where. I was delighted when I heard this: There, says I, I always thought so when I liv'd at home! Now if I had wings like an Eagle I would fly to tell my dear mother that God is greater than the sun, moon, and stars; and that they were made by Him.

I was exceedingly pleas'd with this information of my master's, because it corresponded so well with my own opinion; I thought now if I could but get home, I should be wiser than all my country-folks, my grandfather, or father, or mother, or any of them —But though I was somewhat enlighten'd by this information of my master's, yet, I had no other knowledge of God but that He was a GOOD SPIRIT, and created every body, and every thing— I never was sensible in myself, nor had any one ever told me, that He would punish the wicked, and love the just. I was only glad that I had been told there was a God because I had always thought so.

My dear kind master grew very fond of me, as was his Lady; she put me to School, but I was uneasy at that, and did not like to go; but my master and mistress requested me to learn in the gentlest terms, and persuaded me to attend my school without any anger at all; that, at last, I came to like it better, and learnt to read pretty well. My schoolmaster was a good man, his

---

[11]Theodorus Jacobus Frelinghuysen (1691–c. 1748), an evangelical minister of the Reformed Dutch church in colonial New Jersey.

name was Vanosdore,[12] and very indulgent to me. — I was in this state when, one sunday, I heard my master preach from these words out of the Revelations, chap. i. v. 7. "*Behold, He cometh in the clouds and every eye shall see him and they that pierc'd Him.*" These words affected me excessively; I was in great agonies because I thought my master directed them to me only; and, I fancied, that he observ'd me with unusual earnestness — I was farther confirm'd in this belief as I look'd round the church, and could see no one person beside myself in such grief and distress as I was; I began to think that my master hated me, and was very desirous to go home, to my own country; for I thought that if God did come (as he said) He would be sure to be most angry with *me,* as I did not know what He was, nor had ever heard of him before.

I went home in great trouble, but said nothing to any body. — I was somewhat afraid of my master; I thought he disliked me. — The next text I heard him preach from was, Heb. xii. 14. "*follow peace with all men, and holiness, without which no man shall see the LORD.*" he preached the law so severely, that it made me tremble. — he said, that GOD would judge the whole world; Ethiopia, Asia, and Africa, and every where. — I was now excessively perplexed, and undetermined what to do; as I had now reason to believe my situation would be equally bad to go, as to stay. — I kept these thoughts to myself, and said nothing to any person whatever.

I should have complained to my good mistress of this great trouble of mind, but she had been a little strange to me for several days before this happened, occasioned by a story told of me by one of the maids. The servants were all jealous, and envied me the regard, and favour shewn me by my master and mistress; and the Devil being always ready, and diligent in wickedness, had influenced this girl, to make a lye on me. — This happened about hay-harvest, and one day when I was unloading the waggon to put the hay into the barn, she watched an opportunity, in my absence, to take the fork out of the stick, and hide it: when I came again to my work, and could not find it, I was a good deal vexed, but I concluded it was dropt somewhere among the hay; so I went and bought another with my own money: when the girl saw that I had another, she was so malicious that she told my mistress I was very unfaithful, and not the person she took me for; and that she knew, I had, without my master's permission, order'd many things in his name, that he must pay for; and as a proof of my carelessness produc'd the fork she had taken out of the stick, and said, she had found it out of doors — My Lady, not knowing the truth of these things, was a little

---

make a lye on: tell a lie about.

[12]Most likely Peter Van Arsdalen, one of Frelinghuysen's assistants.

shy to me, till she mention'd it, and then I soon cleared myself, and convinc'd her that these accusations were false.

I continued in a most unhappy state for many days. My good mistress insisted on knowing what was the matter. When I made known my situation she gave me John Bunyan on the holy war, to read;[13] I found his experience similar to my own, which gave me reason to suppose he must be a bad man; as I was convinc'd of my own corrupt nature, and the misery of my own heart: and as he acknowledg'd that he was likewise in the same condition, I experienc'd no relief at all in reading his work, but rather the reverse. —I took the book to my lady, and inform'd her I did not like it at all, it was concerning a wicked man as bad as myself; and I did not chuse to read it, and I desir'd her to give me another, wrote by a better man that was holy and without sin. —She assur'd me that John Bunyan was a good man, but she could not convince me; I thought him to be too much like myself to be upright, as his experience seem'd to answer with my own.

I am very sensible that nothing but the great power and unspeakable mercies of the Lord could relieve my soul from the heavy burden it laboured under at that time. —A few days after my master gave me Baxter's *Call to the unconverted.*[14] This was no relief to me neither; on the contrary it occasioned as much distress in me as the other had before done, *as it* invited all to come to *Christ;* and I found myself so wicked and miserable that I could not come—This consideration threw me into agonies that cannot be described; in so much that I even attempted to put an end to my life—I took one of the large case-knives, and went into the stable with an intent to destroy myself; and as I endeavoured with all my strength to force the knife into my side, it bent double. I was instantly struck with horror at the thought of my own rashness, and my conscience told me that had I succeeded in this attempt I should probably have gone to hell.

I could find no relief, nor the least shadow of comfort; the extreme distress of my mind so affected my health that I continued very ill for three Days, and Nights; and would admit of no means to be taken for my recovery, though my lady was very kind, and sent many things to me; but I rejected every means of relief and wished to die—I would not go into my own bed, but lay in the stable upon straw—I felt all the horrors of a troubled conscience, so hard to be born, and saw all the vengeance of God

---

[13]John Bunyan (1628–1688), author of *The Holy War* (1682), *The Pilgrim's Progress* (1678–1684), and a classic Protestant conversion narrative, *Grace Abounding to the Chief of Sinners* (1666).

[14]Richard Baxter (1615–1691), author of *Call to the Unconverted* (1657) and (like Bunyan) an important writer in the Nonconformist Protestant tradition.

ready to overtake me—I was sensible that there was no way for me to be saved unless I came to *Christ*, and I could not come to Him: I thought that it was impossible He should receive such a sinner as me.

The last night that I continued in this place, in the midst of my distress these words were brought home upon my mind, "*Behold the Lamb of God.*" I was something comforted at this, and began to grow easier and wished for day that I might find these words in my bible—I rose very early the following morning, and went to my school-master, Mr. Vanosdore, and communicated the situation of my mind to him; he was greatly rejoiced to find me enquiring the way to Zion,[15] and blessed the Lord who had worked so wonderfully for me a poor heathen.—I was more familiar with this good gentleman than with my master, or any other person; and found myself more at liberty to talk to him: he encouraged me greatly, and prayed with me frequently, and I was always benefited by his discourse.

About a quarter of a mile from my Master's house stood a large remarkably fine Oak-tree, in the midst of a wood; I often used to be employed there in cutting down trees, (a work I was very fond of) I seldom failed going to this place every day; sometimes twice a day if I could be spared. It was the highest pleasure I ever experienced to set under this Oak; for there I used to pour out all my complaints to the LORD: and when I had any particular grievance I used to go there, and talk to the tree, and tell my sorrows, as if it had been to a friend.

Here I often lamented my own wicked heart, and undone state; and found more comfort and consolation than I ever was sensible of before. —Whenever I was treated with ridicule or contempt, I used to come here and find peace. I now began to relish the book my Master gave me, Baxter's *Call to the unconverted,* and took great delight in it. I was always glad to be employ'd in cutting wood, 'twas a great part of my business, and I follow'd it with delight, as I was then quite alone and my heart lifted up to GOD, and I was enabled to pray continually; and blessed for ever be his Holy Name, he faithfully answer'd my prayers. I can never be thankful enough to Almighty GOD for the many comfortable opportunities I experienced there.

It is possible the circumstance I am going to relate will not gain credit with many; but this I know, that the joy and comfort it conveyed to me, cannot be expressed and only conceived by those who have experienced the like.

---

set: sit.

[15] That is, the way to salvation.

I was one day in a most delightful frame of mind; my heart so overflowed with love and gratitude to the Author of all my comforts.—I was so drawn out of myself, and so fill'd and awed by the Presence of God that I saw (or thought I saw) light inexpressible dart down from heaven upon me, and shone around me for the space of a minute.—I continued on my knees, and joy unspeakable took possession of my soul.—The peace and serenity which filled my mind after this was wonderful, and cannot be told.—I would not have changed situations, or been any one but myself for the whole world. I blest God for my poverty, that I had no worldly riches or grandeur to draw my heart from Him. I wish'd at that time, if it had been possible for me, to have continued on that spot for ever. I felt an unwillingness in myself to have any thing more to do with the world, or to mix with society again. I seemed to possess a full assurance that my sins were forgiven me. I went home all my way rejoicing, and this text of scripture came full upon my mind. *"And I will make an everlasting convenant with them, that I will not turn away from them, to do them good; but I will put my fear in their hearts that they shall not depart from me."* The first opportunity that presented itself, I went to my old school-master, and made known to him the happy state of my soul who joined with me in praise to God for his mercy to me the vilest of sinners.—I was now perfectly easy, and had hardly a wish to make beyond what I possess'd, when my temporal comforts were all blasted by the death of my dear and worthy Master Mr. Freelandhouse, who was taken from this world rather suddenly: he had but a short illness, and died of a fever. I held his hand in mine when he departed; he told me he had given me my freedom. I was at liberty to go where I would.—He added that he had always pray'd for me and hop'd I should be kept unto the end. My master left me by his will ten pounds, and my freedom.

I found that if he had lived 'twas his intention to take me with him to Holland, as he had often mention'd me to some friends of his there that were desirous to see me; but I chose to continue with my Mistress who was as good to me as if she had been my mother.

The loss of Mr. Freelandhouse distress'd me greatly, but I was render'd still more unhappy by the clouded and perplex'd situation of my mind; the great enemy of my soul being ready to torment me, would present my own misery to me in such striking light, and distress me with doubts, fears, and such a deep sense of my own unworthiness, that after all the comfort and encouragement I had received, I was often tempted to believe I should be a Cast-away at last.—The more I saw of the Beauty and Glory of God, the

---

Cast-away: unredeemed sinner, condemned to damnation.

more I was humbled under a sense of my own vileness. I often repair'd to my old place of prayer; I seldom came away without consolation. One day this Scripture was wonderfully apply'd to my mind, *"And ye are compleat in Him which is the Head of all principalities and power."* —The Lord was pleas'd to comfort me by the application of many gracious promises at times when I was ready to sink under my trouble. *"Wherefore He is able also to save them to the uttermost that come unto God by Him seeing He ever liveth to make intercession for them.* Hebrews x. ver. 14. *For by one offering He hath perfected for ever them that are sanctified.*

My kind, indulgent Mistress liv'd but two years after my Master. Her death was a great affliction to me. She left five sons, all gracious young men, and Ministers of the Gospel.—I continued with them all, one after another, till they died; they liv'd but four years after their parents, when it pleased God to take them to Himself. I was left quite destitute, without a friend in the world. But I who had so often experienced the Goodness of GOD, trusted in Him to do what He pleased with me.—In this helpless condition I went in the wood to prayer as usual; and tho' the snow was a considerable height, I was not sensible of cold, or any other inconveniency.—At times indeed when I saw the world frowning round me, I was tempted to think that the LORD had forsaken me. I found great relief from the contemplation of these words in Isaiah xlix. v. 16. *"Behold I have graven thee on the palms of my hands; thy walls are continually before me."* And very many comfortable promises were sweetly applied to me. The lxxxix. Psalm and 34th verse, *"My covenant will I not break nor alter the thing that is gone out of my lips."* Hebrews, chap. xvi. v. 17, 18. Phillipians, chap. i. v. 6; and several more.

As I had now lost all my dear and valued friends every place in the world was alike to me. I had for a great while entertain'd a desire to come to EN-GLAND.—I imagined that all the Inhabitants of this Island were *Holy*; because all those that had visited my Master from thence were good, (Mr. Whitefield[16] was his particular friend) and the authors of the books that had been given me were all English. But above all places in the world I wish'd to see Kidderminster,[17] for I could not but think that on the spot where Mr. Baxter had liv'd, and preach'd, the people must be all *Righteous*.

---

[16] George Whitefield (1714–1770), leader of the Calvinist group within the Methodist movement and immensely popular as a preacher both in Britain and in colonial North America.

[17] Town where Gronniosaw eventually settled, located in the midlands region of England (near Birmingham) and associated with Nonconformist Protestantism.

The situation of my affairs requir'd that I should tarry a little longer in NEW-YORK, as I was something in debt, and was embarrass'd how to pay it. —About this time a young Gentleman that was a particular acquaintance of one of my young Master's, pretended to be a friend to me, and promis'd to pay my debts, which was three pounds; and he assur'd me he would never expect the money again. —But, in less than a month, he came and demanded it; and when I assur'd him I had nothing to pay, he threatened to sell me. —Though I knew he had no right to do that, yet as I had no friend in the world to go to, it alarm'd me greatly. —At length he purpos'd my going a Privateering, that I might by these means, be enabled to pay him, to which I agreed. —Our Captain's name was ———— ———— I went in Character of Cook to him. —Near St. Domingo [18] we came up to five French ships, Merchant-men. —We had a very smart engagement that continued from eight in the morning till three in the afternoon; when victory declar'd on our side. —Soon after this we were met by three English ships which join'd us, and that encourag'd us to attack a fleet of 36 Ships. —We boarded the three first and then follow'd the others; and had the same success with twelve; but the rest escap'd us. —There was a great deal of blood shed, and I was near death several times, but the LORD preserv'd me.

I met with many enemies, and much persecution, among the sailors; one of them was particularly unkind to me, and studied ways to vex and teaze me. —I can't help mentioning one circumstance that hurt me more than all the rest, which was, that he snatched a book out of my hand that I was very fond of, and used frequently to amuse myself with, and threw it into the sea. —But what is remarkable he was the first that was killed in our engagement. —I don't pretend to say that this happen'd because he was not my friend; but I thought 'twas a very awful Providence to see how the enemies of the LORD are cut off.

Our Captain was a cruel hard-hearted man. I was excessively sorry for the prisoners we took in general; but the pitiable case of one young Gentleman grieved me to the heart. —He appear'd very amiable; was strikingly handsome. Our Captain took four thousand pounds from him; but that did not satisfy him, as he imagin'd he was posses'd of more, and had somewhere conceal'd it, so that the Captain threatened him with death, at which he appear'd in the deepest distress, and took the buckles out of his shoes, and untied his hair, which was very fine, and long; and in which several very valuable rings were fasten'd. He came into the Cabbin to me, and in

---

Privateering: a legalized form of piracy directed against hostile nations during wartime.

[18] Island in the Caribbean then divided between the French (St. Domingue, present-day Haiti) and Spanish (Santo Domingo, present-day Dominican Republic).

the most obliging terms imaginable ask'd for something to eat and drink; which when I gave him, he was so thankful and pretty in his manner that my heart bled for him; and I heartily wish'd that I could have spoken in any language in which the ship's crew would not have understood me; that I might have let him know his danger; for I heard the Captain say he was re- solv'd upon his death; and he put his barbarous design into execution, for he took him on shore with one of the sailors, and there they shot him.

This circumstance affected me exceedingly, I could not put him out of my mind a long while. — When we return'd to NEW-YORK the Captain di- vided the prize-money among us, that we had taken. When I was call'd upon to receive my part, I waited upon Mr. ———, (the Gentleman that paid my debt and was the occasion of my going abroad) to know if he chose to go with me to receive my money or if I should bring him what I owed. — He chose to go with me; and when the Captain laid my money on the table ('twas an hundred and thirty-five pounds) I desir'd Mr. ——— to take what I was indebted to him; and he swept it all into his handkerchief, and would never be prevail'd on to give a farthing of money, nor any thing at all be- side. — And he likewise secur'd a hogshead of sugar which was my due from the same ship. The Captain was very angry with him for this piece of cruelty to me, as was every other person that heard it. — But I have reason to believe (as he was one of the Principal Merchants in the city) that he transacted business for him and on that account did not chuse to quarrel with him.

At this time a very worthy Gentleman, a Wine Merchant, his name Dunscum, took me under his protection, and would have recovered my money for me if I had chose it; but I told him to let it alone; that I wou'd rather be quiet. — I believed that it would not prosper with him, and so it happen'd, for by a series of losses and misfortunes he became poor, and was soon after drowned, as he was on a party of pleasure. — The vessel was driven out to sea, and struck against a rock by which means every soul perished.

I was very much distress'd when I heard it, and felt greatly for his fam- ily who were reduc'd to very low circumstances. — I never knew how to set a proper value on money. If I had but a little meat and drink to supply the present necessaries of life, I never wish'd for more; and when I had any I al- ways gave it if ever I saw an object in distress. If it was not for my dear Wife and Children I should pay as little regard to money now as I did at that time. — I continu'd some time with Mr. Dunscum as his servant; he was very kind to me. — But I had a vast inclination to visit ENGLAND, and wish'd

---

hogshead: a large cask.

continually that it would please Providence to make a clear way for me to see this Island. I entertain'd a notion that if I could get to ENGLAND I should never more experience either cruelty or ingratitude, so that I was very desirous to get among Christians. I knew Mr. Whitefield very well.—I had heard him preach often at NEW-YORK. In this disposition I listed in the twenty eighth Regiment of Foot, who were design'd for Martinico in the late war.—We went in Admiral Pocock's fleet from New-York to Barbadoes; from thence to Martinico.—When that was taken we proceded to the Havannah, and took that place likewise.—There I got discharged.[19]

I was then worth about thirty pounds, but I never regarded money in the least, nor would I tarry to receive my prize-money least I should lose my chance of going to England.—I went with the Spanish prisoners to Spain; and came to Old-England with the English prisoners.—I cannot describe my joy when we were within sight of Portsmouth.[20] But I was astonished when we landed to hear the inhabitants of that place curse and swear, and otherwise profane. I expected to find nothing but goodness, gentleness and meekness in this Christian Land, I then suffer'd great perplexities of mind.

I enquir'd if any serious Christian people resided there, the woman I made this enquiry of, answer'd me in the affirmative; and added that she was one of them.—I was heartily glad to hear her say so. I thought I could give her my whole heart: she kept a Public-House. I deposited with her all the money that I had not an immediate occasion for; as I thought it would be safer with her.—It was 25 guineas but 6 of them I desired her to lay out to the best advantage, to buy me some shirts, hat and some other necessaries. I made her a present of a very handsome large looking glass that I brought with me from Martinico, in order to recompence her for the trouble I had given her. I must do this woman the justice to acknowledge that she did lay out some little for my use, but the 19 guineas and part of the 6, with my watch, she would not return, but denied that I ever gave it her.

I soon perceived that I was got among bad people, who defrauded me of my money and watch; and that all my promis'd happiness was blasted. I

---

listed: enlisted.

Public-House: pub, tavern.

[19] Admiral George Pocock (1706–1792) was an important commander in the British fleet who led the siege against Havana, Cuba (then a Spanish colony) during the course of the Seven Years' War (1756–1763); the siege of Martinique (then a French colony) was led by Admiral G. B. Rodney.

[20] Portsmouth was an important (and rough) naval town and shipping center on the southern coast of England, across from the Isle of Wight.

had no friend but GOD and I pray'd to Him earnestly. I could scarcely believe it possible that the place where so many eminent Christians had lived and preached could abound with so much wickedness and deceit. I thought it worse than *Sodom*[21] (considering the great advantages they have) I cryed like a child and that almost continually: at length GOD heard my prayers and rais'd me a friend indeed.

This publican had a brother who lived on Portsmouth-common, his wife was a very serious good woman. —When she heard of the treatment I had met with, she came and enquired into my real situation and was greatly troubled at the ill usage I had received, and took me home to her own house. —I began now to rejoice, and my prayer was turned into praise. She made use of all the arguments in her power to prevail on her who had wronged me, to return my watch and money, but it was to no purpose, as she had given me no receipt and I had nothing to show for it, I could not demand it. —My good friend was excessively angry with her and obliged her to give me back four guineas, which she said she gave me out of charity: Though in fact it was my own, and much more. She would have employed some rougher means to oblige her to give up my money, but I would not suffer her, let it go says I "My GOD is in heaven." Still I did not mind my loss in the least; all that grieved me was, that I had been disappointed in finding some Christian friends, with whom I hoped to enjoy a little sweet and comfortable society.

I thought the best method that I could take now, was to go to London, and find out Mr. Whitefield, who was the only living soul I knew in England, and get him to direct me to some way or other to procure a living without being troublesome to any Person. —I took leave of my christian friend at Portsmouth, and went in the stage to London. —A creditable tradesman in the City, who went up with me in the stage, offer'd to show me the way to Mr. Whitefield's Tabernacle.[22] Knowing that I was a perfect stranger, I thought it very kind, and accepted his offer; but he obliged me to give him half-a-crown for going with me, and likewise insisted on my giving him five shillings more for conducting me to Dr. Gifford's Meeting.[23]

I began now to entertain a very different idea of the inhabitants of England than what I had figur'd to myself before I came amongst them.

---

publican: keeper of a public-house (tavern).

[21] City destroyed by God in the Old Testament on account of its wickedness (see Genesis 18–19).

[22] Whitefield had established the "New Tabernacle," for preaching to large London crowds up to four thousand, in 1753.

[23] Andrew Gifford (1700–1784), Nonconformist Protestant minister in London.

—Mr. Whitefield receiv'd me very friendly, was heartily glad to see me, and directed me to a proper place to board and lodge in Petticoat-Lane, till he could think of some way to settle me in, and paid for my lodging, and all my expences. The morning after I came to my new lodging, as I was at breakfast with the gentlewoman of the house, I heard the noise of some looms over our heads: I enquir'd what it was; she told me a person was weaving silk.—I express'd a great desire to see it, and ask'd if I might: She told me she would go up with me; she was sure I should be very welcome. She was as good as her word, and as soon as we enter'd the room, the person that was weaving look'd about, and smiled upon us, and I loved her from that moment.—She ask'd me many questions, and I in turn talk'd a great deal to her. I found she was a member of Mr. Allen's Meeting,[24] and I begun to entertain a good opinion of her, though I was almost afraid to indulge this inclination, least she should prove like all the rest I had met with at Portsmouth, &c. and which had almost given me a dislike to all white women.—But after a short acquaintance I had the happiness to find she was very different, and quite sincere, and I was not without hope that she entertain'd some esteem for me. We often went together to hear Dr. Gifford, and as I had always a propensity to relieve every object in distress as far as I was able, I used to give to all that complain'd to me; sometimes half a guinea at a time, as I did not understand the real value of it.—This gracious, good woman took great pains to correct and advise me in that and many other respects.

After I had been in London about six weeks I was recommended to the notice of some of my late Master Mr. Freelandhouse's acquaintance, who had heard him speak frequently of me. I was much persuaded by them to go to Holland.—My Master lived there before he bought me, and used to speak of me so respectfully among his friends there, that it raised in them a curiosity to see me; particularly the Gentlemen engaged in the Ministry, who expressed a desire to hear my experience and examine me. I found that it was my good old Master's design that I should have gone if he had lived; for which reason I resolved upon going to Holland, and informed my dear friend Mr. Whitefield of my intention; he was much averse to my going at first, but after I gave him my reasons appeared very well satisfied. I likewise informed my Betty (the good woman that I have mentioned above) of my determination to go to Holland and I told her that I believed she was to be my Wife: that if it was the LORD's Will I desired it, but not else.—She made me very little answer, but has since told me, she did not think it at that time.

---

[24]John Allen, Nonconformist minister in the Spitalfields district of London.

I embarked at Tower-wharf at four o'clock in the morning, and arriv'd at Amsterdam the next day by three o'clock in the afternoon. I had several letters of recommendation to my old master's friends, who receiv'd me very graciously. Indeed, one of the chief Ministers was particularly good to me; he kept me at his house a long while, and took great pleasure in asking questions, which I answer'd with delight, being always ready to say, "*Come unto me all ye that fear GOD, and I will tell what he hath done for my Soul.*"[25] I cannot but admire the footsteps of Providence; astonish'd that I should be so wonderfully preserved! Though the Grandson of a King, I have wanted bread, and should have been glad of the hardest crust I ever saw. I who, at home, was surrounded and guarded by slaves, so that no indifferent person might approach me, and clothed with gold, have been inhumanely threatened with death; and frequently wanted clothing to defend me from the inclemency of the weather; yet I never murmured, nor was I discontented. —I am willing, and even desirous to be counted as nothing, a stranger in the world, and a pilgrim here; for "*I know that my* REDEEMER *liveth,*"[26] and I'm thankful for every trial and trouble that I've met with, as I am not without hope that they have been all sanctified to me.

The Calvinist Ministers desired to hear my Experience from myself, which proposal I was very well pleased with: So I stood before 38 Ministers every Thursday for seven weeks together, and they were all very well satisfied, and persuaded I was what I pretended to be. —They wrote down my experience as I spoke it; and the LORD ALMIGHTY was with me at that time in a remarkable manner, and gave me words and enabled me to answer them; so great was his mercy to take me in hand a poor blind heathen.

At this time a very rich Merchant at AMSTERDAM offered to take me into his family in the capacity of his Butler, and I very willingly accepted it. — He was a gracious worthy Gentleman and very good to me. —He treated me more like a friend than a servant. —I tarried there a twelvemonth but was not thoroughly contented, I wanted to see my wife; (that is now) and for that reason I wished to return to ENGLAND. I wrote to her once in my absence, but she did not answer my letter; and I must acknowledge if she had, it would have given me a less opinion of her. —My Master and Mistress persuaded me much not to leave them and likewise their two Sons who entertained a good opinion of me; and if I had found my Betty married on my arrival in ENGLAND, I should have returned to them again immediately.

---

[25] See Psalms 16:66.

[26] See Job 19:25.

My Lady purposed my marrying her maid; she was an agreeable young woman, had saved a good deal of money, but I could not fancy her, though she was willing to accept of me, but I told her my inclinations were engaged in ENGLAND, and I could think of no other Person. — On my return home, I found my Betty disengaged. — She had refused several offers in my absence, and told her sister that, she thought, if ever she married I was to be her husband.

Soon after I came home, I waited on Doctor Gifford who took me into his family and was exceedingly good to me. The character of this pious worthy Gentleman is well known; my praise can be of no use or signification at all. — I hope I shall ever gratefully remember the many favours I have received from him. — Soon after I came to Doctor Gifford I expressed a desire to be admitted into their Church, and set down with them; they told me I must first be baptized; so I gave in my experience before the Church, with which they were very well satisfied, and I was baptized by Doctor Gifford with some others. I then made known my intentions of being married; but I found there were many objections against it because the person I had fixed on was poor. She was a widow, her husband had left her in debt, and with a child, so that they persuaded me against it out of real regard to me. — But I had promised and was resolved to have her; as I knew her to be a gracious woman, her poverty was no objection to me as they had nothing else to say against her. When my friends found that they could not alter my opinion respecting her, they wrote to Mr. Allen, the Minister she attended, to persuade her to leave me; but he replied that he would not interfere at all, that we might do as we would. I was resolved that all my wife's little debt should be paid before we were married; so that I sold almost every thing I had and with all the money I could raise cleared all that she owed, and I never did any thing with a better will in all my Life, because I firmly believed that we should be very happy together, and so it prov'd, for she was given me from the LORD. And I have found her a blessed partner, and we have never repented, tho' we have gone through many great troubles and difficulties.

My wife got a very good living by weaving, and could do extremely well; but just at that time there was great disturbance among the weavers; so that I was afraid to let my wife work, least they should insist on my joining the rioters which I could not think of, and, possibly, if I had refused to do so they would have knock'd me on the head.[27] — So that by these means my wife could get no employ, neither had I work enough to maintain my fam-

---

[27] The Spitalfields weavers, hit by the postwar depression that followed Britain's victory in the Seven Years' War, rioted in demand of better pay and conditions in 1765.

ily. We had not yet been married a year before all these misfortunes overtook us.

Just at this time a gentleman, that seemed much concerned for us, advised me to go into *Essex* with him and promised to get me employed. — I accepted his kind proposal, and he spoke to a friend of his, a Quaker, a gentleman of large fortune, who resided a little way out of the town of *Colchester;* his name was *Handbarar;* he ordered his steward to set me to work.

There were several employed in the same way with myself. I was very thankful and contented though my wages were but small. — I was allowed but eight pence a day, and found myself; but after I had been in this situation for a fortnight, my Master, being told that a Black was at work for him, had an inclination to see me. He was pleased to talk to me for some time, and at last enquired what wages I had; when I told him he declared, it was too little, and immediately ordered his Steward to let me have eighteen pence a day, which he constantly gave me after; and I then did extremely well.

I did not bring my wife with me: I came first alone and it was my design, if things answered according to our wishes, to send for her — I was now thinking to desire her to come to me when I receiv'd a letter to inform me she was just brought to bed and in want of many necessaries. — This news was a great trial to me and a fresh affliction: but my GOD, *faithful and abundant in mercy,* forsook me not in this trouble. — As I could not read *English,* I was obliged to apply to some one to read the letter I received, relative to my wife. I was directed by the good Providence of GOD to a worthy young gentleman, a Quaker, and friend of my Master. — I desired he would take the trouble to read my letter for me, which he readily comply'd with and was greatly moved and affected at the contents; insomuch that he said he would undertake to make a gathering for me, which he did and was the first to contribute to it himself. The money was sent that evening to LONDON by a person who happen'd to be going there; nor was this All the goodness that I experienced from these kind friends, for, as soon as my wife came about and was fit to travel, they sent for her to me, and were at the whole expence of her coming; so evidently has the love and mercy of GOD appeared through every trouble that ever I experienced. We went on very comfortably all the summer. — We lived in a little cottage near Mr. *Handbarrar's* House; but when the winter came on I was discharged, as he had no further occasion for me. And now the prospect began to darken upon us again. We thought it most adviseable to move our habitation a little nearer

---

was just brought to bed: had just given birth

to the Town, as the house we lived in was very cold, and wet, and ready to tumble down.

The boundless goodness of GOD to me has been so very great, that with the most humble gratitude I desire to prostrate myself before Him; for I have been wonderfully supported in every affliction. My GOD never left me. I perceived light *still* through the thickest darkness.

My dear wife and I were now both unemployed, we could get nothing to do. The winter prov'd remarkably severe, and we were reduc'd to the greatest distress imaginable. —I was always very shy of asking for any thing; I could never beg; neither did I chuse to make known our wants to any person, for fear of offending as we were entire strangers; but our last bit of bread was gone, and I was obliged to think of something to do for our support. —I did not mind for myself at all; but to see my dear wife and children in want pierc'd me to the heart. —I now blam'd myself for bringing her from London, as doubtless had we continued there we might have found friends to keep us from starving. The snow was at this season remarkably deep; so that we could see no prospect of being relieved. In this melancholy situation, not knowing what step to pursue, I resolved to make my case known to a Gentleman's Gardiner that lived near us, and entreat him to employ me: but when I came to him, my courage failed me, and I was ashamed to make known our real situation. —I endeavoured all I could to prevail on him to set me to work, but to no purpose: he assur'd me it was not in his power: but just as I was about to leave him, he asked me if I would accept of some Carrots? I took them with great thankfulness and carried them home: he gave me four, they were very large and fine. —We had nothing to make fire with, so consequently could not boil them: But was glad to have them to eat *raw*. Our youngest child was quite an infant; so that my wife was obliged to chew it, and fed her in that manner for several days. —We allowed ourselves but one every day, least they should not last 'till we could get some other supply. I was unwilling to eat at all myself; nor would I take any the last day that we continued in this situation, as I could not bear the thought that my dear wife and children would be in want of every means of support. We lived in this manner, 'till our carrots were all gone: then my Wife began to lament because of our poor babies: but I comforted her all I could; still hoping, and believing that *my* GOD would not let us die: but that it would please Him to relieve us, which *He* did by almost a Miracle.

We went to bed, as usual, before it was quite dark, (as we had neither fire nor candle) but had not been there long before some person knocked at the door & enquir'd if *James Albert* lived there: I answer'd in the affirmative, and rose immediately; as soon as I open'd the door I found it was the servant of an eminent Attorney who resided at *Colchester.* —He ask'd me how it was with me? if I was not almost starv'd? I burst out a crying, and told him I was indeed. He said his master suppos'd so, and that he wanted to speak with me, and I must return with him. This Gentleman's name was *Danniel,* he was a sincere good christian. He used to stand and talk with me frequently when I work'd in the road for Mr. *Handbarrar,* and would have employed me himself, if I had wanted work.—When I came to his house he told me that he had thought a good deal about me of late, and was apprehensive that I must be in want, and could not be satisfied till he sent to enquire after me. I made known my distress to him, at which he was greatly affected; and generously gave me a guinea; and promis'd to be kind to me in future. I could not help exclaiming. *O the boundless mercies of my God!* I pray'd unto Him, and He has heard me; I trusted in Him and He has preserv'd me: where shall I begin to praise Him, or how shall I love Him enough?

I went immediately and bought some bread and cheese and coal and carried it home. My dear wife was rejoiced to see me return with something to eat. She instantly got up and dressed our Babies, while I made a fire, and the first Nobility in the land never made a more comfortable meal.—We did not forget to thank the LORD for all his goodness to us.—Soon after this, as the spring came on, Mr. Peter *Daniel* employed me in helping to pull down a house, and rebuilding it. I had then very good work, and full employ: he sent for my wife, and children to *Colchester,* and provided us a house where we lived very comfortably.—I hope I shall always gratefully acknowledge his kindness to myself and family. I worked at this house for more than a year, till it was finished; and after that I was employed by several successively, and was never so happy as when I had something to do; but perceiving the winter coming on, and work rather slack, I was apprehensive that we should again be in want or become troublesome to our friends.

I had at this time an offer made me of going to *Norwich* and having constant employ.—My wife seemed pleased with this proposal, as she supposed she might get work there in the weaving-manufactory, being the business she was brought up to, and more likely to succeed there than any other place; and we thought as we had an opportunity of moving to a Town where we could both be employ'd it was most adviseable to do so; and that probably we might settle there for our lives.—When this step was resolv'd on, I went first alone to see how it would answer; which I very much repented after, for it was not in my power immediately to send my wife any supply, as I fell into the hands of a Master that was neither kind nor considerate; and she was reduced to great distress, so that she was oblig'd to sell the few goods that we had, and when I sent for her was under the disagreeable necessity of parting with our bed.

When she came to *Norwich* I hired a room ready furnished. —I experienced a great deal of difference in the carriage of my Master from what I had been accustomed to from some of my other Masters. He was very irregular in his payments to me. —My wife hired a loom and wove all the leisure time she had and we began to do very well, till we were overtaken by fresh misfortunes. Our three poor children fell ill of the small pox; this was a great trial to us; but still I was persuaded in myself we should not be forsaken. —And I did all in my power to keep my dear partner's spirits from sinking. Her whole attention now was taken up with the children as she could mind nothing else, and all I could get was but little to support a family in such a situation, beside paying for the hire of our room, which I was obliged to omit doing for several weeks: but the woman to whom we were indebted would not excuse us, tho' I promised she should have the very first money we could get after my children came about, but she would not be satisfied and had the cruelty to threaten us that if we did not pay her immediately she would turn us all into the street.

The apprehension of this plunged me in the deepest distress, considering the situation of my poor babies: if they had been in health I should have been less sensible of this misfortune. But My GOD, *still faithful to his promise,* raised me a friend. Mr. Henry Gurdney, a Quaker, a gracious gentleman heard of our distress, he sent a servant of his own to the woman we hired the room of, paid our rent, and bought all the goods with my wife's loom and gave it us all.

Some other gentlemen, hearing of his design, were pleased to assist him in these generous acts, for which we never can be thankful enough; after this my children soon came about; we began to do pretty well again; my dear wife work'd hard and constant when she could get work, but it was upon a disagreeable footing as her employ was so uncertain, sometimes she could get nothing to do and at other times when the weavers of *Norwich* had orders from LONDON they were so excessively hurried, that the people they employ'd were often oblig'd to work on the *Sabbath-day;* but this my wife would never do, and it was matter of uneasiness to us that we could not get our living in a regular manner, though we were both diligent, industrious, and willing to work. I was far from being happy in my Master, he did not use me well. I could scarcely ever get my money from him; but I continued patient 'till it pleased GOD to alter my situation.

My worthy friend Mr. Gurdney advised me to follow the employ of chopping chaff and bought me an instrument for that purpose. There were but few people in the town that made this their business beside myself; so

---

chopping chaff: chopping up hay, straw, or other cut grains or grasses for animal fodder.

that I did very well indeed and we became easy and happy.—But we did not continue long in this comfortable state: Many of the inferior people were envious and ill-natur'd and set up the same employ and work'd under price on purpose to get my business from me, and they succeeded so well that I could hardly get any thing to do, and became again unfortunate: Nor did this misfortune come alone, for just at this time we lost one of our little girls who died of a fever; this circumstance occasion'd us new troubles, for the Baptist Minister refused to bury her because we were not their members. The Parson of the parish denied us because she had never been baptized. I applied to the Quakers, but met with no success; this was one of the greatest trials I ever met with, as we did not know what to do with our poor baby.—At length I resolv'd to dig a grave in the garden behind the house, and bury her there; when the Parson of the parish sent for me to tell me he would bury the child, but did not chuse to read the burial service over her. I told him I did not mind whether he would or not, as the child could not hear it.

We met with a great deal of ill treatment after this, and found it very difficult to live.—We could scarcely get work to do, and were obliged to pawn our cloaths. We were ready to sink under our troubles.—When I purposed to my wife to go to *Kidderminster* and try if we could do there. I had always an inclination for that place, and now more than ever as I had heard *Mr. Fawcet*[28] mentioned in the most respectful manner, as a pious worthy Gentleman, and I had seen his name in a favourite book of mine, Baxter's *Saints everlasting rest;* and as the Manufactory of *Kidderminster* seemed to promise my wife some employment, she readily came into my way of thinking.

I left her once more, and set out for *Kidderminster* in order to judge if the situation would suit us.—As soon as I came there I waited immediately on *Mr. Fawcet,* who was pleased to receive me very kindly and recommended me to *Mr. Watson* who employed me in twisting silk and worsted together. I continued here about a fortnight, and when I thought it would answer our expectation, I returned to *Norwich* to fetch my wife; she was then near her time, and too much indisposed. So we were obliged to tarry until she was brought to bed, and as soon as she could conveniently travel we came to *Kidderminster,* but we brought nothing with us as we were obliged to sell all we had to pay our debts and the expences of my wife's illness, *&c.*

---

near her time: soon to give birth.

[28] Benjamin Fawcett (1715–1780), Nonconformist minister and religious author with a chapel in Kidderminster.

Such is our situation at present.—My wife, by hard labor at the loom, does every thing that can be expected from her towards the maintenance of our family; and GOD is pleased to incline the hearts of his People at times to yield us their charitable assistance; being myself through age and infirmity able to contribute but little to their support. As Pilgrims, and very poor Pilgrims, we are travelling through many difficulties towards our HEAVENLY HOME, and waiting patiently for his gracious call, when the LORD shall deliver us out of the evils of this present world and bring us to the EVERLASTING GLORIES of the world to come.—To HIM be PRAISE for EVER and EVER, AMEN.

FINIS.

From Thoughts and Sentiments on the Evil and Wicked Traffic of the Slavery and Commerce of the Human Species, Humbly Submitted to the Inhabitants of Great Britain by Ottobah Cugoano, A Native of Africa

Ottobah Cugoano

Ottobah Cugoano (born c. 1757), also called John Stuart, provided the first extended attack on colonial slavery and the slave trade by a "native of Africa" who had endured the system at first hand. Although not nearly so popular as the *Interesting Narrative* written by his colleague Olaudah Equiano, *Thoughts and Sentiments* piqued enough curiosity on its appearance in 1787 that a first-person sketch of Cugoano's life was printed up to be inserted in various copies. According to the sketch, as supplemented by surviving letters and the autobiographical passages included in *Thoughts and Sentiments* itself, Cugoano was kidnapped by African slave merchants at about thirteen years of age in 1770, indicating a birth year near 1757. He was born in Ajumako, a region of present-day Ghana on the west coast of Africa, where his father and relations were "chief men" and Cugoano himself was taken in by the king's family. After his capture in 1770, he was brought to an unnamed trading depot, transferred to the major slaving fort at Cape Coast Castle, and brought to the island of Grenada in the British West Indies. There he spent close to a year in a "slave-gang," evidently working on a sugar plantation. Bought by Alexander Campbell, Cugoano spent another year in various parts of the West Indies before coming with his master to England at the end of 1772. Hoping that Christian baptism would prevent his being sent back into plantation slavery, Cugoano went to a Dr. Skinner for religious instruction and was duly baptized at St. James's Church, Westminster, in 1773.

Spotty records and references indicate that Cugoano remained in London at least until 1791. In the mid-1780s Cugoano worked as a free servant for the fashionable painter Richard Cosway. In 1786, Cugoano sent a letter on the slavery question to the Prince of Wales and during the same period he cosigned various letters and petitions from the "Sons of Africa," a group of at least two dozen Black British activists that notably included Olaudah Equiano. Equiano may have helped Cugoano with the editing and revision of *Thoughts and Sentiments* in 1787, or so scholars have surmised, based on similarities in phrasing and thought between the two writers and on the rough character of Cugoano's English in his surviving letters. The work was translated into French the following year and issued in an abbreviated version in 1791 (signed "Quobna Ottobah Cugoano"). That version included a proposal by Cugoano to open a school for "*all such of his* Complexion *as are desirous of being acquainted with the Knowledge of the Christian Religion and the* Laws *of* Civilization" (Fryer 1984, 101). In a letter of the same year addressed to the prominent abolitionist Granville Sharp, Cugoano mentions preparations to leave for New Brunswick in Nova Scotia, Canada, where a sizeable group of former American slaves had emigrated after supporting the British during the United States War of Independence. A good number of these left Nova Scotia to found Freetown in the British freed slave colony of Sierra Leone in January 1792, so the last part of the eighteenth century may have found Cugoano emigrating to Canada, toiling on in London, or even resettling in Africa.

Thoughts and Sentiments attacks the slave system on a number of fronts. Cugoano deploys a triple strategy in assailing the moral basis of slavery, invalidating it on Enlightenment grounds (affirming "universal natural rights"), emphasizing its "Antichristian" unlawfulness, and appealing to the humane "sensibility" of his readership. He dissects British stereotypes concerning both Africa and the British residents of African descent, arguing against racial prejudice and insisting that European slavers are the true barbarians. (When first brought among Europeans, Cugoano fully expects to be eaten by them.) He draws on his own experiences as an African captive to engage his readers on a human level, contrasting the "innocence and freedom" of his West African childhood with the despair of captivity (he and his fellow captives attempt to blow up a slave ship before it can take them to the Americas) and the brutality of life in the slave-gang. Cugoano's varied appeals to reason, religion, and feeling show a marked intellectual agility as he critically addresses one proslavery argument after another. His willingness to make pragmatic appeals to British self-interest should be balanced against his stark condemnation of the slave system and his radical critique of European imperialism.

THOUGHTS AND SENTIMENTS
ON THE
EVIL AND WICKED TRAFFIC
OF THE
SLAVERY AND COMMERCE
OF THE
HUMAN SPECIES,
HUMBLY SUBMITTED TO
The INHABITANTS of *GREAT-BRITAIN,*
BY
OTTOBAH CUGOANO,
A NATIVE of *AFRICA.*

He that stealeth a man and selleth him, or maketh merchandize of him, or if he be found in his hand: then that thief shall die.

—LAW OF GOD.[1]

LONDON:

PRINTED IN THE YEAR

M.DCC.LXXXVII.

---

[1] Based on Deuteronomy 24:7.

Thoughts and Sentiments on the Evil of Slavery.

One law, and one manner shall be for you, and for
the stranger that sojourneth with you; and therefore,
all things whatsoever ye would that men should do to
you, do ye even so to them.

—Numb. xv. 16.—Math. vii. 12.

As several learned gentlemen of distinguished abilities, as well as eminent for their great humanity, liberality and candour, have written various essays against that infamous traffic of the African Slave Trade, carried on with the West-India planters and merchants, to the great shame and disgrace of all Christian nations wherever it is admitted in any of their territories, or in any place or situation amongst them; it cannot be amiss that I should thankfully acknowledge these truly worthy and humane gentlemen with the warmest sense of gratitude, for their beneficent and laudable endeavours towards a total suppression of that infamous and iniquitous traffic of stealing, kid-napping, buying, selling, and cruelly enslaving men!

Those who have endeavoured to restore to their fellow-creatures the common rights of nature, of which especially the poor unfortunate Black People have been so unjustly deprived, cannot fail in meeting with the applause of all good men, and the approbation of that which will for ever redound to their honor; they have the warrant of that which is divine: *Open thy mouth, judge righteously, plead the cause of the poor and needy; for the liberal deviseth liberal things, and by liberal things shall stand.*[2] And they can say with the pious Job, *Did not I weep for him that was in trouble; was not my soul grieved for the poor?*[3]

The kind exertions of many benevolent and humane gentlemen, against the iniquitous traffic of slavery and oppression, has been attended with much good to many, and must redound with great honor to themselves, to

---

From Ottobah Cugoano, *Thoughts and Sentiments on the Evil and Wicked Traffic of the Slavery and Commerce of the Human Species, Humbly Submitted to the Inhabitants of Great-Britain, by Ottobah Cugoano, A Native of Africa* (London, 1787)

[2] Isaiah 32:8.

[3] Job 30:25.

humanity and their country; their laudable endeavours have been productive of the most beneficent effects in preventing that savage barbarity from taking place in free countries at home. In this, as well as in many other respects, there is one class of people (whose virtues of probity and humanity are well known) who are worthy of universal approbation and imitation, because, like men of honor and humanity, they have jointly agreed to carry on no slavery and savage barbarity among them; and, since the last war,[4] some mitigation of slavery has been obtained in some respective districts of America, though not in proportion to their own vaunted claims of freedom; but it is to be hoped, that they will yet go on to make a further and greater reformation. However, notwithstanding all that has been done and written against it, that brutish barbarity, and unparalelled injustice, is still carried on to a very great extent in the colonies, and with an avidity as insidious, cruel and oppressive as ever. The longer that men continue in the practice of evil and wickedness, they grow the more abandoned; for nothing in history can equal the barbarity and cruelty of the tortures and murders committed under various pretences in modern slavery, except the annals of the Inquisition and the bloody edicts of Popish massacres.[5]

It is therefore manifest, that something else ought yet to be done; and what is required, is evidently the incumbent duty of all men of enlightened understanding, and of every man that has any claim or affinity to the name of Christian, that the base treatment which the African Slaves undergo, ought to be abolished; and it is moreover evident, that the whole, or any part of that iniquitous traffic of slavery, can no where, or in any degree, be admitted, but among those who must eventually resign their own claim to any degree of sensibility and humanity, for that of barbarians and ruffians.

But it would be needless to arrange an history of all the base treatment which the African Slaves are subjected to, in order to shew the exceeding wickedness and evil of that insidious traffic, as the whole may easily appear in every part, and at every view, to be wholly and totally inimical to every idea of justice, equity, reason and humanity. What I intend to advance against that evil, criminal and wicked traffic of enslaving men, are only some Thoughts and Sentiments which occur to me, as being obvious from the Scriptures of Divine Truth, or such arguments as are chiefly deduced from thence, with other such observations as I have been able to collect. Some of these observations may lead into a larger field of consideration,

---

[4] The United States War of Independence (1775–1783).

[5] The Roman Catholic Church established the Inquisition in 1231 as a papal judicial institution dedicated to persecuting alleged heretics, including Protestants, Jews, and Muslims. Like that of other early Black British writers, Cugoano's Christianity reveals a decidedly Protestant cast.

than that of the African Slave Trade alone; but those causes from wherever they originate, and become the production of slavery, the evil effects produced by it, must shew that its origin and source is of a wicked and criminal nature.

No necessity, or any situation of men, however poor, pitiful and wretched they may be, can warrant them to rob others, or oblige them to become thieves, because they are poor, miserable and wretched: But the robbers of men, the kid-nappers, ensnarers and slave-holders, who take away the common rights and privileges of others to support and enrich themselves, are universally those pitiful and detestable wretches; for the ensnaring of others, and taking away their liberty by slavery and oppression, is the worst kind of robbery, as most opposite to every precept and injunction of the Divine Law, and contrary to that command which enjoins that *all men should love their neighbours as themselves,* and *that they should do unto others, as they would that men should do to them.* As to any other laws that slave-holders may make among themselves, as respecting slaves, they can be of no better kind, nor give them any better character, than what is implied in the common report—that there may be some honesty among thieves. This may seem a harsh comparison, but the parallel is so coincident that, I must say, I can find no other way of expressing my Thoughts and Sentiments, without making use of some harsh words and comparisons against the carriers on of such abandoned wickedness. But, in this little undertaking, I must humbly hope the impartial reader will excuse such defects as may arise from want of better education; and as to the resentment of those who can lay their cruel lash upon the backs of thousands, for a thousand times less crimes than writing against their enormous wickedness and brutal avarice, is what I may be sure to meet with.

However, it cannot but be very discouraging to a man of my complexion in such an attempt as this, to meet with the evil aspersions of some men, who say, "That an African is not entitled to any competent degree of knowledge, or capable of imbibing any sentiments of probity; and that nature designed him for some inferior link in the chain, fitted only to be a slave."[6] But when I meet with those who make no scruple to deal with the human species, as with the beasts of the earth, I must think them not only brutish, but wicked and base; and that their aspersions are insidious and

---

[6]Many European writers held that God's creatures were arranged in a hierarchical sequence, or "Great Chain of Being," running from animals, through human beings, to angels and other spiritual beings, with God at the pinnacle. Some variants of racialist theory postulated a similar hierarchical "chain" of supposed racial groups within the human species, ranking black Africans at the bottom, or placed black Africans as a distinct species between animals and human beings.

false: And if such men can boast of greater degrees of knowledge, than any African is entitled to, I shall let them enjoy all the advantages of it unenvied, as I fear it consists only in a greater share of infidelity, and that of a blacker kind than only skin deep. And if their complexion be not what I may suppose, it is at least the nearest in resemblance to an infernal hue. A good man will neither speak nor do as a bad man will; but if a man is bad, it makes no difference whether he be a black or a white devil.

By some of such complexion, as whether black or white it matters not, I was early snatched away from my native country, with about eighteen or twenty more boys and girls, as we were playing in a field. We lived but a few days journey from the coast where we were kid-napped, and as we were decoyed and drove along, we were soon conducted to a factory, and from thence, in the fashionable way of traffic, consigned to Grenada.[7] Perhaps it may not be amiss to give a few remarks, as some account of myself, in this transposition of captivity.

I was born in the city of Agimaque, on the coast of Fantyn,[8] my father was a companion to the chief in that part of the country of Fantee, and when the old king died I was left in his house with his family; soon after I was sent for by his nephew, Ambro Accasa, who succeeded the old king in the chiefdom of that part of Fantee known by the name of Agimaque and Assinee. I lived with his children, enjoying peace and tranquillity, about twenty moons, which, according to their way of reckoning time, is two years. I was sent for to visit an uncle, who lived at a considerable distance from Agimaque. The first day after we set out we arrived at Assinee, and the third day at my uncle's habitation, where I lived about three months, and was then thinking of returning to my father and young companion at Agimaque; but by this time I had got well acquainted with some of the children of my uncle's hundreds of relations, and we were some days too ventursome in going into the woods to gather fruit and catch birds, and such amusements as pleased us. One day I refused to go with the rest, being rather apprehensive that something might happen to us; till one of my play-fellows said to me, because you belong to the great men, you are afraid to venture your carcase, or else of the *bounsam*, which is the devil. This enraged me so much, that I set a resolution to join the rest, and we went into

---

factory: trading center, here a slave-trading station.

moons: months.

[7] An island one hundred miles north of Venezuela in the Caribbean and at this time a British possession.

[8] Agimaque (Ajumako) was a region of the West African coast (in present-day Ghana) dominated by the Fanti people.

the woods as usual; but we had not been above two hours before our troubles began, when several great ruffians came upon us suddenly, and said we had committed a fault against their lord, and we must go and answer for it ourselves before him.

Some of us attempted in vain to run away, but pistols and cutlasses were soon introduced, threatening, that if we offered to stir we should all lie dead on the spot. One of them pretended to be more friendly than the rest, and said, that he would speak to their lord to get us clear, and desired that we should follow him; we were then immediately divided into different parties, and drove after him. We were soon led out of the way which we knew, and towards the evening, as we came in sight of a town, they told us that this great man of theirs lived there, but pretended it was too late to go and see him that night. Next morning there came three other men, whose language differed from ours, and spoke to some of those who watched us all the night, but he that pretended to be our friend with the great man, and some others, were gone away. We asked our keepers what these men had been saying to them, and they answered, that they had been asking them, and us together, to go and feast with them that day, and that we must put off seeing the great man till after; little thinking that our doom was so nigh, or that these villains meant to feast on us as their prey. We went with them again about half a day's journey, and came to a great multitude of people, having different music playing; and all the day after we got there, we were very merry with the music, dancing and singing. Towards the evening, we were again persuaded that we could not get back to where the great man lived till next day; and when bed-time came, we were separated into different houses with different people. When the next morning came, I asked for the men that brought me there, and for the rest of my companions; and I was told that they were gone to the sea side to bring home some rum, guns and powder, and that some of my companions were gone with them, and that some were gone to the fields to do something or other. This gave me strong suspicion that there was some treachery in the case, and I began to think that my hopes of returning home again were all over. I soon became very uneasy, not knowing what to do, and refused to eat or drink for whole days together, till the man of the house told me that he would do all in his power to get me back to my uncle; then I eat a little fruit with him, and had some thoughts that I should be sought after, as I would be then missing at home about five or six days. I enquired every day if the men had come back, and for the rest of my companions, but could get no answer of any satisfaction. I was kept about six days at this man's house, and in the evening there was another man came and talked with him a good while, and I heard the one say to the other he must go, and the other said the sooner the better; that man came out and told me that he knew my relations at

Agimaque, and that we must set out to-morrow morning, and he would convey me there. Accordingly we set out next day, and travelled till dark, when we came to a place where we had some supper and slept. He carried a large bag with some gold dust, which he said he had to buy some goods at the sea side to take with him to Agimaque. Next day we travelled on, and in the evening came to a town, where I saw several white people, which made me afraid that they would eat me, according to our notion as children in the inland parts of the country. This made me rest very uneasy all the night, and next morning I had some victuals brought, desiring me to eat and make haste, as my guide and kid-napper told me that he had to go to the castle with some company that were going there, as he had told me before, to get some goods. After I was ordered out, the horrors I soon saw and felt, cannot be well described; I saw many of my miserable countrymen chained two and two, some hand-cuffed, and some with their hands tied behind. We were conducted along by a guard, and when we arrived at the castle, I asked my guide what I was brought there for, he told me to learn the ways of the *browfow,* that is the white faced people. I saw him take a gun, a piece of cloth, and some lead for me, and then he told me that he must now leave me there, and went off. This made me cry bitterly, but I was soon conducted to a prison, for three days, where I heard the groans and cries of many, and saw some of my fellow-captives. But when a vessel arrived to conduct us away to the ship, it was a most horrible scene; there was nothing to be heard but rattling of chains, smacking of whips, and the groans and cries of our fellow-men. Some would not stir from the ground, when they were lashed and beat in the most horrible manner. I have forgot the name of this infernal fort; but we were taken in the ship that came for us, to another that was ready to sail from Cape Coast.[9] When we were put into the ship, we saw several black merchants coming on board, but we were all drove into our holes, and not suffered to speak to any of them. In this situation we continued several days in sight of our native land; but I could find no good person to give any information of my situation to Accasa at Agimaque. And when we found ourselves at last taken away, death was more preferable than life, and a plan was concerted amongst us, that we might burn and blow up the ship, and to perish all together in the flames; but we were betrayed by one of our own countrywomen, who slept with some of the head men of the ship, for it was common for the dirty filthy sailors to take the African women and lie upon their bodies; but the

---

castle: slaving fort.

[9]Cape Coast Castle, a major center for the European slave trade located on the Gold Coast (in present-day Ghana).

men were chained and pent up in holes. It was the women and boys which were to burn the ship, with the approbation and groans of the rest; though that was prevented, the discovery was likewise a cruel bloody scene.

But it would be needless to give a description of all the horrible scenes which we saw, and the base treatment which we met with in this dreadful captive situation, as the similar cases of thousands, which suffer by this infernal traffic, are well known. Let it suffice to say, that I was thus lost to my dear indulgent parents and relations, and they to me. All my help was cries and tears, and these could not avail; nor suffered long, till one succeeding woe, and dread, swelled up another. Brought from a state of innocence and freedom, and, in a barbarous and cruel manner, conveyed to a state of horror and slavery: This abandoned situation may be easier conceived than described. From the time that I was kid-napped and conducted to a factory, and from thence in the brutish, base, but fashionable way of traffic, consigned to Grenada, the grievous thoughts which I then felt, still pant in my heart; though my fears and tears have long since subsided. And yet it is still grievous to think that thousands more have suffered in similar and greater distress, under the hands of barbarous robbers, and merciless task-masters; and that many even now are suffering in all the extreme bitterness of grief and woe, that no language can describe. The cries of some, and the sight of their misery, may be seen and heard afar; but the deep sounding groans of thousands, and the great sadness of their misery and woe, under the heavy load of oppressions and calamities inflicted upon them, are such as can only be distinctly known to the ears of Jehovah Sabaoth.[10]

This Lord of Hosts, in his great Providence, and in great mercy to me, made a way for my deliverance from Grenada.—Being in this dreadful captivity and horrible slavery, without any hope of deliverance, for about eight or nine months, beholding the most dreadful scenes of misery and cruelty, and seeing my miserable companions often cruelly lashed, and as it were cut to pieces, for the most trifling faults; this made me often tremble and weep, but I escaped better than many of them. For eating a piece of sugarcane, some were cruelly lashed, or struck over the face to knock their teeth out. Some of the stouter ones, I suppose often reproved, and grown hardened and stupid with many cruel beatings and lashings, or perhaps faint and pressed with hunger and hard labour, were often committing trespasses of this kind, and when detected, they met with exemplary punishment. Some told me they had their teeth pulled out to deter others, and to prevent them from eating any cane in future. Thus seeing my miserable

---

[10] Old Testament term for God transliterated from Hebrew, translated by Cugoano in the next sentence as "Lord of Hosts."

companions and countrymen in this pitiful, distressed and horrible situation, with all the brutish baseness and barbarity attending it, could not but fill my little mind with horror and indignation. But I must own, to the shame of my own countrymen, that I was first kid-napped and betrayed by some of my own complexion, who were the first cause of my exile and slavery; but if there were no buyers there would be no sellers. So far as I can remember, some of the Africans in my country keep slaves, which they take in war, or for debt; but those which they keep are well fed, and good care taken of them, and treated well; and, as to their cloathing, they differ according to the custom of the country. But I may safely say, that all the poverty and misery that any of the inhabitants of Africa meet with among themselves, is far inferior to those inhospitable regions of misery which they meet with in the West-Indies, where their hard-hearted overseers have neither regard to the laws of God, nor the life of their fellow-men.

Thanks be to God, I was delivered from Grenada, and that horrid brutal slavery. — A gentleman coming to England, took me for his servant, and brought me away, where I soon found my situation become more agreeable. After coming to England, and seeing others write and read, I had a strong desire to learn, and getting what assistance I could, I applied myself to learn reading and writing, which soon became my recreation, pleasure, and delight; and when my master perceived that I could write some, he sent me to a proper school for that purpose to learn. Since, I have endeavoured to improve my mind in reading, and have sought to get all the intelligence I could, in my situation of life, towards the state of my brethren and countrymen in complexion, and of the miserable situation of those who are barbarously sold into captivity, and unlawfully held in slavery.

But, among other observations, one great duty I owe to Almighty God, (the thankful acknowledgement I would not omit for any consideration) that, although I have been brought away from my native country, in that torrent of robbery and wickedness, thanks be to God for his good providence towards me; I have both obtained liberty, and acquired the great advantages of some little learning, in being able to read and write, and, what is still infinitely of greater advantage, I trust, to know something of HIM *who is that God whose providence rules over all, and who is the only Potent One that rules in the nations over the children of men. It is unto Him, who is the Prince of the Kings of the earth, that I would give all thanks.*[11] And, in some manner, I may say with Joseph, as he did with respect to the evil intention of his brethren, when they sold him into Egypt, that whatever evil intentions and bad motives those insidious robbers had in carrying me

---

[11] From I Timothy 6:15 and Revelation 1:5.

away from my native country and friends, I trust, was what the Lord intended for my good.[12] In this respect, I am highly indebted to many of the good people of England for learning and principles unknown to the people of my native country. But, above all, what have I obtained from the Lord God of Hosts, the God of the Christians! in that divine revelation of the only true God, and the Saviour of men, what a treasure of wisdom and blessings are involved? How wonderful is the divine goodness displayed in those invaluable books the Old and New Testaments, that inestimable compilation of books, the Bible? And, O what a treasure to have, and one of the greatest advantages to be able to read therein, and a divine blessing to understand![13]...

But again, when he[14] draws a comparison of the many hardships that the poor in Great-Britain and Ireland labour under, as well as many of those in other countries; that their various distresses are worse than the West India slaves—It may be true, in part, that some of them suffer greater hardships than many of the slaves; but, bad as it is, the poorest in England would not change their situation for that of slaves. And there may be some masters, under various circumstances, worse off than their servants; but they would not change their own situation for theirs: Nor as little would a rich man wish to change his situation of affluence, for that of a beggar: and so, likewise, no freeman, however poor and distressing his situation may be, would resign his liberty for that of a slave, in the situation of a horse or a dog. The case of the poor, whatever their hardships may be, in free countries, is widely different from that of the West-India slaves. For the slaves, like animals, are bought and sold, and dealt with as their capricious owners may think fit, even in torturing and tearing them to pieces, and wearing them out with hard labour, hunger and oppression; and should the death of a slave ensue by some other more violent way than that which is commonly the death of thousands, and tens of thousands in the end, the haughty tyrant, in that case, has only to pay a small fine for the murder and death of his slave. The brute creation in general may fare better than man, and some dogs may refuse the crumbs that the distressed poor would be glad of; but the nature and situation of man is far superior to that of beasts; and, in like manner, whatever circumstances poor freemen may be in, their

---

[12] The story of Joseph's betrayal into slavery is told in Genesis 37–45.

[13] Here Cugoano includes a note quoting passages from Edward Young (1683–1765), *Night Thoughts on Life, Death, and Immortality* (1742–1745), *Night* VIII, 769–773, and *Night* VII, 1360–1365, 1368.

[14] Cugoano here is critically addressing a proslavery work by James Tobin (?–1817), *Cursory Remarks upon the Reverend Mr. Ramsay's Essay on the Treatment and Conversion of African Slaves in the Sugar Colonies* (1785).

situation is much superior, beyond any proportion, to that of the hardships and cruelty of modern slavery. But where can the situation of any freeman be so bad as that of a slave; or, could such be found, or even worse, as he would have it, what would the comparison amount to? Would it plead for his craft of slavery and oppression? Or, rather, would it not cry aloud for some redress, and what every well regulated society of men ought to hear and consider, that none should suffer want or be oppressed among them? And this seems to be pointed out by the circumstances which he describes; that it is the great duty, and ought to be the highest ambition of all governors, to order and establish such policy, and in such a wise manner, that every thing should be so managed, as to be conducive to the moral, temporal and eternal welfare of every individual from the lowest degree to the highest; and the consequence of this would be, the harmony, happiness and good prosperity of the whole community.

But this crafty author has also, in defence of his own or his employer's craft in the British West-India slavery, given sundry comparisons and descriptions of the treatment of slaves in the French islands and settlements in the West-Indies and America. And, contrary to what is the true case, he would have it supposed that the treatment of the slaves in the former, is milder than the latter; but even in this, unwarily for his own craft of slavery, all that he has advanced, can only add matter for its confutation, and serve to heighten the ardour and wish of every generous mind, that the whole should be abolished. An equal degree of enormity found in one place, cannot justify crimes of as great or greater enormity committed in another. The various depredations committed by robbers and plunderers, on different parts of the globe, may not be all equally alike bad, but their evil and malignancy, in every appearance and shape, can only hold up to view the just observation, that

> *Virtue herself hath such peculiar mein,*
> *Vice, to be hated, needs but to be seen.*[15]

The farther and wider that the discovery and knowledge of such an enormous evil, as the base and villainous treatment and slavery which the poor unfortunate Black People meet with, is spread and made known, the cry for justice, even virtue lifting up her voice, must rise the louder and higher, for the scale of equity and justice to be lifted up in their defence. *And doth not wisdom cry, and understanding put forth her voice?* But who will regard the voice and hearken to the cry? Not the sneaking advocates for

---

[15]Not identified.

slavery, though a little ashamed of their craft; like the monstrous crocodile weeping over their prey with fine concessions (while gorging their own rapacious appetite) to hope for universal freedom taking place over the globe. Not those inebriated with avarice and infidelity, who hold in defiance every regard due to the divine law, and who endeavour all they can to destroy and take away the natural and common rights and privileges of men. . . .

But such is the insensibility of men, when their own craft of gain is advanced by the slavery and oppression of others, that after all the laudable exertions of the truly virtuous and humane, towards extending the beneficence of liberty and freedom to the much degraded and unfortunate Africans, which is the common right and privilege of all men, in every thing that is just, lawful and consistent, we find the principles of justice and equity, not only opposed, and every duty in religion and humanity left unregarded; but that unlawful traffic of dealing with our fellow-creatures, as with the beasts of the earth, still carried on with as great assiduity as ever; and that the insidious piracy of procuring and holding slaves is countenanced and supported by the government of sundry Christian nations. This seems to be the fashionable way of getting riches, but very dishonourable; in doing this, the slave-holders are meaner and baser than the African slaves, for while they subject and reduce them to a degree with brutes, they seduce themselves to a degree with devils.

"Some pretend that the Africans, in general, are a set of poor, ignorant, dispersed, unsociable people; and that they think it no crime to sell one another, and even their own wives and children; therefore they bring them away to a situation where many of them may arrive to a better state than ever they could obtain in their own native country." This specious pretence is without any shadow of justice and truth, and, if the argument was even true, it could afford no just and warrantable matter for any society of men to hold slaves. But the argument is false; there can be no ignorance, dispersion, or unsociableness so found among them, which can be made better by bringing them away to a state of a degree equal to that of a cow or a horse.

But let their ignorance in some things (in which the Europeans have greatly the advantage of them) be what it will, it is not the intention of those who bring them away to make them better by it; nor is the design of slave-holders of any other intention, but that they may serve them as a kind of engines and beasts of burden; that their own ease and profit may be advanced, by a set of poor helpless men and women, whom they despise and rank with brutes, and keep them in perpetual slavery, both themselves and children, and merciful death is the only release from their toil. By the benevolence of some, a few may get their liberty, and by their own industry and ingenuity, may acquire some learning, mechanical trades, or useful business; and some may be brought away by different gentlemen to free countries, where they get their liberty, but no thanks to slave-holders for it. But amongst those who get their liberty, like all other ignorant men, are generally more corrupt in their morals, than they possibly could have been amongst their own people in Africa; for, being mostly amongst the wicked and apostate Christians, they sooner learn their oaths and blasphemies, and their evil ways, than any thing else. Some few, indeed, may eventually arrive at some knowledge of the Christian religion, and the great advantages of it. Such was the case of Ukawsaw Groniosaw, an African prince, who lived in England.[16] He was a long time in a state of great poverty and distress, and must have died at one time for want, if a good and charitable Attorney had not supported him. He was long after in a very poor state, but he would not have given his faith in the Christian religion, in exchange for all the kingdoms of Africa, if they could have been given to him, in place of his poverty, for it. And such was A. Morrant in America.[17] When a boy, he could stroll away into a desart, and prefer the society of wild beasts to the absurd Christianity of his mother's house. He was conducted to the king of the Cherokees, who, in a miraculous manner, was induced by him to embrace the Christian faith. This Morrant was in the British service last war, and his royal convert, the king of the Cherokee Indians, accompanied General Clinton at the siege of Charles Town. . . .

In a Christian æra, in a land where Christianity is planted, where every one might expect to behold the flourishing growth of every virtue, extending their harmonious branches with universal philanthropy wherever they came; but, on the contrary, almost nothing else is to be seen abroad but the bramble of ruffians, barbarians and slave-holders, grown up to a powerful luxuriance in wickedness. I cannot but wish, for the honor of Christianity, that the bramble grown up amongst them, was known to the heathen nations by a different name, for sure the depredators, robbers and ensnarers of men can never be Christians, but ought to be held as the abhorence of all men, and the abomination of all mankind, whether Christians or heathens. Every man of any sensibility, whether he be a Christian or an heathen, if he has any discernment at all, must think, that for any man, or any class of men, to deal with their fellow-creatures as with the beasts of the field; or to account them as such, however ignorant they may be, and in whatever situation, or wherever they may find them, and whatever country

---

[16] Gronniosaw's *Narrative* is included in full in this volume, pages 47–78.

[17] John Marrant (1755–1791), *A Narrative of the Lord's Wonderful Dealings with John Marrant, a Black* (1785).

or complexion they may be of, that those men, who are the procurers and holders of slaves, are the greatest villains in the world. And surely those men must be lost to all sensibility themselves, who can think that the stealing, robbing, enslaving, and murdering of men can be no crimes; but the holders of men in slavery are at the head of all these oppressions and crimes. And, therefore, however unsensible they may be of it now, and however long they may laugh at the calamity of others, if they do not repent of their evil way, and the wickedness of their doings, by keeping and holding their fellow-creatures in slavery, and trafficking with them as with the brute creation, and to give up and surrender that evil traffic, with an awful abhorrence of it, that this may be averred, if they do not, and if they can think, they must and cannot otherwise but expect in one day at last, to meet with the full stroke of the long suspended vengeance of heaven when death will cut them down to a state as mean as that of the most abjected slave, and to a very eminent danger of a far more dreadful fate hereafter, when they have the just reward of their iniquities to meet with.

And now, as to the Africans being dispersed and unsociable, if it was so, that could be no warrant for the Europeans to enslave them; and even though they may have many different feuds and bad practices among them, the continent of Africa is of vast extent, and the numerous inhabitants are divided into several kingdoms and principalities, which are governed by their respective kings and princes, and those are absolutely maintained by their free subjects. Very few nations make slaves of any of those under their government; but such as are taken prisoners of war from their neighbours, are generally kept in that state, until they can exchange and dispose of them otherwise; and towards the west coast they are generally procured for the European market, and sold. They have a great aversion to murder, or even in taking away the lives of those which they judge guilty of crimes; and, therefore, they prefer disposing of them otherwise better than killing them.* This gives their merchants and procurers of slaves a power to travel a great way into the interior parts of the country to buy such as are wanted to be disposed of. These slave-procurers are a set of as great villains as any in the world. They often steal and kidnap many more than they buy at first, if they can meet with them by the way; and they have only their certain boundaries to go to, and sell them from one to another; so that if they are sought after and detected, the thieves are seldom found, and the others

---

*It may be true, that some of the slaves transported from Africa, may have committed crimes in their own country, that require some slavery as a punishment; but, according to the laws of equity and justice, they ought to become free, as soon as their labour has paid for their purchase in the West-Indies or elsewhere. [Cugoano's note.]

only plead that they bought them so and so. These kid-nappers and slave-procurers, called merchants, are a species of African villains, which are greatly corrupted; and even viciated by their intercourse with the Europeans; but, wicked and barbarous as they certainly are, I can hardly think, if they knew what horrible barbarity they were sending their fellow-creatures to, that they would do it. But the artful Europeans have so deceived them, that they are bought by their inventions of merchandize, and beguiled into it by their artifice; for the Europeans, at their factories, in some various manner, have always kept some as servants to them, and with gaudy cloaths, in a gay manner, as decoy ducks to deceive others, and to tell them that they want many more to go over the sea, and be as they are. So in that respect, wherein it may be said that they will sell one another, they are only ensnared and enlisted to be servants, kept like some of those which they see at the factories, which, for some gew-gaws, as presents given to themselves and friends, they are thereby enticed to go; and something after the same manner that East-India soldiers are procured in Britain; and the inhabitants here, just as much sell themselves, and one another, as they do; and the kid-nappers here, and the slave-procurers in Africa, are much alike: But many other barbarous methods are made use of by the vile instigators, procurers and ensnarers of men; and some of the wicked and profligate princes and chiefs of Africa accept of presents, from the Europeans, to procure a certain number of slaves; and thereby they are wickedly instigated to go to war with one another on purpose to get them, which produces many terrible depredations; and sometimes when those engagements are entered into, and they find themselves defeated of their purpose, it has happened that some of their own people have fallen a sacrifice to their avarice and cruelty. And it may be said of the Europeans, that they have made use of every insidious method to procure slaves whenever they can, and in whatever manner they can lay hold of them, and that their forts and factories are the avowed dens of thieves for robbers, plunderers and depredators.

But again, as to the Africans selling their own wives and children, nothing can be more opposite to every thing they hold dear and valuable; and nothing can distress them more, than to part with any of their relations and friends. Such are the tender feelings of parents for their children, that, for the loss of a child, they seldom can be rendered happy, even with the intercourse and enjoyment of their friends, for years. For any man to think that it should be otherwise, when he may see a thousand instances of a natural instinct, even in the brute creation, where they have a sympathetic feeling for their offspring; it must be great want of consideration not to think, that much more than merely what is natural to animals, should in a higher degree be implanted in the breast of every part of the rational creation of man. And what man of feeling can help lamenting the loss of parents, friends, liberty, and perhaps property and other valuable and dear connections. Those people annually brought away from Guinea, are born as free, and are brought up with as great a predilection for their own country, freedom and liberty, as the sons and daughters of fair Britain. Their free subjects are trained up to a kind of military service, not so much by the desire of the chief, as by their own voluntary inclination. It is looked upon as the greatest respect they can shew to their king, to stand up for his and their own defence in time of need. Their different chieftains, which bear a reliance on the great chief, or king, exercise a kind of government something like that feudal institution which prevailed some time in Scotland. In this respect, though the common people are free, they often suffer by the villainy of their different chieftains, and by the wars and feuds which happen among them. Nevertheless, their freedom and rights are as dear to them, as those privileges are to other people. And it may be said that freedom, and the liberty of enjoying their own privileges, burns with as much zeal and fervour in the breast of an Æthiopian, as in the breast of any inhabitant on the globe.

But the supporters and favourers of slavery make other things a pretence and an excuse in their own defence; such as, that they find that it was admitted under the Divine institution by Moses, as well as the long continued practice of different nations for ages; and that the Africans are peculiarly marked out by some signal prediction in nature and complexion for that purpose.

This seems to be the greatest bulwark of defence which the advocates and favourers of slavery can advance, and what is generally talked of in their favour by those who do not understand it. I shall consider it in that view, whereby it will appear, that they deceive themselves and mislead others. Men are never more liable to be drawn into error, than when truth is made use of in a guileful manner to seduce them. Those who do not believe the scriptures to be a Divine revelation, cannot, consistently with themselves, make the law of Moses, or any mark or prediction they can find respecting any particular set of men, as found in the sacred writings, any reason that one class of men should enslave another. In that respect, all that they have to enquire into should be, whether it be right, or wrong, that any part of the human species should enslave another; and when that is the case, the Africans, though not so learned, are just as wise as the Europeans; and when the matter is left to human wisdom, they are both liable to err. But what the light of nature, and the dictates of reason, when rightly

---

Æthiopian: here, connotes dark-skinned African.

considered, teach, is, that no man ought to enslave another; and some, who have been rightly guided thereby, have made noble defences for the universal natural rights and privileges of all men. But in this case, when the learned take neither revelation nor reason for their guide, they fall into as great, and worse errors, than the unlearned; for they only make use of that system of Divine wisdom, which should guide them into truth, when they can find or pick out any thing that will suit their purpose, or that they can pervert to such—the very means of leading themselves and others into error. And, in consequence thereof, the pretenses that some men make use of for holding of slaves, must be evidently the grossest perversion of reason, as well as an inconsistent and diabolical use of the sacred writings. For it must be a strange perversion of reason, and a wrong use or disbelief of the sacred writings, when any thing found there is so perverted by them, and set up as a precedent and rule for men to commit wickedness. They had better have no reason, and no belief in the scriptures, and make no use of them at all, than only to believe, and make use of that which leads them into the most abominable evil and wickedness of dealing unjustly with their fellow men.

But this will appear evident to all men that believe the scriptures, that every reason necessary is given that they should be believed; and, in this case, that they afford us this information: "That all mankind did spring from one original, and that there are no different species among men. For God who made the world, hath made of one blood all the nations of men that dwell on all the face of the earth." Wherefore we may justly infer, as there are no inferior species, but all of one blood and of one nature, that there does not an inferiority subsist, or depend, on their colour, features or form, whereby some men make a pretence to enslave others; and consequently, as they have all one creator, one original, made of one blood, and all brethren descended from one father, it never could be lawful and just for any nation, or people, to oppress and enslave another. . . .

They that can stand and look on and behold no evil in the infamous traffic of slavery must be sunk to a wonderful degree of insensibility; but surely those that can delight in that evil way for their gain, and be pleased with the wickedness of the wicked, and see no harm in subjecting their fellow-creatures to slavery, and keeping them in a state of bondage and subjection as a brute, must be wretchedly brutish indeed. But so bewitched are the general part of mankind with some sottish or selfish principle, that they care nothing about what is right or wrong, any farther than their own interest leads them to; and when avarice leads them on they can plead a thousand excuses for doing wrong, or letting others do wickedly, so as they have any advantage by it, to their own gratification and use. That sottish and selfish principle, without concern and discernment among men is such, that if they can only prosper themselves, they care nothing about the miserable situation of others: and hence it is, that even those who are elevated to high rank of power and affluence, and as becoming their eminent stations, have opportunity of extending their views afar, yet they can shut their eyes at this enormous evil of the slavery and commerce of the human species; and, contrary to all the boasted accomplishments, and fine virtues of the civilized and enlightened nations, they can sit still and let the torrent of robbery, slavery, and oppression roll on.

There is a way which seemeth good unto a man, but the end thereof are the ways of death. Should the enslavers of men think to justify themselves in their evil way, or that it can in any possible way be right for them to subject others to slavery; it is but charitable to evince and declare unto them, that they are those who have gone into that evil way of brutish stupidity as well as wickedness, that they can behold nothing of moral rectitude and equity among men but in the gloomy darkness of their own hemisphere, like the owls and night-hawks, who can see nothing but mist and darkness in the meridian blaze of day. When men forsake the paths of virtue, righteousness, justice, and mercy, and become vitiated in any evil way, all their pretended virtues, sensibility, and prudence among men, however high they may shine in their own, and of others estimation, will only appear to be but specious villainy at last. That virtue which will ever do men any good in the end, is as far from that which some men call such, as the gaudy appearance of a glow-worm in the dark is to the intrinsic value and lustre of a diamond: for if a man hath not love in his heart to his fellow-creatures, with a generous philanthropy diffused throughout his whole soul, all his other virtues are not worth a straw.

The whole law of God is founded upon love, and the two grand branches of it are these: *Thou shalt love the Lord thy God with all thy heart and with all thy soul, and thou shalt love thy neighbour as thyself.*[18] And so it was when man was first created and made: they were created male and female, and pronounced to be in the image of God, and, as his representative, to have dominion over the lower creation: and their Maker, who is love, and the intellectual Father of Spirits, blessed them, and commanded them to arise in a bond of union of nature and of blood, each being a brother and a sister together, and each the lover and the loved of one another. But when they were envied and invaded by the grand enslaver of men, all their jarring incoherency arose, and those who adhered to their pernicious usurper soon became envious, hateful, and hating one another. And those who go on to injure, ensnare, oppress, and enslave their

---

[18] Matthew 22:37–39.

fellow-creatures, manifest their hatred to men, and maintain their own infamous dignity and vassalage, as the servants of sin and the devil: but the man that has any honour as a man scorns their ignominious dignity: the noble philanthropist looks up to his God and Father as his only sovereign; and he looks around on his fellow men as his brethren and friends; and in every situation and case, however mean and contemptible they may seem, he endeavours to do them good: and should he meet with one in the desert, whom he never saw before, he would hail him my brother! my sister! my friend! how fares it with thee? And if he can do any of them any good it would gladden every nerve of his soul.

But as there is but *one law and one manner* prescribed universally for all mankind, *for you, and for the stranger that sojourneth with you,* and wheresoever they may be scattered throughout the face of the whole earth, the difference of superiority and inferiority which are found subsisting amongst them is no way incompatible with the universal law of love, honor, righteousness, and equity; so that a free, voluntary, and sociable servitude, which is the very basis of human society, either civil or religious, whereby we serve one another that we may be served, or do good that good may be done unto us, is in all things requisite and agreeable to all law and justice. But the taking away the natural liberties of men, and compelling them to any involuntary slavery, or compulsory service, is an injury and robbery contrary to all law, civilization, reason, justice, equity, and humanity: therefore when men break through the laws of God, and the rules of civilization among men, and go forth to steal, to rob, to plunder, to oppress and to enslave, and to destroy their fellow-creatures, the laws of God and man require that they should be suppressed, and deprived of their liberty, or perhaps their lives.

But justice and equity does not always reside among men, even where some considerable degree of civilization is maintained; if it had, that most infamous reservoir of public and abandoned merchandizers and enslavers of men would not have been suffered so long, nor the poor unfortunate Africans, that never would have crossed the Atlantic to rob them, would not have become their prey. But it is just as great and as heinous a transgression of the law of God to steal, kidnap, buy, sell, and enslave any one of the Africans, as it would be to ensnare any other man in the same manner, let him be who he will. And suppose that some of the African pirates had been as dextrous as the Europeans, and that they had made excursions on the coast of Great-Britain or elsewhere, and though even assisted by some of your own insiduous neighbours, for there may be some men even among you vile enough to do such a thing if they could get money by it; and that they should carry off your sons and your daughters, and your wives and friends, to a perpetual and barbarous slavery, you would certainly think that those African pirates were justly deserving of any punishment that could be put upon them.[19] But the European pirates and merchandizers of the human species, let them belong to what nation they will, are equally as bad; and they have no better right to steal, kidnap, buy, and carry away and sell the Africans, than the Africans would have to carry away any of the Europeans in the same barbarous and unlawful manner. . . .

None but men of the most brutish and depraved nature, led on by the invidious influence of infernal wickedness, could have made their settlements in the different parts of the world discovered by them, and have treated the various Indian nations, in the manner that the barbarous inhuman Europeans have done: and their establishing and carrying on that most dishonest, unjust and diabolical traffic of buying and selling, and of enslaving men, is such a monstrous, audacious and unparallelled wickedness, that the very idea of it is shocking, and the whole nature of it is horrible and infernal. It may be said with confidence as a certain general fact, that all their foreign settlements and colonies were founded on murders and devastations, and that they have continued their depredations in cruel slavery and oppression to this day: for where such predominant wickedness as the African slave-trade, and the West Indian slavery, is admitted, tolerated and supported by them, and carried on in their colonies, the nations and people who are the supporters and encouragers thereof must be not only guilty themselves of that shameful and abandoned evil and wickedness, so very disgraceful to human nature, but even partakers in those crimes of the most vile combinations of various pirates, kidnappers, robbers and thieves, the ruffians and stealers of men, that ever made their appearance in the world. . . .

The Spaniards began their settlements in the West Indies and America, by depredations of rapine, injustice, treachery and murder; and they have continued in the barbarous practice of devastation, cruelty, and oppression ever since: and their principles and maxims in planting colonies have been adopted, in some measure, by every other nation in Europe. This guiltful method of colonization must undoubtedly and imperceptibly have hardened men's hearts, and led them on from one degree of barbarity and cruelty to another: for when they had destroyed, wasted and desolated the native inhabitants, and when many of their own people, enriched with plunder, had retired, or returned home to enjoy their ill-gotten wealth, other resources for men to labour and cultivate the ground, and such other

---

[19]Muslim pirates from the north coast of Africa (the "Barbary pirates") posed a major problem for European shipping from the seventeenth century through the 1820s, taking numerous Europeans captive and selling them for ransom or into slavery.

laborious employments were wanted. Vast territories and large posses-sions, without getting inhabitants to labour for them, were of no use. A general part of what remained of the wretched fugitives, who had the best native right to those possessions, were obliged to make their escape to places more remote, and such as could not, were obliged to submit to the hard labour and bondage of their invaders; but as they had not been used to such harsh treatment and laborious employment as they were then sub-jected to, they were soon wasted away and became few. Their proud in-vaders found the advantage of having their labour done for nothing, and it became their general practice to pick up the unfortunate strangers that fell in their way, when they thought they could make use of them in their ser-vice. That base traffic of kidnapping and stealing men was begun by the Portuguese on the coast of Africa, and as they found the benefit of it for their own wicked purposes, they soon went on to commit greater depre-dations. The Spaniards followed their infamous example, and the African slave-trade was thought most advantageous for them, to enable themselves to live in ease and affluence by the cruel subjection and slavery of others. The French and English, and some other nations in Europe, as they founded settlements and colonies in the West Indies, or in America, went on in the same manner, and joined hand in hand with the Portuguese and Spaniards, to rob and pillage Africa, as well as to waste and desolate the in-habitants of the western continent. But the European depredators and pi-rates have not only robbed and pillaged the people of Africa themselves; but, by their instigation, they have infested the inhabitants with some of the vilest combinations of fraudulent and treacherous villains, even among their own people; and have set up their forts and factories as a reservoir of public and abandoned thieves, and as a den of desperadoes, where they may ensnare, entrap and catch men. So that Africa has been robbed of its inhabitants; its free-born sons and daughters have been stole, and kid-napped, and violently taken away, and carried into captivity and cruel bondage. And it may be said, in respect to that diabolical traffic which is still carried on by the European depredators, that Africa has suffered as much and more than any other quarter of the globe. O merciful God! when will the wickedness of man have an end? . . .

But whereas the people of Great-Britain having now acquired a greater share in that iniquitous commerce than all the rest together, they are the first that ought to set an example, lest they have to repent for their wicked-ness when it becomes too late; lest some impending calamity should speed-ily burst forth against them, and lest a just retribution for their enormous crimes, and a continuance in committing similar deeds of barbarity and injustice should involve them in ruin. For we may be assured that God will certainly avenge himself of such heinous transgressors of his law, and of all those planters and merchants, and of all others, who are the authors of the Africans graves, severities, and cruel punishments, and no plea of any absolute necessity can possibly excuse them. And as the inhabitants of Great-Britain, and the inhabitants of the colonies, seem almost equally guilty of the oppression, there is great reason for both to dread the severe vengeance of Almighty God upon them, and upon all such notorious workers of wickedness; for it is evident that the legislature of Great-Britain patronises and encourages them, and shares in the infamous profits of the slavery of the Africans. It is therefore necessary that the inhabitants of the British nation should seriously consider these things for their own good and safety, as well as for our benefit and deliverance, and that they may be sensible of their own error and danger, lest they provoke the vengeance of the Almighty against them. For what wickedness was there ever risen up so monstrous, and more likely to bring a heavy rod of destruction upon a nation, than the deeds committed by the West-Indian slavery, and the African slave trade. And even in that part of it carried on by the Liverpool and Bristol merchants, the many shocking and inhuman instances of their barbarity and cruelty are such, that every one that heareth thereof has reason to tremble, and cry out, *Should not the land tremble for this, and every one mourn that dwelleth therein?*

The vast carnage and murders committed by the British instigators of slavery, is attended with a very shocking, peculiar, and almost unheard of conception, according to the notion of the perpetrators of it; they either consider them as their own property, that they may do with as they please, in life or death; or that the taking away the life of a black man is of no more account than taking away the life of a beast. A very melancholy instance of this happened about the year 1780, as recorded in the courts of law;[20] a master of a vessel bound to the Western Colonies, selected 132 of the most sickly of the black slaves, and ordered them to be thrown overboard into the sea, in order to recover their value from the insurers, as he had perceived that he was too late to get a good market for them in the West-Indies. On the trial, by the counsel for the owners of the vessel against the underwriters, their argument was, that the slaves were to be considered the same as horses; and their plea for throwing them into the sea, was nothing better

---

[20] In 1781 the captain of the *Zong,* a British-owned slaving ship en route to Jamaica from West Africa, instructed his crew to throw 133 slaves overboard rather than risk losing them to disease, as the ship's insurers would cover the value of slaves murdered for alleged reasons of safety but not of those dying from natural causes. All but one of the slaves perished. When Olaudah Equiano learned of the massacre, he alerted the antislavery activist Granville Sharp, who publicized the incident and pressed (unsuccessfully) for judicial prosecution.

than that it might be more necessary to throw them overboard to lighten their vessel than goods of greater value, or something to that effect. These poor creatures, it seems, were tied two and two together when they were thrown into the sea, lest some of them might swim a little for the last gasp of air, and, with the animation of their approaching exit, breath their souls away to the gracious Father of spirits. Some of the last parcel, when they saw the fate of their companions, made their escape from tying by jumping overboard, and one was saved by means of a rope from some in the ship. The owners of the vessel, I suppose, (inhuman connivers of robbery, slavery, murder and fraud) were rather a little defeated in this, by bringing their villainy to light in a court of law; but the inhuman monster of a captain was kept out of the way of justice from getting hold of him. Though such perpetrators of murder and fraud should have been sought after from the British Dan in the East-Indies to her Beershebah in the West.[21] . . .

But why should a total abolition, and an universal emancipation of slaves, and the enfranchisement of all the Black People employed in the culture of the Colonies, taking place as it ought to do, and without any hesitation, or delay for a moment, even though it might have some seeming appearance of loss either to government or to individuals, be feared at all? Their labour, as freemen, would be as useful in the sugar colonies as any other class of men that could be found; and should it even take place in such a manner that some individuals, at first, would suffer loss as a just reward for their wickedness in slave-dealing, what is that to the happiness and good of doing justice to others, and, I must say, to the great danger, otherwise, that must eventually hang over the whole community? It is certain, that the produce of the labour of slaves, together with all the advantages of the West-India traffic, bring in an immense revenue to government; but let that amount be what it will, there might be as much or more expected from the labour of an equal increase of free people, and without the implication of any guilt attending it, and which, otherwise, must be a greater burden to bear, and more ruinous consequences to be feared from it, than if the whole national debt was to sink at once, and to rest upon the heads of all that might suffer by it. Whereas, if a generous encouragement were to be given to a free people, peaceable among themselves, intelligent and industrious, who by art and labour would improve the most barren situations and make the most of that which is fruitful; the free and

---

culture: agriculture.

[21] "From Dan even to Beersheba" is a stock phrase in the Old Testament to express the full extent of Israel; Cugoano modifies it to convey the reach of the growing British empire from India in the East to the West Indian colonies in the Caribbean.

voluntary labour of many, would soon yield to any government, many greater advantages than any thing that slavery can produce. And this should be expected, wherever a Christian government is extended, and the true religion is embraced, that the blessings of liberty should be extended likewise, and that it should diffuse its influences first to fertilize the mind, and then the effects of its benignity would extend, and arise with exuberant blessings and advantages from all its operations. Was this to be the case, every thing would increase and prosper at home and abroad, and ten thousand times greater and greater advantages would arise to the state, and more permanent and solid benefit to individuals from the service of freemen, than ever they can reap, or in any possible way enjoy, by the labour of slaves. . . .

And now that blessings may come instead of a curse, and that many beneficent purposes of good might speedily arise and flow from it, and be more readily promoted: I would hereby presume to offer the following considerations, as some outlines of a general reformation which ought to be established and carried on. And first, I would propose, that there ought to be days of mourning and fasting appointed, to make enquiry into that great and pre-eminent evil for many years past carried on against the Heathen nations, and the horrible iniquity of making merchandize of us, and cruelly enslaving the poor Africans: and that you might seek grace and repentance, and find mercy and forgiveness before God Omnipotent; and that he may give you wisdom and understanding to devise what ought to be done.

Secondly, I would propose that a total abolition of slavery should be made and proclaimed; and that an universal emancipation of slaves should begin from the date thereof, and be carried on in the following manner: That a proclamation should be caused to be made, setting forth the Antichristian unlawfulness of the slavery and commerce of the human species; and that it should be sent to all the courts and nations in Europe, to require their advice and assistance, and as they may find it unlawful to carry it on, let them whosoever will join to prohibit it. And if such a proclamation be found advisable to the British legislature, let them publish it, and cause it to be published, throughout all the British empire, to hinder and prohibit all men under their government to traffic either in buying or selling men; and, to prevent it, a penalty might be made against it of one thousand pounds, for any man either to buy or sell another man. And that it should require all slave-holders, upon the immediate information thereof, to mitigate the labour of their slaves to that of a lawful servitude, without tortures or oppression; and that they should not hinder, but cause and procure some suitable means of instruction for them in the knowledge of the Christian religion. And agreeable to the late *royal Proclamation, for the En-*

couragement of Piety and Virtue, and for the preventing and punishing of Vice, Profaneness and Immorality;[22] that by no means, under any pretence whatsoever, either for themselves or their masters, the slaves under their subjection should not be suffered to work on the Sabbath days, unless it be such works as necessity and mercy may require. But that those days, as well as some other hours selected for the purpose, should be appropriated for the time of their instruction; and that if any of their owners should not provide such suitable instructors for them, that those slaves should be taken away from them and given to others who would maintain and instruct them for their labour. And that it should be made known to the slaves, that those who had been above seven years in the islands or elsewhere, if they had obtained any competent degree of knowledge of the Christian religion, and the laws of civilization, and had behaved themselves honestly and decently, that they should immediately become free; and that their owners should give them reasonable wages and maintenance for their labour, and not cause them to go away unless they could find some suitable employment elsewhere. And accordingly, from the date of their arrival to seven years, as they arrive at some suitable progress in knowledge, and behaved themselves honestly, that they should be getting free in the course of that time, and at the end of seven years to let every honest man and woman become free; for in the course of that time, they would have sufficiently paid their owners by their labour, both for their first purpose, and for the expences attending their education. By being thus instructed in the course of seven years, they would become tractable and obedient, useful labourers, dutiful servants and good subjects; and Christian men might have the honor and happiness to see many of them vieing with themselves to praise the God of their salvation. And it might be another necessary duty for Christians, in the course of that time, to make enquiry concerning some of their friends and relations in Africa: and if they found any intelligent persons amongst them, to give them as good education as they could, and find out a way of recourse to their friends; that as soon as they had made any progress in useful learning and the knowledge of the Christian religion, they might be sent back to Africa, to be made useful there as soon, and as many of them as could be made fit for instructing others. The rest would become useful residentors in the colonies; where there might be employment enough given to all free people, with suitable wages according to their

---

residentors: residents.

[22]Published in 1787 as *By the King, a Proclamation, for the Encouragement of Piety and Virtue* . . . ; keeping the Sabbath day holy (making Sunday a day of rest, churchgoing, and prayer) was a cause that appealed to laborers as well as to both Evangelical Church of England and Nonconformist Protestants.

usefulness, in the improvement of land; and the more encouragement that could be given to agriculture, and every other branch of useful industry, would thereby encrease the number of the inhabitants; without which any country, however blessed by nature, must continue poor.

And, thirdly, I would propose, that a fleet of some ships of war should be immediately sent to the coast of Africa, and particularly where the slave trade is carried on, with faithful men to direct that none should be brought from the coast of Africa without their own consent and the approbation of their friends, and to intercept all merchant ships that were bringing them away, until such a scrutiny was made, whatever nation they belonged to. And, I would suppose, if Great-Britain was to do any thing of this kind, that it would meet with the general approbation and assistance of other Christian nations; but whether it did or not, it could be very lawfully done at all the British forts and settlements on the coast of Africa; and particular remonstrances could be given to all the rest, to warn them of the consequences of such an evil and enormous wicked traffic as is now carried on. The Dutch have some crocodile settlers at the Cape,[23] that should be called to a particular account for their murders and inhuman barbarities. But all the present governors of the British forts and factories should be dismissed, and faithful and good men appointed in their room; and those forts and factories, which at present are a den of thieves, might be turned into shepherd's tents, and have good shepherds sent to call the flocks to feed beside them. Then would doors of hospitality in abundance be opened in Africa to supply the weary travellers, and that immense abundance which they are enriched with, might be diffused afar; but the character of the inhabitants on the west coast of Africa, and the rich produce of their country, have been too long misrepresented by avaricious plunderers and merchants who deal in slaves; and if that country was not annually ravished and laid waste, there might be a very considerable and profitable trade carried on with the Africans. And, should the noble Britons, who have often supported their own liberties with their lives and fortunes, extend their philanthropy to abolish the slavery and oppression of the Africans, they might have settlements and many kingdoms united in a friendly alliance with themselves, which might be made greatly to their own advantage, as well as they might have the happiness of being useful to promoting the prosperity and felicity of others, who have been cruelly injured and wrongfully dealt with. Were the Africans to be dealt with in a friendly manner, and kind

---

crocodile: hypocritical (from the proverbial "crocodile tears").

[23] The Dutch colony on the Cape of Good Hope at the southern tip of Africa, centered in Cape Town in present-day South Africa.

instruction to be administered unto them, as by degrees they became to love learning, there would be nothing in their power, but what they would wish to render their service in return for the means of improving their understanding; and the present British factories, and other settlements, might be enlarged to a very great extent. And as Great-Britain has been remarkable for ages past, for encouraging arts and sciences, and may now be put in competition with any nation in the known world, if they would take compassion on the inhabitants of the coast of Guinea, and to make use of such means as would be needful to enlighten their minds in the knowledge of Christianity, their virtue, in this respect, would have its own reward. And as the Africans became refined and established in light and knowledge, they would imitate their noble British friends, to improve their lands, and make use of that industry as the nature of their country might require, and to supply those that would trade with them, with such productions as the nature of their climate would produce; and, in every respect, the fair Britons would have the preference with them to a very great extent; and, in another respect, they would become a kind of first ornament to Great-Britain for her tender and compassionate care of such a set of distressed poor ignorant people. And were the noble Britons, and their august Sovereign, to cause protection and encouragement to be given to those Africans, they might expect in a short time, if need required it, to receive from thence great supplies of men in a lawful way, either for industry or defence; and of other things in abundance, from so great a source, where every thing is luxurious and plenty, if not laid waste by barbarity and gross ignorance. Due encouragement being given to so great, so just, and such a noble undertaking, would soon bring more revenue in a righteous way to the British nation, than ten times its share in all the profits that slavery can produce*; and such a laudable example would inspire every generous and enterprizing mind to imitate so great and worthy a nation, for establishing religion, justice, and equity to the Africans, and, in doing this, would be held in the highest esteem by all men, and be admired by all the world.

Guinea: West Africa.

*A gentleman of my acquaintance told me that, if ever he hears tell of any thing of this kind taking place, he has a plan in contemplation, which would, in some equitable manner, produce from one million to fifteen millions sterling to the British government annually, as it might be required; of which a due proportion of that revenue would be paid by the Africans; and that it would prevent all smuggling and illicit traffic; in a great measure, prevent running into debt, long imprisonment, and all unlawful bankruptcies; effectually prevent all dishonesty and swindling, and almost put an end to all robbery, fraud and theft. [Cugoano's note.]

These three preceding considerations may suffice at present to shew, that some plan might be adopted in such a manner as effectually to relieve the grievances and oppression of the Africans, and to bring great honour and blessings to that nation, and to all men whosoever would endeavour to promote so great good to mankind; and it might render more conspicuous advantages to the noble Britons, as the first doers of it, and greater honour than the finding of America was at first to those that made the discovery: Though several difficulties may seem to arise at first, and the good to be sought after may appear as remote and unknown, as it was to explore the unknown regions of the Western Ocean; should it be sought after, like the intrepid Columbus,[24] if they do not find kingdoms of wealth by the way, they may be certain of finding treasures of happiness and peace in the end. . . .

Particular thanks is due to every one of that humane society of worthy and respectful gentlemen whose liberality hath supported many of the Black poor about London.[25] *Those that honor their Maker have mercy on the poor; and many blessings are upon the head of the just: may the fear of the Lord prolong their days, and cause their memory to be blessed, and may their number be encreased to fill their expectation with gladness;* for they have not only commiserated the poor in general, *but even those which are accounted as beasts, and imputed as vile in the sight of others.* The part that the British government has taken, to co-operate with them, has certainly a flattering and laudable appearance of doing some good; and the fitting out ships to supply a company of Black People with clothes and provisions, and to carry them to settle at Sierra Leona, in the West coast of Africa, as a free colony to Great-Britain, in a peaceable alliance with the inhabitants, has every appearance of honour, and the approbation of friends.[26] According to the plan, humanity hath made its appearance in a more honorable way of colonization, than any Christian nation have ever done before, and may be productive of much good, if they continue to encourage and support them.

---

[24]Christopher Columbus (1451–1506), whose expeditions to the Americas in the 1490s and early 1500s opened the way for the European exploration and colonization of the New World.

[25]The Committee for the Relief of the Black Poor, established in 1786.

[26]In 1786 the British government and the Committee for the Relief of the Black Poor joined in supporting a plan to relocate large numbers of the "Black Poor" in Sierra Leone on the West Coast of Africa. Many of the intended settlers were loyalists who had been promised their freedom for supporting the British during the American Revolution. There was a good deal of skepticism regarding the Sierra Leone scheme, which was implemented only through a good deal of coercion and ended in disaster.

But after all, there is some doubt whether their own flattering expectation in the manner as set forth to them, and the hope of their friends may not be defeated and rendered abortive; and there is some reason to fear, that they never will be settled as intended, in any permanent and peaceable way at Sierra Leona.

This prospect of settling a free colony to Great-Britain in a peaceable alliance with the inhabitants of Africa at Sierra Leona, has neither altogether met with the credulous approbation of the Africans here, nor yet been sought after with any prudent and right plan by the promoters of it. Had a treaty of agreement been first made with the inhabitants of Africa, and the terms and nature of such a settlement fixed upon, and its situation and boundary pointed out; then might the Africans, and others here, have embarked with a good prospect of enjoying happiness and prosperity themselves, and have gone with a hope of being able to render their services, in return, of some advantage to their friends and benefactors of Great-Britain. But as this was not done, and as they were to be hurried away at all events, come of them after what would; and yet, after all, to be delayed in the ships before they were set out from the coast, until many of them have perished with cold, and other disorders, and several of the most intelligent among them are dead, and others that, in all probability, would have been most useful for them were hindered from going, by means of some disagreeable jealousy of those who were appointed as governors, the great prospect of doing good seems all to be blown away.[27] And so it appeared to some of those who are now gone, and at last, hap hazard, were obliged to go; who endeavoured in vain to get away by plunging into the water, that they might, if possible wade ashore, as dreading the prospect of their wretched fate, and as beholding their perilous situation, having every prospect of difficulty and surrounding danger.

What with the death of some of the original promoters and proposers of this charitable undertaking, and the death and deprivation of others that were to share the benefit of it, and by the adverse motives of those employed to be the conductors thereof, we think it will be more than what can be well expected, if we ever hear of any good in proportion to so great, well designed, laudable and expensive charity. Many more of the Black People still in this country would have, with great gladness, embraced the opportunity, longing to reach their native land; but as the old saying is, A burnt child dreads the fire, some of these unfortunate sons and daughters of

---

[27] Cugoano's friend Olaudah Equiano was among those who abandoned the Sierra Leone expedition as its poor planning and corrupt management became evident; see Equiano's account on pages 172–175.

Africa have been severally unlawfully dragged away from their native abodes, under various pretences, by the insidious treachery of others, and have been brought into the hands of barbarous robbers and pirates, and, like sheep to the market, have been sold into captivity and slavery, and thereby have been deprived of their natural liberty and property, and every connection that they held dear and valuable, and subjected to the cruel service of the hard-hearted brutes called planters. But some of them, by various services either to the public or to individuals, as more particularly in the course of last war, have gotten their liberty again in this free country. They are thankful for the respite, but afraid of being ensnared again; for the European seafaring people in general, who trade to foreign parts, have such a prejudice against Black People, that they use them more like asses than men, so that a Black Man is scarcely ever safe among them. Much assiduity was made use to perswade the Black People in general to embrace the opportunity of going with this company of transports; but the wiser sort declined from all thoughts of it, unless they could hear of some better plan taking place for their security and safety. For as it seemed prudent and obvious to many of them taking heed to that sacred enquiry, *Doth a fountain send forth at the same place sweet water and bitter?*[28] They were afraid that their doom would be to drink of the bitter water. For can it be readily conceived that government would establish a free colony for them nearly on the spot, while it supports its forts and garrisons, to ensnare, merchandize, and to carry others into captivity and slavery. . . .

And let me now hope that you will pardon me in all that I have been thus telling you, O ye inhabitants of Great-Britain! to whom I owe the greatest respects; to your king! to yourselves! and to your government! And tho' many things which I have written may seem harsh, it cannot be otherwise evaded when such horible iniquity is transacted: and tho' to some what I have said may appear as the rattling leaves of autumn, that may soon be blown away and whirled in a vortex where few can hear and know: I must yet say, although it is not for me to determine the manner, that the voice of our complaint implies a vengeance, because of the great iniquity that you have done, and because of the cruel injustice done unto us Africans; and it ought to sound in your ears as the rolling waves around your circumambient shores; and if it is not hearkened unto, it may yet arise with a louder voice, as the rolling thunder, and it may encrease in the force of its volubility, not only to shake the leaves of the most stout in heart, but to rend the mountains before them, and to cleave in pieces the rocks under

---

circum-ambient: encompassing.

[28] James 3:11.

them, and to go on with fury to smite the stoutest oaks in the forest; and even to make that which is strong, and wherein you think that your strength lieth, to become as stubble, and as the fibres of rotten wood, that will do you no good, and your trust in it will become a snare of infatuation to you!

FINIS.

From The Interesting Narrative of the Life of Olaudah Equiano, or Gustavus Vassa, the African: Written by Himself

Olaudah Equiano

Olaudah Equiano (c. 1745–1797), also known by his slave name, Gustavus Vassa, provided in *The Interesting Narrative* the most popular Black British autobiography of its time and an influential model for slave narratives to follow. Equiano's fascinating, garrulous text has also contributed most of the material for later reconstructions of his life, supplemented by letters, minor publications, and public records that usually—but not invariably—confirm the account given in his narrative. As he himself tells it, Equiano was born around 1745 to a highly placed family in the Igbo village of Essaka (in present-day Nigeria). Kidnapped with his sister at the age of eleven by African slave traders, Equiano proceeded through a long journey that brought him into contact with a number of distinct regions and cultures and separated him from his sister. After arriving at the coast, Equiano endured the grueling Middle Passage to the Americas, where he landed at the British West Indian island of Barbados and soon found himself on his way to the North American colonies, under the name Michael. Sold to a Mr. Campbell, who renamed him Jacob, Equiano worked on a Virginia slave plantation until he was again sold, sometime around 1756, to the British naval captain Michael Henry Pascal. Pascal renamed him Gustavus Vassa, after the sixteenth-century Swedish hero, a name that Equiano would use exclusively in his private dealings for the rest of his life, as Vincent Carretta has stressed ("Olaudah Equiano"). Carretta has also turned up records that place Equiano—or Vassa—with Pascal in 1754 (two years earlier than

Equiano has it); that suggest that he was taken from Africa around the age of seven, not eleven; and (in the muster book for the ship *Racehorse*) that indicate a birthplace in South Carolina, not Africa (1997, 101–103). This new research has revived old doubts—going back to the contemporary reception of *The Interesting Narrative*—that Equiano exaggerated the extent of, and filled in some of the details of, his African past or even invented it altogether from travel accounts and other sources. Equiano vigorously combatted such suspicions during his lifetime, and scholars of West African culture have been impressed by the accuracy of his reports on Igbo life and customs (Acholonu 1989).

Sometime between late 1754 and early 1757, then, Pascal brought Equiano to England, where he worked for several families in Falmouth and Guernsey, taking advantage of chance opportunities to learn to read and write. He was baptized (as Gustavas Vassa) in February 1759 at St. Margaret's Church in Westminster. Following Pascal into active duty, Equiano served on various naval ships in the Mediterranean and the Americas, hoping that his service in the Seven Years' War (1756–1763) would lead to his freedom. Instead, much to his dismay, at the end of 1762 Equiano was sold to Captain James Doran, who took him to the Caribbean island of Montserrat and sold him in turn to the Quaker merchant Robert King some months later. Equiano worked out of Montserrat as a small trader with Captain Thomas Farmer for the next four years, sailing around the West Indies and up the North American coast to Savannah, Charleston, and Philadelphia. Taking advantage of every opportunity these journeys presented to trade on his own behalf, Equiano accumulated sufficient capital to purchase his own freedom, for £40, in July 1766.

For a time, Equiano remained in the West Indies, working for King as a free agent, but returned to London in 1767 to study hairdressing and learn to play the French horn. (Gentleman's servant and musician were, along with seafaring, among the better careers open to free Blacks in England.) He soon returned to the sea, sailing with various captains in the Mediterranean (where he took a fancy to Turkish customs) and the Caribbean. In May 1773 he accompanied Constantine Phipps on a voyage to the North Pole, sailed to Spain in 1775, and accompanied Dr. Charles Irving to the Mosquito Coast of Central America in 1775–1776. There he worked for Irving as a slave purchaser and plantation overseer before quitting in despair in the face of colonial corruption, returning to London in early 1777.

At this stage in his life, Equiano began to take an increasingly active role in criticizing the slave system, seeking better conditions for freed slaves and other Blacks living in England, and promoting better relations with Africa. In 1779 he petitioned the Bishop of London, without success, to be sent to Africa as a missionary. He brought the massacre of 132 African captives aboard the slave ship *Zong* to the attention of the antislavery activist Granville Sharp in 1783, helping to make the *Zong* incident a notorious example of the evils of the slave trade. In 1786, Equiano was appointed Commissary for Stores for the expedition to repatriate freed slaves to the Sierra Leone colony on the West African coast, but was forced out of his position after he protested at the corruption and poor planning that spelled disaster for the expedition. Impelled by the Sierra Leone debacle to defend his reputation in print, Equiano now began publishing letters critical of the slave system and attacking proslavery arguments in periodicals like the *Public Advertiser* and the *Morning Chronicle*. Some of these are cosigned by the "Sons of Africa," a group of perhaps two dozen Black British activists that included Equiano's friend Ottobah Cugoano. Equiano may have contributed to Cugoano's *Thoughts and Sentiments* against the slave trade, published in 1787. Two years later, he published his own outspoken critique of slavery, *The Interesting Narrative*.

Equiano's unprecedented book, addressed to both houses of the British Parliament, reveals the power of weaving arguments against the slave trade, plantation slavery, racial discrimination, and European chauvinism, earlier developed by Cugoano and a number of White abolitionists, into a narrative of captivity, cultural dislocation, slavery, the struggle for freedom and literacy, and emancipation work. No less importantly, however, Equiano's text frequently exceeds its abolitionist mandate to recount incidents, observations, and speculations that overtly have little to do with the antislavery cause. These seeming digressions, often revealing an arch sense of humor, give *The Interesting Narrative* a variety and complexity that render it at once more entertaining and more convincing. The narrator's rich humanity is everywhere evident, implicitly adding weight to his arguments for the African's title to full equality and thus to equal rights and treatment. The work was a popular success, going through nine editions in the author's lifetime along with translations into German, Dutch, and Russian. Equiano, whose letters to various periodicals had helped publicize his book, took an increasingly active role in the marketing and publishing of *The Interesting Narrative*. He went on book tours throughout Great Britain, advocating abolition and gaining an ever-longer list of subscribers to offset pub-lication costs in advance and add to the author's profits. Equiano married Susanna Cullen, an Englishwoman from a Cambridgeshire family, in 1792, and the couple had two daughters together, Ann Maria (who did not survive childhood) and Joanna. Equiano died in 1797, leaving Joanna a then considerable bequest amounting to £950 by the time she received it on her twenty-first birthday in 1816.

THE
INTERESTING NARRATIVE

OF

THE LIFE

OF

OLAUDAH EQUIANO,

OR

GUSTAVUS VASSA,

THE AFRICAN.

WRITTEN BY HIMSELF.

VOL I.

Behold, God is my salvation; I will trust and not be afraid, for the Lord Jehovah is my strength and my song; he also is become my salvation.

And in that day shall ye say, Praise the Lord, call upon his name, declare his doings among the people. Isaiah xii, 2, 4.

LONDON:

Printed for and sold by the AUTHOR, No. 10, Union-Street, Middlesex Hospital;

Sold also by Mr. Johnson, St. Paul's Church-Yard; Mr. Murray, Fleet-Street; Messrs. Robson and Clark, Bond-Street; Mr. Davis, opposite Gray's Inn, Holborn; Messrs. Shepperson and Reynolds, and Mr. Jackson, Oxford-Street; Mr. Lackington, Chiswell-Street; Mr. Mathews, Strand; Mr. Murray, Prince's-Street, Soho; Mess. Taylor and Co. South Arch, Royal Exchange; Mr. Button, Newington-Causeway; Mr. Parsons, Paternoster-Row; and may be had of all the Booksellers in Town and Country.

[Entered at Stationer's Hall.]

To the Lords Spiritual and Temporal, and the Commons of the Parliament of Great Britain.[1]

My Lords and Gentlemen,

PERMIT me, with the greatest deference and respect, to lay at your feet the following genuine Narrative; the chief design of which is to excite in your august assemblies a sense of compassion for the miseries which the Slave-Trade has entailed on my unfortunate countrymen. By the horrors of that trade was I first torn away from all the tender connexions that were naturally dear to my heart; but these, through the mysterious ways of Providence, I ought to regard as infinitely more than compensated by the introduction I have thence obtained to the knowledge of the Christian religion, and of a nation which, by its liberal sentiments, its humanity, the glorious freedom of its government, and its proficiency in arts and sciences, has exalted the dignity of human nature.

I am sensible I ought to entreat your pardon for addressing to you a work so wholly devoid of literary merit; but, as the production of an unlettered African, who is actuated by the hope of becoming an instrument towards the relief of his suffering countrymen, I trust that *such a man,* pleading in *such a cause,* will be acquitted of boldness and presumption.

May the God of heaven inspire your hearts with peculiar benevolence on that important day when the question of Abolition is to be discussed, when thousands, in consequence of your Determination, are to look for Happiness or Misery!

I am,
MY LORDS AND GENTLEMEN,
Your most obedient,
And devoted humble Servant,
OLAUDAH EQUIANO,
OR
GUSTAVUS VASSA.

Union-Street, Mary-le-bone,
   March 24, 1789.

From Olaudah Equiano, *The Interesting Narrative of the Life of Olaudah Equiano, or Gustavus Vassa, the African* (London: Printed for the author, 1789).

[1] In addressing his narrative to both Houses of the British Parliament, the hereditary House of Lords and the elective House of Commons, Equiano underscores its status as an intervention in the antislavery cause.

The Life, &c.

VOLUME I, CHAPTER I.

I believe it is difficult for those who publish their own memoirs to escape the imputation of vanity; nor is this the only disadvantage under which they labour: it is also their misfortune, that what is uncommon is rarely, if ever, believed, and what is obvious we are apt to turn from with disgust, and to charge the writer with impertinence. People generally think those memoirs only worthy to be read or remembered which abound in great or striking events, those, in short, which in a high degree excite either admiration or pity: all others they consign to contempt and oblivion. It is therefore, I confess, not a little hazardous in a private and obscure individual, and a stranger too, thus to solicit the indulgent attention of the public; especially when I own I offer here the history of neither a saint, a hero, nor a tyrant. I believe there are few events in my life, which have not happened to many: it is true the incidents of it are numerous; and, did I consider myself an European, I might say my sufferings were great: but when I compare my lot with that of most of my countrymen, I regard myself as a *particular favourite of Heaven,* and acknowledge the mercies of Providence in every occurrence of my life. If then the following narrative does not appear sufficiently interesting to engage general attention, let my motive be some excuse for its publication. I am not so foolishly vain as to expect from it either immortality or literary reputation. If it affords any satisfaction to my numerous friends, at whose request it has been written, or in the smallest degree promotes the interests of humanity, the ends for which it was undertaken will be fully attained, and every wish of my heart gratified. Let it therefore be remembered, that, in wishing to avoid censure, I do not aspire to praise.

That part of Africa, known by the name of Guinea, to which the trade for slaves is carried on, extends along the coast above 3400 miles, from the Senegal to Angola, and includes a variety of kingdoms. Of these the most considerable is the kingdom of Benen, both as to extent and wealth, the richness and cultivation of the soil, the power of its king, and the number and warlike disposition of the inhabitants. It is situated nearly under the line, and extends along the coast about 170 miles, but runs back into the interior part of Africa to a distance hitherto I believe unexplored by any

---

Benen: Benin.
the line: the equator.

traveller; and seems only terminated at length by the empire of Abyssinia, near 1500 miles from its beginning. This kingdom is divided into many provinces or districts: in one of the most remote and fertile of which, called Eboe, I was born, in the year 1745, in a charming fruitful vale, named Essaka.² The distance of this province from the capital of Benin and the sea coast must be very considerable; for I had never heard of white men or Europeans, nor of the sea: and our subjection to the king of Benin was little more than nominal; for every transaction of the government, as far as my slender observation extended, was conducted by the chiefs or elders of the place. The manners and government of a people who have little commerce with other countries are generally very simple; and the history of what passes in one family or village may serve as a specimen of a nation. My father was one of those elders or chiefs I have spoken of, and was styled Embrenche; a term, as I remember, importing the highest distinction, and signifying in our language a *mark* of grandeur. This mark is conferred on the person entitled to it, by cutting the skin across at the top of the forehead, and drawing it down to the eye-brows; and while it is in this situation applying a warm hand, and rubbing it until it shrinks up into a thick *weal* across the lower part of the forehead. Most of the judges and senators were thus marked; my father had long born it: I had seen it conferred on one of my brothers, and I was also *destined* to receive it by my parents. Those Embrenche, or chief men, decided disputes and punished crimes; for which purpose they always assembled together. The proceedings were generally short; and in most cases the law of retaliation prevailed. I remember a man was brought before my father, and the other judges, for kidnapping a boy; and, although he was the son of a chief or senator, he was condemned to make recompense by a man or woman slave. Adultery, however, was sometimes punished with slavery or death; a punishment which I believe is inflicted on it throughout most of the nations of Africa³: so sacred among them is the honour of the marriage bed, and so jealous are they of the fidelity of their wives. Of this I recollect an instance:—a woman was convicted before the judges of adultery, and delivered over, as the custom was, to her husband to be punished. Accordingly he determined to put her to death: but it being found, just before her execution, that she had an infant at her breast; and no woman being prevailed on to perform the part of a nurse, she was spared on account of the child. The men, however, do not

---

Abyssinia: Ethiopia.

²The Eboe or Igbo region is in present-day Nigeria; Essaka may be the modern Nigerian village of Iseke.

³See Benezet's "Account of Guinea" throughout. [Equiano's note; Anthony Benezet, *Some Historical Account of Guinea . . .* (1772). Eds.]

preserve the same constancy to their wives, which they expect from them; for they indulge in a plurality, though seldom in more than two. Their mode of marriage is thus:—both parties are usually betrothed when young by their parents, (though I have known the males to betroth themselves). On this occasion a feast is prepared, and the bride and bridegroom stand up in the midst of all their friends, who are assembled for the purpose, while he declares she is thenceforth to be looked upon as his wife, and that no other person is to pay any addresses to her. This is also immediately proclaimed in the vicinity, on which the bride retires from the assembly. Some time after she is brought home to her husband, and then another feast is made, to which the relations of both parties are invited: her parents then deliver her to the bridegroom, accompanied with a number of blessings, and at the same time they tie round her waist a cotton string of the thickness of a goose-quill, which none but married women are permitted to wear: she is now considered as completely his wife; and at this time the dowry is given to the new married pair, which generally consists of portions of land, slaves, and cattle, household goods, and implements of husbandry. These are offered by the friends of both parties; besides which the parents of the bridegroom present gifts to those of the bride, whose property she is looked upon before marriage; but after it she is esteemed the sole property of her husband. The ceremony being now ended the festival begins, which is celebrated with bonefires, and loud acclamations of joy, accompanied with music and dancing.

We are almost a nation of dancers, musicians, and poets. Thus every great event, such as a triumphant return from battle, or other cause of public rejoicing is celebrated in public dances, which are accompanied with songs and music suited to the occasion. The assembly is separated into four divisions, which dance either apart or in succession, and each with a character peculiar to itself. The first division contains the married men, who in their dances frequently exhibit feats of arms, and the representation of a battle. To these succeed the married women, who dance in the second division. The young men occupy the third; and the maidens the fourth. Each represents some interesting scene of real life, such as a great achievement, domestic employment, a pathetic story, or some rural sport; and as the subject is generally founded on some recent event, it is therefore ever new. This gives our dances a spirit and variety which I have scarcely seen elsewhere.[4] We have many musical instruments, particularly drums of

---

husbandry: agriculture.

[4]When I was in Smyrna I have frequently seen the Greeks dance after this manner. [Equiano's note; Smyrna is the modern city of Izmir in Turkey. Eds.]

different kinds, a piece of music which resembles a guitar, and another much like a stickado. These last are chiefly used by betrothed virgins, who play on them on all grand festivals.

As our manners are simple, our luxuries are few. The dress of both sexes is nearly the same. It generally consists of a long piece of callico, or muslin, wrapped loosely round the body, somewhat in the form of a highland plaid. This is usually dyed blue, which is our favourite colour. It is extracted from a berry, and is brighter and richer than any I have seen in Europe. Besides this, our women of distinction wear golden ornaments; which they dispose with some profusion on their arms and legs. When our women are not employed with the men in tillage, their usual occupation is spinning and weaving cotton, which they afterwards dye, and make it into garments. They also manufacture earthen vessels, of which we have many kinds. Among the rest tobacco pipes, made after the same fashion, and used in the same manner, as those in Turkey.[5]

Our manner of living is entirely plain; for as yet the natives are unacquainted with those refinements in cookery which debauch the taste: bullocks, goats, and poultry, supply the greatest part of their food. These constitute likewise the principal wealth of the country, and the chief articles of its commerce. The flesh is usually stewed in a pan; to make it savoury we sometimes use also pepper, and other spices, and we have salt made of wood ashes. Our vegetables are mostly plantains, eadas, yams, beans, and Indian corn. The head of the family usually eats alone; his wives and slaves have also their separate tables. Before we taste food we always wash our hands: indeed our cleanliness on all occasions is extreme; but on this it is an indispensable ceremony. After washing, libation is made, by pouring out a small portion of the food, in a certain place, for the spirits of departed relations, which the natives suppose to preside over their conduct, and guard them from evil. They are totally unacquainted with strong or spirituous liquors; and their principal beverage is palm wine. This is gotten from a tree of that name by tapping it at the top, and fastening a large gourd to it; and sometimes one tree will yield three or four gallons in a night. When just drawn it is of a most delicious sweetness; but in a few days it acquires a tartish and more spirituous flavour: though I never saw any one intoxicated by it. The same tree also produces nuts and oil. Our

---

stickado: a kind of xylophone.

eada: eddoe, a West African root vegetable.

[5]The bowl is earthen, curiously figured, to which a long reed is fixed as a tube. This tube is sometimes so long as to be born by one, and frequently out of grandeur by two boys. [Equiano's note.]

principal luxury is in perfumes; one sort of these is an odoriferous wood of delicious fragrance: the other a kind of earth; a small portion of which thrown into the fire diffuses a most powerful odour.[6] We beat this wood into powder, and mix it with palm oil; with which both men and women perfume themselves.

In our buildings we study convenience rather than ornament. Each master of a family has a large square piece of ground, surrounded with a moat or fence, or enclosed with a wall made of red earth tempered; which, when dry, is as hard as brick. Within this are his houses to accommodate his family and slaves; which, if numerous, frequently present the appearance of a village. In the middle stands the principal building, appropriated to the sole use of the master, and consisting of two apartments; in one of which he sits in the day with his family, the other is left apart for the reception of his friends. He has besides these a distinct apartment in which he sleeps, together with his male children. On each side are the apartments of his wives, who have also their separate day and night houses. The habitations of the slaves and their families are distributed throughout the rest of the enclosure. These houses never exceed one story in height: they are always built of wood, or stakes driven into the ground, crossed with wattles, and neatly plastered within, and without. The roof is thatched with reeds. Our day-houses are left open at the sides; but those in which we sleep are always covered, and plastered in the inside, with a composition mixed with cowdung, to keep off the different insects, which annoy us during the night. The walls and floors also of these are generally covered with mats. Our beds consist of a platform, raised three or four feet from the ground, on which are laid skins, and different parts of a spungy tree called plaintain. Our covering is calico or muslin, the same as our dress. The usual seats are a few logs of wood; but we have benches, which are generally perfumed, to accommodate strangers: these compose the greater part of our household furniture. Houses so constructed and furnished require but little skill to erect them. Every man is a sufficient architect for the purpose. The whole neighbourhood afford their unanimous assistance in building them and in return receive, and expect no other recompense than a feast.

As we live in a country where nature is prodigal of her favours, our wants are few and easily supplied; of course we have few manufactures. They consist for the most part of calicoes, earthern ware, ornaments, and

---

wattles: interwoven twigs or branches.

[6]When I was in Smyrna I saw the same kind of earth, and brought some of it with me to England; it resembles musk in strength, but is more delicious in scent, and is not unlike the smell of a rose. [Equiano's note.]

instruments of war and husbandry. But these make no part of our commerce, the principal articles of which, as I have observed, are provisions. In such a state money is of little use; however we have some small pieces of coin, if I may call them such. They are made something like an anchor; but I do not remember either their value or denomination. We have also markets, at which I have been frequently with my mother. These are sometimes visited by stout mahogany-coloured men from the south west of us: we call them Oye-Eboe, which term signifies red men living at a distance. They generally bring us fire-arms, gunpowder, hats, beads, and dried fish. The last we esteemed a great rarity, as our waters were only brooks and springs. These articles they barter with us for odoriferous woods and earth, and our salt of wood ashes. They always carry slaves through our land; but the strictest account is exacted of their manner of procuring them before they are suffered to pass. Sometimes indeed we sold slaves to them, but they were only prisoners of war, or such among us as had been convicted of kidnapping, or adultery, and some other crimes, which we esteemed heinous. This practice of kidnapping induces me to think, that, notwithstanding all our strictness, their principal business among us was to trepan our people. I remember too they carried great sacks along with them, which not long after I had an opportunity of fatally seeing applied to that infamous purpose.

Our land is uncommonly rich and fruitful, and produces all kinds of vegetables in great abundance. We have plenty of Indian corn, and vast quantities of cotton and tobacco. Our pine apples grow without culture; they are about the size of the largest sugar-loaf, and finely flavoured. We have also spices of different kinds, particularly pepper; and a variety of delicious fruits which I have never seen in Europe; together with gums of various kinds, and honey in abundance. All our industry is exerted to improve those blessings of nature. Agriculture is our chief employment; and every one, even the children and women, are engaged in it. Thus we are all habituated to labour from our earliest years. Every one contributes something to the common stock; and as we are unacquainted with idleness, we have no beggars. The benefits of such a mode of living are obvious. The West India planters prefer the slaves of Benin or Eboe to those of any other part of Guinea, for their hardiness, intelligence, integrity, and zeal. Those benefits are felt by us in the general healthiness of the people, and in their vigour and activity; I might have added too in their comeliness.

---

trepan: entrap.
sugar-loaf: refined sugar shaped into a cone.
planters: plantation owners.

Deformity is indeed unknown amongst us, I mean that of shape. Numbers of the natives of Eboe now in London might be brought in support of this assertion: for, in regard to complexion, ideas of beauty are wholly relative. I remember while in Africa to have seen three negro children, who were tawny, and another quite white, who were universally regarded by myself, and the natives in general, as far as related to their complexions, as deformed. Our women too were in my eyes at least uncommonly graceful, alert, and modest to a degree of bashfulness; nor do I remember to have ever heard of an instance of incontinence amongst them before marriage. They are also remarkably cheerful. Indeed cheerfulness and affability are two of the leading characteristics of our nation.

Our tillage is exercised in a large plain or common, some hours walk from our dwellings, and all the neighbours resort thither in a body. They use no beasts of husbandry; and their only instruments are hoes, axes, shovels, and beaks, or pointed iron to dig with. Sometimes we are visited by locusts, which come in large clouds, so as to darken the air, and destroy our harvest. This however happens rarely, but when it does, a famine is produced by it. I remember an instance or two wherein this happened. This common is often the theatre of war; and therefore when our people go out to till their land, they not only go in a body, but generally take their arms with them for fear of a surprise; and when they apprehend an invasion they guard the avenues to their dwellings, by driving sticks into the ground, which are so sharp at one end as to pierce the foot, and are generally dipt in poison. From what I can recollect of these battles, they appear to have been irruptions of one little state or district on the other, to obtain prisoners or booty. Perhaps they were incited to this by those traders who brought the European goods I mentioned amongst us. Such a mode of obtaining slaves in Africa is common; and I believe more are procured this way, and by kidnaping, than any other.[7] When a trader wants slaves, he applies to a chief for them, and tempts him with his wares. It is not extraordinary, if on this occasion he yields to the temptation with as little firmness, and accepts the price of his fellow creature's liberty with as little reluctance as the enlightened merchant. Accordingly he falls on his neighbours, and a desperate battle ensues. If he prevails and takes prisoners, he gratifies his avarice by selling them; but, if his party be vanquished, and he falls into the hands of the enemy, he is put to death: for, as he has been known to foment their quarrels, it is thought dangerous to let him survive, and no ransom can save him, though all other prisoners may be redeemed. We have firearms, bows and arrows, broad two-edged swords and javelins: we have

---

[7] See Benezet's Account of Africa throughout. [Equiano's note.]

shields also which cover a man from head to foot. All are taught the use of these weapons; even our women are warriors, and march boldly out to fight along with the men. Our whole district is a kind of militia: on a certain signal given, such as the firing of a gun at night, they all rise in arms and rush upon their enemy. It is perhaps something remarkable, that when our people march to the field a red flag or banner is borne before them. I was once a witness to a battle in our common. We had been all at work in it one day as usual, when our people were suddenly attacked. I climbed a tree at some distance, from which I beheld the fight. There were many women as well as men on both sides; among others my mother was there, and armed with a broad sword. After fighting for a considerable time with great fury, and after many had been killed our people obtained the victory, and took their enemy's Chief prisoner. He was carried off in great triumph, and, though he offered a large ransom for his life, he was put to death. A virgin of note among our enemies had been slain in the battle, and her arm was exposed in our market-place, where our trophies were always exhibited. The spoils were divided according to the merit of the warriors. Those prisoners which were not sold or redeemed we kept as slaves: but how different was their condition from that of the slaves in the West Indies! With us they do no more work than other members of the community, even their masters; their food, clothing and lodging were nearly the same as theirs, (except that they were not permitted to eat with those who were free-born); and there was scarce any other difference between them, than a superior degree of importance which the head of a family possesses in our state, and that authority which, as such, he exercises over every part of his household. Some of these slaves have even slaves under them as their own property, and for their own use.

As to religion, the natives believe that there is one Creator of all things, and that he lives in the sun, and is girted round with a belt that he may never eat or drink; but, according to some, he smokes a pipe, which is our own favourite luxury. They believe he governs events, especially our deaths or captivity; but, as for the doctrine of eternity, I do not remember to have ever heard of it: some however believe in the transmigration of souls in a certain degree. Those spirits, which are not transmigrated, such as our dear friends or relations, they believe always attend them, and guard them from the bad spirits or their foes. For this reason they always before eating, as I have observed, put some small portion of the meat, and pour some of their drink, on the ground for them; and they often make oblations of the blood of beasts or fowls at their graves. I was very fond of my mother, and almost constantly with her. When she went to make these oblations at her mother's tomb, which was a kind of small solitary thatched house, I sometimes attended her. There she made her libations, and spent most of the night in cries and lamentations. I have been often extremely terrified on these occasions. The loneliness of the place, the darkness of the night, and the ceremony of libation, naturally awful and gloomy, were heightened by my mother's lamentations; and these, concuring with the cries of doleful birds, by which these places were frequented, gave an inexpressible terror to the scene.

We compute the year from the day on which the sun crosses the line, and on its setting that evening there is a general shout throughout the land; at least I can speak from my own knowledge throughout our vicinity. The people at the same time make a great noise with rattles, not unlike the basket rattles used by children here, though much larger, and hold up their hands to heaven for a blessing. It is then the greatest offerings are made; and those children whom our wise men foretel will be fortunate are then presented to different people. I remember many used to come to see me, and I was carried about to others for that purpose. They have many offerings, particularly at full moons; generally two at harvest before the fruits are taken out of the ground: and when any young animals are killed, sometimes they offer up part of them as a sacrifice. These offerings, when made by one of the heads of a family, serve for the whole. I remember we often had them at my father's and my uncle's, and their families have been present. Some of our offerings are eaten with bitter herbs. We had a saying among us to any one of a cross temper, 'That if they were to be eaten, they should be eaten with bitter herbs.'

We practised circumcision like the Jews, and made offerings and feasts on that occasion in the same manner as they did. Like them also, our children were named from some event, some circumstance, or fancied foreboding at the time of their birth. I was named *Olaudah*, which, in our language, signifies vicissitude or fortune also; one favoured, and having a loud voice and well spoken. I remember we never polluted the name of the object of our adoration; on the contrary, it was always mentioned with the greatest reverence; and we were totally unacquainted with swearing, and all those terms of abuse and reproach which find their way so readily and copiously into the languages of more civilized people. The only expressions of that kind I remember were 'May you rot, or may you swell, or may a beast take you.'

I have before remarked that the natives of this part of Africa are extremely cleanly. This necessary habit of decency was with us a part of religion, and therefore we had many purifications and washings; indeed almost as many, and used on the same occasions, if my recollection does not fail me, as the Jews. Those that touched the dead at any time were obliged to wash and purify themselves before they could enter a dwelling-house. Every woman too, at certain times, was forbidden to come into a dwelling-house, or touch any person, or any thing we ate. I was so fond of my mother I could not keep from her, or avoid touching her at some of those periods, in consequence of which I was obliged to be kept out with her, in a little house made for that purpose, till offering was made, and then we were purified.

Though we had no places of public worship, we had priests and magicians, or wise men. I do not remember whether they had different offices, or whether they were united in the same persons, but they were held in great reverence by the people. They calculated our time, and foretold events, as their name imported, for we called them Ah-affoe-way-cah, which signifies calculators or yearly men, our year being called Ah-affoe. They wore their beards, and when they died they were succeeded by their sons. Most of their implements and things of value were interred along with them. Pipes and tobacco were also put into the grave with the corpse, which was always perfumed and ornamented, and animals were offered in sacrifice to them. None accompanied their funerals but those of the same profession or tribe. These buried them after sunset, and always returned from the grave by a different way from that which they went.

These magicians were also our doctors or physicians. They practised bleeding by cupping; and were very successful in healing wounds and expelling poisons. They had likewise some extraordinary method of discovering jealousy, theft, and poisoning; the success of which no doubt they derived from their unbounded influence over the credulity and superstition of the people. I do not remember what those methods were, except that as to poisoning: I recollect an instance or two, which I hope it will not be deemed impertinent here to insert, as it may serve as a kind of specimen of the rest, and is still used by the negroes in the West Indies. A virgin had been poisoned, but it was not known by whom: the doctors ordered the corpse to be taken up by some persons, and carried to the grave. As soon as the bearers had raised it on their shoulders, they seemed seized with some [8] sudden impulse, and ran to and fro unable to stop themselves. At last, after having passed through a number of thorns and prickly bushes unhurt, the corpse fell from them close to a house, and defaced it in the fall; and, the owner being taken up, he immediately confessed the poisoning.[9]

---

[8] See also Leut. Matthew's Voyage, p. 123. [Equiano's note; John Matthews, *A Voyage to the River Sierra-Leone . . .* (1788). Eds.]

[9] An instance of this kind happened at Montserrat in the West Indies in the year 1763. I then belonged to the Charming Sally, Capt. Doran.—The chief mate, Mr. Mansfield, and some of the crew being one day on shore, were present at the burying of a poisoned negro girl. Though they had often heard of the circumstance of the running in such cases, and had even seen it, they imagined it to be a trick of the corpse-bearers. The mate

The natives are extremely cautious about poison. When they buy any eatable the seller kisses it all round before the buyer, to shew him it is not poisoned; and the same is done when any meat or drink is presented, particularly to a stranger. We have serpents of different kinds, some of which are esteemed ominous when they appear in our houses, and these we never molest. I remember two of those ominous snakes, each of which was as thick as the calf of a man's leg, and in colour resembling a dolphin in the water, crept at different times into my mother's night-house, where I always lay with her, and coiled themselves into folds, and each time they crowed like a cock. I was desired by some of our wise men to touch these, that I might be interested in the good omens, which I did, for they were quite harmless, and would tamely suffer themselves to be handled; and then they were put into a large open earthen pan, and set on one side of the highway. Some of our snakes, however, were poisonous: one of them crossed the road one day when I was standing on it, and passed between my feet without offering to touch me, to the great surprise of many who saw it; and these incidents were accounted by the wise men, and therefore by my mother and the rest of the people, as remarkable omens in my favour.

Such is the imperfect sketch my memory has furnished me with of the manners and customs of a people among whom I first drew my breath. And here I cannot forbear suggesting what has long struck me very forcibly, namely, the strong analogy which even by this sketch, imperfect as it is, appears to prevail in the manners and customs of my countrymen and those of the Jews, before they reached the Land of Promise, and particularly the patriarchs while they were yet in that pastoral state which is described in Genesis—an analogy, which alone would induce me to think that the one people had sprung from the other. Indeed this is the opinion of Dr. Gill,[10] who, in his commentary on Genesis, very ably deduces the pedigree of the Africans from Afer and Afra, the descendants of Abraham by Keturah his wife and concubine (for both these titles are applied to her). It is also conformable to the sentiments of Dr. John Clarke, formerly Dean of

---

therefore desired two of the sailors to take up the coffin, and carry it to the grave. The sailors, who were all of the same opinion, readily obeyed; but they had scarcely raised it to their shoulders, before they began to run furiously about, quite unable to direct themselves, till, at last, without intention, they came to the hut of him who had poisoned the girl. The coffin then immediately fell from their shoulders against the hut, and damaged part of the wall. The owner of the hut was taken into custody on this, and confessed the poisoning.—I give this story as it was related by the mate and crew on their return to the ship. The credit which is due to it I leave with the reader. [Equiano's note.]
eatable: food.
[10]John Gill, *An Exposition of the Old Testament* . . . (1788).

Sarum, in his Truth of the Christian Religion:[11] both these authors concur in ascribing to us this original. The reasonings of these gentlemen are still further confirmed by the scripture chronology; and if any further corroboration were required, this resemblance in so many respects is a strong evidence in support of the opinion. Like the Israelites in their primitive state, our government was conducted by our chiefs or judges, our wise men and elders; and the head of a family with us enjoyed a similar authority over his household with that which is ascribed to Abraham and the other patriarchs. The law of retaliation obtained almost universally with us as with them: and even their religion appeared to have shed upon us a ray of its glory, though broken and spent in its passage, or eclipsed by the cloud with which time, tradition, and ignorance might have enveloped it; for we had our circumcision (a rule I believe peculiar to that people): we had also our sacrifices and burnt-offerings, our washings and purifications, on the same occasions as they had.

As to the difference of colour between the Eboan Africans and the modern Jews, I shall not presume to account for it. It is a subject which has engaged the pens of men of both genius and learning, and is far above my strength. The most able and Reverend Mr. T. Clarkson, however, in his much admired Essay on the Slavery and Commerce of the Human Species, has ascertained the cause, in a manner that at once solves every objection on that account, and, on my mind at least, has produced the fullest conviction. I shall therefore refer to that performance for the theory,[12] contenting myself with extracting a fact as related by Dr. Mitchel.[13] "The Spaniards, who have inhabited America, under the torrid zone, for any time, are become as dark coloured as our native Indians of Virginia; of which *I myself have been a witness.*" There is also another instance[14] of a Portuguese settlement at Mitomba, a river in Sierra Leona; where the inhabitants are bred from a mixture of the first Portuguese discoverers with the natives, and are now become in their complexion, and in the woolly quality of their hair, *perfect negroes,* retaining however a smattering of the Portuguese language.

---

torrid zone: the tropics, global region between the tropic of Cancer and the tropic of Capricorn.

[11] *The Truth of the Christian Religion,* a work by Hugo Grotius, translated by John Clarke in 1711.

[12] Page 178 to 216. [Equiano's note; Equiano refers to Thomas Clarkson, *An Essay on the Slavery and Commerce of the Human Species* (1786).]

[13] Philos. Trans. No. 476, Sect. 4, cited by Mr. Clarkson, p. 205. [Equiano's note; Equiano cites Clarkson citing John Mitchell in the *Philosophical Transactions* for 1744.]

[14] Same page. [Equiano's note.]

These instances, and a great many more which might be adduced, while they shew how the complexions of the same persons vary in different climates, it is hoped may tend also to remove the prejudice that some conceive against the natives of Africa on account of their colour. Surely the minds of the Spaniards did not change with their complexions! Are there not causes enough to which the apparent inferiority of an African may be ascribed, without limiting the goodness of God, and supposing he forbore to stamp understanding on certainly his own image, because "carved in ebony." Might it not naturally be ascribed to their situation? When they come among Europeans, they are ignorant of their language, religion, manners, and customs. Are any pains taken to teach them these? Are they treated as men? Does not slavery itself depress the mind, and extinguish all its fire and every noble sentiment? But, above all, what advantages do not a refined people possess over those who are rude and uncultivated. Let the polished and haughty European recollect that his ancestors were once, like the Africans, uncivilized, and even barbarous. Did Nature make *them* inferior to their sons? and should *they too* have been made slaves? Every rational mind answers, No. Let such reflections as these melt the pride of their superiority into sympathy for the wants and miseries of their sable brethren, and compel them to acknowledge, that understanding is not confined to feature or colour. If, when they look round the world, they feel exultation, let it be tempered with benevolence to others, and gratitude to God, "who hath made of one blood all nations of men for to dwell on all the face of the earth;[15] and whose wisdom is not our wisdom, neither are our ways his ways."

Chapter II.

I HOPE the reader will not think I have trespassed on his patience in introducing myself to him with some account of the manners and customs of my country. They had been implanted in me with great care, and made an impression on my mind, which time could not erase, and which all the adversity and variety of fortune I have since experienced served only to rivet and record; for, whether the love of one's country be real or imaginary, or a lesson of reason, or an instinct of nature, I still look back with pleasure on the first scenes of my life, though that pleasure has been for the most part mingled with sorrow.

I have already acquainted the reader with the time and place of my birth. My father, besides many slaves, had a numerous family, of which

---

[15] Acts, c. xvii, v. 26. [Equiano's note.]

seven lived to grow up, including myself and a sister, who was the only daughter. As I was the youngest of the sons, I became, of course, the greatest favourite with my mother, and was always with her; and she used to take particular pains to form my mind. I was trained up from my earliest years in the art of war; my daily exercise was shooting and throwing javelins; and my mother adorned me with emblems, after the manner of our greatest warriors. In this way I grew up till I was turned the age of eleven, when an end was put to my happiness in the following manner:—Generally when the grown people in the neighbourhood were gone far in the fields to labour, the children assembled together in some of the neighbours' premises to play; and commonly some of us used to get up a tree to look out for any assailant, or kidnapper, that might come upon us; for they sometimes took those opportunities of our parents' absence to attack and carry off as many as they could seize. One day, as I was watching at the top of a tree in our yard, I saw one of those people come into the yard of our next neighbour but one, to kidnap, there being many stout young people in it. Immediately on this I gave the alarm of the rogue, and he was surrounded by the stoutest of them, who entangled him with cords, so that he could not escape till some of the grown people came and secured him. But alas! ere long it was my fate to be thus attacked, and to be carried off, when none of the grown people were nigh. One day, when all our people were gone out to their works as usual, and only I and my dear sister were left to mind the house, two men and a woman got over our walls, and in a moment seized us both, and, without giving us time to cry out, or make resistance, they stopped our mouths, and ran off with us into the nearest wood. Here they tied our hands, and continued to carry us as far as they could, till night came on, when we reached a small house, where the robbers halted for refreshment, and spent the night. We were then unbound, but were unable to take any food; and, being quite overpowered by fatigue and grief, our only relief was some sleep, which allayed our misfortune for a short time. The next morning we left the house, and continued travelling all the day. For a long time we had kept the woods, but at last we came into a road which I believed I knew. I had now some hopes of being delivered; for we had advanced but a little way before I discovered some people at a distance, on which I began to cry out for their assistance: but my cries had no other effect than to make them tie me faster and stop my mouth, and then they put me into a large sack. They also stopped my sister's mouth, and tied her hands; and in this manner we proceeded till we were out of the sight of these people. When we went to rest the following night they offered us

---

delivered: rescued.

some victuals; but we refused it; and the only comfort we had was in being in one another's arms all that night, and bathing each other with our tears. But alas! we were soon deprived of even the small comfort of weeping together. The next day proved a day of greater sorrow than I had yet experienced; for my sister and I were then separated, while we lay clasped in each other's arms. It was in vain that we besought them not to part us; she was torn from me, and immediately carried away, while I was left in a state of distraction not to be described. I cried and grieved continually; and for several days I did not eat any thing but what they forced into my mouth. At length, after many days travelling, during which I had often changed masters, I got into the hands of a chieftain, in a very pleasant country. This man had two wives and some children, and they all used me extremely well, and did all they could to comfort me; particularly the first wife, who was something like my mother. Although I was a great many days journey from my father's house, yet these people spoke exactly the same language with us. This first master of mine, as I may call him, was a smith, and my principal employment was working his bellows, which were the same kind as I had seen in my vicinity. They were in some respects not unlike the stoves here in gentlemen's kitchens; and were covered over with leather; and in the middle of that leather a stick was fixed, and a person stood up, and worked it, in the same manner as is done to pump water out of a cask with a hand pump. I believe it was gold he worked, for it was of a lovely bright yellow colour, and was worn by the women on their wrists and ancles. I was there I suppose about a month, and they at last used to trust me some little distance from the house. This liberty I used in embracing every opportunity to inquire the way to my own home: and I also sometimes, for the same purpose, went with the maidens, in the cool of the evenings, to bring pitchers of water from the springs for the use of the house. I had also remarked where the sun rose in the morning, and set in the evening, as I had travelled along; and I had observed that my father's house was towards the rising of the sun. I therefore determined to seize the first opportunity of making my escape, and to shape my course for that quarter; for I was quite oppressed and weighed down by grief after my mother and friends; and my love of liberty, ever great, was strengthened by the mortifying circumstance of not daring to eat with the free-born children, although I was mostly their companion. While I was projecting my escape, one day an unlucky event happened, which quite disconcerted my plan, and put an end to my hopes. I used to be sometimes employed in assisting an elderly woman slave to cook and take care of the poultry; and one morning, while I was feeding some

---

victuals: food.

chickens, I happened to toss a small pebble at one of them, which hit it on the middle and directly killed it. The old slave, having soon after missed the chicken, inquired after it; and on my relating the accident (for I told her the truth, because my mother would never suffer me to tell a lie) she flew into a violent passion, threatened that I should suffer for it; and, my master being out, she immediately went and told her mistress what I had done. This alarmed me very much, and I expected an instant flogging, which to me was uncommonly dreadful; for I had seldom been beaten at home. I therefore resolved to fly; and accordingly I ran into a thicket that was hard by, and hid myself in the bushes. Soon afterwards my mistress and the slave returned, and, not seeing me, they searched all the house, but not finding me, and I not making answer when they called to me, they thought I had run away, and the whole neighbourhood was raised in the pursuit of me. In that part of the country (as in ours) the houses and villages were skirted with woods, or shrubberies, and the bushes were so thick that a man could readily conceal himself in them, so as to elude the strictest search. The neighbours continued the whole day looking for me, and several times many of them came within a few yards of the place where I lay hid. I then gave myself up for lost entirely, and expected every moment, when I heard a rustling among the trees, to be found out, and punished by my master: but they never discovered me, though they were often so near that I even heard their conjectures as they were looking about for me; and I now learned from them, that any attempt to return home would be hopeless. Most of them supposed I had fled towards home; but the distance was so great, and the way so intricate, that they thought I could never reach it, and that I should be lost in the woods. When I heard this I was seized with a violent panic, and abandoned myself to despair. Night too began to approach, and aggravated all my fears. I had before entertained hopes of getting home, and I had determined when it should be dark to make the attempt; but I was now convinced it was fruitless, and I began to consider that, if possibly I could escape all other animals, I could not those of the human kind; and that, not knowing the way, I must perish in the woods. Thus was I like the hunted deer:

— "Ev'ry leaf and ev'ry whisp'ring breath
 "Convey'd a foe, and ev'ry foe a death."[16]

I heard frequent rustlings among the leaves; and being pretty sure they were snakes I expected every instant to be stung by them. This increased

---

[16]Slightly misquoted from John Denham, *Cooper's Hill* (1642), lines 287–288.

my anguish, and the horror of my situation became now quite insupportable. I at length quitted the thicket, very faint and hungry, for I had not eaten or drank any thing all the day; and crept to my master's kitchen, from whence I set out at first, and which was an open shed, and laid myself down in the ashes with an anxious wish for death to relieve me from all my pains. I was scarcely awake in the morning when the old woman slave, who was the first up, came to light the fire, and saw me in the fire place. She was very much surprised to see me, and could scarcely believe her own eyes. She now promised to intercede for me, and went for her master, who soon after came, and, having slightly reprimanded me, ordered me to be taken care of, and not to be ill-treated.

Soon after this my master's only daughter, and child by his first wife, sickened and died, which affected him so much that for some time he was almost frantic, and really would have killed himself, had he not been watched and prevented. However, in a small time afterwards he recovered, and I was again sold. I was now carried to the left of the sun's rising, through many different countries, and a number of large woods. The people I was sold to used to carry me very often, when I was tired, either on their shoulders or on their backs. I saw many convenient well-built sheds along the roads, at proper distances, to accommodate the merchants and travellers, who lay in those buildings along with their wives, who often accompany them; and they always go well armed.

From the time I left my own nation I always found somebody that understood me till I came to the sea coast. The languages of different nations did not totally differ, nor were they so copious as those of the Europeans, particularly the English. They were therefore easily learned; and, while I was journeying thus through Africa, I acquired two or three different tongues. In this manner I had been travelling for a considerable time, when one evening, to my great surprise, whom should I see brought to the house where I was but my dear sister! As soon as she saw me she gave a loud shriek, and ran into my arms—I was quite overpowered: neither of us could speak; but, for a considerable time, clung to each other in mutual embraces, unable to do any thing but weep. Our meeting affected all who saw us; and indeed I must acknowledge, in honour of those sable destroyers of human rights, that I never met with any ill treatment, or saw any offered to their slaves, except tying them, when necessary, to keep them from running away. When these people knew we were brother and sister they indulged us together; and the man, to whom I supposed we belonged, lay with us, he in the middle, while she and I held one another by the hands across his breast all night; and thus for a while we forgot our misfortunes in the joy of being together: but even this small comfort was soon to have an end; for scarcely had the fatal morning appeared, when she was again torn from me for ever! I was now more miserable, if possible, than before. The small relief which her presence gave me from pain was gone, and the wretchedness of my situation was redoubled by my anxiety after her fate, and my apprehensions lest her sufferings should be greater than mine, when I could not be with her to alleviate them. Yes, thou dear partner of all my childish sports! thou sharer of my joys and sorrows! happy should I have ever esteemed myself to encounter every misery for you, and to procure your freedom by the sacrifice of my own. Though you were early forced from my arms, your image has been always rivetted in my heart, from which neither *time nor fortune* have been able to remove it; so that, while the thoughts of your sufferings have damped my prosperity, they have mingled with adversity and increased its bitterness. To that Heaven which protects the weak from the strong, I commit the care of your innocence and virtues, if they have not already received their full reward, and if your youth and delicacy have not long since fallen victims to the violence of the African trader, the pestilential stench of a Guinea ship, the seasoning in the European colonies, or the lash and lust of a brutal and unrelenting overfeer.

I did not long remain after my sister. I was again sold, and carried through a number of places, till, after travelling a considerable time, I came to a town called Tinmah, in the most beautiful country I had yet seen in Africa. It was extremely rich, and there were many rivulets which flowed through it, and supplied a large pond in the centre of the town, where the people washed. Here I first saw and tasted cocoa-nuts, which I thought superior to any nuts I had ever tasted before; and the trees, which were loaded, were also interspersed amongst the houses, which had commodious shades adjoining, and were in the same manner as ours, the insides being neatly plastered and whitewashed. Here I also saw and tasted for the first time sugar-cane. Their money consisted of little white shells, the size of the finger nail. I was sold here for one hundred and seventy-two of them by a merchant who lived and brought me there. I had been about two or three days at his house, when a wealthy widow, a neighbour of his, came there one evening, and brought with her an only son, a young gentleman about my own age and size. Here they saw me; and, having taken a fancy to me, I was bought of the merchant, and went home with them. Her house and premises were situated close to one of those rivulets I have mentioned, and were the finest I ever saw in Africa: they were very extensive, and she had a number of slaves to attend her. The next day I was washed and

---

seasoning: often fatal period of acclimatization to the rigors of colonial slavery and the pathogens of a new disease environment.

perfumed, and when meal-time came I was led into the presence of my mistress, and ate and drank before her with her son. This filled me with astonishment; and I could scarce help expressing my surprise that the young gentleman should suffer me, who was bound, to eat with him who was free; and not only so, but that he would not at any time either eat or drink till I had taken first, because I was the eldest, which was agreeable to our custom. Indeed every thing here, and all their treatment of me, made me forget that I was a slave. The language of these people resembled ours so nearly, that we understood each other perfectly. They had also the very same customs as we. There were likewise slaves daily to attend us, while my young master and I with other boys sported with our darts and bows and arrows, as I had been used to do at home. In this resemblance to my former happy state I passed about two months; and I now began to think I was to be adopted into the family, and was beginning to be reconciled to my situation, and to forget by degrees my misfortunes, when all at once the delusion vanished; for, without the least previous knowledge, one morning early, while my dear master and companion was still asleep, I was wakened out of my reverie to fresh sorrow, and hurried away even amongst the uncircumcised.

Thus, at the very moment I dreamed of the greatest happiness, I found myself most miserable; and it seemed as if fortune wished to give me this taste of joy, only to render the reverse more poignant. The change I now experienced was as painful as it was sudden and unexpected. It was a change indeed from a state of bliss to a scene which is inexpressible by me, as it discovered to me an element I had never before beheld, and till then had no idea of, and wherein such instances of hardship and cruelty continually occurred as I can never reflect on but with horror.

All the nations and people I had hitherto passed through resembled our own in their manners, customs, and language: but I came at length to a country, the inhabitants of which differed from us in all those particulars. I was very much struck with this difference, especially when I came among a people who did not circumcise, and are without washing their hands. They cooked also in iron pots, and had European cutlasses and cross bows, which were unknown to us, and fought with their fists amongst themselves. Their women were not so modest as ours, for they ate, and drank, and slept, with their men. But, above all, I was amazed to see no sacrifices or offerings among them. In some of those places the people ornamented themselves with scars, and likewise filed their teeth very sharp. They wanted sometimes to ornament me in the same manner, but I would not suffer them; hoping that I might some time be among a people who did not thus disfigure themselves, as I thought they did. At last I came to the banks of a large river, which was covered with canoes, in which the people appeared to live with their household utensils and provisions of all kinds. I was beyond measure astonished at this, as I had never before seen any water larger than a pond or a rivulet: and my surprise was mingled with no small fear when I was put into one of these canoes, and we began to paddle and move along the river. We continued going on thus till night; and when we came to land, and made fires on the banks, each family by themselves, some dragged their canoes on shore, others stayed and cooked in theirs, and laid in them all night. Those on the land had mats, of which they made tents, some in the shape of little houses: in these we slept; and after the morning meal we embarked again and proceeded as before. I was often very much astonished to see some of the women, as well as the men, jump into the water, dive to the bottom, come up again, and swim about. Thus I continued to travel, sometimes by land, sometimes by water, through different countries and various nations, till, at the end of six or seven months after I had been kidnapped, I arrived at the sea coast. It would be tedious and uninteresting to relate all the incidents which befell me during this journey, and which I have not yet forgotten; of the various hands I passed through, and the manners and customs of all the different people among whom I lived: I shall therefore only observe, that in all the places where I was the soil was exceedingly rich; the pomkins, eadas, plantains, yams, &c. &c. were in great abundance, and of incredible size. There were also vast quantities of different gums, though not used for any purpose; and every where a great deal of tobacco. The cotton even grew quite wild; and there was plenty of red-wood. I saw no mechanics whatever in all the way, except such as I have mentioned. The chief employment in all these countries was agriculture, and both the males and females, as with us, were brought up to it, and trained in the arts of war.

The first object which saluted my eyes when I arrived on the coast was the sea, and a slave ship, which was then riding at anchor, and waiting for its cargo. These filled me with astonishment, which was soon converted into terror when I was carried on board. I was immediately handled and tossed up to see if I were sound by some of the crew; and I was now persuaded that I had gotten into a world of bad spirits, and that they were going to kill me. Their complexions too differing so much from ours, their long hair, and the language they spoke, (which was very different from any I had ever heard) united to confirm me in this belief. Indeed such were the

---

pomkins: pumpkins.
red-wood: various red-colored woods used for making dyes.
mechanics: skilled craftspersons.
saluted: greeted.

horrors of my views and fears at the moment, that, if ten thousand worlds had been my own, I would have freely parted with them all to have exchanged my condition with that of the meanest slave in my own country. When I looked round the ship too and saw a large furnace or copper boiling, and a multitude of black people of every description chained together, every one of their countenances expressing dejection and sorrow, I no longer doubted of my fate; and, quite overpowered with horror and anguish, I fell motionless on the deck and fainted. When I recovered a little I found some black people about me, who I believed were some of those who brought me on board, and had been receiving their pay; they talked to me in order to cheer me, but all in vain. I asked them if we were not to be eaten by those white men with horrible looks, red faces, and loose hair. They told me I was not; and one of the crew brought me a small portion of spirituous liquor in a wine glass; but, being afraid of him, I would not take it out of his hand. One of the blacks therefore took it from him and gave it to me, and I took a little down my palate, which, instead of reviving me, as they thought it would, threw me into the greatest consternation at the strange feeling it produced, having never tasted any such liquor before. Soon after this the blacks who brought me on board went off, and left me abandoned to despair. I now saw myself deprived of all chance of returning to my native country, or even the least glimpse of hope of gaining the shore, which I now considered as friendly; and I even wished for my former slavery in preference to my present situation, which was filled with horrors of every kind, still heightened by my ignorance of what I was to undergo. I was not long suffered to indulge my grief; I was soon put down under the decks, and there I received such a salutation in my nostrils as I had never experienced in my life: so that, with the loathsomeness of the stench, and crying together, I became so sick and low that I was not able to eat, nor had I the least desire to taste any thing. I now wished for the last friend, death, to relieve me; but soon, to my grief, two of the white men offered me eatables; and, on my refusing to eat, one of them held me fast by the hands, and laid me across I think the windlass, and tied my feet, while the other flogged me severely. I had never experienced any thing of this kind before; and although, not being used to the water, I naturally feared that element the first time I saw it, yet nevertheless, could I have got over the nettings, I would have jumped over the side, but I could not; and, besides, the crew used to watch us very closely who were not chained down to the decks, lest we should leap into the water: and I have seen some of these poor African

---

windlass: horizontal roller, beam, or barrel cranked by hand to draw a rope, chain, or anchor cable up and down.

prisoners most severely cut for attempting to do so, and hourly whipped for not eating. This indeed was often the case with myself. In a little time after, amongst the poor chained men, I found some of my own nation, which in a small degree gave ease to my mind. I inquired of these what was to be done with us; they gave me to understand we were to be carried to these white people's country to work for them. I then was a little revived, and thought, if it were no worse than working, my situation was not so desperate: but still I feared I should be put to death, the white people looked and acted, as I thought, in so savage a manner; for I had never seen among any people such instances of brutal cruelty; and this not only shewn towards us blacks, but also to some of the whites themselves. One white man in particular I saw, when we were permitted to be on deck, flogged so unmercifully with a large rope near the foremast, that he died in consequence of it; and they tossed him over the side as they would have done a brute. This made me fear these people the more; and I expected nothing less than to be treated in the same manner. I could not help expressing my fears and apprehensions to some of my countrymen: I asked them if these people had no country, but lived in this hollow place (the ship): they told me they did not, but came from a distant one. 'Then,' said I, 'how comes it in all our country we never heard of them?' They told me because they lived so very far off. I then asked where were their women? had they any like themselves? I was told they had: 'and why,' said I, 'do we not see them?' they answered, because they were left behind. I asked how the vessel could go? they told me they could not tell; but that there were cloths put upon the masts by the help of the ropes I saw, and then the vessel went on; and the white men had some spell or magic they put in the water when they liked in order to stop the vessel. I was exceedingly amazed at this account, and really thought they were spirits. I therefore wished much to be from amongst them, for I expected they would sacrifice me: but my wishes were vain; for we were so quartered that it was impossible for any of us to make our escape. While we stayed on the coast I was mostly on deck; and one day, to my great astonishment, I saw one of these vessels coming in with the sails up. As soon as the whites saw it, they gave a great shout, at which we were amazed; and the more so as the vessel appeared larger by approaching nearer. At last she came to an anchor in my sight, and when the anchor was let go I and my countrymen who saw it were lost in astonishment to observe the vessel stop; and were now convinced it was done by magic. Soon after this the other ship got her boats out, and they came on board of us, and the people of both ships seemed very glad to see each other. Several of the strangers also shook hands with us black people, and made motions

---

brute: animal.

with their hands, signifying I suppose we were to go to their country; but we did not understand them. At last, when the ship we were in had got in all her cargo, they made ready with many fearful noises, and we were all put under deck, so that we could not see how they managed the vessel. But this disappointment was the least of my sorrow. The stench of the hold while we were on the coast was so intolerably loathsome, that it was dangerous to remain there for any time, and some of us had been permitted to stay on the deck for the fresh air; but now that the whole ship's cargo were confined together, it became absolutely pestilential. The closeness of the place, and the heat of the climate, added to the number in the ship, which was so crowded that each had scarcely room to turn himself, almost suffocated us. This produced copious perspirations, so that the air soon became unfit for respiration, from a variety of loathsome smells, and brought on a sickness among the slaves, of which many died, thus falling victims to the improvident avarice, as I may call it, of their purchasers. This wretched situation was again aggravated by the galling of the chains, now become insupportable; and the filth of the necessary tubs, into which the children often fell, and were almost suffocated. The shrieks of the women, and the groans of the dying, rendered the whole a scene of horror almost inconceivable. Happily perhaps for myself I was soon reduced so low here that it was thought necessary to keep me almost always on deck; and from my extreme youth I was not put in fetters. In this situation I expected every hour to share the fate of my companions, some of whom were almost daily brought upon deck at the point of death, which I began to hope would soon put an end to my miseries. Often did I think many of the inhabitants of the deep much more happy than myself. I envied them the freedom they enjoyed, and as often wished I could change my condition for theirs. Every circumstance I met with served only to render my state more painful, and heighten my apprehensions, and my opinion of the cruelty of the whites. One day they had taken a number of fishes; and when they had killed and satisfied themselves with as many as they thought fit, to our astonishment who were on the deck, rather than give any of them to us to eat as we expected, they tossed the remaining fish into the sea again, although we begged and prayed for some as well as we could, but in vain; and some of my countrymen, being pressed by hunger, took an opportunity, when they thought no one saw them, of trying to get a little privately; but they were discovered, and the attempt procured them some very severe floggings. One day, when we had a smooth sea and moderate wind, two of my wearied countrymen who were chained together (I was near them at the

---

necessary tubs: latrines.

time), preferring death to such a life of misery, somehow made through the nettings and jumped into the sea: immediately another quite dejected fellow, who, on account of his illness, was suffered to be out of irons, also followed their example; and I believe many more would very soon have done the same if they had not been prevented by the ship's crew, who were instantly alarmed. Those of us that were the most active were in a moment put down under the deck, and there was such a noise and confusion amongst the people of the ship as I never heard before, to stop her, and get the boat out to go after the slaves. However two of the wretches were drowned, but they got the other, and afterwards flogged him unmercifully for thus attempting to prefer death to slavery. In this manner we continued to undergo more hardships than I can now relate, hardships which are inseparable from this accursed trade. Many a time we were near suffocation from the want of fresh air, which we were often without for whole days together. This, and the stench of the necessary tubs, carried off many. During our passage I first saw flying fishes, which surprised me very much: they used frequently to fly across the ship, and many of them fell on the deck. I also now first saw the use of the quadrant; I had often with astonishment seen the mariners make observations with it, and I could not think what it meant. They at last took notice of my surprise; and one of them, willing to increase it, as well as to gratify my curiosity, made me one day look through it. The clouds appeared to me to be land, which disappeared as they passed along. This heightened my wonder; and I was now more persuaded than ever that I was in another world, and that every thing about me was magic. At last we came in sight of the island of Barbadoes,[17] at which the whites on board gave a great shout, and made many signs of joy to us. We did not know what to think of this; but as the vessel drew nearer we plainly saw the harbour, and other ships of different kinds and sizes; and we soon anchored amongst them off Bridge Town. Many merchants and planters now came on board, though it was in the evening. They put us in separate parcels, and examined us attentively. They also made us jump, and pointed to the land, signifying we were to go there. We thought by this we should be eaten by these ugly men, as they appeared to us; and, when soon after we were all put down under the deck again, there was much dread and trembling among us, and nothing but bitter cries to be heard all the night from these apprehensions, insomuch that at last the white people got some old slaves from the land to pacify us. They told us we were not to be eaten, but to work, and were soon to go on land, where we should see many of our

---

quadrant: navigation instrument used to determine latitude by measuring the altitude of the sun or another star.

[17] Barbados, British West Indian island, with its capital at Bridgetown.

country people. This report eased us much; and sure enough, soon after we were landed, there came to us Africans of all languages. We were conducted immediately to the merchant's yard, where we were all pent up together like so many sheep in a fold, without regard to sex or age. As every object was new to me every thing I saw filled me with surprise. What struck me first was that the houses were built with stories, and in every other respect different from those in Africa: but I was still more astonished on seeing people on horseback. I did not know what this could mean; and indeed I thought these people were full of nothing but magical arts. While I was in this astonishment one of my fellow prisoners spoke to a countryman of his about the horses, who said they were the same kind they had in their country. I understood them, though they were from a distant part of Africa, and I thought it odd I had not seen any horses there; but afterwards, when I came to converse with different Africans, I found they had many horses amongst them, and much larger than those I then saw. We were not many days in the merchant's custody before we were sold after their usual manner, which is this:—On a signal given, (as the beat of a drum) the buyers rush at once into the yard where the slaves are confined, and make choice of that parcel they like best. The noise and clamour with which this is attended, and the eagerness visible in the countenances of the buyers, serve not a little to increase the apprehensions of the terrified Africans, who may well be supposed to consider them as the ministers of that destruction to which they think themselves devoted. In this manner, without scruple, are relations and friends separated, most of them never to see each other again. I remember in the vessel in which I was brought over, in the men's apartment, there were several brothers, who, in the sale, were sold in different lots; and it was very moving on this occasion to see and hear their cries at parting. O, ye nominal Christians! might not an African ask you, learned you this from your God, who says unto you, Do unto all men as you would men should do unto you? Is it not enough that we are torn from our country and friends to toil for your luxury and lust of gain? Must every tender feeling be likewise sacrificed to your avarice? Are the dearest friends and relations, now rendered more dear by their separation from their kindred, still to be parted from each other, and thus prevented from cheering the gloom of slavery with the small comfort of being together and mingling their sufferings and sorrows? Why are parents to lose their children, brothers their sisters, or husbands their wives? Surely this is a new refinement in cruelty, which, while it has no advantage to atone for it, thus aggravates distress, and adds fresh horrors even to the wretchedness of slavery.

---

devoted: doomed.

From CHAPTER III.

I NOW totally lost the small remains of comfort I had enjoyed in conversing with my countrymen; the women too, who used to wash and take care of me, were all gone different ways, and I never saw one of them afterwards.

I stayed in this island for a few days; I believe it could not be above a fortnight; when I and some few more slaves, that were not saleable amongst the rest, from very much fretting, were shipped off in a sloop for North America. On the passage we were better treated than when we were coming from Africa, and we had plenty of rice and fat pork. We were landed up a river a good way from the sea, about Virginia county, where we saw few or none of our native Africans, and not one soul who could talk to me. I was a few weeks weeding grass, and gathering stones in a plantation; and at last all my companions were distributed different ways, and only myself was left. I was now exceedingly miserable, and thought myself worse off than any of the rest of my companions; for they could talk to each other, but I had no person to speak to that I could understand. In this state I was constantly grieving and pining, and wishing for death rather than any thing else. While I was in this plantation the gentleman, to whom I suppose the estate belonged, being unwell, I was one day sent for to his dwelling house to fan him; when I came into the room where he was I was very much affrighted at some things I saw, and the more so as I had seen a black woman slave as I came through the house, who was cooking the dinner, and the poor creature was cruelly loaded with various kinds of iron machines; she had one particularly on her head, which locked her mouth so fast that she could scarcely speak; and could not eat nor drink. I was much astonished and shocked at this contrivance, which I afterwards learned was called the iron muzzle. Soon after I had a fan put into my hand, to fan the gentleman while he slept; and so I did indeed with great fear. While he was fast asleep I indulged myself a great deal in looking about the room, which to me appeared very fine and curious. The first object that engaged my attention was a watch which hung on the chimney, and was going. I was quite surprised at the noise it made, and was afraid it would tell the gentleman any thing I might do amiss: and when I immediately after observed a picture hanging in the room, which appeared constantly to look at me, I was still more affrighted, having never seen such things as these before. At one time I thought it was something relative to magic; and not seeing it move I thought it might be some way the whites had to keep their great men when they died, and offer them libation as we used to do to our friendly spirits.

---

sloop: small single-masted sailing ship.

In this state of anxiety I remained till my master awoke, when I was dismissed out of the room, to my no small satisfaction and relief; for I thought that these people were all made up of wonders. In this place I was called Jacob; but on board the African snow I was called Michael. I had been some time in this miserable, forlorn, and much dejected state, without having any one to talk to, which made my life a burden, when the kind and unknown hand of the Creator (who in very deed leads the blind in a way they know not) now began to appear, to my comfort; for one day the captain of a merchant ship, called the Industrious Bee, came on some business to my master's house. This gentleman, whose name was Michael Henry Pascal, was a lieutenant in the royal navy, but now commanded this trading ship, which was somewhere in the confines of the county many miles off. While he was at my master's house it happened that he saw me, and liked me so well that he made a purchase of me. I think I have often heard him say he gave thirty or forty pounds sterling for me; but I do not now remember which. However, he meant me for a present to some of his friends in England: and I was sent accordingly from the house of my then master, one Mr. Campbell, to the place where the ship lay; I was conducted on horseback by an elderly black man, (a mode of travelling which appeared very odd to me). When I arrived I was carried on board a fine large ship, loaded with tobacco, &c. and just ready to sail for England. I now thought my condition much mended; I had sails to lie on, and plenty of good victuals to eat; and every body on board used me very kindly, quite contrary to what I had seen of any white people before; I therefore began to think that they were not all of the same disposition. A few days after I was on board we sailed for England. I was still at a loss to conjecture my destiny. By this time, however, I could smatter a little imperfect English; and I wanted to know as well as I could where we were going. Some of the people of the ship used to tell me they were going to carry me back to my own country, and this made me very happy. I was quite rejoiced at the sound of going back; and thought if I should get home what wonders I should have to tell. But I was reserved for another fate, and was soon undeceived when we came within sight of the English coast. While I was on board this ship, my captain and master named me *Gustavus Vasa*.[18] I at that time began to understand him a little, and refused to be called so, and told him as well as I could that I would be called Jacob; but he said I should not, and still called me

---

snow: two-masted ship.

[18] After Gustav Eriksson Vasa (c. 1496–1560), hero of Swedish independence and king Gustav I of Sweden. Slaves were frequently named (with a tone of mockery) after kings, conquerors, and civic or military heroes, such as Caesar and Pompey.

Gustavus; and when I refused to answer to my new name, which at first I did, it gained me many a cuff; so at length I submitted, and was obliged to bear the present name, by which I have been known ever since. The ship had a very long passage; and on that account we had very short allowance of provisions. Towards the last we had only one pound and a half of bread per week, and about the same quantity of meat, and one quart of water a-day. We spoke with only one vessel the whole time we were at sea, and but once we caught a few fishes. In our extremities the captain and people told me in jest they would kill and eat me; but I thought them in earnest, and was depressed beyond measure, expecting every moment to be my last. While I was in this situation one evening they caught, with a good deal of trouble, a large shark, and got it on board. This gladdened my poor heart exceedingly, as I thought it would serve the people to eat instead of their eating me; but very soon, to my astonishment, they cut off a small part of the tail, and tossed the rest over the side. This renewed my consternation; and I did not know what to think of these white people, though I very much feared they would kill and eat me. There was on board the ship a young lad who had never been at sea before, about four or five years older than myself: his name was Richard Baker. He was a native of America, had received an excellent education, and was of a most amiable temper. Soon after I went on board he shewed me a great deal of partiality and attention, and in return I grew extremely fond of him. We at length became insepa-rable; and, for the space of two years, he was of very great use to me, and was my constant companion and instructor. Although this dear youth had many slaves of his own, yet he and I have gone through many sufferings together on shipboard; and we have many nights lain in each other's bo-soms when we were in great distress. Thus such a friendship was cemented between us as we cherished till his death, which, to my very great sorrow, happened in the year 1759, when he was up the Archipelago,[19] on board his majesty's ship the Preston: an event which I have never ceased to regret, as I lost at once a kind interpreter, an agreeable companion, and a faithful friend; who, at the age of fifteen, discovered a mind superior to prejudice; and who was not ashamed to notice, to associate with, and to be the friend and instructor of one who was ignorant, a stranger, of a different com-plexion, and a slave! My master had lodged in his mother's house in Amer-ica: he respected him very much, and made him always eat with him in the cabin. He used often to tell him jocularly that he would kill me to eat.

---

cuff: slap.

[19] Chain of islands off mainland Greece.

Sometimes he would say to me — the black people were not good to eat, and would ask me if we did not eat people in my country. I said, No: then he said he would kill Dick (as he always called him) first, and afterwards me. Though this hearing relieved my mind a little as to myself, I was alarmed for Dick and whenever he was called I used to be very much afraid he was to be killed; and I would peep and watch to see if they were going to kill him: nor was I free from this consternation till we made the land. One night we lost a man overboard; and the cries and noise were so great and confused, in stopping the ship, that I, who did not know what was the matter, began, as usual, to be very much afraid, and to think they were going to make an offering with me, and perform some magic; which I still believed they dealt in. As the waves were very high I thought the Ruler of the seas was angry, and I expected to be offered up to appease him. This filled my mind with agony, and I could not any more that night close my eyes again to rest. However, when daylight appeared I was a little eased in my mind; but still every time I was called I used to think it was to be killed. Some time after this we saw some very large fish, which I afterwards found were called grampusses. They looked to me extremely terrible, and made their appearance just at dusk; and were so near as to blow the water on the ship's deck. I believed them to be the rulers of the sea; and, as the white people did not make any offerings at any time, I thought they were angry with them: and, at last, what confirmed my belief was, the wind just then died away, and a calm ensued, and in consequence of it the ship stopped going. I supposed that the fish had performed this, and I hid myself in the fore part of the ship, through fear of being offered up to appease them, every minute peeping and quaking: but my good friend Dick came shortly towards me, and I took an opportunity to ask him, as well as I could, what these fish were. Not being able to talk much English, I could but just make him understand my question; and not at all, when I asked him if any offerings were to be made to them: however, he told me these fish would swallow any body; which sufficiently alarmed me. Here he was called away by the captain, who was leaning over the quarter-deck railing and looking at the fish; and most of the people were busied in getting a barrel of pitch to light, for them to play with. The captain now called me to him, having learned some of my apprehensions from Dick; and having diverted himself and others for some time with my fears, which appeared ludicrous enough in my crying and trembling, he dismissed me. The barrel of pitch was now lighted and put over the side into the water: by this time it was just dark, and the fish went after it; and, to my great joy, I saw them no more.

---

grampusses: small toothed whales such as orcas.

However, all my alarms began to subside when we got sight of land; and at last the ship arrived at Falmouth,[20] after a passage of thirteen weeks. Every heart on board seemed gladdened on our reaching the shore, and none more than mine. The captain immediately went on shore, and sent on board some fresh provisions, which we wanted very much: we made good use of them, and our famine was soon turned into feasting, almost without ending. It was about the beginning of the spring 1757 when I arrived in England, and I was near twelve years of age at that time. I was very much struck with the buildings and the pavement of the streets in Falmouth; and, indeed, any object I saw filled me with new surprise. One morning, when I got upon deck, I saw it covered all over with the snow that fell over-night: as I had never seen any thing of the kind before, I thought it was salt; so I immediately ran down to the mate and desired him, as well as I could, to come and see how somebody in the night had thrown salt all over the deck. He, knowing what it was, desired me to bring some of it down to him: accordingly I took up a handful of it, which I found very cold indeed; and when I brought it to him he desired me to taste it. I did so, and I was surprised beyond measure. I then asked him what it was; he told me it was snow: but I could not in anywise understand him. He asked me if we had no such thing in my country; and I told him, No. I then asked him the use of it, and who made it; he told me a great man in the heavens, called God: but here again I was to all intents and purposes at a loss to understand him; and the more so, when a little after I saw the air filled with it, in a heavy shower, which fell down on the same day. After this I went to church; and having never been at such a place before, I was again amazed at seeing and hearing the service. I asked all I could about it; and they gave me to understand it was worshipping God, who made us and all things. I was still at a great loss, and soon got into an endless field of inquiries, as well as I was able to speak and ask about things. However, my little friend Dick used to be my best interpreter; for I could make free with him, and he always instructed me with pleasure: and from what I could understand by him of this God, and in seeing these white people did not sell one another, as we did, I was much pleased; and in this I thought they were much happier than we Africans. I was astonished at the wisdom of the white people in all things I saw; but was amazed at their not sacrificing, or making any offerings, and eating with unwashed hands, and touching the dead. I likewise could not help remarking the particular slenderness of their women, which I did not at first like; and I thought they were not so modest and shamefaced as the African women.

---

[20] Port on southwest coast of England in Cornwall.

I had often seen my master and Dick employed in reading; and I had a great curiosity to talk to the books, as I thought they did; and so to learn how all things had a beginning: for that purpose I have often taken up a book, and have talked to it, and then put my ears to it, when alone, in hopes it would answer me; and I have been very much concerned when I found it remained silent.

My master lodged at the house of a gentleman in Falmouth, who had a fine little daughter about six or seven years of age, and she grew prodigiously fond of me; insomuch that we used to eat together, and had servants to wait on us. I was so much caressed by this family that it often reminded me of the treatment I had received from my little noble African master. After I had been here a few days, I was sent on board of the ship; but the child cried so much after me that nothing could pacify her till I was sent for again. It is ludicrous enough, that I began to fear I should be betrothed to this young lady; and when my master asked me if I would stay there with her behind him, as he was going away with the ship, which had taken in the tobacco again, I cried immediately, and said I would not leave her. At last, by stealth, one night I was sent on board the ship again; and in a little time we sailed for Guernsey[21] where she was in part owned by a merchant, one Nicholas Doberry. As I was now amongst a people who had not their faces scarred, like some of the African nations where I had been, I was very glad I did not let them ornament me in that manner when I was with them. When we arrived at Guernsey, my master placed me to board and lodge with one of his mates, who had a wife and family there; and some months afterwards he went to England, and left me in care of this mate, together with my friend Dick. This mate had a little daughter, aged about five or six years, with whom I used to be much delighted. I had often observed that when her mother washed her face it looked very rosy; but when she washed mine it did not look so: I therefore tried oftentimes myself if I could not by washing make my face of the same colour as my little playmate (Mary), but it was all in vain; and I now began to be mortified at the difference in our complexions. This woman behaved to me with great kindness and attention; and taught me every thing in the same manner as she did her own child, and indeed in every respect treated me as such. I remained here till the summer of the year 1757; when my master, being appointed first lieutenant of his majesty's ship the Roebuck, sent for Dick and me, and his old mate: on this we all left Guernsey, and set out for England in a sloop bound for London. As we were coming up towards the

---

[21] One of the (British) Channel Islands lying between England and France in the English Channel.

Nore,[22] where the Roebuck lay, a man-of-war's boat came alongside to press our people; on which each man ran to hide himself. I was very much frightened at this, though I did not know what it meant, or what to think or do. However I went and hid myself also under a hencoop. Immediately afterwards the press-gang came on board with their swords drawn, and searched all about, pulled the people out by force, and put them into the boat. At last I was found out also: the man that found me held me up by the heels while they all made their sport of me, I roaring and crying out all the time most lustily: but at last the mate, who was my conductor, seeing this, came to my assistance, and did all he could to pacify me; but all to very little purpose, till I had seen the boat go off. Soon afterwards we came to the Nore, where the Roebuck lay; and, to our great joy, my master came on board to us, and brought us to the ship. When I went on board this large ship, I was amazed indeed to see the quantity of men and the guns. However my surprise began to diminish as my knowledge increased; and I ceased to feel those apprehensions and alarms which had taken such strong possession of me when I first came among the Europeans, and for some time after. I began now to pass to an opposite extreme; I was so far from being afraid of any thing new which I saw, that, after I had been some time in this ship, I even began to long for a battle.

FROM CHAPTER IV.

IT was now between two and three years since I first came to England, a great part of which I had spent at sea; so that I became inured to that service, and began to consider myself as happily situated; for my master treated me always extremely well; and my attachment and gratitude to him were very great. From the various scenes I had beheld on ship-board, I soon grew a stranger to terror of every kind, and was, in that respect at least, almost an Englishman. I have often reflected with surprise that I never felt half the alarm at any of the numerous dangers I have been in, that I was filled with at the first sight of the Europeans, and at every act of theirs, even the most trifling, when I first came among them, and for some time afterwards. That fear, however, which was the effect of my ignorance, wore away as I began to know them. I could now speak English tolerably well, and I perfectly understood every thing that was said. I now not only felt

---

man-of-war: naval warship.

press: impress, force into military service.

[22] Area near the mouth of the Thames River, which leads from the English coast into London.

myself quite easy with these new countrymen, but relished their society and manners. I no longer looked upon them as spirits, but as men superior to us; and therefore I had the stronger desire to resemble them; to imbibe their spirit, and imitate their manners; I therefore embraced every occasion of improvement; and every new thing that I observed I treasured up in my memory. I had long wished to be able to read and write; and for this purpose I took every opportunity to gain instruction, but had made as yet very little progress. However, when I went to London with my master, I had soon an opportunity of improving myself, which I gladly embraced. Shortly after my arrival, he sent me to wait upon the Miss Guerins, who had treated me with much kindness when I was there before; and they sent me to school.

While I was attending these ladies their servants told me I could not go to Heaven unless I was baptized. This made me very uneasy; for I had now some faint idea of a future state: accordingly I communicated my anxiety to the eldest Miss Guerin, with whom I was become a favourite, and pressed her to have me baptized; when to my great joy she told me I should. She had formerly asked my master to let me be baptized, but he had refused; however she now insisted on it; and he being under some obligation to her brother complied with her request; so I was baptized in St. Margaret's church, Westminster, in February 1759, by my present name.[23] The clergyman, at the same time, gave me a book, called a Guide to the Indians, written by the Bishop of Sodor and Man.[24] On this occasion Miss Guerin did me the honour to stand as godmother, and afterwards gave me a treat. I used to attend these ladies about the town, in which service I was extremely happy; as I had thus many opportunities of seeing London, which I desired of all things. I was sometimes, however, with my master at his rendezvous-house, which was at the foot of Westminster-bridge. Here I used to enjoy myself in playing about the bridge stairs, and often in the watermen's wherries, with other boys. On one of these occasions there was another boy with me in a wherry, and we went out into the current of the river: while we were there two more stout boys came to us in another wherry, and, abusing us for taking the boat, desired me to get into the other wherry boat. Accordingly I went to get out of the wherry I was in; but just as I had got one of my feet into the other boat the boys shoved it off, so that

---

rendezvous-house: place for lodging and recruiting seamen.

watermen: boatmen, ferrymen.

wherries: long, light rowboats designed for rivers and harbors.

[23] That is, Gustavus Vassa.

[24] Thomas Wilson, *An Essay Towards an Instruction for the Indians* (1740).

I fell into the Thames; and, not being able to swim, I should unavoidably have been drowned, but for the assistance of some watermen who providentially came to my relief.

The Namur being again got ready for sea, my master, with his gang, was ordered on board; and, to my no small grief, I was obliged to leave my school-master, whom I liked very much, and always attended while I stayed in London, to repair on board with my master. Nor did I leave my kind patronesses, the Miss Guerins, without uneasiness and regret. They often used to teach me to read, and took great pains to instruct me in the principles of religion and the knowledge of God. I therefore parted from those amiable ladies with reluctance; after receiving from them many friendly cautions how to conduct myself, and some valuable presents.

When I came to Spithead, I found we were destined for the Mediterranean, with a large fleet, which was now ready to put to sea. We only waited for the arrival of the admiral, who soon came on board; and about the beginning of the spring 1759, having weighed anchor, and got under way, sailed for the Mediterranean; and in eleven days, from the Land's End, we got to Gibraltar.[25] While we were here I used to be often on shore, and got various fruits in great plenty, and very cheap.

I had frequently told several people, in my excursions on shore, the story of my being kidnapped with my sister, and of our being separated, as I have related before; and I had as often expressed my anxiety for her fate, and my sorrow at having never met her again. One day, when I was on shore, and mentioning these circumstances to some persons, one of them told me he knew where my sister was, and, if I would accompany him, he would bring me to her. Improbable as this story was I believed it immediately, and agreed to go with him, while my heart leaped for joy: and, indeed, he conducted me to a black young woman, who was so like my sister, that, at first sight, I really thought it was her: but I was quickly undeceived; and, on talking to her, I found her to be of another nation.

While we lay here the Preston came in from the Levant. As soon as she arrived, my master told me I should now see my old companion, Dick, who had gone in her when she sailed for Turkey. I was much rejoiced at this news, and expected every minute to embrace him; and when the captain

---

gang: crew.

Levant: collective term for the countries bordering the eastern Mediterrenean, from Greece to Egypt, then a Muslim region under Ottoman control.

[25]Equiano's ship touches at Spithead (between Portsmouth and the Isle of Wight); rounds Land's End (the southwestern tip of Cornwall); and sails to Gibraltar, a fortified British possession on the Mediterranean coast of Spain, strategically situated on the narrow Strait of Gibraltar and facing Tangier in North Africa.

came on board of our ship, which he did immediately after, I ran to inquire after my friend; but, with inexpressible sorrow, I learned from the boat's crew that the dear youth was dead! and that they had brought his chest, and all his other things, to my master: these he afterwards gave to me, and I regarded them as a memorial of my friend, whom I loved, and grieved for, as a brother. . . .

While I was here, I met with a trifling incident, which surprised me agreeably. I was one day in a field belonging to a gentleman who had a black boy about my own size; this boy having observed me from his master's house, was transported at the sight of one of his own countrymen, and ran to meet me with the utmost haste. I not knowing what he was about turned a little out of his way at first, but to no purpose: he soon came close to me and caught hold of me in his arms as if I had been his brother, though we had never seen each other before. After we had talked together for some time he took me to his master's house, where I was treated very kindly. This benevolent boy and I were very happy in frequently seeing each other till about the month of March 1761, when our ship had orders to fit out again for another expedition. When we got ready, we joined a very large fleet at Spithead, commanded by Commodore Keppel, which was destined against Belle-Isle,[26] and with a number of transport ships with troops on board to make a descent on the place. We sailed once more in quest of fame. I longed to engage in new adventures and see fresh wonders. . . .

. . . Our ship having arrived at Portsmouth, we went into the harbour, and remained there till the latter end of November, when we heard great talk about peace; and, to our very great joy, in the beginning of December we had orders to go up to London with our ship to be paid off. We received this news with loud huzzas, and every other demonstration of gladness; and nothing but mirth was to be seen throughout every part of the ship. I too was not without my share of the general joy on this occasion. I thought now of nothing but being freed, and working for myself, and thereby getting money to enable me to get a good education; for I always had a great desire to be able at least to read and write; and while I was on ship-board I had endeavoured to improve myself in both. While I was in the Ætna particularly, the captain's clerk taught me to write, and gave me a smattering of arithmetic as far as the rule of three. There was also one Daniel Queen, about forty years of age, a man very well educated, who messed with me on board this ship, and he likewise dressed and attended the captain. Fortunately this man soon became very much attached to me, and took very

---

messed: took meals.
[26] Island off France in the Bay of Quiberon.

great pains to instruct me in many things. He taught me to shave and dress hair a little, and also to read in the Bible, explaining many passages to me, which I did not comprehend. I was wonderfully surprised to see the laws and rules of my country written almost exactly here; a circumstance which I believe tended to impress our manners and customs more deeply on my memory. I used to tell him of this resemblance; and many a time we have sat up the whole night together at this employment. In short, he was like a father to me; and some even used to call me after his name; they also styled me the black Christian. Indeed I almost loved him with the affection of a son. Many things I have denied myself that he might have them; and when I used to play at marbles or any other game, and won a few halfpence, or got any little money, which I sometimes did, for shaving any one, I used to buy him a little sugar or tobacco, as far as my stock of money would go. He used to say, that he and I never should part; and that when our ship was paid off, as I was as free as himself or any other man on board, he would instruct me in his business, by which I might gain a good livelihood. This gave me new life and spirits; and my heart burned within me, while I thought the time long till I obtained my freedom. For though my master had not promised it to me, yet, besides the assurances I had received that he had no right to detain me, he always treated me with the greatest kindness, and reposed in me an unbounded confidence; he even paid attention to my morals; and would never suffer me to deceive him, or tell lies, of which he used to tell me the consequences; and that if I did so God would not love me; so that, from all this tenderness, I had never once supposed, in all my dreams of freedom, that he would think of detaining me any longer than I wished.

In pursuance of our orders we sailed from Portsmouth for the Thames, and arrived at Deptford the 10th of December, where we cast anchor just as it was high water. The ship was up about half an hour, when my master ordered the barge to be manned; and all in an instant, without having before given me the least reason to suspect any thing of the matter, he forced me into the barge; saying, I was going to leave him, but he would take care I should not. I was so struck with the unexpectedness of this proceeding, that for some time I did not make a reply, only I made an offer to go for my books and chest of clothes, but he swore I should not move out of his sight; and if I did he would cut my throat, at the same time taking his hanger. I began, however, to collect myself; and, plucking up courage, I told him I was free, and he could not by law serve me so. But this only enraged him the more; and he continued to swear, and said he would soon let me know

---

hanger: small sword worn hanging from the belt.

whether he would or not, and at that instant sprung himself into the barge from the ship, to the astonishment and sorrow of all on board. The tide, rather unluckily for me, had just turned downward, so that we quickly fell down the river along with it, till we came among some outward-bound West Indiamen; for he was resolved to put me on board the first vessel he could get to receive me. The boat's crew, who pulled against their will, became quite faint different times, and would have gone ashore; but he would not let them. Some of them strove then to cheer me, and told me he could not sell me, and that they would stand by me, which revived me a little; and I still entertained hopes; for as they pulled along he asked some vessels to receive me, but they could not. But, just as we had got a little below Gravesend, we came alongside of a ship which was going away the next tide for the West Indies; her name was the Charming Sally, Captain James Doran; and my master went on board and agreed with him for me; and in a little time I was sent for into the cabin. When I came there Captain Doran asked me if I knew him; I answered that I did not; 'Then,' said he 'you are now my slave.' I told him my master could not sell me to him, nor to any one else. 'Why,' said he, 'did not your master buy you?' I confessed he did. 'But I have served him,' said I, 'many years, and he has taken all my wages and prize-money, for I only got one sixpence during the war; besides this I have been baptized; and by the laws of the land no man has a right to sell me:' And I added, that I had heard a lawyer and others at different times tell my master so.[27] They both then said that those people who told me so were not my friends; but I replied—it was very extraordinary that other people did not know the law as well as they. Upon this Captain Doran said I talked too much English; and if I did not behave myself well, and be quiet, he had a method on board to make me. I was too well convinced of his power over me to doubt what he said; and my former sufferings in the slave-ship presenting themselves to my mind, the recollection of them made me shudder. However, before I retired I told them that as I could not get any right among men here I hoped I should hereafter in Heaven; and I immediately left the cabin, filled with resentment and sorrow. The only coat I had with

---

West Indiamen: ships engaged in the West Indian trade.

agreed: arrived at a price.

prize-money: money from ships and cargoes captured in wartime, shared unequally among the captain, officers, and crew.

[27] Especially in the years before Judge Mansfield's decision on the Somerset case (1772), the legal status of slaves brought to England was uncertain. Though many held that slaves were automatically considered free once on English soil, slaves continued to be bought and sold in England and forcibly returned to colonial slavery into the early nineteenth century.

me my master took away with him, and said if my prize-money had been 10,000l. he had a right to it all, and would have taken it. I had about nine guineas, which, during my long sea-faring life, I had scraped together from trifling perquisites and little ventures; and I hid it that instant, lest my master should take that from me likewise, still hoping that by some means or other I should make my escape to the shore; and indeed some of my old shipmates told me not to despair, for they would get me back again; and that, as soon as they could get their pay, they would immediately come to Portsmouth to me, where this ship was going: but, alas! all my hopes were baffled, and the hour of my deliverance was yet far off. My master, having soon concluded his bargain with the captain, came out of the cabin, and he and his people got into the boat and put off; I followed them with aching eyes as long as I could, and when they were out of sight I threw myself on the deck, while my heart was ready to burst with sorrow and anguish.

FROM CHAPTER V.

THUS, at the moment I expected all my toils to end, was I plunged, as I supposed, in a new slavery; in comparison of which all my service hitherto had been 'perfect freedom;' and whose horrors, always present to my mind, now rushed on it with tenfold aggravation. I wept very bitterly for some time: and began to think that I must have done something to displease the Lord, that he thus punished me so severely. This filled me with painful reflections on my past conduct; I recollected that on the morning of our arrival at Deptford I had rashly sworn that as soon as we reached London I would spend the day in rambling and sport. My conscience smote me for this unguarded expression: I felt that the Lord was able to disappoint me in all things, and immediately considered my present situation as a judgment of Heaven on account of my presumption in swearing: I therefore, with contrition of heart, acknowledged my transgression to God, and poured out my soul before him with unfeigned repentance, and with earnest supplications I besought him not to abandon me in my distress, nor cast me from his mercy for ever. In a little time my grief, spent with its own violence, began to subside; and after the first confusion of my thoughts was over I reflected with more calmness on my present condition: I considered that trials and disappointments are sometimes for our good, and I thought God might perhaps have permitted this in order to teach me wisdom and resignation; for he had hitherto shadowed me with the wings of his mercy, and by his invisible but powerful hand brought me the way I knew not.

---

perquisites: casual wages or tips.

These reflections gave me a little comfort, and I rose at last from the deck with dejection and sorrow in my countenance, yet mixed with some faint hope that the *Lord would appear* for my deliverance. . . .

Mr. King[28] dealt in all manner of merchandize, and kept from one to six clerks. He loaded many vessels in a year; particularly to Philadelphia, where he was born, and was connected with a great mercantile house in that city. He had besides many vessels and droggers, of different sizes, which used to go about the island; and others to collect rum, sugar, and other goods. I understood pulling and managing those boats very well; and this hard work, which was the first that he set me to, in the sugar seasons used to be my constant employment. I have rowed the boat, and slaved at the oars, from one hour to sixteen in the twenty-four; during which I had fifteen pence sterling per day to live on, though sometimes only ten pence. However this was considerably more than was allowed to other slaves that used to work with me, and belonged to other gentlemen on the island: those poor souls had never more than nine pence per day, and seldom more than six pence, from their masters or owners, though they earned them three or four pisterines:[29] for it is a common practice in the West Indies for men to purchase slaves though they have not plantations themselves, in order to let them out to planters and merchants at so much a piece by the day, and they give what allowance they chuse out of this produce of their daily work to their slaves for subsistence; this allowance is often very scanty. My master often gave the owners of these slaves two and a half of these pieces per day, and found the poor fellows in victuals himself, because he thought their owners did not feed them well enough according to the work they did. The slaves used to like this very well; and, as they knew my master to be a man of feeling, they were always glad to work for him in preference to any other gentleman: some of whom, after they had been paid for these poor people's labours, would not give them their allowance out of it. Many times have I even seen these unfortunate wretches beaten for asking for their pay; and often severely flogged by their owners if they did not bring them their daily or weekly money exactly to the time; though the poor creatures were obliged to wait on the gentlemen they had worked for sometimes for more than half the day before they could get

---

droggers: drogher, a slow-going West Indian coasting craft.

[28] Equiano is now on the West Indian island of Montserrat (at this time a British possession), where Captain Doran has sold him to the Quaker merchant Robert King, described by Equiano as amiable, charitable, and humane.

[29] These pisterines are of the value of a shilling. [Equiano's note; a shilling was worth twelve pence.]

their pay; and this generally on Sundays, when they wanted the time for themselves. In particular, I knew a countryman of mine who once did not bring the weekly money directly that it was earned; and though he brought it the same day to his master, yet he was staked to the ground for this pretended negligence, and was just going to receive a hundred lashes, but for a gentleman who begged him off fifty. This poor man was very industrious; and, by his frugality, had saved so much money by working on shipboard, that he had got a white man to buy him a boat, unknown to his master. Some time after he had this little estate the governor wanted a boat to bring his sugar from different parts of the island; and, knowing this to be a negro-man's boat, he seized upon it for himself, and would not pay the owner a farthing. The man on this went to his master, and complained to him of this act of the governor; but the only satisfaction he received was to be damned very heartily by his master, who asked him how dared any of his negroes to have a boat. If the justly-merited ruin of the governor's fortune could be any gratification to the poor man he had thus robbed, he was not without consolation. Extortion and rapine are poor providers; and some time after this the governor died in the King's Bench[30] in England, as I was told, in great poverty. The last war favoured this poor negro-man, and he found some means to escape from his Christian master: he came to England; where I saw him afterwards several times. Such treatment as this often drives these miserable wretches to despair, and they run away from their masters at the hazard of their lives. Many of them, in this place, unable to get their pay when they have earned it, and fearing to be flogged, as usual, if they return home without it, run away where they can for shelter, and a reward is often offered to bring them in dead or alive. My master used sometimes, in these cases, to agree with their owners, and to settle with them himself; and thereby he saved many of them a flogging.

Once, for a few days, I was let out to fit a vessel, and I had no victuals allowed me by either party; at last I told my master of this treatment, and he took me away from it. In many of the estates, on the different islands where I used to be sent for rum or sugar, they would not deliver it to me, or any other negro; he was therefore obliged to send a white man along with me to those places; and then he used to pay him from six to ten pisterines a day. From being thus employed, during the time I served Mr. King, in going about the different estates on the island, I had all the opportunity I could

---

directly that: as soon as.
[30] A debtors' prison in London.

wish for to see the dreadful usage of the poor men; usage that reconciled me to my situation, and made me bless God for the hands into which I had fallen.

I had the good fortune to please my master in every department in which he employed me; and there was scarcely any part of his business, or household affairs, in which I was not occasionally engaged. I often supplied the place of a clerk, in receiving and delivering cargoes to the ships, in tending stores, and delivering goods: and, besides this, I used to shave and dress my master when convenient, and take care of his horse; and when it was necessary, which was very often, I worked likewise on board of different vessels of his. By these means I became very useful to my master; and saved him, as he used to acknowledge, above a hundred pounds a year. Nor did he scruple to say I was of more advantage to him than any of his clerks; though their usual wages in the West Indies are from sixty to a hundred pounds current a year.

I have sometimes heard it asserted that a negro cannot earn his master the first cost; but nothing can be further from the truth. I suppose nine tenths of the mechanics throughout the West Indies are negro slaves; and I well know the coopers among them earn two dollars a day; the carpenters the same, and oftentimes more; as also the masons, smiths, and fishermen, &c. and I have known many slaves whose masters would not take a thousand pounds current for them. But surely this assertion refutes itself; for, if it be true, why do the planters and merchants pay such a price for slaves? And, above all, why do those who make this assertion exclaim the most loudly against the abolition of the slave trade? So much are men blinded, and to such inconsistent arguments are they driven by mistaken interest! I grant, indeed, that slaves are some times, by half-feeding, half-clothing, over-working and stripes, reduced so low, that they are turned out as unfit for service, and left to perish in the woods, or expire on a dunghill.

My master was several times offered by different gentlemen one hundred guineas for me; but he always told them he would not sell me, to my great joy: and I used to double my diligence and care for fear of getting into the hands of those men who did not allow a valuable slave the common support of life. Many of them even used to find fault with my master for feeding his slaves so well as he did; although I often went hungry, and an Englishman might think my fare very indifferent; but he used to tell them

---

first cost: purchase price.

coopers: makers and repairers of casks and barrels.

guineas: gold coins worth twenty-one shillings (a pound was worth twenty shillings).

he always would do it, because the slaves thereby looked better and did more work.

While I was thus employed by my master I was often a witness to cruelties of every kind, which were exercised on my unhappy fellow slaves. I used frequently to have different cargoes of new negroes in my care for sale; and it was almost a constant practice with our clerks, and other whites, to commit violent depredations on the chastity of the female slaves; and these I was, though with reluctance, obliged to submit to at all times, being unable to help them. When we have had some of these slaves on board my master's vessels to carry them to other islands, or to America, I have known our mates to commit these acts most shamefully, to the disgrace, not of Christians only, but of men. I have even known them gratify [to] their brutal passion with females not ten years old; and these abominations some of them practised to such scandalous excess, that one of our captains discharged the mate and others on that account. And yet in Montserrat I have seen a negro man staked to the ground, and cut most shockingly, and then his ears cut off bit by bit, because he had been connected with a white woman who was a common prostitute: as if it were no crime in the whites to rob an innocent African girl of her virtue; but most heinous in a black man only to gratify a passion of nature, where the temptation was offered by one of a different colour, though the most abandoned woman of her species. . . .

The small account in which the life of a negro is held in the West Indies is so universally known, that it might seem impertinent to quote the following extract, if some people had not been hardy enough of late to assert that negroes are on the same footing in that respect as Europeans. By the 329th Act, page 125, of the Assembly of Barbadoes, it is enacted 'That if any negro, or other slave, under punishment by his master, or his order, for running away, or any other crime or misdemeanor towards his said master, unfortunately shall suffer in life or member, no person whatsoever shall be liable to a fine; but if any man shall out of *wantonness, or only of bloody-mindedness, or cruel intention, wilfully kill a negro, or other slave, of his own, he shall pay into the public treasury fifteen pounds sterling.'* And it is the same in most, if not all, of the West India islands. Is not this one of the many acts of the islands which call loudly for redress? And do not the assembly which enacted it deserve the appellation of savages and brutes rather than of Christians and men? It is an act at once unmerciful, unjust, and unwise;

---

wantonness: caprice.

which for cruelty would disgrace an assembly of those who are called barbarians; and for its injustice and *insanity* would shock the morality and common sense of a Samaide or a Hottentot.[31]

Shocking as this and many more acts of the bloody West India code at first view appear, how is the iniquity of it heightened when we consider to whom it may be extended! Mr. James Tobin,[32] a zealous labourer in the vineyard of slavery, gives an account of a French planter of his acquaintance, in the island of Martinico,[33] who shewed him many mulattoes working in the fields like beasts of burden; and he told Mr. Tobin these were all the produce of his own loins! And I myself have known similar instances. Pray, reader, are these sons and daughters of the French planter less his children by being begotten on a black woman? And what must be the virtue of those legislators, and the feelings of those fathers, who estimate the lives of their sons, however begotten, at no more than fifteen pounds; though they should be murdered, as the act says, *out of wantonness and bloody-mindedness!* But is not the slave trade entirely a war with the heart of man?[34] And surely that which is begun by breaking down the barriers of virtue involves in its continuance destruction to every principle, and buries all sentiments in ruin!

I have often seen slaves, particularly those who were meagre, in different islands, put into scales and weighed; and then sold from three pence to six pence or nine pence a pound. My master, however, whose humanity was shocked at this mode, used to sell such by the lump. And at or after a sale it was not uncommon to see negroes taken from their wives, wives taken from their husbands, and children from their parents, and sent off to other islands, and wherever else their merciless lords chose; and probably never more during life to see each other! Oftentimes my heart has bled at these partings; when the friends of the departed have been at the water side, and, with sighs and tears, have kept their eyes fixed on the vessel till it went out of sight. . . .

---

[31] Samaide (or Samoyed) was a name for one of the Mongolian peoples of Siberia; Hottentot was a name for one of the Khoisan peoples of southern Africa.

[32] James Tobin, a West Indian plantation owner and notable apologist for slavery.

[33] Martinique, an island in the Caribbean and at the time a French colony.

[34] In later editions this reads, "at war with the heart of man."

VOLUME II, *FROM* CHAPTER VII.

...We set sail once more for Montserrat, and arrived there safe; but much out of humour with our friend the silversmith.[35] When we had unladen the vessel, and I had sold my venture, finding myself master of about forty-seven pounds, I consulted my true friend, the Captain, how I should proceed in offering my master the money for my freedom. He told me to come on a certain morning, when he and my master would be at breakfast together. Accordingly, on that morning I went, and met the Captain there, as he had appointed. When I went in I made my obeisance to my master, and with my money in my hand, and many fears in my heart, I prayed him to be as good as his offer to me, when he was pleased to promise me my freedom as soon as I could purchase it. This speech seemed to confound him; he began to recoil: and my heart that instant sunk within me. 'What,' said he, 'give you your freedom? Why, where did you get the money? Have you got forty pounds sterling?' 'Yes, sir,' I answered. 'How did you get it?' replied he. I told him, very honestly. The Captain then said he knew I got the money very honestly and with much industry, and that I was particularly careful. On which my master replied, I got money much faster than he did; and said he would not have made me the promise he did if he had thought I should have got money so soon. 'Come, come,' said my worthy Captain, clapping my master on the back, 'Come, Robert, (which was his name) I think you must let him have his freedom; you have laid your money out very well; you have received good interest for it all this time, and here is now the principal at last. I know Gustavus has earned you more than an hundred a-year, and he will still save you money, as he will not leave you: — Come, Robert, take the money.' My master then said, he would not be worse than his promise; and, taking the money, told me to go to the Secretary at the Register Office, and get my manumission drawn up. These words of my master were like a voice from heaven to me: in an instant all my trepidation was turned into unutterable bliss; and I most reverently bowed myself with gratitude, unable to express my feelings, but by the overflowing of my eyes, while my true and worthy friend, the Captain, congratulated us both with a peculiar degree of heart-felt pleasure. As soon as

---

manumission: official emancipation from slavery.

[35] By this point in the narrative, Equiano has been working for some time as a small trader with King's employee Captain Thomas Farmer, trading on the side on his own account, around the West Indies and the coast of North America. In what Equiano calls a "ludicrous" episode, he and Farmer have just been cheated of a promised legacy from a silversmith who turned out to be penniless.

the first transports of my joy were over, and that I had expressed my thanks to these my worthy friends in the best manner I was able, I rose with a heart full of affection and reverence, and left the room, in order to obey my master's joyful mandate of going to the Register Office. As I was leaving the house I called to mind the words of the Psalmist, in the 126th Psalm, and like him, 'I glorified God in my heart, in whom I trusted.' These words had been impressed on my mind from the very day I was forced from Deptford to the present hour, and I now saw them, as I thought, fulfilled and verified. My imagination was all rapture as I flew to the Register Office, and, in this respect, like the apostle Peter,[36] (whose deliverance from prison was so sudden and extraordinary, that he thought he was in a vision) I could scarcely believe I was awake. Heavens! who could do justice to my feelings at this moment! Not conquering heroes themselves, in the midst of a triumph—Not the tender mother who has just regained her long-lost infant, and presses it to her heart—Not the weary hungry mariner, at the sight of the desired friendly port—Not the lover, when he once more embraces his beloved mistress, after she had been ravished from his arms!—All within my breast was tumult, wildness, and delirium! My feet scarcely touched the ground, for they were winged with joy, and, like Elijah, as he rose to Heaven, they 'were with lightning sped as I went on.' Every one I met I told of my happiness, and blazed about the virtue of my amiable master and captain.

When I got to the office and acquainted the Register with my errand he congratulated me on the occasion, and told me he would draw up my manumission for half price, which was a guinea. I thanked him for his kindness; and, having received it and paid him, I hastened to my master to get him to sign it, that I might be fully released. Accordingly he signed the manumission that day, so that, before night, I who had been a slave in the morning, trembling at the will of another, was become my own master, and completely free. I thought this was the happiest day I had ever experienced; and my joy was still heightened by the blessings and prayers of the sable race, particularly the aged, to whom my heart had ever been attached with reverence.

As the form of my manumission has something peculiar in it, and expresses the absolute power and dominion one man claims over his fellow, I shall beg leave to present it before my readers at full length:

Montserrat.—To all men unto whom these presents shall come: I Robert King, of the parish of St. Anthony in the said island, merchant, send

---

[36] Acts, chap. xii, ver. 9. [Equiano's note.]

greeting: Know ye, that I the aforesaid Robert King, for and in consideration of the sum of seventy pounds current money of the said island, to me
in hand paid, and to the intent that a negro man-slave, named Gustavus
Vassa, shall and may become free, have manumitted, emancipated, enfranchised, and set free, and by these presents do manumit, emancipate, en-
franchise, and set free, the aforesaid negro man-slave, named Gustavus
Vassa, for ever, hereby giving, granting, and releasing unto him, the said
Gustavus Vassa, all right, title, dominion, sovereignty, and property, which,
as lord and master over the aforesaid Gustavus Vassa, I had, or now I have,
or by any means whatsoever I may or can hereafter possibly have over him
the aforesaid negro, for ever. In witness whereof I the above-said Robert
King have unto these presents set my hand and seal, this tenth day of July,
in the year of our Lord one thousand seven hundred and sixty-six.

ROBERT KING.

Signed, sealed, and delivered in the presence of
Terry Legay, Montserrat.

Registered the within manumission at full length, this eleventh day of
July, 1766, in liber D.

TERRY LEGAY, Register.

In short, the fair as well as black people immediately styled me by a new
appellation, to me the most desirable in the world, which was Freeman,
and at the dances I gave my Georgia superfine blue clothes made no indifferent appearance, as I thought. Some of the sable females, who formerly
stood aloof, now began to relax and appear less coy; but my heart was still
fixed on London, where I hoped to be ere long. . . .

FROM CHAPTER IX.

. . . We had a most prosperous voyage, and, at the end of seven weeks, arrived at Cherry-Garden stairs.[37] Thus were my longing eyes once more
gratified with a sight of London, after having been absent from it above
four years. I immediately received my wages, and I never had earned seven
guineas so quick in my life before; I had thirty-seven guineas in all, when I

---

these presents: the present document.
[37] A landing spot on the south bank of the Thames River in London. After working for
King some months as a free sailor, during which time he suffers a series of shipwrecks as
well as being cheated, abused, and nearly kidnapped, Equiano has returned to England.

got cleared of the ship. I now entered upon a scene, quite new to me, but full of hope. In this situation my first thoughts were to look out for some of my former friends, and amongst the first of those were the Miss Guerins. As soon, therefore, as I had regaled myself I went in quest of those kind ladies, whom I was very impatient to see; and with some difficulty and perseverance, I found them at May's-hill, Greenwich.[38] They were most agreeably surprised to see me, and I quite overjoyed at meeting with them. I told them my history, at which they expressed great wonder, and freely acknowledged it did their cousin, Capt. Pascal, no honour. He then visited there frequently; and I met him four or five days after in Greenwich park. When he saw me he appeared a good deal surprised, and asked me how I came back? I answered, 'In a ship.' To which he replied dryly, 'I suppose you did not walk back to London on the water.' As I saw, by his manner, that he did not seem to be sorry for his behaviour to me, and that I had not much reason to expect any favour from him, I told him that he had used me very ill, after I had been such a faithful servant to him for so many years; on which, without saying any more, he turned about and went away. A few days after this I met Capt. Pascal at Miss Guerin's house, and asked him for my prize-money. He said there was none due to me; for, if my prize money had been 10,000l. he had a right to it all. I told him I was informed otherwise; on which he bade me defiance; and, in a bantering tone, desired me to commence a lawsuit against him for it: 'There are lawyers enough,' said he, 'that will take the cause in hand, and you had better try it.' I told him then that I would try it, which enraged him very much; however, out of regard to the ladies, I remained still, and never made any farther demand of my right. Some time afterwards these friendly ladies asked me what I meant to do with myself, and how they could assist me. I thanked them, and said, if they pleased, I would be their servant; but if not, as I had thirty-seven guineas, which would support me for some time, I would be much obliged to them to recommend me to some person who would teach me a business whereby I might earn my living. They answered me very politely, that they were sorry it did not suit them to take me as their servant, and asked me what business I should like to learn? I said, hair-dressing. They then promised to assist me in this; and soon after they recommended me to a gentleman whom I had known before, one Capt. O'Hara, who treated me with much kindness, and procured me a master, a hair-dresser, in Coventry-court, Haymarket,[39] with whom he placed me. I was with this man from September till the February following. In that time we had a

---

[38] Borough of southeast London.

[39] Area of central London quite near where Picadilly Circus lies today.

neighbour in the same court who taught the French horn. He used to blow it so well that I was charmed with it, and agreed with him to teach me to blow it. Accordingly he took me in hand, and began to instruct me, and I soon learned all the three parts. I took great delight in blowing on this instrument, the evenings being long; and besides that I was fond of it, I did not like to be idle, and it filled up my vacant hours innocently. At this time also I agreed with the Rev. Mr. Gregory, who lived in the same court, where he kept an academy and an evening-school, to improve me in arithmetic. This he did as far as barter and alligation; so that all the time I was there I was entirely employed. In February 1768 I hired myself to Dr. Charles Irving, in Pall-mall, so celebrated for his successful experiments in making sea water fresh; and here I had plenty of hair-dressing to improve my hand. This gentleman was an excellent master; he was exceedingly kind and good tempered; and allowed me in the evenings to attend my schools, which I esteemed a great blessing; therefore I thanked God and him for it, and used all my diligence to improve the opportunity. This diligence and attention recommended me to the notice and care of my three preceptors, who on their parts bestowed a great deal of pains in my instruction, and besides were all very kind to me. My wages, however, which were by two thirds less than I ever had in my life (for I had only 12l. per annum) I soon found would not be sufficient to defray this extraordinary expense of masters, and my own necessary expenses; my old thirty-seven guineas had by this time worn all away to one. I thought it best, therefore, to try the sea again in quest of more money, as I had been bred to it, and had hitherto found the profession of it successful. I had also a very great desire to see Turkey, and I now determined to gratify it. Accordingly, in the month of May, 1768, I told the doctor my wish to go to sea again, to which he made no opposition; and we parted on friendly terms. The same day I went into the city in quest of a master. I was extremely fortunate in my inquiry; for I soon heard of a gentleman who had a ship going to Italy and Turkey, and he wanted a man who could dress hair well. I was overjoyed at this, and went immediately on board of his ship, as I had been directed, which I found to be fitted up with great taste, and I already foreboded no small pleasure in sailing in her. Not finding the gentleman on board, I was directed to his lodgings, where I met with him the next day, and gave him a specimen of my dressing. He liked it so well that he hired me immediately, so that I was perfectly happy; for the ship, master, and voyage, were entirely to my mind. The ship

---

barter and alligation: arithmetical methods used in business.
per annum: yearly.
master: shipmaster.

was called the Delawar, and my master's name was John Jolly, a neat smart good humoured man, just such an one as I wished to serve. We sailed from England in July following, and our voyage was extremely pleasant. We went to Villa Franca, Nice, and Leghorn;[40] and in all these places I was charmed with the richness and beauty of the countries, and struck with the elegant buildings with which they abound. We had always in them plenty of extraordinary good wines and rich fruits, which I was very fond of; and I had frequent occasions of gratifying both my taste and curiosity; for my captain always lodged on shore in those places, which afforded me opportunities to see the country around. I also learned navigation of the mate, which I was very fond of. When we left Italy we had delightful sailing among the Archipelago islands, and from thence to Smyrna in Turkey.[41] This is a very ancient city; the houses are built of stone, and most of them have graves adjoining to them; so that they sometimes present the appearance of churchyards. Provisions are very plentiful in this city, and good wine less than a penny a pint. The grapes, pomegranates, and many other fruits, were also the richest and largest I ever tasted. The natives are well looking and strong made, and treated me always with great civility. In general I believe they are fond of black people; and several of them gave me pressing invitations to stay amongst them, although they keep the franks, or Christians, separate, and do not suffer them to dwell immediately amongst them. I was astonished in not seeing women in any of their shops, and very rarely any in the streets; and whenever I did they were covered with a veil from head to foot, so that I could not see their faces, except when any of them out of curiosity uncovered them to look at me, which they sometimes did. I was surprised to see how the Greeks are, in some measure, kept under by the Turks, as the negroes are in the West Indies by the white people. The less refined Greeks, as I have already hinted, dance here in the same manner as we do in my nation. On the whole, during our stay here, which was about five months, I liked the place and the Turks extremely well. I could not help observing one very remarkable circumstance there: the tails of the sheep are flat, and so very large, that I have known the tail even of a lamb to weigh from eleven to thirteen pounds. The fat of them is very white and rich, and is excellent in puddings, for which it is much used. Our ship being at length richly loaded with silk, and other articles, we sailed for England. . . .

---

[40] Sailing along the western shore of the Mediterranean after passing through the Strait of Gibraltar, the ship visits the port cities of Villa Franca in Spain, Nice in France, and Leghorn (Livorno) in Italy.

[41] Now called Izmir, Smyrna is a major port in western Turkey that had been a principal Greek city in Classical times, was conqured by the Turks in the fourteenth century, and was annexed to the Ottoman empire in the fifteenth century.

FROM CHAPTER X.

OUR voyage to the North Pole being ended, I returned to London with Doctor Irving,[42] with whom I continued for some time, during which I began seriously to reflect on the dangers I had escaped, particularly those of my last voyage, which made a lasting impression on my mind, and, by the grace of God, proved afterwards a mercy to me; it caused me to reflect deeply on my eternal state, and to seek the Lord with full purpose of heart ere it was too late. I rejoiced greatly; and heartily thanked the Lord for directing me to London, where I was determined to work out my own salvation, and in so doing procure a title to heaven, being the result of a mind blinded by ignorance and sin.

In process of time I left my master, Doctor Irving, the purifier of waters, and lodged in Coventry-court, Haymarket, where I was continually oppressed and much concerned about the salvation of my soul, and was determined (in my own strength) to be a first-rate Christian. I used every means for this purpose; and, not being able to find any person amongst my acquaintance that agreed with me in point of religion, or, in scripture language, 'that would shew me any good;' I was much dejected, and knew not where to seek relief; however, I first frequented the neighbouring churches, St. James's, and others, two or three times a day, for many weeks: still I came away dissatisfied; something was wanting that I could not obtain, and I really found more heartfelt relief in reading my bible at home than in attending the church; and, being resolved to be saved, I pursued other methods still. First I went among the quakers, where the word of God was neither read or preached, so that I remained as much in the dark as ever. I then searched into the Roman catholic principles, but was not in the least satisfied. At length I had recourse to the Jews, which availed me nothing, for the fear of eternity daily harassed my mind, and I knew not where to seek shelter from the wrath to come. However this was my conclusion, at all events, to read the four evangelists, and whatever sect or party I found adhering thereto such I would join.[43] Thus I went on heavily without any guide to direct me the way that leadeth to eternal life. I asked different people questions about the manner of going to heaven, and was told different ways. Here I was much staggered, and could not find any at that time

---

[42] Equiano has returned to London after voyages to Portugal, the Mediterranean, the West Indies, and a nearly fatal exploration voyage to the Arctic region with Charles Irving in quest of a northern passage to the Pacific.

[43] The gospels of Matthew, Mark, Luke, and John in the New Testament.

more righteous than myself, or indeed so much inclined to devotion. I thought we should not all be saved (this is agreeable to the holy scriptures), nor would all be damned. I found none among the circle of my acquaintance that kept wholly the ten commandments. So righteous was I in my own eyes, that I was convinced I excelled many of them in that point, by keeping eight out of ten; and finding those who in general termed themselves Christians not so honest or so good in their morals as the Turks, I really thought the Turks were in a safer way of salvation than my neighbours:[44] so that between hopes and fears I went on, and the chief comforts I enjoyed were in the musical French horn, which I then practised, and also dressing of hair. Such was my situation some months, experiencing the dishonesty of many people here. I determined at last to set out for Turkey, and there to end my days. It was now early in the spring 1774. I sought for a master, and found a captain John Hughes, commander of a ship called Anglicania, fitting out in the river Thames, and bound to Smyrna in Turkey. I shipped myself with him as a steward; at the same time I recommended to him a very clever black man, John Annis, as a cook. This man was on board the ship near two months doing his duty: he had formerly lived many years with Mr. William Kirkpatrick, a gentleman of the island of St. Kitts,[45] from whom he parted by consent, though he afterwards tried many schemes to inveigle the poor man. He had applied to many captains who traded to St. Kitts to trepan him; and when all their attempts and schemes of kidnapping proved abortive, Mr. Kirkpatrick came to our ship at Union Stairs[46] on Easter Monday, April the fourth, with two wherry boats and six men, having learned that the man was on board; and tied, and forcibly took him away from the ship, in the presence of the crew and the chief mare, who had detained him after he had notice to come away. I believe that this was a combined piece of business: but, at any rate, it certainly reflected great disgrace on the mate and captain also, who, although they had desired the oppressed man to stay on board, yet he did not in the least assist to recover him, or pay me a farthing of his wages, which was about five pounds. I proved the only friend he had, who attempted to regain him his liberty if possible, having known the want of liberty myself. I sent as soon as I could to Gravesend,[47] and got knowledge of the ship in which he was;

[44]The Turks were, of course, Muslims; Equiano may well have been aware of the long history of Islam in sub-Saharan Africa, predating European influence by many centuries.
[45]An island near Montserrat in the British West Indies.
[46]A landing spot on the north bank of the Thames River.
[47]Port near the mouth of the Thames.

but unluckily she had sailed the first tide after he was put on board. My intention was then immediately to apprehend Mr. Kirkpatrick, who was about setting off for Scotland; and, having obtained a *habeas corpus* for him, and got a tipstaff to go with me to St. Paul's church-yard,[48] where he lived, he, suspecting something of this kind, set a watch to look out. My being known to them occasioned me to use the following deception: I whitened my face, that they might not know me, and this had its desired effect. He did not go out of his house that night, and next morning I contrived a well plotted stratagem notwithstanding he had a gentleman in his house to personate him. My direction to the tipstaff, who got admittance into the house, was to conduct him to a judge, according to the writ. When he came there, his plea was, that he had not the body in custody, on which he was admitted to bail. I proceeded immediately to that philanthropist, Granville Sharp, Esq.[49] who received me with the utmost kindness, and gave me every instruction that was needful on the occasion. I left him in full hope that I should gain the unhappy man his liberty, with the warmest sense of gratitude towards Mr. Sharp for his kindness; but, alas! my attorney proved unfaithful; he took my money, lost me many months employ, and did not do the least good in the cause: and when the poor man arrived at St. Kitts, he was, according to custom, staked to the ground with four pins through a cord, two on his wrists, and two on his ancles, was cut and flogged most unmercifully, and afterwards loaded cruelly with irons about his neck. I had two very moving letters from him, while he was in this situation; and also was told of it by some very respectable families now in London, who saw him in St. Kitts, in the same state in which he remained till kind death released him out of the hands of his tyrants. . . .

. . . Now every leading providential circumstance that happened to me, from the day I was taken from my parents to that hour, was then in my view, as if it had but just then occurred.[50] I was sensible of the invisible

---

tipstaff: sheriff's officer, constable, or officer of the court.

personate: impersonate.

[48] A *habeas corpus* is a legal order demanding that a restrained or imprisoned person be produced so that proper authorities can determine whether that person is being held legally; widely seen as a hallmark of British liberty.

[49] Granville Sharp (1735–1813), a leading abolitionist, had been the prime mover behind the case of James Somerset, leading to Judge Mansfield's 1772 decision declaring that slavery had no legal standing in England.

[50] Having once more considered leaving England for good and emigrating to Turkey, Equiano goes through a long and profound crisis of faith. This passage finds him in a ship's cabin on a return voyage from Spain, at the point of accepting Christian salvation through the "free grace" of Christ.

hand of God, which guided and protected me when in truth I knew it not: still the Lord pursued me although I slighted and disregarded it; this mercy melted me down. When I considered my poor wretched state I wept, seeing what a great debtor I was to sovereign free grace. Now the Ethiopian was willing to be saved by Jesus Christ, the sinner's only surety, and also to rely on none other person or thing for salvation. Self was obnoxious, and good works he had none, for it is God that worketh in us both to will and to do. The amazing things of that hour can never be told—it was joy in the Holy Ghost! I felt an astonishing change; the burden of sin, the gaping jaws of hell, and the fears of death, that weighed me down before, now lost their horror; indeed I thought death would now be the best earthly friend I ever had. Such were my grief and joy as I believe are seldom experienced. I was bathed in tears, and said, What am I that God should thus look on me the vilest of sinners? I felt a deep concern for my mother and friends, which occasioned me to pray with fresh ardour; and, in the abyss of thought, I viewed the unconverted people of the world in a very awful state, being without God and without hope.

It pleased God to pour out on me the Spirit of prayer and the grace of supplication, so that in loud acclamations I was enabled to praise and glorify his most holy name. When I got out of the cabin, and told some of the people what the Lord had done for me, alas, who could understand me or believe my report!—None but to whom the arm of the Lord was revealed. I became a barbarian to them in talking of the love of Christ: his name was to me as ointment poured forth; indeed it was sweet to my soul, but to them a rock of offence. I thought my case singular, and every hour a day until I came to London, for I much longed to be with some to whom I could tell of the wonders of God's love towards me, and join in prayer to him whom my soul loved and thirsted after. I had uncommon commotions within, such as few can tell aught about. Now the bible was my only companion and comfort; I prized it much, with many thanks to God that I could read it for myself, and was not left to be tossed about or led by man's devices and notions. The worth of a soul cannot be told.—May the Lord give the reader an understanding in this....

Ethiopian: here, dark-skinned African.

FROM CHAPTER XI.

. . . I was happy once more amongst my friends and brethren, till November, when my old friend, the celebrated Doctor Irving, bought a remarkable fine sloop, about 150 tons. He had a mind for a new adventure in cultivating a plantation at Jamaica and the Musquito Shore;[51] asked me to go with him, and said that he would trust me with his estate in preference to any one. By the advice, therefore, of my friends, I accepted of the offer, knowing that the harvest was fully ripe in those parts, and hoped to be the instrument, under God, of bringing some poor sinner to my well beloved master, Jesus Christ. Before I embarked, I found with the Doctor four Musquito Indians, who were chiefs in their own country, and were brought here by some English traders for some selfish ends. One of them was the Musquito king's son; a youth of about eighteen years of age; and whilst he was here he was baptized by the name of George. They were going back at the government's expense, after having been in England about twelve months, during which they learned to speak pretty good English. When I came to talk to them about eight days before we sailed, I was very much mortified in finding that they had not frequented any churches since they were here, to be baptized, nor was any attention paid to their morals. I was very sorry for this mock Christianity, and had just an opportunity to take some of them once to church before we sailed. We embarked in the month of November 1775, on board of the sloop Morning Star, Captain David Miller, and sailed for Jamaica. In our passage, I took all the pains that I could to instruct the Indian prince in the doctrines of Christianity, of which he was entirely ignorant; and, to my great joy, he was quite attentive, and received with gladness the truths that the Lord enabled me to set forth to him. I taught him in the compass of eleven days all the letters, and he could put even two or three of them together and spell them. I had Fox's Martyrology with cuts,[52] and he used to be very fond of looking into it, and would ask many questions about the papal cruelties he saw depicted there, which I explained to him. I made such progress with this youth, especially in religion, that when I used to go to bed at different hours of the night, if

---

cuts: woodcut illustrations.

papal: Roman Catholic.

[51] The Mosquito Coast, located in present-day Nicaragua and Honduras on the Caribbean shore of Central America, named after the Moskito Amerindians (with whom the British then had an alliance).

[52] John Foxe (1516–1587), *Actes and Monuments,* commonly known as *The Book of Martyrs* (1563), a popular work with pronounced anti-Catholic tendencies that was especially valued by Nonconformist (or Dissenting) Protestants.

he was in his bed, he would get up on purpose to go to prayer with me, without any other clothes than his shirt; and before he would eat any of his meals amongst the gentlemen in the cabin, he would first come to me to pray, as he called it. I was well pleased at this, and took great delight in him, and used much supplication to God for his conversion. I was in full hope of seeing daily every appearance of that change which I could wish; not knowing the devices of satan, who had many of his emissaries to sow his tares as fast as I sowed the good seed, and pull down as fast as I built up. Thus we went on nearly four fifths of our passage, when satan at last got the upper hand. Some of his messengers, seeing this poor heathen much advanced in piety, began to ask him whether I had converted him to Christianity, laughed, and made their jest at him, for which I rebuked them as much as I could; but this treatment caused the prince to halt between two opinions. Some of the true sons of Belial,[53] who did not believe that there was any hereafter, told him never to fear the devil, for there was none existing; and if ever he came to the prince, they desired he might be sent to them. Thus they teazed the poor innocent youth, so that he would not learn his book any more! He would not drink nor carouse with these ungodly actors, nor would he be with me, even at prayers. This grieved me very much. I endeavoured to persuade him as well as I could, but he would not come; and entreated him very much to tell me his reasons for acting thus. At last he asked me, 'How comes it that all the white men on board who can read and write, and observe the sun, and know all things, yet swear, lie, and get drunk, only excepting yourself?' I answered him, the reason was, that they did not fear God; and that if any one of them died so they could not go to, or be happy with God. He replied, that if these persons went to hell he would go to hell too. I was sorry to hear this; and, as he sometimes had the tooth-ach, and also some other persons in the ship at the same time, I asked him if their tooth-ach made his easy: he said, No. Then I told him if he and these people went to hell together, their pains would not make his any lighter. This answer had great weight with him: it depressed his spirits much; and he became ever after, during the passage, fond of being alone. . . .

---

[53] In John Milton's (1608–1674) Christian epic *Paradise Lost* (1667), the "sons / Of Belial" (a demon) are depicted as drunkards and rapists (Book I, lines 501–505).

FROM CHAPTER XII.

SUCH were the various scenes which I was a witness to, and the fortune I experienced until the year 1777.[54] Since that period my life has been more uniform, and the incidents of it fewer, than in any other equal number of years preceding; I therefore hasten to the conclusion of a narrative, which I fear the reader my think already sufficiently tedious.

I had suffered so many impositions in my commercial transactions in different parts of the world, that I became heartily disgusted with the seafaring life, and I was determined not to return to it, at least for some time. I therefore once more engaged in service shortly after my return, and continued for the most part in this situation until 1784.

Soon after my arrival in London, I saw a remarkable circumstance relative to African complexion, which I thought so extraordinary, that I beg leave just to mention it: A white negro woman, that I had formerly seen in London and other parts, had married a white man, by whom she had three boys, and they were every one mulattoes, and yet they had fine light hair. In 1779 I served Governor Macnamara, who had been a considerable time on the coast of Africa. In the time of my service, I used to ask frequently other servants to join me in family prayers; but this only excited their mockery. However, the Governor, understanding that I was of a religious turn, wished to know of what religion I was; I told him I was a protestant of the church of England, agreeable to the thirty-nine articles of that church, and that whomsoever I found to preach according to that doctrine, those I would hear. A few days after this, we had some more discourse on the same subject: the Governor spoke to me on it again, and said that he would, if I chose, as he thought I might be of service in converting my countrymen to the Gospel faith, get me sent out as a missionary to Africa. I at first refused going, and told him how I had been served on a like occasion by some white people the last voyage I went to Jamaica, when I attempted (if it were the will of God) to be the means of converting the Indian prince; and I said I supposed they would serve me worse than Alexander the coppersmith did St. Paul, if I should attempt to go amongst them in Africa. He told me not to fear, for he would apply to the Bishop of London to get me ordained. On these terms I consented to the Governor's

---

[54]Equiano has just returned to London. Irving's Mosquito Coast plantation scheme has failed (after Equiano, initially serving as slave purchaser and overseer, leaves and is replaced by a cruel and incompetent White overseer). Working his passage to Jamaica, Equiano is again cheated and abused in the Americas before once more leaving for England, where he arrives in January 1777.

proposal to go to Africa, in hope of doing good if possible amongst my countrymen. . . .[55]

. . . On my return to London in August I was very agreeably surprised to find that the benevolence of government had adopted the plan of some philanthropic individuals to send the Africans from hence to their native quarter; and that some vessels were then engaged to carry them to Sierra Leone; an act which redounded to the honour of all concerned in its promotion, and filled me with prayers and much rejoicing.[56] There was then in the city a select committee of gentlemen for the black poor, to some of whom I had the honour of being known;[57] and, as soon as they heard of my arrival they sent for me to the committee. When I came there they informed me of the intention of government; and as they seemed to think me qualified to superintend part of the undertaking, they asked me to go with the black poor to Africa. I pointed out to them many objections to my going; and particularly I expressed some difficulties on the account of the slave dealers, as I would certainly oppose their traffic in the human species by every means in my power. However these objections were over-ruled by the gentlemen of the committee, who prevailed on me to go, and recommended me to the honourable Commissioners of his Majesty's Navy as a proper person to act as commissary for government in the intended expedition; and they accordingly appointed me in November 1786 to that office, and gave me sufficient power to act for the government in the ca-pacity of commissary, having received my warrant and the following order.

By the principal Officers and Commissioners of his Majesty's Navy.

Whereas you were directed, by our warrant of the 4th of last month, to receive into your charge from Mr. Irving the surplus provisions remaining of what was provided for the voyage, as well as the provisions for the support of the black poor, after the landing at Sierra Leone, with the cloathing, tools, and all other articles provided at government's ex-pense; and as the provisions were laid in at the rate of two months for the voyage, and for four months after the landing, but the number

---

[55] After his request to the bishop of London is turned down, Equiano abandons his plan to go to Africa as a missionary, makes several more voyages to the Americas, and returns to London in August 1786.

[56] On the Sierra Leone scheme see page 108, note 26, and compare Cugoano's discussion on pages 108–10.

[57] The Committee for the Relief of the Black Poor, established in 1786.

embarked being so much less than was expected, whereby there may be a considerable surplus of provisions, cloathing, &c. These are, in addition to former orders, to direct and require you to appropriate or dispose of such surplus to the best advantage you can for the benefit of government, keeping and rendering to us a faithful account of what you do herein. And for your guidance in preventing any white persons going, who are not intended to have the indulgence of being carried thither, we send you herewith a list of those recommended by the Committee for the black poor as proper persons to be permitted to embark, and acquaint you that you are not to suffer any others to go who do not produce a certificate from the committee for the black poor, of their having their permission for it. For which this shall be your warrant. Dated at the Navy Office, January 16, 1787.

> J. Hinslow,
> Geo. Marsh,
> W. Palmer.

To Mr. Gustavus Vassa,
    Commissary of Provi-
    sions and Stores for
    the Black Poor going
    to Sierra Leone.

I proceeded immediately to the execution of my duty on board the vessels destined for the voyage, where I continued till the March following.

During my continuance in the employment of government, I was struck with the flagrant abuses committed by the agent, and endeavoured to remedy them, but without effect. One instance, among many which I could produce, may serve as a specimen. Government had ordered to be provided all necessaries (slops, as they are called, included) for 750 persons; however, not being able to muster more than 426, I was ordered to send the superfluous slops, &c. to the king's stores at Portsmouth; but, when I demanded them for that purpose from the agent, it appeared they had never been bought, though paid for by government. But that was not all, government were not the only objects of peculation; these poor people suffered infinitely more; their accommodations were most wretched; many of them wanted beds, and many more cloathing and other necessaries. For the truth of this, and much more, I do not seek credit from my own assertion. I appeal to the testimony of Capt. Thompson, of the Nautilus, who

---

slops: cheap clothing and other furnishings for seafarers.
peculation: embezzlement.

convoyed us, to whom I applied in February 1787 for a remedy, when I had remonstrated to the agent in vain, and even brought him to be a witness of the injustice and oppression I complained of. I appeal also to a letter written by these wretched people, so early as the beginning of the preceding January, and published in the Morning Herald of the 4th of that month, signed by twenty of their chiefs.

I could not silently suffer government to be thus cheated, and my countrymen plundered and oppressed, and even left destitute of the necessaries for almost their existence. I therefore informed the Commissioners of the Navy of the agent's proceeding; but my dismission was soon after procured, by means of a gentleman in the city, whom the agent, conscious of his peculation, had deceived by letter, and whom, moreover, empowered the same agent to receive on board, at the government expense, a number of persons as passengers, contrary to the orders I received. By this I suffered a considerable loss in my property: however, the commissioners were satisfied with my conduct, and wrote to Capt. Thompson, expressing their approbation of it.

Thus provided, they proceeded on their voyage; and at last, worn out by treatment, perhaps not the most mild, and wasted by sickness, brought on by want of medicine, cloaths, bedding, &c. they reached Sierra Leone just at the commencement of the rains. At that season of the year it is impossible to cultivate the lands; their provisions therefore were exhausted before they could derive any benefit from agriculture; and it is not surprising that many, especially the lascars, whose constitutions are very tender, and who had been cooped up in ships from October to June, and accommodated in the manner I have mentioned, should be so wasted by their confinement as not long to survive it.

Thus ended my part of the long-talked-of expedition to Sierra Leone; an expedition which, however unfortunate in the event, was humane and politic in its design, nor was its failure owing to government: every thing was done on their part; but there was evidently sufficient mismanagement attending the conduct and execution of it to defeat its success.

I should not have been so ample in my account of this transaction, had not the share I bore in it been made the subject of partial animadversion, and even my dismission from my employment thought worthy of being made by some a matter of public triumph.[58] The motives which might influence any person to descend to a petty contest with an obscure African,

---

lascars: discharged sailors originally from India and other parts of the East, who made part of the Black British population.

[58] See the Public Advertiser, July 14, 1787. [Equiano's note.]

and to seek gratification by his depression, perhaps it is not proper here to inquire into or relate, even if its detection were necessary to my vindication; but I thank Heaven it is not.[59] . . .

March the 21st, 1788, I had the honour of presenting the Queen with a petition on behalf of my African brethren, which was received most graciously by her Majesty:[60]

To the QUEEN's *most Excellent*
Majesty.

MADAM,

YOUR Majesty's well known benevolence and humanity emboldens me to approach your royal presence, trusting that the obscurity of my situation will not prevent your Majesty from attending to the sufferings for which I plead.

Yet I do not solicit your royal pity for my own distress; my sufferings, although numerous, are in a measure forgotten. I supplicate your Majesty's compassion for millions of my African countrymen, who groan under the lash of tyranny in the West Indies.

The oppression and cruelty exercised to the unhappy negroes there, have at length reached the British legislature, and they are now deliberating on its redress; even several persons of property in slaves in the West Indies, have petitioned parliament against its continuance, sensible that it is as impolitic as it is unjust—and what is inhuman must ever be unwise.

Your Majesty's reign has been hitherto distinguished by private acts of benevolence and bounty; surely the more extended the misery is, the greater claim it has to your Majesty's compassion, and the greater must be your Majesty's pleasure in administering to its relief.

I presume, therefore, gracious Queen, to implore your interposition with your royal consort, in favour of the wretched Africans; that, by your Majesty's benevolent influence, a period may now be put to their misery; and that they may be raised from the condition of brutes, to which they are at present degraded, to the rights and situation of freemen, and admitted to partake of the blessings of your Majesty's happy government; so shall your Majesty enjoy the heart-felt pleasure of procuring happiness to millions, and be rewarded in the grateful prayers of themselves, and of their posterity.

---

[59] Equiano inserts a copy of his petition to the commissioners of the state treasury, and notes that he was awarded £50 in back wages.

[60] At the request of some of my most particular friends, I take the liberty of inserting it here. [Equino's note; Her Majesty is Queen Charlotte (1744–1818), wife ("Royal Consort") of George III, who ruled Great Britain from 1760 to 1820.]

And may the all-bountiful Creator shower on your Majesty, and the Royal Family, every blessing that this world can afford, and every fulness of joy which divine revelation has promised us in the next.

I am your Majesty's most dutiful and devoted servant to command,

GUSTAVUS VASSA,

The Oppressed Ethiopean.

No. 53, Baldwin's Gardens.

The negro consolidated act, made by the assembly of Jamaica last year, and the new act of amendment now in agitation there, contain a proof of the existence of those charges that have been made against the planters relative to the treatment of their slaves.[61]

I hope to have the satisfaction of seeing the renovation of liberty and justice resting on the British government, to vindicate the honour of our common nature. These are concerns which do not perhaps belong to any particular office: but, to speak more seriously to every man of sentiment, actions like these are the just and sure foundation of future fame; a reversion, though remote, is coveted by some noble minds as a substantial good. It is upon these grounds that I hope and expect the attention of gentlemen in power. These are designs consonant to the elevation of their rank, and the dignity of their stations: they are ends suitable to the nature of a free and generous government; and, connected with views of empire and dominion, suited to the benevolence and solid merit of the legislature. It is a pursuit of substantial greatness. —May the time come—at least the speculation to me is pleasing—when the sable people shall gratefully commemorate the auspicious æra of extensive freedom. Then shall those persons[62] particularly be named with praise and honour, who generously proposed and stood forth in the cause of humanity, liberty, and good policy; and brought to the ear of the legislature designs worthy of royal patronage and adoption. May Heaven make the British senators the dispersers of light, liberty, and science, to the uttermost parts of the earth: then will be glory to God on the highest, on earth peace, and good-will to men: —Glory, honour, peace, &c. to every soul of man that worketh good, to the Britons first, (because to them the Gospel is preached) and also to the nations. 'Those that honour their Maker have mercy on the poor.' 'It is righteousness

---

science: then a term for general knowledge.

[61] Limited reform acts of 1787 and 1792.

[62] Grenville Sharp, Esq; the Reverend Thomas Clarkson; the Reverend James Ramsay; our approved friends, men of virtue, are an honour to their country, ornamental to human nature, happy in themselves, and benefactors to mankind! [Equianor's note.]

exalteth a nation; but sin is a reproach to any people; destruction shall be to the workers of iniquity, and the wicked shall fall by their own wickedness.'[63] May the blessings of the Lord be upon the heads of all those who commiserated the cases of the oppressed negroes, and the fear of God prolong their days; and may their expectations be filled with gladness! 'The liberal devise liberal things, and by liberal things shall stand,' Isaiah xxxii. 8. They can say with pious Job, 'Did not I weep for him that was in trouble? was not my soul grieved for the poor?' Job xxx. 25.

As the inhuman traffic of slavery is to be taken into the consideration of the British legislature, I doubt not, if a system of commerce was established in Africa, the demand for manufactures would most rapidly augment, as the native inhabitants will insensibly adopt the British fashions, manners, customs, &c. In proportion to the civilization, so will be the consumption of British manufactures.

The wear and tear of a continent, nearly twice as large as Europe, and rich in vegetable and mineral productions, is much easier conceived than calculated.

A case in point. —It cost the Aborigines of Britain little or nothing in clothing, &c. The difference between their forefathers and the present generation, in point of consumption, is literally infinite. The supposition is most obvious. It will be equally immense in Africa—The same cause, viz. civilization, will ever have the same effect.

It is trading upon safe grounds. A commercial intercourse with Africa opens an inexhaustible source of wealth to the manufacturing interests of Great Britain, and to all which the slave trade is an objection.

If I am not misinformed, the manufacturing interest is equal, is not superior, to the landed interest, as to the value, for reasons which will soon appear. The abolition of slavery, so diabolical, will give a most rapid extension of manufactures, which is totally and diametrically opposite to what some interested people assert.

The manufacturers of this country must and will, in the nature and reason of things, have a full and constant employ by supplying the African markets.

Population, the bowels and surface of Africa, abound in valuable and useful returns; the hidden treasures of centuries will be brought to light and into circulation. Industry, enterprize, and mining, will have their full scope, proportionably as they civilize. In a word, it lays open an endless field of commerce to the British manufactures and merchant adventurer.

---

viz.: namely.

[63] An amalgam of Proverbs 14:31, 14:34, 10:29, and 11:5.

The manufacturing interest and the general interests are synonymous. The abolition of slavery would be in reality an universal good.

Tortures, murder, and every other imaginable barbarity and iniquity, are practised upon the poor slaves with impunity. I hope the slave trade will be abolished. I pray it may be an event at hand. The great body of manufacturers, uniting in the cause, will considerably facilitate and expedite it; and, as I have already stated, it is most substantially their interest and advantage, and as such the nation's at large, (except those persons concerned in the manufacturing neck-yokes, collars, chains, hand-cuffs, leg-bolts, drags, thumb-screws, iron muzzles, and coffins; cats, scourges, and other instruments of torture used in the slave trade). In a short time one sentiment alone will prevail, from motives of interest as well as justice and humanity. Europe contains one hundred and twenty millions of inhabitants. Query—How many millions doth Africa contain? Supposing the Africans, collectively and individually, to expend 5l. a head in raiment and furniture yearly when civilized, &c. an immensity beyond the reach of imagination!

This I conceive to be a theory founded upon facts, and therefore an infallible one. If the blacks were permitted to remain in their own country, they would double themselves every fifteen years. In proportion to such increase will be the demand for manufactures. Cotton and indigo grow spontaneously in most parts of Africa; a consideration this of no small consequence to the manufacturing towns of Great [Britain]. It opens a most immense, glorious, and happy prospect—the clothing, &c. of a continent ten thousand miles in circumference, and immensely rich in productions of every denomination in return for manufactures.

I have only therefore to request the reader's indulgence and conclude. I am far from the vanity of thinking there is any merit in this narrative: I hope censure will be suspended, when it is considered that it was written by one who was as unwilling as unable to adorn the plainness of truth by the colouring of imagination. My life and fortune have been extremely chequered, and my adventures various. Even those I have related are considerably abridged. If any incident in this little work should appear uninteresting and trifling to most readers, I can only say, as my excuse for mentioning it, that almost every event of my life made an impression on my mind and influenced my conduct. I early accustomed myself to look for the hand of God in the minutest occurrence, and to learn from it a lesson of morality and religion; and in this light every circumstance I have

---

drags: clogs, weights attached to the leg or neck to hamper mobility.

cats: cat-o'-nine-tails, whip with nine knotted lashes used in the navy and army as well as on slave plantations.

related was to me of importance. After all, what makes any event important, unless by its observation we become better and wiser, and learn 'to do justly, to love mercy, and to walk humbly before God ?'[65] To those who are possessed of this spirit, there is scarcely any book or incident so trifling that does not afford some profit, while to others the experience of ages seems of no use; and even to pour out to them the treasures of wisdom is throwing the jewels of instruction away.

THE END.

From The Life, History, and Unparalleled Sufferings of John Jea, the African Preacher: Compiled and Written by Himself

John Jea

Little has been discovered regarding John Jea (c. 1773–?) aside from what can be gleaned from his autobiography. Jea writes that he was born in Old Callabar, an established slaving port near the southern border of present-day Nigeria, in 1773. At two-and-a-half years of age, Jea was captured and sent to North America with his parents, brothers, and sisters. Sold to a Dutch family in New York, they worked as field slaves under brutally harsh conditions. As Jea grew older, his resistance to slavery began to work itself out in relation to religious practice. At first he refused to attend religious services, then began his own program of private prayer and meditation, and still later struggled to attend the same chapel services he had earlier regarded as punitive torment. At fifteen, Jea underwent a dark night of the soul (aggravated by savage beatings for disobedience), emerging with a conviction of his personal salvation and a missionary desire to convert his fellow slaves. Jea's evangelical zeal did not sit well with his masters, and he was sold three times before presenting himself for baptism to a local minister, Peter Lowe. His current master, enraged by Jea's act of religious independence, had him hauled up before a group of religious magistrates, who were satisfied by Jea's understanding of Christian belief and, according to Jea, ordered him freed.

---

[65] Micah 6:8.

(Christian baptism would not have guaranteed Jea his freedom, though he seems to have thought so at the time.) Instead, Jea's master taunted him with his inability to read the Bible, assuming that this would put an end to the question of Jea's freedom.

What happened next counts as perhaps the most remarkable (not to say incredible) instance of the "talking book" motif in the slave narrative tradition. After trying and failing to hear the Bible talk to him—a gesture that can be found in the narratives of Gronniosaw (page 58) and Equiano (page 147) as well—Jea prayed for six weeks until an angel appeared to him in a vision, teaching him to read the Book of John. Jea successfully demonstrated his miraculous reading skills (confined to Scripture) to his minister, Lowe, and then to a group of New York City magistrates, who decreed that Jea be granted his freedom and gave him an implicit mandate to preach. His new life as an itinerant preacher—at first in New York and New Jersey, then increasingly far afield—brought Jea to Boston, Massachusetts, for several years. Returning to New York, Jea married a Native American servant named Elizabeth, who went mad, beat her mother to death, and then murdered her child by Jea. She was tried and put to death. After several more years in New York and Massachusetts, Jea signed on as cook to the *Superb of Boston*, sailing the North American Atlantic coast before heading for England.

Jea spent a number of years preaching in Liverpool and other parts of England, then working his passage as ship's cook and steward to preach in Boston, New York, and New Orleans, and in the Dutch cities of Amsterdam and Rotterdam. While in Holland he was married to Charity, a woman from the Mediterranean island of Malta who, in contrast to Elizabeth, died a "natural death." Jea's voyaging then took him to the West Indies and to the Atlantic coast of South America, where his ship was caught up in the unsuccessful British invasion of Buenos Aires (1806–1807). Returning to Britain, Jea preached in Ireland, where he again got married (this time to a woman named Mary) before returning to England and shipping out from Portsmouth. Captured by a French privateer, Jea spent time as a prisoner in various parts of France, refusing to join the American cause in the War of 1812 as a condition for his freedom. Managing to return to England through sheer persistence, Jea settled in the rough Portsea neighborhood of Portsmouth, preaching and putting together his autobiography (published sometime around 1815) and a book of hymns (1816), excerpted below (pages 304–308).

Like the narratives of Ukawsaw Gronniosaw and Mary Prince, Jea's life was taken down by an amanuensis (despite the book's subtitle, Jea never learned to write). Also like Gronniosaw's, Jea's narrative closely follows the pattern of the Protestant spiritual autobiography, featuring long passages of religious exhortation (not included here) and weaving together the quest for spiritual freedom and freedom from slavery. Like Equiano, another sailor and inveterate voyager, Jea comes to prefer England to the Americas (where he, too, is nearly betrayed back into slavery). His staunch refusal to fight with the young American republic against "Old England" carries a note of something like patriotism, or perhaps appreciation for Britain's divestment from the slave trade in 1807. Two references in public archives place Jea in England in the period shortly following the appearance of his *Life*. In October 1816, he married yet again, to an Englishwoman named Jemima Davis at High Wycombe, Buckinghamshire. The following year their daughter, Hephzabah, was baptized (September 25) at St. John's, an Anglican chapel in Portsea. Nothing is currently known about Jea's life after 1817.

The Life and History of John Jea.

I, JOHN JEA, the subject of this narrative, was born in the town of Old Callabar, in Africa, in the year 1773.[1] My father's name was Hambleton Robert Jea, my mother's name Margaret Jea; they were of poor, but industrious parents. At two years and a half old, I and my father, mother, brothers, and sisters, were stolen, and conveyed to North America, and sold for slaves; we were then sent to New York, the man who purchased us was very cruel, and used us in a manner, almost too shocking to relate; my master and mistress's names were Oliver and Angelika Triehues,[2] they had seven children—three sons and four daughters; he gave us a very little food or raiment, scarcely enough to satisfy us in any measure whatever; our food was what is called Indian corn pounded, or bruised and boiled with water, the same way burgo is made, and about a quart of sour butter-milk poured on it; for one person two quarts of this mixture, and

---

From John Jea, *The Life, History, and Unparalleled Sufferings of John Jea, The African Preacher* (Portsea, Eng.: Printed for the Author, c. 1815).

burgo: burgoo, oatmeal gruel.

[1] Calabar, a slaving port located in the southwest corner of what is now Nigeria.

[2] Identified by Hodges (Jea's modern editor) as Albert and Anetje Terhune, a Dutch couple then living in Flatbush (Brooklyn), New York (Hodges 1993, 45).

about three ounces of dark bread, per day, the bread was darker than that usually allowed to convicts, and greased over with very indifferent hog's lard; at other times when he was better pleased, he would allow us about half-a-pound of beef for a week, and about half-a-gallon of potatoes; but that was very seldom the case, and yet we esteemed ourselves better used than many of our neighbours.

Our labour was extremely hard, being obliged to work in the summer from about two o'clock in the morning, till about ten or eleven o'clock at night, and in the winter from four in the morning, till ten at night. The horses usually rested about five hours in the day, while we were at work; thus did the beasts enjoy greater privileges than we did. We dared not murmur, for if we did we were corrected with a weapon an inch and-a-half thick, and that without mercy, striking us in the most tender parts, and if we complained of this usage, they then took four large poles, placed them in the ground, tied us up to them, and flogged us in a manner too dreadful to behold; and when taken down, if we offered to lift up our hand or foot against our master or mistress, they used us in a most cruel manner; and often they treated the slaves in such a manner as caused their death, shooting them with a gun, or beating their brains out with some weapon, in order to appease their wrath, and thought no more of it than if they had been brutes: this was the general treatment which slaves experienced. After our master had been treating us in this cruel manner, we were obliged to thank him for the punishment he had been inflicting on us, quoting that Scripture which saith, "Bless the rod, and him that hath appointed it."[3] But, though he was a professor of religion, he forgot *that* passage which saith "God is love, and whoso dwelleth in love dwelleth in God, and God in him."[4] And, again, we are commanded to love our enemies; but it appeared evident that his wretched heart was hardened; which led us to look up unto him as our god, for we did not know him who is able to deliver and save all who call upon him in truth and sincerity. Conscience, that faithful monitor, (which either excuses or accuses) caused us to groan, cry, and sigh, in a manner which cannot be uttered.

We were often led away with the idea that our masters were our gods; and at other times we placed our ideas on the sun, moon, and stars, looking unto them, as if they could save us; at length we found, to our great disappointment, that these were nothing else but the works of the Supreme Being; this caused me to wonder how my master frequently expressed that all his houses, land, cattle, servants, and every thing which he possessed was

---

[3] Cf. Micah 6:9.

[4] 1 John 4:16.

his own; not considering that it was the Lord of Hosts, who has said that the gold and the silver, the earth, and the fullness thereof, belong to him.

Our master told us, that when we died, we should be like the beasts that perish; not informing us of God, heaven, or eternal punishments, and that God hath promised to bring the secrets of every heart into judgment, and to judge every man according to his works.

From the following instances of the judgments of God, I was taught that he is God, and there is none besides him, neither in the heavens above, nor in the earth beneath, nor in the waters under the earth; for he doth with the armies of heaven and the inhabitants of the earth as seemeth him good; and there is none that can stay his hand, nor say unto him, with a prevailing voice, *what dost thou?*

My master was often disappointed in his attempts to increase the produce of his lands; for oftentimes he would command us to carry out more seed into the field to insure a good crop, but when it sprang up and promised to yield plentifully, the Almighty caused the worms to eat it at the root, and destroyed nearly the whole produce; God thus showing him his own inability to preserve the fruits of the earth.

At another time he ordered the trees to be pruned, that they might have brought forth more fruit, to have increased his worldly riches, but God, who doth not as man pleaseth, sent the caterpillar, the canker-worm, and the locust, when the trees bore a promising appearance, and his fond hopes were blasted, by the fruits being all destroyed. Thus was he again disappointed, but still remained ignorant of the hand of God being in these judgments.

Notwithstanding he still went on in his wickedness until another calamity befel him; for when the harvest was fully ripe, the corn cut down, and standing in shocks ready to be carried into the barn, it pleased God to send a dreadful storm of thunder and lightning, hail and rain, which compelled them to leave it out, till it rotted on the ground. Often were his cattle destroyed by distempers of various kinds; yet he hearkened not unto the voice of the Lord.

At one time, when his barns and storehouses were filled with all sorts of grain, and he rejoiced in the greatness of his harvest, it pleased the Almighty to send a very dreadful storm of thunder and lightning, which consumed a great part of his property; such scenes as these occurred several times, yet he regarded not the power of the Almighty, nor the strength of his arm; for when we poor slaves were visited by the hand of God, and he took us from time to eternity, he thought no more of our poor souls than if we had had none, but lamented greatly the loss of the body; which caused me very much to wonder at his actions, I being very young, not above eight or nine years of age, and seeing the hand of the Almighty, though I did not at that time know it was his works, in burning up the pastures, in permitting the cattle to die for want of water, and in causing the fruits of the earth to be blighted. At the same time a most violent storm of thunder and lightning was experienced, which, in the space of thirty or forty miles, consumed about thirteen houses, barns, and store-houses, which terrified us poor slaves in a terrible manner, not knowing what these things meant. Even my master and mistress were very much terrified, fearful of being destroyed by the violence of the weather.

About two or three days after this awful scene a day of fasting, prayer, and thanksgiving, was commanded by General Washington,[5] to pray to Almighty God to withdraw his anger from us; which day was observed by all, but us poor slaves, for we were obliged to fast, but were not exempted from work; our masters thinking us not worthy to go to a place of worship; which surprised me a great deal, being very ignorant, and I asked my parents what all this meant, but they could not tell me, but supposed, from what they had heard them say, they were worshipping their god; then I began to enquire how this could be, having heard my master often say, that all he possessed was his own, and he could do as he pleased with it; which, indeed, was the saying of all those who had slaves. My curiosity being thus raised, I made bold to speak to my master's sons, and asked them the reason they prayed and called upon God, and they told me because of the awful judgments that had happened on the land; then I asked what awful judgments they meant, and they said unto me, have you not seen how the Lord hath destroyed all things from off the face of the earth? and I answered yes; I then asked them who did this, and they told me God; then, said I, ought not God to be feared, seeing that he can build up and he can cast down, he can create and he can destroy, and though we may cultivate our lands and sow our seed, we can never secure the crop without the favour of Him who, is the sovereign disposer of all things? They answered, yes. From this I observed that there were those who feared God when the weather was tempestuous, but feared him not when it was fine.

Seeing them act in such a wicked manner, I was encouraged to go on in my sins, being subject to all manner of iniquity that could be mentioned; not knowing there was a God, for they told us that we poor slaves had no God. As I grew up, my desire to know who their God was increased, but I did not know who to apply to, not being allowed to be taught by any one whatever, which caused me to watch their actions very closely; and in so

---

[5]George Washington (1732–1799), American general and commander in chief of the Revolutionary armies during the United States War of Independence (1775–1783), later becoming the first president of the United States (1789–1797).

doing, I, at one time, perceived that something was going forward which I could not comprehend, at last I found out that they were burying a slave master, who was very rich; they appeared to mourn and lament for his death, as though he had been a good man, and I asked them why they let him die; they said they could not help it, for God killed him: I said unto them, what, could you not have taken him away from God? They said, no, for he killed whomsoever he pleased. I then said he must be a dreadful God, and was led to fear least he should kill me also; although I had never seen death, but at a distance. But this fear did not last long, for seeing others full of mirth, I became so too.

A short time after this, there were great rejoicings on account of a great victory obtained by the Americans over the poor Indians,[6] who had been so unfortunate as to lose their possessions, and they strove against the Americans, but they over-powered and killed thousands of them, and numbers were taken prisoners, and for this cause they greatly rejoiced. They expressed their joy by the ringing of bells, firing of guns, dancing and singing, while we poor slaves were hard at work. When I was informed of the cause of these rejoicings, I thought, *these* people made a great mourning when *God* killed one man, but they rejoice when *they* kill so many. I was thus taught that though they talked much about their God, they did not regard him as they ought. They had forgotten that sermon of our blessed Saviour's on the mount, which you find in St. Matthew's gospel, v. *chap, 43, 44, v.*; and I had reason to think their hearts were disobedient, not obeying the truth, though it was read and preached to them; their hearts being carnal, as the Scriptures saith, were at enmity with God, not subject to the law of God, neither indeed could be; for they gave themselves up to the works of the flesh, to fulfil it in the lusts thereof.

* * *

I was sold to three masters, all of whom spoke ill of me, and said that I should spoil the rest of the slaves, by my talking and preaching.[7] The last master I was sold to, I ran from to the house of God, and was baptized unknown to him; and when the minister[8] made it known to him, he was like a man that had lost his reason, and swore that I should not belong to any society; but the minister informed him it was too late, for the work was al-

---

[6]Probably the actions against the Iroquois, then loosely allied with the British, led by General John Sullivan ("Sullivan's March"), culminating in the Battle of Newtown, New York (August 29, 1779).

[7]After his conversion experience at "about fifteen years of age," Jea becomes increasingly unruly and impatient of control.

[8]The Dutch Reformed minister Peter Lowe.

ready finished, and according to the spiritual law of liberty, I was considered a worthy member of society. My master then beat me most cruelly, and threatened to beat the minister over the head with a cane. He then took me before the magistrates, who examined me, and inquired what I knew about God and the Lord Jesus Christ. Upon this I made a public acknowledgment before the magistrates, that God, for Christ's sake, had pardoned my sins and blotted out all mine iniquities, through our Lord Jesus Christ, whereby he was become my defence and deliverer; and that there is no other name under heaven, given to man, whereby he shall be saved, but only in the name of our Lord Jesus Christ. On hearing this, the magistrates told me I was free from my master, and at liberty to leave him; but my cruel master was very unwilling to part with me, because he was of the world.

"They are of the world: therefore speak they of the world, and the world heareth them." I John iv. 5. This was evident, for if my master had been of God he would have instructed me in the Scriptures, as God had given him ability, and according to the oracles of the living God; for we have all one father, and if any man teach let him do it as God gives him ability; so saith the Scriptures. But my master strove to battle me, and to prevent me from understanding the Scriptures: so he used to tell me that there was a time to every purpose under the sun, to do all manner of work, that slaves were in duty bound to do whatever their masters commanded them, whether it was right or wrong; so that they must be obedient to a hard spiteful master as to a good one. He then took the bible and showed it to me, and said that the book talked with him. Thus he talked with me endeavouring to convince me that I ought not to leave him, although I had received my full liberty from the magistrates, and was fully determined, by the grace of God, to leave him; yet he strove to the uttermost to prevent me; but thanks be to God, his strivings were all in vain.

My master's sons also endeavored to convince me, by their reading in the behalf of their father; but I could not comprehend their dark sayings, for it surprised me much, how they could take that blessed book into their hands, and to be so superstitious as to want to make me believe that the book did talk with them; so that every opportunity when they were out of the way, I took the book, and held it up to my ears, to try whether the book would talk with me or not, but it proved to be all in vain, for I could not hear it speak one word, which caused me to grieve and lament, that after God had done so much for me as he had, in pardoning my sins, and blotting out my iniquities and transgressions, and making me a new creature, the book would not talk with me; but the Spirit of the Lord brought this passage of Scripture to my mind, where Jesus Christ says, *"Whatsoever ye shall ask the Father in my name, ye shall receive. Ask in faith nothing doubting: for according unto your faith it shall be unto you. For unto him that believeth, all things are possible."* [9] Then I began to ask God in faithful and fervent prayer, as the Spirit of the Lord gave me utterance, begging earnestly of the Lord to give me the knowledge of his word, that I might be enabled to understand it in its pure light, and be able to speak it in the Dutch and English languages, that I might convince my master that he and his sons had not spoken to me as they ought, when I was their slave.

Thus I wrestled with God by faithful and fervent prayer, for five or six weeks, like Jacob of old, Gen. xxxii. 24. Hosea xii. 4. My master and mistress, and all people, laughed me to scorn, for being such a fool, to think that God would hear my prayer and grant unto me my request. But I gave God no rest day nor night, and I was so earnest, that I can truly say, I shed as many tears for this blessing, as I did when I was begging God to grant me the pardon and forgiveness of my sins. During the time I was pouring out my supplications and prayers unto the Lord, my hands were employed, labouring for the bread that perisheth, and my heart within me still famishing for the word of God; as spoken of in the Scriptures, *"There shall be a famine in the land; not a famine of bread, nor of water, but of the word of God."* [10] And thus blessed be the Lord, that he sent a famine into my heart, and caused me to call upon him by his Spirit's assistance, in the time of my trouble.

The Lord heard my groans and cries at the end of six weeks, and sent the blessed angel of the convenant to my heart and soul, to release me from all my distress and troubles, and delivered me from all mine enemies, which were ready to destroy me; thus the Lord was pleased in his infinite mercy, to send an angel, in a vision, in shining raiment, and his countenance shining as the sun, with a large bible in his hands, and brought it unto me, and said, *"I am come to bless thee, and to grant thee thy request,"* as you read in the Scriptures. Thus my eyes were opened at the end of six weeks, while I was praying, in the place where I slept, although the place was as dark as a dungeon, I awoke, as the Scripture saith, and found it illuminated with the light of the glory of God, and the angel standing by me, with the large book open, which was the Holy Bible, and said unto me, *"Thou hast desired to read and understand this book, and to speak the language of it both in English and in Dutch; I will therefore teach thee, and now read;"* and then he taught me to read the first chapter of the gospel according to St. John; and when I had read the whole chapter, the angel and the book were both gone in the twinkling of an eye, which astonished me very much, for the place was dark immediately; being about four o'clock in the morning in the winter season.

---

[9] An amalgam of John 16:23, James 1:6, and Mark 9:23.

[10] Amos 8:11.

After my astonishment had a little subsided, I began to think whether it was a fact that an angel had taught me to read, or only a dream; for I was in such a strait, like Peter was in the prison, when the angel smote him on the side, and said unto Peter, "*Arise, Peter, and take thy garment, and spread it around thee, and follow me.*"[11] And Peter knew not whether it was a dream or not; and when the angel touched him the second time, Peter arose, took his garment, folded it around him, and followed the angel, and the gates opened unto him of their own accord. So it was with me when the room was darkened again, that I wondered within myself whether I could read or not but the Spirit of the Lord convinced me that I could; I then went out of the house to a secret place, and there rendered thanksgivings and praises unto God's holy name, for his goodness in showing me to read his holy word, to understand it, and to speak it, both in the English and Dutch languages.

I tarried at a distance from the house, blessing and praising God, until the dawning of the day, and by that time the rest of the slaves were called to their labour; they were all very much surprised to see me there so early in the morning, rejoicing as if I had found a pearl of great price, for they used to see me very sad and grieved on other mornings, but now rejoicing, and they asked me what was the reason of my rejoicing more now than at other times, but I answered I would not tell them. After I had finished my day's work I went to the minister's house, and told him that I could read, but he doubted greatly of it, and said unto me, "How is it possible that you can read? For when you were a slave your master would not suffer any one, whatever, to come near you to teach you, nor any of the slaves, to read; and it is not long since you had your liberty, not long enough to learn to read." But I told him, that the Lord had learnt me to read last night. He said it was impossible. I said, "Nothing is impossible with God, for all things are possible with him; but the thing impossible with man is possible with God: for he doth with the host of heaven, and with the inhabitants of the earth, as he pleaseth, and there is none that can withstay his hand, nor dare to say what dost thou? And so did the Lord with me as it pleased him, in shewing me to read his word, and to speak it, and if you have a large bible, as the Lord showed me last night I can read it." But he said, "No, it is not possible that you can read." This grieved me greatly, which caused me to cry. His wife then spoke in my behalf, and said unto him, "You have a large bible, fetch it, and let him try and see whether he can read it or not, and you will then be convinced." The minister then brought the bible to me, in order that I should read; and as he opened the bible for me to read, it appeared

---

[11] Acts 12:7.

unto me, that a person said, "That is the place, read it." Which was the first chapter of the gospel of St. John, the same the Lord had taught me to read. So I read to the minister; and he said to me, "You read very well and very distinct;" and asked me who had learnt me. I said the Lord had learnt me last night. He said that it was impossible; but, if it were so, he should find it out. On saying this he went and got other books, to see whether I could read *them;* I tried, but could not. He then brought a spelling book, to see if I could spell; but he found to his great astonishment, that I could not. This convinced him and his wife that it was the Lord's work, and it was marvelous in their eyes.

This caused them to spread a rumour all over the city of New York, saying, that the Lord had worked great miracles on a poor black man. The people flocked from all parts to know whether it was true or not; and some of them took me before the magistrates, and had me examined concerning the rumour that was spread abroad, to prevent me, if possible, from saying the Lord had taught me to read in one night, in about fifteen minutes; for they were afraid that I should teach the other slaves to call upon the name of the Lord, as I did aforetime, and that they should come to the knowledge of the truth.

The magistrates examined me strictly, to see if I could read, as the report stated; they brought a bible for me to read in, and I read unto them the same chapter the Lord had taught me, as before-mentioned, and they said I read very well and very distinct, and asked me who had taught me to read. I still replied, that the Lord had taught me. They said that it was impossible; but brought forth spelling and other books, to see if I could read them, or whether I could spell, but they found to their great surprise, that I could not read other books, neither could I spell a word; then they said, it was the work of the Lord, and a very great miracle indeed; whilst others exclaimed and said that it was not right that I should have my liberty. The magistrates said that it was right and just that I should have my liberty, for they believed that I was of God, for they were persuaded that no man could read in such a manner, unless he was taught of God.

From that hour, in which the Lord taught me to read, until the present, I have not been able to read in any book, nor any reading whatever, but such as contain the word of God.

Through the report of the minister (whose name was the REVEREND PETER LOWE, a pastor of the Presbyterian church) and the magistrates, I was permitted to go on in the strength of the Lord, and to proclaim the glad tidings of salvation by Jesus Christ, unto every one, both great small, saying unto those that were christians, *"Rejoice with me, for the Lord hath liberated my soul from all my enemies."* I was so over-joyed that I cried out,

"Make a joyful noise unto God, all ye lands: Sing forth the honour of his name: make his praise glorious, &c." as in the lxvith Psalm.

I was now enabled, by the assistance of the Holy Spirit, to go from house to house, and from plantation to plantation, warning sinners, in the name of Jesus, to flee from the wrath to come; teaching and admonishing them to turn from their evil course of life; whilst some mocked and others scoffed at me, many said that I was mad, others pointed at me, and said there goes *"the preacher,"* in a mocking and jeering manner. Sometimes after I had been preaching in a house, and was leaving it, some of the people, who were assembled together, without the door, would beat and use me in a very cruel manner, saying, as the Jews of old did to Jesus Christ, when they smote him with the palms of their hands, *"Prophesy unto us who it was that smote thee?"* [12]

* * *

Thus we went on preaching in the name of the Lord, and it pleased God to bless our feeble efforts, by adding unto our number such as should be saved.

At this time the Lord was pleased to raise up some white friends, who were benevolent and kind to us, when they saw our simpleness, and that God prospered us in our manner and way of worship; who joined their mites with our's, and purchased a piece of ground, and built upon it a meeting-house, in the city of New York, for us poor black Africans to worship in, which held about *fifteen hundred people!* They also procured white preachers twice a week to preach, to assist the other black man and myself.

Being thus highly favoured, we now had preaching three times on the Sabbath-day, and every night in the week; and the number of them that were added unto the society, was about *nine hundred and fifty souls!*

I continued at this place four years after that, preaching with the other preachers; for we were appointed to preach in rotation. The word of the Lord grew and multiplied exceedingly, for it pleased the Lord, sometimes at one service, to add to our number *fifteen souls!* and, sometimes *more!* At our watch nights and camp meetings, I have known one hundred and fifty, or two hundred, awakened at one time; by which it was evident that the time was like the day of Pentecost; which you have an account of in the second chapter of Acts.

Thus, when we were assembled together with one accord, the Lord was pleased to send down his convincing and converting spirit, to convince and convert the congregation, and they were filled with the spirit of prayer, which caused them to groan and cry unto God, begging him to have mercy

---

[12] Matthew 26:68.

upon their never-dying souls, to such a degree, that it caused some to say, that the people were drunk, others said they were possessed with devils, many said they were mad, and others laughing, mocking, and scoffing at them; while the people came running in out of the streets and houses to see what was the matter; and many of *them* were convinced of sin, and of righteousness, and of judgment to come; crying out with the jailor of old, "*What shall we do to be saved?*" We still continued speaking as the Spirit gave us utterance.

It was our heart's desire, and prayer to God, that every sinner might be saved; so we went on in the strength of God, by the aid of his Spirit, warning sinners every where to repent and believe the gospel, that their souls might be saved through grace, by faith in the Lord Jesus Christ. When the congregation grew numerous, and there were enough preachers besides myself, I was then constrained by the Spirit, and the love of God, to go about four hundred miles from hence, to preach the everlasting gospel to the people there, at a place called Boston, in North America. I continued preaching there about three years and a half, and the Lord crowned my feeble endeavors with great success, and gave me souls for my hire, and seals to my ministry.

After being at Boston three years and a half, I returned to New York, to see my mother, sisters, brothers, and friends, and after arriving there, I thought it necessary to enter into the state of matrimony, and we lived very comfortably together about two years, being of one heart and one mind, both of us belonging to the Methodist society in New York. My wife was of the Indian colour. To add to our comfort the Lord was pleased to give us a daughter.

But a circumstance transpired which interrupted our felicity, and made me very unhappy: My wife's mistress had been trying to persuade her not to be so religious, for she would make herself melancholy to be so much at the house of God, and she did not like it; she told her she thought it was no harm to sing songs, and to do as the rest of the people of the world did, and said there was a time for every purpose under the sun: a time to be born, and a time to die; a time to plant, and a time to pluck up that which is planted; a time to kill, and a time to heal; a time to break down, and a time to build up; a time to weep, and a time to laugh; a time to mourn, and a time to dance; a time to cast away stones, and a time to gather stones together; a time to embrace, and a time to refrain from embracing; a time to get, and a time to lose; a time to keep, and a time to cast away; a time to rend, and a time to sew; a time to keep silence, and a time to speak; a time to love, and a time to hate; a time of war, and a time of peace. Thus her mistress spoke, not thinking that these were spiritual times, nor considering that the Scriptures were wrote by inspiration and that they must be understood by the Spirit; "*For what man knoweth the things of a man, save the spirit of man which is in him? even so the things of God knoweth no man, but the Spirit of God. Now we have received, not the spirit of the world, but the spirit which is of God; that we might know the things that are freely given to us of God. Which things also we speak, not in the words which man's wisdom teacheth, but which the Holy Ghost teacheth; comparing spiritual things with spiritual. But the natural man receiveth not the things of the Spirit of God: for they are foolishness unto him: neither can he know them, because they are spiritually discerned.*" I Cor. ii. 12, 13, 14.

From this it appeared that her mistress did not understand the things which were of God, although she was a professor of religion; for she was continually attempting to persuade her, to turn to the ways of the world, and said that so much religion was not required. By these persuasions, my wife began to listen to the advice of her mistress, and to the temptations of the Devil's cunning arts, and began neither to fear God, nor regard man; and wanted me to turn to the beggarly elements of the world; but I told her I was determined by the grace of God, to live and die for God, so that whether I lived or died I should be the Lord's; begging and beseeching her to turn unto God, with full purpose of heart, that he might have mercy on her poor heart; informing her, that "Thus saith the Lord, turn ye even to me with all your heart, and with fasting, and with weeping, and with mourning; And rend your heart, and not your garments, and turn unto the Lord your God: for he is gracious and merciful, slow to anger, and of great kindness, and repenteth him of the evil. Who knoweth if he will return and repent, and leave a blessing behind him; even a meat offering and a drink offering unto the Lord your God?" Joel ii. 12, 13, 14. But she would not hearken unto me, for she was led away by the advice of her mistress, and the temptations of Satan. She now used her poor little innocent and harmless infant very cruel, in order to prevent me from going to the house of God: during my absence from home, she used to try every method in her power to make the poor little babe suffer; her mother always took the child's part, and endeavoured as much as possible to hinder her from using it ill, and when I returned home she would acquaint me of my wife's transactions. On account of this she beat her mother in such a manner, that it caused her death, being pregnant at the time, so that she was not able to resist her wicked undertakings. Thus if she had been dealt with according to the law of God, she would have been put to death, for the Scriptures saith, "He that smiteth his father or mother, shall be surely put to death." Exod. xxi. 15.

---

professor of religion: religious adherent.

Thus, my wife treated her mother, that she died by her cruel usage. Her mistress on this took her to task, and beat her very much, for using her mother in such a manner, particularly in her situation; and told her that she was become a hardened sinner, desiring her to turn unto the Lord, that he might have mercy upon her, or else she would certainly perish; but she was so hardened in her heart, that she could not bear to hear the name of the Lord mentioned; for she would curse and swear, and break and destroy every thing she could get at. It now seemed as if the devil had taken full possession of her heart, and now her master and mistress persuaded me to intreat her to go to the house of God, but she would not, the more I entreated her, the worse she was, and abused and ill-used me as she did the poor infant.

One day while I was gone to my mother's house, which was about nine miles from home, she was so overpowered by the temptation of the Devil, that she *murdered the poor little infant!* by squeezing it between her hands. When I returned home, I was greatly surprised to see a number of people assembled together at the door of my house; and on enquiring what was the matter, they told me that my wife had killed the child. I said unto her, "What hast thou been doing?" She replied, "I have killed the child, and I mean to kill you, if I possibly can." I then said to her, "My dear wife, what is the reason of your doing this horrid deed? what do you think will become of your never-dying soul?" She said, that she expected to go to eternal misery; and therefore she was determined to do all the mischief she could.

She was taken before the judge, and found guilty of the crime laid to her charge, that murdering of her infant. She acknowledged that she had committed the horrid deed; and therefore suffered according to the law. Before her punishment took place, I frequently visited her, to endeavour to convince her of the state of her soul, and begged her to pray unto God to have mercy upon her soul, and strengthen her in her dying moments; but her heart was so hardened by sin, that it was all in vain.

This, my dear reader, you must think, was a fiery trial for me to endure; it almost cast me down to the ground, and to make shipwreck of faith and a good conscience: indeed, my state of mind was such, that it caused me to go to a river, several times, in order to make away with myself; thus the old lion would have devoured me; but, thanks be to God, he gave me grace to withstand the temptations of the Devil at last. . . .

By the assistance of God, I took ship at Boston for Venneliea, in the East Indies;[13] not to please myself, but for the glory of God, and the good of

---

[13] Evidently, Venezuela in the West (not East) Indies — that is, on the Caribbean coast of northeastern South America.

souls; as the Scriptures saith, "*Let no man seek his own, but every man another's wealth. Whatsoever is sold in the shambles, that eat, asking no question for conscience sake: For the earth is the Lord's, and the fullness thereof. If any of them that believe not bid you to a feast, and ye be disposed to go; whatsoever is set before you, eat, asking no question for conscience sake. But if any man say unto you, This is offered in sacrifice unto idols, eat not for his sake that shewed it, and for conscience sake: for the earth is the Lord's, and the fullness thereof: Conscience, I say, not thine own, but of the other: for why is my liberty judged of another man's conscience? For if I by grace be a partaker, why am I evil spoken of for that for which I give thanks? Whether therefore ye eat, or drink, or whatsoever ye do, do all to the glory of God. Give none offence, neither to the Jews, nor to the Gentiles, nor to the church of God: Even as I please all men in all things, not seeking mine own profit, but the profit of many, that they may be saved.*" I Cor. x. 24, to the end.

This was my motive in going to the East Indies, that whatsoever I did, to do it for the honour and glory of God; not to seek mine own interest, but the interest of my Lord and Master Jesus Christ; not for the honour and riches of this world, but the riches and honours of that which is to come: I say, not for the riches of this world, which fadeth away; neither for the glory of man; nor for golden treasure; but my motive and great concern was for the sake of my Lord and Master, who went about doing good, in order to save poor wicked and sinful creatures.

We had a good passage to Venneliea, but were not permitted to land, although the ship remained there a fortnight. We then received orders to sail to Buones Ayres, where we arrived all safe and well, excepting me, for I was ill a fortnight with pains in my legs. We laid at Buones Ayres about eight months, but I had not the pleasure of preaching the gospel there, on account of the war between the Spaniards and the English; it was the period that General Achmet took Monte Video, and General Whitelock came to assist him with his army.[14] So I still continued preaching on board of our own ship, by God's assistance.

During the time we laid there, one of the sailors, a young man about eighteen or nineteen years of age, having considerable property on board of the ship, which he wanted to smuggle on shore, (which indeed was the traffic of the whole ship's crew, both officers and men) was boasting of his

[14]In 1806–1807, the British initiated military operations in the Rio de la Plata area of the South American Atlantic coast, supporting colonial independence efforts against the Spanish, seeking to open trade routes, and hoping to forestall Napoleon's global ambitions. Sir Samuel Auchmuty invaded Montevideo (capital of present-day Uruguay) in February 1807, and Lieutenant General John Whitelock attacked Buenos Aires (capital of present-day Argentina) with disastrous results in July of the same year.

money, and that he would go on shore, and get intoxicated, and when we got to our destined port, he would visit every place of riot and vice. So I said unto him, "You had better think about a dying hour; for though you are young you must die, and you do not know how soon; for there is nothing more certain than death, and nothing more uncertain than life." But he said, that he did not want any of my preaching, and that he should live till we arrived at our destined port, and enjoy his pleasure; but to his great surprise he never lived to see it, for that same day he went to go on shore, and from our ship he went alongside of another, when he fell out of the boat, and sunk immediately, not having time to say one word; the whole of the ship's company being eye-witnesses of it. That ship's name was *The Arrow of Boston, in North America;* and the ship to which he and I belonged, was *The Prince of Boston, in North America.* We remained at Buones Ayres eight months, when all the vessels that were there, were ordered to the different ports to which they belonged: we accordingly made for Boston, where we all safely arrived, except the young man who was drowned.

I had engaged myself on board of the above ship, as cook, for seventeen Spanish dollars per month, in order that I should not be burdensome to the church of God; and this was the way I acted whenever I travelled; for, as St. Paul saith, "*I would rather labour with my hands than be burdensome to the church.*" [15]

When we arrived at Boston I was involved in trouble by the captain wanting to wrong me out of my wages, for he entered a law-suit against me in order to cast me into prison; but thank God it was not in his power, for "*There is no condemnation to them which are in Christ Jesus who walk not after the flesh, but after the Spirit;*" [16] and this the captain found to his sorrow, for God, by his blessed Spirit, delivered me out of his hands, and from the power of the law; the captain and mates having to pay all costs and charges of the court, for injuring my character, which amounted to two thousand dollars for the captain; eight hundred for the chief mate; and eight hundred for the second mate. The amount of which, a man, whom I took for my friend, received for me, and went away with, and I never saw him any more, which distressed me greatly.

The remainder of my troubles and distresses during my stay in the West Indies, in the different islands, and also in the State of Virginia and Baltimore, where I was put in prison, and they strove to make me a slave, (for it was a slave country) were very severe; but God delivered me by his grace, for he has promised to be with us in six troubles, and in the seventh he will

---

[15] Cf. 2 Corinthians 11:9.

[16] Romans 8:1.

not leave us nor forsake us; and that there shall be nothing to harm or hurt us, if we are followers of that which is good. By these promises I was encouraged not to repine at the losses and crosses I had met with.

I staid at Boston about four months, and preached the gospel there with great success, by the aid and assistance of God's Spirit. After that time I had a desire to go to Ireland to preach the gospel; so I parted with the dear people at Boston in body, but not in mind, our minds continuing one, for it grieved them a great deal that I would go from them, but I was constrained by the Spirit of God, although I had not forgotten the troubles and difficulties that God had brought me through. . . .

I therefore embarked at Boston for Ireland, and arrived safe at Limerick, where the brethren and sisters in Christ gladly received me. The prosperity of the work of the Lord in this place, was a memorial, like unto the day of Pentecost;[17] for God showered down righteousness into the hearts of the people in copious showers, so that many of the people thought that miracles were wrought, by the weak instrumentality of my preaching the everlasting gospel. By this means the fame of my preaching spread through the country, even from Limerick to Cork. I preached in Limerick and in the country villages round, and by the Spirit of God, many people were convinced and converted. I also preached to the regiment, at the request of the commanding officer and the mayor of Limerick. The mayor was so kind as to go with me to protect me from the Romans; for they were very much inveterate against me, and said they would have my life. And when the mayor did not go with me, a guard of soldiers was sent. By the command of the mayor and the commanding officer, five of the Roman priests were brought before them, and ordered to give a reason why they were so malicious against me. They could only say, that I would not believe their doctrine, neither would they believe mine; and one of the head priests said, that I was going to hell. The mayor and commanding officer then said, that they would defy any person in Limerick to dispute my doctrine. Then three of the priests said unto them, "We cannot deny or dispute his doctrine." They then went out full of rage and fury, and determined to lay in wait for my life. After this I had greater success than ever, although running greater hazard of losing my life, but I said,

I am not ashamed to own my Lord,
    Nor to defend his cause;

Romans: Roman Catholics.

[17] The day that the original disciples of Jesus Christ, following his death and resurrection, were filled with the Holy Spirit (recounted in Acts 2).

Maintain the honour of his word,
    The glory of his cross.

Jesus, my God, I know his name,
    His name is all my trust;
Nor will he put my soul to shame,
    Nor let my hope be lost.

Firm as his throne his promise stands,
    And he can well secure,
What I have committed to his hands,
    Till the decisive hour.

Before my departure from Ireland, I took to me a partner in life, who is still alive and with me. Her name is Mary Jea, a native of Ireland. This was my third time of marriage. My second wife died a natural death, while I was at Holland; she was a Malteese woman; and her name was Charity Jea. My first wife's name was Elizabeth Jea, of whom mention has been made before. I have had several children, none of whom are alive, but I hope they are all in heaven, where I expect to see them, by the grace of God, and spend an endless day of praise around his dazzling throne, where parting shall be no more for ever.

I and my wife accordingly took ship at the Cove Cork for St. John's in Hallifax,[18] but after we were on board, we found we were obliged to come to England, to take convoy from Portsmouth. When we arrived at Portsmouth, my wife was taken ill; and the friends in Christ thought it necessary that she should remain until her health was restored, and then to follow me, or else for me to return for her. But to our sad disappointment we set sail from Portsmouth in the evening with a breeze of wind, which lasted till near the morning, when about eight or nine o'clock we were becalmed; and as we were laying to becalmed off Torbay, about five or six miles from the land of Torbay, and striving to get up with the convoy, we were taken by a French privateer, who carried us into Pampoole in France.[19] Our vessel was the brig *Iscet of Liverpool*, HENRY PATTERSON, Master.

After we landed at Pampoole, we were marched to Cambrai,[20] which was seven hundred miles from Pampoole. After a long march we arrived

---

Malteese: Maltese, from the island of Malta in the Mediterranean.

[18] Evidently, St. John's, New Brunswick, a port on the Bay of Fundy across from Nova Scotia (capital, Halifax) in Canada.

[19] Tor Bay is on the southern coast of England, west of Portsmouth; Paimpol is a fishing village across the Channel in the Bretagne region of France.

[20] Cambrai, town located north of Paris in France.

safe at Cambrai, after many severe troubles and trials. Here I remained five years in the prison at that place; and was constrained by the love of God to preach to the people there, the unsearchable riches of Jesus Christ, and God was pleased to crown my feeble endeavours with great success; and, in eighteen months, the Lord was pleased to add to my number two hundred souls; the number of the people in the prison was about three thousand: and I had liberty from the commissary general of the Depot, to preach to all of them.

After I had been there eighteen months, orders came from the minister of Paris, that all who were called Americans, were to go away; we were accordingly marched away to Brest,[21] seven hundred miles from Cambrai; and all the dear prisoners in the depot were very sorry to part with me, the same as if I had been their own father; but I was forced to go. This was the Lord's doings and it was marvellous in our eyes. I told them that God had promised me in his word that he would deliver me from all my enemies, both temporal and spiritual, by his blessed Spirit; but they would not believe me, until they saw me going away; they then were exceedingly sorrowful, and made a subscription for me, which amounted to about nine crowns. On the morning before I went away, I preached my farewell sermon, which was from the 2 Cor. xiii. II. "Finally, brethren, farewel. Be perfect, be of good comfort, be of one mind, live in peace; and the God of love and peace shall be with you."

We arrived safe at Brest, thanks be to God, but we had great trials and difficulties on our march thither, being obliged to walk without shoes, and having no more provisions than what we could buy by our scanty allowance, which was a half-penny per mile; and when our feet were so sore that we could not march, we were not allowed any thing. Some of us had no clothes to cover our nakedness; and our lodgings at nights were in barns and cow-houses, and we were obliged to lay down the same as beasts, and indeed not so comfortable, for we were not allowed straw nor any thing else to lay on.

As soon as we arrived at Brest we were sent on board of a French corvette, under American colours, to go and fight against the English,[22] but twenty, out of near two hundred that were sent on board, would not enlist under the banner of the tyrants of this world; for far be it from *me* ever to fight against Old England, unless it be with the sword of the gospel, under

---

corvette: two-masted French naval vessel.

[21] French city on the westernmost coast of Bretagne.

[22] The French were allied with the American Republic during the War of 1812 (1812–1814).

the captain of our salvation, Jesus Christ. Those of us who would not fight against the English, were sent on board of a French man of war, that they should punish us, but they would not, but sent us to Morlaix, about thirty miles from Brest, where they put us in prison, and kept us upon bread and water for a fortnight, then all the rest consented to go back on board of the corvette, rather than be sent again to the depot, for we were to be sent back loaded with chains, and under joint arms. I was the only one that stood out; and I told them I was determined not to fight against any one and that I would rather suffer any thing than do it. They said they would send me back to Cambrai, and they would keep me upon bread and water, until the wars were over. I said I was willing to suffer any thing, rather than fight. They then took me before the council and the head minister of the Americans, to examine me. They asked me which I liked to do, to go back to the ship, or to be marched to Cambrai. I told them they might send me on board of the vessel, if they liked; but if they did I was determined not to do any work, for I would rather suffer any thing than fight or kill any one. They then consulted together what they should do with me; and made up their minds to turn me out of prison. The head minister then asked me what I was at, that I would not fight for my country. I told him that I was not an American, but that I was a poor black African, *a preacher of the gospel.* He said, "Cannot you go on board, and preach the gospel there?" — "No, Sir," said I, "it is a floating hell, and therefore I cannot preach there." Then said the council, "We will cool your Negro temper, and will not suffer any of your insolence in our office." So they turned me out of their office; and said that I had liberty to go any where in the town, but not out of the town; that they would not give me any work, provisions, or lodgings, but that I should provide it myself. Thus was I left upon the mercy of God, but was enabled to cast my care and dependance on the Lord Jesus; for he has promised to deliver those who call upon him in the time of trouble; and I did call upon him in the time of my trouble and distress, and he delivered me.

I was two days without food, walking about without any home, and I went into the hospitals, gaols, and open streets, preaching the gospel unto every creature, as Christ hath commanded us.

Thus I went about preaching the gospel of our Lord and Saviour Jesus Christ. Often, at the conclusion of my sermons, many of the nobility and gentry came to me, and said, "We are much edified by your preaching; when do you preach again?" I told them, in the mornings at nine o'clock, and in the afternoons at three, by God's assistance. Thus I did both Sundays and other days, when the weather would permit, during the time I was at Morlaix.

It pleased God to raise up a friend unto me on the second day of my distress, after I was turned out of Morlaix prison into the streets, by order of the American counsellor Mr. Dyeott, and Mr. Veal the American minister of France. The French commissary-general gave me liberty to preach every where God would permit me; so I went on in the name of the Lord, preaching and exhorting the people to put their trust in the Lord, and serve him truly with fear, reverence, and godly sincerity. This dear friend, whom God was pleased to raise up unto me, was so alarmed by my preaching, that he was constrained by the love of God to come and speak unto me, and asked me where I lived. I told him no where. He asked me if I had any place to stay at. I told him no; for I had been turned out of prison two days, and was not suffered to work, and was not allowed to go farther than the bounds of the town; that I might humble myself to the order of the American counsellor, to go on board of the corvette, to fight against the English. Thus they strove to punish me; but it was utterly in vain, for this friend took me to his house and family; his family consisted of a wife and four children; who received me into their house as an angel of God, and gave me food, raiment, and lodging, for fourteen months, and charged me nothing for it, but said, that the Lord would repay them seven-fold for what they had done. Thus they gladly received me into their house, as Lot did the angels, Genesis xix.

But Mr. Dyeott, the American counsellor, told the people that received me into their house, that they should turn me out of doors, in order that I should go on board of the corvette, to fight against England; and if they would not order me out of their house, they should not have any satisfaction for what they were doing for me; for they were preventing me from going on board the corvette. Thus he endeavoured to lay every obstacle in my way, by trying to prevent those people from doing for me; but the dear man and woman said, that if no person satisfied them for their doings, God would, and as for me I should not perish, for as long as they had a mouthful of victuals, I should have part of it, and such as they had I should be welcome to, the same as their own children. Some said that I was imposing on these people, for Mr. Tangey had only one shilling and three-pence per day, which he earned by hard labour, and said it would be far better for me to go on board of the corvette, for thereby I should be enabled to obtain a great sum of prize-money. But I told them, as I had Mr. Dyeott, that I would not go on board if they would give me a guinea for every breath I drew, and that I would sooner starve and die first, than I would go on board; and that if they carried me on board in irons I would lay there and die before I would do the least work. I had been on board four weeks before, laying upon the bare deck, without bed or blankets; and I counted it a floating hell, for the evil language of the officers and sailors, continually cursing and swearing; and my humble supplications and petitions were unto God that he would deliver me from this vessel; and God did deliver me.

Some persons said unto those of the house where I was staying, that they were wrong in keeping me, but they would not hearken unto them, and kept me, until peace was proclaimed between France and Great Britain, and all the soldiers were out of France. I then made application to Mr. Dyeott for a passport to England, but he denied me, and said that he would keep me in France until he could send me to America, for he said that I was an American, that I lied in saying I was married in England, and that I was no African. I told him with a broken heart, and crying, that I was an African, and that I was married in England. But he contradicted me three times. When I told the people where I lived, they said that he was rich, and that it was impossible for me to get clear, and asked me if *I* thought I should. I told them yes, for all things were possible with God, and to him that believed all things were possible, and according to our faith it should be unto us; and my faith was such, that I believed God would deliver me.

A captain of an English ship of war, laying at Morlaix, advised me to go to the French commissary, to get a passport to England, and that if I succeeded, he would take me in his ship. Accordingly I went to the French commissary, who sent me to the mayor, and I asked him if his honour would have the goodness to grant me a passport to England, to see my wife. The mayor answered and said unto me, "You must go to Mr. Dyeott, the American counsellor, to get a passport." I said unto him, "Sir, it is no use; I have been to him three times, and he pushed me out of doors, and would not suffer me to speak to him." Then the mayor said, "Stop a moment, and I will send a letter to him;" he then wrote a letter, and gave it me, saying, "Take this to Mr. Dyeott." I accordingly carried the letter to Mr. Dyeott, who opened the letter and read it; after he had so done, he said unto me, "Had you the impudence to go to the mayor?" I said, "Yes, sir, for I was compelled to do it." He then took me by the shoulders, and pushed me out of doors, and said that he would keep me as long as he possibly could. I then returned to the house where I lived, crying and mourning, and my spirit within me was troubled; and the people asked me what made me cry. I told them that I had been to the counsellor, and he would not let me go, and said that he would keep me as long as he could. They said it was what they expected. I said that God had told me to call upon him in the time of trouble, and he would deliver me. So I passed that night in fasting and prayer unto God, and wrestled with him as Jacob did with the angel; and blessed be God, I *did* prevail. I went to the mayor in the morning, and asked him if Mr. Dyeott had said any thing to him concerning me. He said no; and asked me what Mr. Dyeott said unto me. I said that he would not give me any thing, for he would not suffer me to work, or to go to England; but said he would keep me perishing in France, until he could send me to America. The mayor said, "Stop awhile, and I will send a gentleman with you to Mr. Dyeott." The gentleman accordingly went with me to him, and asked him what he meant to do with me. He said that he meant to keep me, and send me to America, for I was an American. The gentleman then said, "You must not keep this poor black man in this manner; you have kept him already fourteen months without food or employment; and if he be an American, why do you not give him American support?" He said, "Because he will not go on board the vessel I have provided for him." At that moment the mayor came in, and said, "What do you mean to do with this man?" He said, "I mean to keep him in France until I can send him to America." The mayor said, "You cannot keep him in this manner, you must give him a passport to England." But he said he would not. The mayor said if he would not, he would; and told me to come with him to his office: I went with him, and he gave me a passport to embark at St. Maloes²³ on board of any vessel that was going to England.

As I was going to St. Maloes I met with an English captain, whose brig was laying at Morlaix, and he said that he was going to Guernsey,²⁴ in three hours time; and as he had heard me preach at Morlaix, he would give me my passage for nothing.

Then I told the dear people at the house where I had lived, who were exceedingly glad, and thankful to God for my deliverance. I also was thankful to God our blessed Lord and Saviour Jesus Christ, that brotherly love had continued.

I arrived safe at Guernsey, and brotherly love did not withdraw itself from me there, for the brethren in Christ gladly received me, and gave me the right-hand of fellowship, treated me as a brother, and gave me liberty to preach in the different chapels; and I can say with truth, there was no chapel large enough to hold the congregations. I remained there fifteen days, and during that time there were many souls convinced and converted to God. After that I departed from them in the Guernsey packet, for Southampton, and they furnished me with every thing convenient for me; and thank God, I arrived there in safety, and was cordially received by the brethren, who gave me the use of their chapels to preach in, and much good was done during my stay. They kindly furnished me with every thing that was necessary. But I did not stay there any more than four days, because I wanted to come to Portsmouth. I arrived safe at Portsmouth, and

---

²³ Saint-Malo, another coastal town in Bretagne.

²⁴ One of the (British) Channel Islands lying between England and France.

found my wife well, which I bless God for; I was gladly received by the brethren in Christ, and preached for several of them; and I can say with truth, that all those who have received me in the name of Christ, are brethren unto me, and I pray that the Lord will bless them, and give them all a happy admittance into his kingdom, there to sing the song of Moses and the Lamb, for ever and ever.

My dear reader, I would now inform you, that I have stated this in the best manner I am able, for I cannot write, therefore it is not quite so correct as if I had been able to have written it myself; not being able to notice the time and date when I left several places, in my travels from time to time, as many do when they are travelling; nor would I allow alterations to be made by the person whom I employed to print this Narrative.

Now, dear reader, I trust by the grace of God, that the small house in Hawk Street, which the Lord hath been pleased to open unto me, for the public worship of his great and glorious name, will be filled with converts, and that my feeble labours will be crowned with abundant success.

The Axe Laid to the Root, or a Fatal Blow to Oppressors, Being an Address to the Planters and Negroes of the Island of Jamaica, No. 1
and
The Horrors of Slavery; Exemplified in the Life and History of the Rev. Robert Wedderburn, V.D.M.

Robert Wedderburn

The child of a Jamaican slave and her owner, Robert Wedderburn (c. 1761–c. 1835) came to England as a sailor and went through a number of overlapping careers in London: tailor, preacher, radical activist and propagandist, antislavery agitator, and brothel keeper. Thanks to his notoriety as a radical politician during a repressive era, Wedderburn's autobiographical accounts can be supplemented by the reports of government spies and reformers (Fryer 1984, 220–227,

McCalman, 114–128). His father, Dr. James Wedderburn (1730–1807), was a Scottish physician living as a planter, slave doctor, and slave dealer in Jamaica at the time of Robert's birth. His mother, Rosanna, was a house slave on the estate of Wedderburn's father, who bought her (through an intermediary) primarily for sexual purposes and sold her when she was five months pregnant. Wedderburn spent his childhood in the care of his grandmother, Talkee Amy, an African-born small trader living in Kingston, who dabbled on the side in smuggling and "obeah" (an Afro-Caribbean religious belief system, associated with sorcery and ritual practices). While still a child, Wedderburn had the indelible experiences of seeing his grandmother flogged for witchcraft and his mother flogged while pregnant.

At age seventeen, around 1778, Wedderburn joined the British navy, serving as a gunner, and came to England. He lived in the rougher areas of London, such as St. Giles, and somehow managed to learn tailoring despite the restrictive apprenticeship rules of the time. He married Elizabeth Ryan on November 5, 1781, in St. Katherine Creechurch on Leadenhall Street (in central London); they had at least seven children together. Sometime around 1786, Wedderburn was profoundly affected by a London Methodist preacher and took out a license to preach (as a Unitarian) himself. Along with nonconformist religion, Wedderburn developed an interest in radical politics, reading Thomas Paine's *Rights of Man* (1791–1792) and eventually meeting the radical utopian thinker Thomas Spence (1750–1814) around 1813, some nine months before Spence's death. By then, years of waging the Revolutionary and Napoleonic Wars (1793–1815) had taken a toll on the British economy, which would only grow worse during the coming period of postwar depression. Wedderburn no longer worked as a journeyman tailor but as a "jobber," doing piecework and patching. Wedderburn was only one of many London artisans whose livelihoods were diminished at this time and whose independent spirits were galled by the years of repressive wartime legislation, but he became one of the most outspoken.

After Spence's death in 1814, Thomas Evans took on the leadership of the Spencean movement, which advocated the expropriation of privately held land, to be communally held and managed instead, and also demanded universal (male) suffrage, religious toleration, and the abolition of colonial slavery. Wedderburn worked closely with Evans and in 1817, when Evans was imprisoned for a year, became the group's effective leader. Wedderburn promoted and developed Spence's ideas in the two magazines he published that year, *The Forlorn Hope* and *The Axe Laid to the Root,* the latter (ostensibly addressed to the "Planters and Negroes" of Jamaica, and perhaps distributed there) tying Spence's agrarian utopianism to the cause of colonial emancipation. He also developed a reputation as a brilliant and fiery orator, giving spontaneous, rousing, witty, and often blasphemous speeches to Spenceans, assorted radicals, hangers-on, and government spies in taverns, radical chapels, and other meeting places.

In 1817 Wedderburn and Evans, now out of prison, obtained a license to open a dissenting chapel in the Haymarket district, promoting radical politics under the guise of a "Christian Philanthropy" society with greater protection from government interference. By April 1819, however, Wedderburn had broken with Evans to set up his own radical chapel in Soho, where he could address groups of up to three hundred in a huge and semiruinous hayloft. Radical agitation—and government attempts to repress it—heated up considerably in the aftermath of the "Peterloo" massacre in August of that year, when a local militia supported by government troops turned on a massive but peaceful demonstration in St. Peter's Field, Manchester, slashing and bayoneting some four hundred of the demonstrators (men and women alike) and killing eleven. Wedderburn, prominent among the advocates for a revolutionary response, was arrested late in 1819 on the charge of seditious blasphemy, successfully tried the next year, and sentenced to two years in Dorchester Gaol on May 11, 1820.

One of Wedderburn's visitors in prison was the prominent abolitionist William Wilberforce, who may have helped plant the seed for Wedderburn's autobiographical *Horrors of Slavery* (1824), dedicated to Wilberforce. The immediate provocation for that outspoken, collagelike tract, however, seems to have been an antislavery squib in the colorful sporting magazine, *Bell's Life in London,* which printed a flurry of exchanges among Wedderburn, his half-brother, Andrew Colvile, and *Bell's* editors in 1824. This material was augmented and published by Wedderburn later in the year, with assistance from William Dugdale, a radical and pornographer. With little in the way of formal schooling, Wedderburn depended on such collaborators throughout his writing career, including Evans; George Cannon ("Erasmus Perkins"), a radical preacher and retailer of pirated editions and pornography; and Richard Carlile, a prominent radical politician, publisher, and bookseller who served time with Wedderburn in Dorchester Gaol. In 1828 Wedderburn started a new chapel in Chancery Lane, this one devoted to the practice of "Christian

Diabolism," but his career as a radical preacher seems to have fizzled. Two years later Wedderburn was arrested for running a brothel in Featherbed Lane (not far from the Christian Diabolist meeting house) and for brawling outside of it. Now in his late sixties, Wedderburn served two years of hard labor at Newcastle prison. He died in obscurity sometime around 1835.

The Axe Laid to the Root, or a Fatal Blow to Oppressors, Being an Address to the Planters and Negroes of the Island of Jamaica

Robert Wedderburn

To the Editor.[1]

Be it known to the world, that, I Robert Wedderburn, son of James Wedderburn, esq. of Inveresk, near Musselborough, by Rosannah his slave, whom he sold to James Charles Shalto Douglas, esq. in the parish of St. Mary, in the island of Jamaica, while pregnant with the said Wedderburn, who was not held as a slave, (a provision being made in the agreement, that the child when born should be free.) This Wedderburn, doth charge all potentates, governors, and governments of every description with felony, who does wickedly violate the sacred rights of man—by force of arms, or otherwise, seizing the persons of men and dragging them from their native country, and selling their stolen persons and generations— Wedderburn demands, in the name of God, in the name of natural justice, and in the name of humanity, that all slaves be set free; for innocent individuals are entitled to the protection of civil society; and that all stealers, receivers, and oppressors in this base practic[e] be forgiven, as the crime commenced in the days of ignorance, and is now exposed in the enlightened age of reason.

From Robert Wedderburn, *The Axe Laid to the Root, or a Fatal Blow to Oppressors, Being an Address to the Planters and Negroes of the Island of Jamaica* (London: Wedderburn [1817]).

[1] Wedderburn himself.

Oh, ye oppressed, use no violence to your oppressors, convince the world you are rational beings, follow not the example of St. Domingo,[2] let not your jubilee, which will take place, be stained with the blood of your oppressors, leave revengeful practices for European kings and ministers.

My advice to you, is, to appoint a day wherein you will all pretend to sleep one hour beyond the appointed time of your rising to labour; let the appointed day be twelve months before it takes place; let it be talked of in your market place, and on the roads. The universality of your sleeping and non-resistance, will strike terror to your oppressors. Go to your labour peaceably after the hour is expired; and repeat it once a year, till you obtain your liberty. Union among you, will strike tremendous terror to the receivers of stolen persons. But do not petition, for it is degrading to human nature to petition your oppressors. Above all, mind and keep possession of the land you now possess as slaves; for without that, freedom is not worth possessing; for if you once give up the possession of your lands, your oppressors will have power to starve you to death, through making laws for their own accommodation; which will force you to commit crimes in order to obtain subsistance: as the landholders in Europe are serving those that are disposessed of lands; for it is a fact, that thousands of families are now in a starving state; the prisons are full: humanity impells the executive power to withdraw the sentence of death on criminals, whilst the landholders, in fact, are surrounded with every necessary of life. Take warning by the sufferings of the European poor, and never give up your lands you now possess, for it is your right by God and nature, for the "earth was given to the children of men."

Oh, ye christians, you are convinced of the crime of stealing human beings; and some have put a stop to it. By law, give up the stolen families in possession, and perfect your repentance. I call on a mighty people, and their sovereign, to burst the chains of oppression, and let the oppressed go free, says "the Lord;" and so says Wedderburn the deluded Spencean. Oh, ye Africans and relatives now in bondage to the Christians, because you are innocent and poor; receive this the only tribute the offspring of an African can give, for which, I may ere long be lodged in a prison, without even a trial; for it is a crime now in England to speak against oppression.

Dear countrymen and relatives, it is natural to expect you will enquire what is meant by a deluded Spencean; I must inform you it is a title given

---

[2] Saint Domingue, the French-governed half of the Caribbean island of Hispaniola, where a massive and notoriously violent slave revolution began in 1791, eventually leading to the creation in 1804 of Haiti, the first independent Black republic in the Americas.

by ignorant or self-interested men, to the followers of one Thomas Spence,[3] who knew that the earth was given to the children of men, making no difference for colour or character, just or unjust; and that any person calling a piece of land his own private property, was a criminal; and though they may sell it, or will it to their children, it is only transferring of that which was first obtained by force or fraud. This old truth, newly discovered, has completely terrified the landholders in England, and confounded the Attorney General and the Crown Lawyers; and what is more alarming, it is not in the power of the legislature, with all their objections to the doctrines to make a law to prevent the publishing of self evident truths, while a shadow of the British Constitution remains. The landholders, whose interest it is to oppose, is driven to the necessity of falsefying and misrepresenting the motives of the disciples of Spence; but truth once known, will dispel falsehood, as the rising sun excludes darkness.

Your humble servant being a Spencean Philanthropist, is proud to wear the name of a madman; if the landholders please, they may call me a traitor, or one who is possessed with the spirit of Beelzebub.[4] What can the landholders, priests or lawyers say, or do more than they did against Christ; yet his doctrine is on record, which says "woe unto them that add house to house, or field to field."[5] When you are exorted to hold the land, and never give it up to your oppressors, you are not told to hold it as private property, but as tenants at will to the sovereignty of the people.

Beware of the clergy of every description, they are bound by law and interest, in all countries, to preach agreable to the will of the governor under whom they live: as proof of which, they must have a licence, if not of the established church. Listen to them as far as your reason dictates of a future state, but never suffer them to interfere in your worldly affairs; for they are cunning, and therefore are more capable of vice than you are; for instance, one was hung at Kingston, for coining; one in London, for forgery; one for a rape; one for murder; one was detected throwing the sleave of his surplice over the plate, while he robbed it, even at the time he was administering the Lord's supper, in the Borough; and Bishop Burn, of Kent, who had 800l. per annum, confessed on his death bed, he had practised the same offence for 40 years, and all these were college bred men, and of course gentlemen. You know also they buy and sell your persons as well as others, and thereby encouraging that base practice. This is not doing as they would be done by.

---

[3] For Thomas Spence (founder of the Spencean movement) see page 205 of this volume.
[4] The devil.
[5] Isaiah 5:8.

Adieu, for the present, my afflicted countrymen and relatives yet in bondage, though the prince, lords, and commons, are convinced it is a crime deserving of death, to steal and hold a man in bondage.

I am a West-Indian, a lover of liberty, and would dishonour human nature if I did not shew myself a friend to the liberty of others.

ROBERT WEDDERBURN.

To the Editor.

As the present state of affairs will not afford matters of importance to fill up your paper, I am encouraged to hope for your indulgance in granting me an opportunity to contend with all our enemies, who may be disposed to enter into a paper war respecting the Spencean doctrine.

It appears to me very necessary, for it is only by rational contention, that truth is to be attained. It is not right to take for granted that the Spenceans are fools, and mad traitors:—it is their opinion they are wise, loyal, and in their senses, and they alone, respecting landed property. While they hold such opinions, they will naturally be disposed to believe it is their duty before God and man, to preach Spenceanism at all times, and in all countries. Persecutions, whether legal or permiscous, has failed to put a stop to opinions in all ages, whether such be true or false; for it holds the human mind in chains which cannot be broken but by argument. It is my intention to conduct myself in a becoming manner to all opposers.

It is necessary that the doctrine should be stated fairly, that the opposers may make their attact as seems most to their own advantage. The Spenceans presume that the earth cannot be justly the private property of individuals, because it was never manufactured by man; therefore whoever first sold it, sold that which was not his own, and of course there cannot be a title deed produced consistent with natural and universal justice. Secondly, that it is inconsistent with justice, that a few should have the power to till or not to till the earth, thereby holding the existence of the whole population in their hands. They can cause a famine, or create abundance; they, the landholders, can say to a great majority of any nation:—I may grow, till, or destroy at my will, as occasion serves my interest; is not Ireland sufficient to support its inhabitants? Is England able to support its population? The Spenceans say it will, if the land was not held as private property. Furthermore, the Spenceans say, that land monopoly is the cause of unequal laws.

---

permiscous: promiscuous.
attact: attack.

The majority are thereby deprived of the power of having a pure government. All reformation attempted by the most virtuous, whether Major Cartwright, or Sir Francis Burdett,[6] or any other virtuous character,—is only an attempt to heal, without extracting the core.

To have a parliament, and every man to vote, is just and right; a nation without it, may be charged with ignorance and cowardice: but without an equal share in the soil, no government can be pure, let its name or form be what it may. The Spenceans recommend a division of rents, in preference to a division of lands:—as Moses's failed, Spence's plan is an improvement upon that system which came from heaven. It admits no mortgages; it needs no jubilee.[7]

It is natural to expect the doctrine will spread, and the army of the rising generation may be composed of Spenceans.

Therefore the landholders, who are our despots, will do well to use arguments in time, and convince the Spenceans; though it has been said that the bayonet is necessary to enforce the law; but that will not be used in a bad cause, when men are better taught. The Spenceans say, the clergy must be wilfully blind, or under a servile fear of man, that will not preach Spenceanism; for it is not contrary to the old and new testament.

Spenceanism admits no withholding an equal share of the rents from any one, not even from a criminal, much less from persons of different political or religious opinions; birth or death is the alpha and omega right or exclusion.

The opponants, however they may be armed with the powerful means of education, whether laiety or clergy, will find that a simple Spencean, who cannot write his name, will receive his opponant as David did the giant Goliah;[8] and with simple means destroy his gigantic impositions.

Spenceanism cannot be confined in a dungeon, if the Evans' are.[9] Hector Campbel, in particular is requested to renew the attact. No private correspondence will be held, while the British government is under the necessity of allowing fortunes to false swearing informers.

* * *

---

[6] Major John Cartwright (1740–1824) and Sir Francis Burdett (1770–1844) were prominent radical politicians advocating the reform of government and the extension of the voting franchise (then limited to a minority of men, mainly property holders).

[7] In Leviticus 25, God instructs Moses to declare a jubilee every fiftieth year as a period of slave emancipation, land redistribution, and debt forgiveness.

[8] For the story of David's combat with the giant Goliath, see 1 Samuel 17.

[9] Thomas Evans, the leader of the Spencean movement after Spence's death in 1814, was imprisoned during 1817 after being arrested on suspicion of treason.

To all who love to hear of the increase of liberty, are these few lines directed.

The slaves of Jamaica, are ready now to demand a day of their masters, in addition to the day and a half that was allowed before, being taught by the methodists that it is a crime to labour on the sabbath day; and it is the opinion of many, that they will have it.

This information is by my brother's wife, who is held as a slave by a clergyman of the church of England; whether she obtained this information from the conversation which passed at her master's table, or whether it is her own observation, on what she had heard among her fellow slaves, I will not avow; but this information is confirmed by a letter from a book-keeper to his mother, who informed me, that it is the opinion of her son, that the island of Jamaica will be in the hands of the blacks within twenty years. Prepare for flight, ye planters, for the fate of St. Domingo awaits you. Get ready your blood hounds, the allies which you employed against the Maroons.[10] Recollect the fermentation will be universal. Their weapons are their bill-hooks; their store of provision is every where in abundance; you know they can live upon sugar canes, and a vast variety of herbs and fruits, — yea, even upon the buds of trees. You cannot cut off their supplies. They will be victorious in their flight, slaying all before them; they want no turnpike roads: they will not stand to engage organized troops, like the silly Irish rebels. Their method of fighting is to be found in the scriptures, which they are now learning to read. They will slay man, woman, and child, and not spare the virgin, whose interest is connected with slavery, whether black, white, or tawny. O ye planters, you know this has been done; the cause which produced former bloodshed still remains, — of necessity similar effects must take place. The holy alliance of Europe,[11] cannot prevent it, they have enough to do at home, being compelled to keep a standing army in the time of peace, to enforce the civil law.

My heart glows with revenge, and cannot forgive. Repent ye christians, for flogging my aged grandmother before my face, when she was accused of witchcraft by a silly European. O Boswell, ought not your colour and

---

bill-hooks: Thick, heavy knives with hooked ends, used for pruning and cutting through brushwood.

[10] "Maroons" were escaped slaves who formed independent communities in the hills, forests, or swamps where they were most difficult to track and capture; sometimes they collaborated with colonial governments in hunting down more recently escaped slaves, and at other times they harbored escaped slaves or seconded slave revolts.

[11] A number of European sovereigns formed the Holy Alliance in 1815, following the final defeat of Napoleon, to promote Christian government, to restore or buttress hereditary monarchies, and to combat revolution.

countrymen to be visited with wrath, for flogging my mother before my face, at the time when she was far advanced in pregnancy.[12] What was her crime? did not you give her leave to visit her aged mother; (she did not acquaint her mistress at her departure,) this was her fault. But it originates in your crime in holding her as a slave—could not you wait till she returned, but travel 15 miles to punish her on that visit. You set a pattern to your slaves to treat your wife with contempt, by taking your negro wenches to your adultrous bed, in preference to your wedded wife. It being a general practice in the island, is no excuse for you,—who was a scholar and professed to be a christian—how can I forgive you? Oh! my father, what do you deserve at my hands? Your crimes will be visited upon your legitimate offspring: for the sins of a wicked father will be visited upon his children, who continues in the practice of their father's crimes. Ought I not to encourage your slaves, O my brother, to demand their freedom even at the danger of your life, if it could not be obtained without. Do not tell me you hold them by legal right. No law can be just which deprives another of his liberty, except for criminal offences: such law-makers according to the rules of equity, are felons of the deepest dye; for they attempt to justify wickedness. The time is fast approaching, when such rulers must act righteously, or be drawn from their seats; for truth and justice must prevail—combined armies cannot stop their progress—religious superstition, the support of tyrants, gives way.

The priesthood who took the lead, are compelled to sculk in the rear, and take shelter under Bell's system of education, to impress on the minds of youth their nonsensical creed; dreading the purity of the Lancasterian mode.[13] But you my countrymen, can act without education; the equality of your present station in slavery, is your strength. You all feel the injury— you are all capable of making resistance. Your oppressors know—they dread you—they can foresee their downfal when you determine to obtain your liberty, and possess your natural right—that is freedom. Beware, and offend not your God, like the jews of old, in choosing a king; agrandize no man by forms of law. He who preserves your liberty, will of necessity

---

[12] See Wedderburn's account below on page 223 of this volume.

[13] Andrew Bell (1753–1832) and Joseph Lancaster (1778–1838) had developed similar "monitorial" methods for cheaply educating the "children of the poor" in the early nineteenth century, emphasizing drill, repetition, routine, and mutual instruction—and surveillance. Lancaster (a Quaker), however, was preferred by nonconformists and radicals, who suspected Bell's Church of England credentials and harsher disciplinary methods.

receive universal praise, like Washington,[14] to endless generations, without the aid of hireling priests to celebrate his fame.

Check if possible by law and practice, that avarice in man, which is never satisfied. If you suffer any among you to become emensly rich, he will want homage, and a title; yea, he will dispose of your lives, liberty, and property; and to support his divine right, he will establish a priesthood—he will call in foreign usurpers to assist him to oppress you. Under the protection of foreign bayonets, he will threaten to erect a gallows at every door. France is reduced to this state of humiliation. A black king is capable of wickedness, as well as a white one.

WEDDERBURN.

---

emensly: immensely.

[14] George Washington (1732–99), hero of American independence and first president of the United States (1789–97).

Dedicated to W. WILBERFORCE, M.P.

The Horrors of Slavery;

Exemplified in
The Life and History
of the
Rev. ROBERT WEDDERBURN, V.D.M.

(Late a Prisoner in His Majesty's Gaol at Dorchester, for Conscience-Sake,)

*Son of the late JAMES WEDDERBURN, Esq. of Inveresk, Slave-Dealer,
by one of his Slaves in the Island of Jamaica:*

IN WHICH IS INCLUDED

The Correspondence of the Rev. ROBERT WEDDERBURN
and his Brother, A. COLVILLE, Esq. *alias* WEDDERBURN,
of 35, Leadenhall Street.

With Remarks on, and Illustrations of the Treatment of the Blacks,

AND

A VIEW OF THEIR DEGRADED STATE,
AND THE
DISGUSTING LICENTIOUSNESS OF THE PLANTERS.

LONDON:
PRINTED AND PUBLISHED BY R. WEDDERBURN,
23, RUSSELL COURT, DRURY LANE;
And Sold by R. Carlile, 84, *Fleet Street; and* T. Davison, *Duke Street,
West Smithfield.*
1824.

To

WILLIAM WILBERFORCE, Esq. M.P.[1]

Respected Sir,

AN oppressed, insulted, and degraded African—to whom but you can I dedicate the following pages, illustrative of the treatment of my poor countrymen? Your name stands high in the list of the glorious benefactors of the human race; and the slaves of the earth look upon you as a tower of strength in their behalf. When in prison, for conscience-sake, at Dorchester, you visited me, and you gave me—your advice, for which I am still your debtor, and likewise for the two books beautifully bound in calf, from which I have since derived much ghostly consolation. Receive, Sir, my thanks for what you have done; and if, from the following pages, you should be induced to form any motion in parliament, I am ready to prove their contents before the bar of that most Honourable House.

I remain, Sir,

Your most obedient, and
most devoted Servant,

Robert Wedderburn.

23, Russel Court,
Drury Lane.

Life of the
Rev. ROBERT WEDDERBURN.

THE events of my life have been few and uninteresting. To my unfortunate origin I must attribute all my miseries and misfortunes. I am now upwards

---

From Robert Wedderburn, *The Horrors of Slavery; Exemplified in the Life and History of the Rev. Robert Wedderburn, V.D.M.* (London: Wedderburn, 1824).

ghostly: spiritual.

[1] William Wilberforce (1759–1833), antislavery writer, activist, and member of Parliament who indefatigably pushed for the abolition first of the slave trade, then of colonial slavery.

of sixty years of age, and therefore I cannot long expect to be numbered amongst the living. But, before I pass from this vale of tears, I deem it an act of justice to myself, to my children, and to the memory of my mother, to say what I am, and who were the authors of my existence; and to shew the world, that, not to my own misconduct is to be attributed my misfortunes, but to the inhumanity of a MAN, whom I am compelled to call by the name of FATHER. I am the offspring of a slave, it is true; but I am a man of free thought and opinion; and though I was immured for two years in his Majesty's gaol at Dorchester, for daring to express my sentiments as a free man, I am still the same in mind as I was before, and imprisonment has but confirmed me that I was right. They who know me, will confirm this statement.

To begin then with the beginning—I was born in the island of Jamaica, about the year 1762, on the estate of a Lady Douglas, a distant relation of the Duke of Queensbury. My mother was a woman of colour, by name ROSANNA, and at the time of my birth a slave to the above Lady Douglas. My father's name was JAMES WEDDERBURN, Esq. of Inveresk, in Scotland, an extensive proprietor, of sugar estates in Jamaica, which are now in the possession of a younger brother of mine, by name, A. COLVILLE, Esq. of No. 35, Leadenhall Street.

I must explain at the outset of this history—what will appear unnatural to some—the reason of my abhorrence and indignation at the conduct of my father. From him I have received no benefit in the world. By him my mother was made the object of his brutal lust, then insulted, abused, and abandoned; and, within a few weeks from the present time, a younger and more fortunate brother of mine, the aforesaid A. Colville, Esq. has had the insolence to revile her memory in the most abusive language, and to stigmatize her for that which was owing to the deep and dark iniquity of my father. Can I contain myself at this? or, have I not the feelings of human nature within my breast? Oppression I can bear with patience, because it hath always been my lot; but when to this is added insult and reproach from the authors of my miseries, I am forced to take up arms in my own defence, and to abide the issue of the conflict.

My father's name, as I said before, was JAMES WEDDERBURN, of Inveresk, in Scotland, near Musselborough, where, if my information is correct, the Wedderburn family have been seated for a long time. My grandfather was a staunch Jacobite, and exerted himself strenuously in the cause of the

---

gaol: jail.

Pretender, in the rebellion of the year 1745.[2] For his aiding to restore the exiled family to the throne of England, he was tried, condemned, and executed. He was hung by the neck till he was dead; his head was then cut off, and his body was divided into four quarters. When I first came to England, in the year 1779, I remember seeing the remains of a rebel's skull which had been affixed over Temple Bar; but I never yet could fully ascertain whether it was my dear grandfather's skull, or not. Perhaps my dear brother, A. COLVILLE, can lend me some assistance in this affair. For this act of high treason, our family estates were confiscated to the King, and my dear father found himself destitute in the world, or with no resource but his own industry. He adopted the medical profession; and in Jamaica he was Doctor and Man-Midwife, and turned an honest penny by drugging and physicing the poor blacks, where those that were cured, he had the credit for, and for those he killed, the fault was laid to their own obstinacy. In the course of time, by dint of *booing* and *booing,* my father was restored to his father's property, and he became the proprietor of one of the most extensive sugar estates in Jamaica. While my dear and honoured father was poor, he was chaste as any Scotchman, whose poverty made him virtuous; but the moment he became rich, he gave loose to his carnal appetites, and indulged himself without moderation, but as parsimonious as ever. My father's mental powers were none of the brightest, which may account for his libidinous excess. It is a common practice, as has been stated by Mr. Wilberforce in parliament, for the planters to have lewd intercourse with their female slaves; and so inhuman are many of these said planters, that many well-authenticated instances are known, of their selling their slaves while pregnant, and making that a pretence to enhance their value. A father selling his offspring is no disgrace there. A planter letting out his prettiest female slaves for purposes of lust, is by no means uncommon. My father ranged through the whole of his household for his own lewd purposes; for they being his personal property, cost nothing extra; and if any one proved with child—why, it was an acquisition which might one day fetch something in the market, like a horse or pig in Smithfield.

---

booing and booing: fussing.
Smithfield: proverbial London meat market.
[2] Jacobites supported the restoration of the line of James II (1685–1689), deprived of the British throne during the "Glorious Revolution" of 1688–1689. Jacobite rebellions occurred in 1715 and 1745, each time finding support in Scotland, where the Jacobite line had originated (James I of England was already James VI of Scotland when he succeeded Elizabeth I and the thrones of England and Scotland were combined). The "Pretender" was Charles Edward, "Bonnie Prince Charlie," grandson of James II.

In short, amongst his own slaves my father was a perfect parish bull; and his pleasure was the greater, because he at the same time increased his profits.

I now come to speak of the infamous manner with which JAMES WED-DERBURN, Esq. of Inveresk, and father to A. COLVILLE, Esq. No. 35, Leadenhall Street, entrapped my poor mother in his power. My mother was a lady's maid; and had received an education which perfectly qualified her to conduct a household in the most agreeable manner. She was the property of Lady Douglas, whom I have before mentioned; and, prior to the time she met my father, was chaste and virtuous. After my father had got his estate, he did not renounce the pestle and mortar, but, in the capacity of Doctor, he visited Lady Douglas. He there met my mother for the first time, and was determined to have possession of her. His character was known; and therefore he was obliged to go *covertly* and *falsely* to work. In Jamaica, slaves that are esteemed by their owners have generally the power of refusal, whether they will be sold to a particular planter, or not; and my father was aware, that if *he* offered to purchase her, he would meet with a refusal. But his brutal lust was not to be stopped by trifles; my father's conscience would stretch to any extent; and he was a firm believer in the doctrine of "grace abounding to the chief of sinners."[3] For this purpose, he employed a fellow of the name of Cruikshank, a brother doctor and Scotchman, to strike a bargain with Lady Douglas for my mother; and this scoundrel of a Scotchman bought my mother for the use of my father, in the name of another planter, a most respectable and highly esteemed man. I have often heard my mother express her indignation at this base and treacherous conduct of my father—a treachery the more base, as it was so calm and premeditated. Let my brother COLVILLE deny this if he can; let him bring me into court, and I will prove what I here advance. To this present hour, while I think of the treatment of my mother, my blood boils in my veins; and, had I not some connections for which I was bound to live, I should long ago have taken ample revenge of my father. But it is as well as it is; and I will not leave the world without some testimony to the injustice and inhumanity of my father.

From the time my mother became the property of my father, she assumed the direction and management of his house; for which no woman was better qualified. But her station there was very disgusting. My father's

---

pestle and mortar: used to mix drugs and remedies.

[3] Ironic allusion to John Bunyan's classic spiritual autobiography, *Grace Abounding to the Chief of Sinners* (1666).

house was full of female slaves, all objects of his lusts; amongst whom he strutted like Solomon in his grand seraglio,[4] or like a bantam cock upon his own dunghill. My good father's slaves did increase and multiply, like Jacob's kine; and he cultivated those talents well which God had granted so amply.[5] My poor mother, from being the housekeeper, was the object of their envy, which was increased by her superiority of education over the common herd of female slaves. While in this situation, she bore my father two children, one of whom, my brother James, a millwright, I believe, is now living in Jamaica, upon the estate. Soon after this, my father introduced a new concubine into his seraglio, one ESTHER TROTTER, a free tawny, whom he placed over my mother, and to whom he gave the direction of his affairs. My brother COLVILLE asserts, that my mother was of a violent and rebellious temper. I will leave the reader now to judge for himself, whether she had not some reason for her conduct. Hath not a slave feelings? If you starve them, will they not die? If you wrong them, will they not revenge?[6] Insulted on one hand, and degraded on the other, was it likely that my poor mother could practice the Christian virtue of humility, when her Christian master provoked her to wrath? She shortly afterwards became again pregnant; and I have not the least doubt but that from her rebellious and violent temper during that period, that I have inherited the same disposition — the same desire to see justice overtake the oppressors of my country-men — and the same determination to lose no stone unturned, to accomplish so desirable an object. My mother's state was so unpleasant, that my father at last consented to sell her back to Lady Douglas; but not till the animosity in my father's house had grown to such an extent, that my uncle, Sir JOHN WEDDERBURN, my father's elder brother, had given my mother an asylum in his house, against the brutal treatment of my father. At the time of sale, my mother was five months gone in pregnancy; and one of the stipulations of the bargain was, that the child which she then bore should be FREE from the moment of its birth. I was that child. When about four months old, the ill-treatment my mother had experienced had such an effect upon her, that I was obliged to be weaned, to save her life. Lady Douglas, at my admission into the Christian church, stood my godmother,

---

[4] Seraglio, an Italianized Turkish term, connotes a Muslim harem, the group of wives and slaves who inhabit the *haram* (sacred or forbidden precinct) within the *serai* (large enclosed dwelling). Solomon, king of Israel in the Old Testament, had one thousand wives and concubines (see 1 Kings 11:3).

[5] Ironic biblical references to Jacob's miraculously fertile cattle (Genesis 30:43) and Christ's parable of the talents (Matthew 25:14–30).

[6] Reworking of Shylock's well-known soliloquy ("Hath not a Jew eyes? . . .") in Act III, scene 1, of Shakespeare's *The Merchant of Venice* (c. 1597).

and, as long as she lived, never deserted me. She died when I was about four years old.

From my mother I was delivered over to the care of my grandmother, who lived at Kingston, and who earned her livelihood by retailing all sorts of goods, hard or soft, smuggled or not, for the merchants of Kingston. My grandmother was the property of one JOSEPH PAYNE, at the east end of Kingston; and her place was to sell his property—cheese, checks, chintz, milk, gingerbread, &c; in doing which, she trafficked on her own account with the goods of other merchants, having an agency of half-a-crown in the pound allowed her for her trouble. No woman was perhaps better known in Kingston than my grandmother, by the name of "*Talkee Amy,*" signifying a chattering old woman. Though a slave, such was the confidence the merchants of Kingston had in her honesty, that she could be trusted to any amount; in fact, she was the regular agent for selling smuggled goods.

I never saw my dear father but once in the island of Jamaica, when I went with my grandmother to know if he meant to do any thing for me, his son. Giving her some abusive language, my grandmother called him a mean Scotch rascal, thus to desert his own flesh and blood; and declared, that as she had kept me hitherto, so she would yet, without his paltry assistance. This was the parental treatment I experienced from a Scotch West-India planter and slave-dealer.

When I was about eleven years of age, my poor old grandmother was flogged for a witch by her master, the occasion of which I must relate in this place. Joseph Payne, her master, was an old and avaricious merchant, who was concerned in the smuggling trade. He had a vessel manned by his own slaves, and commanded by a Welchman of the name of Lloyd, which had made several profitable voyages to Honduras for mahogany, which was brought to Jamaica, and from thence forwarded to England. The old miser had some notion, that Lloyd cheated him in the adventure, and therefore resolved to go himself as a check upon him. Through what means I know not, but most likely from information given by Lloyd out of revenge and jealousy, the Spaniards surprised and captured the vessel; and poor old Payne, at seventy years of age, was condemned to carry stones at Fort Homea, in the Bay of Honduras, for a year and a day; and his vessel and his slaves were confiscated to the Spaniards. On his way home he died, and was tossed overboard to make food for fishes. His nephew succeeded to his property; and a malicious woman-slave, to curry favour with him, persuaded him, that the ill-success of old Payne's adventures was owing to my

---

checks, chintz: kinds of fabric.

grandmother's having bewitched the vessel. The old miser had liberated five of his slaves before he set out on his unlucky expedition; and my grandmother's new master being a believer in the doctrine of Witchcraft, conceived that my grandmother had bewitched the vessel, out of revenge for her not being liberated also. To punish her, therefore, he tied up the poor old woman of seventy years, and flogged her to that degree, that she would have died, but for the interference of a neighbour. Now, what aggravated the affair was, that my grandmother had brought up this young villain from eight years of age, and, till now, he had treated her as a mother. But my grandmother had full satisfaction soon afterwards. The words of our blessed Lord and Saviour Jesus Christ were fulfilled in this instance: "Do good to them that despitefully use you, and in so doing you shall heap coals of fire upon their heads."[7] This woman had an only child, which died soon after this affair took place (plainly a judgment of God); and the mother was forced to come and beg pardon of my grandmother for the injury she had done her, and solicit my grandmother to assist her in the burial of her child. My grandmother replied, "I can forgive you, but I can never forget the flogging;" and the good old woman instantly set about assisting her in her child's funeral, it being as great an object to have a decent burial with the blacks in Jamaica, as with the lower classes in Ireland. This same woman, who had so wickedly calumniated my grandmother, afterwards made public confession of her guilt in the market-place at Kingston, on purpose to ease her guilty conscience, and to make atonement for the injury she had done. I mention this, to show upon what slight grounds the planters exercise their cowskin whips, not sparing even an old woman of seventy years of age. But to return —

After the death of Lady Douglas, who was brought to England to be buried, James Charles Sholto Douglas, Esq. my mother's master, promised her her freedom on his return to Jamaica; but his covetous heart would not let him perform his promise He told my mother to look out for another master to purchase her; and that her price was to be £100. The villain Cruikshank, whom I have mentioned before, offered Douglas £10 more for her; and Douglas was so mean as to require £110 from my mother; otherwise he would have sold her to Cruikshank against her will, for purposes the reader can guess. One Doctor Campbell purchased her; and in consequence of my mother having been a companion of, and borne children to my father, Mrs. Campbell used to upbraid her for not being humble enough to her, who was but a doctor's wife. This ill-treatment had such an

[7] Romans 12:20.

effect on my mother, that she resolved to starve herself to death; and, though a cook, abstained from victuals for six days. When her intention was discovered, Doctor Campbell became quite alarmed for his £110, and gave my mother leave to look out for another owner; which she did, and became the property of a Doctor Boswell. The following letter, descriptive of her treatment in this place, appeared in "BELL'S LIFE IN LONDON," a Sunday paper, on the 29th February, 1824: —

"TO THE EDITOR OF 'BELL'S LIFE IN LONDON.'"

"*February 20th, 1824.*

"SIR, — Your observations on the Meeting of the Receivers of Stolen Men call for my sincere thanks, I being a descendant of a Slave by a base Slave-Holder, the late JAMES WEDDERBURN, Esq. of Inveresk, who sold my mother when she was with child of me, HER THIRD SON BY HIM!!! She was FORCED to submit to him, being *his Slave*, THOUGH HE KNEW SHE DISLIKED HIM ! She knew that he was mean, and, when gratified, would not give her her freedom, which is the custom for those, *as a reward,* who have preserved their persons, with Gentlemen (if I may call a Slave-Dealer a Gentleman). I HAVE SEEN MY POOR MOTHER STRETCHED ON THE GROUND, TIED HANDS AND FEET, AND FLOGGED IN THE MOST INDECENT MANNER, THOUGH PREGNANT AT THE SAME TIME!!! her *fault* being the not acquainting her mistress that her master had *given her leave to go to see her mother in town!* So great was the anger of this Christian Slave-Dealer, that he went fifteen miles to punish her while on the visit! Her master was then one BOSWELL; his chief companion was CAPTAIN PARR, who *chained a female Slave to a stake, and starved her to death!* Had it not been for a British Officer in the Army, who had her dug up and proved it, this fact would not have been known. *The murderer was sentenced to transport himself for one year.* He came to England, and returned in the time — this was *his punishment.* My uncle and aunt were sent to America, and sold by their father's brother, who said that he sent them to be educated. *He had a little shame,* for the law in Jamaica allowed him to sell them, or even had they been his children — *so much for humanity and Christian goodness.* As for these men, who wished that the King would proclaim that there was no intention of emancipation, — Oh, what barbarism ! —

"ROBERT WEDDERBURN.

"*No. 27, Crown Street, Soho.*"

I little expected, when I sent this letter, that my dear brother, A. COLVILLE, Esq. of No. 35, Leadenhall Street, would have dared to reply to it. But he did; and what all my letters and applications to him, and my visit to my father, could not accomplish, was done by the above plain letter. The following is the letter of Andrew, as it appeared in the same paper on the 21st of March last, with the Editor's comments: —

BROTHER or NO BROTHER—"THAT IS THE QUESTION?"[8]

A LETTER FROM ANOTHER SON OF THE LATE SLAVE-DEALER,
JAMES WEDDERBURN, ESQ.

Our readers will recollect, that on the 29th ult. we published a letter signed ROBERT WEDDERBURN, in which the writer expressed his feelings in bitter terms of reproach against the atrocities of the man he called his FATHER, practised, as he declared them to have been, upon his unhappy Mother, and who was, as he stated, at once the victim of his Father's lust and subsequent barbarity. When we inserted the Letter alluded to, we merely treated on the horrors of the station generally, to which Slavery reduced our fellow-beings, but without pledging ourselves to the facts of the statements in question, as narrated by the son, against so inhuman a parent. But we are now more than ever inclined to believe them literally true; since we have received the following letter by the hands of *another son*—apparently, however, a greater favourite with his father than ROBERT—and in which the brutalities stated by the latter to have been practised upon his mother, are not attempted to be denied. The following letter we publish verbatim et literatim as we received it—a remark or two upon its contents presently: —

"TO THE EDITOR OF 'BELL'S LIFE IN LONDON.'"

"SIR,—Your Paper of the 29th ult. containing a Letter signed ROBERT WEDDERBURN, was put into my hands only yesterday, otherwise I should have felt it to be my duty to take earlier notice of it.

"In answer to this most slanderous publication, I have to state, that the person calling himself Robert Wedderburn is NOT a son of the late Mr. James Wedderburn, of Inveresk, who never had any child by, or any connection of *that kind* with the mother of this man. The pretence of his using the name of Wedderburn at all, arises out of the following circumstances: —The late Mr. James Wedderburn, of Inveresk, had, when he resided in the parish of Westmoreland, in the Island of Jamaica, a negro woman-*slave*, whom he employed as a cook; this woman had so violent a

---

ult.: *ultimo,* of last month.
verbatim et literatim: word for word and letter for letter.
[8] Allusion to Hamlet's famous soliloquy ("To be or not to be…") in Shakespeare's *Hamlet* (c. 1601), Act III, scene 1.

temper that she was continually quarrelling with the other servants, and occasioning a disturbance in the house. He happened to make some observation upon her troublesome temper, when a gentleman in company said, he would be very glad to *purchase* her if she was a good cook. The *sale accordingly took place,* and the woman was removed to the residence of the gentleman, in the parish of Hanover. Several years afterwards, this woman was delivered of a mulatto child, and as *she could not tell who was the father,* her master, in a foolish joke, named the child Wedderburn. About twenty-two or twenty-three years ago, this man applied to me for money upon the *strength of his name,* claiming to be a son of Mr. James Wedderburn, of Inveresk, which occasioned me to write to my father, when he gave me the above explanation respecting this person; adding, that a few years after he had returned to this country, and married, this same person importuned him with the same story that he now tells; and as he persisted in annoying him after the above explanation was given to him, that he found it necessary to have him brought before the Sheriff of the county of Edinburgh. But whether the man was punished, or only discharged upon promising not to repeat the annoyance, *I do not now recollect.*

"Your conduct, Sir, is most unjustifiable in thus lending yourself to be the vehicle of such foul slander upon the character of the respected dead — when the story is so improbable in itself—when upon the slightest enquiry you would have discovered that it referred to a period of between sixty and seventy years ago, and *therefore* is not applicable to any argument upon the present condition of the West India Colonies—and when, upon a little further enquiry, you might easily have obtained the above contradiction and explanation.

"I have only to add, that in the event of your not inserting this letter in your Paper of Sunday next, or of your repeating or insinuating any further slander upon the character of my father, the late Mr. James Wedderburn, of Inveresk, I have instructed my Solicitor to take immediate measures for obtaining legal redress against you.

"I am, Sir, your humble Servant,

"A. COLVILLE.

"*35, Leadenhall Street, March 17th, 1824.*"

As to our Correspondent's threat of prosecuting us, &c. we have not time just at present to say any thing further on this subject, than to remind him that HE IS NOT in *Jamaica,* and that we are not alarmed at trifles; so, trust he will summon to his aid all the *temperance* he is master of, whilst we proceed to the task he has himself imperatively *forced* upon us. Our Correspondent, A. COLVILLE, says, that *he is* the son of the late

JAMES WEDDERBURN, and that our other Correspondent, ROBERT WED-
DERBURN, is *not* so; that the said ROBERT WEDDERBURN was so called in a
jest; and that *his own mother did not know who was the father of her own
child.* — All this may be good *Slave-Dealers'* logic, for aught we know — but
how stands the case at issue? Two parties say that each is the son of JAMES
WEDDERBURN; and, without knowing either of them, the assertion of the
one is equally good as the assertion of the other, as far as *bare assertion* will
go. But ROBERT states that he was the "THIRD son" of JAMES WEDDERBURN
by the same mother; and here we must seriously ask Mr. COLVILLE, if such
statement be correct, whether he means to tell us that *the whole family was
made by accident,* or that the mother herself could not, owing to "her violence of temper," on oath, positively swear *whether she had any children or
not?* As to the "foolish joke" of calling a child after its father, we are ready
to admit that many a Slave-Dealer would feel himself offended at such a liberty taken with his name; and the more especially where he *intended to turn
him into ready money by disposing of him* — a practice with Slave-Dealers, of
which our present Correspondent, we presume, is not entirely ignorant.
However, if he be in reality, as he says, one of WEDDERBURN'S children, it
is evident that the ceremony of calling a child by the name of its father has
been dispensed within his own case, of which the difference between the
name of his father and himself are striking proofs. But, it seems, that ROB-
ERT WEDDERBURN is not *entirely unknown* to A. COLVILE, nor was he to
JAMES WEDDERBURN, "having applied for money" to them both, "on the
strength of his name" — This matter, as it aimed at the *pocket,* A. COLVILE
perfectly remembers, "but whether the *man was punished*" — a consideration of much less importance certainly — he "does not now recollect."

But we must now call the attention of A. COLVILE — "the real Simon
Pure,"[9] — and more particularly of our readers, to the next paragraph of his
letter, in which we are informed that we have been guilty of "lending ourselves" to "foul slander upon the character of the respected dead," *because* — what? — why, because "*the story is so improbable in itself,*" and refers
"*to a period of between sixty and seventy years ago, and* THEREFORE not
applicable to any argument upon the West India Colonies!" Although
this is excellent reasoning — inasmuch as it has stood the test of *time,*
having been urged between sixty or seventy years *past,* — yet it is of that
obvious description that spares us the necessity of replying to it. But
wherein we appear most culpable in the eyes of this affirmed son of JAMES

---

[9]Mocking term for the real person or genuine article, from the comic character Simon
Pure (a "Quaking preacher") in Susannah Centlivre's play, *A Bold Stroke for a Wife*
(1718).

WEDDERBURN, is, that we did not, by "inquiry," obtain the "contradiction," which we have now so fortunately, obtained?—But we are really too busily employed to hunt out the Solicitors of Slave-Dealers' children, for the purpose of inquiring who are so fortunate as to be acknowledged as such, and who are so unfortunate as to be disowned by them.—Yet, after all, the intelligence we *have* obtained by the above letter, is *but* a "contradiction" of an assertion, *without one single* PROOF that the assertion is untrue.

We now flatter ourselves that A. COLVILE will entertain a more favourable opinion of our love of equity than he appears to have done hitherto? We have inserted his letter, as it was his wish we should do, although we assure him it has not been from fear of any "dread instructions" which he may have confided to his Solicitor.

One word more, by way of advice, and we have done:—Concerning ROBERT WEDDERBURN and A. COLVILE, each tells us that he is the son of JAMES WEDDERBURN. Slave-Buyers, we are aware, frequently have many children born to them by this dreadful species of female *property*—when the dearest ties of consanguinity are trampled upon by a sordid thirst of interest, we had almost said *inherent,* in the *Slaver.* Yet, let not this unnatural feeling extend to the offspring of such connections—an offspring that should be the more closely cemented by the ties of affection, as mutual sorrows are attendant on their births;—let, then, the bonds of sympathy lighten the bondage to which they were (however unjustly) born; and if PROVIDENCE favours the one, let him strive to meliorate the distresses of the other. A father's marriage makes him *not the less the father of his own children,* in the EYE OF HEAVEN, though borne to him by his Slaves; and we should feel much greater pleasure to hear if A. COLVILE were to *relieve* R. WEDDERBURN (who, by the way, has not mentioned *his* name), than in *his* attempt to prove that a mother does not know the father of her child, and *that* child, as we are informed, the THIRD she had borne to him!

The next Sunday, 28th March, I replied to brother Andrew's statement; and I will leave the reader to judge which had the best of the argument. BROTHER OR NO BROTHER—"THAT IS THE QUESTION?"

"We this day publish a third letter upon this, certainly not uninteresting, subject—from him who declares himself to be the elder branch of the general stock; and if this be true, we must—*en passant*—in the first place, address a word or two to the younger scion—a Mr. Colvile—(we here insert

---

en passant: in passing.

the name as he himself has spelt it) will perceive by our publishing the annexed letter, that we do *not* "lend ourselves to foul slander, &c." as in a moment of ridiculous petulance he was, last week, pleased to aver—but we shall hope that our publication of the little vituperative anathemas denounced against us in the epistle with which he honoured us, has, ere this, convinced him how grossly he libelled us in the assertion. However, we forgive his irritability, and will venture, once more, to give him a little advice as to his future literary communications. If, as he has asserted, the writer of the following letter be *not his brother,* instead of using idle threats of setting his Solicitor upon us, let him seat himself soberly down in his closet, and send us the result of his temperate reflections upon the subject in question. Let him remember also, that his argument will lose nothing by *good language,* nor be the less convincing by being urged in terms not unbecoming a gentleman. It may not, perhaps, be improper, once more to remind Mr. Colvile that the publication which first offended him made no allusion to *himself*—and he must make great allowances for the warmth of feeling expressed by a man whose natural sympathies have been so deeply wounded as those (according to his own statement—and of which he adduces corroborative facts) of Robert Wedderburn. Let Mr. Colvile send us a statement of *facts* that will *disprove* the statements of Robert Wedderburn, and Mr. C. shall soon be convinced that—to speak in his own phrase—"we do not lend ourselves to be the vehicle of foul slander," but are really what we pretend ourselves to be, and what every public journalist *ought* to be— *the Advocates of Truth and Justice.* Mr. C. cannot think that we ever had the least intention of injuring or offending him, aware as he is that we did not know that there was such a being as himself in existence until he told us so; and as we are of no party, our columns are as open to one part of his father's family as to another.

But *Mr. Colvile* asserts in his letter of the 17th instant, that the case therein referred to, as published by us, "was not applicable to any argument upon the present condition of the West India Colonies."—As to a matter of opinion, we must beg leave to differ with him: *length of time* is no argument against the inhumanities of Slave-Dealers, as practised against the unprotected Slave. Many years ago it was acknowledged that the power of the West-India Slave Dealer *had* been by him abused, but that the condition of his *live stock* was now [then] meliorated. The self-same argument is urged with equal vehemence at the present day; and such *would be* the never-failing *salvo* for ages to come, were the wretched captives to be left

---

vituperative anathemas: abusive curses.
instant: of the current month.

to the mercy—we beg pardon—to the *cruelty* of their fiend-like masters: and here we must remind Mr. Colvile that this is not merely our own opinion upon the subject, but was the language of British Senators when commencing the benevolent work of casting off the chains of their fellow men. We would wish to act with *becoming* delicacy to Mr. C. or to Mr. Anybody-else, under similar circumstances, unless forced to cast it aside by him or them—but we say (for we have made *certain* inquiries since we published his letter) that we should have expected that *he* would have been one of the *last* to have spoken with indifference on the *sale* of his fellow creatures. Let us merely suppose that his own mother had been treated as many of the unhappy mothers of Slave-Dealers' children *have* been treated, what, then, we would ask, *must* have been the feelings of any man not lost to all sense of humanity?—And is it not a matter of *chance*, where *interest* preponderates to induce him to marry—*who* of a Slave-Dealer's children is born to him in wedlock, and who is not? Mr. C. has not yet informed us whether or not *he* was born in wedlock, nor do we either know or care.— We will repeat to Mr. Colvile what we have often before repeated, *viz.* our unalterable conviction that the man who accumulates wealth by the blood of his fellows, must ever be dead to the feelings common to our nature. But although we have said we would never cease to exclaim against the horrible traffic in human flesh until there was an amelioration of the condition of Slavery; yet, unjust as is the argument of force against the force of argument, we wished not an *instantaneous* emancipation, although we could have wished our Ministers to have gone farther than they have done, and extended their object to the other Colonies, as they have already commenced it in Trinidad. However, as it is, we rejoice to find that there is a *beginning* to soften the rigour of captivity and fetters; but, as Mr. Wilberforce truly observed, the consequence of disappointed hope might be to drive the Negroes to "*take the cause into their own hands.*" With him, we trust that such may not be the case!

We now return to the point from which we have so far, and not unnecessarily, we think, digressed. The columns of our journal are ever open to redress any wrong we may have unintentionally committed; but we are not to be threatened into silence upon a subject, the truth of which, in some material points, is not even attempted to be *denied,* or *disproved* by *corroborative circumstances;* and if Mr. Colvile will not follow the good advice we have already bestowed upon him, he would do well to address himself to that Ultra-Radical or Loyalist,—who so jumbles his extremes we know not which to call him—the *Infamous John Bull.*[10]—In *his* columns Mr. C. may

---

[10] *John Bull,* a satirical, antiradical, scurrilous Sunday newspaper, edited by Theodore Hook from 1820 to 1841.

hack, cut, and quarter the Slaves *ad libitum*. It is true, indeed, that thus, many thousands of *our* readers may not *see* the ink-engulphed massacre, but perhaps the general carnage may make amends for this deficiency? However, Mr. Colvile will please himself in his future operations; and, just hinting to him (should he address the *Infamous John Bull*) the propriety of passing by the *Scotch Cow,* alluded to in the following letter, we recommend it to his perusal without further ceremony: —

"TO THE EDITOR OF 'BELL'S LIFE IN LONDON."

"SIR, —I did not expect, when I communicated my statement, as it appeared in your Paper of the 29th ult. that any person would have had the temerity, not to say audacity, to have contradicted my assertion, and thereby occasion me to PROVE the deep depravity of the man to whom I owe my existence. I deem it now an imperative duty to reply to the infamous letter of A. COLVILE, *alias* WEDDERBURN, and to defend the memory of my unfortunate mother, a woman virtuous in principle, but a Slave, and a sacrifice to the unprincipled lust of my father. —Your Correspondent, *my dear and affectionate brother,* will, doubtless, laugh, when he hears of the VIRTUES of SLAVES, *unless such as will enhance their price—*but I shall leave it to your readers to decide on the *laugh* of a Slave-Dealer after the picture of lust and cruelty and avarice, which I mean to lay before them. *My dear brother's statement* is FALSE, when he says that I was not born till several years after my mother was sold by my father: —but let me tell him, that my mother was pregnant at the time of *sale,* and that I was born within four months after it took place. One of the conditions of the sale was, that her offspring, your humble servant, was to be free, from its birth, and I thank my GOD, that through a long life of hardship and adversity, I have ever been free both in mind and body: and have always raised my voice in behalf of my enslaved countrymen! My mother had, previously to my birth, borne two other sons to JAMES WEDDERBURN, Esq. of Inveresk, Slave-Dealer, one of whom, a mill-wright, works now upon the family estate in Jamaica, and has done his whole life-time; and so far was my father from doubting me to be his son, that he recorded my freedom, and that of my brother JAMES, the millwright, himself, in the Government Secretary's Office; where it may be seen to this day. *My dear brother* states that my mother was of a violent temper, which was the reason of my father selling her; —yes, and I glory in her *rebellious* disposition, and which I have inherited from her. My honoured father's house was, in fact, nothing more than a *Seraglio of Black Slaves,* miserable objects of an abandoned lust, guided by avarice; and it

---

ad libitum: at will

was from this den of iniquity that she (my mother) was determined to escape. A Lady Douglas, of the parish of St. Mary, was my mother's purchaser, and also stood my godmother. Perhaps, *my dear brother* knows nothing of one Esther Trotter, a free tawny, who bore my father two children, a boy and a girl, and which children my inhuman father *transported to Scotland*, to gratify his malice, because their mother refused to be any longer the object of his lust, and because she claimed support for herself and offspring? Those children *my dear and loving brother* knows under the name of Graham, being brought up in the same house with them at Inveresk. It is true that I did apply to *my dear brother,* A. Colvile—as he signs himself, but his real name is Wedderburn—for some pecuniary assistance; but it was upon the ground of *right,* according to *Deuteronomy,* xxi. 10, 17.

"'If a man have two wives, one beloved and another hated, and they have borne him children, both the beloved and the hated, and if the first-born son be her's that was hated;

"'Then it shall be, when he maketh his sons to inherit that which he hath, that he may not make the son of the beloved first-born before the son of the hated, which is, indeed, the first-born;

"'But he shall acknowledge the son of the hated for the first-born, by giving him a double portion of all that he hath, for he is the beginning of his strength, the right of the first-born is his."

"I was at that time, Mr. Editor, in extreme distress; the quartern loaf was then 1s. 10½ d., I was out of work, and my wife was lying in, which I think was some excuse for applying to an *affectionate brother,* who refused to relieve me. He says that he knew nothing of me before that time; but he will remember seeing me at his father's house five years before—the precise time I forget, but A. Colvile will recollect it, when I state, that it was the very day on which one of our *dear* father's cows died in calving, and when a butcher was sent for from Musselburgh, *to kill the dead beast,* and take it to market—a perfect specimen of Scotch economy. It was seven years after my arrival in England that I visited my father, who had the inhumanity to threaten to send me to gaol if I troubled him. I never saw my worthy father in Britain but this time, and then he did not abuse my mother, as my dear brother, A. Colvile, has done; nor did he deny me to be his son, but called me a *lazy fellow,* and said he would do nothing for me. From his cook I had one draught of small beer, and his footman gave me a cracked sixpence—and these are all the obligations I am under to my *worthy* father and *my dear brother,* A. Colvile. It is false where my brother says I was taken

---

quartern loaf: four-pound loaf (of bread).

before the Sheriff of the County—I applied to the Council of the City of Edinburgh for assistance, and they gave me 16*d.* and a travelling pass; and for my passage up to London I was indebted to the Captain of a Berwick smack.

"In conclusion, Mr. Editor, I have to say, that if *my dear brother* means to *show fight* before the Nobs at Westminster, I shall soon give him an opportunity, as I mean to publish my whole history in a cheap pamphlet, and to give the public a specimen of the inhumanity, cruelty, avarice, and diabolical lust of the West-India Slave-Holders; and in the Courts of Justice I will defend and prove my assertions.

> "*I am, Sir, your obedient Servant;*
>
> "ROBERT WEDDERBURN.

"*23, Russell Court, Drury Lane.*"

I could expatiate at great length on the inhumanity and cruelty of the West-India planters were I not fearful that I should become wearisome on so notorious a subject. My brother, ANDREW COLVILE, is a tolerable specimen of them, as may be seen by his letter, his cruelty venting itself in slandering my mother's memory, and his bullying in threatening the Editor with a prosecution. I have now fairly given him the challenge; let him meet it if he dare. My readers can form some idea what Andrew is in a free country, and what he would be in Jamaica, on his sugar estates, amongst his own slaves. Verily, he is "a chip of the old block." To make one exception to this family, I must state, that ANDREW COLVILE'S elder brother, who is now dead, when he came over to Jamaica, acknowledged his father's tawny children, and, amongst them, my brothers as his brothers. He once invited them all to a dinner, and behaved very free and familiar to them. I was in England at that time. Let my dear brother Andrew deny this, if he can, also.

I should have gone back to Jamaica, had I not been fearful of the planters; for such is their hatred of any one having black blood in his veins, and who dares to think and act as a free man, that they would most certainly have trumped up some charge against me, and hung me. With them I should have had no mercy. In a future part of my history I shall give some particulars of the treatment of the blacks in the West Indies, and the prospect of a general rebellion and massacre there, from my own experience. In the mean time, I bid my readers farewell.

> R. WEDDERBURN.

23, Russell Court, Drary Lane.

Nobs: persons of (or pretending to) high social status.

The History of Mary Prince, A West-Indian Slave: Related by Herself

Mary Prince

Mary Prince (c. 1788 – c. 1833) occupies a singular place in the history of Black British writing: not only was she the first black woman to escape slavery and publish her narrative but her work remains the only known English-language narrative written by a West Indian slave woman. Furthermore, scholars regard Prince's *History* as a unique cultural production. Sandra Pouchet Paquet (1992) holds that despite the constraints placed on Prince and her text, her narrative nevertheless retains a "qualitative uniqueness," one that is "distinctly West Indian, distinctly a black woman's and distinctly a slave's" (131), while Sukhdev Sandhu and David Dabydeen (1999) remark that against other Black British slave writings, Prince's narrative stands out for its visceral quality. They rightly contrast the monosyllabic, "witness stand simplicity" of Prince's account with the long-winded, moralistic tone of polemic that creeps into some other British slave narratives (liv). In the tradition of Black British writing, Prince's text proves that less can be more: the less she accuses and moralizes, the more she tells about the effects of slavery on real lives. In fact, of all the Black writers of this period, none takes readers more swiftly and more shrewdly into the horrors of slavery than Prince. Readers remain fascinated with the amount of authorial control Prince possessed as narrator of the *History*, just as they continue to be intrigued by the amount of political control she exercised in her role as slave.

Mary Prince was born in 1788 in Bermuda, a British colony. Turk's Island (far south of Bermuda in the West Indies), where Prince spent a particularly horrific time, was the center of the Bermuda salt industry. As she chronicles in her account, Prince spent her first twelve years with Captain Williams and was then sold to the abusive Captain I——. Prince relates the abuse she suffered under Captain I—— (at one point he gave her "a hundred lashes with his own hand" and continued beating her "until he was quite wearied, and so hot that he sank back in his chair, almost like to faint" [page 247]), as well as the trauma she suffered under his jealous wife. Her next owner, Mr. D——, was less violent but in many ways more brutal than Captain I——. He would repeatedly hang her by the wrists, strip her naked, then methodically, with an eerie sense of self-control, beat her. The working conditions, as well as Mr. D——'s treatment of her, became so unbearable that she finally convinced Mr. D——to sell her to the merchant John Wood and his wife, who brought her to their home in Antigua as a house slave.

Mary Prince arrived in London in 1828, as a servant still under the putative ownership of Mr. and Mrs. Wood. Once in Britain she left the Woods and took refuge at the Anti-Slavery Society office in Aldermanbury. When Prince arrived on the Society's doorsteps, she was alone and in poverty, her body aching with rheumatism and pain brought on by the harsh labor and physical abuse she had endured in the Caribbean. Although the Anti-Slavery Society did not rescue every former slave who came to their door, they took a special interest in Prince and gave her a job working for Thomas Pringle, the society's secretary. In return, Prince narrated her riveting story, which the society immediately recognized as a bestseller, even for an audience already saturated with antislavery sentiment. (The *History* went through three editions in 1831, its first year of publication.) It may be impossible to tell how much of the narrative Prince authorized, since it was "taken down from Mary's own lips by a lady who happened to be at the time residing" with the Pringles, the poet and Methodist convert Susanna Strickland. Pringle himself then "went over the whole" manuscript and "pruned" it "into its present shape" (page 237). Yet even though the narrative was designed as a tool for the Anti-Slavery Society and mediated by both an amanuensis and an editor, it manages to capture the orality of Prince's retelling. For example, there are places in the text where Prince says, "But I must go on with the thread of my story" (page 246), and other places where she finds English language and sentiment inadequate. She cannot describe some of her experiences because they are "too, too bad to speak in England" (page 247). Often she is at a loss to "find words to tell you all I then felt and suffered" (page 241).

Although defeating proslavery arguments does not appear to be a major purpose behind Prince's *History*, its lyrical smoothness and gut-wrenching honesty manage to overturn even the most stubborn proslavery claims, such as the planters' repeated insistence that slave working conditions were humane. More importantly, Prince's self-representation revised a central antislavery icon: the slave woman. Utterly sentimentalized and in need of pity and salvation, the image of the slave woman had served British poets and abolitionists since the early days of agitation against the slave trade in the 1780s. The slave women in Prince's text are active, productive, intelligent, nuanced figures, notably including the slave woman Hetty, Prince's own mother, and Prince herself.

Very little is known of Prince's life after the *History* was published. An addendum to the preface to the third edition indicates that she was going blind. What did happen after publication was a heated public controversy between Prince's antislavery supporters and the proslavery lobby headed by James Macqueen, which culminated in two court cases, both of which were settled the same year the Emancipation Act was passed in Parliament, 1833. The documents attached by Pringle as a "Supplement" to Prince's *History*, reproduced here, preserve the public fervor her *History* evoked.

HISTORY OF MARY PRINCE,

A WEST-INDIAN SLAVE.

RELATED BY HERSELF.

WITH A SUPPLEMENT BY THE EDITOR.

To which is added

THE NARRATIVE OF ASA–ASA
A CAPTURED AFRICAN.

By our sufferings, since ye brought us
To the man-degrading mart, —
All sustain'd by patience, taught us
Only by a broken heart, —
Deem our nation brutes no longer,
Till some reason ye shall find,
Worthier of regard, and stronger
Than the colour of our kind.

Cowper[1]

LONDON:
PUBLISHED BY F. WESTLEY AND H. DAVIS
1831.

---

[1] From William Cowper (1731–1800), "The Negro's Complaint" (1788).

PREFACE.

THE idea of writing Mary Prince's history was first suggested by herself. She wished it to be done, she said, that good people in England might hear from a slave what a slave had felt and suffered; and a letter of her late master's, which will be found in the Supplement, induced me to accede to her wish without farther delay. The more immediate object of the publication will afterwards appear.

The narrative was taken down from Mary's own lips by a lady who happened to be at the time residing in my family as a visitor.[2] It was written out fully, with all the narrator's repetitions and prolixities, and afterwards pruned into its present shape; retaining, as far as was practicable, Mary's exact expressions and peculiar phraseology. No fact of importance has been omitted, and not a single circumstance or sentiment has been added. It is essentially her own, without any material alteration farther than was requisite to exclude redundances and gross grammatical errors, so as to render it clearly intelligible.

After it had been thus written out, I went over the whole, carefully examining her on every fact and circumstance detailed; and in all that relates to her residence in Antigua I had the advantage of being assisted in this scrutiny by Mr. Joseph Phillips, who was a resident in that colony during the same period, and had known her there.

The names of all the persons mentioned by the narrator have been printed in full, except those of Capt. I —— and his wife,[3] and that of Mr. D ——, to whom conduct of peculiar atrocity is ascribed. These three individuals are now gone to answer at a far more awful tribunal than that of public opinion, for the deeds of which their former bondwoman accuses them; and to hold them up more openly to human reprobation could no longer affect themselves, while it might deeply lacerate the feelings of their surviving and perhaps innocent relatives, without any commensurate public advantage.

From Mary Prince, *The History of Mary Prince, a West Indian Slave, Related by Herself. With a Supplement by the Editor* [Thomas Pringle] (London: Westley and Davis, 1831).

[2] Prince's amanuensis was Susanna Strickland, author of *Enthusiasm; and Other Poems* (1831) and a recent convert to Methodism.

[3] In her scholarly edition of Prince's *History*, Ferguson identifies Captain I—— and his wife as John Ingham and Mary Spencer Ingham, married in 1789 and residents of Spanish Point, Bermuda (Prince 1997, 34–35).

Without detaining the reader with remarks on other points which will be adverted to more conveniently in the Supplement, I shall here merely notice farther, that the Anti-Slavery Society have no concern whatever with this publication, nor are they in any degree responsible for the statements it contains. I have published the tract, not as their Secretary, but in my private capacity; and any profits that may arise from the sale will be exclusively appropriated to the benefit of Mary Prince herself.

Tho. Pringle[4]

7, Solly Terrace, Claremont Square,
    January 25, 1831.

P. S. Since writing the above, I have been furnished by my friend Mr. George Stephen, with the interesting narrative of Asa-Asa, a captured African, now under his protection; and have printed it as a suitable appendix to this little history.[5]

T. P.

The
History of Mary Prince,

A WEST INDIAN SLAVE.
(Related by herself.)

I WAS born at Brackish-Pond, in Bermuda,[6] on a farm belonging to Mr. Charles Myners. My mother was a household slave; and my father, whose name was Prince, was a sawyer belonging to Mr. Trimmingham, a shipbuilder at Crow-Lane. When I was an infant, old Mr. Myners died,

---

sawyer: a workman who saws lumber.

[4] Thomas Pringle (1789–1834), a magazine editor, poet, and antislavery activist who had lived in South Africa before returning to London in 1826, becoming secretary to the Anti-Slavery Society the following year.

[5] The brief "Narrative of Louis Asa-Asa" is not included here. [Eds.]

[6] Bermuda, then (as now) a British colony, is an archipelago of seven main, and many smaller, islands off the Atlantic coast of North America, located well north of the West Indies at about the latitude of Charleston, South Carolina.

and there was a division of the slaves and other property among the family. I was bought along with my mother by old Captain Darrel, and given to his grandchild, little Miss Betsey Williams. Captain Williams, Mr. Darrel's son-in-law, was master of a vessel which traded to several places in America and the West Indies, and he was seldom at home long together.

Mrs. Williams was a kind-hearted good woman, and she treated all her slaves well. She had only one daughter, Miss Betsey, for whom I was purchased, and who was about my own age. I was made quite a pet of by Miss Betsey, and loved her very much. She used to lead me about by the hand, and call me her little nigger. This was the happiest period of my life; for I was too young to understand rightly my condition as a slave, and too thoughtless and full of spirits to look forward to the days of toil and sorrow.

My mother was a household slave in the same family. I was under her own care, and my little brothers and sisters were my play-fellows and companions. My mother had several fine children after she came to Mrs. Williams,—three girls and two boys. The tasks given out to us children were light, and we used to play together with Miss Betsey, with as much freedom almost as if she had been our sister.

My master, however, was a very harsh, selfish man; and we always dreaded his return from sea. His wife was herself much afraid of him; and, during his stay at home, seldom dared to shew her usual kindness to the slaves. He often left her, in the most distressed circumstances, to reside in other female society, at some place in the West Indies of which I have forgot the name. My poor mistress bore his ill-treatment with great patience, and all her slaves loved and pitied her. I was truly attached to her, and, next to my own mother, loved her better than any creature in the world. My obedience to her commands was cheerfully given; it sprung solely from the affection I felt for her, and not from fear of the power which the white people's law had given her over me.

I had scarcely reached my twelfth year when my mistress became too poor to keep so many of us at home; and she hired me out to Mrs. Pruden, a lady who lived about five miles off, in the adjoining parish, in a large house near the sea. I cried bitterly at parting with my dear mistress and Miss Betsey, and when I kissed my mother and brothers and sisters, I thought my young heart would break, it pained me so. But there was no help; I was forced to go. Good Mrs. Williams comforted me by saying that I should still be near the home I was about to quit, and might come over and see her and my kindred whenever I could obtain leave of absence from Mrs. Pruden. A few hours after this I was taken to a strange house, and found myself among strange people. This separation seemed a sore trial to me then; but oh! 'twas light, light to the trials I have since endured!—'twas nothing—nothing to be mentioned with them; but I was a child then, and it was according to my strength.

I knew that Mrs. Williams could no longer maintain me; that she was fain to part with me for my food and clothing; and I tried to submit myself to the change. My new mistress was a passionate woman; but yet she did not treat me very unkindly. I do not remember her striking me but once, and that was for going to see Mrs. Williams when I heard she was sick, and staying longer than she had given me leave to do. All my employment at this time was nursing a sweet baby, little Master Daniel; and I grew so fond of my nursling that it was my greatest delight to walk out with him by the sea-shore, accompanied by his brother and sister, Miss Fanny and Master James.—Dear Miss Fanny! She was a sweet, kind young lady, and so fond of me that she wished me to learn all that she knew herself; and her method of teaching me was as follows:—Directly she had said her lessons to her grandmamma, she used to come running to me, and make me repeat them one by one after her; and in a few months I was able not only to say my letters but to spell many small words. But this happy state was not to last long. Those days were too pleasant to last. My heart always softens when I think of them.

At this time Mrs. Williams died. I was told suddenly of her death, and my grief was so great that, forgetting I had the baby in my arms, I ran away directly to my poor mistress's house; but reached it only in time to see the corpse carried out. Oh, that was a day of sorrow.—a heavy day! All the slaves cried. My mother cried and lamented her sore; and I (foolish creature!) vainly entreated them to bring my dear mistress back to life. I knew nothing rightly about death then, and it seemed a hard thing to bear. When I thought about my mistress I felt as if the world was all gone wrong; and for many days and weeks I could think of nothing else. I returned to Mrs. Pruden's; but my sorrow was too great to be comforted, for my own dear mistress was always in my mind. Whether in the house or abroad, my thoughts were always talking to me about her.

I staid at Mrs. Pruden's about three months after this; I was then sent back to Mr. Williams to be sold. Oh, that was a sad sad time! I recollect the day well. Mrs. Pruden came to me and said, "Mary, you will have to go home directly; your master is going to be married, and he means to sell you and two of your sisters to raise money for the wedding." Hearing this I burst out a crying,—though I was then far from being sensible of the full weight of my misfortune, or of the misery that waited for me. Besides, I did not like to leave Mrs. Pruden, and the dear baby, who had grown very fond of me. For some time I could scarcely believe that Mrs. Pruden was in earnest, till I received orders for my immediate return.—Dear Miss Fanny!

how she cried at parting with me, whilst I kissed and hugged the baby, thinking I should never see him again. I left Mrs. Pruden's, and walked home with a heart full of sorrow. The idea of being sold away from my mother and Miss Betsey was so frightful, that I dared not trust myself to think about it. We had been bought of Mr. Myners, as I have mentioned, by Miss Betsey's grandfather, and given to her, so that we were by right *her* property, and I never thought we should be separated or sold away from her.

When I reached the house, I went in directly to Miss Betsey. I found her in great distress; and she cried out as soon as she saw me, "Oh, Mary! my father is going to sell you all to raise money to marry that wicked woman. You are *my* slaves, and he has no right to sell you; but it is all to please her." She then told me that my mother was living with her father's sister at a house close by, and I went there to see her. It was a sorrowful meeting; and we lamented with a great and sore crying our unfortunate situation. "Here comes one of my poor picaninnies!" she said, the moment I came in, "one of the poor slave-brood who are to be sold to-morrow."

Oh dear! I cannot bear to think of that day, — it is too much. — It recalls the great grief that filled my heart, and the woeful thoughts that passed to and fro through my mind, whilst listening to the pitiful words of my poor mother, weeping for the loss of her children. I wish I could find words to tell you all I then felt and suffered. The great God above alone knows the thoughts of the poor slave's heart, and the bitter pains which follow such separations as these. All that we love taken away from us — Oh, it is sad, sad! and sore to be borne! — I got no sleep that night for thinking of the morrow; and dear Miss Betsey was scarcely less distressed. She could not bear to part with her old playmates, and she cried sore and would not be pacified.

The black morning at length came; it came too soon for my poor mother and us. Whilst she was putting on us the new osnaburgs in which we were to be sold, she said, in a sorrowful voice, (I shall never forget it!) "See, I am *shrouding* my poor children; what a task for a mother!" — She then called Miss Betsey to take leave of us. "I am going to carry my little chickens to market," (these were her very words,) "take your last look of them; may be you will see them no more." "Oh, my poor slaves! my own slaves!" said dear Miss Betsey, "you belong to me; and it grieves my heart to part with you." — Miss Betsey kissed us all, and, when she left us, my

---

picaninnies: a term then used in the Americas to refer to young children of black African ancestry.

osnaburgs: garments made of coarse linen.

mother called the rest of the slaves to bid us good bye. One of them, a woman named Moll, came with her infant in her arms. "Ay!" said my mother, seeing her turn away and look at her child with the tears in her eyes, "your turn will come next." The slaves could say nothing to comfort us; they could only weep and lament with us. When I left my dear little brothers and the house in which I had been brought up, I thought my heart would burst.

Our mother, weeping as she went, called me away with the children Hannah and Dinah, and we took the road that led to Hamble Town, which we reached about four o'clock in the afternoon. We followed my mother to the market-place, where she placed us in a row against a large house, with our backs to the wall and our arms folded across our breasts. I, as the eldest, stood first, Hannah next to me, then Dinah; and our mother stood beside, crying over us. My heart throbbed with grief and terror so violently, that I pressed my hands quite tightly across my breast, but I could not keep it still, and it continued to leap as though it would burst out of my body. But who cared for that? Did one of the many by-standers, who were looking at us so carelessly, think of the pain that wrung the hearts of the negro woman and her young ones? No, no! They were not all bad, I dare say, but slavery hardens white people's hearts towards the blacks; and many of them were not slow to make their remarks upon us aloud, without regard to our grief—though their light words fell like cayenne on the fresh wounds of our hearts. Oh those white people have small hearts who can only feel for themselves.

At length the vendue master, who was to offer us for sale like sheep or cattle, arrived, and asked my mother which was the eldest. She said nothing, but pointed to me. He took me by the hand, and led me out into the middle of the street, and, turning me slowly round, exposed me to the view of those who attended the vendue. I was soon surrounded by strange men, who examined and handled me in the same manner that a butcher would a calf or a lamb he was about to purchase, and who talked about my shape and size in like words—as if I could no more understand their meaning than the dumb beasts. I was then put up to sale. The bidding commenced at a few pounds, and gradually rose to fifty-seven,[7] when I was knocked down to the highest bidder; and the people who stood by said that I had fetched a great sum for so young a slave.

---

cayenne: hot red pepper.

vendue master: auctioneer, superintends vendue (sale) of slaves.

[7] Bermuda currency; about £38 sterling. [Pringle's note.]

I then saw my sisters led forth, and sold to different owners; so that we had not the sad satisfaction of being partners in bondage. When the sale was over, my mother hugged and kissed us, and mourned over us, begging of us to keep up a good heart, and do our duty to our new masters. It was a sad parting; one went one way, one another, and our poor mammy went home with nothing.[8]

My new master was a Captain I——, who lived at Spanish Point. After parting with my mother and sisters, I followed him to his store, and he gave me into the charge of his son, a lad about my own age, Master Benjy, who took me to my new home. I did not know where I was going, or what my new master would do with me. My heart was quite broken with grief, and my thoughts went back continually to those from whom I had been so suddenly parted. "Oh, my mother! my mother!" I kept saying to myself, "Oh, my mammy and my sisters and my brothers, shall I never see you again!"

Oh, the trials! the trials! they make the salt water come into my eyes when I think of the days in which I was afflicted—the times that are gone; when I mourned and grieved with a young heart for those whom I loved.

---

[8] Let the reader compare the above affecting account, taken down from the mouth of this negro woman, with the following description of a vendue of slaves at the Cape of Good Hope, published by me in 1826, from the letter of a friend,—and mark their similarity in several characteristic circumstances. The resemblance is easily accounted for: slavery wherever it prevails produces similar effects. — "Having heard that there was to be a sale of cattle, farm stock, &c. by auction, at a Veld-Cornet's in the vicinity, we halted our waggon one day for the purpose of procuring a fresh spann of oxen. Among the stock of the farm sold, was a female slave and her three children. The two eldest children were girls, the one about thirteen years of age, and the other about eleven; the youngest was a boy. The whole family were exhibited together, but they were sold separately, and to different purchasers. The farmers examined them as if they had been so many head of cattle. While the sale was going on, the mother and her children were exhibited on a table, that they might be seen by the company, which was very large. There could not have been a finer subject for an able painter than this unhappy group. The tears, the anxiety, the anguish of the mother, while she met the gaze of the multitude, eyed the different countenances of the bidders, or cast a heart-rending look upon the children; and the simplicity and touching sorrow of the young ones, while they clung to their distracted parent, wiping their eyes, and half concealing their faces,—contrasted with the marked insensibility and jocular countenances of the spectators and purchasers,—furnished a striking commentary on the miseries of slavery, and its debasing effects upon the hearts of its abettors. While the woman was in this distressed situation she was asked, 'Can you feed sheep?' Her reply was so indistinct that it escaped me; but it was probably in the negative, for her purchaser rejoined, in a loud and harsh voice, 'Then I will teach you with the sjamboc,' (a whip made of the rhinoceros' hide.) The mother and her three children were sold to three separate purchasers; and they were literally torn from each other."—*Ed.* [Pringle's note.]

It was night when I reached my new home. The house was large, and built at the bottom of a very high hill; but I could not see much of it that night. I saw too much of it afterwards. The stones and the timber were the best things in it; they were not so hard as the hearts of the owners.[9]

Before I entered the house, two slave women, hired from another owner, who were at work in the yard, spoke to me, and asked who I belonged to? I replied, "I am come to live here." "Poor child, poor child!" they both said; "you must keep a good heart, if you are to live here." — When I went in, I stood up crying in a corner. Mrs. I—— came and took off my hat, a little black silk hat Miss Pruden made for me, and said in a rough voice, "You are not come here to stand up in corners and cry, you are come here to work." She then put a child into my arms, and, tired as I was, I was forced instantly to take up my old occupation of a nurse. — I could not bear to look at my mistress, her countenance was so stern. She was a stout tall woman with a very dark complexion, and her brows were always drawn together into a frown. I thought of the words of the two slave women when I saw Mrs. I——, and heard the harsh sound of her voice.

The person I took the most notice of that night was a French Black called Hetty, whom my master took in privateering from another vessel, and made his slave. She was the most active woman I ever saw, and she was tasked to her utmost. A few minutes after my arrival she came in from milking the cows, and put the sweet-potatoes on for supper. She then fetched home the sheep, and penned them in the fold; drove home the cattle, and staked them about the pond side;[10] fed and rubbed down my master's horse, and gave the hog and the fed cow[11] their suppers; prepared the beds, and undressed the children, and laid them to sleep. I liked to look at her and watch all her doings, for her's was the only friendly face I had as yet seen, and I felt glad that she was there. She gave me my supper of potatoes and milk, and a blanket to sleep upon, which she spread for me in the passage before the door of Mrs. I——'s chamber.

I got a sad fright, that night. I was just going to sleep, when I heard a noise in my mistress's room; and she presently called out to inquire if some work was finished that she had ordered Hetty to do. "No, Ma'am, not yet," was Hetty's answer from below. On hearing this, my master started up from his bed, and just as he was, in his shirt, ran down stairs with a long

---

[9] These strong expressions, and all of a similar character in this little narrative, are given verbatim as uttered by Mary Prince. — *Ed.* [Pringle's note.]

[10] The cattle on a small plantation in Bermuda are, it seems, often thus staked or tethered, both night and day, in situations where grass abounds. [Pringle's note.]

[11] A cow fed for slaughter. [Pringle's note.]

cow-skin [12] in his hand. I heard immediately after, the cracking of the thong, and the house rang to the shrieks of poor Hetty, who kept crying out, "Oh, Massa! Massa! me dead. Massa! have mercy upon me—don't kill me outright."—This was a sad beginning for me. I sat up upon my blanket, trembling with terror, like a frightened hound, and thinking that my turn would come next. At length the house became still, and I forgot for a little while all my sorrows by falling fast asleep.

The next morning my mistress set about instructing me in my tasks. She taught me to do all sorts of household work; to wash and bake, pick cotton and wool, and wash floors, and cook. And she taught me (how can I ever forget it!) more things than these; she caused me to know the exact difference between the smart of the rope, the cart-whip, and the cow-skin, when applied to my naked body by her own cruel hand. And there was scarcely any punishment more dreadful than the blows I received on my face and head from her hard heavy fist. She was a fearful woman, and a savage mistress to her slaves.

There were two little slave boys in the house, on whom she vented her bad temper in a special manner. One of these children was a mulatto, called Cyrus, who had been bought while an infant in his mother's arms; the other, Jack, was an African from the coast of Guinea, whom a sailor had given or sold to my master. Seldom a day passed without these boys receiving the most severe treatment, and often for no fault at all. Both my master and mistress seemed to think that they had a right to ill-use them at their pleasure; and very often accompanied their commands with blows, whether the children were behaving well or ill. I have seen their flesh ragged and raw with licks.—Lick—lick—they were never secure one moment from a blow, and their lives were passed in continual fear. My mistress was not contented with using the whip, but often pinched their cheeks and arms in the most cruel manner. My pity for these poor boys was soon transferred to myself; for I was licked, and flogged, and pinched by her pitiless fingers in the neck and arms, exactly as they were. To strip me naked—to hang me up by the wrists and lay my flesh open with the cow-skin, was an ordinary punishment for even a slight offence. My mistress often robbed me too of the hours that belong to sleep. She used to sit up very late, frequently even until morning; and I had then to stand at a bench and wash during the greater part of the night, or pick wool and cotton; and often I have dropped down overcome by sleep and fatigue, till roused from a state of stupor by the whip, and forced to start up to my tasks.

---

[12] A thong of hard twisted hide, known by this name in the West Indies. [Pringle's note.]

Poor Hetty, my fellow slave, was very kind to me, and I used to call her my Aunt; but she led a most miserable life, and her death was hastened (at least the slaves all believed and said so,) by the dreadful chastisement she received from my master during her pregnancy. It happened as follows. One of the cows had dragged the rope away from the stake to which Hetty had fastened it, and got loose. My master flew into a terrible passion, and ordered the poor creature to be stripped quite naked, notwithstanding her pregnancy, and to be tied up to a tree in the yard. He then flogged her as hard as he could lick, both with the whip and cow-skin, till she was all over streaming with blood. He rested, and then beat her again and again. Her shrieks were terrible. The consequence was that poor Hetty was brought to bed before her time, and was delivered after severe labour of a dead child. She appeared to recover after her confinement, so far that she was repeatedly flogged by both master and mistress afterwards; but her former strength never returned to her. Ere long her body and limbs swelled to a great size; and she lay on a mat in the kitchen, till the water burst out of her body and she died. All the slaves said that death was a good thing for poor Hetty; but I cried very much for her death. The manner of it filled me with horror. I could not bear to think about it; yet it was always present to my mind for many a day.

After Hetty died all her labours fell upon me, in addition to my own. I had now to milk eleven cows every morning before sunrise, sitting among the damp weeds; to take care of the cattle as well as the children; and to do the work of the house. There was no end to my toils—no end to my blows. I lay down at night and rose up in the morning in fear and sorrow; and often wished that like poor Hetty I could escape from this cruel bondage and be at rest in the grave. But the hand of that God whom then I knew not, was stretched over me; and I was mercifully preserved for better things. It was then, however, my heavy lot to weep, weep, weep, and that for years; to pass from one misery to another, and from one cruel master to a worse. But I must go on with the thread of my story.

One day a heavy squall of wind and rain came on suddenly, and my mistress sent me round the corner of the house to empty a large earthen jar. The jar was already cracked with an old deep crack that divided it in the middle, and in turning it upside down to empty it, it parted in my hand. I could not help the accident, but I was dreadfully frightened, looking forward to a severe punishment. I ran crying to my mistress, "O mistress, the jar has come in two." "You have broken it, have you?" she replied; "come directly here to me." I came trembling: she stripped and flogged me long and severely with the cow-skin; as long as she had strength to use the lash, for she did not give over till she was quite tired.—When my master came home at night, she told him of my fault; and oh, frightful! how he fell a swearing. After abusing me with every ill name he could think of, (too, too bad to speak in England,) and giving me several heavy blows with his hand, he said, "I shall come home to-morrow morning at twelve, on purpose to give you a round hundred." He kept his word—Oh sad for me! I cannot easily forget it. He tied me up upon a ladder, and gave me a hundred lashes with his own hand, and master Benjy stood by to count them for him. When he had licked me for some time he sat down to take breath; then after resting, he beat me again and again, until he was quite wearied, and so hot (for the weather was very sultry), that he sank back in his chair, almost like to faint. While my mistress went to bring him drink, there was a dreadful earthquake. Part of the roof fell down, and every thing in the house went—clatter, clatter, clatter. Oh I thought the end of all things near at hand; and I was so sore with the flogging, that I scarcely cared whether I lived or died. The earth was groaning and shaking; every thing tumbling about; and my mistress and the slaves were shrieking and crying out, "The earthquake! the earthquake!" It was an awful day for us all.

During the confusion I crawled away on my hands and knees, and laid myself down under the steps of the piazza, in front of the house. I was in a dreadful state—my body all blood and bruises, and I could not help moaning piteously. The other slaves, when they saw me, shook their heads and said, "Poor child! poor child!"—I lay there till the morning, careless of what might happen, for life was very weak in me, and I wished more than ever to die. But when we are very young, death always seems a great way off, and it would not come that night to me. The next morning I was forced by my master to rise and go about my usual work, though my body and limbs were so stiff and sore, that I could not move without the greatest pain.— Nevertheless, even after all this severe punishment, I never heard the last of that jar; my mistress was always throwing it in my face.

Some little time after this, one of the cows got loose from the stake, and eat one of the sweet-potatoe slips. I was milking when my master found it out. He came to me, and without any more ado, stooped down, and taking off his heavy boot, he struck me such a severe blow in the small of my back, that I shrieked with agony, and thought I was killed; and I feel a weakness in that part to this day. The cow was frightened at his violence, and kicked down the pail and split the milk all about. My master knew that this accident was his own fault, but he was so enraged that he seemed glad of an excuse to go on with his ill usage. I cannot remember how many licks he gave me then, but he beat me till I was unable to stand, and till he himself was weary.

After this I ran away and went to my mother, who was living with Mr. Richard Darrel. My poor mother was both grieved and glad to see me; grieved because I had been so ill used, and glad because she had not seen me for a long, long while. She dared not receive me into the house, but she hid me up in a hole in the rocks near, and brought me food at night, after every body was asleep. My father, who lived at Crow-Lane, over the salt-water channel, at last heard of my being hid up in the cavern, and he came and took me back to my master. Oh I was loth, loth to go back; but as there was no remedy, I was obliged to submit.

When we got home, my poor father said to Capt. I——, "Sir, I am sorry that my child should be forced to run away from her owner; but the treatment she has received is enough to break her heart. The sight of her wounds has nearly broke mine. —I entreat you, for the love of God, to forgive her for running away, and that you will be a kind master to her in future." Capt. I—— said I was used as well as I deserved, and that I ought to be punished for running away. I then took courage and said that I could stand the floggings no longer; that I was weary of my life, and therefore I had run away to my mother; but mothers could only weep and mourn over their children, they could not save them from cruel masters—from the whip, the rope, and the cow-skin. He told me to hold my tongue and go about my work, or he would find a way to settle me. He did not, however, flog me that day.

For five years after this I remained in his house, and almost daily received the same harsh treatment. At length he put me on board a sloop, and to my great joy sent me away to Turk's Island.[13] I was not permitted to see my mother or father, or poor sisters and brothers, to say good bye, though going away to a strange land, and might never see them again. Oh the Buckra people who keep slaves think that black people are like cattle, without natural affection. But my heart tells me it is far otherwise.

We were nearly four weeks on the voyage, which was unusually long. Sometimes we had a light breeze, sometimes a great calm, and the ship made no way; so that our provisions and water ran very low, and we were put upon short allowance. I should almost have been starved had it not been for the kindness of a black man called Anthony, and his wife, who had brought their own victuals, and shared them with me.

When we went ashore at the Grand Quay, the captain sent me to the house of my new master, Mr. D——, to whom Captain I—— had sold me. Grand Quay is a small town upon a sandbank; the houses low and built of wood. Such was my new master's. The first person I saw, on my arrival, was

---

Buckra: a term for people of European ancestry in various Black dialects of the Americas.

[13] The Turks Islands (Grand Turk and Salt Cay), now part of the Turks and Caicos Islands in the West Indies, had been settled by Bermudans in the mid-seventeenth century in order to establish a salt industry there.

Mr. D——, a stout sulky looking man, who carried me through the hall to show me to his wife and children. Next day I was put up by the vendue master to know how much I was worth, and I was valued at one hundred pounds currency.

My new master was one of the owners or holders of the salt ponds, and he received a certain sum for every slave that worked upon his premises, whether they were young or old. This sum was allowed him out of the profits arising from the salt works. I was immediately sent to work in the salt water with the rest of the slaves. This work was perfectly new to me. I was given a half barrel and a shovel, and had to stand up to my knees in the water, from four o'clock in the morning till nine, when we were given some Indian corn boiled in water, which we were obliged to swallow as fast as we could for fear the rain should come on and melt the salt. We were then called again to our tasks, and worked through the heat of the day; the sun flaming upon our heads like fire, and raising salt blisters in those parts which were not completely covered. Our feet and legs, from standing in the salt water for so many hours, soon became full of dreadful boils, which eat down in some cases to the very bone, afflicting the sufferers with great torment. We came home at twelve; ate our corn soup, called *blawly*, as fast as we could, and went back to our employment till dark at night. We then shovelled up the salt in large heaps, and went down to the sea, where we washed the pickle from our limbs, and cleaned the barrows and shovels from the salt. When we returned to the house, our master gave us each our allowance of raw Indian corn, which we pounded in a mortar and boiled in water for our suppers.

We slept in a long shed, divided into narrow slips, like the stalls used for cattle. Boards fixed upon stakes driven into the ground, without mat or covering, were our only beds. On Sundays, after we had washed the salt bags, and done other work required of us, we went into the bush and cut the long soft grass, of which we made trusses for our legs and feet to rest upon, for they were so full of the salt boils that we could get no rest lying upon the bare boards.

Though we worked from morning till night, there was no satisfying Mr. D——. I hoped, when I left Capt. I——, that I should have been better off, but I found it was but going from one butcher to another. There was this difference between them: my former master used to beat me while raging and foaming with passion; Mr. D—— was usually quite calm. He would stand by and give orders for a slave to be cruelly whipped, and assist in the punishment, without moving a muscle of his face; walking about and

---

pickle: salt brine.

taking snuff with the greatest composure. Nothing could touch his hard heart—neither sighs, nor tears, nor prayers, nor streaming blood; he was deaf to our cries, and careless of our sufferings.—Mr. D —— has often stripped me naked, hung me up by the wrists, and beat me with the cow-skin, with his own hand, till my body was raw with gashes. Yet there was nothing very remarkable in this; for it might serve as a sample of the common usage of the slaves on that horrible island.

Owing to the boils in my feet, I was unable to wheel the barrow fast through the sand, which got into the sores, and made me stumble at every step; and my master, having no pity for my sufferings from this cause, rendered them far more intolerable, by chastising me for not being able to move so fast as he wished me. Another of our employments was to row a little way off from the shore in a boat, and dive for large stones to build a wall round our master's house. This was very hard work; and the great waves breaking over us continually, made us often so giddy that we lost our footing, and were in danger of being drowned.

Ah, poor me!—my tasks were never ended. Sick or well, it was work—work—work!—After the diving season was over, we were sent to the South Creek, with large bills, to cut up mangoes to burn lime with. Whilst one party of slaves were thus employed, another were sent to the other side of the island to break up coral out of the sea.

When we were ill, let our complaint be what it might, the only medicine given to us was a great bowl of hot salt water, with salt mixed with it, which made us very sick. If we could not keep up with the rest of the gang of slaves, we were put in the stocks, and severely flogged the next morning. Yet, not the less, our master expected, after we had thus been kept from our rest, and our limbs rendered stiff and sore with ill usage, that we should still go through the ordinary tasks of the day all the same.—Sometimes we had to work all night, measuring salt to load a vessel; or turning a machine to draw water out of the sea for the salt-making. Then we had no sleep—no rest—but were forced to work as fast as we could, and go on again all next day the same as usual. Work—work—work—Oh that Turk's Island was a horrible place! The people in England, I am sure, have never found out what is carried on there. Cruel, horrible place!

Mr. D —— had a slave called old Daniel, whom he used to treat in the most cruel manner. Poor Daniel was lame in the hip, and could not keep up with the rest of the slaves; and our master would order him to be stripped and laid down on the ground, and have him beaten with a rod of rough briar till his skin was quite red and raw. He would then call for a

---

bills: bill-hooks, thick knives with hooked ends used for cutting and pruning.

bucket of salt, and fling upon the raw flesh till the man writhed on the ground like a worm, and screamed aloud with agony. This poor man's wounds were never healed, and I have often seen them full of maggots, which increased his torments to an intolerable degree. He was an object of pity and terror to the whole gang of slaves, and in his wretched case we saw, each of us, our own lot, if we should live to be as old.

Oh the horrors of slavery!—How the thought of it pains my heart! But the truth ought to be told of it; and what my eyes have seen I think it is my duty to relate; for few people in England know what slavery is. I have been a slave—I have felt what a slave feels, and I know what a slave knows; and I would have all the good people in England to know it too, that they may break our chains, and set us free.

Mr. D—— had another slave called Ben. He being very hungry, stole a little rice one night after he came in from work, and cooked it for his supper. But his master soon discovered the theft; locked him up all night; and kept him without food till one o'clock the next day. He then hung Ben up by his hands, and beat him from time to time till the slaves came in at night. We found the poor creature hung up when we came home; with a pool of blood beneath him, and our master still licking him. But this was not the worst. My master's son was in the habit of stealing the rice and rum. Ben had seen him do this, and thought he might do the same, and when master found out that Ben had stolen the rice and swore to punish him, he tried to excuse himself by saying that Master Dickey did the same thing every night. The lad denied it to his father, and was so angry with Ben for informing against him, that out of revenge he ran and got a bayonet, and whilst the poor wretch was suspended by his hands and writhing under his wounds, he run it quite through his foot. I was not by when he did it, but I saw the wound when I came home, and heard Ben tell the manner in which it was done.

I must say something more about this cruel son of a cruel father—He had no heart—no fear of God; he had been brought up by a bad father in a bad path, and he delighted to follow in the same steps. There was a little old woman among the slaves called Sarah, who was nearly past work; and, Master Dickey being the overseer of the slaves just then, this poor creature, who was subject to several bodily infirmities, and was not quite right in her head, did not wheel the barrow fast enough to please him. He threw her down on the ground, and after beating her severely, he took her up in his arms and flung her among the prickly-pear bushes, which are all covered over with sharp venomous prickles. By this her naked flesh was so grievously wounded, that her body swelled and festered all over, and she died a few days after. In telling my own sorrows, I cannot pass by those of my fellow-slaves—for when I think of my own griefs, I remember theirs.

I think it was about ten years I had worked in the salt ponds at Turk's Island, when my master left off business, and retired to a house he had in Bermuda, leaving his son to succeed him in the island. He took me with him to wait upon his daughters; and I was joyful, for I was sick, sick of Turk's Island, and my heart yearned to see my native place again, my mother, and my kindred.

I had seen my poor mother during the time I was a slave in Turk's Island. One Sunday morning I was on the beach with some of the slaves, and we saw a sloop come in loaded with slaves to work in the salt water. We got a boat and went aboard. When I came upon the deck I asked the black people, "Is there any one here for me?" "Yes," they said, "your mother." I thought they said this in jest—I could scarcely believe them for joy; but when I saw my poor mammy my joy was turned to sorrow, for she had gone from her senses. "Mammy," I said, "is this you?" She did not know me. "Mammy," I said, "what's the matter?" She began to talk foolishly, and said that she had been under the vessel's bottom. They had been overtaken by a violent storm at sea. My poor mother had never been on the sea before, and she was so ill, that she lost her senses, and it was long before she came quite to herself again. She had a sweet child with her—a little sister I had never seen, about four years of age, called Rebecca. I took her on shore with me, for I felt I should love her directly; and I kept her with me a week. Poor little thing! her's has been a sad life, and continues so to this day. My mother worked for some years on the island, but was taken back to Bermuda some time before my master carried me again thither.[14]

After I left Turk's Island, I was told by some negroes that came over from it, that the poor slaves had built up a place with boughs and leaves, where they might meet for prayers, but the white people pulled it down twice, and would not allow them even a shed for prayers. A flood came down after and washed away many houses, filled the place with sand, and overflowed the ponds: and I do think that this was for their wickedness; for the Buckra men[15] there were very wicked. I saw and heard much that was very very bad at that place.

---

[14] Of the subsequent lot of her relatives she can tell but little. She says, her father died while she and her mother were at Turk's Island; and that he had been long dead and buried before any of his children in Bermuda knew of it, they being slaves on other estates. Her mother died after Mary went to Antigua. Of the fate of the rest of her kindred, seven brothers and three sisters, she knows nothing further than this—that the eldest sister, who had several children to her master, was taken by him to Trinidad; and that the youngest, Rebecca, is still alive, and in slavery in Bermuda. Mary herself is now about forty-three years of age.—*Ed.* [Pringle's note.]

[15] Negro term for white people. [Pringle's note.]

I was several years the slave of Mr. D —— after I returned to my native place. Here I worked in the grounds. My work was planting and hoeing sweet-potatoes, Indian corn, plaintains, bananas, cabbages, pumpkins, onions, &c. I did all the household work, and attended upon a horse and cow besides, — going also upon all errands. I had to curry the horse — to clean and feed him — and sometimes to ride him a little. I had more than enough to do — but still it was not so very bad as Turk's Island.

My old master often got drunk, and then he would get in a fury with his daughter, and beat her till she was not fit to be seen. I remember on one occasion, I had gone to fetch water, and when I was coming up the hill I heard a great screaming; I ran as fast as I could to the house, put down the water, and went into the chamber, where I found my master beating Miss D —— dreadfully. I strove with all my strength to get her away from him; for she was all black and blue with bruises. He had beat her with his fist, and almost killed her. The people gave me credit for getting her away. He turned round and began to lick me. Then I said, "Sir, this is not Turk's Island." I can't repeat his answer, the words were too wicked — too bad to say. He wanted to treat me the same in Bermuda as he had done in Turk's Island.

He had an ugly fashion of stripping himself quite naked, and ordering me then to wash him in a tub of water. This was worse to me than all the licks. Sometimes when he called me to wash him I would not come, my eyes were so full of shame. He would then come to beat me. One time I had plates and knives in my hand, and I dropped both plates and knives, and some of the plates were broken. He struck me so severely for this, that at last I defended myself, for I thought it was high time to do so. I then told him I would not live longer with him, for he was a very indecent man — very spiteful, and too indecent; with no shame for his servants, no shame for his own flesh. So I went away to a neighbouring house and sat down and cried till the next morning, when I went home again, not knowing what else to do.

After that I was hired to work at Cedar Hills, and every Saturday night I paid the money to my master. I had plenty of work to do there — plenty of washing; but yet I made myself pretty comfortable. I earned two dollars and a quarter a week, which is twenty pence a day.

During the time I worked there, I heard that Mr. John Wood was going to Antigua. I felt a great wish to go there, and I went to Mr. D ——, and asked him to let me go in Mr. Wood's service. Mr. Wood did not then want to purchase me; it was my own fault that I came under him, I was so anxious to go. It was ordained to be, I suppose; God led me there. The truth is, I did not wish to be any longer the slave of my indecent master.

Mr. Wood took me with him to Antigua,[16] to the town of St. John's, where he lived. This was about fifteen years ago. He did not then know whether I was to be sold; but Mrs. Wood found that I could work, and she wanted to buy me. Her husband then wrote to my master to inquire whether I was to be sold? Mr. D—— wrote in reply, "that I should not be sold to any one that would treat me ill." It was strange he should say this, when he had treated me so ill himself. So I was purchased by Mr. Wood for 300 dollars, (or £100 Bermuda currency.)[17]

My work there was to attend the chambers and nurse the child, and to go down to the pond and wash clothes. But I soon fell ill of the rheumatism, and grew so very lame that I was forced to walk with a stick. I got the Saint Anthony's fire, also, in my left leg, and became quite a cripple. No one cared much to come near me, and I was ill a long long time; for several months I could not lift the limb. I had to lie in a little old out-house, that was swarming with bugs and other vermin, which tormented me greatly; but I had no other place to lie in. I got the rheumatism by catching cold at the pond side, from washing in the fresh water; in the salt water I never got cold. The person who lived in next yard, (a Mrs. Greene,) could not bear to hear my cries and groans. She was kind, and used to send an old slave woman to help me, who sometimes brought me a little soup. When the doctor found I was so ill, he said I must be put into a bath of hot water. The old slave got the bark of some bush that was good for the pains, which she boiled in the hot water, and every night she came and put me into the bath, and did what she could for me: I don't know what I should have done, or what would have become of me, had it not been for her.—My mistress, it is true, did send me a little food; but no one from our family came near me but the cook, who used to shove my food in at the door, and say, "Molly, Molly, there's your dinner." My mistress did not care to take any trouble about me; and if the Lord had not put it into the hearts of the neighbours to be kind to me, I must, I really think, have lain and died.

It was a long time before I got well enough to work in the house. Mrs. Wood, in the meanwhile, hired a mulatto woman to nurse the child; but she was such a fine lady she wanted to be mistress over me. I thought it very hard for a coloured woman to have rule over me because I was a slave and she was free. Her name was Martha Wilcox; she was a saucy woman, very saucy; and she went and complained of me, without cause, to my mistress,

---

Saint Anthony's fire: name for various inflammatory or gangrenous skin diseases.

[16] Antigua, an island in the Caribbean, then a British possession largely devoted to sugar cultivation.

[17] About £67. 10s. sterling. [Pringle's note.]

and made her angry with me. Mrs. Wood told me that if I did not mind what I was about, she would get my master to strip me and give me fifty lashes: "You have been used to the whip," she said, "and you shall have it here." This was the first time she threatened to have me flogged; and she gave me the threatening so strong of what she would have done to me, that I thought I should have fallen down at her feet, I was so vexed and hurt by her words. The mulatto woman was rejoiced to have power to keep me down. She was constantly making mischief; there was no living for the slaves—no peace after she came.

I was also sent by Mrs. Wood to be put in the Cage one night, and was next morning flogged, by the magistrate's order, at her desire; and this all for a quarrel I had about a pig with another slave woman. I was flogged on my naked back on this occasion: although I was in no fault after all; for old Justice Dyett, when we came before him, said that I was in the right, and ordered the pig to be given to me. This was about two or three years after I came to Antigua.

When we moved from the middle of the town to the Point, I used to be in the house and do all the work and mind the children, though still very ill with the rheumatism. Every week I had to wash two large bundles of clothes, as much as a boy could help me to lift; but I could give no satisfaction. My mistress was always abusing and fretting after me. It is not possible to tell all her ill language.—One day she followed me foot after foot scolding and rating me. I bore in silence a great deal of ill words; at last my heart was quite full, and I told her that she ought not to use me so;—that when I was ill I might have lain and died for what she cared; and no one would then come near me to nurse me, because they were afraid of my mistress. This was a great affront. She called her husband and told him what I had said. He flew into a passion: but did not beat me then; he only abused and swore at me; and then gave me a note and bade me go and look for an owner. Not that he meant to sell me; but he did this to please his wife and to frighten me. I went to Adam White, a cooper, a free black, who had money, and asked him to buy me. He went directly to Mr. Wood, but was informed that I was not to be sold. The next day my master whipped me.

Another time (about five years ago) my mistress got vexed with me, because I fell sick and I could not keep on with my work. She complained to her husband, and he sent me off again to look for an owner. I went to a Mr. Burchell, showed him the note, and asked him to buy me for my own benefit; for I had saved about 100 dollars, and hoped, with a little help, to

---

cooper: one who makes and repairs casks and barrels.

purchase my freedom. He accordingly went to my master:—"Mr. Wood," he said, "Molly has brought me a note that she wants an owner. If you intend to sell her, I may as well buy her as another." My master put him off and said that he did not mean to sell me. I was very sorry at this, for I had no comfort with Mrs. Wood, and I wished greatly to get my freedom.

The way in which I made my money was this.—When my master and mistress went from home, as they sometimes did, and left me to take care of the house and premises, I had a good deal of time to myself, and made the most of it. I took in washing, and sold coffee and yams and other provisions to the captains of ships. I did not sit still idling during the absence of my owners; for I wanted, by all honest means, to earn money to buy my freedom. Sometimes I bought a hog cheap on board ship, and sold it for double the money on shore; and I also earned a good deal by selling coffee. By this means I by degrees acquired a little cash. A gentleman also lent me some to help to buy my freedom—but when I could not get free he got it back again. His name was Captain Abbot.

My master and mistress went on one occasion into the country, to Date Hill, for change of air, and carried me with them to take charge of the children, and to do the work of the house. While I was in the country, I saw how the field negroes are worked in Antigua. They are worked very hard and fed but scantily. They are called out to work before daybreak, and come home after dark; and then each has to heave his bundle of grass for the cattle in the pen. Then, on Sunday morning, each slave has to go out and gather a large bundle of grass; and, when they bring it home, they have all to sit at the manager's door and wait till he come out: often have they to wait there till past eleven o'clock, without any breakfast. After that, those that have yams or potatoes, or fire-wood to sell, hasten to market to buy a dog's worth[18] of salt fish, or pork, which is a great treat for them. Some of them buy a little pickle out of the shad barrels, which they call sauce, to season their yams and Indian corn. It is very wrong, I know, to work on Sunday or go to market; but will not God call the Buckra men to answer for this on the great day of judgment—since they will give the slaves no other day?

While we were at Date Hill Christmas came; and the slave woman who had the care of the place (which then belonged to Mr. Roberts the marshal), asked me to go with her to her husband's house, to a Methodist meeting for prayer, at a plantation called Winthorps. I went; and they were the first prayers I ever understood. One woman prayed; and then they all

---

[18] A dog is the 72nd part of a dollar. [Pringle's note.]

sung a hymn; then there was another prayer and another hymn; and then they all spoke by turns of their own griefs as sinners. The husband of the woman I went with was a black driver. His name was Henry. He confessed that he had treated the slaves very cruelly; but said that he was compelled to obey the orders of his master. He prayed them all to forgive him, and he prayed that God would forgive him. He said it was a horrid thing for a ranger[19] to have sometimes to beat his own wife or sister; but he must do so if ordered by his master.

I felt sorry for my sins also. I cried the whole night, but I was too much ashamed to speak. I prayed God to forgive me. This meeting had a great impression on my mind, and led my spirit to the Moravian church[20] so that when I got back to town, I went and prayed to have my name put down in the Missionaries' book; and I followed the church earnestly every opportunity. I did not then tell my mistress about it; for I knew that she would not give me leave to go. But I felt I *must* go. Whenever I carried the children their lunch at school, I ran round and went to hear the teachers.

The Moravian ladies (Mrs. Richter, Mrs. Olufsen, and Mrs. Sauter) taught me to read in the class; and I got on very fast. In this class there were all sorts of people, old and young, grey headed folks and children; but most of them were free people. After we had done spelling, we tried to read in the Bible. After the reading was over, the missionary gave out a hymn for us to sing. I dearly loved to go to the church, it was so solemn. I never knew rightly that I had much sin till I went there. When I found out that I was a great sinner, I was very sorely grieved, and very much frightened. I used to pray God to pardon my sins for Christ's sake, and forgive me for every thing I had done amiss; and when I went home to my work, I always thought about what I had heard from the missionaries, and wished to be good that I might go to heaven. After a while I was admitted a candidate for the holy Communion. — I had been baptized long before this, in August 1817, by the Rev. Mr. Curtin, of the English Church, after I had been taught to repeat the Creed and the Lord's Prayer. I wished at that time to attend a Sunday School taught by Mr. Curtin, but he would not receive me without a written note from my master, granting his permission. I did not ask my owner's permission, from the belief that it would be

---

[19]The head negro of an estate — a person who has the chief superintendence under the manager. [Pringle's note.]

[20]The Moravians were an evangelical Protestant denomination founded in the eighteenth century, who had begun sending missionaries to convert the Black slaves in the West Indies as early as 1732.

refused; so that I got no farther instruction at that time from the English Church.[21]

Some time after I began to attend the Moravian Church, I met with Daniel James, afterwards my dear husband. He was a carpenter and cooper to his trade; an honest, hard-working, decent black man, and a widower. He had purchased his freedom of his mistress, old Mrs. Baker, with money he had earned whilst a slave. When he asked me to marry him, I took time to consider the matter over with myself, and would not say yes till he went to church with me and joined the Moravians. He was very industrious after he bought his freedom; and he had hired a comfortable house, and had convenient things about him. We were joined in marriage, about Christmas 1826, in the Moravian Chapel at Spring Gardens, by the Rev. Mr. Olufsen. We could not be married in the English Church. English marriage is not allowed to slaves; and no free man can marry a slave woman.

When Mr. Wood heard of my marriage, he flew into a great rage, and sent for Daniel, who was helping to build a house for his old mistress. Mr. Wood asked him who gave him a right to marry a slave of his? My husband said, "Sir, I am a free man, and thought I had a right to choose a wife; but if I had known Molly was not allowed to have a husband, I should not have asked her to marry me." Mrs. Wood was more vexed about my marriage than her husband. She could not forgive me for getting married, but stirred up Mr. Wood to flog me dreadfully with the horsewhip. I thought it very hard to be whipped at my time of life for getting a husband—I told her so. She said that she would not have nigger men about the yards and premises, or allow a nigger man's clothes to be washed in the same tub where hers were washed. She was fearful, I think, that I should lose her time, in order to wash and do things for my husband: but I had then no time to wash for myself; I was obliged to put out my own clothes, though I was always at the wash-tub.

I had not much happiness in my marriage, owing to my being a slave. It made my husband sad to see me so ill-treated. Mrs. Wood was always abusing me about him. She did not lick me herself, but she got her husband to do it for her, whilst she fretted the flesh off my bones. Yet for all this she would not sell me. She sold five slaves whilst I was with her; but though she

---

[21] She possesses a copy of Mrs. [Sarah] Trimmer's "Charity School Spelling Book," presented to her by the Rev. Mr. Curtin, and dated August 30, 1817. In this book her name is written "Mary, Princess of Wales"—an appellation which, she says, was given her by her owners. It is a common practice with the colonists to give ridiculous names of this description to their slaves; being, in fact, one of the numberless modes of expressing the habitual contempt with which they regard the negro race. — In printing this narrative we have retained Mary's paternal name of Prince. — *Ed.* [Pringle's note.]

was always finding fault with me, she would not part with me. However, Mr. Wood afterwards allowed Daniel to have a place to live in our yard, which we were very thankful for.

After this, I fell ill again with the rheumatism, and was sick a long time; but whether sick or well, I had my work to do. About this time I asked my master and mistress to let me buy my own freedom. With the help of Mr. Burchell, I could have found the means to pay Mr. Wood; for it was agreed that I should afterwards serve Mr. Burchell a while, for the cash he was to advance for me. I was earnest in the request to my owners; but their hearts were hard—too hard to consent. Mrs. Wood was very angry—she grew quite outrageous—she called me a black devil, and asked me who had put freedom into my head. "To be free is very sweet," I said: but she took good care to keep me a slave. I saw her change colour, and I left the room.

About this time my master and mistress were going to England to put their son to school, and bring their daughters home; and they took me with them to take care of the child. I was willing to come to England: I thought that by going there I should probably get cured of my rheumatism, and should return with my master and mistress, quite well, to my husband. My husband was willing for me to come away, for he had heard that my master would free me,—and I also hoped this might prove true; but it was all a false report.

The steward of the ship was very kind to me. He and my husband were in the same class in the Moravian Church. I was thankful that he was so friendly, for my mistress was not kind to me on the passage; and she told me, when she was angry, that she did not intend to treat me any better in England than in the West Indies—that I need not expect it. And she was as good as her word.

When we drew near to England, the rheumatism seized all my limbs worse than ever and my body was dreadfully swelled. When we landed at the Tower,[22] I shewed my flesh to my mistress, but she took no great notice of it. We were obliged to stop at the tavern till my master got a house; and a day or two after, my mistress sent me down into the wash-house to learn to wash in the English way. In the West Indies we wash with cold water—in England with hot. I told my mistress I was afraid that putting my hands first into the hot water and then into the cold, would increase the pain in my limbs. The doctor had told my mistress long before I came from the West Indies, that I was a sickly body and the washing did not agree with me. But Mrs. Wood would not release me from the tub, so I was forced to do as I could. I grew worse, and could not stand to wash. I was then forced to sit

---

[22] Tower Stairs on the north bank of the Thames near the Tower of London.

down with the tub before me, and often through pain and weakness was reduced to kneel or to sit down on the floor, to finish my task. When I complained to my mistress of this, she only got into a passion as usual, and said washing in hot water could not hurt any one;—that I was lazy and insolent, and wanted to be free of my work; but that she would make me do it. I thought her very hard on me, and my heart rose up within me. However I kept still at that time, and went down again to wash the child's things; but the English washerwomen who were at work there, when they saw that I was so ill, had pity upon me and washed them for me.

After that, when we came up to live in Leigh Street, Mrs. Wood sorted out five bags of clothes which we had used at sea, and also such as had been worn since we came on shore, for me and the cook to wash. Elizabeth the cook told her, that she did not think that I was able to stand to the tub, and that she had better hire a woman. I also said myself, that I had come over to nurse the child, and that I was sorry I had come from Antigua, since mistress would work me so hard, without compassion for my rheumatism. Mr. and Mrs. Wood, when they heard this, rose up in a passion against me. They opened the door and bade me get out. But I was a stranger, and did not know one door in the street from another, and was unwilling to go away. They made a dreadful uproar, and from that day they constantly kept cursing and abusing me. I was obliged to wash, though I was very ill. Mrs. Wood, indeed once hired a washerwoman, but she was not well treated, and would come no more.

My master quarrelled with me another time, about one of our great washings, his wife having stirred him up to do so. He said he would compel me to do the whole of the washing given out to me, or if I again refused, he would take a short course with me: he would either send me down to the brig in the river, to carry me back to Antigua, or he would turn me at once out of doors, and let me provide for myself. I said I would willingly go back, if he would let me purchase my own freedom. But this enraged him more than all the rest: he cursed and swore at me dreadfully, and said he would never sell my freedom—if I wished to be free, I was free in England, and I might go and try what freedom would do for me, and be d——d. My heart was very sore with this treatment, but I had to go on. I continued to do my work, and did all I could to give satisfaction, but all would not do.

Shortly after, the cook left them, and then matters went on ten times worse. I always washed the child's clothes without being commanded to do it, and any thing else that was wanted in the family; though still I was very sick—very sick indeed. When the great washing came round, which was

---

d——d: damned.

every two months, my mistress got together again a great many heavy things, such as bed-ticks, bed-coverlets, &c, for me to wash. I told her I was too ill to wash such heavy things that day. She said, she supposed I thought myself a free woman, but I was not; and if I did not do it directly I should be instantly turned out of doors. I stood a long time before I could answer, for I did not know well what to do. I knew that I was free in England, but I did not know where to go, or how to get my living; and therefore, I did not like to leave the house. But Mr. Wood said he would send for a constable to thrust me out; and at last I took courage and resolved that I would not be longer thus treated, but would go and trust to Providence. This was the fourth time they had threatened to turn me out, and, go where I might, I was determined now to take them at their word; though I thought it very hard, after I had lived with them for thirteen years, and worked for them like a horse, to be driven out in this way, like a beggar. My only fault was being sick, and therefore unable to please my mistress, who thought she never could get work enough out of her slaves; and I told them so: but they only abused me and drove me out. This took place from two to three months, I think, after we came to England.

When I came away, I went to the man (one Mash) who used to black the shoes of the family, and asked his wife to get somebody to go with me to Hatton Garden to the Moravian Missionaries: these were the only persons I knew in England. The woman sent a young girl with me to the mission house, and I saw there a gentleman called Mr. Moore. I told him my whole story, and how my owners had treated me, and asked him to take in my trunk with what few clothes I had. The missionaries were very kind to me — they were sorry for my destitute situation, and gave me leave to bring my things to be placed under their care. They were very good people, and they told me to come to the church.

When I went back to Mr. Wood's to get my trunk, I saw a lady, Mrs. Pell, who was on a visit to my mistress. When Mr. and Mrs. Wood heard me come in, they set this lady to stop me, finding that they had gone too far with me. Mrs. Pell came out to me, and said, "Are you really going to leave, Molly? Don't leave, but come into the country with me." I believe she said this because she thought Mrs. Wood would easily get me back again. I replied to her, "Ma'am, this is the fourth time my master and mistress have driven me out, or threatened to drive me — and I will give them no more occasion to bid me go. I was not willing to leave them, for I am a stranger in this country, but now I must go — I can stay no longer to be so used." Mrs. Pell then went up stairs to my mistress, and told that I would go, and

---

bed-ticks: bedtick, large bag or case stuffed with feathers, straw, or the like for bedding.

that she could not stop me. Mrs. Wood was very much hurt and frightened when she found I was determined to go out that day. She said, "If she goes the people will rob her, and then turn her adrift." She did not say this to me, but she spoke it loud enough for me to hear; that it might induce me not to go, I suppose. Mr. Wood also asked me where I was going to. I told him where I had been, and that I should never have gone away had I not been driven out by my owners. He had given me a written paper some time before, which said that I had come with them to England by my own desire; and that was true. It said also that I left them of my own free will, because I was a free woman in England; and that I was idle and would not do my work—which was not true. I gave this paper afterwards to a gentleman who inquired into my case.[23]

I went into the kitchen and got my clothes out. The nurse and the servant girl were there, and I said to the man who was going to take out my trunk, "Stop, before you take up this trunk, and hear what I have to say before these people. I am going out of this house, as I was ordered; but I have done no wrong at all to my owners, neither here nor in the West Indies. I always worked very hard to please them, both by night and day; but there was no giving satisfaction, for my mistress could never be satisfied with reasonable service. I told my mistress I was sick, and yet she has ordered me out of doors. This is the fourth time; and now I am going out."

And so I came out, and went and carried my trunk to the Moravians. I then returned back to Mash the shoe-black's house, and begged his wife to take me in. I had a little West Indian money in my trunk; and they got it changed for me. This helped to support me for a little while. The man's wife was very kind to me. I was very sick, and she boiled nourishing things up for me. She also sent for a doctor to see me, and he sent me medicine, which did me good, though I was ill for a long time with the rheumatic pains. I lived a good many months with these poor people, and they nursed me, and did all that lay in their power to serve me. The man was well acquainted with my situation, as he used to go to and fro to Mr. Wood's house to clean shoes and knives; and he and his wife were sorry for me.

About this time, a woman of the name of Hill told me of the Anti-Slavery Society, and went with me to their office, to inquire if they could do any thing to get me my freedom, and send me back to the West Indies. The gentlemen of the Society took me to a lawyer, who examined very strictly into my case; but told me that the laws of England could do nothing to

---

[23] See page [266]. [Pringle's note.]

make me free in Antigua.[24] However they did all they could for me: they gave me a little money from time to time to keep me from want; and some of them went to Mr. Wood to try to persuade him to let me return a free woman to my husband; but though they offered him, as I have heard, a large sum for my freedom, he was sulky and obstinate, and would not consent to let me go free.

This was the first winter I spent in England, and I suffered much from the severe cold, and from the rheumatic pains, which still at times torment me. However, Providence was very good to me, and I got many friends — especially some Quaker ladies, who hearing of my case, came and sought me out, and gave me good warm clothing and money. Thus I had great cause to bless God in my affliction.

When I got better I was anxious to get some work to do, as I was unwilling to eat the bread of idleness. Mrs. Mash, who was a laundress, recommended me to a lady for a charwoman. She paid me very handsomely for what work I did, and I divided the money with Mrs. Mash; for though very poor, they gave me food when my own money was done, and never suffered me to want.

In the spring, I got into service with a lady, who saw me at the house where I sometimes worked as a charwoman. This lady's name was Mrs. Forsyth. She had been in the West Indies, and was accustomed to Blacks, and liked them. I was with her six months, and went with her to Margate. She treated me well, and gave me a good character when she left London.[25]

After Mrs. Forsyth went away, I was again out of place, and went to lodgings, for which I paid two shillings a week, and found coals and candle. After eleven weeks, the money I had saved in service was all gone, and I was forced to go back to the Anti-Slavery office to ask a supply, till I could get another situation. I did not like to go back — I did not like to be idle. I would rather work for my living than get it for nothing. They were very good to give me a supply, but I felt shame at being obliged to apply for relief whilst I had strength to work.

At last I went into the service of Mr. and Mrs. Pringle, where I have been ever since, and am as comfortable as I can be while separated from my dear husband, and away from my own country and all old friends and connections. My dear mistress teaches me daily to read the word of God, and takes

---

charwoman: lower household servant, hired by the day for chores and odd jobs.

[24] She came first to the Anti-Slavery Office in Aldermanbury, about the latter end of November 1828; and her case was referred to Mr. George Stephen to be investigated. More of this hereafter. — Ed. [Pringle's note.]

[25] She refers to a written certificate which will be inserted afterwards. [Pringle's note.]

great pains to make me understand it. I enjoy the great privilege of being enabled to attend church three times on the Sunday; and I have met with many kind friends since I have been here, both clergymen and others. The Rev. Mr. Young, who lives in the next house, has shown me much kindness, and taken much pains to instruct me, particularly while my master and mistress were absent in Scotland. Nor must I forget, among my friends, the Rev. Mr. Mortimer, the good clergyman of the parish, under whose ministry I have now sat for upwards of twelve months. I trust in God I have profited by what I have heard from him. He never keeps back the truth, and I think he has been the means of opening my eyes and ears much better to understand the word of God. Mr. Mortimer tells me that he cannot open the eyes of my heart, but that I must pray to God to change my heart, and make me to know the truth, and the truth will make me free.

I still live in the hope that God will find a way to give me my liberty, and give me back to my husband. I endeavour to keep down my fretting, and to leave all to Him, for he knows what is good for me better than I know myself. Yet, I must confess, I find it a hard and heavy task to do so.

I am often much vexed, and I feel great sorrow when I hear some people in this country say, that the slaves do not need better usage, and do not want to be free.[26] They believe the foreign people,[27] who deceive them, and say slaves are happy. I say, Not so. How can slaves be happy when they have the halter round their neck and the whip upon their back? and are disgraced and thought no more of than beasts? — and are separated from their mothers, and husbands, and children, and sisters, just as cattle are sold and separated? Is it happiness for a driver in the field to take down his wife or sister or child, and strip them, and whip them in such a disgraceful manner? — women that have had children exposed in the open field to shame! There is no modesty or decency shown by the owner to his slaves; men, women, and children are exposed alike. Since I have been here I have often wondered how English people can go out into the West Indies and act in such a beastly manner. But when they go to the West Indies, they forget God and all feeling of shame, I think, since they can see and do such things. They tie up slaves like hogs—moor[28] them up like cattle, and they lick them, so as hogs, or cattle, or horses never were flogged,—and yet they

---

[26] The whole of this paragraph especially, is given as nearly as was possible in Mary's precise words. [Pringle's note.]

[27] She means West Indians. [Pringle's note.]

[28] A West Indian phrase: to fasten or tie up. [Pringle's note.]

come home and say, and make some good people believe, that slaves don't want to get out of slavery. But they put a cloak about the truth. It is not so. All slaves want to be free—to be free is very sweet. I will say the truth to English people who may read this history that my good friend, Miss S——, is now writing down for me. I have been a slave myself—I know what slaves feel—I can tell by myself what other slaves feel, and by what they have told me. The man that says slaves be quite happy in slavery—that they don't want to be free—that man is either ignorant or a lying person. I never heard a slave say so. I never heard a Buckra man say so, till I heard tell of it in England. Such people ought to be ashamed of themselves. They can't do without slaves, they say. What's the reason they can't do without slaves as well as in England? No slaves here—no whips—no stocks—no punishment, except for wicked people. They hire servants in England; and if they don't like them, they send them away: they can't lick them. Let them work ever so hard in England, they are far better off than slaves. If they get a bad master, they give warning and go hire to another. They have their liberty. That's just what *we* want. We don't mind hard work, if we had proper treatment, and proper wages like English servants, and proper time given in the week to keep us from breaking the Sabbath. But they won't give it: they will have work—work—work, night and day, sick or well, till we are quite done up; and we must not speak up nor look amiss, however much we be abused. And then when we are quite done up, who cares for us, more than for a lame horse? This is slavery. I tell it, to let English people know the truth; and I hope they will never leave off to pray God, and call loud to the great King of England, till all the poor blacks be given free, and slavery done up for evermore.

Supplement to the
History of Mary Prince.

By the Editor.

LEAVING Mary's narrative, for the present, without comment to the reader's reflections, I proceed to state some circumstances connected with her case which have fallen more particularly under my own notice, and which I consider it incumbent now to lay fully before the public.

About the latter end of November, 1828, this poor woman found her way to the office of the Anti-Slavery Society in Aldermanbury, by the aid of a person who had become acquainted with her situation, and had advised her to apply there for advice and assistance. After some preliminary examination into the accuracy of the circumstances related by her, I went along with her to Mr. George Stephen, solicitor, and requested him to investigate and draw up a statement of her case, and have it submitted to counsel, in order to ascertain whether or not, under the circumstances, her freedom could be legally established on her return to Antigua. On this occasion, in Mr. Stephen's presence and mine, she expressed, in very strong terms, her anxiety to return thither if she could go as a free person, and, at the same time, her extreme apprehensions of the fate that would probably await her if she returned as a slave. Her words were, "I would rather go into my grave than go back a slave to Antigua, though I wish to go back to my husband very much—very much—very much! I am much afraid my owners would separate me from my husband, and use me very hard, or perhaps sell me for a field negro;—and slavery is too too bad. I would rather go into my grave!"

The paper which Mr. Wood had given her before she left his house, was placed by her in Mr. Stephen's hands. It was expressed in the following terms:—

"I have already told Molly, and now give it her in writing, in order that there may be no misunderstanding on her part, that as I brought her from Antigua at her own request and entreaty, and that she is consequently now free, she is of course at liberty to take her baggage and go where she pleases. And, in consequence of her late conduct, she must do one of two things— either quit the house, or return to Antigua by the earliest opportunity, as she does not evince a disposition to make herself useful. As she is a stranger in London, I do not wish to turn her out, or would do so, as two female servants are sufficient for my establishment. If after this she does remain, it will be only during her good behaviour: but on no consideration will I allow her wages or any other remuneration for her services.

"JOHN A. WOOD."

"London, August 18, 1828."

This paper, though not devoid of inconsistencies, which will be apparent to any attentive reader, is craftily expressed; and was well devised to serve the purpose which the writer had obviously in view, namely, to frustrate any appeal which the friendless black woman might make to the sympathy of strangers, and thus prevent her from obtaining an asylum, if she left his house, from any respectable family. As she had no one to refer to for a character in this country except himself, he doubtless calculated securely on her being speedily driven back, as soon as the slender fund she had in her possession was expended, to throw herself unconditionally upon his tender mercies; and his disappointment in this expectation appears to have exasperated his feelings of resentment towards the poor woman, to a degree which few persons alive to the claims of common justice, not to speak of christianity or common humanity, could easily have anticipated. Such, at least, seems the only intelligible inference that can be drawn from his subsequent conduct.

The case having been submitted, by desire of the Anti-Slavery Committee, to the consideration of Dr. Lushington and Mr. Sergeant Stephen, it was found that there existed no legal means of compelling Mary's master to grant her manumission; and that if she returned to Antigua, she would inevitably fall again under his power, or that of his attorneys, as a slave. It was, however, resolved to try what could be effected for her by amicable negotiation; and with this view Mr. Ravenscroft, a solicitor, (Mr. Stephen's relative,) called upon Mr. Wood, in order to ascertain whether he would consent to Mary's manumission on any reasonable terms, and to refer, if required, the amount of compensation for her value to arbitration. Mr. Ravenscroft with some difficulty obtained one or two interviews, but found Mr. Wood so full of animosity against the woman, and so firmly bent against any arrangement having her freedom for its object, that the negotiation was soon broken off as hopeless. The angry slave-owner declared "that he would not move a finger about her in this country, or grant her manumission on any terms whatever; and that if she went back to the West Indies, she must take the consequences."

This unreasonable conduct of Mr. Wood, induced the Anti-Slavery Committee, after several other abortive attempts to effect a compromise, to think of bringing the case under the notice of Parliament. The heads of Mary's statement were accordingly engrossed in a Petition, which Dr. Lushington offered to present, and to give notice at the same time of his intention to bring in a Bill to provide for the entire emancipation of all slaves brought to England with the owner's consent. But before this step was taken, Dr. Lushington again had recourse to negociation with the master; and, partly through the friendly intervention of Mr. Manning, partly by personal conference, used every persuasion in his power to induce Mr. Wood to relent and let the bondwoman go free. Seeing the matter thus seriously taken up, Mr. Wood became at length alarmed, — not relishing, it appears, the idea of having the case publicly discussed in the House of Commons; and to avert this result he submitted to temporize — assumed a demeanour of unwonted civility, and even hinted to Mr. Manning (as I was given to understand) that if he was not driven to utter hostility by the threatened exposure, he would probably meet our wishes "in his own time and way." Having gained time by these manœuvres, he adroitly endeavoured to cool the ardour of Mary's new friends, in her cause, by representing her as an abandoned and worthless woman, ungrateful towards him, and undeserving of sympathy from others; allegations which he supported

268 // MARY PRINCE

by the ready affirmation of some of his West India friends, and by one or two plausible letters procured from Antigua. By these and like artifices he appears completely to have imposed on Mr. Manning, the respectable West India merchant whom Dr. Lushington had asked to negotiate with him; and he prevailed so far as to induce Dr. Lushington himself (actuated by the benevolent view of thereby best serving Mary's cause,) to abstain from any remarks upon his conduct when the petition was at last presented in Parliament. In this way he dextrously contrived to neutralize all our efforts, until the close of the Session of 1829; soon after which he embarked with his family for the West Indies.

Every exertion for Mary's relief having thus failed; and being fully convinced from a twelvemonth's observation of her conduct, that she was really a well-disposed and respectable woman; I engaged her, in December 1829, as a domestic servant in my own family. In this capacity she has remained ever since; and I am thus enabled to speak of her conduct and character with a degree of confidence I could not have otherwise done. The importance of this circumstance will appear in the sequel.

From the time of Mr. Wood's departure to Antigua, in 1829, till June or July last, no farther effort was attempted for Mary's relief. Some faint hope was still cherished that this unconscionable man would at length relent, and "in his own time and way," grant the prayer of the exiled negro woman. After waiting, however, nearly twelvemonths longer, and seeing the poor woman's spirits daily sinking under the sickening influence of hope deferred, I resolved on a final attempt in her behalf, through the intervention of the Moravian Missionaries, and of the Governor of Antigua. At my request, Mr. Edward Moore, agent of the Moravian Brethren in London, wrote to the Rev. Joseph Newby, their Missionary in that island, empowering him to negotiate in his own name with Mr. Wood for Mary's manumission, and to procure his consent, if possible, upon terms of ample pecuniary compensation. At the same time the excellent and benevolent William Allen, of the Society of Friends,[29] wrote to Sir Patrick Ross, the Governor of the Colony, with whom he was on terms of friendship, soliciting him to use his influence in persuading Mr. Wood to consent: and I confess I was sanguine enough to flatter myself that we should thus at length prevail. The result proved, however, that I had not yet fully appreciated the character of the man we had to deal with.

---

[29]The Society of Friends or "Quakers," a dissenting Christian denomination dating to the seventeenth century and long associated with social reform efforts, were among the first to enlist in the antislavery cause.

Mr. Newby's answer arrived early in November last, mentioning that he had done all in his power to accomplish our purpose, but in vain; and that if Mary's manumission could not be obtained without Mr. Wood's consent, he believed there was no prospect of its ever being effected.

A few weeks afterwards I was informed by Mr. Allen, that he had received a letter from Sir Patrick Ross, stating that he also had used his best endeavours in the affair, but equally without effect. Sir Patrick at the same time inclosed a letter, addressed by Mr. Wood to his Secretary, Mr. Taylor, assigning his reasons for persisting in this extraordinary course. This letter requires our special attention. Its tenor is as follows: —

"My dear Sir,

"In reply to your note relative to the woman Molly, I beg you will have the kindness to oblige me by assuring his Excellency that I regret exceedingly my inability to comply with his request, which under other circumstances would afford me very great pleasure.

"There are many and powerful reasons for inducing me to refuse my sanction to her returning here in the way she seems to wish. It would be to reward the worst species of ingratitude, and subject myself to insult whenever she came in my way. Her moral character is very bad, as the police records will shew; and she would be a very troublesome character should she come here without any restraint. She is not a native of this country, and I know of no relation she has here. I induced her to take a husband, a short time before she left this, by providing a comfortable house in my yard for them, and prohibiting her going out after 10 to 12 o'clock (our bed-time) without special leave. This she considered the greatest, and indeed the only, grievance she ever complained of, and all my efforts could not prevent it. In hopes of inducing her to be steady to her husband, who was a free man, I gave him the house to occupy during our absence; but it appears the attachment was too loose to bind her, and he has taken another wife: so on that score I do her no injury. — In England she made her election, and quitted my family. This I had no right to object to; and I should have thought no more of it, but not satisfied to leave quietly, she gave every trouble and annoyance in her power, and endeavoured to injure the character of my family by the most vile and infamous falsehoods, which was embodied in a petition to the House of Commons, and would have been presented, had not my friends from this island, particularly the Hon. Mr. Byam and Dr. Coull, come forward, and disproved what she had asserted.

"It would be beyond the limits of an ordinary letter to detail her baseness, though I will do so should his Excellency wish it; but you may judge of her depravity by one circumstance, which came out before Mr. Justice Dyett, in a quarrel with another female.

✦   ✦   ✦

"Such a thing I could not have believed possible.[30]

"Losing her value as a slave in a pecuniary point of view I consider of no consequence; for it was our intention, had she conducted herself properly and returned with us, to have given her freedom. She has taken her freedom; and all I wish is, that she would enjoy it without meddling with me.

"Let me again repeat, if his Excellency wishes it, it will afford me great pleasure to state such particulars of her, and which will be incontestably proved by numbers here, that I am sure will acquit me in his opinion of acting unkind or ungenerous towards her. I'll say nothing of the liability I should incur, under the Consolidated Slave Law, of dealing with a free person as a slave.

"My only excuse for entering so much into detail must be that of my anxious wish to stand justified in his Excellency's opinion.

"*I am, my dear Sir,*
Yours very truly,
JOHN A. WOOD.
"20th Oct. 1830."

"*Charles Taylor, Esq.*
&c. &c. &c.

"I forgot to mention that it was at her own special request that she accompanied me to England—and also that she had a considerable sum of money with her, which she had saved in my service. I knew of £36 to £40, at least, for I had some trouble to recover it from a white man, to whom she had lent it.

"*J.A.W.*"

Such is Mr. Wood's justification of his conduct in thus obstinately refusing manumission to the Negro-woman who had escaped from his "house of bondage."

Let us now endeavour to estimate the validity of the excuses assigned, and the allegations advanced by him, for the information of Governor Sir Patrick Ross, in this deliberate statement of his case.

1. To allow the woman to return home free, would, he affirms "be to reward the worst species of ingratitude."

He assumes, it seems, the sovereign power of pronouncing a virtual sentence of banishment, for the alleged crime of ingratitude. Is this then a power which any man ought to possess over his fellow-mortal? or which any good man would ever wish to exercise? And, besides, there is no evidence whatever, beyond Mr. Wood's mere assertion, that Mary Prince owed him or his family the slightest mark of gratitude. Her account of the

---

[30] I omit the circumstance here mentioned, because it is too indecent to appear in a publication likely to be perused by females. It is, in all probability, a vile calumny; but even if it were perfectly true, it would not serve Mr. Wood's case one straw.—Any reader who wishes it, may see the passage referred to, in the autograph letter in my possession. T.P. [Pringle's note.]

treatment she received in his service, *may* be incorrect; but her simple statement is at least supported by minute and feasible details, and, unless rebutted by positive facts, will certainly command credence from impartial minds more readily than his angry accusation, which has something absurd and improbable in its very front. Moreover, is it not absurd to term the assertion of her *natural rights* by a slave,—even supposing her to have been kindly dealt with by her "owners," and treated in every respect the reverse of what Mary affirms to have been her treatment by Mr. Wood and his wife,—"the *worst* species of ingratitude?" This may be West Indian ethics, but it will scarcely be received as sound doctrine in Europe.

2. To permit her return would be "to subject himself to insult whenever she came in his way."

This is a most extraordinary assertion. Are the laws of Antigua then so favourable to the free blacks, or the colonial police so feebly administered, that there are no sufficient restraints to protect a rich colonist like Mr. Wood,—a man who counts among his familiar friends the Honourable Mr. Byam, and Mr. Taylor the Government Secretary,—from being insulted by a poor Negro-woman? It is preposterous.

3. Her moral character is so bad, that she would prove very troublesome should she come to the colony "without any restraint."

"Any restraint?" Are there no restraints (supposing them necessary) short of absolute slavery to keep "troublesome characters" in order? But this, I suppose, is the *argumentum ad gubernatorem*—to frighten the governor. She is such a termagant, it seems, that if she once gets back to the colony *free,* she will not only make it too hot for poor Mr. Wood, but the police and courts of justice will scarce be a match for her! Sir Patrick Ross, no doubt, will take care how he intercedes farther for so formidable a virago! How can one treat such arguments seriously?

4. She is not a native of the colony, and he knows of no relation she has there.

True: But was it not her home (so far as a slave can have a home) for thirteen or fourteen years? Were not the connexions, friendships, and associations of her mature life formed there? Was it not there she hoped to spend her latter years in domestic tranquillity with her husband, free from the lash of the taskmaster? These considerations may appear light to Mr. Wood, but they are every thing to this poor woman.

---

termagant: violent, quarrelsome woman.
virago: overbearing, powerful, manlike woman.

5. He induced her, he says, to take a husband, a short time before she left Antigua, and gave them a comfortable house in his yard, &c. &c.

This paragraph merits attention. He "*induced her to take a husband?*" If the fact were true, what brutality of mind and manners does it not indicate among these slave-holders? They refuse to legalize the marriages of their slaves, but *induce* them to form such temporary connexions as may suit the owner's conveniency, just as they would pair the lower animals; and this man has the effrontery to tell us so! Mary, however, tells a very different story, (see page [258];) and her assertion, independently of other proof, is at least as credible as Mr. Wood's. The reader will judge for himself as to the preponderance of internal evidence in the conflicting statements.

6. He alleges that she was, before marriage, licentious, and even depraved in her conduct, and unfaithful to her husband afterwards.

These are serious charges. But if true, or even partially true, how comes it that a person so correct in his family hours and arrangements as Mr. Wood professes to be, and who expresses so edifying a horror of licentiousness, could reconcile it to his conscience to keep in the bosom of his family so *depraved,* as well as so *troublesome* a character for at least thirteen years, and confide to her for long periods too the charge of his house and the care of his children—for such I shall shew to have been the facts? How can he account for not having rid himself with all speed, of so disreputable an inmate—he who values her loss so little "in a pecuniary point of view?" How can he account for having sold *five other slaves* in that period, and yet have retained this shocking woman—nay, even have refused to sell her, on more than one occasion, when offered her full value? It could not be from ignorance of her character, for the circumstance which he adduces as a proof of her shameless depravity, and which I have omitted on account of its indecency, occurred, it would appear, not less than *ten years ago.* Yet, notwithstanding her alleged ill qualities and habits of gross immorality, he has not only constantly refused to part with her; but after thirteen long years, brings her to England as an attendant on his wife and children, with the avowed intention of carrying her back along with his maiden daughter, a young lady returning from school! Such are the extraordinary facts; and until Mr. Wood shall reconcile these singular inconsistencies between his actions and his allegations, he must not be surprised if we in England prefer giving credit to the former rather than the latter; although at present it appears somewhat difficult to say which side of the alternative is the more creditable to his own character.

7. Her husband, he says, has taken another wife; "so that on that score," he adds, "he does her no injury."

Supposing this fact be true, (which I doubt, as I doubt every mere assertion from so questionable a quarter,) I shall take leave to put a question or two to Mr. Wood's conscience. Did he not write from England to his friend Mr. Darrel, soon after Mary left his house, directing him to turn her husband, Daniel James, off his premises, on account of her offence; telling him to inform James at the same time that his wife had *taken up* with another man, who had robbed her of all she had—a calumny as groundless as it was cruel? I further ask if the person who invented this story (whoever he may be,) was not likely enough to impose similar fabrications on the poor negro man's credulity, until he may have been induced to prove false to his marriage vows, and to "take another wife," as Mr. Wood coolly expresses it? But withal, I strongly doubt the fact of Daniel James' infidelity; for there is now before me a letter from himself to Mary, dated in April 1830, couched in strong terms of conjugal affection; expressing his anxiety for her speedy return, and stating that he had lately "received a grace" (a token of religious advancement) in the Moravian church, a circumstance altogether incredible if the man were living in open adultery, as Mr. Wood's assertion implies.

8. Mary, he says, endeavoured to injure the character of his family by infamous falsehoods, which were embodied in a petition to the House of Commons, and would have been presented, had not his friends from Antigua, the Hon. Mr. Byam, and Dr. Coull, disproved her assertions.

I can say something on this point from my own knowledge. Mary's petition contained simply a brief statement of her case, and, among other things, mentioned the treatment she had received from Mr. and Mrs. Wood. Now the principal facts are corroborated by other evidence, and Mr. Wood must bring forward very different testimony from that of Dr. Coull before well-informed persons will give credit to his contradiction. The value of that person's evidence in such cases will be noticed presently. Of the Hon. Mr. Byam I know nothing, and shall only at present remark that it is not likely to redound greatly to his credit to appear in such company. Furthermore, Mary's petition *was* presented, as Mr. Wood ought to know; though it was not discussed, nor his conduct exposed as it ought to have been.

9. He speaks of the liability he should incur, under the Consolidated Slave Law, of dealing with a free person as a slave.

Is not this pretext hypocritical in the extreme? What liability could he possibly incur by voluntarily resigning the power, conferred on him by an iniquitous colonial law, of re-imposing the shackles of slavery on the bondwoman from whose limbs they had fallen when she touched the free soil of

England?—There exists no liability from which he might not have been easily secured, or for which he would not have been fully compensated.

He adds in a postscript that Mary had a considerable sum of money with her,—from £36 to £40 at least, which she had saved in his service. The fact is, that she had at one time 113 dollars in cash; but only a very small portion of that sum appears to have been brought by her to England, the rest having been partly advanced, as she states, to assist her husband, and partly lost by being lodged in unfaithful custody.

Finally, Mr. Wood repeats twice that it will afford him great pleasure to state for the governor's satisfaction, if required, such particulars of "the woman Molly," upon incontestable evidence, as he is sure will acquit him in his Excellency's opinion "of acting unkind or ungenerous towards her."

This is well: and I now call upon Mr. Wood to redeem his pledge;—to bring forward facts and proofs fully to elucidate the subject;—to reconcile, if he can, the extraordinary discrepancies which I have pointed out between his assertions and the actual facts, and especially between his account of Mary Prince's character and his own conduct in regard to her. He has now to produce such a statement as will acquit him not only in the opinion of Sir Patrick Ross, but of the British public. And in this position he has spontaneously placed himself, in attempting to destroy, by his deliberate criminatory letter, the poor woman's fair fame and reputation,—an attempt but for which the present publication would probably never have appeared.

Here perhaps we might safely leave the case to the judgment of the public; but as this negro woman's character, not the less valuable to her because her condition is so humble, has been so unscrupulously blackened by her late master, a party so much interested and inclined to place her in the worst point of view,—it is incumbent on me, as her advocate with the public, to state such additional testimony in her behalf as I can fairly and conscientiously adduce.

My first evidence is Mr. Joseph Phillips, of Antigua. Having submitted to his inspection Mr. Wood's letter and Mary Prince's narrative, and requested his candid and deliberate sentiments in regard to the actual facts of the case, I have been favoured with the following letter from him on the subject:—

"London, January 18, 1831.

"Dear Sir,

"In giving you my opinion of Mary Prince's narrative, and of Mr. Wood's letter respecting her, addressed to Mr. Taylor, I shall first mention my opportunities of forming a proper estimate of the conduct and character of both parties.

"I have known Mr. Wood since his first arrival in Antigua in 1803. He was then a poor young man, who had been brought up as a ship carpenter in Bermuda. He was afterwards raised to be a clerk in the Commissariat department, and realised sufficient capital to commence business as a merchant. This last profession he has followed successfully for a good many years, and is understood to have accumulated very considerable wealth. After he entered into trade, I had constant intercourse with him in the way of business; and in 1824 and 1825, I was regularly employed on his premises as his clerk; consequently, I had opportunities of seeing a good deal of his character both as a merchant and as a master of slaves. The former topic I pass over as irrelevant to the present subject: in reference to the latter, I shall merely observe that he was not, in regard to ordinary matters, more severe than the ordinary run of slave owners; but, if seriously offended, he was not of a disposition to be easily appeased, and would spare no cost or sacrifice to gratify his vindictive feelings. As regards the exaction of work from domestic slaves, his wife was probably more severe than himself—it was almost impossible for the slaves ever to give her entire satisfaction.

"Of their slave Molly (or Mary) I know less than of Mr. and Mrs. Wood; but I saw and heard enough of her, both while I was constantly employed on Mr. Wood's premises, and while I was there occasionally on business, to be quite certain that she was viewed by her owners as their most respectable and trust-worthy female slave. It is within my personal knowledge that she had usually the charge of the house in their absence, was entrusted with the keys, &c.; and was always considered by the neighbours and visitors as their confidential household servant, and as a person in whose integrity they placed unlimited confidence,—although when Mrs. Wood was at home, she was no doubt kept pretty closely at washing and other hard work. A decided proof of the estimation in which she was held by her owners exists in the fact that Mr. Wood uniformly refused to part with her, whereas he sold five other slaves while she was with them. Indeed, she always appeared to me to be a slave of superior intelligence and respectability; and I always understood such to be her general character in the place.

"As to what Mr. Wood alleges about her being frequently before the police, &c. I can only say I never heard of the circumstance before; and as I lived for twenty years in the same small town, and in the vicinity of their residence, I think I could scarcely have failed to become acquainted with it, had such been the fact. She might, however, have been occasionally before the magistrate in consequence of little disputes among the slaves, without any serious imputation on her general respectability. She says she was twice summoned to appear as a witness on such occasions; and that she was once sent by her mistress to be confined in the Cage, and was afterwards flogged by her desire. This cruel practice is very common in Antigua; and, in my opinion, is but little creditable to the slave owners and magistrates by whom such arbitrary punishments are inflicted, frequently for very trifling faults. Mr. James Scotland is the only magistrate in the colony who invariably refuses to sanction this reprehensible practice.

"Of the immoral conduct ascribed to Molly by Mr. Wood, I can say nothing further than this—that I have heard she had at a former period (previous to her marriage) a connexion with a white person, a Capt. ———, which I have no doubt was broken off when she became seriously impressed with religion. But, at any rate, such connexions are so common, I might almost say universal, in our slave colonies, that except by the missionaries and a few serious persons, they are considered, if faults at all, so very venial as scarcely to deserve the name of immorality. Mr. Wood knows this colonial estimate of such connexions as well as I do; and, however false such an estimate must be allowed to be, especially when applied to their own conduct by persons of education, pretending to adhere to the pure Christian rule of morals,—yet when he ascribes to a negro slave, to whom legal marriage was denied, such great criminality for laxity of this sort, and professes to be so exceedingly shocked and amazed at the tale he himself relates, he must, I am confident, have had a farther object in view than the information of Mr. Taylor or Sir Patrick Ross. He must, it is evident, have been aware that his letter would be sent to Mr. Allen, and accordingly adapted it, as more important documents from the colonies are often adapted, *for effect in England.* The tale of the slave Molly's immoralities, be assured, was not intended for Antigua so much as for Stoke Newington, and Peckham, and Aldermanbury.

"In regard to Mary's narrative generally, although I cannot speak to the accuracy of the details, except in a few recent particulars, I can with safety declare that I see no reason to question the truth of a single fact stated by her, or even to suspect her in any instance of intentional exaggeration. It bears in my judgment the genuine stamp of truth and nature. Such is my unhesitating opinion, after a residence of twenty-seven years in the West Indies.

To T. Pringle, Esq.   "I remain, &c.   "JOSEPH PHILLIPS."

"P.S. As Mr. Wood refers to the evidence of Dr. T. Coull in opposition to Mary's assertions, it may be proper to enable you justly to estimate the worth of that person's evidence in cases connected with the condition and treatment of slaves. You are aware that in 1829, Mr. M'Queen of Glasgow, in noticing a Report of the "Ladies' Society of Birmingham for the relief of British Negro Slaves," asserted with his characteristic audacity, that the statement which it contained respecting distressed and deserted slaves in Antigua was "an abominable falsehood." Not contented with this, and with insinuating that I, as agent of the society in the distribution of their charity in Antigua, had fraudulently duped them out of their money by a fabricated tale of distress, Mr. M'Queen proceeded to libel me in the most opprobrious terms, as "a man of the most worthless and abandoned character."[31] Now I know from good authority that it was *upon Dr. Coull's information* that Mr. M'Queen founded this impudent contradiction of notorious facts, and this audacious libel of my personal character. From this single circumstance you may judge of the value of his evidence in the case of Mary Prince. I can furnish further infor-

---

[31] In elucidation of the circumstances above referred to, I subjoin the following extracts from the Report of the Birmingham Ladies' Society for 1830:—

"As a portion of the funds of this association has been appropriated to assist the benevolent efforts of a society which has for fifteen years afforded relief to distressed and deserted slaves in Antigua, it may not be uninteresting to our friends to learn the manner in which the agent of this society has been treated for simply obeying the command of our Saviour, by ministering, like the good Samaritan, to the distresses of the helpless and the desolate. The society's proceedings being adverted to by a friend of Africa, at one of the public meetings held in this country, a West Indian planter, who was present, wrote over to his friends in Antigua, and represented the conduct of the distributors of this charity in such a light, that it was deemed worthy of the cognizance of the House of Assembly. Mr. Joseph Phillips, a resident of the island, who had most kindly and disinterestedly exerted himself in the distribution of the money from England among the poor deserted slaves, was brought before the Assembly, and most severely interrogated: on his refusing to deliver up his private correspondence with his friends in England, he was thrown into a loathsome jail, where he was kept for nearly five months; while his loss of business, and the oppressive proceedings instituted against him, were involving him in poverty and ruin. On his discharge by the House of Assembly, he was seized in their lobby for debt, and again imprisoned."

"In our report for the year 1826, we quoted a passage from the 13th Report of the Society for the relief of deserted Slaves in the island of Antigua, in reference to a case of great distress. This statement fell into the hands of Mr. M'Queen, the Editor of the Glasgow Courier. Of the consequences resulting from this circumstance we only gained information through the Leicester Chronicle, which had copied an article from the Weekly Register of Antigua, dated St. John's, September 22, 1829. We find from this that Mr. M'Queen affirms, that 'with the exception of the fact that the society is, as it deserves to be, duped out of its money, the whole tale' (of the distress above referred to) 'is an abominable falsehood.' This statement, which we are informed has appeared in many of the public papers, is COMPLETELY REFUTED in our Appendix, No. 4, to which we refer our readers. Mr. M'Queen's statements, we regret to say, would lead many to believe that there are no deserted Negroes to assist; and that the case mentioned was a perfect fabrication. He also distinctly avers, that the disinterested and humane agent of the society, Mr. Joseph Phillips, is 'a man of the most worthless and abandoned character.' In opposition to this statement, we learn the good character of Mr. Phillips from those who have long been acquainted with his laudable exertions in the cause of humanity, and from the Editor of the Weekly Register of Antigua, who speaks, on his own knowledge, of more than twenty years back; confidently appealing at the same time to the inhabitants of the colony in which he resides for the truth of his averments, and producing a testimonial to Mr. Phillips's good character signed by two members of the Antigua House of Assembly, and by Mr. Wyke, the collector of his Majesty's customs, and by Antigua merchants, as follows—'that they have been acquainted with him the last four years and upwards, and he has always conducted himself in an upright becoming manner—his character we know to be unimpeached, and his morals unexceptionable.'

(Signed)　　　　　　"Thomas Saunderson　　　　John D. Taylor
　　　　　　　　　　　John A. Wood　　　　　　　　George Wyke
　　　　　　　　　　　Samuel L. Darrel　　　　　　Giles S. Musson
　　　　　　　　　　　　　Robert Grant."

"St. John's, Antigua, June 28, 1825."

In addition to the above testimonies, Mr. Phillips has brought over to England with him others of a more recent date, from some of the most respectable persons in Antigua—sufficient to cover with confusion all his unprincipled calumniators. See also his account of his own case in the Anti-Slavery Reporter, No. 74, p. 69. [Pringle's note.]

278 // MARY PRINCE

mation respecting Dr. Coull's colonial proceedings, both private and judicial, should circumstances require it." "J. P."

I leave the preceding letter to be candidly weighed by the reader in opposition to the inculpatory allegations of Mr. Wood—merely remarking that Mr. Wood will find it somewhat difficult to impugn the evidence of Mr. Phillips, whose "upright," "unimpeached," and "unexceptionable" character, he has himself vouched for in unqualified terms, by affixing his signature to the testimonial published in the Weekly Register of Antigua in 1825. (See Note [31].)

The next testimony in Mary's behalf is that of Mrs. Forsyth, a lady in whose service she spent the summer of 1829.—(See page [263].) This lady, on leaving London to join her husband, voluntarily presented Mary with a certificate, which, though it relates only to a recent and short period of her history, is a strong corroboration of the habitual respectability of her character. It is in the following terms:—

"Mrs. Forsyth states, that the bearer of this paper (Mary James,) has been with her for the last six months; that she has found her an excellent character, being honest, industrious, and sober; and that she parts with her on no other account than this— that being obliged to travel with her husband, who has lately come from abroad in bad health, she has no farther need of a servant. Any person wishing to engage her, can have her character in full from Miss Robson, 4, Keppel Street, Russel Square, whom Mrs. Forsyth has requested to furnish particulars to any one desiring them.

"4, Keppel Street, 28th Sept. 1829."

In the last place, I add my own testimony in behalf of this negro woman. Independently of the scrutiny, which, as Secretary of the Anti-Slavery Society, I made into her case when she first applied for assistance, at 18, Aldermanbury, and the watchful eye I kept upon her conduct for the ensuing twelvemonths, while she was the occasional pensioner of the Society, I have now had the opportunity of closely observing her conduct for fourteen months, in the situation of a domestic servant in my own family; and the following is the deliberate opinion of Mary's character, formed not only by myself, but also by my wife and sister-in-law, after this ample period of observation. We have found her perfectly honest and trustworthy in all respects; so that we have no hesitation in leaving every thing in the house at her disposal. She had the entire charge of the house during our absence in Scotland for three months last autumn, and conducted herself in that charge with the utmost discretion and fidelity. She is not, it is true, a very expert housemaid, nor capable of much hard work, (for her constitution appears to be a good deal broken,) but she is careful, industrious, and anxious to do her duty and to give satisfaction. She is capable of strong attachments, and feels deep, though unobtrusive, gratitude for real kindness shown her. She possesses considerable natural sense, and has much quickness of observation and discrimination of character. She is remarkable for *decency* and *propriety* of conduct—and her *delicacy*, even in trifling minutiæ, has been a trait of special remark by the females of my family. This trait, which is obviously quite unaffected, would be a most inexplicable anomaly, if her former habits had been so indecent and depraved as Mr. Wood alleges. Her chief faults, so far as we have discovered them, are, a somewhat violent and hasty temper, and a considerable share of natural pride and self-importance; but these defects have been but rarely and transiently manifested, and have scarcely occasioned an hour's uneasiness at any time in our household. Her religious knowledge, notwithstanding the pious care of her Moravian instructors in Antigua, is still but very limited, and her views of christianity indistinct; but her profession, whatever it may have of imperfection, I am convinced, has nothing of insincerity. In short, we consider her on the whole as respectable and well-behaved a person in her station, as any domestic, white or black, (and we have had ample experience of both colours,) that we have ever had in our service.

But after all, Mary's character, important though its exculpation be to her, is not really the point of chief practical interest in this case. Suppose all Mr. Wood's defamatory allegations to be true—suppose him to be able to rake up against her out of the records of the Antigua police, or from the veracious testimony of his brother colonists, twenty stories as bad or worse than what he insinuates—suppose the whole of her own statement to be false, and even the whole of her conduct since she came under our observation here to be a tissue of hypocrisy;—suppose all this—and leave the negro woman as black in character as in complexion,[32]—yet it would affect not the main facts—which are these.—1. Mr. Wood, not daring in England to punish this woman arbitrarily, as he would have done in the West Indies, drove her out of his house, or left her, at least, only the alternative of returning instantly to Antigua, with the certainty of severe treatment there, or submitting in silence to what she considered intolerable usage in his household. 2. He has since obstinately persisted in refusing her manumission, to enable her to return home in security, though repeatedly offered more than ample compensation for her value as a slave; and this on

---

[32] If it even were so, how strong a plea of palliation might not the poor negro bring, by adducing the neglect of her various owners to afford religious instruction or moral discipline, and the habitual influence of their evil *example* (to say the very least,) before her eyes? What moral good could she possibly learn—what moral evil could she easily escape, while under the uncontrolled power of such masters as she describes Captain T—— and Mr. D—— of Turk's Island? All things considered, it is indeed wonderful to find her such as she now is. But as she has herself piously expressed it, "that God whom then she knew not mercifully preserved her for better things."

various frivolous pretexts, but really, and indeed not unavowedly, in order to *punish* her for leaving his service in England, though he himself had professed to give her that option. These unquestionable facts speak volumes.[33]

---

[33] Since the preceding pages were printed off, I have been favoured with a communication from the Rev. J. Curtin, to whom among other acquaintances of Mr. Wood's in this country, the entire proof sheets of this pamphlet had been sent for inspection. Mr. Curtin corrects some omissions and inaccuracies in Mary Prince's narrative (see [pages 257–258],) by stating, 1. That she was baptized, not in August, but on the 6th of April, 1817; 2. That sometime before her baptism, on her being admitted a catechumen, preparatory to that holy ordinance, she brought a note from her owner, Mr. Wood, recommending her for religious instruction, &c.; 3. That it was his usual practice, when any adult slaves came on *week days* to school, to require their owners' permission for their attendance; but that on *Sundays* the chapel was open indiscriminately to all.—Mary, after a personal interview with Mr. Curtin, and after hearing his letter read by me, still maintains that Mr. Wood's note recommended her for baptism merely, and that she never received any religious instruction whatever from Mr. and Mrs. Wood, or from any one else at that period beyond what she has stated in her narrative. In regard to her non-admission to the Sunday school without permission from her owners, she admits that she may possibly have mistaken the clergyman's meaning on that point, but says that such was certainly her impression at the time, and the actual cause of her non-attendance.

Mr. Curtin finds in his books some reference to Mary's connection with a Captain———, (the individual, I believe, alluded to by Mr. Phillips at page [276]); but he states that when she attended his chapel she was always decently and becomingly dressed, and appeared to him to be in a situation of trust in her mistress's family.

Mr. Curtin offers no comment on any other part of Mary's statement; but he speaks in very favourable, though general terms of the respectability of Mr. Wood, whom he had known for many years in Antigua; and of Mrs. Wood, though she was not personally known to him, he says, that he had "heard her spoken of by those of her acquaintance, as a lady of very mild and amiable manners."

Another friend of Mr. and Mrs. Wood, a lady who had been their guest both in Antigua and England, alleges that Mary has grossly misrepresented them in her narrative; and says that she "can vouch for their being the most benevolent, kind-hearted people that can possibly live." She has declined, however, to furnish me with any written correction of the misrepresentations she complains of, although I offered to insert her testimony in behalf of her friends, if sent to me in time. And having already kept back the publication a fortnight waiting for communications of this sort, I will not delay it longer. Those who have withheld their strictures have only themselves to blame.

Of the general character of Mr. and Mrs. Wood, I would not designedly give any *unfair* impression. Without implicitly adopting either the *ex parte* view of Mary Prince, or the unmeasured encomiums of their friends, I am willing to believe them to be, on the whole, fair, perhaps favourable, specimens of colonial character. Let them even be rated, if you will, in the very highest and most benevolent class of slaveholders; and, laying every thing else entirely out of view, let Mr. Wood's conduct in this affair be tried exclusively by the facts established beyond dispute, and by his own statement of the case in his letter to Mr. Taylor. But then, I ask, if the very *best* and *mildest* of your slave-owners can act as Mr. Wood is proved to have acted, what is to be expected of persons whose

The case affords a most instructive illustration of the true spirit of the slave system, and of the pretensions of the slaveholders to assert, not merely their claims to a "vested right" in the *labour* of their bondmen, but to an indefeasible property in them as their "absolute chattels." It furnishes a striking practical comment on the assertions of the West Indians that self-interest is a sufficient check to the indulgence of vindictive feelings in the master; for here is a case where a man (a *respectable* and *benevolent* man as his friends aver,) prefers losing entirely the full price of the slave, for the mere satisfaction of preventing a poor black woman from returning home to her husband! If the pleasure of thwarting the benevolent wishes of the Anti-Slavery Society in behalf of the deserted negro, be an additional motive with Mr. Wood, it will not much mend his wretched plea.

I may here add a few words respecting the earlier portion of Mary Prince's narrative. The facts there stated must necessarily rest entirely, — since we have no collateral evidence, — upon their intrinsic claims to probability, and upon the reliance the reader may feel disposed, after perusing the foregoing pages, to place on her veracity. To my judgment, the internal evidence of the truth of her narrative appears remarkably strong. The circumstances are related in a tone of natural sincerity, and are accompanied in almost every case with characteristic and minute details, which must, I conceive, carry with them full conviction to every candid mind that this negro woman has actually seen, felt, and suffered all that she so impressively describes; and that the picture she has given of West Indian slavery is not less true than it is revolting.

But there may be some persons into whose hands this tract may fall, so imperfectly acquainted with the real character of Negro Slavery, as to be shocked into partial, if not absolute incredulity, by the acts of inhuman oppression and brutality related of Capt. I —— and his wife, and of Mr. D ——, the salt manufacturer of Turk's Island. Here, at least, such persons may be disposed to think, there surely must be *some* exaggeration; the facts are too shocking to be credible. The facts are indeed shocking, but unhappily not the less credible on that account. Slavery is a curse to the oppressor scarcely less than to the oppressed: its natural tendency is to

---

mildness, or equity, or common humanity no one will dare to vouch for? If such things are done in the green tree, what will be done in the dry? — And what else then can Colonial Slavery possibly be, even in its best estate, but a system incurably evil and iniquitous? — I require no other data — I need add no further comment. [Pringle's note.]

absolute chattels: inalienable property.

brutalize both. After a residence myself of six years in a slave colony, I am inclined to doubt whether, as regards its *demoralizing* influence, the master is not even a greater object of compassion than his bondman. Let those who are disposed to doubt the atrocities related in this narrative, on the testimony of a sufferer, examine the details of many cases of similar barbarity that have lately come before the public, on unquestionable evidence. Passing over the reports of the Fiscal of Berbice, and the Mauritius horrors recently unveiled, let them consider the case of Mr. and Mrs. Moss, of the Bahamas, and their slave Kate, so justly denounced by the Secretary for the Colonies;—the cases of Eleanor Mead—of Henry Williams—and of the Rev. Mr. Bridges and Kitty Hylton, in Jamaica.[34] These cases alone might suffice to demonstrate the inevitable tendency of slavery as it exists in our colonies, to brutalize the master to a truly frightful degree—a degree which would often cast into the shade even the atrocities related in the narrative of Mary Prince; and which are sufficient to prove, independently of all other evidence, that there is nothing in the revolting character of the facts to affect their credibility; but that on the contrary, similar deeds are at this very time of frequent occurrence in almost every one of our slave colonies. The system of coercive labour may vary in different places; it may be more destructive to human life in the cane culture of Mauritius and Jamaica, than in the predial and domestic bondage of Bermuda or the Bahamas,—but the spirit and character of slavery are every where the same, and cannot fail to produce similar effects. Wherever slavery prevails, there will inevitably be found cruelty and oppression. Individuals who have preserved humane, and amiable, and tolerant dispositions towards their black dependents, may doubtless be found among slave-holders; but even where a happy instance of this sort occurs, such as Mary's first mistress, the kind-hearted Mrs. Williams, the favoured condition of the slave is still as precarious as it is rare: it is every moment at the mercy of events; and must always be held by a tenure so proverbially uncertain as that of human prosperity, or human life. Such examples, like a feeble and flickering streak of light in a gloomy picture, only serve by contrast to exhibit the depth of the prevailing shades. Like other exceptions, they only prove the general rule:

---

predial: adjective referring here to field slavery.

[34] Pringle refers to reports of atrocities against slaves in Berbice, a Dutch colony on the Caribbean coast of South America that became British Guiana (present-day Guyana) in 1831; Mauritius, an island in the Indian Ocean (east of Madagascar) colonized by the Dutch, French, and (from 1810) British; and the British West Indian colonies of the Bahamas and Jamaica. Pringle's notes (omitted here) refer to numbers 5, 16, 44, 47, 64, 65, 66, 69, 71, and 76 of the *Anti-Slavery Reporter* for details.

the unquestionable tendency of the system is to vitiate the best tempers, and to harden the most feeling hearts. "Never be kind, nor speak kindly to a slave," said an accomplished English lady in South Africa to my wife: "I have now," she added, "been for some time a slave-owner, and have found, from vexatious experience in my own household, that nothing but harshness and hauteur will do with slaves."

I might perhaps not inappropriately illustrate this point more fully by stating many cases which fell under my own personal observation, or became known to me through authentic sources, at the Cape of Good Hope[35]—a colony where slavery assumes, as it is averred, a milder aspect than in any other dependency of the empire where it exists; and I could shew, from the judicial records of that colony, received by me within these few weeks, cases scarcely inferior in barbarity to the worst of those to which I have just specially referred; but to do so would lead me too far from the immediate purpose of this pamphlet, and extend it to an inconvenient length. I shall therefore content myself with quoting a single short passage from the excellent work of my friend Dr. Walsh, entitled "Notices of Brazil,"—a work which, besides its other merits, has vividly illustrated the true spirit of Negro Slavery, as it displays itself not merely in that country, but wherever it has been permitted to open its Pandora's box of misery and crime.

Let the reader ponder on the following just remarks, and compare the facts stated by the Author in illustration of them, with the circumstances related at pages [244–46] of Mary's narrative:—

"If then we put out of the question the injury inflicted on others, and merely consider the deterioration of feeling and principle with which it operates on ourselves, ought it not to be a sufficient, and, indeed, unanswerable argument, against the permission of Slavery?

"The exemplary manner in which the paternal duties are performed at home, may mark people as the most fond and affectionate parents; but let them once go abroad, and come within the contagion of slavery, and it seems to alter the very nature of a man; and the father has sold, and still sells, the mother and his children, with as little compunction as he would a sow and her litter of pigs; and he often disposes of them together.

"This deterioration of feeling is conspicuous in many ways among the Brazilians. They are naturally a people of a humane and good-

---

[35] Pringle had lived from 1820 to 1826 at the Cape of Good Hope, a Dutch colony located at the southern tip of Africa, seized by the British in 1795, officially established as a British colony in 1814, and today forming part of the Republic of South Africa.

natured disposition, and much indisposed to cruelty or severity of any kind. Indeed, the manner in which many of them treat their slaves is a proof of this, as it is really gentle and considerate; but the natural tendency to cruelty and oppression in the human heart, is continually evolved by the impunity and uncontrolled licence in which they are exercised. I never walked through the streets of Rio, that some house did not present to me the semblance of a bridewell, where the moans and the cries of the sufferers, and the sounds of whips and scourges within, announced to me that corporal punishment was being inflicted. Whenever I remarked this to a friend, I was always answered that the refractory nature of the slave rendered it necessary, and no house could properly be conducted unless it was practised. But this is certainly not the case; and the chastisement is constantly applied in the very wantonness of barbarity, and would not, and dared not, be inflicted on the humblest wretch in society, if he was not a slave, and so put out of the pale of pity.

"Immediately joining our house was one occupied by a mechanic, from which the most dismal cries and moans constantly proceeded. I entered the shop one day, and found it was occupied by a saddler, who had two negro boys working at his business. He was a tawny, cadaverous-looking man, with a dark aspect; and he had cut from his leather a scourge like a Russian knout, which he held in his hand, and was in the act of exercising on one of the naked children in an inner room: and this was the cause of the moans and cries we heard every day, and almost all day long.

"In the rear of our house was another, occupied by some women of bad character, who kept, as usual, several negro slaves. I was awoke early one morning by dismal cries, and looking out of the window, I saw in the back yard of the house, a black girl of about fourteen years old; before her stood her mistress, a white woman, with a large stick in her hand. She was undressed except her petticoat and chemise, which had fallen down and left her shoulders and bosom bare. Her hair was streaming behind, and every fierce and malevolent passion was depicted in her face. She too, like my hostess at Governo [another striking illustration of the *dehumanising* effects of Slavery,] was the very representation of a fury. She was striking the poor girl, whom she had driven up into a corner, where she was on her knees appealing for mercy. She shewed her none, but continued to strike her on the head and thrust the stick into her face, till she was herself exhausted, and her poor victim covered with blood. This scene was renewed every morning, and the cries and moans of the poor suffering blacks, announced that they were enduring the penalty of slavery, in being the objects on which the irritable and malevolent passions of the whites are allowed to vent themselves with impunity; nor could I help deeply deploring that state of society in which the vilest characters in the community are allowed an almost uncontrolled power of life and death, over their innocent, and far more estimable fellow-creatures." — (Notices of Brazil, vol. ii. p. 354–356.)

In conclusion, I may observe that the history of Mary Prince furnishes a corollary to Lord Stowell's decision in the case of the slave Grace[36] and that it is most valuable on this account. Whatever opinions may be held by some readers on the grave question of immediately abolishing Colonial Slavery, nothing assuredly can be more repugnant to the feelings of Englishmen than that the system should be permitted to extend its baneful influence to this country. Yet such is the case, when the slave landed in England still only possesses that qualified degree of freedom, that a change of domicile will determine it. Though born a British subject, and resident within the shores of England, he is cut off from his dearest natural rights by the sad alternative of regaining them at the expence of liberty, and the certainty of severe treatment. It is true that he has the option of returning; but it is a cruel mockery to call it a voluntary choice, when upon his return depend his means of subsistence and his re-union with all that makes life valuable. Here he has tasted "the sweets of freedom," to quote the words of the unfortunate Mary Prince; but if he desires to restore himself to his family, or to escape from suffering and destitution, and the other evils of a climate uncongenial to his constitution and habits, he must abandon the enjoyment of his late-acquired liberty, and again subject himself to the arbitrary power of a vindictive master.

The case of Mary Prince is by no means a singular one; many of the same kind are daily occurring: and even if the case were singular, it would still loudly call for the interference of the legislature. In instances of this kind no injury can possibly be done to the owner by confirming to the slave his resumption of his natural rights. It is the master's spontaneous act to bring him to this country; he knows when he brings him that he divests himself of his property; and it is, in fact, a minor species of slave trading, when he has thus enfranchised his slave, to *re-capture* that slave by the necessities of his condition, or by working upon the better feelings of his heart. Abstractedly from all legal technicalities, there is no real difference between thus compelling the return of the enfranchised negro, and trepanning a free native of England by delusive hopes into perpetual slavery. The

---

trepanning: entrapping.

[36] William Scott, Lord Stowell (1745–1836), Judge of the High Court of Admiralty, had ruled in the case of the Antiguan slave Grace in 1827 that a colonial slave brought to Great Britain, although considered free while on British soil, lost any claim to freedom upon voluntarily returning to the colonies.

most ingenious casuist could not point out any essential distinction between the two cases. Our boasted liberty is the dream of imagination, and
no longer the characteristic of our country, if its bulwarks can thus be
thrown down by colonial special pleading. It would well become the character of the present Government to introduce a Bill into the Legislature
making perpetual that freedom which the slave has acquired by his passage
here, and thus to declare, in the most ample sense of the words, (what indeed we had long fondly believed to be the fact, though it now appears that
we have been mistaken,) THAT NO SLAVE CAN EXIST WITHIN THE SHORES OF
GREAT BRITAIN.

Part Two

POETRY

From Poems on Various Subjects, Religious and Moral

Phillis Wheatley

Phillis Wheatley (c. 1753–1784) presents a study in improbability. From beginning to end her career could not have been predicted, and that perhaps is why her life and her poetry remain so difficult to explain. From slave child to literary acclaim, from fame to poverty and desperation, Phillis Wheatley endured.

On July 11, 1761, when Wheatley was approximately eight years old, she arrived in Boston from the coast of West Africa on board the slave ship the *Phillis*. She was purchased shortly afterwards by John Wheatley (1703–1778) and his wife, Susanna Wheatley (1709–1774). The Wheatleys, who were part of a Boston mercantile family, had two children (Mary and Nathaniel) and were devout Christians, well educated, and (by colonial standards) refined.

Much has been made of the Wheatleys' influence on and care of Phillis Wheatley. It has even been claimed that she was "treated almost as a member of the family" (Wheatley 1982, 5). Certainly, she was provided with what would have been considered an exceptional education for a colonial woman of the time. Mary and Susanna Wheatley tutored her in English language and literature, history, astronomy, geography, and Latin. Scholars have shown that she had light duties as a slave. Many sources note that she was allowed heat and light in her room at night—both for her delicate health and to aid in her production of poetry.

Yet, despite these significant benefits granted her beyond what would normally have been the lot of a slave, it is important to remember that she remained, in fact, a slave. She wrote most of her significant poetry prior to her manumission. Central to her poetic achievement is her *Poems on Various Subjects, Religious and Moral*, published in England in 1773 by the bookseller Archibald Bell under the patronage of the philanthropist Lady Huntingdon, when Wheatley was not more than twenty years old (Wheatley 1982, 6). Her trip to England that year marked the pinnacle of Phillis Wheatley's career. She was introduced in London society and received gifts of money and books. Unfortunately, she was not able to meet Lady Huntingdon, who was away from London when she arrived. News of Susanna Wheatley's grave illness brought Phillis back to America earlier than intended, although a letter survives expressing her regret at not having met Lady Huntingdon. Another letter to her friend Obour Tanner (a fellow servant in Boston), dated October 30, 1773 states, "I can't say but my voyage to England has conduced to the recovery (in a great measure) of my Health. The Friends I found there among the Nobility and Gentry. Their Benevolent conduct towards me, the unexpected, and unmerited civility and Complaisance with which I was treated by all, fills me with astonishment, I can scarcely Realize it" (Wheatley 1982, 198). She returned from England happier and healthier than she ever would be again.

Over the next few years Phillis Wheatley's life would change dramatically. She was freed sometime after she returned from England, likely a few months before her mentor Susanna Wheatley's death in 1774. Phillis was allowed to stay on in the house until she married John Peters (a free Black) on April 1, 1778. By the fall of 1778 both John and Mary Wheatley had died, and as Nathaniel Wheatley had married and permanently relocated to England, all of her early supports were gone. Accounts of Phillis's husband, John Peters, vary considerably. Certainly, he had his share of financial difficulties, and living conditions for the couple deteriorated over the course of the marriage. Phillis published only sporadically and worked as a domestic. She gave birth to three children, none of whom lived past early childhood. By December 1784 John Peters was running from his creditors, and Phillis, whose health had never been good, died in poverty and squalor at around the age of thirty. Her last child died shortly thereafter and was buried with its mother. At the time of her death she had written proposals for a second book of poetry; and the evidence suggests that she had kept up with some of her foreign correspondents as well.

In her own lifetime, reception of her poetry was decidedly mixed. Thomas Jefferson harshly criticized her work, while Benjamin Franklin found merit in it (Williams 1986, 257). Reviews in magazines were sometimes glowing, sometimes deprecating. Modern critics have failed to resolve this tradition of ambivalence. Many see her poems as largely imitative and unoriginal. She has been criticized roundly for what strikes readers as a deficit of personal feeling and a lack of explicit engagement with the issue of slavery.

Many of these criticisms could be leveled at eighteenth-century poetry in general. True, Wheatley wrote in a style derivative of Alexander Pope's heroic couplets, as did most of the poets of the day. It is also true that her poetry is suffused with Christian piety. It must be remembered that the Age of Reason applauded imitation of older, fixed poetic forms. Also, if one examines Wheatley's use of religious symbolism closely, an implicit critique of slavery can readily be elicited among the various interpretations that arise.

In short, Wheatley was an extraordinary woman, frail in body but quick-witted and intelligent. She did flourish in the environment provided by the Wheatleys; yet, amazingly, when that environment was gone and she experienced the depths of poverty and pain, she continued to create. Like her name, the composite of the name of a slave ship and a cultured educated family, her poetry reveals a composite character. That this poetry was written at all is not only an improbability, but a marvel, and a testament to what the intelligent mind and tenacious spirit can accomplish.

To the KING's Most Excellent Majesty, 1768.[1]

YOUR subjects hope, dread Sire —
The crown upon your brows may flourish long,
And that your arm may in your God be strong!
O may your sceptre num'rous nations sway,
5   And all with love and readiness obey!

But how shall we the *British* king reward!
Rule thou in peace, our father, and our lord!
Midst the remembrance of thy favours past,
The meanest peasants most admire the last.*

From Phillis Wheatley, *Poems on Various Subjects, Religious and Moral* (London: Bell, 1773).

[1] King George III of Great Britain and Ireland (1738–1820) ruled Britain from 1760 to 1820.
* The Repeal of the Stamp Act. [Note in original ed.][2]
[2] The Stamp Act was imposed by England in 1765 to raise money for the colonies' defense. All legal papers were required to bear an official stamp. Mob resistance to the act ensued, and George III was persuaded to relent. However, the repeal of the Stamp Act did not pacify the colonists but instead actually encouraged and solidified American resistance to British rule.

10 May *George*, belov'd by all the nations round,
Live with heav'ns choicest constant blessings crown'd!
Great God, direct, and guard him from on high,
And from his head let ev'ry evil fly!
And may each clime with equal gladness see
15 A monarch's smile can set his subjects free!

An HYMN to Morning.

ATTEND my lays, ye ever honour'd nine,[1]
Assist my labours, and my strains refine;
In smoothest numbers pour the notes along,
For bright *Aurora* now demands my song.[2]

5   *Aurora* hail, and all the thousands dies,
Which deck thy progress through the vaulted skies:
The morn awakes, and wide extends her rays,
On ev'ry leaf the gentle zephyr plays;
Harmonious lays the feather'd race resume,
10 Dart the bright eye, and shake the painted plume.

Ye shady groves, your verdant gloom display
To shield your poet from the burning day:
Calliope awake the sacred lyre,[3]
While thy fair sisters fan the pleasing fire:
15 The bow'rs, the gales, the variegated skies
In all their pleasures in my bosom rise.

See in the east th' illustrious king of day!
His rising radiance drives the shades away—
But Oh! I feel his fervid beams too strong,
20 And scarce begun, concludes th' abortive song.

---

zephyr: gentle breeze from the west.

verdant: green and lush.

[1] The nine Muses, daughters of Mnemosyne and Zeus, said in classical mythology to inspire works of art.

[2] The Roman goddess of dawn, Aurora is the daughter of Uranus and Gaea. Her Greek equivalent is Eos.

[3] Calliope is the muse of epic poetry, which tells of heroic deeds.

An HYMN to the Evening.

SOON as the sun forsook the eastern main
The pealing thunder shook the heav'nly plain;
Majestic grandeur! From the zephyr's wing,
Exhales the incense of the blooming spring.
5 Soft purl the streams, the birds renew their notes,
And through the air their mingled music floats.

Through all the heav'ns what beauteous dies are spread!
But the west glories in the deepest red:
So may our breasts with ev'ry virtue glow,
10 The living temples of our God below!

Fill'd with the praise of him who gives the light,
And draws the sable curtains of the night,
Let placid slumbers sooth each weary mind,
At morn to wake more heav'nly, more refin'd;
15 So shall the labours of the day begin
More pure, more guarded from the snares of sin.

Night's leaden sceptre seals my drowsy eyes,
Then cease, my song, till fair *Aurora* rise.

To the Right Honourable WILLIAM, Earl of Dartmouth, His Majesty's Principal Secretary of State for North America, &c.[1]

HAIL, happy day, when, smiling like the morn,
Fair *Freedom* rose *New-England* to adorn:
The northern clime beneath her genial ray,
Dartmouth, congratulates thy blissful sway:
5 Elate with hope her race no longer mourns,
Each soul expands, each grateful bosom burns,
While in thine hand with pleasure we behold
The silken reins, and *Freedom's* charms unfold.

---

main: ocean.

[1] William Legge (1731–1801), second Earl of Dartmouth, as British secretary of state for the North American colonies from 1772 to 1775, initially supported a policy of conciliation (opposing, for example, the imposition of the Stamp Tax), although he became a proponent of harsh measures toward the colonies after the Boston Tea Party in December 1773.

Long lost to realms beneath the northern skies
10   She shines supreme, while hated *faction* dies:
Soon as appear'd the *Goddess* long desir'd,
Sick at the view, she languish'd and expir'd;
Thus from the splendors of the morning light
The owl in sadness seeks the caves of night.

15   No more, *America,* in mournful strain   ⎫
Of wrongs, and grievance unredress'd complain,   ⎬
No longer shall thou dread the iron chain,   ⎭
Which wanton *Tyranny* with lawless hand
Had made, and with it meant t'enslave the land.

20   Should you, my lord, while you peruse my song,
Wonder from whence my love of *Freedom* sprung,
Whence flow these wishes for the common good,
By feeling hearts alone best understood,
I, young in life, by seeming cruel fate
25   Was snatch'd from *Afric's* fancy'd happy seat:
What pangs excruciating must molest,
What sorrows labour in my parent's breast?
Steel'd was that soul and by no misery mov'd
That from a father seiz'd his babe belov'd:
30   Such, such my case. And can I then but pray
Others may never feel tyrannic sway?

For favours past, great Sir, our thanks are due,
And thee we ask thy favours to renew,
Since in thy pow'r, as in thy will before,
35   To sooth the griefs, which thou did'st once deplore.
May heav'nly grace the sacred sanction give
To all thy works, and thou for ever live
Not only on the wings of fleeting *Fame,*
Though praise immortal crowns the patriot's name,
40   But to conduct to heav'ns refulgent fane,
May fiery coursers sweep th' ethereal plain,
And bear thee upwards to that blest abode,
Where, like the prophet, thou shalt find thy God.

---

coursers: swift horses.

To a Gentleman on his Voyage to
Great-Britain for the Recovery of
his Health.

WHILE others chant of gay *Elysian* scenes,[1]
Of balmy zephyrs, and of flow'ry plains,
My song more happy speaks a greater name,
Feels higher motives and a nobler flame.
5 For thee, O R——,[2] the muse attunes her strings,
And mounts sublime above inferior things.

   I sing not now of green embow'ring woods,
I sing not now the daughters of the floods,
I sing not of the storms o'er ocean driv'n,
10 And how they howl'd along the waste of heav'n,
But I to R—— would paint the *British* shore,
And vast *Atlantic,* not untry'd before:
Thy life impair'd commands thee to arise,
Leave these bleak regions, and inclement skies,
15 Where chilling winds return the winter past,
And nature shudders at the furious blast.

   O thou stupendous, earth-enclosing main
Exert thy wonders to the world again!
If ere thy pow'r prolong'd the fleeting breath,
20 Turn'd back the shafts, and mock'd the gates of death,
If ere thine air dispens'd an healing pow'r,
Or snatch'd the victim from the fatal hour,
This equal case demands thine equal care,
And equal wonders may this patient share.
25 But unavailing, frantic is the dream
To hope thine aid without the aid of him
Who gave thee birth, and taught thee where to flow,
And in thy waves his various blessings show.

   May R—— return to view his native shore
30 Replete with vigour not his own before,
Then shall we see with pleasure and surprize,
And own thy work, great Ruler of the skies!

----

[1] The Elysian fields, or Elysium, said in classical mythology to be the home of the Blessed after death. Interestingly, it is sometimes placed in the north of Africa.
[2] R—— is Joseph Rotch Jr., whose 1772 voyage from Boston to London in search of recovery did not turn out well: he died in England in 1773.

To S. M. a young *African* Painter, on
seeing his Works.[1]

TO show the lab'ring bosom's deep intent,
And thought in living characters to paint,
When first thy pencil did those beauties give,
And breathing figures learnt from thee to live,
5 How did those prospects give my soul delight,
A new creation rushing on my sight?
Still, wond'rous youth! each noble path pursue,
On deathless glories fix thine ardent view:
Still may the painter's and the poet's fire
10 To aid thy pencil, and thy verse conspire!
And may the charms of each seraphic theme
Conduct thy footsteps to immortal fame!
High to the blissful wonders of the skies
Elate thy soul, and raise thy wishful eyes.
15 Thrice happy, when exalted to survey
That splendid city, crown'd with endless day,
Whose twice six gates on radiant hinges ring:
Celestial *Salem* blooms in endless spring.[2]

Calm and serene thy moments glide along,
20 And may the muse inspire each future song!
Still, with the sweets of contemplation bless'd,
May peace with balmy wings your soul invest!
But when these shades of time are chas'd away,
And darkness ends in everlasting day,
25 On what seraphic pinions shall we move,
And view the landscapes in the realms above?
There shall thy tongue in heav'nly murmurs flow,
And there my muse with heav'nly transport glow;
No more to tell of *Damon's* tender sighs,

---

seraphic: angelic.

pinions: wings.

[1] Scipio Moorhead, a Black painter and etcher and a slave, was active in Boston in 1773. He is generally credited with the portrait that served as model for the engraving of Wheatley featured on the frontispiece of *Poems on Various Subjects*.

[2] Salem ("peace") here connotes Jerusalem; the "celestial" Jerusalem is the heavenly city described in Revelation 21.

30 Or rising radiance of *Aurora's* eyes,[3]
For nobler themes demand a nobler strain,
And purer language on th' ethereal plain.
Cease, gentle muse! the solemn gloom of night
Now seals the fair creation from my sight.

A FAREWEL TO AMERICA. TO MRS. S. W.[1]

I.

ADIEU, *New-England's* smiling meads,
   Adieu, the flow'ry plain:
I leave thine op'ning charms, O spring,
   And tempt the roaring main.

II.

5 In vain for me the flow'rets rise,
   And boast their gaudy pride,
While here beneath the northern skies
   I mourn for *health* deny'd.

III.

Celestial maid of rosy hue,
10   O let me feel thy reign!
I languish till thy face I view,
   Thy vanish'd joys regain.

IV.

Susannah mourns, nor can I bear
   To see the crystal show'r,
15 Or mark the tender falling tear
   At sad departure's hour;

V.

Not unregarding can I see
   Her soul with grief opprest:

---

[3] Here, Damon and Aurora evoke the stock lover and beloved of pastoral poetry, understood as an inferior poetic genre in comparison with religious poetry.
[1] Susanna Wheatley, the poet's owner and mentor.

But let no sighs, no groans for me,
20   Steal from her pensive breast.

VI.

In vain the feather'd warblers sing,
    In vain the garden blooms,
And on the bosom of the spring
    Breathes out her sweet perfumes.

VII.

25 While for *Britannia's* distant shore
    We sweep the liquid plain,
And with astonish'd eyes explore
    The wide-extended mein.

VIII.

Lo! *Health* appears! celestial dame!
30   Complacent and serene,
With *Hebe's* mantle o'er her Frame,[2]
    With soul-delighting mein.

IX.

To mark the vale where *London* lies
    With misty vapours crown'd,
35 Which cloud *Aurora's* thousand dyes,
    And veil her charms around,

X.

Why, *Phœbus*, moves thy car so slow?[3]
    So slow thy rising ray?
Give us the famous town to view,
40   Thou glorious king of day!

---

mein: mien, demeanor or appearance.
[2] Hebe, child of Zeus and Hera and goddess of eternal youth in classical mythology.
[3] Phoebus is the Roman name for Apollo, the sun god and patron of the Muses in classical mythology, said to preside over the oracle at Delphi.

XI.

For thee, *Britannia,* I resign
  New-England's smiling fields;
To view again her charms divine,
  What joy the prospect yields!

XII.

45 But thou! Temptation hence away,
  With all thy fatal train
Nor once seduce my soul away,
  By thine enchanting strain.

XIII.

Thrice happy they, whose heav'nly shield
50 Secures their souls from harms,
And fell *Temptation* on the field
  Of all its pow'r disarms!

Boston, May 7, 1773.

From The Interesting Narrative

Olaudah Equiano

Although Equiano's *Interesting Narrative* remains one of the major texts of modern literary scholarship (for an introduction, see pages 111–14 of this volume), his poetry has gone virtually unnoted. Equiano's poetry in the *Narrative* falls into two distinct categories. He composes original verses, and he also quotes the poetry of other British writers. His original work consists primarily of the poem "Miscellaneous Verses, or Reflections on the State of My Mind During My First Convictions; of the Necessity of Believing the Truth, and Experiencing the Inestimable Benefits of Christianity." Equiano (1789) also inserted a poetic stanza, most likely of his own composition, into Chapter 6 of the *Interesting Narrative* to illustrate his remark "I was now completely disgusted with the West Indies, and thought I never should be entirely free until I had left them" (1:250).

Besides these original verses, Equiano prominently quotes British poetry, including John Bicknell and Thomas Day's abolitionist poem *The Dying Negro, a Poetical Epistle,* Milton's *Paradise Lost,* and the popular dramatist Colly Cibber's play *Love's Last Shift.* However, it is worth noting that in ten places where Equiano does quote the poetry of others, always to emphasize a strategic point about his experience, he misquotes or adapts nine out of the ten times. In each case, he changes the meaning of the original poetry to reflect the slave's experience. For instance, although Equiano adopts Alexander Pope's translation of Homer's *Iliad,* he creatively misquotes in order to make the poem speak to the issue of slavery. While Pope's version reads:

> O King! oh Father! Hear my humble pray'r . . .
> If *Greece* must perish, we thy will obey,
> But let us perish in the face of Day! (5:68)

Equiano's lines differ significantly:

> Oh Jove! O father! If it be thy will
> That we must perish, we thy will obey,
> But let us perish by the light of day. (1789, 1:145)

Equiano's persistent altering of canonical and popular poetry suggests that he not only imports British literature into his discourse, but transforms it and thus gives it a new authority.

FROM VOLUME I, CHAPTER VI.

"With thoughts like these my anxious boding mind
"Recall'd those pleasing scenes I left behind;
"Scenes where fair Liberty in bright array
"Makes darkness bright, and e'en illumines day;
5 "Where nor complexion, wealth, or station, can
"Protect the wretch who makes a slave of man."

From Olaudah Equiano, *The Interesting Narrative of the Life of Olaudah Equiano, or Gustavus Vassa, the African* (London: Printed for the author, 1789).

From Volume II, Chapter X.

Micellaneous Verses,

OR

Reflections on the State of my mind
during my first Convictions; of the
Necessity of believing the Truth,
and experiencing the inestimable
Benefits of Christianity.

WELL may I say my life has been
One scene of sorrow and of pain;
From early days I griefs have known,
And as I grew my griefs have grown:

5 Dangers were always in my path;
And fear of wrath, and sometimes death;
While pale dejection in me reign'd
I often wept, by grief constrain'd.

When taken from my native land,
10 By an unjust and cruel band,
How did uncommon dread prevail!
My sighs no more I could conceal.

'To ease my mind I often strove,
'And tried my trouble to remove:
15 'I sung, and utter'd sighs between—
'Assay'd to stifle guilt with sin.

'But O! not all that I could do
'Would stop the current of my woe;
'Conviction still my vileness shew'd;
20 'How great my guilt—how lost from God!

'Prevented, that I could not die,
'Nor might to one kind refuge fly;
'An orphan state I had to mourn,—
'Forsook by all, and left forlorn.'

25 Those who beheld my downcast mien
Could not guess at my woes unseen:
They by appearance could not know
The troubles that I waded through.

'Lust, anger, blasphemy, and pride,
30 'With legions of such ills beside,
'Troubled my thoughts,' while doubts and fears
Clouded and darken'd most my years.

'Sighs now no more would be confin'd—
'They breath'd the trouble of my mind:
35 'I wish'd for death, but check'd the word,
'And often pray'd unto the Lord.'

Unhappy, more than some on earth,
I thought the place that gave me birth—
Strange thoughts oppress'd—while I replied
40 "Why not in Ethiopia died?"

And why thus spared, nigh to hell?—
God only knew—I could not tell!
'A tott'ring fence, a bowing wall,'
'I thought myself ere since the fall.'

45 'Oft times I mused, nigh despair,
'While birds melodious fill'd the air:
'Thrice happy songsters, ever free,
'How bless'd were they compar'd to me!'

Thus all things added to my pain,
50 While grief compell'd me to complain;
When sable clouds began to rise
My mind grew darker than the skies.

The English nation call'd to leave,
How did my breast with sorrows heave!
55 I long'd for rest—cried "Help me, Lord!
"Some mitigation, Lord, afford!"

Yet on, dejected, still I went—
Heart-throbbing woes within were pent;
Nor land, nor sea, could comfort give,
60 Nothing my anxious mind relieve.

Weary with travail, yet unknown
To all but God and self alone,
Numerous months for peace I strove,
And numerous foes I had to prove.

65 Inur'd to dangers, griefs, and woes,
Train'd up 'midst perils, deaths, and foes,

I said "Must it thus ever be? —
"No quiet is permitted me."

Hard hap, and more than heavy lot!
70 I pray'd to God "Forget me not —
"What thou ordain'st willing I'll bear;
"But O! deliver from despair!"

Strivings and wrestlings seem'd in vain;
Nothing I did could ease my pain:
75 Then gave I up my works and will,
Confess'd and own'd my doom was hell!

Like some poor pris'ner at the bar,
Conscious of guilt, of sin and fear,
Arraign'd, and self-condemned, I stood —
80 'Lost in the world, and in my blood!'

Yet here, 'midst blackest clouds confin'd,
A beam from Christ, the day-star, shin'd;
Surely, thought I, if Jesus please,
He can at once sign my release.

85 I, ignorant of his righteousness,
Set up my labours in its place;
'Forgot for why his blood was shed,
'And pray'd and fasted in its stead.'

He dy'd for sinners — I am one!
90 Might not his blood for me atone?
Tho' I am nothing else but sin,
Yet surely he can make me clean!

Thus light came in, and I believ'd;
Myself forgot, and help receiv'd!
95 My Saviour then I know I found,
For, eas'd from guilt, no more I groan'd.

O, happy hour, in which I ceas'd
To mourn, for then I found a rest!
My soul and Christ were now as one —
100 Thy light, O Jesus, in me shone!

Bless'd be thy name, for now I know
I and my works can nothing do;
"The Lord alone can ransom man —
"For this the spotless Lamb was slain!"

105 When sacrifices, works, and pray'r,
    Prov'd vain, and ineffectual were,
    "Lo, then I come!" the Saviour cry'd,
    And, bleeding, bow'd his head and dy'd!

    He dy'd for all who ever saw
110 No help in them, nor by the law:—
    I this have seen; and gladly own
    "Salvation is by Christ alone*!"

From A Collection of Hymns: Compiled and Selected by John Jea, African Preacher of the Gospel

John Jea

One of the more obscure early Black British writers, Jea has drawn attention mainly for his autobiographical narrative, the *Life, History, and Unparalleled Sufferings* (1815) (for an introduction, see pages 180–82 of this volume). A second work by Jea, however, *A Collection of Hymns,* published in Portsea, Portsmouth, in 1816, survives in a single known copy. Consisting of over three hundred hymns in all, Jea's collection includes twenty-eight hymns attributed to the Methodist Charles Wesley; eighteen to the poet, early children's writer, and Dissenting minister Isaac Watts; and some twenty-nine that have been ascribed by Graham Russell Hodges (1993) to Jea himself (165–167). As Hodges points out, a collection of hymns would have been indispensable to an itinerant preacher like Jea, who traveled about over three continents preaching and singing in chapels, meeting houses, and outdoor rallies in the woods and open fields (165). Hymns punctuated and gave variety to the preaching and, more importantly, brought preacher and congregants into rhythmic, charismatic fellowship. Familiar hymns, like those of Watts and Wesley, would give a chapel service or camp meeting common touchstones to help unify the congregation and tie the present service to religious experiences past. The hymn form, however, in its comparative metrical simplicity and its large repertoire of standard melodies, phrases,

---

* Acts iv. 12. [Equiano's note.]

and motifs, could also lend itself to the spirit of creative improvisation that marked itinerant gospel preaching generally.

Among the hymns ascribed to Jea, several deal with issues of captivity and slavery, mingling confessional and political statements and linking religious salvation to personal freedom. Composed orally (Jea remarks in his narrative that he "cannot write" [page 204]), these hymns reveal Jea manipulating his public persona as the "African preacher" in ways that allow him to inject antislavery sentiment into religious worship. Lacking the neoclassical polish and mythological references of Wheatley's poems, they belong instead to the beginnings of an oral, sung Black poetic tradition that remains vibrant as "Gospel" music in the contemporary United States.

---

252. WORKS OF CREATION

AFRICA nations, great and small,
   Upon this earthly ball,
Give glory to the God above,
   And crown him Lord of all.

5 'Tis God above, who did in love
   Your souls and bodies free,
By British men with life in hand,
   The gospel did decree.

By God's free grace they run the race,
10 And did his glory see,
   To preach the gospel to our race,
   The gospel Liberty.

His wisdom did their souls inspire,
   His heavenly riches spread;
15 And by the Spirit of the Lord,
   They in his footsteps tread.

280. CONFESSION

WHEN I from Africa did come,
  I was both small and young;
I did not know where I did go,
  Because I was so young.

5 My father and my mother too,
  We all were stole away;
My sisters and my brothers too.
  Were took by the ship's crew.

We were took on board, and there we laid,
10   And knew not what to do;
The God above to us in love,
  Did his kind aid afford.

When we were carried 'cross the main,
  To great America,
15 There we were sold, and then were told
  That we had not a soul.

Thanks be to God who did in love
  To us his mercy show,
Did to my soul his gospel show,
20   By grace, almighty power.

281. CONFESSION OF MASTER AND MISTRESS

OUR master and our mistress too,
  To us they did confess,
That we were theirs, and not our own,
  They bought us with a price.

5 The price of silver and of gold,
  Which they did call their own,
The sons and daughters did the same,
  As their grandfathers did.

They did not think that God well knew
10   All they did think and say
Against us poor African slaves,
  As they do every day.

But God who did poor Joseph save,
  Who was in Egypt sold,

15 So did he unto us poor slaves,
　　And he'll redeem the whole.

　Then shall we give him all the praise,
　　And glory to his name;
　Redeeming love shall be our song,
20　And end with endless days.

284. Trusting in Christ

　I thank God, that did set
　　My soul at liberty;
　My body freed from men below,
　　By his almighty grace.

5 I will be slave no more,
　　Since Christ has set me free,
　He nail'd my tyrants to his cross,
　　And bought my liberty.

　I bless the Lord that he
10　Has made my spirit whole,
　Therefore to him my heart I'll give,
　　And all I have and hold.

　The world's glittering wealth,
　　I bid it all farewell;
15 The gold, the silver, and all things
　　That is upon this land.

　Dear Saviour, O how long,
　　Shall this bright hour delay?
　Fly swifter round, ye wheels of time,
20　And bring the welcome day.

289. Encouragement

　HARK! poor slave, it is the Lord,
　It is the Saviour, hear his word;
　Jesus speaks and speaks to thee, —
　"Say, poor sinner, lovest thou me?"

5 Thou dost say "I'm not a slave,
　"I was born on British ground;"
　O remember when thou wast
　In chains of sin and mis'ry bound.

I, the Lord, did thee deliver,
10 And when wounded heal'd thy wounds,
Sought thee wandering, set thee right,
Turn'd thy darkness into light.

Can a man so hardened be,
As not to remember me?
15 Yes, he may forgetful be,
Yet will I remember thee.

Thou shalt see my glory soon,
When the work of grace is done;
Partners of my throne shall be, —
20 "Say, poor sinner, lovest thou me?"

From Poems by a Slave in the Island of Cuba, Recently Liberated; Translated from the Spanish, by R. R. Madden, M.D.

Juan Francisco Manzano

Through an accident of literary history, one of the most important slave narratives in Spanish was first published in an English translation and long remained available only in English. The autobiography of Juan Francisco Manzano (c. 1797–1854) first appeared with an English translation of his poems published in London in 1840. The translator, Richard Robert Madden (1798–1886), was an Irish physician and a prominent member of the Anti-Slavery Society based in London. In the wake of the emancipation legislation of 1833, Madden was employed by the British Colonial Office to help administer the emancipation statutes from 1833 to 1839, first as a special magistrate in Jamaica and then in the Spanish colony of Cuba, where the British hoped to curtail the Spanish slave trade. While in Cuba, Madden learned of Manzano, a largely self-taught slave who had attracted the notice of the local gentry through publishing poetry in various Cuban literary magazines. Given a collection of Manzano's poems in 1838 by the Cuban writer Domingo del Monte (1804–1853), as well as the first part of Manzano's autobiography (the second part was lost), Madden translated them into English. He published Manzano's works along with related texts of his own in conjunction with the

British and Foreign Anti-Slavery Society, wishing both to highlight Manzano's accomplishment and to advertise the cruelties of the Cuban slave system in the cause of the international antislavery movement.

Manzano's parents, Maria del Pilar Manzano and Toribio de Castro, were both slaves in the service of a Cuban aristocrat, the Marquesa de Santa Ana (Mullen 1981, 14). Born around 1797, Manzano passed with his family into the possession of the Marquesa de Prado Ameno, a much harsher mistress, at about the age of ten. What Manzano recalled as an idyllic childhood, despite his enslaved status, now became a series of removals from one situation to another, many of them involving difficult working conditions and sadistic punishments. Eventually, at about his twentieth year, Manzano absconded to Havana, where he worked as a tailor, housepainter, confectioner, and personal chef. In 1835 he married Delia, a pianist of mixed African and European ancestry, and was able to purchase his freedom the next year with help from del Monte and other Cuban literary figures. Although he taught himself to write in his late teens, copying scraps of writing discarded by his master, Manzano had already begun versifying by the age of twelve, composing by memory and reciting his poems for a fellow servant to write down. He read his poem "Mis trenta anos" ("My Thirty Years," included below, page 309–10), at del Monte's salon in 1835, launching a literary career that included poetry, a tragedy (*Zafira*) in 1841, and the autobiographical narrative that he completed in 1839. The publication the next year of his poetry and autobiography in London attests to the persistence of antislavery sentiment and activism in Britain in the years following full emancipation in the British West Indian colonies in 1838.

THIRTY YEARS.

When I think on the course I have run,
From my childhood itself to this day,
I tremble, and fain would I shun,
The remembrance its terrors array.

From Juan Francisco Manzano, *Poems by a Slave in the Island of Cuba, Recently Liberated; Translated from the Spanish, by R. R. Madden, M.D.* (London: Ward, 1840).

5   I marvel at struggles endured,
    With a destiny frightful as mine,
    At the strength for such efforts: — assured
    Tho' I am, 'tis in vain to repine.

    I have known this sad life thirty years,
10 And to me, thirty years it has been
    Of suff'ring, of sorrow and tears,
    Ev'ry day of its bondage I've seen.

    But 'tis nothing the past — or the pains,
    Hitherto I have struggled to bear,
15 When I think, oh, my God! on the chains,
    That I know I'm yet destined to wear.

THE DREAM
"Addressed to My Younger Brother"

Thou knowest, dear Florence, my sufferings of old,
The struggles maintained with oppression for years,
We shared them together, and each was consoled
With the whispers of love that were mingled with tears.

5   But now, far apart, this sad pleasure is gone,
    We mingle our sighs and our sorrows no more;
    The course is a new one that each has to run,
    And dreary the prospect for either in store.

    But in slumber, our spirits, at least, shall commune,
10 Behold, how they meet in the visions of sleep;
    In dreams that recall early days, like the one
    In my brother's remembrance, I fondly would keep.

    For solitude pining, in anguish of late
    The heights of Quintana I sought, for repose,
15 And there of seclusion enamoured, the weight
    Of my cares was forgotten, I felt not my woes.

    Exhausted and weary, the spell of the place
    Soon weighed down my eyelids, and slumber then stole
    So softly o'er nature, it left not a trace
20 Of trouble or sorrow, o'ercasting my soul.

    I seemed to ascend like a bird in the air,
    And the pinions that bore me, amazed me the more;

I gazed on the plumage of beauty so rare,
As they waved in the sun, at each effort to soar.

25 My spirit aspired to a happier sphere,
The buoyancy even of youth was surpassed;
One effort at flight not divested of fear,
And the flutter ensued, was successful at last.

And leaving the earth and its toils, I look down,
30 Or upwards I glance, and behold with surprise,
The wonders of God, and the firmament strewn
With myriads of brilliants, that spangle the skies.

The ocean of ether around me, each star
Of the zodiac shining, above either pole,
35 Of the earth as a point in the distance afar,
And one flap of the wing, serves to traverse the whole.

The bounds which confine the wide sea, and the height
Which separates earth from the heavenly spheres;
The moon as a shield I behold in my flight,
40 And each spot on its surface distinctly appears.

The valley well known of Matanzas[1] is nigh,
And trembling, my brother, I gaze on that place,
Where, cold and forgotten, the ashes now lie
Of the parents we clung to in boyhood's embrace.

45 How the sight of that place sent the blood to my heart,
I shudder e'en now to recall it, and yet
I'd remind you of wrongs we were wont to impart,
And to weep o'er in secret at night when we met.

I gazed on that spot, where together we played,
50 Our innocent pastimes came fresh to my mind;
Our mother's caresses, the fondness displayed,
In each word and each look of a parent so kind.

The ridge of that mountain, whose fastnesses wild
The fugitives seek, I beheld, and around
55 Plantations were scattered of late where they toiled,
And the graves of their comrades are now to be found.

---

[1] Matanzas, on the north coast of Cuba not too far west of Havana, was the scene of Manzano's childhood with the Marquesa de Santa Ana.

The mill-house was there and its turmoil of old,
But sick of these scenes, for too well they were known;
I looked for the stream, where in childhood I strolled
60 By its banks when a moment of peace was my own.

But no recollections of pleasure or pain
Could drive the remembrance of thee from my core;
I sought my dear brother, embraced him again,
But found him a slave, as I left him before.

65 "Oh, Florence," I cried, "let us fly from this place,
The gloom of a dungeon is here to affright!
'Tis dreadful as death or its terrors to face,
And hateful itself as the scaffold to sight.

"Let us fly on the wings of the wind, let us fly,
70 And for ever abandon so hostile a soil
As this place of our birth, where our doom is to sigh
In hapless despair, and in bondage to toil."

To my bosom I clasped him, and winging once more
My flight in the air, I ascend with my charge,
75 The sultan I seem of the winds, as I soar,
A monarch whose will, sets the pris'ner at large.

Like Icarus[2] boldly ascending on high,
I laugh at the anger of Minos,[3] and see
A haven of freedom aloft, where I fly,
80 And the place where the slave from his master is free.

The rapture which Daedalus inly approved
To Athens from Crete, when pursuing his flight,
On impetuous pinions, I felt when I moved
Through an ocean of ether, so boundless and bright.

85 But the moment I triumphed o'er earth and its fears,
And dreamt of aspiring to heavenly joys:

---

[2] Son of the miraculous inventor Daedalus in Greek mythology, Icarus escaped imprisonment with his father using wings made of feathers and wax, which melted when he ignored Daedalus's warning and flew too near the sun. Icarus fell into the Aegean Sea and drowned.

[3] Minos, son of Zeus and Europa and mythical ruler of the island of Crete, where he imprisoned Daedalus and Icarus.

Of hearing the music divine of the spheres,[4]
And tasting of pleasure that care never cloys.

I saw in an instant, the face of the skies
90   So bright and serene but a moment before;
Enveloped in gloom, and there seemed to arise
The murmur preceding the tempest's wild roar.

Beneath me, the sea into fury was lashed,
Above me, the thunder rolled loudly, and now
95   The hurricane round me in turbulence dashed,
And the glare of the lightning e'en flashed on my brow.

The elements all seemed in warfare to be,
And succour or help there was none to be sought;
That fate of poor Icarus seemed now for me,
100   And my daring attempt its own punishment brought.

'Twas then, oh, my God! that a thunder-clap came,
And the noise of its crash broke the slumbers so light,
That stole o'er my senses and fettered my frame,
And the dream was soon over, of freedom's first flight.

105   And waking, I saw thee, my brother, once more,
The sky was serene and my terrors were past;
But doubt there was none of the tempests of yore
And the clouds that of old, our young hopes overcast.

---

[4] In ancient cosmology, the Earth was thought to be surrounded by a nested series of rotating spheres, which produced a divine or celestial harmony as they revolved at different speeds.

Part Three

VOICES

Letter to James Rogers

James Harris

In 1787, James Rogers received this letter from James Harris, a Black man living in London. Rogers ran a slaving business out of Bristol and, not surprisingly, does not appear to have been a man of character. According to Madge Dresser (who discovered Harris's letter and has read through Rogers's correspondence), Rogers violated both his slaves and the laws governing the slave trade. For instance, Parliament passed the "Dolben Act" in 1788, limiting the number of slaves that ships could carry. Rogers's correspondence shows that he immediately sought to violate the new law by proposing to sail his ship under French colors and thus evade policing by the British navy. In addition, historical records show that on board his ship Rogers permitted the sexual abuse of female slaves, as well as physical violence against males (Dresser 2001, 152–153).

James Harris's connection to Rogers remains unclear. Harris may have been a servant of one of Rogers's associates, or he may have lived in Bristol for a while and met Rogers there. At any rate, Harris felt enough of a connection to ask Rogers for help in contacting his former employer, Mr. Gibbs. Apparently, Gibbs had promised to free Harris, but failed to follow through (Dresser 2001, 169–170).

The difficulties Harris mentions reflect the quandary Blacks found themselves in while living in London, when racial profiling — characterizing Blacks as dishonest, lazy, sexually licentious — had begun in earnest. First, Harris cannot find employment in England because of the White population's "aversion to black servants." He wishes to return to Jamaica, and has been offered a situation at £50 a year, but he cannot accept it because he does not yet own manumission papers, and as he says, the people of Jamaica "generally takes very great advantage of the poor black people so that even a free man is scarce Amongs them." Harris's dilemma plays out in other "officially" published texts in this anthology — Ukawsaw Gronniosaw, Olaudah Equiano, and most notably, Mary Prince. When transported to London, Prince and her owners, the Woods, undergo a series of arguments, with the Woods threatening to dismiss Prince and Prince refusing to leave. Reflecting James Harris's predicament here about how to live in England outside of the institution of slavery, Prince reveals: "I was sorry I had come from Antigua," and when her owners hear this they "opened the door and bade me get out. But I was a stranger, and did not know one door in the street from another, and was unwilling to go away" (page 260). In fact, Prince declares more than once that as a free Black in England, she counts as a "stranger" (page 261). Freedom thus remains a precarious state for former slaves in England, as Prince states: "I was free in England, but I did not know where to go, or how to get my living; and therefore, I did not like to leave the house" (page 261).

Since the details of Harris's life are unknown, beyond those hinted at in the letter, his text stands as a singular instance reflecting the situations of the ten thousand Black Britons who did not have the chance, as did Cugoano, Equiano, or Prince, to publish and profit from their accounts. Harris's letter bears witness to the poverty, dubious chances of employment, and uncertain title to freedom experienced by countless other Blacks, who remain silent in the historical records.

LETTER TO JAMES ROGERS

Most worthy Sir

I hope your goodness will pardon this great liberty which I have Presume to take to write to so worthy a gentleman as yourself but having No friend in this great and good Kingdom I have Sir form'd an opinion in My mind that I shall find one in you so that you will take my humble Pition into cinsideration—I am Sir at this present in the greatest Distress Immagenable wanting of bread and cloaths for the quality in General have such an aversion to black servants so that their is not one In a hundred that will imploy or take one into their service but For what reason I cannot say—this Sir I have represented to my old Master Mr Hicks for some releaf and Craved his

From *Slavery, Abolition, and Emancipation*, vol. 1: *Black Writers*, edited by Sukhdev Sandhu and David Dabydeen (London: Pickering and Chatto, 1999).

Charity to give me My free monimition that I may go to Jamaica without being Molisted when I am there by any of the inhabitance of the Island as the people of that Country generally takes very great advantage of the poor black people so that even a free man is scarce Amongs them—Mr Hicks did promise me when I quited his Service that he will give me my freedom that I might go to any Part of the world unmolisted and I have applyd several times to Him by Letters and have never receivd an answer from either of the Letters as I could wish to go to Jamaica for a Little while and Try what I Can do their as I Cannot gett my Living in England to support my poor family so I takes it very hard sir that He will not grant me that one favour but keeping me Here to perish for want—good Sir I shall ever be in duty bound to pray for you now and for hereafter if you will be so Kind as to speak to Mr Hicks to grant me that one favor I will never Trouble him more—Sir a gentleman has offered me £50 per year about four months agone to go with him to Jamaica but for want of this free pass I could not go with Him, being apprehencive that he or some other persons might Take advantage of me and having nothing to show I might be Deprived of my Liberty—so most worthy Sir be so kind as to Represent this to my dear master—as I have gott a wife and Two Children who suffers as well as myself for want of this Monimition—

So pardon good Sir this very great freedom that I have taking—and except of my pittion—

I am duty bound to pray and say I am Your poor and very humble Ser^t,

Ja^s, Brit^n, Harris

London Nov^r, 10, 1787
N° 2 William Street Manchester Square

Letters from Sierra Leone Settlers

After the American Revolution, about three thousand former slaves, who had gained their freedom by fighting for the British, settled in Nova Scotia with the promise of land grants. However, the promised land never materialized. Consequently, in 1791, Thomas Peters traveled from Nova Scotia to England to petition in person for redress. He asked to be allowed to settle in Sierra Leone, a request that was readily granted. The Sierra Leone Company, a commercial venture established by antislavery advocates, was sponsoring a settlement to be called Freetown. The plan for Freetown, initially conceived by Granville Sharp in 1786, entailed a self-governing community of slaves resettled in their West African homeland. The scheme was, however, a recipe for failure from the beginning. The Sierra Leone Company was loosely formed and underfunded, and the land upon which the settlement was to be built was already occupied by a local tribe, the Temnes. The Crown would be trying to govern yet another colony from afar, this time with only ideology (and a desire to keep Black Loyalists far from the streets of London) as an incentive to succeed. An initial expedition, which left England for Sierra Leone in February 1787, had failed disastrously—as both Ottobah Cugoano and Oloudah Equiano had predicted (see pages 109 and 174 of this volume)—with 314 of the initial 374 settlers dead by 1791. Peters' bold trip to London ended by giving the Sierra Leone colony a second chance at success.

Lt. John R. Clarkson, a naval officer and brother to Thomas Clarkson (British philanthropist and antislavery agitator) offered his services to the Sierra Leone Company when he became disillusioned with warfare. Clarkson organized the transport of 1,190 Nova Scotian Black loyalists to Sierra Leone in January 1792. Unfortunately, he all but assured them free title to a piece of land, although this was outside both the scope of his authority and the stated purpose of the Sierra Leone Company. The company was not in fact offering land, which quickly became a major point of contention. Along with the establishment of quitrents (annual fixed rental fees) on farmland worked by the settlers, Clarkson's unfulfilled promise gave the settlers a bitter sense of disppointment and betrayal. Most of the letters reprinted here were written by the settlers to Clarkson.

The first three letters were written to Clarkson while settlers were still in Halifax preparing to emigrate. They demonstrate the problems and anxieties that began arising even before departure. First, almost 1,200 Loyalists chose to leave Nova Scotia, three times the number anticipated by Clarkson. The unexpected numbers reflected mainly the influence of a charismatic Black minister who supported the idea of resettling.

When the settlers arrived in Sierra Leone, heavy rains began; malaria and dysentery broke out, and about a hundred settlers died in the epidemic. Two-thirds of the accompanying Whites also died, and many more left the colony to return home. Clarkson himself became ill. Clarkson's illness, coupled with the strain of insubordination of White colleagues and the continued demands of the settlers, produced severe emotional distress as demonstrated in letters 4, 5, 6, and 7.

In December 1792 Clarkson returned to England on sick leave. He had intended to marry and return to Sierra Leone but never did. Two of his men, William Dawes and Zachary Macaulay, took charge during his absence. The settlers found this turn of events disturbing; although they were disappointed they had not received the land promised to them by Clarkson, they were later to think of him as the only White person they could trust. Letters 8, 10, and 11 bear this out. Reverence for Clarkson continued; the prayer he offered in 1792 when he departed Sierra Leone "has over the years acquired almost divine attributes" (Foray 1977, 41).

As the complaints of the settlers grew, their representatives, Cato Perkins and Isaac Anderson, sailed to London to speak to the directors of the Sierra Leone Company and to beg Clarkson to return. The directors, who had become increasingly suspicious of and dissatisfied with Clarkson, now fired him. Perkins and Anderson were not allowed to see Clarkson and returned to Sierra Leone without redress (letter 8). Nevertheless, Clarkson continued to receive letters of complaint from the settlers for another five years (letters 10 and 11).

Trouble continued to grow in Clarkson's absence. When Britain went to war with France in 1793, the French sacked Freetown. The settlers, as they rebuilt, suggested that the French attack had brought company rule to an end. Over time their discontent solidified, and intense fights broke out. Thomas Ludlum, the new governor, and Isaac Anderson, a rebel leader, disagreed violently over the future of the colony. The final letter in this collection, number 13, is from Anderson to Ludlum, and the only copy of it is actually a transcription, which appears in the Freetown council minutes. In it Anderson demands that Ludlum either release rebel settlers being held as captives or send the women and children out of the fort in anticipation of a rebel attack. Previously, the form of the letter had been reserved for legal redress; now, it played a role in direct resistance. Daring to send such a letter constituted a capital crime under English law, for which Isaac Anderson was duly tried, convicted, and hanged.

For the fullest treatment of the history of the founding of Freetown, see Christopher Fyfe's *A History of Sierra Leone* (1963), which details the coming of Europeans, the rise of the slave trade, the principal expeditions, and the eventual liberation of Sierra Leone from the Crown in 1961. The history of the settlement of Sierra Leone is both tragic and heroic, idealistic and venial. For a complete volume of the Sierra Leone Settlers' letters, see Fyfe's 1991 "*Our Children Free* and Happy": Letters from Black Settlers in Africa in the 1790s. The letters pulsate with the pathos of the people struggling under terrible conditions.

———

1. To Clarkson from the Inhabitants of Birchtown, 20 December 1791
British Library, Clarkson Papers, Vol. I, Add. MS 41262A folio 23

To the Honble. m^r. Clarkson[1] Agent to the Sierra Leona Society.
Whereas a Number of us Formerly,
Where Inhabitants of Birch Town near Shelburne
Nova Scotia, But now intending under your
Inspection to imbarque to Sierra Leona—Would
Therefore humbly Solicit. that on our arrival
You will be pleased to settle us as near as Possible
To the Inhabitants of Preston, as they and us
Are Intimately acquaint'd—so in Order to
Render us Unanimous, would be Glad to be
As Nearly Connected as possible when the Tract
Or Tracts of Land shall be Laid out, humbly
Relying up on your Interest in this matter, and
In Compliance with this request will be bound To Pray———

The Inhabitants of Birch Town

———

[1] In January 1792, Lt. John R. Clarkson transported the 1,190 Black loyalists who founded Freetown from Nova Scotia to Sierra Leone. Clarkson was appointed governor later the same year. He supported granting this petition.

2. To Clarkson from Thomas Peters and David Edmon, 23 December 1791[2]
British Library, Clarkson Papers, Vol. I, Add. MS 41262A folio 24

halefax   december the 23 1791

the humbel petion of the Black peple lying in mr wisdoms Store Called the anoplus[3] Compnay humbely bag that if it is Consent to your honer as it is the larst Christmas day that we ever Shall see in the amaraca that it may please your honer to grant us one days alowance of frish Beef for a Christmas diner that if it is agreabel to you and the rest of the Gentlemon to whom it may Consern

> *thomas petus*
> *david Edmon*
> *In behalf of the Black People of at Halifax bound to Sierra Leone*

3. To Clarkson from Peter Richardson, 12 January 1792[4]
Sierra Leone Collection, Special Collections, Section II (Lt. John Clarkson), folder 5, The University Library, University of Illinois at Chicago

Jan 12, 1792

Dear Sir the Ill behaviour Of Some Of the People that Went Against Orders Not Agreeable to the Rules Of the Law for One Of Our Woman Goes by the Name Of Sally Pone Mentions Some Expression that Other People May

---

[2]Thomas Peters was a runaway slave who fought for the British during the American Revolution. In 1791 he went to England to request the land promised to the Nova Scotian Loyalists. He requested to go to Sierra Leone, where he died in an epidemic in 1792. In 1795 David Edmon was a leading settler elected as a tythingman in 1795 and as a hundredor in 1798. (For these elective positions, see note 19, below.) Edmon was wounded in the insurrection of 1799–1800 while arresting Nathaniel Wansey.

[3]Those settlers coming from Annapolis, Nova Scotia.

[4]Written on board the ship *Mary* in anticipation of leaving Halifax for Sierra Leone.

take Some holt And do As She has Done And Said for She Says that she do not Care for You and I Nor for Any Of the laws that Is made by Your Orders for Sir this Morning There was some Of the People that did not behave And did what was not Agreeable to the Rules of Our Law and we was Exammining Of them and this Woman Sally Pone came in when we was Exammining them And She say what i have mention Obove And not Only but Call us a pack of Deavils And Mention many Expressions that was very Scandilous And we Egreed to lett You Know that She may be Justifyed Acording to the Rules of the Law

<table>
<tr><td>Peter Richardson</td><td>Mr William</td></tr>
<tr><td>On board of the Mary</td><td>Clarkson Esqr</td></tr>
<tr><td>1 Syman Addams</td><td>Of his Magisty Navy</td></tr>
<tr><td>2 Warrick francies</td><td>Halifax</td></tr>
<tr><td>3 John Prince</td><td></td></tr>
<tr><td>4 franck Patrick</td><td></td></tr>
<tr><td>5 George Black</td><td></td></tr>
</table>

Was in Preasant When theese Words was
Mention by Sally Pone

4. To Clarkson from Susane Smith, 12 May 1792
Sierra Leone Collection, Special Collections, Section II (Lt. John Clarkson), folder 5, The University Library, University of Illinois at Chicago

Sierra Leone May 12th 1792

Sir I your hum bel Servent begs the faver of your Excelence to See if you will Pleas to Let me hav Som Sope for I am in great want of Some I hav not had aney Since I hav bin to this plais I hav bin Sick and I want to git Som Sope verry much to wash my famely Clos for we ar not fit to be Sean for dirt —

your hum   Susane Smith
bel Servet

5. To Clarkson from Daniel Cary,
16 June 1792
Sierra Leone Collection, Special Collections, Section II (Lt. John Clarkson), folder 5, The University Library, University of Illinois at Chicago

Sir

I have wrote you these few Lines to informed you that I should wished to get married this afternoon if it is not unconvenient to you to do it for me from

your Servt
Dannail Cary

Freetown
June 16th = 92

6. To Clarkson from Andrew Moor,
24 August 1792[5]
Sierra Leone Collection, Special Collections, Section II (Lt. John Clarkson), folder 5, The University Library, University of Illinois at Chicago

To The Right Honourable John Clarkeson Esq
Captan Generall and Commander in Chief In and Over the Free Colony of Searra
Leone and Its Dependancys and Vice-
Admaral of the Same etc etc

Whereas you Honours Memorilist Andrew Moors Wife being brought to bed this morning and Delivered of a Daughter and now Stands in need of Some Nourishment for her and the Child your Excellancys Memorialest begeth that out your Humanity and Geantle Goodness you Will take it Int your honours Consideration to Give Orders that She and the Child have

---

[5] Andrew Moor was brought as a slave to Georgia in colonial North America. As a farmer in the Sierra Leone settlement he was the first to discover indigenous coffee, which was later cultivated around Freetown. He eventually became a church clerk until he retired in 1839 at the age of 77.

Some Nourishmen Such as Oat meal Molassis or Shugger a Little Wine and Spirits and Some Nut mig and your Memorialest as in Dutey bound Shall Ever Pray

NB and one lb Candles for Light

7. TO CLARKSON FROM INHABITANTS OF FREETOWN, 19 NOVEMBER 1792

Sierra Leone Collection, Special Collections, Section II (Lt. John Clarkson), folder 5, The University Library, University of Illinois at Chicago

Free Town November 19ᵗʰ 1792
To His Excellency John Clarkson Esqr

Sir we would wish by this Oppertunity to inform you that we are Ready in anything that his in our power for the preservation of this Colony we lay down our case open before you which If you pleases to peruse it we hope you'll take in Consideration that we are under a very presd situation in the first place we labours hard with very small wages—which is very loo for the Expence of tools runs hard as we are Oblidge to have a good many therefore we are Come to a Rasatition[6] to lay it before you in hopes yr honour will take in Consideration towards us we dont wish to offend, we Could wish as we only works for three Shillings pr. day to have our provision free or else have our wages raisd and pay for it by free grace we wish to have our full provision as work men ought to have and our wages to be half in hard Cash and the other part in the Colony mony[7] by which there will be no grumbling—there is one thing more that is our allowance in liqr. in our time of working for the Climate has a very Requisite Call for it[8]

—*Witness our hands*—

John Duncome X

Cato Perkins X

Thomas Baccas X

---

[6] "Rasatition" is translated by Fyfe (1991, 29) as "Rasalition," as in "resolution." However, in the manuscript, it is spelled "Rasatition."

[7] The Sierra Leone Company issued its money for use in the company store.

[8] Clarkson continued their existing pay but refused their requests for liquor.

Peter Frances X

Isaac Anderson X

Cato Burder X

Boston King X

Thos Hogg X

Summerset Loghan X

Ceser Smith X

Steven Peters X

Abram Smith X

Thos Quiper X

Luke Dixon X

Thos Jackson X

Wm Furguson X

John Townsen X

Miles Dixon X

Richard Webb X

Joseph Williams X

John Johnson X

Daniel Prophet X

Robert Morris X

Phillip Lawrance X

Anthony Steven X

Dem Sillavan X

Henry Cook X

John Cooper X

Sighn by the above
names Munday
November 19th 1792

8. To Clarkson from Cato Perkins and
Isaac Anderson, 30 October 1793
The British Library, Clarkson Papers,
Vol. I, Add. MS 41263 folio 101

Mr John Clarkson   London Octr 30 1793
                                                    N° 13 Finch Lane

Hon^d. Sir

We send you the Petition which we brought from our Fellow Settlers at Free
Town and we hope you will not see any thing in it that is not true for we
declare Sir we want nothing but what you Promised us, and we look upon
you so much our Friend that we think you will see us done Justice by

Lady Ann Huntingdon[9] has put Mr Perkins to Colledge till he leaves this
Country we are

                          Sir your Faithful
                          Humble Servants

                          Cato Perkins

                          Issac Anderson

9. To Clarkson from Richard
Corankeapoan, 13 December 1793[10]
Sierra Leone Collection, Special Collections, Section II
(Lt. John Clarkson), folder 5, The University Library,
University of Illinois at Chicago

Sierra leon [piece of letter missing, torn off with the seal] the 13 1793

honered Sir I take this oppertunety to wright to your honer to let you know
that I am well and I hope that thes Lines may find your honer well and your
good Ladey Sir I am verey glad to hear from your honer and to hear that

---

[9]Lady Ann Erskine, who succeeded Selina, Countess of Huntingdon (influential early
Methodist and advocate for slaves and former slaves), in 1791.

[10]Richard Corankeapoan (Crankapone) emigrated to Nova Scotia in 1792. In Sierra
Leone he served as a marshal and arrested settlers who opposed the government in 1800.
On November 18, 1801, he was killed defending Fort Thornton.

you got Safe home and to hear of your good Suckces in your marain I gave your Joy honer Joy and god Bless you and gave you Long Life and may you Both Live hapey for ever Sir we are the most of us is verey hartey thear is not maney sick a mong us we have the most of us drowd our town Lots and are a Buldn our houses the pepol is much desatfied with the goods and the proveisons have got to such a price it is verey dear sence your honer have Left us Sir Cap[t] deboise [11] is left us four days ago

thear is some of our pepol will not Be Contented with aney thing Som fue but we donot mind what everey one Says But the Body of the Colleney is Bent for your honer to Com and Be our govener thear is two men a goin to England to See the Companey with som papers Isaac Anderson and Cato purkins and to return a gain as soon as thea have ansur [12] Sir Rember me to Davied georg [13] his wife is well and all the famley John Cutbuth [14] and his fameley and I Remain you ever duteyfull Servent

Richard Corankeapoan

10. To Clarkson from Settlers in Sierra Leone, 19 November 1794
British Library, Clarkson Papers, Vol. I, Add. MS 41263 folios 114–115

Sierra Leone Novr 19. 1794

To John Clarkson Esq[r]

A Most Respectable Friend to Us the Settlers in Sierra Leone—In Your Being here We wance did call it Free town but since your Absence—We have A Reason to call it A Town Of Slavery————Be not Offended of our Saying so—We take it our duty to write unto to You letting you know the French have Attacked us and Destroy all the Compy—Property and

---

[11] Isaac Dubois was a White loyalist who took employment with the Sierra Leone Company. He was dismissed with Clarkson in 1793. He was married to Anna Maria Falconbridge, the author of *Two Voyages to Sierra Leone* (1794).

[12] Isaac Anderson, a spokesperson for the settlers, was elected hundredor in 1796. He became a leader in the rebellion against quitrents in 1799. The rebellion was put down, and Anderson was hanged. Cato Perkins, a leading preacher in the colony, did not take part in the rebellion.

[13] Davied georg (David George), a Baptist elder, was elected hundredor in 1792 and made marshal. Although he did not fight in the rebellion, he was banished from the colony.

[14] John Cutbuth (Cuthbert) was a captain who eventually turned against the company.

likewise our Little Affects. But thanks be God I Raly Believed that God see the tyranny and Oppression that are upon us—and send the Message of his Power to Attack the Barbarous Task Masters in the Hight of their Pomp and Oppression and furthermore after the Enemy have pity Our Case and Bestowed A little few Necessary upon us the Superintended are Desirous to take away from us by Empression and Signify to say that we have took the Company Property—may it please your honour Sir—but wonce Consider—if any man see A place is to be Destroyed by fire and Run the Risk of his life to care of that Ruin Afore it is Destroyed do you not think the Protector of these articles have A just Right to these property altho the Articles is not of much Consequence Which is A few Boards and one little Notion A Nother—but may it please your honour if the Superintended had the least Consideration to come as Ask Us in a fare Manner if we will Bestow these things to the Company—God only knows we would give it up with all Respect—but in stead of thad he came With that Empression to tell us if We did not give them up we should Never be Employ'd in the Comp^y Work nor not any more to be look'd upon but shall be Blotted Out of the Companys Book—but However we look unto God— furthermore he never was the man that Ever gav'd us any Amanition to Protect our Selves or Else the French should have never plundered the Place as thay did for we would run the Risk of saving some of the Companys Property he had the Enteligence three days Afore the French Attacked Us—and after seeing the Enemy of the Cape he never would fire nor give us leave but lett the Enemy come in Broad side of the town and fire upon us then all hopes was taken Away by firing kild one person and Wounded two that one dyed the day After and it was the means of Cutting the Others mans legs—we do Raly look to see you with ever Longing Eyes—Our Only Friend—John Clarkson Esqr it Raly will give us pleasure to see you Or hear from your Excellancy—

Your Well Wishers—

Luke Jordan	*Moses Wilkinson preacher*
Jn Jordan	*Isaac Anderson*
Rubin Simmons	*Stephen Peters*
Amarica Tolbert	*Jas. Hutcherson*
A great many More	*Sierra Leone*
the Paper wont afford[15]	

---

[15]The names signed to this letter are in the hand of the letter writer and not individual signatures. Most were active in Moses Wilkinson's Methodist church, with America

11. To Clarkson from Luke Jordan and Nathaniel Snowball, 29 July 1796[16]
British Library, Clarkson Papers, Vol. III, MS 41263 folio 131

Free town July 29, 1796
Very Dear & honored Sir

We are persuaded from that affection which you have already discovered towards us that you will be Glad to hear we & the Colony people at large are in good health & spirits.

We have to lament that such an union as is very desireable for persons in our situation does not exist among us. There are as there always have been divisions among us; indeed Mr. George & some of his people seem to think they can do no greater service for the Company or Colony than to invent & carry all the lies in their Power to the Governor against those who differ from them in things which pertain to religion.

The land which we understand you gave us we have had difficulty to hold in our possession. There have been two tryals concerning it & in the last the jury gave it in our favour but as yet the matter is not quite settled.

We could say many things but after all it will amount to no more than this that we love you, & remember your Labours of love & compassion towards us with Gratitude, & pray that Heaven may always smile on you & yours. We have the honor & happiness to be, Sir your Most obedient & humble servants

Luke Jordan
Nathaniel Snowball

Daddy Moses[17] wishes his love to you

Tolbert and Stephen Peters serving as elders. Tolbert later left to join the Pirate's Bay colony. Rubin Simmons lived outside the colony for several years when it was discovered that he was involved with the rebellion.

[16]This letter differs from the others both in style and in handwriting. According to Fyfe (1963, 75), it may have been written for Jordan and Snowball by John Garvin, a Methodist schoolmaster, or by Jacob Grigg, a Baptist missionary, White residents of the settlement who opposed the Sierra Leone Company policies.

[17]Moses Wilkinson, the Methodist minister (see note 15, above).

12. To Captain Ball from Ishmael York,[18] Stephen Peters and Isaac Anderson, in the name of the colonists, 16 January 1798

Public Record Office, London, CO series 270/4 folios 103–104

To the Honorable Captn Ball Esqr
Commander of his majesty Ship the Dudless

Honour Sir

We the hundreors & tithing[19] of this place having find ourselves opresed would wish to address your honour with these few lines to lay frefore your honour all our grievances and our Distresses which we are incontring with here. First we received a Proclamation from goverment for our good behaviour in the last war, which was brought to us by one Mr John Clarksonn & told us that goverment had heard of our Complaints been in a Cold Country would remove us to Sierra Leone where we may be Comfortable This when we received it from Mr Clarkson we gladly exsepted of the offer from his Majesty. And found shiping & Provision & brought us here. And hoving now find we are oppressed we would wish to know whether we are shut out from goverment or whether we remained his subject or not which if we are his subject we be glad to know from your honour if we has not a right to appleyed to goverment to see ourselves righted in all the wrongs which are Done to us here since we been, Now if your honour will take a view & see how Dissalute we are, What petty forts you see a long the water side Done out of our own expence been poor not able to make the place sufficantly strong to protect us again we have all the roads to Clean ourselves and all our poor are upon ourselves and after all this been burden with our poor roads Bridges & all the burden of the place we are

---

[18] Ishmael York was born in Carolina, North America. He was an elder, tythingman, and hundredor. He was banished from the colony even though he did not take part in the rebellion. The letter is copied into the Freetown council minutes and is prefaced by the following remarks: "16 January, 1798. Captn Ball of his Majestys Ship Dadalus presented to Mr Macaulay a Letter full of complaints addressed to him by Ishmael York, Stephen Peters, and Isaac Anderson in the name of the Colonists, and which he had declined to reply to. Resolved—That the said Letter which contains important Matter be inserted in the minutes of council. The letter is literally as follows. viz."

[19] According to Sharp's system of government for the settlement, every ten households formed a tything, every ten tythings a hundred. Each tything elected a tythingman. Every ten tythings elected a hundredor. These officials helped keep order and mediated small disputes.

shamefully Called upon to pay a quit-rent[20] of a shilling a actr for the land which we hold Sir we are sorry to informed your honour that we are not used here as free settlers we humbly beges an answer to this —

Freetown	*We are Sir*
Jany 15th 1798	*your honour most humble servts*
Hundreors	*Ishmael (X) York &*
	Stephen Peters &
	Isaac H. Anderson

P.S. We shall take it kind if your honour will Called a meeting to have a hearing between us & the Governor. —

13. TO MR LUDLOW FROM ISAAC ANDERSON, UNDATED (SOMETIME AROUND THE END OF SEPTEMBER, 1800).[21]
Public Record Office, CO series 270/5, Appendix to Narrative, No. 8

Sunday

September Sunday Mr Ludlow Sir we we de sire to now wether you will let our Mends out if not turn out the womans and Chill Dren.

Slave Complaints

British Guiana (present-day Guyana) sits on the northern coast of South America and arose from the 1831 unification of the colonies of Demerara, Essequibo, and Berbice. The British had occupied these slave colonies, formerly under Dutch control, from 1796. British amalgamation and control resulted in a complex, multilayered slave system, including elements established by the Dutch, still earlier elements adapted by the Dutch from the Spanish, and the institutions, administration, and procedures imposed by the British.

---

[20] Quit-rent: rent in money or kind for land. The Freetown settlers were asked to pay 1 shilling per acre. These unexpected rents were a major contributing factor to the 1799 insurrection.

[21] The letter is unsigned and undated and was inserted into the Freetown council minutes sequentially, at the end of September 1800. Sending anonymous threatening letters to a governor carried the death penalty at this time.

However complex the rules on plantations, both slaves and masters regularly violated them (da Costa 1994, 45). Slaves would wander around without permission or take property that did not belong to them; masters would not adequately feed and clothe slaves or would force them to work on Sunday (the official Sabbath, or day of rest). But Demerara and Berbice differed. These colonies had an official position called the fiscal, established to make sure that rules were followed. The fiscal was in charge of hearing and investigating cases and maintaining order in the colony; both masters and slaves could appeal to him for redress. Yet the fiscal's records are filled to an overwhelming degree with slave voices (not surprisingly, given the overwhelming imbalance of power, masters did not choose to complain too often).

An institution that the Spanish had adapted from the Romans, the office of the fiscal included functions similar to those of the protector of Indians in the Spanish colonies. An analogous position had featured in the Dutch South African colony of the Cape of Good Hope. After 1824, the fiscal's functions in Demerara and Berbice merged with those of the protector of slaves created by the British government as part of its goal to ameliorate colonial slave conditions. Records like these can provide a hidden history of slave resistance. Most histories, of course, were written by Europeans or White creoles, and although the records of slave complaints were written down by White officials, they generally include the voices of slaves, often recorded in the first person. The documents reveal an uncanny ability to catch the edge of the slave voice, and thus allow one at least to glimpse the world that the slaves created for themselves in the face of colonial oppression. In each one of these complaints, readers will find more than initially meets the eye. As the historian Emilia Viotti da Costa (1994) observes, most of the slave complaints have to do with "aspects of slave culture that slaveowners were troubled by, and it was usually only when the slaves' traditions led to conflict that they found their way into the documentary record. That is why we know something about slaves' notions about family, nursing practices, and 'obeah'" (77).

Slaves complained about ill treatment by managers, drivers, and overseers; they complained about inadequate food and clothing allowances; they complained about sexual improprieties taken with slave women; they complained about the amount of work they were expected to do; and they complained about sickness. A manager who lived in Demerara gave witness in the 1820s to the slaves' own consciousness of their "rights": "No class of people are more alive to their own rights than the slave population of this country; and when these happen at any time, or in any way, to be the least infringed upon, they do not hesitate to seek for redress. . . . If slaves are curtailed in the least, either by mistake or design, of the time allowed them for breakfast and dinner, or made to work at improper hours, or punished on trivial occasions, they do not fail to make complaint of it . . . sometimes they are very trivial in nature, being hardly worth noticing, and are only brought forward by some of the ignorant of the slaves, who have been urged on by the more artful and vicious, for the purpose of forwarding their own private designs" (*Royal Gazette,* June 29, 1820; quoted in da Costa 1994, 64). Slave complaints thus constituted a form of resistance and a powerful tool for slaves seeking to control their working conditions. Just as important, complaints gave slaves a voice within the official discourse on slavery. On the more troubling side, the slave complaint records indicate how high the stakes were for slaves bringing their concerns to the fiscal, since most of the time their complaints brought them severe punishment, sometimes in the public marketplace. Still, they continued to speak out.

Just one year after many of the complaints registered here, one of the major uprisings in the history of the Caribbean occurred in Demerara, as a direct result of the slaves' knowledge of their rights. In March 1823, the abolitionist William Wilberforce published an influential pamphlet calling for better treatment of slaves. At the same time, the Anti-Slavery Society (which still exists) was formed, and on May 15, another abolitionist and member of Parliament introduced a motion advocating the gradual abolition of slavery. Consequently, Parliament issued an Order in Council insisting on certain minimal rights for slaves, including a limitation of work hours and the abolition of female flogging. In Berbice, the Order in Council was explained from the pulpit, while in Demerara it was discussed in the Court of Policy. News of the order spread quickly among the slave population, and the slaves in Demerara became convinced that the colonial governor and planters were deliberately withholding their rights granted by the British Parliament itself. At this point, a rebellion broke out. The colony's well-established plantocracy was overwhelmed by some thirty thousand rebel slaves. Although it began on just two plantations, the revolt quickly spread over fifty estates, covering most of the land between Demerara's two major coastal cities, with rebel leaders announcing the negroes are determined to have nothing more or less than their freedom. In retaliation, the planters arrested the White minister John Smith, declared martial law, and then killed over one hundred slaves, set fire to their huts, and sentenced many to a thousand lashes or to lives of hard labor in chain gangs.

Only after the Demerara uprising of 1823 did the British government decide to intervene in the management of the slave population; the fiscals became somewhat more responsive to slave complaints and insisted on punishing or fining at least a few masters. The uprising also had a wider impact. It received great publicity in England, and many historians believe it represented the turning point in British emancipation of slaves in the colonies, for from 1824 on, the campaign for final emancipation began in earnest.

REPORT MADE TO HIS HONOR THE PRESIDENT RESPECTING THE NEGRO *HOPE,* SAYING TO BELONG TO MR. NIEWERKIRK, ON A COMPLAINT OF A. SCHLAPFER, 8 FEBRUARY 1819

EXAMINATION of Negro *Hope,* belonging to *J. G. Cloot de Niewerkirk:*— Says, That he was sent with a letter to town by his master, that he went to sleep at the colony house, knowing his master when in town to put up there; that next morning, passing through the house, he saw two pieces of calico, a pair of ear-rings, and a red handkerchief in one of the rooms, and no person being present he took them;[1] that he left the house and was met on the road by a boy, who seeing the red handkerchief in his hand claimed it as his property, and on opening it, the said boy perceived the calico and ear-rings, which he, Hope, had tied up in the handkerchief, and took him to Mr. Schlapfer, who took him to the barracks. On being asked what induced him to take these articles, he replied, that seeing them, and no one present, he had taken them with the view of giving them to his mother on the estate.

A. Schlapfer examined, and indentified the articles as the property of Henrietta Enderman, his housekeeper; that he was informed by the boy, his

---

From *Further Papers Relating to Slaves in the West Indies* (ordered by the House of Commons to be printed, 23 June 1825).

[1] Slave owners constantly complained of slave theft, often seen as a blatant form of resistance.

master ordered him to wait at the colony house till he came on Monday morning. I saw the ear-rings on Saturday night; boy went away very early on Sunday morning. Quamina, belonging to Dr. Leslie, brought the boy Hope about nine o'clock this morning, and asked what he had in his lap to make it look so big, he said he was ruptured, Quamina pulled the lap open, and the handkerchief and two pieces of calico dropped out. Henrietta seeing some stolen articles on Hope went and examined, and found a pair of ear-rings missing, and on examining Hope's trowsers pocket the ear-rings were found in it; the boy Hope ran away, I pursued, and taking hold of him, he bit my hand; I called out to Mr. White for assistance, and having secured him I carried him to the barracks.

NEGRO *TOMMY*, BELONGING TO WILLIAM FRASER, COMPLAINANT, 9 FEBRUARY 1819

Negro *Tommy*, belonging to William Fraser, complainant:—Says, he is a cooper by trade, and employed as such by his master on plantation Goldstone Hall; that on Friday morning last he went in the boiling-house for nails, and there saw another cooper, by name George, heading up sugars; complainant went to one of the casks and took a lump of sugar for the purpose of sweetening three gallons of hot water; did not hide the same, but proceeded with it in his hand from the boiling-house; was met by his master, Mr. Fraser, who inquired where he got the sugar, complainant informed him of his having taken it, and for what purpose, his master immediately ordered him to be laid down, tied to stakes, put two drivers over him,[2] and one hundred lashes inflicted upon him;[3] on inquiring how complainant knew that one hundred lashes had been put upon him, he said, that persons standing by had counted them was required to state the names of such persons, says, that Barbary, Shaw and Billy counted them, the overseer, lately come on the estate, was present; after receiving

---

cooper: craftsman who makes and repairs casks and barrels.

boiling-house: building for boiling sugar, a process that clarifies and evaporates the cane juice into sugar crystals.

[2] Drivers (slave drivers) were policemen and mediators, but they were also slaves and potentially rebel leaders. Drivers got bigger rations of food and clothing, and they had the authority to command other slaves. However, their precarious position as Blacks in the favor of White owners made it increasingly dangerous for planters to upset the driver's authority once it had been established with the slaves.

[3] Thirty-nine lashes was the legal limit of the colony.

this punishment Mr. Fraser went to complainant's house and searched it, found in his tool chest a quantity of old nails, among which were also a very few new ones; Mr. Fraser went to the trouble of weighing them, there were fourteen pounds; accounts for having these nails in his possession, by stating that having been employed by Mr. B. Jeffery to cooper some casks, he according to his custom had kept all the old nails; that on his quitting Mr. Jeffery he had omitted to give these nails over; to this quantity, so procured, he was also in the custom of putting up any old nails which passed through his hand at Goldstone Hall; he had no particular view in keeping these nails; some few were occasionally used by him to repair his house, some in his work, when occasion required; and trusts from the quantity found in his tool chest, which was frequently opened to the view of other persons, that it cannot be construed they were selected and reserved for sale. Complains of not being sufficiently fed, nor clothed; has but one bunch of plantains a week. Says, he has belonged to Mr. Fraser about five years, during which period he has had clothing only twice; does not belong to plantation Goldstone Hall, but to Mr. Fraser. Exhibits his posteriors, few lashes appear, not more in appearance to sanction a supposition he had been punished beyond the limit of lashes prescribed by law. On this being represented to complainant, he said he had been favoured by the drivers, who threw the whips over him; names of the drivers, Tommy and Acawa. Says that after being flogged, Mr. Fraser had his buttocks washed with brine, and ordered to be locked up every night in the stocks; was confined Friday night, Saturday night, and all Sunday.

Presidency, 10th February.

Examination of *Samuel Willcox*, overseer on plantation Goldstone Hall:—States, that the negro Tommy was flogged on Friday for stealing sugar: Tommy came to me and asked for nails; I went with him to the store for the nails (the store is not in the boiling-house); after delivering the nails, and returning with him, I was met on my way to the boiling-house by another negro, who also asked for nails; I had therefore to return to the store. Tommy, I learnt from Gift, (a boy in the still-house), that Tommy had gone in the boiling-house. Gift gave notice of Tommy the cooper being in the boiling-house to Tommy the driver. Mr. Fraser met Tommy the cooper, and brought him to me with the sugar, asking me if I knew any thing of it. I said no; but supposed he must have got it out of the

---

plantains: tropical plant closely related to the banana and a staple slave food.
still-house: distillery where molasses is converted into rum, the staple Caribbean liquor and a valuable export commodity.

boiling-house during my absence. The sugar, I suppose, was about the quantity of half a pound, more or less. Mr. Fraser then ordered the drivers, Tommy and Acawa, to flog the cooper Tommy: he was tied down to stakes and flogged; to the best of my knowledge forty-one lashes were given; I counted them, there were neither more nor less than forty-one: he appeared much cut. I have seen negroes flogged before, but never with so much severity. He was released, and went about his work directly. Mr. Fraser then went, as I was informed, and searched Tommy's house to see if he could find anything else: I learnt this from the driver who went with Mr. Fraser. The above-mentioned drivers returned with a box to the boiling-house door from Tommy the cooper's house. I saw a napkin, having about a pound or two of sugar, and some nails, old and new ones; about fifteen pounds weight of nails; I believe the old ones were the largest proportion. The coopers come daily for nails, and take as many as is deemed necessary for the work they have to perform. I never knew him to be guilty of stealing nails. I have heard from the drivers, Tommy the cooper was not to be trusted. Mr. Fraser, in consequence of finding these nails, directed him to be confined in the stocks at night till next Christmas. He was put in the stocks at night since the flogging. I believe he gets his weekly allowance as the other negroes, and they are all well fed. During my residence on the estate he has conducted himself with propriety; the negroes do not speak so well of him: they are never allowed to take sugar out of the boiling-house; they get molasses almost every Sunday. I do not know whether he was confined in the stocks on Sunday last or not; I believe I have not seen him on the estate since last Monday forenoon. I did not count the previous cracks of the whip; but the forty-one lashes, which I can correctly speak to, I counted as those which cut him on the bottom.

Examination of *W. Fraser*, proprietor of plantation Goldstone Hall:— I was amongst the carpenters on Friday, at the Stoke Holes, aback of the boiling-house; I saw Tommy passing with something in his apron: I asked him, "What have you got there. Tommy?" he replied, "nails." I said, "So many nails for you alone:" he replied, it was for himself and another. I requested to see them. After some delay or hesitation on his part, I took hold of the apron and looked into it, and found sugar and nails mixed together; I asked him where he got the sugar, and he said, in the boiling-house; the nails he had got for his work from the store, and not out of the boiling-house. I asked him who gave him the sugar. He said he had taken it. I observed, "Do you not know that you are not permitted to go into the boiling-house to take sugar? you also know, if I found you at such work I would punish you; had you come and asked me for the sugar I would have given it you: you also know I never forgive lying or stealing, and therefore

I must punish you." The overseers and drivers were about the door, I ordered the drivers to flog him; they tied him to the stakes and flogged him, and in consequence of the fault he had committed I gave him such a punishment that I, as owner of that slave, considered myself in duty bound to do, always bearing in mind the laws of the colony with respect, and I gave him thirty-nine lashes.

PLANTATION GELDERLAND: — *NETTELJE, JULIA, LEA,* AND *MIETJE,* 11 MARCH 1819

Plantation Gelderland: — *Nettelje, Julia, Lea,* and *Mietje,* each with an infant in arms,[4] complain that no time is allowed them to nurse their children; that during the crop an equal quantity of coffee is expected and required of them as from other women having no children, or of the men; that a similar task is given them in weeding grass with the rest of the gang, which they are not able to perform, in consequence of carrying their children on their backs; in the event of failing, they are beaten in his presence with the handle of the whip by the driver Esperance.[5] Nettelje and also Mietje were flogged the day before yesterday by the carpenter La Fleur; they, with others, were weeding the dam; they had made a fire to drive away the sand-flies; they were seen by Mr. Toel, the manager, suckling their infants, he inquired if they had no work to do; they replied they had just taken their children up, who were crying; they were laid down and flogged, their coats were stained with blood. Mr. Toel took the fire up, and threw it in the trench. Julia was locked up in the stocks because she did not keep with the rest of the gang, and threatened to be flogged next morning; she is a young girl, with her first child. Lea complains that she is not allowed to suckle her child during her work; she was threatened to be flogged next day by Mr. Toel, at same time with Julia.

---

[4] Slave mothers were a highly charged issue both in the colonies and in Britain, especially during this time. After the British slave trade was abolished in 1807, plantations relied on slave births to keep up their work force. Slave mothers thus exercised a great deal of personal power through their control over reproduction and slave children.

[5] This demonstrates the slaves' keen awareness of a debate raging on both sides of the Atlantic regarding the issue of female flogging. The imperial legislature opposed female flogging partly because of indecency, partly to protect women who could reproduce the labor force. In 1823, George Canning, the speaker of the House of Commons, abolished female flogging altogether.

JANE, BELONGING TO MR. BOURMESTER, 11 MARCH 1819

Jane, belonging to Mr. Bourmester, says her master gave her to his house-keeper Grace,[6] who is constantly abusing and ill-treating her; she is often in the habit of kicking her, and beating her with any thing that comes to hand, sometimes with a fire-stick, sometimes with a piece of wood. Monday morning she was sent by Grace to look for wood; when she returned she took a piece of crab-wood she had brought, and beat her with it, and kicked her. Her master was not at home; she got breakfast for her mistress and a gentleman, Mr. Harvey. After breakfast, sent me for wood; I had just recovered from a fit of sickness, having had a blister on my belly, which was not yet healed; I felt faint, and was under the necessity of sitting down to recover myself. When I came home with the wood it was about 11 o'clock; as soon as I returned she began to beat and kick me, saying she hated to see me; a boy belonging to Mr. De George, named Alexander, saw when she beat me, and a girl named Sophia, belonging to Sue Austerhem.

COMPLAINT OF THE SAMBO GIRL *BETSY,* BELONGING TO MR. J. F. OBERMULLER, BERBICE, 8 MAY 1819

Complaint of the sambo girl *Betsey,* belonging to Mr. J. F. Obermuller, inhabitant of this town:—Says, that she was washing a frock her mother had sent her a few Sundays ago; her mistress seeing her so occupied, took the said frock from her.[7] Complainant stated it was hard; she never gave her any clothes, and now that she was washing her frock she should take it away; her mistress went and complained to her husband that complainant had been insolent; her master flew in a passion, and kicked her on her belly so that she could scarcely draw her breath; the next morning, or morning

---

sambo: then a term for the offspring of one parent of full African ancestry and one "mulatto" parent of half-African, half-European ancestry.

[6]Often relationships between Black women who held various positions in the White household grew difficult. House slaves often identified with the power of their owners, and some exercised their control over slaves they regarded as having lower status.

[7]This complaint registers the fairly common struggle between White mistresses and Black slaves. The privileges of this mistress over the slave Betsey were embodied in these pieces of clothing, since White women possessed relatively few forms of power and control compared to men. This mistress may well also have harbored sexual jealousy toward Betsey, since many slave owners viewed their slave women as sexual property.

after, her mistress saw her with a jacket, and tore it off her, saying she did not wish her to wear a jacket, or appear dressed; she, the complainant, again stated the hardship she experienced in having her clothes torn off her, as she, her mistress, never gave her any; mistress again complained to master that complainant was impudent; master had her flogged with a rope; her brother Jacob flogged her; she gave her mistress no cause of complaint; she never will allow them to have any thing decent. She says, that for the least trifle she and her sister are locked up in the stocks, sometimes for three weeks, and fed with only two plantains a day; her mistress had her sister locked up for a fortnight, saying that she had made the bed improperly, thereby causing the child to fall; her sister denied it; she was locked up in the stocks.

Heard a complaint of the Negro Greenock, belonging to plantation Cotton-Tree, 19 May 1819

Heard a complaint of the negro *Greenock,* belonging to plantation Cotton-Tree: — States, that he was not well fed; that the plantains given them were remaining in their houses, and quite yellow; that the manager was constantly in the field. The appearance of the negro indicating that he must have been well fed, and the further complaint appearing that the manager performed his duty towards his employer and frivolous, he was directed to receive fifty lashes; which were inflicted in my presence in the market-place same day.[8]

Complaint of the negroes Brutus, Goodluck, and Ambrose, belonging to plantation Cotton-Tree, West Coast, Berbice, 22 May 1819

Complaint of the negroes *Brutus, Goodluck* and *Ambrose,* belonging to plantation Cotton-Tree, West Coast: — That they are not allowed time for breakfast; that they sleep in the field, work in said place till gun-fire, and then have to cut grass, and go to the field before cock-crow; that they are confined in the stocks, and not allowed to go out even for the common calls of nature; that they went to their master, Mr. Katz, to complain, and he flogged them; the plantains given them for allowance rot in their

---

[8] Public punishment was a common outcome of slave complaints.

houses, not having time to eat them. Inquired what work they do at eight o'clock at night; reply, Cut canes.

Mr. W. W. Kernon, the manager of the estate Cotton-Tree, being in attendance, denies the charges preferred:—Declares that the negroes are allowed from eleven o'clock till one every day to get their breakfast; that they are turned out between five and six o'clock, just at day-break, and turn in at dusk in the evening; after which they cut or bring the grass which they, according to the general customs of negroes, have cut at noon. That Cotton-Tree estate is in sugar; that whenever they cut canes the tops are brought home instead of grass: denies the charge of cutting canes till eight, as very improbable; first, from the dread of the negroes cutting themselves; secondly, from the fear of cutting a field of canes improperly. Says, that Goodluck and Ambrose having run away about three weeks ago, on being taken up they were confined in the stocks at night; and positive they never were confined in the day, as that would be a loss of labour, and no punishment to an idle negro. Brutus was placed watchman over them, and the three have been absent from the estate since Tuesday evening, to the best of my recollection. Refers himself to the overseers of the estate for proof of the above assertions, and to Mr. Katz, the proprietor, who frequently visits the estate, and would not sanction any oppression of his slaves.

The negroes being admitted, and inquired when they absented themselves from the estate, Brutus says they left the estate on the evening, and went to N° 2; took a small punt and came over at night. Goodluck prevaricates, saying that they took the small punt from N° 2, but the tide turning against them at breakfast-time, they got to the mouth of Carye, and remained there all day. They intended to go to the master; but being afraid, did not go: they slept in the punt all night, and came to the fiscal next morning; say yesterday, Friday morning.

The charge preferred by the negroes being contradicted by the manager, and the negroes prevaricating as to the time of quitting the estate, I directed the attendance of one of the overseers of Cotton-Tree; and he having attended about two o'clock on Saturday the 22d, he, to my inquiry, gave the following information, declaring himself ready to affirm the same by solemn oath:—*Thomas Kelley,* overseer on Cotton-Tree, declares, That the negroes are turned out between five and six o'clock, or a quarter past five; that the bell is regularly rung at eleven o'clock to turn in, and at one to turn out; that he has known some of the negroes work at breakfast-time, but by order of the driver; that the manager has in his presence reprimanded the driver for so doing, and on one occasion punished him; that he never knew the negroes work after dusk; that two of complainants were ordered to be locked up every night for three weeks, for running away twice; that neither of them ever was locked up during the day, to his knowledge, for this above crime; could not have been confined without his knowledge, he being field-overseer. That he read the list of negroes to throw grass on Tuesday evening past; that Brutus on that occasion not bringing grass, he inquired the cause of such neglect, and was informed he was employed confining Goodluck and Ambrosius in the stocks; that some time after, but on that very evening, the driver came and reported Brutus, Goodluck and Ambrosius had absconded, which he (the overseer) communicated to the manager.

Found complaint of the negroes unfounded; for which, and for absenting themselves from Tuesday evening to Friday morning, directed each seventy-five lashes; inflicted Monday morning, 24th.

Sir,   *May 24th.*

I have maturely investigated the complaint preferred by three of your negroes attached to plantation Cotton-Tree against their manager, Mr. Kernan; and having found their complaint without foundation, I have deemed it my duty to order the said three slaves to be exemplarily punished at the public market-place, which was done this morning in my presence.[9] I have endeavoured, and I hope succeeded in impressing on their minds, that as much as it is my duty to attend to any complaint of negroes, and to cause redress in all cases of oppression, so also it is my duty to inflict punishment on all slaves who prefer false and ungrounded complaints against their employers; and I have moreover pointed out the duty incumbent on a slave, in the event of a supposed grievance, to represent the same to the proprietor, their master, previous to the immediate application to my office.

I feel pleasure in stating, that I have every reason to believe that the punishment inflicted on them has been deserving. In returning them to plantation Cotton-Tree, I flatter myself it will be unnecessary for me to state that the manager is to receive them again in favour, resting satisfied that the punishment inflicted by me has been and is proportionate to the offence committed.

I have the honour to be, Sir, your most obedient and humble servant,

(*signed*)   *M. S. Bennett,*

Honourable W. Katz, Esq.   *Fiscal of the Colony.*

---

[9] Bennett, the fiscal of the colony, explains in a letter to H. Beard, the governor of the colony, that he "kept a book of minutes, but without recording my decisions on the same, unless in such cases as appeared necessary to be investigated before Commissaries, or the full Court of Criminal Justice."

COMPLAINT OF *A. J. GLASIUS*, PLANTATION RECUMZIGT, BERBICE, 2 JUNE 1819

Investigation of a Complaint preferred by *A. J. Glasius,* Esq. Proprietor of the above Estate, against part of the Gang for insubordinate Conduct on Whitsunday past, on the occasion of Clothing and Rations being delivered the Gang on the above day. This investigation held in presence of the honourable William Helder, member of the court of Criminal Justice.

Complaint of *A. J. Glasius:*—States, that knowing Sunday was the only day on which slaves are allowed to dance at the ensuing holidays, he intentionally omitted to have coffee picked, as great part of Saturday evening and Sunday morning would be taken up in washing and putting it away. He also directed the drivers to omit bringing home fuel on Sunday morning, but directed that some of the negroes should get grass, and as Monday was a holiday, but not a dancing day, fuel should be brought home then. The negroes all appeared satisfied: they each received a dram at the overseer's house, and four large flasks of rum to take to the negro-houses with them, as customary in holiday-time. The evening and great part of the night were spent by them in dancing. On the Sunday morning, about half-past six, I directed the overseer to give the negroes their rations, namely, a tierce of beef, fifty stockfish, half a cask of barley, each a hand of tobacco, two pipes, and salt: the drivers to have rations, and the men three ells of osnaburgs, the women five, and the house people six, and the children one and a half ells. Jackets, hats, &c. had been given last Easter. After the rations were laid out, the overseer called on me, and inquired whether I would be present myself; but breakfast being on the table I declined doing so, after ascertaining from him that every thing was laid out as had been directed by me. About half an hour after, the overseer with the drivers came up, and informed me that after eighteen or twenty negroes had received their allowance, and on its coming to the turn of negro August to receive his, he had taken up the osnaburgs, and, after examining it, had exclaimed, "Is this the osnaburgs we are to receive? I will not have it;" that his example had been followed by most of the others, and particularly by the negroes

---

dram: a small amount.

tierce: a third part.

ells: measurement of length varying from about 24 to 48 inches; the English ell is about 45 inches.

osnaburgs: a coarse, plain, strong fabric of linen or cotton.

Conraad and Virtus. I inquired again if the quantity I had directed had been cut off; and in order to satisfy myself the better, I sent for it, measured it, and found it full three ells; the same quantity I have ever given since I have resided on the property, a period of sixteen years. I ordered the drivers to go to August, and direct him to come to me; the drivers returned, saying he refused to do so. The overseer then went to the negro-houses, to direct August to come to me to account for his conduct, and explain the cause of his refusing the osnaburgs. The overseer, however, returned, saying, August, on his coming up, cried out, "Come, my lads, let us be off;" and he was immediately joined by five-and-twenty others, who proceeded on the estate towards the back. They took the beef, fish, barley, tobacco and pipes, and went off.

I inquired in the evening of the drivers if the negroes had returned, and was informed a few had. The next morning the drivers informed me that the rest also had returned during the night. As soon as the insubordinate part of the gang had quitted the negro-houses with a shout, I gave notice to the burgher captain of the same, and requested he would apprise the fiscal of it. The fiscal attended on the estate on the Monday morning, and having directed six to be confined in the stocks for examination, he cautioned the gang to return to duty and attend to the orders that should be given them; after which he quitted the estate and the six ringleaders remained in confinement.

Mr. Glasius produced the journal of the estate. It appeared osnaburgs and checks had been served to the gang May 1815.

Osnaburgs and checks December 1815, on account of getting no jackets.

December 1816, jackets and hats.

Ditto 1817, double allowance, 586 ells osnaburgs, and 427 ditto checks, in consequence of no jackets.

January 1819, jackets and hats.

May ———, osnaburgs, which great part of the gang objected to.
The osnaburgs refused by the gang was examined and found of an excellent quality, and a few pieces taken out of the heap were measured and found to contain three ells, five ells.

The negro *August* being admitted, states, that he is not the only one that refused to take the osnaburgs; that they received no clothing since Mr.

---

burgher: a Dutch term often understood to refer to those descended from unions between Europeans and local residents (creoles).

checks: fabrics woven in a check patterns.

Staal's time, about five years ago; that their master constantly tells them that when his ship comes he will give them checks and osnaburgs; that lately jackets and hats had been given them on account of the arrival of their young mistress, but no checks nor osnaburgs; and therefore seeing so small a quantity given last Sunday, he with some others got dissatisfied and refused to take it. Denies having been sent for by his master on Sunday; but confronted with the overseer B. Dorr, the latter declared that the drivers having been sent for to call August, and returning without him, he went and met them, inquired why he did not come; the drivers stated that August positively denied; he the overseer therefore went himself, and they were then just going away; he reported it to the proprietor.

The head driver *William* states, that he received orders from his master last Sunday to go and bring August. He went to the negro-house, and seeing August, acquainted him with his master's orders. August replied "I will not come, for he will lock me up in the stocks." Returning from the negro-houses he was met by the overseer and returned with him, August, whilst a number of others then went off. The driver was then questioned respecting the delivery of osnaburgs, checks, jackets and hats; states that osnaburgs, checks, jackets and hats had been yearly furnished them; sometimes jackets and hats, at others, osnaburgs and checks.

Negro *Conraad:*—Says, that he has no cause of complaint, but that his master has been for many years promising them jackets, blankets, osnaburgs and checks; that they have had no clothing for years, and therefore seeing the quantity of three ells put out for them last Sunday after so many years disappointment, he with others had refused to take the osnaburgs, but had taken the beef, stockfish, pipes and tobacco. States, since Messrs. Schwiel's administration they have had no clothing. We got three ells checks and three ells salemporis from Mr. Staal. It appears from information of Mr. Glasius, that the estate had been released from sequestration about two years ago. A piece of Dutch osnaburgs was produced by Mr. Glasius, and he inquired of Conraad whether this osnaburgs had not been given to the negroes since his administration: denies it.

Negro *Virtus:*—Says, he took his osnaburgs, but seeing his mattys refuse to take it, he threw it down also. His master has continually amused them with promise of clothing, now for five holidays, but has given them nothing; has had no clothing since Mr. Staal's time.

---

salemporis: a novelty cotton fabric with small checks made with fancy colors.

Negro *Adonis:*—Corroborates the evidence of the above negroes as to promise and time of not having received clothing. Being confronted with the driver William, admits he received checks the last year of Mr. Staal's administration, 1816; admits he received osnaburgs another time, 1817; also that he had received a jacket and hat previous to this. Admits he lately received a jacket and hat, and that three ells of osnaburgs were offered him last Sunday.

Negro *Moy:*—Corroborates the former evidence respecting the promise and length of time they had had no clothing: says, he did not represent to his master that the quantity of cloth was not enough, because the others did; had no clothing for five years; other negroes get every year. The driver having a shirt of checks on, which he says was given him by his master, witness was called upon to state whether he had received any; says he got three ells of checks, a cap of which he now has on: a remnant of Dutch osnaburgs produced, and inquired if he got any of that; he says, he got three ells of the same: a lined jacket was also produced, which he also acknowledged to have got one of, also a hat; admits lately to have received a Dutch jacket and hat, holiday before last.

Negro woman *Jenny:*—States, that she refused to take the five ells of osnaburgs because it was not sufficient for a coat; admits that her master gave her three ells a few weeks ago on account of her having a young infant; one and a half ells were laid out new for the child; got six ells checks and six ells osnaburgs three years ago, three new years. Confronted with the drivers, it appears this was issued in December 1817; admits she got a lined jacket with a hat in December 1816, and a jacket and hat last Easter; the five ells osnaburgs laid out Whitsunday, but refused.

After examination of the complaint preferred by the proprietor and the defence and evidence of the negroes accused, the honourable member and myself took into consideration that it did not appear from the month of May 1815 to the 1st January 1817, that the negroes had received the clothing customarily given on estates. This having been represented to Mr. Glasius, he replied, that he was not amenable for the acts or intermissions of sequesters of the estate appointed by the court; that his estate, Recumzigt, was released from sequestration in the month of June or July 1817; that he has on the estate,—43 men, 33 women, 15 boys, and 13 girls,—total 104: That he proves from his books that up to the present date he has delivered to his negroes, in December 1817, 586 ells osnaburgs, 427 ells checks, 88 jackets, and 370 ells of osnaburgs now to be issued, making together 1,383 ells of clothing, an average of 13 ells for negroes of every description for the space of 18 months, with one jacket and a hat. States, that if any proper representation had been made to him that his slaves required some little additional supply, it ought to have been duly represented; and if any grievance did exist and not redressed by him, they should have preferred it to the fiscal; but that insubordinate conduct of several of his slaves, and in particular that of the negro August and Conraad, were such during the late holidays as to create much uneasiness, and evince a spirit of disobedience which ought to be checked, to prevent a recurrence of such conduct; and therefore prays that an example should be made of the ringleaders. Mr. Glasius further proves, that 88 jackets and 88 hats were delivered to his negroes in December 1816 by the co-sequester, H. Staal.

Taking the above into consideration, and the negro August having during his examination evinced much disrespectful conduct, and it appearing from the evidence of the overseer that he was first to object and induce to refuse taking the clothing offered them, and that he also had positively refused to comply with the declarations of his master, delivered to him by the driver, and therefore guilty of insolent and unbecoming conduct; it was resolved, that the negro August should be exemplarily punished; and the negro Conraad, for disrespectful conduct in presence of the fiscal on Monday last, to receive a few lashes.

To His Honor H. Beard, President Courts Justice, Berbice, 3 June 1819

His Honor H. Beard, President Courts Justice.

Sir,   *Berbice, 3d June 1819.*

I beg leave to represent, for your Honor's information, that I received, on the 30th ultimo, a letter from Captain Favre, of the Burgher Militia, stating that Mr. Glasius, the proprietor of plantation Recumzigt, had requested of him, by letter on Whitsunday, the assistance of a militia guard, in consequence of the insubordinate conduct of twenty-six negroes attached to his estate. In consequence of this information, I attended on the 31st on plantation Recumzigt, and learned that the said slaves had refused to receive the quantity of osnaburgs allowed them by their said proprietor; and that he was fearful they intended to quit the estate for the bush,[10] and would probably endeavour to induce others to follow. Having confined six,

---

[10] An implicit reference to the maroons, or "bush Negroes." The greatest and most permanent success of rebel Africans was achieved in Guyana by runaway slaves—or maroons—from the earliest days of Dutch colonization in the area.

represented as of the most unruly of these negroes, I returned to town; and yesterday, with the honourable A. Helder, member of the court of Criminal Justice, I again attended on plantation Recumzigt.

We examined the negroes confined by me on the 31st May, and found that they were very much dissatisfied with the quantity of osnaburgs allowed them, say three ells for the men, five for the women, and one and a half for the children; and although the honourable member and myself were of opinion that the quantity allowed them was not sufficient, we are nevertheless satisfied that the conduct of the slaves examined, and in particular that of the negro August, was highly reprehensible, and had evinced a spirit of insubordination by taking the osnaburgs served out to him, throwing it in the trench, prohibiting the other slaves from taking their allowance, and positively refusing to comply with his master's directions to attend and account for his reprehensible conduct. We deemed it necessary, for this unbecoming manner, to direct him to be punished in presence of the gang, as an example. The other negroes examined appearing sensible of their improper conduct, were dismissed, after being reprimanded for their past behaviour; and informed, that in the event of any grievance existing, it was the duty of the slave to represent and seek redress from his master, and if not succeeding, then to look for such redress from higher authority. The whole gang appeared satisfied with this argument; and the negro August, after punishment, acknowledged the impropriety of his conduct, and begged his master's forgiveness.

I have the honour to be, Sir,

Your Honor's obliged and humble servant.

Beerenstein Complaint. — *Rosetta* v. *Zealand*, Berbice, 4 June 1819

Berbice, 4th June 1819.

Examination of the negro woman *Rosetta*,[11] belonging to plantation Beerenstein: — The complainant says she has nothing to say against the manager nor her owner, but that the driver Zealand is the person which made her go to town; that he is continually licking and cursing her, and even cut her with a cutlass once in the arm, which mark is very visible, and once knocked her with a cutlass in her teeth, that Zealand is the ruler of the estate, so that the manager has less to say than he; that Zealand has a wash-

---

licking: beating.

[11] Rosetta is also called Susetta.

erwoman, and the use of the milk of the cows, (even tell to throw the same away), and that the manager has not the least authority to hinder him in his proceedings, he being allowed the use of every thing; that in consequence of some licks lately received from Zealand she left the estate, she hid herself a few days in the bush, went to the colony hospital and miscarried there; the sick nurse Elias,[12] with Mooalla, Mandrienna and Betze, being witnesses to this occurrence; which miscarriage she attributes to the several misbehaviours of Zealand against her.

Rosetta objects to the witnesses brought in by Zealand, as the one is his boy, and the other his assistant driver; says the remainder of the gang will substantiate her declaration.

Berbice, June 4th, 1819.

Examination of the negro *Zealand,* belonging to plantation Beerenstein: — Says Saturday week they were employed in loading plantains in the punts; that he, as driver of the estate, directed the good bunches to be taken out for sale, and the bad ones to be brought home for plantation use; that on this occasion he told Rosetta to take a bad bunch which she put in the punt, out of the same; that the woman turned her head to him; upon which he, observing her to look very red in the eyes, asked her why she looked so; to which she gave him a very cross and disgusting answer; which vexing him, he went up to her with a thin piece of bush-rope, telling her not to be insolent, and licking her at the same time with this said instrument of correction on her mouth, stating, that as her mouth was so bad the same only deserved to be punished. Upon which Finch, sitting there at that time, directed him to put her in the stocks; upon which she pushed at Finch, who, standing, threw, by the consequence of her pushing, a negro in the trench. Afterwards he laid hold of her and put her in the stocks, but requested from Finch to release her again, to which he consented; and after which she made her way to town.

June 4th, 1819.

Examination of *Jack,* also of Beerenstein, a witness in the case of driver Zealand: — Says, that he saw Zealand strike Rosetta with the bush-rope on her mouth, so that it made the blood come out, and swelled the lips. Says further, he never saw Zealand strike Rosetta with a cutlass. Lastly, states that he never saw Zealand lick Rosetta but only on the occasion of loading plantains Saturday week.

---

[12] A Black doctor at the hospital.

Examination of *Primo*, also from Beerenstein, and witness *for* Zealand, driver of said estate:—Says, that he saw Zealand strike Rosetta with a carracarra on her mouth till the blood came out of the same; says, never to have seen that the driver ill-used the woman with a cutlass; and further states, that on the occasion of loading plantains on Saturday, it was the first time he ever saw Zealand to strike Rosetta.—Direct attendance of manager, Dr. Beresford, and other witnesses called by her.

John Beresford, medical practitioner, and attendant of the hospital belonging to the Winkle department, being questioned whether it was to his knowledge that the woman Susetta had miscarried in the hospital during her late confinement, states, that he was requested by Mr. Scott to examine the said woman, who had complained that she had miscarried in consequence of the ill-treatment experienced from Zealand; that he, the medical practitioner, had examined the said woman Susetta very minutely, and could not discover any appearance of miscarriage which she stated had occurred a few days before; and finding nothing the matter with her, he reported her fit for work.

Examination *Elias*, cause Rosetta, alias Susetta; witness doctor of hospital:—Says, that Rosetta has been in the hospital four or five weeks ago; she came from the estate to complain no physic was given her; she was put in the stocks by Mr. Scott's order; she was examined by the doctor, but he ordered no physic; she one morning showed me a pot half full of blood and water; she said she had miscarried; the appearance was of a thick substance; I directed her to put it up carefully till the doctor came; she put it under the hospital; it was destroyed by the pigs; doctor never saw it; I never told him, because it was made away with by the pigs, and she did not because she was in the stocks; she had been about a week in the stocks when this occurrence took place; I never knew she was pregnant.

Mandorina, witness cause Rosetta:—Says she was in the hospital at the time Susetta was there; saw a pewter pot, which had blood in it; Susetta said she had passed it; I did not examine it; Susetta did not say in my hearing she had miscarried; being sick, I paid little attention; the doctor came there every morning; it was never told to him.

Mocalla, witness cause Rosetta, or Susetta:—Says, Susetta, or Rosetta, was confined in the stocks whilst I was sick in the hospital; I understood

---

carracarra: an instrument used in flogging slaves, apparently made of bamboo.

one day that she had miscarried; I saw a pot which she showed to Elias, the hospital black doctor; I did not examine it being sick; the doctor did not attend this day; I heard Rosetta say she had miscarried; I saw her clothes; there was blood on them, and I believe she did miscarry; neither this, nor former witness, knows how long Rosetta had been confined when this occurrence took place.

W. Scott, agent, having heard the above evidence, states that the woman Rosetta, alias Susetta, came to him to complain against the manager; that she reported she had absconded in consequence of ill-treatment received from Zealand, and had miscarried during the short stay he made in the bush, for which reason he, agent, requested Dr. Beresford to attend her; states further, that she has a complaint of the bladder. —Reprimanded.

COMPLAINT *JONAS* VERSUS *GRADE,* MANAGER, PLANTATION L'ESPÉRANCE, 10 JUNE 1819

Complaint *Jonas* versus *Grade,* manager: —States, that two women, named Diana and Cornelia, were in the hospital, having small sores in their feet; complainant is sick-nurse, and occasionally employed as house-servant; the said women were directed by the manager to go to the negro-houses to split leaves; the overseer, seeing one of them he conceived able to go to the field, sent her there; manager saw her in the field with a piece of rag round her foot, and observed, as the coffee crop was coming in he was wishful of no sores being on the estate; directed me to confine them in the sick-house till well; I told them of this, and they absented themselves.

There was also a woman named Roosje;[13] she was employed in the Logie picking coffee; she was big with child; wanted one month of her time;[14] the manager sent the overseer to see her; she with the others were coming on; the overseer informed him that they were not picking enough or well; and the manager, standing at his window up stairs, directed the driver Zindeg to flog them; the driver did this with his whip doubled;[15] whether they were flogged so by the manager's order I do not know, but he saw it; the woman Rosa was flogged either on Friday or Saturday, I am not certain; Sunday she complained of pain in her belly and back, and Sunday night I think she

---

[13] Roosje is also called Rosa.

[14] Although this suggests that she is eight months pregnant, the other complainants corroborate that she is five months pregnant.

[15] A common form of punishment and torture in the Caribbean, a doubled whip could deliver a more severe lashing.

miscarried; the doctor of the estate came to visit and attend her next day, and directed physic; she remained some weeks in her house.

In consequence of my not bringing the two women above stated, the manager directed I should be locked up in the stocks every night; he went to town, and the overseer put me watchman at the water-side; the manager came home the evening I was placed there, and inquired who was watchman; I answered it was I, Jonas; he inquired who put me watchman; I informed him it was the overseer; he directed me to call the overseer; on the overseer's coming, he said, "Did I not direct that Jonas should be locked up in the stocks every night? take him, and do so now." On hearing this order, I availed myself of the darkness of the evening and started off, and went to town to seek redress, not knowing what I had done to deserve this punishment.

Evidence of the woman *Rosa:*—States, that she was sent by the manager's order to pick coffee in the Logie. The complainant represented to the manager that she was too big to stoop. The manager directed her to comply with the order; she went to pick coffee on her knees. At eleven o'clock their work was examined, and the driver Zondag directed to flog them by the manager; this was done with the whip doubled. When Zondag the driver came to her, he said to the manager, this woman is rather big with child; the manager replied, "Give it to her till the blood flies out." I was flogged; the whip broke, and I was flogged with carracarras, this happened on a Friday; I was sent to the field on Saturday. I told the driver I could not work, as I had pains in my loins; he directed me to go to the manager. I went to him: he sent me to the hospital; I remained there a day. The doctor examined me, and said there was nothing the matter with me, and sitting down was not good for me. I went to the field, and was put on a row with another to help. On Sunday evening I miscarried; I was five months gone with child; the labour was hard. The midwife had to force it; the child was dead; one eye was out, the arm broken, and a stripe visible over the head, which must have been done with the double whip. The doctor came to attend me on Monday morning; the child was not seen by him, it had been buried. He prescribed for me. The child was seen by Ariaantje, Claritje and Marianna. I was assisted by my sister Claritje; the regular midwife did not attend me, as I was taken suddenly. She was sent for however, and saw the child; it was buried by Marianna.

Evidence of *J. H. Eenhuys,* assistant surgeon to Dr. Westervild, practitioner of and medical attendant on plantation L'Espérance:—States, that he visited the woman Rosa early in the morning on the 14th March; she informed him she had miscarried that evening before I examined and prescribed for her. A few days previous to this occurrence I saw Rosa in the sick-house; she was pregnant and complaining; I thought between three and four months gone. I experience that many miscarriages arise from the women taking no exercise and contracting lazy habits;[16] and thinking this was her case, I directed her to take exercise. I did not see the child, it was buried. I believe I inquired if she had been delivered of the after-birth, and being informed by an old woman, the midwife, I directed something for her and went away.

Evidence of the negro woman *Marianna:*—States, I was sent for in the night to come to Rosa, who was taken in labour, (trouble had come,) I went; she was not yet delivered. I assisted another woman to deliver her. The child's arm was broken; one eye out bruised and sunk in the head; it was a fine male child, quite formed; in every respect perfect.[17] Thinks the child was more than five months from its perfect form and appearance. Claritje and George reported it to the manager that Roosje had miscarried, and as he gave no directions respecting it I buried it. The child was seen by the father and the two other women, Claritje and Ariantje. The woman Roosje told the doctor the state the child was in. He replied, "I suppose you have been eating green pines."[18] Roosje denied it, saying it was from the flogging she got.

Evidence of *Ariaantje:*—States that Roosje is her sister, witness was called in the night by Claritje to come to Roosje, who was in labour. I went, and found her in said state; I got there before Marianna was present. When the child fell, the child was a male, perfect; the arm broken, the eye out, the head broken and bruised. After the miscarriage I went away. Being asked why it was not mentioned to the manager, the doctor, or the burgher officer, she says it was not her business.

Evidence of *George:*—States he is husband to Roosje; corroborates her evidence as to the flogging she received, and the expressions made use of by the manager to the driver about flogging her. This happened on a Thursday; Sunday night she miscarried. The child was a male, perfect; it was born dead; the arm was broken, one of the eyes out, and the head

---

[16] Plantation owners, doctors, and overseers suspected that slave women regularly gave themselves abortions or induced miscarriages, and the suspected methods used by slave women were thus a constant focus of medical investigation.

[17] Marianna is emphasizing the value of the child to the plantation work force.

[18] One suspected method of inducing miscarriage.

bruised. States this to have been occasioned from the blows his wife received from the driver Zindeg with the doubled whip. Reported this miscarriage to Mr. Grade, the manager, who told him to bring it. Did not mention to him the state it was in. Roosje did give this information to the doctor, the little one; he replied, "You must tell a lie: you have been eating green pines I believe." Inquired why he had not gone to complain either to the burgher officer or fiscal; says he was cook; and therefore could not leave his work.

Evidence of the driver *Zondag:*—States, that the women were put to pick coffee; a certain quantity was to be got, which did not take place. The overseer told me by order of the manager, Mr. Grade, to range the women out on the drogery planker: I did so. The manager came out, and told me to begin and flog them, from one to the other; I began and went on till I came to the woman Roosje. I observed to the manager, "This woman is pregnant:" the manager said, "Go; that is my business." I did so; she did not get more than the rest. I did not flog Roosje with a carracarra; it had broken before I came to her: she received her punishment with the whip doubled; she miscarried a few nights after this punishment took place. The punishment was inflicted at eleven o'clock, breakfast time. I did not see the child. Claritje told me the state the child was in. The question being put to him, "*Whether the manager, on his (the driver's) representation that Roosje was pregnant, had made use of the expression, "Never mind; flog her till the blood comes?"* He replied, "Yes."

Evidence of the negro woman *Claritje:*—States that she is elder sister or shipmate of Roosje; that she was sent for at night to Roosje, who was taken in labour. The child was born dead; it was a male, perfect. Marianna was there; Ariaantje also. The arm was broken, one eye was bruised and hurt; it could be seen it was done with the whip; and the head broken. The father reported the death of it. Manager said to bury it: the father dug the grave. Marianna took it out. Reason she did not tell the manager of the state the child was in was because she thought Marianna would have done it. George mentioned it to Mr. Grade: does not know what he said.

George again called in, and inquired whether he had mentioned to Mr. Grade the state the child was in; said, he told Mr. Grade the arm was broken, and that it was in consequence of the flogging she got. Mr. Grade said, "It is a lie." Says the overseer was present; the manager asked him how

---

drogery planker: the plank flooring of a West Indian trading vessel.

it was his wife had miscarried: he replied, it was from the flogging you gave her. Manager says, "You lie; I did not flog her." The overseer said, "I did not either." I then observed, "If neither of you did, who did then?" Says his wife has had seven children for him, and never miscarried before.

Examination of *Justus Von Steiniss,* overseer of plantation L'Espérance: — I was present when the women were ranged out on the drogery; they were flogged by Zondag. Mr. Grade said, if they did not pick coffee enough, he the (driver) should be confined in the stocks. I saw him punish some of the women. Mr. Grade was not present. I did not hear Zondag say any thing to Mr. Grade respecting this child having a broken arm. Never said any thing to him himself.

On inquiry, the manager states that Jonas absented himself from the estate on the 30th of April last.

W. ROSS, ATTORNEY, PLANTATION DEMTICHEM, COMPLAINANT, AGAINST THE NEGRO HANS, BELONGING TO BEERENSTEIN, ON CHARGE OF OBIAH,[19] PLANTATION DEMTICHEM, 17 JUNE 1819

Gabriel, a girl about nine or ten years of age, daughter of Isaac and Nancy:—States, that she was employed in her father's house on Monday night boiling plantains, by direction of her mother; that whilst so occupied, La Rose and Amsterdam came to her, and took her to January's house, where she saw a strange negro, who she knew was named Hans, having seen him formerly at Buses Lust; he told me not to cry; if I did, he would flog me; he then took a piece of salemporis, and put it over my head; he told me that if I saw any thing, I should die; he directed Lindsay Harry to take me on his shoulders; Hans, Amsterdam and La Rose went to Frederick's; we were joined by my father; they called Frederick's wife to open the

---

[19] Also known as "obeah" and "obi," obiah is an Afro-Caribbean religious system akin to voodoo, then found throughout the British West Indies. It involved ritual practices and was often associated with the manufacture of charms and poisons and was sometimes implicated in slave revolts. While some Whites dismissed obeah as superstitious nonsense, most considered it a dangerous slave practice, one that could cause fatal epidemics on plantations and otherwise affect control over the slave population. Many islands established laws against its practice, often holding obeah trials. And in 1788–1789, a special Privy Council was established in Britain to investigate the practice (see Richardson 1993).

door; Frederick was in the stocks; the door was opened by Pompadore, Frederick's wife; we went in, my eyes still blindfolded; the piece of salemporis went over my head; I held the pot in my hands, being on the back of Lindsay Harry, the salemporis descending over the pot. She was taken off Lindsay Harry's shoulders, and sat down on a small bench; Hans went and lay down on Pompadore's bed; he lay on the bed till the people had done grinding coffee; all the people came to Frederick's house; Hans then got up, took the pot from me, and gave it to my father; Pompadore did not see that I had the pot in my hands; it was so covered with the salemporis she could not see it; nobody spoke to me; the pot, when I received it, had nothing but a little water in it.

The overseer, *Boaz,* states: — That the negroes being employed grinding coffee, he had missed the two carpenters, La Rose and Amsterdam, who were working at the Friends that day, but still one employed to grind coffee. The driver said, "Perhaps they are not yet come from the Friends," with which answer I was at that moment satisfied. I make particular inquiry for the carpenters at work at the Friends.

W. *Ross,* attorney of plantation Demtichem: — States, that on Sunday forenoon the negro Frederick, the head carpenter, and a man of good character, came crying to the overseer, Mr. Boaz, to complain that the negroes were breaking open his house, and digging up the ground, accusing him of being a poisoner, and consequently that poison must be secreted in the house;[20] the overseer immediately proceeded to the negro yard, and brought the drivers January, La Fleur, Benjamin and Frederick up to the door; the driver January commenced justifying himself by stating, that several sudden deaths had lately taken place on the estate, and that he, with others, had sent for the negro Hans, who was a good negro, and with whom he was acquainted, to find out the cause of these sudden deaths; immediately on hearing that it was with the knowledge of the drivers that this man had been sent for, I declined further investigation, directed them to be locked up in the stocks, and reported the circumstance to the burgher officer and the Fiscal. It appeared that the minds of the negroes must have

---

[20] Slaves poisoning masters and their children or other slaves, was a central fear throughout the colonies, as well as in the literature written about slavery during this period. The 1788 Privy Council documents state: "the Skill of some Negroes in the Art of Poisoning has been noticed ever since the Colonists became acquainted with them. . . . The secret and insidious Manner in which this Crime is generally perpetrated, makes the legal Proof of it extremely difficult. Suspicions therefore have been frequent, but Detections rare" (Lambert 1995, 215–221).

been greatly agitated, they having thrown themselves on the ground, biting the grass, tearing the earth with their hands, and conducting themselves like maniacs. I had this information from Mr. Boaz, the overseer; did not witness it myself, being confined to my room from indisposition. On Tuesday I had information from the girl Gabriel that the negro Hans was in the negro house; I went there with the overseers, but could not find him; yesterday morning the same little girl pointed out to the overseer, saying, "The man that gave me the pot is now passing;" the overseer came and reported it to me; I directed him immediately to follow him with some of the negroes; William, the stable boy, went; the overseer succeeded in bringing him to me. States, that the minds of the people were in such a state of ecstasy, and conducted themselves as possessed to that degree as to attract the attention of three gentlemen passing, who came in and inquired the cause of this uncommon agitation, just as Frederick was reporting the circumstance to the overseer.

Evidence of *S. Boaz,* overseer of plantation Demtichem:—States, that yesterday, having received orders from Mr. Ross to take the negro Hans from the public road, he pursued him with the stable boy, William; who, on coming near to Hans, and being desired to seize him, had declared he was afraid to do so. In consequence of this information I went and took hold of the man, who made an attempt to get away; but not being able to run as fast as I, I seized and brought him to the attorney. I received orders to take him to town, with numerous articles found on his person; I did so, and took him to the Fiscal, who directed one of the dienaaren of justice to take him to gaol. When Hans was brought to the door he had on a shirt and trowsers. Mr. Ross directed one of the carpenters and head cooper to undress him; they hesitated, till peremptorily directed to do so by Mr. Ross. The articles were found secreted in his dress, and he had in a handkerchief *s. 50* in money. All the articles, money, &c. were given over at the gaol.

Evidence of *Frederick,* head carpenter:—That on Saturday night he was wakened by the head driver January, who told him to come to his house. On arriving there he found all the men, women and children before January's house. January said, that so many deaths had occurred that he had sent for a man to put every thing to rights; this man was Hans. January then took a ram's horn from above his door and poured a little rum in it,[21] and

---

dienaaren: a Dutch term, here connoting officer of justice.
gaol: jail.
[21] The ram's horn was a common symbol for obeah practitioners.

drank it, saying "that he wished to have the bad people off the estate, and every body must listen well." Hans sang his country song; January drank a second time out of the horn, (witness never saw the horn before,) a bottle of rum was on a table and also a wine glass. Hans pushed the latter off the table and broke it: January got vexed, saying, "this is the second glass you have broken." I said, "never mind, don't get vexed, as you sent for the man; if you want a glass I'll give you one." I sent for one; January directed a dram to be given to the officers. Hans, after singing some time, said he wanted a young girl; he had placed a white feather in the head of all the children. He took a girl named Eve, and lay down on the ground, the girl next to him. She was, however, much alarmed and cried. He then took the girl Gabriel, and she also lay on the ground with Hans. He then got up and said, "these children should point out the persons who administered poison on the estate." He began to sing a country song, and every one must join in chorus.[22] He told January that as he had come to set things right on the estate, every body, big and little, must contribute a bit. The gun fired and I went away.

After grass and fuel had been thrown, the people assembled again at the house of January. Hans told me the driver had engaged to collect this money, but as you are the head man of the estate, I have more confidence in you. You must collect this money, and as soon as I receive it you will see what I shall do for all of you. I said it could do; but why was January not the fittest person, he being the driver and the person who had sent for him. Hans replied he had more confidence in me. The negroes then began to contribute; Hans and January went to another house, leaving me to collect. I received the money; also La Fleur and Benjamin. A sufficient sum having been collected about eleven o'clock, Hans and January joined us. I delivered the money to January; the paper money separate from the silver. He said, "Hans, here is your money." A handkerchief was also contributed; Hantz laid the money in the handkerchief; they went in the open air: Hantz had a tub of water brought, a bundle of wild canes, and also grass; he put the grass in the water and sprinkled their faces; every body was directed to dance, and Hans joined. The negroes became as if crazy; some threw themselves in the mud — others jumped; they that were the most turbulent were flogged with the wild canes by Lindsay Harry, by order of Hans, and recovered; others more furious and not recovering from the stripes of Lindsay Harry, Hans struck with a bamboo, and they immediately recovered.[23]

---

[22] This may refer to one of the many folk songs that were harmless on the surface but implicitly held a message of rebellion.

[23] The obeah ceremony often included rituals that imitated White slave practices, such as flogging, in an effort to undermine them. Notice how the slaves quickly recover from the flogging administered in the obeah ceremony.

He asked me if I was afraid; I said no, but I did not like this sport. He took me round the ring formed twice. He went in the house and drank twice; a circle was again formed. Venus was quite as a crazy person and could not recover the effects, for which she had been struck with the cane and bamboo, but not so as to cure her effectually. She danced in the circle, and coming up to me said, I was the bad man on the estate. I said to Bernard, because we are the eldest on the estate, and that such things were never practised by us, that they want to remove me. He said, "be silent; let us see what is to come." Venus ran out of the circle and said "come, and I show you where the poison is hid." Hans sat on the ground leaning against a table. January went to raise him; he said "stop, stop, let me rest, my eyes are turned." I asked Venus "why do you say I am the bad man, and how do you know it?" She replied, "I see it from the water that has been sprinkled over my face and eyes." They then all followed Venus, shouting and making a noise; they went to my house, threw down two casks of water, broke down my kitchen and fowl-house, and dug up the earth with shovels. Venus said, "it is not here, it must be in the house." I opened the door, they went in. I said, "stop, let some go in; I will give you room." I put my box, hat, &c, on one side, and said, "take care, the poison you look for must be found openly and not by pretence." Benjamin ripped up some of the boards; they dug, but found nothing. Venus said "my eyes are not well washed; I did not accuse the head carpenter, but London." I said, "No, you accused me, and brought the people here; this is not London's house, but mine." Venus then said, "let me go to Hans (who had remained at London's house) to get my eyes properly washed." I said "no; I have been accused, and must insist, as my house has been broken, that this business shall be found out, or I know what to do." Venus then went to Hans and was followed by the gang, and I went and reported this occurrence to the overseer. Says, that Hans, in selecting the child, said it must be the girl who had lost her mother, and Eve was brought to him, but she being so very much alarmed, he said he must have another; if no other child was to be found who had lost its mother, a twin child would do as well. Gabriel was therefore brought to him. When I went to complain, Hantz was removed by some of the negroes to another house.

Evidence of the negro woman *Venus:*—Says that the driver January directed that nobody was to quit the estate; every body must come to his house. I went there, and saw Hantz. January said, every body must bring money and give it to uncle Frederick: every body gave money; I gave two bits (having a child). Hantz said, he would pull off all the poison that was in the ground, which made the people on the estate die so suddenly. A tub of water was brought by Linsey Harry; a handful of grass was put in the water by Hantz, and he stirred up the water: some wild canes also were brought by Harry. Hans sent him. Every person stooped down, and Hans washed their head. They danced first: Hans sang the dance called Water mamma dans. My head began to turn, as if I were mad; don't know how occasioned this: the first dance she ever saw, whose heads turned in such a manner that they fell to the ground. Were flogged with the wild cane first; if not recovered he flogged them with a carracarra, and put guinea pepper in their eyes which he chewed. All this was done to me, but I could not recover. Had not, nor ever does drink rum. I could see and hear every thing, but was exactly as if I were crazy: I recovered a little after this last. Is not aware that she accused Frederick as the bad man. Hans said he would make a little child find where the pot of obiah was hid: did not see the pot. Does not know she took the people to Frederick's house; if I did I am not aware of it. I know I was there, but I am not aware what I did. I was in hysterics; constantly laughing, although nothing was said to make me laugh.[24] Afterwards I went from Frederick's house to January's, where Hans had remained: I went there by myself; he was putting his money in a little pack-all: I stood at the door, he said that something must go out of my head. He chewed some wild cane and put it in my mouth, and I recovered. I returned to Frederick's house. Do not know of any conversation passing between Frederick and myself. I went again to January's house, and found Hans lying on the floor, apparently in a fit; he was shaking and trembling very much. January told Hans he saw the overseer coming. Hans got up; some one held his hand, and he went into the chamber.

Evidence of *Pompadore:*—Says that Isaac came to her on Monday night, and told her to open Frederick's house. She inquired why? He said "Never fear." He came in with Hans, La Rose, and Amsterdam. They lighted a lamp. Linsey Harry had the child Gabriel on his shoulders; a piece of salemporis descending from her head, and covering a pot she held in her hand. Nothing in the pot but water, that I saw. The lamp was lighted, and Hans showed every one present nothing was in the pot but a little water. Hans made Isaac and Amsterdam dig a hole, and he made the child sit on a bench next to the hole, the salemporis hanging over. Hans went and lay on her bed, the hole was near to it: when he got up, he ordered Amsterdam to take the child up, the salemporis still hanging over her head and shoulders, and carry her to the hole. Hans took the salemporis off

---

[24] Venus's "hysterics" suggest the state of obeah "possession," a part of the ritual in which the subject is filled with a god, her whole body shakes with convulsions, and the spirit speaks through her lips. This ritual also mimics and mocks the "possession" of White owners.

the child's head, and then the pot appeared to contain a ram's horn, some fluid, and the bones of some animal. The child fell to the ground immediately as the pot was taken out of her hands; and Hantz said, "See the child is dead." After the child had lain a little it recovered.[25] Did not see any thing administered.

When Hantz lay on the bed, and the child sitting near the hole, all the people were present. Hantz said, the horn, &c. came out of the hole; nobody saw these things come out of the hole.

COMPLAINT OF NEGRO *BRUTUS,* BELONGING TO PLANTATION PROVIDENCE, AGAINST MANAGER, 26 JUNE 1819

Complaint of negro *Brutus,* belonging to plantation Providence, against manager:—Says, that he is watchman of the plantain-walk. Manager told him he was to take two negroes with yaws,[26] and a little boy also with that disease, in his house; complainant objected in consequence of never having had yaws; slept some nights in the open air, then built himself a small hut on the plantain-walk, and covered it with dry leaves. Manager observed it, and said, "Come here, I'll show you where to make a house on the road." He put up a stick to show me where the spot should be. He told me to make the yaws negroes dig a drain near the spot; the negroes said they could not work in consequence of being so completely filled with that malady. I told this to manager; he said, "Lick them." I said if I flogged them with my whip and held it, I shall get yaws too; I am afraid of it. The manager wanted my daughter Peggy; I said "No." He followed her; I said "No." He asked me three times; I said "No." He took Rule's wife, and, after having her a few nights, left her; therefore I refused. Manager asked me Friday night; I refused. Saturday morning he flogged me; it was not for my work. This thing it hurt me, and I come to complain.—Direct attendance of Peggy.

Peggy being sick, *Aqueshaba* her sister attended:—Says, that manager sent aunty Grace to call Peggy, and to say if she would not come I must. We said, daddy said must not go; I was too young. Grace left us and went to daddy; shortly afterwards she returned and tried to coax me to go, but I would not as my daddy had forbid it. Grace went and told manager;

---

[25] Another aspect of the obeah ceremony concerned the practice of raising the dead, thought to be a symbolic act of delivering a given person from the social death of slavery.

[26] A contagious disease found in tropical climates and widespread among the slave populations in the West Indies, characterized by tubercles on the skin.

manager sent to call Fanny; Fanny went. The manager was up in his room; and all of us, the creoles, got orders to be watchmen at manager's door. I was watchman, Peggy, Jenny, Frankey, and many more.

EXAMINATION OF A COMPLAINT PREFERRED BY THE NEGRESS *PRINCESS* AGAINST *ROBERT SEMPLE,* HER OWNER, BERBICE, 11 JUNE 1822

Princess states:—That this morning soon, she saw a woman of the name of Cuba sitting down asleep; she said to her, "What was you doing last night that you did not sleep?" At the same time Mr. Semple came out of his bed-room, and asked me what I said; I told him, "I don't speak with you, I speak with Cuba." Then my master said, "You always have something to say; better you shut your mouth." I answered him again, "Master, I don't speak with you, I speak with Cuba;" and then I came down stairs, and went into the kitchen. Master followed me into the kitchen, and told me I had better go to my work than meddle my tongue; I answered him, "I am doing my work, and you come to trouble me; I was not speaking to you." Then he went to the store and took a horse-whip, and began to flog me. I asked him for what he flogged me? he said, "For badness." I told him, "So long as you flog me for nothing, I shall go to the Fiscal," and I came away.

Sir,   *New Amsterdam, Berbice, 12th June 1822.*

With regard to the complaint preferred against me by the negro woman Princess, I have merely to say, that I charged her of insolence; of which she was guilty, as is apparent by her own statement. To which I have only to add, that it was not when she asked Cuba if she was sick that I spoke to her, but subsequently, on her making some observations respecting my coming out of my bed-room; that when I finished dressing and went down stairs, I found her in the kitchen haranguing her mother, who pushed her out of the kitchen, and desired her to hold her tongue; for doing which she participated in her abuse. I then repeatedly warned her, that unless she was silent and went to her work, I would bring a horse-whip to her; this had no other effect than to make her louder, and to induce her to tell me to bring the horse-whip, which she did, I assure you, several times before I complied with her request; this being the first time, during more than four years that I have owned her, that I have had recourse to such measures.

I have the honour to be, Sir, your most obedient servant,

(signed)   *Robt. Semple.*

To his Honor the Fiscal.

The woman Princess was reprimanded for making this unnecessary complaint; and informed, that if her master complained of her conduct again, she would be punished,

EXAMINATION OF A COMPLAINT PREFERRED BY THE NEGRO *FELIX*, BELONGING TO PLANTATION SCOTLAND, AGAINST THE MANAGER OF SAID ESTATE, BERBICE, 23 AUGUST 1822

Felix states, That he has had a black woman upon the estate for his wife now two years; and the reason of his coming to complain is, that the manager of the estate takes her from him, although he has a wife of his own. He is always taking the negroes wives, particularly his wife (Felix's); for she has had a child for him; and since the child has been born, the manager is always punishing him and his wife without a cause. Some time ago ten of the gang came to complain to their master, (Dr. Broer), to report to him that the manager had connexion with their wives: their master promised to them that he would remove the manager from the estate, and place another one there. Upon this promise the negroes returned to the estate; but since that they have never heard of another manager. Felix and his wife are daily punished, which has compelled him to come to your Honor for redress. He calls upon the whole gang of the estate to prove his assertions to be correct.

On hearing this complaint, the Acting Fiscal proceeded to the estate, accompanied by Dr. Broer, the owner; and on questioning the manager and negroes, in presence of each other, on the subject-matter of the complaint, it appeared that Felix had neglected his work, and was told he would be punished if he did not finish his task the next day, which he did not do; and therefore supposing the manager would punish him, he went to the Fiscal to complain. This being proved, Felix was punished for his misconduct, and the manager severely reprimanded for taking improper liberties with the women on the estate, which it was evident he had done; and Dr. Broer was therefore strongly recommended to discharge him from his employ.

Part Four

RECENT CRITICISM

The Rootless Cosmopolitanism
of the Black Atlantic

Paul Gilroy

Let us imagine that the study of African diaspora identity in the modern, Western world begins with an understanding of the lives of exemplary eighteenth-century figures of whom Olaudah Equiano, Ignatius Sancho, and Phillis Wheatley are the best known.[1] Equiano was a seafarer and a political activist in pursuit of the abolition of slavery who has left us his autobiography, which occupies a primary place in the literary enterprises of this group. He was born in what we would now call Nigeria in the middle of the eighteenth century, then kidnapped as a child and shipped across the Atlantic as a slave. Equiano passed between several masters in different parts of the Americas. His passage from chattel to free man and the processes of self-making that it entailed are communicated in the most obvious way by the proliferation of names under which he was known during different stages of his life—first Michael, then Jacob, and eventually Gustavus Vassa, an appellation borrowed from a celebrated Swedish patriot.

Wheatley, a distinguished poet, celebrity, and eloquent eyewitness to the political upheavals of the American revolutionary war against the British, was Equiano's contemporary. She had been taken from Senegambia as a girl, arrived in Boston in 1761 swathed in a piece of dirty carpet, and was named after the slaver in which she had made her ocean crossing. The absence of her front teeth made observers guess her to be about seven years of age. She was bought by Susannah and John Wheatley for Susannah's use

[1] James Walvin, *An African's Life: The Life and Times of Olaudah Equiano, 1745–1797* (Cassell, 1999); Ola Larsmo, *Maroonberget* (Bonniers, 1996).

in their home. Having noted Phillis's exceptional predisposition to learn, her owners segregated her from other slaves, appointed their eighteen-year-old daughter as the girl's first tutor, and then decided to have her educated more systematically. She repaid their investments in her mental capacity with a torrent of extraordinary poetry that reflects upon her personal transformation from African to American as well as upon the morality of the wider system that had fostered it. Wheatley was the first black person to publish a book. Her 1773 volume *Poems on Various Subjects, Religious and Moral* was published in London by a printer who had been skeptical of the *bona fides* of its black author. It has been placed by many critics at the head of a distinctive tradition of African-American literary creativity.

Like Equiano and many other ex-slaves and their descendants who would follow in their wakes, Wheatley crossed the Atlantic several times, not only as a slave, but as a free woman. Her journeying took her to London, where she moved in some exalted social circles and, as Peter Fryer has pointed out, against the expectations of her hosts bravely made her abolitionist sympathies known.[2] Sir Brook Watson, later to be a Lord Mayor of London, presented her with an edition of *Paradise Lost,* and she received a significant patronage from Selina Hastings, the countess of Huntingdon, a wealthy, prominent, and well-connected figure in the Methodist evangelical movement and the woman to whom Wheatley dedicated her book. Wheatley's poems were widely acclaimed, reviewed, and debated not only for their own qualities, but also, as Henry Louis Gates, Jr., has emphasized, for what they were thought to reveal about the intellectual and imaginative capacities of blacks in general. At the age of twenty-three and after fifteen years as a slave, she was freed on the death of her mistress but was unable to publish a second volume of the poetry that she had hawked door to door to raise money to support herself in freedom. This later work was likely to have been less constrained by the obligations of servitude than its predecessor.

It may be significant for our thinking about the workings of identity that although Equiano was involved in a scheme to resettle eighteenth-century London's unwanted blacks in Sierra Leone, neither he nor Wheatley ever returned to the African homelands from which their long journeys through slavery had begun.

This pair has left an interesting collection of published material through which we can consider the effects of relocation, displacement, and forced

---

[2] Peter Fryer, *Staying Power: The History of Black People in Britain* (Pluto Press, 1984).

transition between cultural codes and habits, language, and religion. Their works are especially valuable for several reasons. The authors belonged to the generation that suffered the trauma of the Middle Passage and in which the physical and psychological effects of that brutal disjunction must have been at their most intense. More significantly, though, through their conspicuous mastery of genre, style, and expressive idiom their texts demand from us a sophisticated grasp of cultural syncretism, adaptation, and intermixture. We can, of course, identify elements in Wheatley's work which betray the residual presence of African animistic religion or sun worship. And although we can locate African words and accurate ethnological detail in Equiano's narrative, his work, like Wheatley's, was also influenced by Pope and Milton. They ask to be evaluated on their own terms as complex, compound formations. They should not be valued only as means to observe the durability of African elements or dismissed as an inadequate mixture, doomed always to be something less than the supposedly pure entities that first combined to produce it. Their legacy is most valuable as a mix, a hybrid. Its recombinant form is indebted to its "parent" cultures but remains assertively and insubordinately a bastard. It reproduces neither of the supposedly anterior purities that gave rise to it in anything like unmodified form. Here, at least, identity must be divorced from purity.

Transcultural mixture alerts us not only to the syncretic complexities of language, culture, and everyday modern life in the torrid areas where racial slavery was practiced, but also to the purity-defying metamorphoses of individual identity in the "contact-zones" of an imperial metropolis.[3] Even under those conditions, identity was the compound result of many accretions. Its protean constitution did not defer to the scripts of ethnic, national, racial, or cultural absolutism.

Like Wheatley's elegies, Equiano's absorbing autobiography yields many precious insights into modern racial slavery and illuminates some of the changes in consciousness and outlook that attended the African slaves as they negotiated the trauma, horror, and violence of forced rupture from home and kin that Orlando Patterson has called "natal alienation."[4] Equiano labored long and hard in a number of different New World locations in order to be able to buy his freedom from his owner. Before this was eventually accomplished in the service of Robert King, a Philadelphia Quaker, he had visited England and served on board warships of the Royal Navy, participating in several battles against the French. He traveled

[3] Mary Louise Pratt, *Imperial Eyes: Travel and Transculturation* (Routledge, 1992).

[4] Orlando Patterson, *Slavery and Social Death: A Comparative Study* (Harvard University Press, 1982).

throughout the Mediterranean, went to the Arctic as part of John Phipps's expedition in 1773, and journeyed among the Musquito Indians of Central America, an encounter that demonstrates to his readers exactly how far the narrator's once-African identity had come from anything that might be described as noble savagery.

No doubt, the rendering of Equiano's life story was tailored to the expectations and conventions of an abolitionist reading public. It certainly describes abuse, injustice, and exploitation, but it also shows him to have been treated with some decency and a measure of trust by masters for whom, both within and against the force of his servitude, he was able to develop significant affection and intimacy. Trapped on a boat on the Thames at Deptford in 1762 and locked in an unexpected confrontation with one master, whom, he tells his readers, he had "loved like a son," Equiano was desperate to gain the safety of the city on the river banks where both men knew that his freedom would be secured. He found himself instead being sold from one owner to another within sight of the shore he was unable to reach.

Equiano gradually acquired not only skills with which to improve his lot as a seaman and a trader but also an elaborate and complex critical consciousness that was able to analyze as well as describe his experiences and the system they exemplified. He became fervently Christian and, exactly as Wheatley had done, used the moral categories of that faith to denounce the immoral trade in human beings that had torn him from Africa and in which he had himself participated as a reluctant crewman on voyages where slaves were the cargo. His economic good fortune and astute management of his own finances made him a free man and a strong advocate on behalf of thrift, diligence, and disciplined Protestant endeavor. A radical Methodism touched his life as well as Wheatley's. It provided an appropriate toolbox with which he could dismantle the Christian pieties that had already been rendered hollow by their indifference to the plight of slaves.

There were other, alternative forms of Christianity around that yield clues as to the ways in which Equiano and Wheatley thought of themselves as children of God and human beings, sinners, workers, and patriots, free men and women whose vivid sense of freedom was conditioned by the fact that they had also been enslaved. The frontispiece of Equiano's 1789 autobiography *The Life of Olaudah Equiano or Gustavus Vassa the African* shows him in his Sunday best holding his Bible open to the Book of Acts 12:4. That citation and the other scriptural references with which he embellished his text are important pointers toward the precise character of Equiano's Protestant outlook. Chapter 7 of his tale describes a formative encounter with the evangelical, "great awakening" Methodism of George Whitefield that had enjoyed a significant presence within antislavery thinking and a pronounced influence upon the black antislavery activism of the time.[5] Wheatley signaled some of the same affiliations in a widely circulated poem commemorating Whitefield's death in August 1772. It recalled that he had made a special point of urging blacks to accept their Christian salvation and reproduced some of his appeals for general recognition of Christ as an "impartial" savior:

> He pray'd that grace in ev'ry heart might dwell,
> He long'd to see America excel;
> He charged its youth that ev'ry grace divine
> Should with full lustre in their conduct shine . . .
> ". . . Take him, ye *Africans*, he longs for you,
> *Impartial Saviour* is his title due:
> Wash'd in the fountain of redeeming blood,
> You shall be sons, and kings, and priests to God."[6]

For Methodists of this group, the Pauline view fully stated in Galatians 3:26–29 was central to the ideal of a properly Christian community:[7]

> For ye are all children of God by faith in Christ Jesus.
> For as many of you as have been baptized into Christ have put on Christ.
> There is neither Jew nor Greek, there is neither bond nor free, there is
> neither male nor female: for ye are all one in Christ Jesus.
> And if ye be Christ's, then are ye Abraham's seed, and heirs according to
> the promise.

One of the most aggressive and unsympathetic whites with whom Equiano came into conflict is presented as abusing him for being "one of St. Paul's men."[8] The superficial differences of gender and social status, race and caste, marked on the body by the trifling order of man, were to be set aside in favor of a relationship with Christ that offered a means to transcend and thereby escape the constraints of mortality and the body-coded

---

[5] Adam Potkay, "Introduction" to Adam Potkay and Sandra Burr, eds., *Black Atlantic Writers of the Eighteenth Century* (St. Martin's Press, 1995), p. 9.

[6] "On the Death of the Rev. Mr. George Whitefield. 1770," lines 20–23 and 34–37; John C. Shields, ed., *The Collected Works of Phillis Wheatley* (Oxford University Press, 1988), p. 23.

[7] Daniel Boyarin has explored elements of the history of this idea in his extraordinary study *A Radical Jew: Paul and the Politics of Identity* (University of California Press, 1995).

[8] Olaudah Equiano, *The Interesting Narrative of the Life of Olaudah Equiano,* 2 vols. (Pall Mall, 1969), vol. 2, p. 195.

order of identification and differentiation we now call "phenotype." There is also here something of a plea for the renunciation of specific defining characteristics associated with and articulated through the body. These are the same qualities that might today be thought of as constituting the most fixed and unchangeable forms of identity. They were lost, or rather left behind, at the point where Equiano's distinctive African body was immersed in the welcoming, baptismal waters of his new Christian faith. Perhaps what we should recognize as a new "identity" was constituted along with a new analysis of slavery in that fateful immersion. For him, slavery became a useful experience, morally and analytically as well as individually. It was a gift from God that redeemed suffering through the provision of wisdom:

> I considered that trials and disappointments are sometimes for our good and I thought God might perhaps have permitted this, in order to teach me wisdom and resignation. For he had hitherto shadowed me with the wings of his mercy and by his invisible, but powerful hand, had brought me the way I knew not. (154)

Thanks to the density of her allusions and the compression of the poetic form in which she wrote, Wheatley's ambivalence about her journeying through cultures and between identities is a more evasive quarry. Her poetry has been argued over in detail precisely because commentators find it hard to assess the relationship between her command of English neo-classicism, her enthusiasm for the American revolutionary struggle, and those few moments when unexpectedly strident denunciations of slavery erupted from her pen. An appreciation of the divine providence that took her from the darkness of her African life is combined with forthright assertions of the injustice and immorality of the slave trade and less frequent affirmations of an autonomy that preceded the fateful contact with whites and their world. The African-American poet and critic June Jordan is surely acute in drawing attention to the powerful assertion of autonomy that leaps out halfway through "On Being Brought from Africa to America," a poem that Wheatley had published when she was only sixteen years old:

> 'Twas mercy brought me from my Pagan land,
> Taught my benighted soul to understand
> That there's a God, that there's a *Saviour* too:
> Once I redemption neither sought nor knew.
> Some view our sable race with scornful eye,
> "Their color is a diabolic die."
> Remember, *Christians*, *Negroes*, black as *Cain*,
> May be refin'd, and join th' angelic train.

Equiano, Wheatley, and their many peers are also important to contemporary considerations of racialized identity because they dwelled in different locations. Significant portions of their itinerant lives were lived on British soil, and it is tempting to speculate here about how an acknowledgment of their political and cultural contributions to England, or perhaps to London's heterocultural life, might complicate the nation's portraits of itself. This decidedly monochromatic representation operates too often to exclude or undermine the significance of black participation and to minimize the power of colonial and imperial circuitry in determining the internal patterns of national life.

Tension about where to put the eighteenth-century blacks is connected not only to a color-coded British nativism that is indifferent if not actively hostile to the presence of slaves and ex-slaves, but also to another conceptual problem. This more profound conflict can be made visible in the contrast between encamped nations, rooted in one spot even if their imperial tendrils extend further, and the very different patterns of itinerant dwelling found in the transnational, maritime adventures of Equiano and celebrated in the cross-cultural creativity of Wheatley. The commemorative modes appropriate to this very different ecology of belonging reveal themselves in the oppositions between geography and genealogy, between land and sea. The latter possibility prompts a partial reversal of the myth in which Britannia held dominion over the waves. We can begin to perceive the sublime force of the ocean, and the associated impact of those who made their temporary homes on it, as a counterpower that confined, regulated, inhibited, and sometimes even defied the exercise of territorial sovereignty.[9]

It is not surprising that in his search to find historical precedents that could explain the character of the African idyll from which he had been snatched by unjust transnational trade in human flesh, Equiano turned once more to his Bible. In an interesting move that also repudiated the race-minded theories of those who used the biblically based Hamitic hypothesis[10] to present blackness as a curse and implicate it in justifications of slavery, he argued that Africans were descended not from Noah's accursed son, whose punishment entailed what could be read as a legitimation for

---

[9]Marcus Rediker, *Between the Devil and the Deep Blue Sea: Merchant Seamen, Pirates and the Anglo-American Maritime World, 1700–1750* (Cambridge University Press, 1987); Janice E. Thomson, *Mercenaries, Pirates, and Sovereigns* (Princeton University Press, 1994); E. E. Rice, ed., *The Sea and History* (Sutton Publishing, 1996), esp. chap. 5; N. A. M. Rodger, "Sea Power and Empire: 1688–1793," in P. J. Marshall, ed., *The Oxford History of The British Empire, Volume Two: The Eighteenth Century* (Oxford, 1998).

[10]Edith R. Sanders, "The Hamitic Hypothesis; Its Origin and Functions in Time Perspective," *Journal of African History*, X, 4 (1969), pp. 521–532.

slavery, but from the union of Abraham and Keturah. This bold claim was backed up with citations from contemporary scholarly work. It is combined with another assertion that recurs in the literature and political commentary produced by enslaved Africans and their descendants. Equiano suggests that there is one significant historical precedent for the mores and conduct of the African people from which he was wrongfully taken:

> . . . here I cannot forbear suggesting what has long struck me very forcibly, namely the strong analogy, which even by this sketch, imperfect as it is, appears to prevail in manners and customs of my countrymen and those of the Jews, before they reached the Land of Promise, and particularly the Patriarchs, while they were yet in that pastoral state which is described in Genesis—an analogy which alone would induce me to think that the one people had sprung from the other . . . As to the difference of colour between Eboan Africans and the modern Jews, I shall not presume to account for it. (127–28) [11]

This "analogy" is evidence that the force of emergent raciology had touched Equiano's modern self-consciousness. It can be used in turn to introduce a discussion of the idea of diaspora, which, transcoded from its biblical sources and often divorced from the Jewish traditions in which it is primarily articulated, proved very useful to black thinkers as they struggled to comprehend the dynamics of identity and belonging constituted between the poles of geography and genealogy. For them, Jewish history in general and the idea of diaspora in particular were a useful means to regulate the conflict between the duties deriving from the place of dwelling and those different obligations, temptations, vices, and pleasures that belonged to the place of sojourn. Diaspora is an especially valuable idea because it points toward a more refined and more wieldy sense of culture than the characteristic notions of rootedness exemplified above in the words of President Mandela. It makes the spatialization of identity problematic and interrupts the ontologization of place.

---

[11] For a ground-breaking discussion of these formulations see Adam Potkay, "Introduction" to *Black Atlantic Writers of the Eighteenth Century*.

Slavery and Sensibility: Phillis Wheatley Within the Fracture

Donna Landry

The laboring-class women poets we have investigated so far may have invoked the metaphor of slavery to characterize their domestic obligations, their confinement to drudgery; Phillis Wheatley writes literally as a slave. The poetic sensibility of her white counterparts may be produced from within the constraints of servitude and class-based attitudes towards plebeian subjugation, but Wheatley's "sensibility" is from the first moment of her poetic enunciation put in question by her status as a slave. Even abolitionist discourse of the period, at the same time as it argues for the emancipation of slaves, is traversed by doubts and hesitations about the slaves' status as "human," and hence discursive, subjects. Wheatley may have found "herself" figured in certain abolitionist texts; she clearly read the Bible as a potentially emancipatory document; to a certain extent her writing seems to have been a liberationary gesture. Yet given the terms of the great debates about slavery in the period, abolitionist discourse itself also functioned as a form of discursive constraint upon Wheatley's literary production.

Even as late as 1788, four years after Wheatley's death, such abolitionist poems as Hannah More's *Slavery, A Poem* and Ann Yearsley's *A Poem On The Inhumanity Of The Slave-Trade*[1] represent the black slave as a crudely patched-together figure, a field of contradictions that reveal the workings of ideology, the desire to naturalize and recuperate the other while remaining uneasily alert to the threat of cultural difference. J. M. S. Tompkins suggests that "it must have been in conscious rivalry that [Yearsley] published her poem ... within a few months of Miss More's *Slavery*."[2] Read as rivals or not, the poems represent quite different takes on the question of abolition. Yearsley writes in blank verse, More in couplets; Yearsley

---

From Donna Landry, *The Muses of Resistance: Laboring-Class Women's Poetry in Britain, 1739–1796*. Reprinted with the permission of Cambridge University Press.

[1] Hannah More, *Slavery, A Poem* (London: T. Cadell, 1788) and Ann Yearsley, *A Poem On The Inhumanity Of The Slave-Trade* (London: G. G. J. and J. Robinson, 1788). In *Subject to Others: British Women Writers and Colonial Slavery 1760–1834* [New York: Routledge, 1992], [Moira] Ferguson analyzes crucial connections between the emergence of feminism and abolitionist politics.

[2] [J. M. S.] Tompkins, *The Polite Marriage* [Cambridge: Cambridge University Press, 1938], p. 77.

appeals to local authority in Bristol and More to London-based parliamentary and so, ostensibly, national authority. Yearsley heroically dramatizes the native characters Luco and Incilanda, while More presents a rational argument against slavery bolstered by an appeal to religion. Yearsley's vision of an emancipated future is a civic one—Bristol uncorrupted—while More represents the end of slavery not geographically or politically but metaphysically. If Yearsley's poem seems rather overwrought, More's rises to occasional argumentative elegance only to fracture disablingly along ideological lines. Imperial conquest equals pillage, we are told, yet Britain can "give" Africa her rightful liberties; colonialism is rendered brutally suspect, yet we are assured that no natives were killed in the settling of Quaker Pennsylvania. For both poets, slave uprisings represent a crisis of legitimacy comparable with contemporary rebellions against monarchy. Yearsley achieves Miltonic eloquence in her attack on "Law" and "Custom" in favor of "Heav'n-born Liberty" ([lines] 15–18):

> ... Custom, Law,
> Ye blessings, and ye curses of mankind,
> What evils do ye cause? We feel enslav'd,
> Yet move in your direction. Custom, thou
> Wilt preach up filial piety; thy sons
> Will groan, and stare with impudence at Heav'n,
> As if they did abjure the act, where Sin
> Sits full on Inhumanity; the church
> They fill with mouthing, vap'rous sighs and tears,
> Which, like the guileful crocodile's, oft fall,
> Nor fall, but at the cost of human bliss. (18–28)

But she also recuperates black resistance by refamiliarizing her slave subjects as affectingly domestic, as if that sameness could save them for white audiences, the same strategy that Wheatley herself employs in her brief autobiographical moments:

> "Parental fondness, and the dear returns
> "Of filial tenderness were thine, till torn
> "From the dissolving scene." —(413–15)

More, however, even as she argues that blacks "have heads to think, and hearts to feel, / And souls to act, with firm, tho' erring zeal" (67–68), falls back on a notion of their cultural difference as savagery:

> Strong, but luxuriant virtues boldly shoot
> From the wild vigour of a savage root. (73–74)

Tho' dark and savage, ignorant and blind,
They claim the common privilege of kind. (137–38)

And while she insists vehemently that blacks can feel as well as whites, she seems less sanguine about their capacity to reason:

Plead not, in reason's palpable abuse,
Their sense of *feeling callous and obtuse:
From heads to hearts lies Nature's plain appeal,
Tho' few can reason, all mankind can feel. (147–50)

Surely the argument that Africans (like white laborers) might not be able to reason is at least as cruel and stupid an argument? But More does not pursue this line of thought. And thus the abolitionist case that would preserve both liberty and difference begins to undermine itself in Enlightenment terms, collapses rational argument back into a matter of Christian faith that must transcend "mere" rationality, and that forever casts the other as a primitive or childlike being in need of civilizing discipline and the Word.

Whether recuperative, effacing difference, or seeking to preserve difference at the expense of the other's rationality, abolitionist discourse is fraught with inconsistency. Though it offers Wheatley a lever to use in opening up discursive space within white colonial culture, abolitionist discourse is far from offering her a utopian projection of alternatives to her fractured semiotic field and her situation of enslavement.

Similarly, Wheatley's relation to the existing discourse of plebeian poets is a complex and not unambiguous one. Her difference from white laboring-class women writers is figured forward from the frontispiece of her volume of verse, a portrait which at once emphasizes her Africanness as exotically other and decorously domesticates it by means of the discipline of writing. Yet the fact that her *Poems On Various Subjects, Religious And Moral* of 1773[3] was first published in London, not Boston, because

---

*Nothing is more frequent than this cruel and stupid argument, that they do not *feel* the miseries inflicted on them as Europeans would do. [More's note.]

[3] *Poems On Various Subjects, Religious And Moral.* By Phillis Wheatley, Negro Servant to Mr. John Wheatley, of Boston, in New England (London: Printed for A. Bell, Aldgate; sold by Cox and Berry, Boston, 1773). The Clark Library copy (shelfmark *PS 866 W5 P7) is inscribed "one of the earliest books by a negro." Wheatley was the first African to publish a book of poetry in English. Juan Latino, a black slave of Granada, published three volumes of verse in Latin between 1573 and 1576; see Charles T. Davis and Henry Louis Gates, Jr. (eds.), *The Slave's Narrative* (Oxford and New York: Oxford University Press, 1985), pp. xxvii–xxviii.

subscribers in England—most influentially Selina Hastings, Countess of Huntingdon, to whom the volume is dedicated—were more forthcoming in support of the productions of a "Negro Servant" than were American colonists, may suggest the extent to which an already existing discourse of laboring-women's poetry legitimated Wheatley's writing and made possible its widest dissemination.

In a sense, then, Wheatley's is the limit case of the plebeian female poet working within and against the dominant culture on all fronts, linguistic, cultural, racial, sexual, and socio-political. Her slavery and her sensibility may remain constitutively different from those of her white British counterparts, her exploitation more totalized and extreme. But we can only know these differences in important, and nuanced, ways if we read her in relation to those other discourses, the plebeian and the abolitionist, that helped constitute and condition the reception of her own.

To make a case for Phillis Wheatley's cultural resistance may not now prove so difficult as it would once have done. Although her work has often been criticized as disablingly conventional and derivative, recent studies are marked by the desire to find in her an authentic African American literary foremother. This recuperative desire produces a consequent strategy of reading in the light of the complex problematics of race her work represents. In one sense at least, the dynamics of race consciousness and literary reception have radically shifted since 1784, when Thomas Jefferson could write, reminding us briefly of More writing about Yearsley's plight:

> Misery is often the parent of the most affecting touches in poetry. Among the blacks is misery enough, God knows, but no poetry. Love is the peculiar oestrum of the poet. Their love is ardent, but it kindles the senses only, not the imagination. Religion, indeed, has produced a Phyllis Whately [sic]; but it could not produce a poet. The compositions published under her name are below the dignity of criticism. The heroes of the Dunciad are to her, as Hercules to the author of that poem.[4]

The crudeness of Jefferson's projection of sensuality without an erotic imaginary onto the ostensible subjectivities of black people may be autobiographically revealing; and his commentary on the *Dunciad* suggests something of the popular penetration that Pope's Grub Street fantasia may have had in late eighteenth-century America. Pope's smallness, slightness, and physical frailty, in contrast with Hercules's superhuman strength, serve as a touchstone for the absurdity, the grotesqueness of Wheatley's

---

[4] Thomas Jefferson, "Query XIV" in *Notes on Virginia* (1784), quoted in Julian D. Mason, Jr., *The Poems of Phillis Wheatley* (Chapel Hill: University of North Carolina Press, 1966), p. xliii.

"pretension" to poetic status. It is gratifying to note that Jefferson's prejudices did not go unchallenged in his lifetime.[5] But the contention that American black culture is somehow debilitatingly imitative of white culture is with us still. Not so baldly stated, perhaps, as in 1878, when Jefferson's views were defended in *The North American Review*, with Wheatley characterized thus:

> She was a poet very much as "Blind Tom" is a musician, her verses being the merest echo of the common jingle of her day . . . A fatal facility of imitation stands in the way of this interesting race, and we cannot fairly deny that facts give support to the opinion of an inherent mental inferiority . . . To the present hour the negro has contributed nothing to the intellectual resources of man.[6]

Even black scholars intent on recovering a tradition of African American literary achievement have often hesitated to read Wheatley as other than subject to "a fatal facility of imitation." Where neoclassical imitation as such is not denigrated as a literary practice, Wheatley still receives faint praise for failing to develop a more "original" or innovative aesthetic, presumably the primary determinant of poetic greatness:

> As I have said, she was not a great poet; but in her way, in her time, and in her locale, she was a fairly good writer of poems generally in imitation of the neoclassical mode made popular by Alexander Pope.[7]

> The *Poems* revealed Phillis to be an imitative poet whose work lacked qualities of greatness; but clearly she had written some of the most interesting verse of colonial America.[8]

---

[5] Ironically, Gilbert Imlay, who enters feminist literary history primarily through his less than enlightened behavior towards Mary Wollstonecraft, defended Wheatley against Jefferson's charges. Citing her poem "On Imagination," Imlay writes: "Indeed, I should be glad to be informed what white upon this continent has written more beautiful lines," in *A Topographical Description of The Western Territory of North America* (New York, 1793), I, pp. 185–86, reprinted in Mason, *The Poems of Phillis Wheatley*, p. xliv. Mason, p. xliv, also reports Henri Grégoire and Samuel Stanhope Smith as challenging Jefferson's racist remarks on Wheatley's behalf in *An Enquiry Concerning The Intellectual and Moral Faculties, And Literature of Negroes & Mulattoes, Distinguished in Science, Literature And The Arts*, trans. D. B. Warden (Brooklyn, 1810), pp. 44–45, and *An Essay on the Causes of the Variety of Complexion and Figure in the Human Species* (New Brunswick and New York, 1810), p. 269, n., respectively.

[6] James Parton, "Antipathy to the Negro," *The North American Review* 127 (November–December 1878), pp. 487–88, quoted in Mason, *The Poems of Phillis Wheatley*, p. xlv.

[7] Mason, *The Poems of Phillis Wheatley*, p. xxxii.

[8] Charles W. Akers, " 'Our Modern Egyptians': Phillis Wheatley and the Whig Campaign Against Slavery in Revolutionary Boston," *The Journal of Negro History* (July 1975), p. 399.

To have written "some of the most interesting verse of colonial America" is not enough: one must still apologize for Wheatley's reliance on imitation. One of the boldest scholarly vindications of Wheatley's aesthetic to date asserts her relative originality:

> Scrutiny of her work will reveal, however, that she was not as derivative of Pope as has been long asserted. In fact, recent scholarship is beginning to detail the extent to which she was not the extensive imitator of anyone.

Yet such a vindication on aesthetic grounds alone cannot be allowed to stand because the political commitments of much black scholarship demand an analysis of a writer's race consciousness as well, and here Wheatley may be defended against previous denigrations—but not entirely vindicated:

> Perhaps the most persistent criticism of Phillis Wheatley has been that based on the usually unaesthetic grounds of her chosen subject matter. She did not write enough about blackness, some charge. She is said by others to have been callously indifferent to her contemporary black life generally, and archly above black slave life in particular. So contending, some see her as the progenitor of a posited black American literary tradition of black self-abnegation, black self-loathing. One writer would have it that so powerfully shaping were the unchallenged New England cultural pressures on a haplessly malleable young Phillis that she was compelled to develop into nothing else but a kind of psychologically malformed grotesquery—a black-white, colonial woman poet. There is perhaps some truth in some of these charges, but a greater truth is that Phillis was very much aware of being a black person, however celebrated a personality, in a world dominated numerically and culturally by white persons, and that she wrote of such matters in her volume of poems, in her miscellaneous poems, and in her letters.[9]

The apologetic caution expressed here—"There is perhaps some truth in some of these charges"—prevents a closer and potentially more radical investigation of how the dominant New England "cultural pressures" are both inscribed in and resisted by Wheatley's literary production. Rather than allowing ourselves to feel a disabling revulsion at the grotesque spectacle of a "black-white, colonial woman poet," and to stop there in our exploration of black colonial female subjectivity, we should look again at

---

[9] William H. Robinson, *Phillis Wheatley and Her Writings* (New York: Garland, 1984), p. 97, p. 108.

the articulation of Wheatley's abolitionist consciousness with her potentially subversive mimicry of white Anglographic cultural forms.[10]

Thanks to recent scholarship, Wheatley need never again be read as a writer unworthy of sophisticated formalist or literary-historical analysis, nor a writer oblivious of or indifferent to the brutal injustices of slavery. Nor need we continue to separate these two considerations as antithetically "aesthetic" and "political." The recovery and republication of her letter of February 11, 1774 to the Rev. Samson Occom, the Amerindian preacher, provides powerful evidence of Wheatley's political acuteness regarding the institution of slavery, and her skill in weaving a texture of allusion and allegorical reference that is keenly critical of—and politely sarcastic about—the hypocrisy of white Christian racism. In her letter, written several months after she became a freed woman, Wheatley praises "the glorious Dispensation of civil and religious Liberty, which are so inseparably united, that there is little or no enjoyment of one without the other." Thus the religious conversion of many Africans to Christianity must lead, ironically if inevitably, to their desire for an emancipated civil and political status. This constitutes a radical reading of Christianity on Wheatley's part, a deployment of religious impulses in the direction of progressive social transformation in spite of the injustices of imperialist conquest and slavery. This utopian impulse points towards concrete social and political equality, not religious consolation in heaven. This is the emancipatory tendency in appropriations of Christian doctrine we might usefully connect to the social radicalism of many sects during the English Civil Wars. Wheatley's Christianity is not the Christianity of political quietism and submissive piety. Just as the Israelites were "solicitous for their Freedom from Egyptian slavery," so African slaves, captive but encouraged by New World ideas of divinity and "natural Rights," rightly desire their liberty:

> God has implanted a Principle, which we call Love of Freedom; it is impatient of oppression, and pants for Deliverance—and by the Leave of our modern Egyptians I will assert that the same principle lives in us. God grant Deliverance in his own Way and Time, and get him honour

---

[10]A recent collection of critical essays not only handily documents this general history of Wheatley criticism, but helps break new ground in the legitimation of Wheatley's *œuvre* as an object of serious study, attending to such questions as Popean influence, the elegiac mode, the sublime, and contemporary definitions of "the Negro." See especially the essays by Albertha Sistrunk, Mukhtar Ali Isani, John C. Shields, and Henry Louis Gates, Jr., in *Critical Essays on Phillis Wheatley,* ed. William H. Robinson (Boston: G. K. Hall and Company, 1982). The collection is usefully reviewed by Valerie Smith in *Early American Literature* 18:1 (Spring 1983), pp. 110–11.

upon all those whose Avaraice impels them to countenance and help forward the Calamities of their fellow Creatures. This I desire not for their Hurt, but to convince them of the strange Absurdity of their Conduct whose Words and Actions are so diametrically opposite. How well the cry for Liberty, and the reverse Disposition for the exercise of oppressive power over others agree I humbly think it does not require the penetration of a Philosopher to determine.[11]

Here Wheatley foregrounds the contradiction between republican theory and oppressive practice in the slave trade. The source of this contradiction, she claims, is economic self-interest or avarice. Only greed perpetuates slavery in defiance of the emancipatory possibilities of republicanism. Just as she pushes the sanctities of republican rhetoric to their limit in this letter, so also her poetry foregrounds the contradictions of colonial experience until even the most pious invocation of Christian faith may be read as the site of hybridity — "the warlike sign of the native."

There may well be a threat disguised as ambiguous gratitude in the autobiographical moment of Wheatley's "To the Right Honourable William, Earl of Dartmouth, His Majesty's Principal Secretary of State for North America, &c.":

> Should you, my lord, while you peruse my song,
> Wonder from whence my love of *Freedom* sprung,
> Whence flow these wishes for the common good,
> By feeling hearts alone best understood,
> I, young in life, by seeming cruel fate
> Was snatch'd from *Afric's* fancy'd happy seat:
> What pangs excruciating must molest,
> What sorrows labour in my parent's breast?
> Steel'd was that soul and by no misery mov'd
> That from a father seiz'd his babe belov'd:
> Such, such my case. And can I then but pray
> Others may never feel tyrannic sway? (20–31)

---

[11] Phillis Wheatley, letter to the Rev. Samson Occom, February 11, 1774, reprinted in Robinson, *Phillis Wheatley and Her Writings*, p. 332, as it appeared in *The Massachusetts Spy* for March 24, 1774. Robinson reminds us that Wheatley had been a freed woman for several months by the time she composed this letter, and notes its "politely sarcastic scoring of the patently absurd Christian racists," pp. 120–21. Akers, in "'Our Modern Egyptians,'" pp. 406–07, reprints the letter as it appeared in the *Boston Post-Boy* (*Massachusetts Gazette*), March 21, 1774, p. 3/2, and the *Boston News-Letter* (*Massachusetts Gazette*), March 24, 1774, p. 1/3. Akers comments, "Thus, in Boston as in Virginia, elitist patriots cried for the rights of man while they continued to enjoy the labor of their African slaves," p. 402.

What if the brutality of imperialist conquest so evident in the slave trade were to produce a generation of freedom-loving rebels amongst its ruthlessly transplanted "native informants"? If the experience of tyranny as forcible transplantation and enslavement produces revolutionary aspirations, they are ironically couched in the language of the slave traders and slaveholders themselves, for whom colonial rebellion will soon prove necessary for preserving their commerce, including the slave trade, as a sign of their much-vaunted liberty. The ostensible humility of Wheatley's pose here ("Even I, a lowly African slave, beseech you, Dartmouth, to be a benevolent administrator lest you produce an anti-imperialist, anti-tyrannical rebellion") does indeed become subtly warlike when we address the question of Wheatley as cultural mimic.

For the terms in which Wheatley can couch her advice to the new secretary of state, the terms in which she can formulate her own experience of slavery, are the white man's terms. That first violent rupture of native community, which leads inexorably towards transportation via slaveship and deracination in the New World, can be projected only retrospectively and speculatively: "*seeming* cruel fate," "*Afric's fancy'd* happy seat," "What pangs excruciating *must* molest" [emphasis Landry's]. Wheatley does not "know" what happened, cannot remember, can only envisage within the master's language what her native prehistory might have been. Except for one detail, which occupies two lines of confident memory and undisputed knowledge, and that is the distinct, reifying brutality and distinctly "unchristian" immunity from compassion that signify the slave-trader as imperial subject: "Steel'd was that soul and by no misery mov'd / That from a father seiz'd his babe belov'd." Of the inhumane instrumentality of the sovereign subject of imperial commerce Wheatley is convinced, and it is a belief reinforced here by an equal conviction of African paternal affection.

As so often in abolitionist discourse, from the anti-slavery poems of Yearsley and More to Harriet Beecher Stowe's *Uncle Tom's Cabin* (1852), the appeal to previously unknowable communities as sites of familial affection attempts to clinch the argument by an act of refamiliarization as refamilialization. Wheatley may not "remember" her father—we have just been led to believe she remembered almost nothing of her life before captivity— but in the Boston of 1772 the notion of paternal affection so rudely violated by the seizure of a child is likely to be read as sympathetic. Here as elsewhere, Wheatley's self-presentation coincides with the representations of slaves' lives manufactured in white, and residually racist, abolitionist discourse. Her self-presentation is often inextricably complicit with the discursive formation in which "freedom" and slavery continue to coexist, and in which "freedom" all too often means the rights of the propertied. Yet this mimicry of a subjectivity recognizable to white readers is explicitly foregrounded in Wheatley's texts as miming, as mimicry—and, as such, it constitutes the grounds for the eventual challenging of the racist formation with which it is deceptively complicit.

Within the fracturing of a semiotic field, Spivak warns, what we are likely to recognize as "great literature" will probably not flourish ("The Rani of Sirmur," p. 130). But the partial erasure and silencing of native cultures wrought by the violence of imperialism may produce strange hybrids. That some profound fracturing of semiotic fields transpires in the Atlantic voyages of eighteenth-century slaveships seems indisputable. We have only to notice that the schooner *Phillis*, owned by Timothy Fitch of Boston, brought Phillis Wheatley to New England to begin to account for some of these discontinuities. The name "Phillis Wheatley" = the slaveship yoked to the white master; a "Christian name" signifying enslavement and a patronymic metonymizing white ownership within the rhetorics of an "extended family."

The cultural amnesia experienced by some transported slaves has been documented, though its interpretation has often been tendentious.[12] Wheatley seems to have suffered from this disarticulation of the memory rather acutely, if we are to believe her nineteenth-century memoirist, Margaretta Matilda Oddell. According to Oddell, the great-grand-niece of Susanna Wheatley, Phillis's mistress, Phillis Wheatley could remember nothing of her previous life before captivity except "the simple circumstance that her mother *poured out water before the sun at his rising*—in reference, no doubt, to an ancient African custom." So she remembers only a stylized glimpse of tribal ritual, her mother propitiating a masculine sun, the "natural" beauty of ritual rendered in a "native" setting. Oddell goes on to speculate that this lack of memories from early childhood might be unusual but does not necessarily indicate a lack of intelligence:

> We cannot know at how early a period she was beguiled from the hut of her mother; or how long a time elapsed between her abduction from her first home and her being transferred to the abode of her benevolent mistress, where she must have felt like one awaking from a fearful dream.

---

[12] See, for example, Anne Lane (ed.), *The Debate Over Slavery: Stanley Elkins and His Critics* (Urbana: University of Illinois Press, 1971), esp. pp. 5–7, pp. 348–61. Erlene Stetson provides a black feminist perspective on the whole question of slavery in "Studying Slavery: Some Literary and Pedagogical Considerations on the Black Female Slave," in *All the Women Are White, All the Blacks Are Men, But Some of Us Are Brave: Black Women's Studies*, ed. Gloria T. Hull, Patricia Bell Scott, Barbara Smith (Old Westbury, N.Y.: The Feminist Press, 1982), pp. 61–84. See also Angela Davis, *Women, Race & Class* (New York: Vintage, 1981).

This interval was, no doubt, a long one; and filled, as it must have been, with various degrees and kinds of suffering, might naturally enough obliterate the recollection of earlier and happier days.[13]

Childishly "beguiled" or, more polemically, violently "seiz'd" as Wheatley puts it in "To Dartmouth": either way, slavery ruptures Wheatley's experience and her semiotic field. But the specific gendering of her memories seems to have much to do with her intended audience: paternal affection for Dartmouth; maternal ritual, a feminized security, for Susanna Wheatley and her great-grand-niece.

What is perhaps most interesting about this lack of early memories, this lack of knowledge of indigenous cultural formations, is that it foregrounds the implantation of imperialist culture on the deracinated subject. Nowhere is this clearer in Wheatley's *œuvre* than in the production of the poem "On Recollection":

The following was occasioned by being in company with some young ladies of family, when one of them said she did not remember, among all the poetic pieces she had seen, ever to have met with a poem upon RECOLLECTION. The African (so let me call her, for so in fact she is) took the hint, went home to her master's, and soon sent the following.[14]

Thus Wheatley explicitly produces a meditation on memory, the "native" materials of which she lacks, for a white colonial patron. Even her "Recollection" is constituted discursively as a function of imperialism, of its power to bestow education and "culture," of its power to solicit the spontaneous poetic expression of colonized subjectivity. Wheatley thus produces a poem on a subject "never before" encountered by the lady patron, proving her poetic genius and authenticity in the very moment of confirming her writerly status as a dependent—indeed subject—construction of imperial discourse. And what are we to make of her single memory of childhood, so legible to white colonial society as exotically cryptic yet true to type—"in reference, no doubt, to an ancient African custom"? Wheatley, whose recollections have been so violently circumscribed, ironically supplements the lack of a poem on "Recollection" for a slave-owning audience.

What Wheatley took to be the function of her writing within white colonial society is far from clear. But in her poem "On Imagination" the contradiction between writing as aesthetic pleasure and writing as a form

---

[13] Oddell, "Memoir," in Robinson, *Phillis Wheatley and Her Writings*, pp. 431–32.
[14] Letter from "L" to the editor, *The London Magazine* (March 1772), quoted in Robinson, *Phillis Wheatley and Her Writings*, p. 25.

of social accommodation to an alien and oppressive culture is disclosed. Elsewhere in her *œuvre*, stashed away in poems ostensibly on other topics, Wheatley figures her relation to writing as ardent, even licentious: like other women poets of the period, and especially those whose pleasures were most restricted by class oppression, Wheatley represents the workings of imagination as erotically charged. She can dare to do so most openly only in brief passages where the context forces other ideas to the fore. Thus, as June Jordan notices, in "To the University of Cambridge, in New-England" it is "an intrinsic ardor" which "bids" Wheatley to write verse: "not to dismiss the extraordinary kindness of the Wheatleys, and not to diminish the wealth of white men's literature with which she found herself quite saturated, but it was none of these extrinsic factors that compelled the labors of her poetry."[15] And in "Thoughts on the Works of Providence," Wheatley's formulation of dream-work renders the unconscious the site of libidinal investment and intellectual freedom:

> Say what is sleep? and dreams how passing strange!
> When action ceases, and ideas range
> Licentious and unbounded o'er the plains. (85–87)

When writing about "imagination" directly, however, Wheatley's representation is no less erotic but distinctly more constrained. Her poem "On Imagination" discloses the contradiction between imaginative "freedom" and the circumstances from which she writes. The discipline of poetic composition, those "silken fetters," keeps her in "soft captivity" that has somehow displaced—not the poet's historical servitude—but a previous state of unbounded imaginative freedom:

> Now here, now there, the roving *Fancy* flies,
> Till some lov'd object strikes her wand'ring eyes,
> Whose silken fetters all the senses bind,
> And soft captivity involves the mind. (9–12)

But why figure the imaginary fixing on an object, the investing of that object with desire and intellectual engagement ("involves the mind") as a form of captivity at all? Surely, ironically, we must read back into the poem what has ostensibly been left out: the situation of servitude from which Wheatley writes, the slavery within which her sensibility is both produced

---

[15] June Jordan, "The Difficult Miracle of Black Poetry in America, or Something Like a Sonnet for Phillis Wheatley," *On Call: Political Essays* (Boston, Mass.: South End Press, 1985), p. 90.

for public consumption and held captive, though a comparatively "soft captivity" it may be: one that allows this slave poetic license.

Wheatley's poetic project may be characterized as one of cultural hybridity with a vengeance. Her most direct allusions to the injustices of her historical situation, and those of other Africans, are always offered, as we have seen, ostensibly in the service of something else: congratulations to university graduates, praise of a new government official, musings on the imagination. Interestingly, in a manuscript poem, "An address to the Deist 1767," Wheatley writes at the age of fourteen:

> Must Ethiopians be employ'd for you?
> Much I rejoice if any good I do. (1–2)[16]

The contradiction between her desire to question, if not refuse outright, conscription into the service of white culture, whether marked by deistical or missionary zeal, and her acknowledgment that to be of service is also intellectually gratifying is broached openly here. A comparable gesture of taking pleasure from the imperialist culture to which she would not be subjected, against which she obliquely protests, but from whose subjection there appears to be no escape, occurs in the ambitious long poem *Niobe in Distress for her Children Slain by Apollo, from Ovid's Metamorphoses, Book VI. and from a View of the Painting of Mr. Richard Wilson.*[17] A single couplet connects this elaborate venture into neoclassical imitation with Wheatley's brief mention of her enslavement in "To Dartmouth" where the brutal implacability of the slave-trader is set against African paternal love. In the very midst of proving herself a true poet in eighteenth-century neoclassical terms, Wheatley represents her poetic heroine in an act of rebellion fuelled by her paternal inheritance and expressed in the paternal language which Wheatley herself has been forbidden to speak, from which her own discourse has been forever ruptured:

> "No reason her imperious temper quells,
> "But all her father in her tongue rebels. (97–98)

---

[16] Wheatley, "An address to the Deist 1767," manuscript in the Massachusetts Historical Society, reprinted in Robinson, *Phillis Wheatley and Her Writings*, pp. 133–34.

[17] Citing this poem as an example, Margaret Doody has suggested in "Augustan *Women?* Four Poets of the Eighteenth Century" that there may be more than mere commonplace wisdom in the idea that classical narratives have an apparently "universal appeal" when we come to such unlikely appropriators of classical sources as Wheatley. I would add that there seems to be a convergence between classical subjects and intellectual ambition in eighteenth-century women's verse, especially for the more "unlikely" imitators.

For this impious queen, this daughter of the desiring, vanquished mortal father, ambition (for her nation, her family) thus articulated succeeds only in producing a disarticulation—the punitive silencing of Niobe through the murder of her children. No "reason" moderates her pride, her desire to rule her people and protest subordination to the gods. And the price of that rebellion is eternal silence: Niobe is turned to stone.

It is precisely "reason," we must assume, that quells Wheatley's own temper, that moderates her discourse and decorously channels the "intrinsic ardor" and "licentious" imagination that drive her to write. And reason is what Wheatley most decisively must prove she possesses if she is to do "any good" as an "Ethiopian" employed by white colonialists, serve the interests of liberty and abolitionism, and write so as to be read as a true poet, thus disproving the assumptions upon which racial prejudice could be based. As Henry Louis Gates has so eloquently argued, writing by Africans was crucial to the eighteenth-century debate over slavery. If an African could write—and especially an African woman—then Africans should not be enslaved, as reasonable, fully human beings. Gates concludes that "writing, for these slaves, was not an activity of mind; rather, it was a commodity which they were forced to trade for their humanity."[18] Understood thus, Wheatley's "soft captivity" as a site of literary production becomes an image not so much of reconciliation and compliance as a sign of hybridity, "the warlike sign of the native." Out of the imperialist fracture, the ruptured native "tongue," comes a mimicry that is more than merely ironical, and far from innocent.

What are we then to make of a poem like "To Maecenas," the poem that introduces Wheatley's volume to the public and explicitly addresses questions of patronage, acculturation, and native poetic desire? How could such a corpus as Wheatley's have been read and not recognized as radically subversive in a cultural climate as skeptical of African writing as eighteenth-century Boston or Britain? "To Maecenas" makes clear by means of its very obscurity how Wheatley's mimicry both represents and conceals rebellion, stages ideological conflict within neoclassical imitation but so obliquely that those possibilities of heteroglossic resistance can only with difficulty be teased out.

In "To Maecenas," Wheatley inadvertently reveals Pope's own hybridization, while asking in Popean language for direct access to classical

---

[18]Henry Louis Gates, Jr., "Editor's Introduction: Writing 'Race' and the Difference It Makes," "Race," Writing, and Difference, pp. 8–9. See also his Figures in Black: Words, Signs, and the "Racial" Self (New York and Oxford: Oxford University Press, 1987), pp. 61–79, and The Signifying Monkey: A Theory of Afro-American Literary Criticism (New York and Oxford: Oxford University Press, 1988), pp. 89–92.

inspiration, like Homer and Virgil. She writes as one who would have Pope's own classical inspiration in spite of the cultural barriers between her and the master texts of Western antiquity. Pope himself is not mentioned in this poem, but his classicized English landscape predominates, and Wheatley addresses Maecenas in conclusion much as Pope addresses Bolingbroke at the close of the *Essay on Man;* we may also think of the last section of *Windsor-Forest* in which Pope envisages global peace as the end of imperialism and slavery:

> As long as *Thames* in streams majestic flows,
> Or *Naiads* in their oozy beds repose,
> While *Phoebus* reigns above the starry train,
> While bright *Aurora* purples o'er the main,
> So long, great Sir, the muse thy praise shall sing,
> So long thy praise shall make *Parnassus* ring:
> Then grant, *Maecenas,* thy paternal rays,
> Hear me propitious, and defend my lays. (48–55)

The epistolary form, with its implied dialogics, is here neither directed amorously towards a lover nor intertextually towards literary precursors, except for Terence, a fellow African (37–42). Rather, Wheatley indirectly addresses her various lacks as an African female slave poet by invoking the ideal type of the patron, neoclassically speaking: Gaius Cilnius Maecenas, Roman statesman and wealthy patron of Virgil and Horace, a rich man of taste who supports the arts, and the patron to whom Virgil's *Georgics* in particular are dedicated. But so obliquely does Wheatley treat the dynamics of patronage in this text, that readers may well share the confusion of one commentator, who notes that Maecenas refers to Gaius Cilnius, only to add in the same note that Wheatley seems to be addressing not a patron but a fellow poet.[19] The paradox of Wheatley's idealization of relations of patronage is that she must conceive of the ideal patron as a poet, as someone blessed equally by the muses, in order to collapse the class-charged distance between patron and poet into imaginary identification:

> MAECENAS, you, beneath the myrtle shade,
> Read o'er what poets sung, and shepherds play'd.
> What felt those poets but you feel the same?
> Does not your soul posses the sacred flame?
> Their noble strains your equal genius shares
> In softer language, and diviner airs. (1–6)

---

[19] See Robinson, *Phillis Wheatley and her Writings,* p. 271, n. 1.

The patron is no sooner assured of poetic genius than Wheatley must hanker after it too. As with Yearsley's and Masters's desires for Pope's rapturous inspiration, so also with Wheatley's desire here; if she could rival Maecenas and Virgil in a single page of verse, or at least lay claim to Virgilian inspiration, she too would experience the rapturous ardor of genius, mounting and soaring above her groveling situation:

> O could I rival thine and *Virgil's* page,
> Or claim the *Muses* with the *Mantuan* Sage;
> Soon the same beauties should my mind adorn,
> And the same ardors in my soul should burn:
> Then should my song in bolder notes arise,
> And all my numbers pleasingly surprize;
> But here I sit, and mourn a grov'ling mind,
> That fain would mount, and ride upon the wind. (23–30)

"Thine and *Virgil's* page": The patron who is himself capable of verse is the patron who does not exploit or feed parasitically upon his protégée. And the greatest praise that Wheatley as a humble protégée can offer is the recognition that her rich and classically educated white male patron, British or colonial, her Maecenas, himself possesses poetic laurels worth stealing:

> While blooming wreaths around thy temples spread,
> I'll snatch a laurel from thine honour'd head,
> While you indulgent smile upon the deed. (45–47)

Thus a coy Phillis Wheatley represents herself audaciously snatching a token sprig of the bays from one whose abundant supply means that he will indulge her in her theft, her audacious imitation. *Les voleuses de langue,* the thieves of language steal but also fly: Wheatley will mount and soar poetically after all, thanks to the indulgence of rich white patrons. And such is the fate of the poet generically, it would seem. Did not Pope himself do much the same in his poetic inscriptions of his friendships with great noblemen in the *Epistles to Several Persons* or *Moral Essays* and the Horatian imitations? Through Wheatley we can even recognize the relatively unacknowledged hybridity of Pope's neoclassicism, the lacks he too experienced in relation to the texts of antiquity, the etiology of his desire in and for writing.

At what possible moment, then, could such egregious flattery become the "warlike sign of the native"? For Wheatley's hybridity is in one sense at least categorically and politically different from Pope's, as we have seen. If we read Wheatley's obliquities scrupulously enough, but do not force the closure of a single referent or role for Maecenas, then this text too speaks of fracture and inscribes a mimicry far from benign. "As long as *Thames* in streams majestic flows, / Or *Naiads* in their oozy beds repose" (48–49): is this a naturalizing simile, a reflex of ideology that accepts British imperialism as given and eternal, and classical culture as rightfully the sign of imperialist dominance? Or is the end of white colonialist hegemony being implicitly insinuated in that "As long as"? "So long as" the imperial regime remains in place, both the muse and Wheatley will celebrate Maecenas' bounty. But after that? Here the Pope of *Windsor-Forest* who predicts a peaceful aftermath to British colonial rule, with native liberties restored, may have particularly appealed to her. The language of contracts, of negotiations that are the products of human agency, subject to revision and change, can be read in the silences surrounding the eternality of a classicized "nature" entirely foreign to Wheatley, entirely consciously learned. As she writes succinctly in the much anthologized "On being brought from Africa to America," "Once I redemption neither sought nor knew" (4). The cultural amnesia consequent upon deracination has made possible her absorption of Christianity, and also of a landscape inhabited by Phoebus and Aurora; but this pre-existing set of native knowledges, however approachable only as negativity or lack, introduces an element of subversion into the tightest of Wheatley's literary imitations.

Whether we read Maecenas primarily as a figure for John Wheatley, paternalist patron, or for Nathaniel, his son, who accompanied Phillis to England in search of a larger public, or more broadly as a figure for the collective type of potential subscribers and readers, who, whether they lived in America or England, were seen by Wheatley as culturally "English," the material conditions of patronage and clientage are obscured. In the gap created by this mystification there arises the possibility of a future undetermined by the majestic Thames, British militarism and commerce, their epiphenomenon, the slave trade, and the neoclassical mythology with which imperialist culture legitimates and sometimes obscures its projects. Until that moment, Wheatley will write, as write she must, and so will continue to find herself subject to the whims of patrons for whom race-, gender-, and class-consciousness strain the old terms of patronage as intimate friendship beyond recognition.

Robert Hayden begins his *American Journal* with "A Letter from Phillis Wheatley, *London*, 1773" (to her black female friend Obour Tanner) in which the crisis of Wheatley's cultural difference from her masters and patrons is dramatized.[20] Hayden's Phillis writes:

> Today, a little Chimney Sweep,
> his face and hands with soot quite Black,
> staring hard at me, politely asked:
> "Does you, M'lady, sweep chimneys too?"
> I was amused, but dear Nathaniel
> (ever Solicitous) was not. (45–50)

Which caused Nathaniel Wheatley greater consternation in his solicitude: the fact that the chimney sweep drew attention to Phillis's color at all ("What cheek!")? The fact that her color, thus recognized as a possible sign of labor, might cast both New World visitors as déclassé colonials, the huckster and the freak, "the Yankee Pedlar / and his Cannibal Mockingbird" (36–37)? Or the fact that the sweep's liberty of speech and the carnivalesque reversal upon which it depends – a lady who sweeps – indicates a certain possible fluidity of class categories, at least imaginatively speaking, that Phillis finds amusing and Nathaniel unthinkable? How Phillis Wheatley's masters must have dreaded even the dimly apprehended possibility of her laughter, and guarded against it through their solicitude.

June Jordan argues that only Wheatley's status as a slave, a dependent, made the publication of her verse safe and acceptable; that the death of Susanna Wheatley in 1774, in the same year as Phillis's twenty-first birthday, meant that she was free, but also without access to publication. Such is the "difficult miracle" of black poetry in America, Jordan claims, for which Phillis Wheatley's history remains the prototype. For Jordan, the strangeness of Wheatley's presence in the historical record can only be evoked by means of incantation and sermonic repetition: "And it was not natural. And she was the first."[21]

It was certainly not "natural" that a female slave wrote and published "verse" in colonial Boston. For Wheatley, every word represented a contest of cultural forces, the most radical kind of heteroglossia inscribed within the fractured, once polyglossic, semiotic field of African American history. But by working within as well as against the logic of abolitionist discourse, by trading the commodity of writing for her humanity, by pushing revolu-

---

[20] Robert Hayden, "A Letter from Phillis Wheatley, *London, 1773*" in *American Journal: Poems* (New York and London: Liveright, 1982), pp. 3–4. My thanks to Anca Vlasopolos for this reference.

[21] Jordan, "The Difficult Miracle," pp. 96–97.

tionary republican principles to their limit without flouting neoclassical decorums, this slave was able to force a "write of way to Western civility," as Houston Baker calls it.[22]

It could be argued that, of the poets examined in this study, Wheatley represents the extremest case of contextual criticism: one whose work may at first sight seem totally conventional, and this perception changes (if it does change) only in the light of biographical knowledge, here the knowledge that the poet was a black, female slave.[23] I would argue, rather, that the material conditions of a text's production, including such "biographical knowledge" and knowledge of relations of patronage, subscription, publication, and reception, are part of the text as such and not "contextual," that is, supplementary or secondary.[24] Particularly in the case of volumes of verse packaged as by "exceptional" figures, as Wheatley's and the collections by the other poets of this study were, such knowledge would be inseparable from the act of reading the poems at all. One would have to posit an ahistorically formalist scene of reading in order for Wheatley's poems to appear stripped of any trace of their conditions of production, and even then some of that biographical knowledge is figured in the poems themselves.

If laboring-class women's poetry published in Britain in the period can be said to constitute a discourse, Wheatley's *Poems* is both related and marginal to it. Read with such texts as Collier's, Leapor's, Yearsley's, Hands's and Little's in mind, Wheatley's *œuvre* becomes a site of resistance where gender oppression specifies but does not comprehend the poet's situation, where gender seems less at stake than race and class in the poet's precarious "soft captivity." Ironically, Wheatley's early death can be attributed directly to those exigencies of gender which her writing tends to ignore. Freed and married to the freedman John Peters at the age of twenty-five, she was dead at thirty-one, worn out by poverty, illness, and childbearing. Read with some attention to the issues raised by postcolonialist criticism, Wheatley's *œuvre* becomes a site not of native or naive servility but of colonial hybridity, in which even the most docile neoclassical allusion, the most pious invocation of Christian faith, may be seen as a warlike sign, as warlike as was possible within this gendered colonial discourse.

---

[22] Houston A. Baker, Jr., "Caliban's Triple Play," in Gates (ed.), *"Race," Writing, and Difference*, p. 383.

[23] I owe this formulation of such an argument to Howard Erskine-Hill.

[24] See Jerome J. McGann, *A Critique of Modern Textual Criticism* (Chicago and London: University of Chicago Press, 1983), p. 81, p. 93.

Tradition and The Interesting Narrative: Capitalism, Abolition, and the Romantic Individual

Sonia Hofkosh

> *The existing order is complete before the new work*
> *arrives; for order to persist after the supervention of*
> *novelty, the* whole *existing order must be, if ever so*
> *slightly, altered; and so the relations, proportions,*
> *values of each work of art toward the whole are*
> *readjusted; and this is conformity between the old*
> *and the new.*
>
> *— T. S. Eliot (1919)* [1]

> *The recognition that tradition bestows is a partial*
> *form of identification. In restaging the past it*
> *introduces other, incommensurable cultural*
> *temporalities into the invention of tradition.*
> *—Homi K. Bhabha (1994)* [2]

In "Out of Africa: Topologies of Nativism," Kwame Anthony Appiah outlines a set of directives for teaching modern African literature to students in Africa, as distinct from teaching that literature in the American academy. African students should read specifically "to connect . . . with their geographical situations," to "value and incorporate the African past,"

---

[1] "Tradition and the Individual Talent," *Selected Prose of T. S. Eliot*, ed. Frank Kermode (New York: Harcourt Brace Jovanovich, 1975), 37–44; 38–39.

[2] Homi K. Bhabha, *The Location of Culture* (London: Routledge, 1994), 2.

whereas the function and effect of reading African writing in the West should be "to extend the American imagination . . . beyond the narrow scope of the United States" and its determining systems of value — economic and political as well as aesthetic.[3] Positing such "different conceptions of reading" (159) aimed alternately at the consolidation of African national identity and tradition and at the translocation of Western self-consciousness and its history of dominance, Appiah's pedagogical correlatives also recognize the dialectical nature of the cultural encounter at issue in African writing. If "the language of empire, of center and periphery, identity and difference, the sovereign subject and her colonies, continues to structure the criticism and reception of African literature *in* Africa as elsewhere," that literature nonetheless can and should be read to challenge such a "rhetoric of alterity" — itself a "Western thematic" — which assumes the polarity of self (indigene) and other (alien) as an "organic" formulation rather than as a set of conventionally (and often violently) occupied positions (163). Thus the mode of reading which Appiah proposes for African students that would "expose the ways in which the systematic character of literary (and, more broadly, aesthetic) judgments of value is the product of certain institutional practices" might constructively motivate readers in the United States as well. Reading African writing here, we too can learn to readjust the "relations, proportions, and values" of our own cultural conformity.

Appiah's critique of the oppositional topos implicit in nativist discourse is elaborated in the context of modern African literature and criticism, particularly as it is exemplified in the writing of Chinua Achebe and Wole Soyinka. With other African writers in the European languages, according to Abiola Irele, these Nigerian authors constitute the main focus of African letters "as a cultural phenomenon and also as an object of academic study," as a discrete and significant body of works, a tradition.[4] For Irele, modern African writing characteristically and fundamentally engages questions of identity—of "presence" (82) or "integrity of being and consciousness" (83)—primarily *as* a question of tradition. Tradition is "felt as the anchor of consciousness, of a presence in the world" (71), and figures as "both theme and determining factor of the very form" of modern African expression (96). But while tradition in this way defines at once the

---

[3] Kwame Anthony Appiah, "Out of Africa: Topologies of Nativism" in *The Bounds of Race: Perspectives on Hegemony and Resistance,* ed. Dominick LaCapra (Ithaca: Cornell University Press, 1991), 134–63.

[4] Abiola Irele, "African Letters: The Making of a Tradition," *The Yale Journal of Criticism,* 5 (Fall 1991), 69–100; 74.

substance and the shape of African writing, it is also associated at the moment of invention with "historical grievance" (76), with the brutal dislocations, the unworlding, compelled by the slave trade and colonialism. Irele traces the tension thus built into the making of an African tradition back to the eighteenth century, specifically to *The Interesting Narrative of the Life of Olaudah Equiano, or Gustavus Vassa, the African,* published in London in 1789. In its introspective mode, Equiano's autobiographical *Interesting Narrative* inaugurates the tradition of African letters, anticipating the emphasis on "self-representation" and "self-reflection" (76) that will become a central feature in the discursive project of modern writers in Africa.

Irele's discussion should remind us once again that tradition is transitional, not a static or always already established structure or syllabus, but on-going, in the process of coming into being through struggle and revision: "It cannot be inherited, and if you want it you must obtain it by great labour."[5] Without denying the central, even originary, place of Equiano's text in the making of a tradition of African letters, nor, alternatively, diffusing the importance of its status as "the prototype of the nineteenth-century slave narrative" and therefore "the very foundation upon which most subsequent Afro-American fictional and nonfictional forms are based,"[6] I want to look at this African writer's participation in, contribution to, and revisionary potential for another history, a romantic history, a history of the individual ("presence" or "consciousness") that has a political as well as an aesthetic unfolding. I want to emphasize that this is not to read Equiano in order to measure the value of his work by trying whether it can be inserted into what Appiah calls "a Great White Tradition of masterpieces."[7] "Fitting in" is not really the issue here.[8] Rather, to read

[5]T. S. Eliot, "Tradition and the Individual Talent," 38.

[6]Henry Louis Gates, Jr., "Introduction," *The Classic Slave Narratives,* ed. Henry Louis Gates (New York: New American Library, 1987), xii, xiv. Cf. Gates's discussion of *The Interesting Narrative* in *The Signifying Monkey: A Theory of African-American Literary Criticism* (New York: Oxford University Press, 1988), 152–58; and Angelo Constanzo, *Surprising Narrative: Olaudah Equiano and the Beginnings of Black Autobiography* (New York: Greenwood, 1987).

[7]"Out of Africa," 142.

[8]"Tradition and the Individual Talent," 39. Here it should be clear that my use of T. S. Eliot does not simply ratify his position in "Tradition and the Individual Talent" or in literary history, so much as it invokes his terms to adapt them toward another purpose. Irele also employs Eliot's critical terminology (81), as do the authors of the nativist polemic Appiah cites in his essay (Chinweizu, Onwuchekwa Jemie, and Ihechukwu Madubuike, *Toward the Decolonization of African Literature* [Enugu, Nigeria, 1980], 106).

Equiano in reference to this other history is to restage the past, to reread that history *as* other, to defamiliarize the terms and tendencies of its elaboration into such an exclusive, capitalized canon. The *Interesting Narrative* is not a "new work" in the sense that T. S. Eliot means when he refers in "Tradition and the Individual Talent" to the supervention of novelty which necessarily alters the existing order of the past. But the relatively recent rediscovery of Equiano's work *in the academy*[9] nonetheless "calls for a reinvention of the radical difference of *our own* cultural past."[10]

One point of examining Equiano's link to the tradition of British romanticism is to suggest the plural and transformative position his text occupies in the very construction of tradition and in the cultural demarcations tradition inscribes. At once spiritual autobiography and abolitionist polemic (among other things), Equiano's text cannot be fully appropriated to conventional categories of literary history. It introduces Homi Bhabha's "incommensurable cultural temporalities" into the narrative of a coherent past. Yet even as it resists the fixity of categorical definitions, such as the difference between an aesthetic of the personal and a political intervention — or between an African text and a British one — *The Interesting Narrative* reveals the investments at stake in establishing principles of difference, investments that both inform and unsettle the account of (generic, national, racial) identity such conventional categories subtend. To say that Equiano's text cannot be fully appropriated to conventional categories is not to suggest that it transcends the definitional rigors of tradition. Rather, it is to suggest that the text casts those rigors into relief; it highlights the way tradition is never simply the same, never simply or consistently itself, that it works through and to contain (include, regulate, subsume) difference. This essay explores the mutual purchase that obtains between tradition and *The Interesting Narrative* through the converging discourses of capitalism, abolition, and individualism that Equiano's text puts into play: that commerce consolidates the force of tradition even while operating within tradition to shift ("if ever so slightly") its terms, its values, and its effects.

> I, who had been a slave in the morning, trembling at the will of another, was become my own master, and completely free.
>
> —Olaudah Equiano (1789)

---

[9] By Paul Edwards in his edition of 1968.

[10] Fredric Jameson, "Third-World Literature in the Era of Multinational Capitalism," in *Social Text* 15 (Fall 1986), 65–88; 66.

Can he who the day before was a trampled slave suddenly become liberal-minded, forebearing, and independent?

—Percy Shelley (1818)[11]

To consider *The Interesting Narrative of the Life of Olaudah Equiano* in the context of the specific conditions of its production ("never singular but always several")[12] is to locate it in the political history of the British abolitionist movement, as a critical contribution to the agitation against the slave trade gathering force in the late eighteenth century. Equiano occupied a significant position in that history. He was a public figure, a "recognized leader of the black community in Britain."[13] He was one among a number of politically visible Africans in London of the 1780s and 1790s, including Ottobah Cugoano, whose polemical *Thoughts and Sentiments on the Evil and Wicked Traffic of the Slavery and Commerce of the Human Species* (1787) Equiano may have helped draft. He served on the London Committee for the Black Poor, had been a government employee, and was a frequent writer of letters to newspapers such as the *Public Advertiser,* to prominent legislators and abolition committees, and even to the queen. He collaborated with a range of influential activists from the reformer Granville Sharp to the republican Thomas Hardy. With the appearance of *The Interesting Narrative,* Equiano traveled to cities throughout England, Scotland, and Ireland to sell copies of his book and to lecture on the cause of antislavery.[14]

---

[11] Olaudah Equiano, *The Interesting Narrative of the Life of Olaudah Equiano, or Gustavus Vassa, the African,* 2 vols. (London, 1789; rpt. London: Dawsons of Pall Mall, 1969), II, 16–17. All references to the text will be to this facsimile edition except where noted. Percy Shelley, "Preface" to "The Revolt of Islam," *Shelley: Poetical Works,* ed. Thomas Hutchinson (Oxford: Oxford University Press, 1970).

[12] Aijaz Ahmad, "Jameson's Rhetoric of Otherness and the 'National Allegory'" in *In Theory: Classes, Nations, Literature* (Verso, 1992), 122.

[13] Victor C. D. Mtubani, "The Black Voice in Eighteenth-Century Britain: African Writers against Slavery and the Slave Trade" in *Pylon: The Atlanta University Review of Race and Culture,* 45 (June 1984), 85–97; 91.

[14] On the contribution of Equiano and other African writers and activists to British abolition, see Wylie Sypher, *Guinea's Captive Kings: British Anti-Slavery Literature of the Eighteenth Century* (Chapel Hill: University of North Carolina Press, 1942); Folarin O. Shyllon, *Black People in Britain 1553–1833* (London: Oxford University Press, 1977) and "Olaudah Equiano: Nigerian Abolitionist and First National Leader of Africans in Britain," in *Journal of African Studies* 4 (1977), 433–51; Peter Fryer, *Staying Power: The History of Black People in Britain* (London: Pluto Press, 1984); Paul Edwards, "Three West African Writers of the 1780s," in *The Slave's Narrative,* ed. Charles T. Davis and Henry Louis Gates, Jr. (Oxford: Oxford University Press, 1985), 175–98; Keith A. Sandiford,

The Interesting Narrative is thus a document generated in the context of a political career. Equiano explicitly situates it as public performance, deflecting the personal implications of writing his life in order to identify that utterance as functional social discourse:

> I am not so foolishly vain as to expect from it either immortality or literary reputation. If it affords any satisfaction to my numerous friends, at whose request it has been written, or in the smallest degree promotes the interests of humanity, the ends for which it was undertaken will be fully attained, and every wish of my heart gratified. (I, 3)

Personal gratification, the author suggests, is motivated by others' pleasure, the "satisfaction of numerous friends." In lieu of vanity and reputation — characteristics of self-interest — Equiano invokes the more universally construed "interests of humanity." What Fredric Jameson calls the "libidinal investment" of this Third World text "is to be read in primarily political and social terms." [15] Addressed in particular to the Lords and Gentlemen of Parliament, Equiano's *Interesting Narrative* claims its place in the public sphere, as a political intervention in a vital national debate, as an "instrument" (I, iv) in the formation of public opinion and legislative policy.

Yet, if the "interest" in *The Interesting Narrative* is public rather than private, national rather than individual, the force of adding his own experience to the academic abolitionist arguments of Anthony Benezet's *Some Historical Account of Guinea* (1771) and Thomas Clarkson's *An Essay on the Slavery and Commerce of the Human Species* (1786), for example, suggests precisely that the instrumentality of Equiano's book *is* the personal:

> Permit me, with the greatest deference and respect, to lay at your feet the following genuine narrative; the chief design of which is to excite in your august assemblies a sense of compassion for the miseries which the Slave-Trade has entailed on my unfortunate countrymen. By the horrors of that trade was I first torn away from all the tender connections that were naturally dear to my heart. . . . (I, iii)

Equiano enters the political debate through personal experience. As the work of "an unlettered African," his "genuine narrative" provides for the abolitionist argument that "something else" Cugoano had called for in

---

Measuring the Moment: Strategies of Protest in Eighteenth-Century Afro-English Writing (London and Toronto: Associated University Presses, 1988). On Equiano's reform activism and the making of the working class, see also Peter Linebaugh, *The London Hanged: Crime and Civil Society in the Eighteenth Century* (London: Penguin Press, 1991), esp. 415.

[15] Jameson, "Third-World Literature," 72.

Thoughts and Sentiments to supplement the efforts of the "learned gentle-men" who write against the slave trade.[16] Equiano speaks in that authentic voice from Africa that Clarkson can only imagine or suppose.[17]

Further, *The Interesting Narrative* seeks to influence ("excite") the collective, political body of Parliament ("august assemblies") through the vocabulary of sentiment and feeling, appealing directly to the very hearts of its individual members: "May the God of Heaven inspire your hearts with peculiar benevolence on that important day when the question of Abolition is to be discussed" (I, v). The preface to the 1814 edition (the twelfth edition of the book printed in Britain) underscores the efficacy of such a personal appeal:

> Being a true relation of occurences which had taken place, and of sufferings which he had endured, it produced a degree of humane feelings in men's minds, to excite which the most animated addresses and the most convincing reasoning would have laboured in vain.[18]

The book is directed not to the reason, an abstract quantity, but seeks rather to register its effect in the very bodies of its readers—at their feet, in their hearts, and in their minds. It represents individual experience to them—both the author's and their own—creating for them an isolate, intimate space through which they can respond sympathetically to its argument. It operates from inside out, self-referentially, narrowing its focus in order to universalize its appeal, claiming its authority on an internal logic ("that *such a man,* pleading in *such a cause* will be acquitted of

---

[16] "The kind exertions of many benevolent and humane gentlemen against the iniquitous traffic of slavery and oppression, has been attended with much good to many. . . . However, nothwithstanding all that has been done and written against it, that brutish barbarity, and unparalleled injustice, is still carried on to a very great extent in the colonies. . . . It is therefore manifest, that something else ought yet to be done." Ottobah Cugoano, *Thoughts and Sentiments on the Evil and Wicked Traffic of the Slavery and Commerce of the Human Species, Humbly Submitted to the Inhabitants of Great Britain* (London, 1787), 1–3.

[17] See the imaginary conversation with an African in *An Essay on the Slavery and Commerce of the Human Species, Particularly the African* (Miami, Florida: Mnemosyne, 1969), 81–86. For early controversy about the issue of authenticity in Equiano's account of himself and his African homeland see *The Interesting Narrative,* appendix A: "To the Reader," and the letters on the *Oracle* article which appeared in the 5th edition of *The Interesting Narrative* in 1792. The controversy continues in S. E. Ogude, "Facts into Fiction: Equiano's Narrative Revisited," *Okike: An African Journal of New Writing,* 22 (Sept. 1982), 57–66.

[18] *The Interesting Narrative* (Leeds: James Nichols, 1814) in *The Classic Slave Narratives,* ed. Henry Louis Gates, Jr. (New York: New American Library, 1987), 5.

boldness and presumption," I, iv). The political dimension of the text is thus itself articulated in libidinal language; in Equiano's abolitionist intervention, his life story, the political is the personal.

But if such a complex embeddedness of public and private might be understood in Jameson's terms as the distinguishing feature of the minority text in an era of (emergent) capitalism, it might also be seen as a crucial factor in the very history of that emergence. Recent debate among economic and political historians about how to explain the progress of the abolitionist movement in late eighteenth-century Britain interrogates the "convergence of humanitarian ideals and capitalist ideology." [19] The ground of that interrogation may shift, "from the direct clash of imperial economic forces [as in C. L. R. James or Eric Williams] to battles for the minds and hearts of metropolitans [as in Roger Anstey or David Brion Davis]," [20] but the question remains largely about "the relation of society to consciousness" [21] —or, to adapt Jameson's terminology, the relation of the public world of classes, economics, and political power to the private domain of subjectivity, sexuality, and the literary.[22] One of the central premises informing much of the current discussion about the history of antislavery is "that the abolition of slavery cannot be explained by direct extrapolation from pure economic motives or mechanisms any more than from pure moral consciousness." [23] Rather, with their various disciplinary emphases and their differing theoretical assumptions, historians tracing the causes and consolidation of the British abolitionist movement uncover the intersection of these opposing categories in early antislavery activity,

---

[19] *British Capitalism and Caribbean Slavery: The Legacy of Eric Williams,* ed. Barbara L. Solow and Stanley L. Engerman (Cambridge: Cambridge University Press, 1987), 18.

[20] Seymour Drescher, "Paradigms Tossed: Capitalism and the Political Sources of Abolition," in *British Capitalism and Caribbean Slavery,* 191–208; 196. See C. L. R. James, *The Black Jacobins: Toussaint L'Ouverture and the San Domingo Revolution* (1938; rev. ed. New York: Vintage, 1963); Eric Williams, *Capitalism and Slavery* (Chapel Hill: University of North Carolina Press, 1944); Roger Anstey, *The Atlantic Slave Trade and British Abolition, 1760–1810* (Atlantic Highlands, N.J.: Humanities Press, 1975); Howard Temperley, "Anti-Slavery as a Form of Cultural Imperialism," in *Anti-Slavery, Religion, and Reform: Essays in Memory of Roger Anstey,* ed. Christine Bolt and Seymour Drescher (Folkestone, Eng., and Camden, Conn.: Archon, 1980), 335–50; David Brion Davis, *The Problem of Slavery in the Age of Revolution, 1770–1823* (Ithaca: Cornell University Press, 1975).

[21] Thomas Bender, "Introduction," in *The Antislavery Debate: Capitalism and Abolitionism as a Problem in Historical Interpretation,* ed. Bender (Berkeley: University of California Press, 1992), 1–13; 2.

[22] Jameson, "Third-World Literature," 69.

[23] Drescher, "Paradigms Tossed," 194–95.

disclosing the operation of a conceptual framework which links rather than separates public and private, economics and ethics, tradition and the individual talent.[24]

Transcribing his own past, Equiano enacts the fundamental and inseparable intersections implicit in the history his text helps mobilize. When he purchases his manumission for forty pounds sterling ("I, who had been a slave in the morning, trembling at the will of another, was become my own master, and completely free"), he demonstrates not only that economic values translate into personal ones, but more precisely that the economic structure of property and power underwrites the very possibility of individual freedom even as that structure is itself girded by an individualist paradigm, the rights of man. Buying his freedom, possessing by that purchase a self "liberal-minded, forbearing, and independent," Equiano dramatizes that in the age of democratic revolution—in America, France, and San Domingo—the rhetoric of rights involves a model of individual agency that relies on the concept of absolute property ("in one's own person") and thus imbricates the economic and the psychological dimensions of self-mastery.[25]

> The only security of property that nature authorizes and reason sanctions is, the right a man has to enjoy the acquisitions which his talents and industry have acquired.
>
> —M. Wollstonecraft (1790)

---

[24] Seymour Drescher's recent work exemplifies the imbrication. Drescher argues against Davis's hegemony of "humanitarian ideals" (or bourgeois ideology) account and for the efficacy of popular, collective agitation. In "Paradigms Tossed," however, he details the way that agitation operates through the "everyday practices of commercial capitalism" (202) and thus through the private sphere, where Wedgewood's medallion and the popular print of a loaded slave ship would have been decoratively displayed, and where the boycott of West Indian sugar by women whose political agency was limited to the domestic realm of consumption would have been implemented. See also Davis's response to Drescher in "Capitalism, Abolitionism, and Hegemony" in Solow and Engerman, *British Capitalism and Caribbean Slavery,* 209–27. For a recent discussion of the role the conception of a privatized domestic virtue played in the politics of Britain's involvement with Caribbean slavery, see Charlotte Sussman, "Women and the Politics of Sugar, 1792," *Representations* 48 (Fall 1994), 48–69.

[25] I draw here on the account of property and individualism in Elizabeth Fox-Genovese and Eugene D. Genovese, *Fruits of Merchant Capital: Slavery and Bourgeois Property in the Rise and Expansion of Capitalism* (New York: Oxford University Press, 1983), esp. 272–98; 298. My discussion is also generally indebted to Elizabeth Fox-Genovese's reminder in *Feminism without Illusions: A Critique of Individualism* (Chapel Hill: University of North Carolina Press, 1991), that individualism and its attendant discourse of rights is the product of a particular historical period—the age of democratic revolution; see esp. 113–38.

Here and there a Napoleon of finance, by luck and industry, could make
enough to purchase his freedom.

—C. L. R. James (1938)[26]

The institution of slavery by which one man could be said to own
another as private property fostered the emerging economics of capitalism
in specific and measurable ways, both in terms of modes of production and
patterns of consumption—of sugar or of cotton textiles, for example.[27] But
so too did capitalism as it developed into the dominant economic system
in Europe depend on the Enlightenment notion of individualism theorized
in John Locke's political philosophy, advanced in the interest-driven
economics of Adam Smith's *The Wealth of Nations* (1776), and put so prof-
itably into practice by many among the entrepreneurial bourgeois who
were active in the agitation to abolish chattel slavery in the British West Indies: "The human essence is freedom from dependence on the will of
others, and freedom is a function of possession."[28] Capitalism derives its
operative logic from the same basic assumption as the liberatory project of
abolition, which posits self-ownership as one of the fundamental, defining
features of human morality.[29] This is the "paradox" that Equiano's *Interesting Narrative* performs.[30] Individualism is two-faced, double-edged;

---

[26] *The Black Jacobins,* 11.

[27] See the specific histories of production and consumption detailed in Part II of *The Atlantic Slave Trade: Effects on Economies, Societies, and Peoples in Africa, the Americas, and
Europe,* ed. Joseph E. Inikori and Stanley L. Engerman (Durham: Duke University Press,
1992).

[28] On the concept of possessive individualism as a moral basis for capitalist ideology see
C. B. Macpherson, *The Political Theory of Possessive Individualism: Hobbes to Locke* (Oxford: Oxford University Press, 1962), 3.

[29] In *An Essay on the Slavery and Commerce of the Human Species,* for example, Clarkson
distinguishes slavery as a punishment for crimes from slavery which involves the idea of
ownership: "Thus then may that slavery, in which only the idea of *labour is* included, be
perfectly equitable, and the delinquent will always receive his punishment as a *man;*
whereas in that, which additionally includes the idea of *property,* and to undergo which,
the delinquent must previously change his nature, and become *a brute,* there is an inconsistency, which no arguments can reconcile, and a contradiction to every principle
of nature, which a man need only appeal to his own feelings immediately to evince" (Miami, Fla.: Mnemosyne, 1969, [76]).

[30] For an attempt to "resolve the paradox" of how capitalism at once promoted the development of slave systems and yet introduced ideology which challenged those systems,
see Robin Blackburn, *The Overthrow of Colonial Slavery, 1776–1848* (London: Verso,
1988), which is concerned primarily to integrate movements of resistance and accommodation among the slaves in "the plantation zone" into the analysis of the metropolitan abolitionist movement. On slave resistance in the colonies, also see Michael Craton,
Testing the Chains: Resistance to Slavery in the British West Indies (Ithaca: Cornell University Press, 1982).

capitalism (the means of exploitation) and abolition (the way to freedom) two sides of the same cognitive coin.[31] Equiano's manumission turns on just such a coin (forty pounds sterling), turns a slave into a master, the trampled and abject into the prototype of independent and creative consciousness.

It is a primary aim of *The Interesting Narrative* to detail the brutalities of chattel slavery and of the racist violence sanctioned by colonial policy. But in the moment that he buys his freedom, Equiano's history might also be seen to literalize the ethos of possessive individualism, exposing even as it does so the double edge that defines the paradigm of the entrepreneurial subject: the self as owner depends on the principle that selves can be owned, freedom on the possibility of alienation, identity on difference. For Houston Baker, the manumission exemplifies Equiano's "adept mercantilism": mastering the economic system empowers a unified subjectivity, "a man who has repossessed himself," an individual.[32] "Having achieved his individuality as a freeman," Joseph Fichtelberg conversely argues, "Equiano can exercise it only in an economic system where humans are commodities, empty markers, ciphers."[33] Two sides of one economy. Taken together, these opposing readings of the economic relations manifest in the moment of liberation suggest that at such a moment Equiano might be at once master and slave, empowered and alienated, subject and object, his own uncanny double: the same and different.

Identity in *The Interesting Narrative* is elaborated in the dynamic of these oppositions, a complex of competing and mutually constitutive positions and values. Identity circulates, changes character, but without wholly occupying or abandoning one position or the other.[34] Instead, at

---

[31] See Homi K. Bhabha's characterization of the "Janus-faced discourse of the nation": "meanings may be partial because they are in *medias res;* and history may be half-made because it is in the process of being made; and the image of cultural authority may be ambivalent because it is caught, uncertainly, in the act of 'composing' its powerful image." "Introduction," *Nation and Narration,* ed. Homi K. Bhabha (London: Routledge, 1990), 1–7; 3.

[32] Houston A. Baker, *Blues, Ideology, and Afro-American Literature: A Vernacular Theory* (Chicago: University of Chicago Press, 1984), 33; 38–39.

[33] "Word Between Worlds: The Economy of Equiano's *Narrative,*" *American Literary History,* 5 (Fall 1993), 459–80; 471.

[34] In her discussion of *The Interesting Narrative,* Susan M. Marren calls this identity "transgressive" and explains it as "a fluid positioning, a mode of articulation of newly imagined, radically nonbinary subjectivities" in "Between Slavery and Freedom: The Transgressive Self in Olaudah Equiano's Autobiography," *PMLA* 108 (Jan. 1993), 94–105; 95. Marren concludes that this transgressive self *transcends* the dynamic of alterity, whereas I suggest an *internalization* that highlights the limits of identity. See Geraldine Murphy's reading of Equiano's "dissident colonialism" as a stance that exposes "the positionality of European—and African—identity" in "Olaudah Equiano, Accidental Tourist," *Eighteenth-Century Studies,* 27 (Summer 1994), 551–68; 557.

the moment he becomes his own master, or, even from the moment when, as "a Napoleon of finance," he makes enough to purchase his freedom, Equiano enacts both the imperial gesture of accumulation and its contrary, the impossibility of such a totalizing, appropriative posture.

> Heavens! who could do justice to my feelings at this moment! Not conquering heroes themselves, in the midst of a triumph—Not the tender mother who has just regained her long-lost infant, and presses it to her heart—Not the weary hungry mariner, at the sight of a desired friendly port—not the lover, when he once more embraces his beloved mistress, after she has been ravished from his arms!—All within my breast was tumult, wildness, and delirium! (II, 15–16)

This moment offers a dynamic at once of affiliation and disavowal. Marshalling multiple figures, none of which can "do justice to [his] feelings," Equiano represents his experience in an excess of contradiction. Not this, not that, nor even the other, his powerful feeling ("tumult, wildness, and delirium") overflows as a series of images of conquest and reunion, loss and gain, images at once conventionally construed and inappropriate, familiar and yet strange. The excess signals the way traditional figures may indeed constitute the very substance of self-expression—what he has "all within," his own discursive property—at the same time that such formulated phrases can never be fully appropriate to individual desire ("my imagination was all rapture . . .") which will always want something else.[35] Extending the boundary of identity ("all within") out to its descriptive limits, Equiano represents individuality *as* delimited by the sheer force of accumulation—accumulated figures, signs of possession—a movement outward that takes in and trades on other('s) desires (the hero, the mother . . .), an internalization of capitalist romance.

Such a scene of internalization aligns the model of identity exemplified at this crucial moment in Equiano's narrative to the romantic tradition as it is articulated in late eighteenth-century culture as a discourse of freedom and individual rights, for instance in the Ur-romanticism of William Godwin's political economy ("The rules by which my actions shall be directed are matters of a consideration entirely personal"), Mary Wollstonecraft's two vindications ("The only security of property that nature authorizes and reason sanctions is, the right a man has to enjoy the acquisitions which his talents and industry have acquired"), or William Blake's allegory of individual man recreating the nation ("I must Create a System or be enslaved

---

[35] His libido liberated with his manumission, Equiano remarks that "some of the sable females, who formerly stood aloof, now began to relax and appear less coy." But he directs his desire elsewhere: "my heart was still fixed on London" (II, 19).

by another Man's").[36] While Equiano shares with these writers notions of the foundational value of the personal, in *The Interesting Narrative*, the discourse of freedom does not simply function in opposition to the coercive rules or directives externally imposed, another man's system over against my own. Equiano's text also works within those structures or, more precisely, it shows how those structures work within. The "inhuman custom"[37] of slavery is clearly the explicit target of Equiano's political polemic, but the narrative simultaneously traces the way humans become accustomed to the terms and values of the dominant system and reproduce them ("mind-forg'd manacles")[38] in their own persons.[39]

For many readers, the central problematic of *The Interesting Narrative* involves exactly this "process of acculturation,"[40] Equiano's internalization of the dominant economy, "mental colonization."[41] But the trajectory that the narrative of Equiano's individual "talents and industry" accomplishes — from slave to master, African to Anglophile, margin to metropole — suggests not only that he adopts forms of culture — "fashions, manners, customs, &c." (II, 250) — that are not natural to him and that therefore go against the indigenous grain, but also that his progress toward freedom, even toward a more perfect grace, discloses the contradictions within

---

[36] William Godwin, *An Inquiry Concerning Political Justice, and Its Influence on General Virtue and Happiness* (London: William Pickering, 1993), 86; Mary Wollstonecraft, *A Vindication of the Rights of Men* (New York: New York University Press, 1989), 24; William Blake, "Jerusalem," I, plate 10 in *The Poetry and Prose of William Blake*, ed. David V. Erdman (Garden City, New York: Doubleday, 1970).

[37] Mary Wollstonecraft, *A Vindication of the Rights of Men*, 14.

[38] William Blake, "London," *The Poetry and Prose of William Blake*, 26.

[39] Orlando Patterson's account of manumission as initiating a new obligation to the master in the form of gratitude can be considered also in terms of the ideology of individualism, which, functioning to internalize constraint, effects a shift from domination by physical force or material conditions (such as in slavery) to the embedded coercion of conscience and responsibility, what Equiano calls "the generous mind . . . struggling between inclination and duty" (II, 20). See *Slavery and Social Death: A Comparative Study* (Cambridge: Harvard University Press, 1982) and Susan M. Marren's application of Patterson's model to Equiano in "Between Slavery and Freedom: The Transgressive Self in Olaudah Equiano's Autobiography," esp. 96, 101.

[40] William L. Andrews, "The First Fifty Years of the Slave Narrative, 1760–1810" in *The Art of the Slave Narrative: Original Essays in Criticism and Theory*, ed. John Sekora and Darwin T. Turner (Western Illinois University, 1982), 6–24; 20.

[41] Chinsole, "Tryin' to Get Over: Narrative Posture in Equiano's Autobiography" in *The Art of the Slave Narrative*, 45–54; 50. Also see M. van Wyk Smith's argument that Equiano "deliberately exploit[s]" orthodoxy to articulate an "antidiscourse of black consciousness" in "Writing the African Diaspora in the Eighteenth Century," *Diaspora* 1:2 (Fall 1991), 127–42; 129; 139.

the notion of the individual that can be subsumed into "the whole existing order" only through a transformative process of displacement. If one of Romanticism's defining characteristics is the will toward "self-possession," [42] then, Equiano's narrative should remind us to consider such a desire neither as a universal value nor as the exclusive territory of a few (white, male) writers undertaking the elaboration and consolidation of a national tradition. Rather, such a model of mastery is deployed within the history of individualism, itself embedded in an economic system that operates at the level of cognition, not just commerce, to produce "relations, proportions, values," not just commodities. Historicized through Equiano's diasporic imagination, the romantic tradition can in this sense hardly be called "anticapitalist," [43] for all its theoretical disdain of "getting and spending." [44] It might instead be seen as complicitous in the development of capitalism even as its emancipatory rhetoric struggles toward reinvention.

Robert Wedderburn and Mulatto Discourse

Helen Thomas

But there comes a time, as it came in my life, when a man is denied the right to live a normal life, when he can only live the life of an outlaw because the government has so decreed to use the law to impose a state of outlawry on him.[1]

From Helen Thomas, *Romanticism and Slave Narratives: Transatlantic Testimonies*, 2000, pp. 255–271 and notes, 320–323. Reprinted with the permission of Cambridge University Press.

[42] For an analysis of "self-possession" as "a crucial element of the larger ideology of romanticism itself," see Marlon B. Ross, *The Contours of Masculine Desire: Romanticism and the Rise of Women's Poetry* (New York: Oxford University Press, 1989), 10.

[43] See Robert Sayre and Michael Lowy, "Figures of Romantic Anticapitalism," in *Spirits of Fire: English Romantic Writers and Contemporary Historical Methods*, ed. G. A. Russo & Daniel P. Watkins (Rutherford, N.J.: Fairleigh Dickinson University Press, 1990), 23–68.

[44] William Wordsworth, "The world is too much with us," *Poetical Works*, ed. Ernest de Selincourt (Oxford: Clarendon Press, 1935).

[1] Nelson Mandela at his first trial in 1962.

Now I have scarcely a drop of black blood left in me,
my blood having so faded with the blood of a Minister,
that I am [becoming] as white as a Mulatto.[2]

Whereas Equiano's narrative of spiritual redemption presents a relatively circumspect demand for political reformation, the accentuation of subversive and millenarian elements of radical dissenting Protestantism provide an overtly militant and confrontational platform for the black British author and rebel, Robert Wedderburn.[3] Born in Jamaica around 1761, Wedderburn was the 'mulatto' offspring of the wealthy Scottish sugar plantation owner, James Wedderburn and his female slave, Rosanna. Separated from his rebellious mother as an infant and never acknowledged by his white father, the near-illiterate Robert was adopted and reared by his African-born maternal grandmother, the Kingston obeah and smuggler, 'Talkee Amy', under whose charge his own prophetic and oratory powers were developed. As slave plantation societies of the West Indies endeavoured to maintain remnants of distinctly African modes of belief, Talkee's position as plantation obeah confirmed her role as transmitter of preslavery epistemologies. She was revered by slaves and indeed, by some of their owners, as a chief communicant with ancestral 'spirits'.[4]

At the age of eleven, Wedderburn witnessed the public flogging of Talkee allegedly for 'witchcraft' by a young boy she had reared herself:

My grandmother's new master being a believer in the doctrine of Witchcraft, conceived that my grandmother had bewitched the vessel [captured by Spaniards], out of revenge for her not being liberated also. To punish her, therefore, he tied up the poor old woman of seventy years, and flogged her to the degree, that she would have died, but for the interference of a neighbour.[5]

---

[2] Furbush, *Dying Confessions,* cited in William Andrews, *To Tell a Free Story: The First Century of Afro-American Autobiography, 1760–1865* (Urbana: Illinois University Press, 1986) 49.

[3] See Iain McCalman's edition, *The Horrors of Slavery and Other Writings by Robert Wedderburn* (Edinburgh: Edinburgh University Press, 1991) and *idem, The Radical Underworld: Prophets, Revolutionaries and Pornographers in London, 1795–1840* (Cambridge: Cambridge University Press, 1988) 5–7, 28–9, 50–3; 149. See also Paul Edwards, *Unreconciled Strivings and Ironic Strategies: Three Afro-British Authors of the Georgian Era: Ignatius Sancho, Olaudah Equiano, Robert Wedderburn* (Edinburgh: Edinburgh University Press, 1992).

[4] McCalman, *The Horrors of Slavery,* 52–3.

[5] Robert Wedderburn, *The Horrors of Slavery: Exemplified in the Life and History of the Revd Robert Wedderburn in Which is Included the Correspondence of Robert Wedderburn and His Brother A[ndrew] Colville, alias Wedderburn.* Printed and published by Robert Wedderburn (London, 1824) 11.

Six years later, in 1778, having served as a fighting seaman in the Royal Navy aboard *HMS Polyphemus* and later as a privateer, Wedderburn arrived in England, aged seventeen.[6] There, he drifted around St Giles as one of the 'London Blackbirds', a community of runaway slaves and immigrants who earned their living as musicians, entertainers, beggars and thieves, until he obtained work as a tailor. According to his semi-autobiographical text, *The Horrors of Slavery: Exemplified in the Life and History of the Revd Robert Wedderburn* (1824), in 1786 Wedderburn underwent what he claims was a profoundly spiritual experience upon hearing the words of a passionate Wesleyan preacher. Having read Thomas Paine's *Rights of Man* (1791), Wedderburn went on to become a licensed Unitarian preacher. The first English Unitarian congregation had been founded seventeen years earlier by Theophilus Lindsey (1723–1808) who, having rejected the Anglican Church's creed restrictions, had established the Essex Street Chapel in London in 1774. These Unitarians practised a system of Christian belief which advocated the unipersonality of God and rejected both the divinity of Christ and the doctrine of the Trinity. Famous Unitarians included Joseph Priestley (1773–1804), the English chemist, political theorist and outstanding Unitarian leader who advocated scriptural rationalism, materialist determinism and humanitarian Christology; Samuel Taylor Coleridge, the poet; and Richard Price (1723–1791), who in 1789 delivered his notorious heretical speech, *A Discourse on the Love of Our Country* at the annual Revolution Society Meeting.

Wedderburn's first publication, a theological tract entitled, *Truth, Self-Supported; Or, A Refutation of Certain Doctrinal Errors, Generally Adopted in the Christian Church* (1790) displayed a complex synthesis of Methodism's principles of redemption and sanctification with elements of West Indian and African culture. His choice of epigraph confirmed his legacy as both a transmitter of (sociopolitical) truths and a creolised voice of radical transformation in the diaspora:

> God hath chosen the foolish things of the world, to confound the wise; and God hath chosen the weak things of the world, to confound the things that are mighty; and base things of the world, and things which are despised hath God chosen, &c. 1 Corinthians 1:27–8[7]

---

[6] Edwards, *Unreconciled Strivings*, 15–19.

[7] Wedderburn, *Truth, Self-Supported; Or, A Refutation of Certain Doctrinal Errors, Generally Adopted in the Christian Church, by Robert Wedderburn (A Creole from Jamaica)* (London, 1790), title page.

Written in the third person rather than the first person characteristic of conversion narratives, Wedderburn's text carefully established a structural framework of spiritual salvation, but with a particular accentuation upon the author's own deliverance from the power of the *law* (the written word of legislation), his empowerment by the *spirit* and the liberty of prophetic oralcy:

> Confident that God had *sealed* him unto the day of redemption, not only sealed, but *removed him* by his power from a legal state of mind, into a state of Gospel liberty, that is to say, a deliverance from the power of authority of the law, considering himself not to be under the power of the law.[8]

Given the ambiguous position of slaves in England during the late eighteenth century under English (colonial and local) law, Wedderburn's claims for self-exclusion from the 'authority of the law' under the aegis of spiritual 'grace' should not be underestimated. William Blackstone's ambitious codification of England's legal constitution, a source of national pride, had been directly encouraged by Lord Mansfield, the Chief Justice. On its publication in 1765, Blackstone's *Commentaries on the Laws of England* was immediately recognised as a lucid and authoritative account of English legislation and government. Of the social rights enjoyed by the 'free-born Englishman', Blackstone had unhesitatingly declared:

> And this spirit of liberty is so implanted in our constitution, and rooted even in our very soil, that a slave or a negro, the moment he lands in England falls under the protection of the laws and becomes *eo instanto* a freeman.[9]

Two years later, having been reminded of the Lord Chancellor's reassurance (formerly the General Attorney, Sir Philip Yorke) to West Indian planters that '*neither baptism nor legislation* could destroy servitude absolutely', Blackstone's unequivocal declaration of English liberty had become one of uncertainty and ambiguity by the time the 1767 edition was printed: 'A slave or negro, the moment he lands in England, falls under the protection of the laws, and so far becomes a freeman; though the master's right to his service may probably still continue'.[10] In spite of this, Blackstone

---

[8] *Ibid.*, 5–6.

[9] Blackstone, *Commentaries on the Laws of England in Four Books,* eighth edn., 4 vols. (Oxford, 1779) cited in Blackburn, *The Overthrow of Colonial Slavery, 1776–1848* (London: Verso, 1990) 81.

[10] Blackburn, *The Overthrow*, 81; Fryer, *Staying Power: The History of Black People in Britain* (London: Pluto, 1984) 114–15; Blackstone, *Commentaries*, vol. i, 123. In the second edition of 1767 the revised formula appears on page 127.

persisted in his attempt to overturn pro-slavery ideologies on the basis that they destroyed the 'very principles upon which all sales are founded'. Yet his systematic and philosophical analysis of the principles of transaction failed to resolve the dichotomy existing between his own textual consolidation of English legislation and the inconsistencies of a social order in which property, acquired neither by purchase, reciprocity nor original title, continued to be recognised.[11]

Granville Sharp's first pamphlet, *A Representation of the Injustice and Dangerous Tendency of Tolerating Slavery; or Of Admitting the Least Claim of Private Property in the Persons of Men*, in *England* (London, 1769) argued that slavery, since it depended upon a definition of a person as a possession, was incompatible with English liberty. But it was Granville's involvement in the judicial test case of *James Somerset* (1771–1772) under the adjudication of the Chief Justice, Lord Mansfield, which seemed to confirm once and for all England's legal position regarding slave status at a time when several thousand slaves resided in the metropolis. Somerset had refused to return with his owners and during the trial, he received considerable support from a coalition of fellow blacks and radical artisans, together with free legal aid from barristers. On the other hand, his master received support from self-interested West Indian planters. Initially Lord Mansfield, reluctant to deprive slave owners in Britain of their rights as masters, attempted to postpone this test case several times. However, his final decision of 1772 prohibited the involuntary deportations of slaves by their masters from England:

> The state of slavery is of such a nature, that *it is incapable of being introduced on any reasons, moral or political; but only [by] positive law,* which preserves its force long after the reasons, occasion, and time itself from whence it was created, is erased from memory: It is so odious, that nothing can be suffered to support it, but positive law. Whatever inconveniences, therefore, may follow from a decision, I cannot say this case is allowed or approved by the law of England; and therefore the black must be discharged.[12]

Although Mansfield ruled against the deportation of slaves back to the colonies, it did not follow that, on arrival in England, slaves by virtue of English law were deemed autonomous emancipated individuals. It was, however, interpreted as such, and indeed in 1778 the Scottish legislature

---

[11] Blackburn, *The Overthrow*, 81.

[12] Michael Craton, James Walvin and David Wright, eds, *Slavery, Abolition and Emancipation: Black Slaves and the British Empire* (London: Longman, 1976) 170; cited in Moira Ferguson, *Subject to Others: British Women Writers and Colonial Slavery, 1670–1834* (London: Routledge, 1992) 116–17; my emphasis.

ruled that no slaveholding rights whatsoever could be upheld within Scotland's borders.

By the time Wedderburn had composed his *Truth, Self-Supported* in 1790, the 'repatriation' Committee for the Relief of the Black Poor (1786) had been in operation for almost four years and Sharp's *Regulation for the New Settlement in Sierra Leone* (1786) had been in circulation for the same amount of time. By 1791, one year after the publication of Wedderburn's tract, slaves had rebelled in the dramatic uprising in St Domingue, the Abolition Bill had been defeated in Parliament and, following the declaration of war between England and France in April 1792, emancipatory demands for slaves were postponed. Although Wedderburn had had no direct experience of slavery, his *Truth, Self-Supported* traced a movement of linguistic and social rebellion by one who considered himself situated on the periphery of a society founded upon principles of binary opposition. For Iain McCalman, Wedderburn's narrative poses a 'crude but sincere attempt to steer an independent course between [the] various doctrinal snags and shoals' of Arminianism, Calvinism and Unitarianism.[13] Yet although Wedderburn's narrative does outline an advancement of radical individualism and nonconformist principles, the route which it follows depends not merely upon a refutation of various theological doctrines, but upon an articulation of cultural ideologies preserved by slave societies in the diaspora.

By situating the journey of his 'desire to become a Christian' alongside his seven year period of transgression 'amongst a set of abandoned reprobates', and his subsequent efforts to abandon 'the road to everlasting ruin', Wedderburn's narrative, in line with that of Equiano, extends the Methodist paradigm of individualism to its furthermost cultural and anarchic extreme. In so doing, Wedderburn's text develops a sustained refutation of established ideological dictates, including that of the legislature by the individual under 'spiritual' inspiration.[14] His interpretation of words by the Wesleyan preacher whom he overhears on passing the Seven Dials in Covent Garden, therefore, functions as a paradigm for the *liberty of grace* (indemnity) prescribed by the suffusion and 'incarnation' of the Holy Spirit:

> [The] Mediator through whom and by whom, the Father performs all his Will, by his own Influence or Essence which is called the Spirit . . .
> *[This] gift of the Spirit is called righteousness* . . . so doth the Spirit *purify and abundantly fill* the soul of the penitent sinner.[15]

---

[13] McCalman, *The Horrors of Slavery*, 58.

[14] Wedderburn, *Truth, Self-Supported*, 3–4.

[15] *Ibid.*, 12, 14–15; my emphases.

Truth, Self-Supported consolidates and imparts an effective paradigm of its author as a prototype of diasporic identity located upon the peripheries of discourse itself, a 'state of Gospel Liberty' situated beyond the authority of the established Church *and* the law. His use of the 'discourse of the spirit' posits a radical *rejection* of the established tenets of the church and society and promotes instead an affirmation of the discourse of the 'self':

> If you enquire of a minister of the church of Rome, he is not allowed to think or speak, but as the Pope dictates, and if you should go to the Pope himself, he must of necessity tell you, that, the doctrine of the Trinity is a truth, because it was first broached by the Church of Rome, which pretends to be an infallible Church, and therefore cannot err; so that according to their sentiments, all that do not believe in their tenets must be damned; *therefore you see the necessity of calling upon God for yourselves*... Instead of the performances required from us under the Law ... believing in Jesus Christ, as the Messiah sent of God, and receiving the grace sent by HIM, is *the only work that God requires of every man.*[16]

As a 'mulatto' son with extremely tenuous legal and social rights, the author's affinity with dissenting Protestantism corresponded to his fervent dedication to a series of social and political demands: indeed, conversion to such unorthodoxy depended upon a verbal testimony of desired amelioration — 'for there is salvation in no other'.[17] Wedderburn's 'conversion' encapsulates a significant moment in the development of his religious and political heterodoxy. His appropriation of the discourse of the spirit not only provides him with spiritual indemnity but identifies him with the 'son' of Jehovah, whose 'possession' of the spirit represents a manifestation of power:

> The Holy Spirit spoken of in Scripture, is not a Being possessing personality as a Jehovah, but an *Influence of Jehovah,* which is possessed by the Son without measure. By the purpose and good-will of the Father, the Spirit qualifies and possesses Jesus Christ with the ability of God.[18]

Wedderburn's proclaimed adherence to radical dissenting Protestantism's faith in the power of the 'spirit' is also endorsed by his citation of a selection of hymns towards the end of his text, including one by Isaac Watts and another by John Wesley.[19] It is possible that the tonal simplicity of the hymns evoked an impression of the sound of 'negro' spirituals and

---

[16] *Ibid.,* 13–14; my emphases.

[17] *Ibid.,* 8–10.

[18] *Ibid.,* 8–9.

[19] Wesley's hymn is identified by McCalman as number 340. John Wesley, *The Works of John Wesley,* ed. Albert Outler, 5 vols. (Nashville: Abingdon Press, 1984).

worksongs reverberating in the plantations. But almost certainly, Methodism's continuum of the African belief in the spirit-world, combined with its obvious antislavery agenda, strategically influenced Wedderburn's claims for 'sanctification' and spiritual indemnity and informed his emphasis upon his *own* powers of exegesis and prophecy, over and beyond those of both the established church and the 'laws' of society. Wedderburn's attestations of 'divine inspiration' and the protection given him by the divine seal thus participate in a paradigm of 'creolised' subversive demands, professing deliverance from the law and 'spiritual immunity' from the perils of sedition and political reformation.

'Acknowledge No King . . . Acknowledge No Priest'[20]

By 1813, Wedderburn had become an ardent follower of Thomas Spence, the leader of an informal political underground, whose doctrines had prophesied an earthly millennium based upon a radical redistribution of land.[21] In 1817, Wedderburn published the first edition of his prophetic *The Axe Laid to the Root, or A Fatal Blow to Oppressors; Being An Address to the Planters and Negroes of the Island of Jamaica* (1817), a text which demanded 'in the name of God, in the name of natural justice and in the name of humanity that all slaves be set free'.[22] Indeed, *The Axe Laid to the Root* advanced claims for land reformation on the plantocratic islands of the West Indies according to Spence's directive and denounced concepts of English liberty as *myths* expounded by priests, kings and lords. Wedderburn's text initially propounds a Spencean vision of *peaceful* sociopolitical transformation by the dissemination of Spencean literature amongst free mulattos —

> Oh, ye oppressed, use no violence to your oppressors, convince the world you are rational beings, follow not the example of St Domingo, let not your jubilee, which will take place, be stained with the blood of your oppressors, leave revengeful practices for European kings and ministers.[23]

---

[20] Wedderburn, *The Trial of the Revd Robert Wedderburn, a Dissenting Minister of the Unitarian Persuasion, for Blasphemy in the Court of the Kings Bench, Westminster, the Sittings after Hilary Term, 1820*, ed. E. Perkins (London: W. Mason, 1820) 5.

[21] See McCalman, *Radical Underworld*. Four years later, the Government arrested Thomas Evans, the founding member of the Society of Spencean Philanthropists set up in 1814.

[22] Wedderburn, *The Axe Laid to the Root, or A Fatal Blow to Oppressors; Being An Address to the Planters and Negroes of the Island of Jamaica* (London, 1817) 4 parts; cited in Ian McCalman ed., *The Horrors of Slavery and Other Writings by Robert Wedderburn* (Edinburgh: Edinburgh University Press, 1991) 81–105.

[23] *Ibid.*, Part 1, 81.

This contrasts however, with the author's demands for violent slave insur-
rections, following the model prescribed by the (in)famous St Domingue
uprising:

> *Jamaica will be in the hands of the blacks within twenty years. Prepare for*
> *flight, ye planters,* for the fate of St Domingo awaits you . . . They [the
> Maroons] will be victorious in their flight, slaying all before them . . .
> *Their method of fighting is to be found in the scriptures, which they are now*
> *learning to read.* They will slay man, woman, and child, and not spare the
> virgin, whose interest is connected with slavery, whether black, white, or
> tawny . . . *My heart glows with revenge, and cannot forgive.*[24]

Wedderburn's call for the emancipation of slaves under the guise of divine guidance ('Wedderburn demands in the name of God . . . that all slaves
be set free') and his vehement denunciation of the established church as a
tyrannical oppressor, are haunted by his memory of the public flogging of
his aged grandmother. For this reason, he portrays himself as a Christ-like
but militantly radical saviour who must reject and disobey his earthly
father (the Scottish James Wedderburn), in order to inherit the kingdom
destined to be his: 'Repent ye christians . . . Oh! my father, what do you
deserve at my hands? Your crimes will be visited upon your legitimate offspring . . . *A black king is capable of wickedness, as well as a white one!*'[25] In
subsequent volumes of his *Axe Laid to the Root*, Wedderburn continued his
antinomian address to the slaves of Jamaica, supplementing it with drastic
calls for a violent transformation of the sociopolitical sphere and advocating the need for the preservation of cultural identity within the diaspora:

> Dear Countrymen, It is necessary for you to know how you may govern
> yourselves without a king, without lords, dukes, earls, or the like; these
> are classes of distinction which tend only to afflict society. I would have
> you know, with all the proud boasting of Europeans they are yet
> ignorant of what political liberty is . . . *Have no white delegate in your*
> *assembly . . . Let every individual learn the art of war, yea, even the females,*
> *for they are capable of displaying courage . . . Teach your children these lines*
> *[from the Desponding Negro], let them be sung on the Sabbath day, in*
> *remembrance of your former sufferings, which will show you what you may*
> *expect from the hands of European Christians, by what they have practised*
> *before.*[26]

---

[24] *Ibid.*, Part 1, 86; my emphases.

[25] *Ibid.*, Part 1, 86–7; my emphasis.

[26] *Ibid.*, Part 2 (1817) 89–90 my emphases.

In the fourth edition of *The Axe Laid to the Root* (1817), Wedderburn incorporated a letter to a Miss Campbell, the heiress to a sugar plantation whom he claimed had been censured by the assembly of Jamaica for freeing her slaves and distributing her land along Spencean lines. By inferring that this 'Miss Campbell' was a descendant of an earlier miscegenetic relationship and more daringly, that she and the author shared the same mother, Wedderburn's text endorsed the paradigm of the mulatto as a radical agent of socioeconomic transformation premised upon apocalyptic stature:

> Dear Miss Campbell . . . I come not to make peace; my fury shall be felt by princes, bidding defiance to pride and prejudice. Truth is my arrow stained with Africans' blood, rendered poisonous by guilt, while they hold my innocent fellow as a slave . . . Fast bound by eternal truth, I have hold of the God of Israel, like a Jacob, and will not let him go. *I will be made a prince by prevailing, though a halter be about my neck.* Jacob, I will excell you in proportion to the present improved state of society. Miss Campbell, though a goddess, I have a command for thee to obey: like the Christians of old, you have fallen from the purity of the Maroons, your original.[27]

In 1819 Wedderburn opened a tavern chapel on the corner of Hopkins Street in Soho, London. In this chapel, which he registered as a Unitarian meeting house for a sect which he later described as 'Christian Diabolists' or 'Devil Worshippers', up to 300 people converged to listen to his potent mixture of religious zeal and popular radicalism, permeated by scriptural symbolism, prophetic rhetoric and personalised testimonies of his 'sleeping visions'.[28] In what we can assume was a unique interplay between performer and audience during his 'farcical theological debates' with the dwarf shoemaker Samuel Waddington, Wedderburn fused theatrical diatribe with anti-clerical blasphemy: he urged his audience to do all that was in their power to overthrow the establishment, even persuading them to participate in dawn drills on Primrose Hill and to tear up iron palisades for use as weapons.[29]

Wedderburn's discourse enigmatically converges with that of the poet and mystic William Blake, whose 'Marriage of Heaven and Hell' (*c.* 1790–3), a 'diabolic' response to Swedenborg, prescribed the 'Voice of the Devil' and the 'Proverbs of Hell' as part of an onslaught against self-righteous members of society and orthodox Christian piety. Blake's account of the ancient

---

[27] *Ibid.*, Part 4 (1817): 96–7; my emphasis.
[28] McCalman, *The Horrors of Slavery*, 132.
[29] *Ibid.*, 136.

poets' receptivity to the gods of nature corresponded closely to the 'animism' of African cults, whilst his text, 'All Religions Are One' (*c.* 1788) stipulated the prime importance of the spirit of prophecy in *all* religions:

> The ancient Poets animated all sensible objects with Gods or Geniuses, calling them by the names and adorning them with the properties of woods, rivers, mountains, lakes, cities, nations, and whatever their enlarged & numerous senses could perceive . . . The Religions of all Nations are derived from each Nations different reception of the Poetic Genius which is every where call'd the Spirit of Prophecy . . . The true Man is the source [of all Religions], he being the Poetic Genius.[30]

The emphasis laid by dissenting Protestantism upon the inspirational role of song, and upon images of rebirth and transformation, made easy transference to the prophetic belief systems prevalent among West Indians and Africans. However, Wedderburn's radical individualism stretched these elements to extreme limits.[31] In 1820, Wedderburn was tried for blasphemy, a trial in which he represented himself, claiming that even if a barrister were to plead his cause gratuitously, 'he would not dare to do it upon principle'. In the written script which formed his defence, and which the author had intended to be read by the preacher and pornographer George Cannon (alias Erasmus Perkins), Wedderburn ridiculed the interrelationship between 'the state religion', the enforcement of the 'law of the land', and the former's enforcement at the expense of 'other opinions or laws'. Wedderburn claimed that the established religion propagated such archaic laws and enactments that if they were 'now resorted to, [they] would be instantly erased from the statute-book as absurd, or inhuman, and totally inconsistent with the enlightenment of the present day'.[32]

In the same manner as Phillis Wheatley's 'evangelical' schema, Wedderburn conflated tenets of spiritual illumination with demands for the

---

[30] William Blake, 'The Marriage of Heaven and Hell', *The Complete Poems of William Blake*, ed. W. H. Stevenson (London: Longman, 1989) III, Plate II. Although it is not known whether Wedderburn knew anything of Blake's writings, Wedderburn's work established a relation to the prophetic example set by his Soho neighbour, Richard Brothers, a contemporary of Blake's who was sent to Bedlam in 1795.

[31] McCalman, *The Horrors of Slavery*, 56. See also Arnold Rattenbury, 'Methodism and the Tatterdemalions', *Popular Culture and Class Conflict, 1590–1914: Explorations in the History of Labour and Leisure*, ed. Eileen and Stephen Yeo (Brighton: Harvester Press, 1981) 28–61; J. Obelkevich, *Religion and Rural Society: South Lindsey, 1825–1875* (Oxford: Clarendon Press, 1976); William Hosking Oliver, *Prophets and Millennialists: The Uses of Biblical Prophecy in England from the 1790s to the 1840s* (Auckland: Auckland University Press, 1978) 11–24, 34–5, 45–7, 50–6.

[32] Wedderburn, *The Trial*, 9.

emancipation of the human mind from 'tyrannical and intolerant laws of darkness, ignorance and the trammels of superstition':

> Therefore I trust that you will not suffer yourselves to be ensnared by that sophistical mode of reasoning which makes me guilty of a crime, merely, because I have offended against opinions or laws originating in times still more bigotted and superstitious than the present. — You will be told that, because christianity, or what *they* choose to call christianity, is a part of the law of the land, or in other words 'the state religion', that those whose opinions differ materially from it, must necessarily be punished if they circulate those opinions.[33]

Moreover, as with the slave confessional narratives discussed above, Wedderburn promotes his oral defence as a *testimony* to the nature of *truth*, a concept which he identified with freedom of religious opinion and liberty of speech. Wedderburn therefore regarded his trial as part of his mission to expose the 'untruths' of legal and theological discourse:

> There is no one who will deny the value and importance of truth, but how is it to be ascertained, if we are not allowed the liberty of free inquiry? Does not Paul tell us to *'prove all things, and to hold fast the best;'* but how are we to be determined in our choice, if we are not allowed to canvas and discuss the merits or demerits of particular systems? . . . I cannot but blush at the weakness and bad policy of those who seek to support their cause by the persecution of an humble individual like myself, when the clergymen of the established church of England alone are 20,000, and their wages amount to two millions annually: in addition to these, there are 50,000 dissenting ministers of different denominations.[34]

In his attempts to identify his own struggles with those of Christ ('He was like myself, one of the lower order, and a genuine radical reformer'), Wedderburn endorses a strategic disassociation of 'genuine Christianity' from the 'state religion' and posits a 're-vision' of Christ as an egalitarian 'who despised the rich for the hardness of their hearts': 'What did he [Jesus Christ] say, *"acknowledge no king."* He was a reformer . . . acknowledge no lord . . . acknowledge no rabbi, (no priest:) no! he knew their tricks, and says, *stand it no longer'*.[35] Wedderburn's spirited defence (which included statements such as 'if, on the contrary, the spirit of bigotry and religious persecution prevails over you, I shall have this satisfaction, that I suffer like Christ' and 'I shall be far happier in the dungeon to which you may consign me, than my persecutors, on their beds of down') ended with an

---

[33] *Ibid.*, 10.

[34] *Ibid.*, 10–12.

[35] *Ibid.*, 5; my emphases.

outrageously ironic 'plea' to (or rather ridicule of) the jury.[36] Not surprisingly, his defence was rejected; Wedderburn was convicted of using 'blasphemous and profane words' and of impiously reviling that book of 'great antiquity' which, it was professed, determined not only the religion of England, but of 'all the civilised and enlightened nations'. The judges severely reprimanded Wedderburn's refusal to repent and consequently denounced his propagation of linguistic and theological deviance as pure 'licentiousness', before proceeding to pass sentence:

> It is our duty then to remove you, at least for a time, from society, that you may be prevented doing it a further injury by the dissemination of your dangerous doctrine. The Court do therefore sentence you to be imprisoned for two years in his majesty's jail at Dorchester.[37]

Wedderburn's (albeit temporary) removal from society (by means of his imprisonment) reflected the serious extent to which the court feared the influential disruption that his 'dangerous doctrine' might cause. As such, Wedderburn's text registers a significant departure from the cultural acquiescence suggested by the slave narratives discussed above.

'Can I Contain Myself at This?': Wedderburn's *Horrors of Slavery*[38]

Seven years after the fourth edition of *Axe Laid to the Root*, Wedderburn published a small pamphlet entitled, *The Horrors of Slavery: Exemplified in the Life and History of the Revd Robert Wedderburn* (1824), dedicated to William Wilberforce. As the subtitle, 'Robert Wedderburn (late Prisoner in his Majesty's Gaol at Dorchester, for Conscience-sake), Son of the Late James Wedderburn, Esq. of Inveresk, Slave Dealer, by One of his Slaves in the Island of Jamaica' explained, Wedderburn had narrowly escaped the more serious charge of high treason. The opening lines of Wedderburn's text suggest a narrative delineating an aged man's humble recollection of past transgressions:

---

[36] *Ibid.,* 19.

[37] Wedderburn, *The Address of the Revd R. Wedderburn, to the Court of the King's Bench at Westminster, on Appealing to Receive Judgement for Blasphemy when he was Sentenced to Two Years Imprisonment in Dorchester Jail on Tuesday 9th of May 1820,* ed. Erasmus Perkins (London, 1820); McCalman, *The Horrors of Slavery,* 141.

[38] Wedderburn, *Horrors of Slavery,* 5.

I am now upwards of sixty years of age, and therefore I cannot long expect to be numbered amongst the living. But, before I pass from this vale of tears, I deem it an act of justice to myself, to my children, and to the memory of my mother, to say what I am, and who were the authors of my existence.[39]

However, what follows is an intense declaration of individual freedom, hinged upon Wedderburn's denunciation of his paternal ancestry and promotion of his maternal cultural heritage: 'To shew the world . . . the inhumanity of a MAN, whom I am compelled to call by the name of FATHER. I am the offspring of a slave, it is true; but I am a man of free thought and opinion'.[40] In a letter to the editor of *Bell's Life in London* of February 1824, Wedderburn identified himself as the progeny of the miscegenetic and deplorable actions of the late James Wedderburn, who he claimed, had 'FORCED' his mother to submit to him 'THOUGH HE KNEW SHE DISLIKED HIM!'[41] The subsequent reply (similarly published in *Bell's Life*) by the author's brother (who had changed his name to A. Colville) dismissed Wedderburn's claims of kinship: 'I have to state, that the person calling himself Robert Wedderburn is NOT a son of the late Mr James Wedderburn, of Inveresk, who never had any child by, or any connection *of that kind* with the mother of that man'.[42]

As part of this endeavour to reclaim his past, Wedderburn attempts to 'reconstruct' and 'de-stigmatise' his mother, Rosanna (whose memory he claimed had been reviled by his white half-brother, A. Colville), and to align his own (rebellious) nature with hers, even to the extent of endorsing her attempted infanticide:

A younger and more fortunate brother of mine, the aforesaid A. Colville, Esq. has had the insolence to revile her memory in the most abusive language, and to stigmatise her for that which was owing to the deep and dark iniquity of my father . . . I have not the least doubt but that from her rebellious and violent temper during that period, that I have inherited the same disposition — the same desire to see justice overtake the oppressors of my country-men — and the same determination to lose [sic] no stone unturned, to accomplish so desirable an object.[43]

---

[39] *Ibid.*, 4.

[40] *Ibid.*, 4.

[41] *Ibid.*, 13.

[42] *Ibid.*, 15.

[43] *Ibid.*, 5, 9. See also Toni Morrison's *Beloved* (1987; London: Chatto and Windus, 1988) for an examination of infanticide in the post-slavery America.

Wedderburn's disenfranchisement had been aggravated by letters to the press which had refuted his claims for inheritance and had sullied his mother's reputation. In a letter to the editor of *Bell's Life in London* it was insinuated that Wedderburn's mother 'was delivered of a mulatto child' and because '*she could not tell who was the father,* her master, in a foolish joke, named the child Wedderburn'.[44] Consequently, Wedderburn's *Horrors of Slavery* endeavours to reestablish his mother's virtue and integrity; furthermore, it interweaves within the dominant network a fabric articulating the proud and rebellious nature of his mixed ancestral and cultural identity, inherited from his African mother and grandmother, and his white grandfather:

> My grandfather was a staunch Jacobite . . . When I first came to England, in the year 1779, I remember seeing the remains of a rebel's skull which had been affixed over Temple Bar; but I never yet could fully ascertain whether it was my dear grandfather's skull, or not.[45]

The text's dedication to William Wilberforce ('Your name stands high in the list of glorious benefactors of the human race; and the slaves of the earth look upon you as a tower of strength') appears to inaugurate an abolitionist polemic in honour of Wilberforce. However, the literary autobiography which follows presents the author as an 'oppressed, insulted and degraded African', whose censure of his paternal father entailed a denunciation of colonialist ideology and of the English legislature.[46] Although ostensibly an autobiographical text, Wedderburn's *Horrors of Slavery* locates addressees other than the 'self' and envisages his audience as including members of the English public, representatives of the powerful propertied class (including the Duke of Queensbury and Lady Douglas) and the legislature, the House of Lords. Wedderburn's 'narrative' therefore not only functions as a striking exposé of a delicate site of taboo (the disclosure of his own sexual genesis) but also as a significant disclosure of the dynamics of miscegenation amongst his audience, the aristocracy and their colonial counterparts, the West Indian planters:

> It is a common practice . . . for the planters to have lewd intercourse with their female slaves; and so inhuman are many of these said planters, that many well-authenticated instances are known, of their selling their slaves while pregnant, and making that a pretence to enhance their value.[47]

---

[44] Wedderburn, *The Horrors of Slavery*, 15–16.

[45] *Ibid.*, 5.

[46] *Ibid.*, 3.

[47] *Ibid.*, 6.

Wedderburn personalised his account of miscegenation by citing details of the licentious and interracial conduct of his father, whose behaviour is encapsulated by the metaphorical title of 'male-midwife'. According to Wedderburn, as soon as his father became rich, 'he gave loose to his carnal appetites, and indulged himself without moderation . . . [in] libidinous excess'. In so doing, he became 'a perfect parish bull [stud]' whose sexual pleasure was the greater since it simultaneously 'increased his profits' and whose house (or harem) was filled with female slaves, such as his mother. Amongst these 'objects of his lust', he strutted 'like Solomon in his grand seraglio', or rather, 'like a bantam cock upon his own dunghill', and his slaves 'did increase and multiply, like Jacob's kine'.[48]

Interestingly, Wedderburn's narrative wavers between an endeavour to denounce his paternal lineage and to fulfil the paradigm of the mulatto identity by reinstating his birthrights from *both* branches of his parentage. On the one hand, therefore, his text presents an effort to valorise his African legacy and redeem the name of the mother whom his 'father' had 'made the object of his brutal lust' and on the other, it presents a narrative of dispossession in terms of his (dis)inheritance of the Wedderburn estate:

> My father's name was JAMES WEDDERBURN, Esq. of Inveresk, in Scotland, an extensive proprietor, of sugar estates in Jamaica, which are now in the possession of a younger brother of mine, by name, A. COLVILLE, Esq. of No. 35, Leadenhall Street. . . From him [my father] I have received no benefit in the world.[49]

Hence Wedderburn's *Horrors of Slavery* can be read not merely as a vilification of slave ideology but as a developed vindication of African cultural legacy. His work registers a further stage of the miscegenetic authenticity and cultural hybridity contained in the works by Wheatley and Equiano. As such, its 'creolised' discourse of fluidity, heterogeneity, movement and change demarcated an illuminating revision of established (static) concepts of power, possession and identity.

Robert's 'brother' changed his name to Colville in order to secure his rights of inheritance on his mother's side; likewise his father changed his name to Wedderburn-Colville. Indeed, a close analysis of Wedderburn's text reveals it to be a narrative saturated with terms of proprietorship—of objects and subjects, slaves and women—and of interrupted

---

[48] *Ibid.*, 6–8.
[49] *Ibid.*, 5.

inheritance: 'estates . . . now in the possession of a younger brother of mine'; 'my father was restored to his father's property'; 'they [female slaves] being his personal property'; '[he] determined to have possession of her'; 'from the time my mother became the property of my father'; and 'she [my mother] was the property of Lady Douglas'. Wedderburn's claims for 'rightful inheritance', however, are not unproblematic, especially when one considers that his father James Wedderburn had made his fortune as a result of his status as an 'extensive proprietor of sugar [slave] estates in Jamaica', and more dubiously, as a result of his acts of self-reproduction by means of his 'rape' of female slaves, Wedderburn's own mother.

Wedderburn's tract draws loosely upon the genre of abolitionist redemption autobiography established by members of London's black literati, such as Cugoano and Equiano, yet its author could not claim to have suffered directly the 'horrors' implied by the title of his pamphlet. Rather, the 'horrors' he locates are those of cultural disenfranchisement, material dispossession and sociopolitical inequality. The narrative of persecution which follows, therefore, details his continued sufferings and injustices beyond the temporal boundaries of plantocratic societies. Whilst his narrative bears comparison with former autobiographies of evangelical conversion and spiritual illumination, it is hinged essentially upon a paradigm of intervention, exposed and manifested by the product of cultural miscegenation—the mulatto figure itself.

Wedderburn's efforts to ridicule government during entertaining public debates invoking provocative calls for his flock of 'Christian Diabolists' or 'Devil Worshippers' to do all that was in their power to overthrow established authority, undoubtedly unsettled the latter, who, as McCalman records, employed spies in order to keep him under strict surveillance. Even from prison, Wedderburn continued his resolute, radical refutation of cultural orthodoxy, evidenced by his tract, *Cast-Iron Parsons: Or 'Hints to the Public and the Legislature, on Political Economy, Clearly Proving the Clergy Can be Entirely Dispensed With, Without Injury to the Christian Religion, or the Established Church, and to the Great Advantage of the State'*:

State Prison, Dorchester, July 28th, 1820:
My Dear Friend, You will naturally suppose that my solitary hours are much occupied with my favorite *hobby*, THEOLOGY; but a subject has at times engaged my attention, which is equally connected with political economy as with religion . . . I shall now give a slight sketch of the operative part of my scheme, which is as follows:—That the legislature pass an act . . . that the order of persons called Clergy, or Priests, Deacons,

Curates, Rectors, Vicars &c. of the Establishment, be totally annihilated, suppressed, and abolished. That every parish shall, immediately after that time, purchase one of the *Cast-Iron Parsons*.[50]

Consequently, Wedderburn's texts and speeches registered a radical challenge to the established authority of England's political legislature and a significant departure from the more subtle 'creolised' strategies contained within the earlier slave narratives.

Wedderburn's last known and most curious tract, 'The Holy Liturgy: Or Divine Science, upon the Principle of Pure Christian Diabolism, Most Strictly Founded upon the Sacred Scriptures', was published before his death at the age of seventy-two (one year before the abolition of slavery in the West Indies) and was partially reproduced on 21 March, 1828 by his fellow inmate, Richard Carlisle, in his journal *The Lion*. Here Wedderburn displayed the same radical demands and parodic anti-establishment critiques which had typified his dynamic performances in his Christian diabolist Chapel in Hopkins Street:

> Startle not, gentle Christian reader, at the name DIABOLICAL CHRISTIANS; but carefully *as thou valuest thine Eternal Salvation,* examine the Scriptural principle of this new sect, and say, if they are not justified, by all that is held sacred, in Christian Revelation, and by the most seriously disposed Christians. *It is not a profane hand, it is not the hand of the reviler, that passeth over this page: but the hand of a most sincere Christian.* . . OUR PRAYERS SHALL BE ALL MOST PROPERLY ADDRESSED TO THE *MAJESTY OF HELL,* to the 'GOD OF THIS WORLD', to that IMPERFECT, that OMNIMALEVOLENT, though POWERFUL BEING, *THE DEVIL.* This it is, that will justify our assumed appellation of CHRISTIAN DIABOLISTS . . . THE GOD OF HELL and 'OF THIS WORLD' partakes *in part* of our character and imperfections, and is, consequently . . . a *Being to be feared, to be worshipped, to be cajoled with prayer.*[51]

---

[50] Wedderburn, *Cast-Iron Parsons: Or 'Hints to the Public and the Legislature, on Political Economy, Clearly Proving the Clergy Can be Entirely Dispensed With Without Injury to the Christian Religion, or the Established Church, and to the Great Advantage of the State'* (London, 1820); cited in McCalman, *The Horrors of Slavery,* 143, 147.

[51] Wedderburn, 'The Holy Liturgy: Or Divine Science, upon the Principle of Pure Christian Diabolism, Most Strictly Founded upon the Sacred Scriptures', *The Lion,* 21 March 1828; cited in McCalman, *The Horrors of Slavery,* 153, 154; my emphases except final sentence. Wedderburn's Christian Diabolist Liturgy found its way to New York where it appeared in *The Correspondent,* ed. George Houston, 4 Oct. 1828, 168–70; McCalman, *The Horrors of Slavery,* 34.

In an enigmatic, if not disquieting way, the obsessiveness of Wedderburn's 'creolised' antinomian rhetoric elucidated, in no ambiguous terms, the psychological effects that the traumatic processes of sexual violence, cultural disturbance, dispossession, denial of rights and displacement had upon the African (now diasporic) slaves. Whereas the Romantics had displayed varying degrees of affinity with abolitionist and political radicalism, yet had stayed, on the whole, within the confines of the law, Wedderburn took such radicalism to a site of 'illegitimate' anarchy. In his hands, the bicultural tactics presented within the earlier narratives by slaves such as Wheatley and Equiano, reached a volatile climax in terms of his radical negation of church/state authority and his demands for ownership and 'cultural' insurrection. Hence Wedderburn's determined struggle for recognition and justice anticipated the concern over citizenship and civil rights which continued to preoccupy blacks on both sides of the Atlantic. As his text completed the translation of the discourse of the spirit into the discourse of legislative power, his endeavour to extend the concepts of individual autonomy and divine election in terms of his political demands took the example established by dissenting Protestantism to a heterodoxical extreme. Accordingly, his work exceeded and, in a sense, exacerbated, the parameters of spiritual discourse contained within the earlier slave narratives and established a conscious fulfilment of the more discrete demands for miscegenetic authenticity and cultural hybridity. The 'diabolic' enterprise of Wedderburn's work thereby endorsed the paradigm of 'creolised' dynamics, not merely as a reflection of the fusion of elements of dissenting Protestantism with fundamental elements of African belief systems, but as narratives of movement, fluidity and heterogeneity characteristic of identity configuration in the black diaspora. As I hope to have demonstrated, this process coincided with the development of hybrid linguistics (such as creole and patois) and the evolution of cross-cultural epistemologies, hinged upon the dynamics of miscegenation during the late eighteenth century. Articulated within the autobiographical works by Wedderburn, Equiano, Phillis Wheatley and others, the diasporic identity emerged as a self-conscious trope of cultural hybridity, premised simultaneously upon both the assimilation and chiasmus of the dominant social and literary order. Such a process was, by its very nature, hinged upon a narrative of incessant movement, of persistent 'translation' and of indeterminate and ceaseless transformation. Most importantly, the conscious expression of this integral process of fluidity and metamorphosis provided a radical challenge to established concepts of culture and race. In its continuous assimilation of and divergence from diverse cultural epistemologies and hermeneutical schemas, the paradigm of identity in the diaspora provided an appropriate framework for the dynamics of discourse itself.

CHRONOLOGY

c. 1710   Ukawsaw Gronniosaw born in present-day Nigeria.

1713   The Treaty of Utrecht, in concluding the War of the Spanish Succession, grants Britain the *asiento* (the exclusive right to supply slaves to Spain's American colonies), leading to Britain's domination of the colonial slave trade through 1807.

1725–1740   Britain engages in a series of wars against the Maroons of Jamaica (autonomous communities of escaped slaves and their descendants).

c. 1729   Ignatius Sancho born at sea en route from Africa to the West Indies.

1739   Following a major slave rebellion (the "Cudjoe" rebellion) in Jamaica, the British strike a treaty with the Maroons.

c. 1745   Olaudah Equiano born in present-day Nigeria.

c. 1753   Phillis Wheatley born in West Africa.

1754   John Woolman, an American Quaker, publishes his early abolitionist tract *Some Considerations on the Keeping of Negroes*.

1756–1763   The Seven Years' War pits Britain against France and other European powers in a contest mainly over colonial possessions and trade domination in the Americas and the East; both Gronniosaw and Equiano take part as seamen sailing under the British.

1757   The British make a treaty with the Maroons of Surinam.

c. 1757   Ottobah Cugoano born in present-day Ghana.

1758   Slavery is condemned by annual meetings of the Society of Friends (Quakers) in both London and Philadelphia.

1760   Tacky's Revolt in Jamaica, leading to the death of over sixty whites and four hundred black rebels. Briton Hammon's *Narrative of the Uncommon Sufferings, and Surprising Deliverance of Briton Hammon, a Negro Man,* the first American slave narrative, published in Boston.

1761   Slave trader *Phillis* arrives in Boston on July 11 carrying the young slave who will be named Phillis Wheatley.

c. 1761   Robert Wedderburn born in Jamaica.

1762   Anthony Benezet, an American Quaker, publishes *A Short Account of That Part of Africa, Inhabited by the Negroes,* including an attack on the slave trade, in Philadelphia.

1767   Benezet publishes *A Caution and Warning to Great Britain and the Colonies.*

1770   Wheatley's *Elegiac Poem* on the death of George Whitefield published in Boston.

1771   Benezet publishes *Some Historical Account of Guinea . . . With an Inquiry into the Rise and Progress of the Slave Trade* in Philadelphia.

1772   Judge Mansfield, deciding in favor of James Somerset, rules that slavery has no legal basis in England. (Colonial slavery and much de facto slavery in England itself remain unaffected.) Ukawsaw Gronniosaw's *Narrative* is first advertised for sale.

1773   Wheatley arrives in England on June 17 to promote her *Poems on Various Subjects,* published in London that year.

c. 1773   John Jea born in present-day Nigeria.

1774   The Methodist leader John Wesley publishes *Thoughts upon Slavery,* an influential antislavery pamphlet.

1775   Sancho's celebrated letter to Laurence Sterne published in a posthumous edition of Sterne's correspondence.

1775–1783   The United States War of Independence breaks out in earnest, leading (with contemporaneous slave revolts in the West Indies and military reversals in India) to a widespread sense of British imperial crisis.

1780   Sancho dies on December 14.

1781   The captain of the slave ship *Zong* has 133 slaves thrown overboard for insurance purposes; 132 perish.

1782   Sancho's *Letters* published posthumously in two volumes, edited by Frances Crewe.

1783   The *Zong* incident, brought to Granville Sharp's attention by Equiano, becomes a notorious legal and political issue.

1784   Wheatley dies at the age of thirty on December 5.

1785   The American slave John Marrant's *Narrative* published in London.

1786   The Committee for the Relief of the Black Poor, established that year in London, begins planning for a freed slave colony in Sierra Leone on the West African coast. Equiano is appointed Commissary for Stores for the initial expedition. Thomas Clarkson publishes his *Essay on the Slavery and Commerce of the Human Species.*

1787   The Society for Effecting the Abolition of the Slave Trade is formed in London. Clarkson begins his mission to discover evidence against the slave trade, visiting Bristol and Liverpool. The first, disastrous expedition to found the Sierra Leone colony departs from London. Cugoano's *Thoughts and Sentiments* published. Equiano, Cugoano, and a group of fellow "Sons of Africa" begin their campaign of jointly sending letters attacking slavery to prominent individuals and various periodicals. James Harris sends his letter asking for help to James Rogers.

1788   Massive petition campaign for the abolition of the slave trade begins in Manchester, England. The Dolben Act, legislation imposing minimal regulation on the slave carrying trade, passes both houses of Parliament.

c. 1788   Mary Prince is born in Bermuda.

1789   Equiano publishes *The Interesting Narrative.*

1790–1791   Formation of the Sierra Leone Company. Civil war breaks out in Saint Domingue (precipitating the Haitian revolution) as the slaves of the north province revolt.

1791   William Wilberforce's bill for abolition of the slave trade is defeated in the House of Commons.

1792   Freetown is founded in Sierra Leone with the arrival of 1190 blacks from Nova Scotia and 119 Europeans from England.

1793   Wilberforce's second abolition bill passes the House of Commons but is defeated in the House of Lords. John Clarkson is dismissed by the directors of the Sierra Leone Company. Britain, now at war with France, captures the French West Indian slave island of Tobago and invades Saint Domingue.

1794 The French attack Freetown, Sierra Leone. Britain captures the French colonies of Martinique, St. Lucia, and Guadeloupe in the West Indies.

1795–1796 Major war in Jamaica between the British colonial powers and the Maroons.

1796 British occupy the colonies of Demerara, Essequibo, and Berbice, taking over from the Dutch.

1797 Equiano dies in London.

c. 1797 Juan Francisco Manzano born in Cuba.

1798 Britain withdraws from Saint Domingue after five years of disastrous casualties fighting Toussaint L'Ouverture and other Haitian revolutionaries.

1799 Sierra Leone Company is granted a royal charter. Nova Scotian settlers openly revolt in Freetown. After five more years of seeing his abolition bills defeated in Parliament, Wilberforce temporarily abandons the annual attempt until 1805. Britain captures the Dutch Caribbean colony of Surinam.

1800 Five hundred and fifty Maroons arrive in Sierra Leone. Toussaint achieves the full control of Saint Domingue.

1802 Betrayed by the French, Toussaint dies in captivity in France.

1804 Inauguration of the Haitian Republic.

1807 In Britain's House of Lords, a bill is passed for abolishing the slave trade within the British colonies. The slave trade becomes illegal from May 1, 1807. The government of Sierra Leone is transferred to the Crown.

1808 Henri Grégoire publishes *De la littérature des négres* (translated into English two years later as *An Enquiry Concerning the Intellectual and Moral Faculties and Literature of Negroes*), including appreciative sketches of Wheatley, Sancho, Cugoano, and Equiano.

1812 War breaks out between Britain and the United States.

1815 The final defeat of Napoleon leaves Britain the dominant global imperial power, while the end of wartime launches a period of economic crisis and increasing agitation for reform in Britain itself.

c. 1815   Jea's *Life, History, and Unparalleled Sufferings* published in Portsea, England.

1816   Bussa's rebellion occurs in Barbados. Jea's *Collection of Hymns* published in Portsea.

1817   Wedderburn publishes two radical magazines, *The Forlorn Hope* and *The Axe Laid to the Root,* in London.

1823   Slaves revolt on Demerara. Slave rebellion also occurs on the east coast of Guyana. The Society for the Mitigation and Gradual Abolition of Slavery is formed by Clarkson and Wilberforce in Britain.

1824   The British House of Commons approves a proposal for the amelioration of slavery and recommends specific reforms for colonial governments. Wedderburn publishes *The Horrors of Slavery* in London.

1828   Lord Stowell rules, in the case of the Antiguan slave Grace, that residence in England does not guarantee freedom for a slave who voluntarily returns to the colonies. Mary Prince arrives in London and escapes her owners, becoming a domestic servant for Thomas Pringle, the secretary of the Anti-Slavery Society.

1829–1830   Mary Prince narrates her story to Susanna Strickland, a poet, recent convert to Methodism, and guest living with the Pringles at the same time as Prince.

1831   The largest and most widespread of all British colonial slave rebellions, "The Christmas Rebellion," led by Samuel Sharpe, takes place in Jamaica. *The History of Mary Prince* published in London and Edinburgh. A public controversy erupts over the *History.*

1833   British Parliament passes the Emancipation Act, requiring former slaves to serve their masters for six years, a plan called "Apprenticeship." The two court cases set in motion by Mary Prince's *History* are settled.

c. 1833   Wedderburn dies in London.

1834   Emancipation, qualified by the apprenticeship provision, comes into effect on August 1 in the British colonies.

1838   Apprenticeship is found to be unworkable and is abandoned. Seven hundred thousand former slaves in the British West Indian colonies finally achieve freedom.

1840   Manzano's *Poems by a Slave in the Island of Cuba*, translated from the Spanish by Richard Robert Madden, published in London.

1854   Manzano dies in Cuba.

1961   Sierra Leone achieves independence from Britain.

WORKS CITED

Acholonu, Catherine Obianuju. 1989. *The Igbo Roots of Olaudah Equiano: An Anthropological Research.* Owerri, Nigeria: AFA.

Appiah, Kwame Anthony. 1992. *In My Father's House: Africa in the Philosophy of Culture.* New York: Oxford University Press.

Austen, Jane. 1966. *Mansfield Park.* Edited by Tony Tanner. Harmondsworth, Eng.: Penguin.

Blackburn, Robin. 1988. *The Overthrow of Colonial Slavery 1776–1848.* London: Verso.

Carretta, Vincent, ed. 1996. *Unchained Voices: An Anthology of Black Authors in the English-Speaking World of the Eighteenth Century.* Lexington: University Press of Kentucky.

Carretta, Vincent, and Philip Gould, eds. 2001. *Genius in Bondage: Literature of the Early Black Atlantic.* Lexington: University Press of Kentucky.

Colley, Linda. 1992a. "Britishness and Otherness: An Argument." *Journal of British Studies* 31: 309–329.

———. 1992b. *Britons: Forging the Nation 1707–1807.* New Haven: Yale University Press.

Constanzo, Angelo. 1987. *Surprising Narrative: Olaudah Equiano and the Beginnings of Black Autobiography.* New York: Greenwood.

Craton, Michael. 1982. *Testing the Chains: Resistance to Slavery in the British West Indies.* Ithaca: Cornell University Press.

Cugoano, Ottobah. 1787. *Thoughts and Sentiments on the Evil and Wicked Traffic of the Slavery and Commerce of the Human Species, Humbly Submitted to the Inhabitants of Great-Britain, by Ottobah Cugoano, a Native of Africa.* London.

————. 1999. *Thoughts and Sentiments on the Evil and Wicked Traffic of the Slavery and Commerce of the Human Species and Other Writings.* Edited by Vincent Carretta. New York: Penguin.

Curtin, Philip. 1969. *The Atlantic Slave Trade: A Census.* Madison: University of Wisconsin Press.

da Costa, Emilia Viotti. 1994. *Crown of Glory, Tears of Blood: The Demerara Slave Rebellion of 1823.* New York: Oxford University Press.

Davis, Charles T., and Henry Louis Gates Jr., eds. 1985. *The Slave's Narrative.* Oxford: Oxford University Press.

Davis, David Brion. 1975. *The Problem of Slavery in the Age of Revolution 1770–1823.* Ithaca: Cornell University Press.

Doyle, Laura. 1996. "The Racial Sublime." In *Romanticism, Race, and Imperial Culture 1780–1834,* edited by Alan Richardson and Sonia Hofkosh, 15–39. Bloomington: Indiana University Press.

Dresser, Madge. 2001. *Slavery Obscured: The Social History of the Slave Trade in an English Provincial Port.* London: Continuum.

Dykes, Eva Beatrice. 1942. *The Negro in Romantic Thought: A Study in Sympathy for the Oppressed.* Washington, D.C.: Associated Publishers.

Echeruo, Michael J. C. 1992. "Theologizing 'Underneath the Tree': An African Topos in Ukawsaw Gronniosaw, William Blake, and William Cole." *Research in African Literatures* 23: 51–58.

Edwards, Paul. 1990. "An African Source of Blake's 'Little Black Boy'?" *Research in African Literatures* 21: 179–182.

Edwards, Paul, and David Dabydeen, eds. 1991. *Black Writers in Britain 1760–1890: An Anthology.* Edinburgh: Edinburgh University Press.

Equiano, Olaudah. 1789. *The Interesting Narrative of the Life of Olaudah Equiano, or Gustavaus Vassa, the African.* 2 vols. London: Equiano.

————. 1995. *The Interesting Narrative and Other Writings.* Edited by Vincent Carretta. Harmondsworth, Eng.: Penguin.

Foray, Cyril P. 1977. *Historical Dictionary of Sierra Leone.* London: Scarecrow Press.

Fryer, Peter. 1984. *Staying Power: The History of Black People in Britain.* London: Pluto Press.

Further Papers Relating to Slaves in the West Indies. 1885. [London]: House of Commons.

Fyfe, Christopher. 1963. *A History of Sierra Leone.* London: Oxford University Press.

———, ed. 1991. *"Our Children Free and Happy": Letters from Black Settlers in Africa in the 1790s.* Edinburgh: Edinburgh University Press.

Gates, Henry Louis. 1988. *The Signifying Monkey: A Theory of Afro-American Literary Criticism.* New York: Oxford University Press.

Gaulter, Henry. 1833. *The Origin & Progress of the Malignant Cholera in Manchester.* London: Longman.

Gilroy, Paul. 2000. *Against Race: Imagining Political Culture Beyond the Color Line.* Cambridge: Harvard University Press.

———. 1993. *The Black Atlantic: Modernity and Double Consciousness.* Cambridge: Harvard University Press.

Grégoire, Henri. 1810. *An Enquiry Concerning the Intellectual and Moral Faculties and Literature of Negroes: Followed with an Account of the Life and Works of Fifteen Negroes and Mulattoes Distinguished in Science, Literature and the Arts.* Translated by D. B. Warren. Brooklyn: T. Kirk.

Gronniosaw, Ukawsaw. [1772.] *A Narrative of the Most Remarkable Particulars in the Life of James Albert Ukawsaw Gronniosaw, An African Prince, As Related by Himself.* Bath, Eng.: W. Gye.

Hammond, Dorothy, and Alta Jablow. 1970. *The Africa That Never Was: Four Centuries of British Writing About Africa.* New York: Twayne.

Henry, Lauren. 1998. "'Sunshine and Shady Groves': What Blake's 'Little Black Boy' Learned from African Writers." In *Romanticism and Colonialism: Writing and Empire, 1780–1830,* edited by Tim Fulford and Peter J. Kitson, 67–86. Cambridge: Cambridge University Press.

Hodges, Graham Russell, ed. 1993. *Black Itinerants of the Gospel: The Narratives of John Jea and George White.* Madison: Madison House.

Hudson, Nicholas. 1996. "From 'Nation' to 'Race': The Origin of Racial Classification in Eighteenth-Century Thought." *Eighteenth-Century Studies* 29: 247–264.

Jea, John. 1816. *A Collection of Hymns. Compiled and Selected by John Jea, African Preacher of the Gospel.* Portsea, Eng.: J. Williams.

———. [c. 1815.] *The Life, History, and Unparalleled Sufferings of John Jea, The African Preacher.* Portsea, Eng.: Jea.

Kitson, Peter J., ed. 1999. *Theories of Race.* Vol. 8 of *Slavery, Abolition, and Emancipation: Writings in the British Romantic Period.* Edited by Kitson and Debbie Lee. London: Pickering and Chatto.

Lambert, Sheila, ed. 1975. *House of Commons Sessional Papers of the Eighteenth Century.* Vol. 69. Wilmington, DE: Scholarly Resources, 1975.

Landry, Donna. 1990. *The Muses of Resistance: Labouring-Class Women's Poetry in Britain, 1739–1796.* Cambridge: Cambridge University Press.

Long, Edward. 1774. *The History of Jamaica.* 3 vols. London: T. Lowndes.

Lovejoy, Paul E. 1982. "The Volume of the Atlantic Slave Trade: A Synthesis." *Journal of African History* 23: 496–497.

Lyons, Charles H. 1975. *To Wash an Aethiop White: British Ideas About Black African Educability, 1530–1960.* New York: Teachers College Press.

Manning, Patrick. 1990. *Slavery and African Life: Occidental, Oriental, and African Slave Trades.* Cambridge: Cambridge University Press.

Manzano, Juan Francisco. 1981. *The Life and Poems of a Cuban Slave.* Edited by Edward J. Mullen. Hamden, Conn.: Archon, 1981.

———. 1840. *Poems by a Slave in the Island of Cuba, Recently Liberated; Translated from the Spanish, by R. R. Madden, M.D.* London: Ward.

Morrison, Toni. 1987. *Beloved.* New York: Knopf.

Myers, Norma. 1996. *Reconstructing the Black Past: Blacks in Britain 1780–1830.* London: Frank Cass.

Paquet, Sandra Pouchet. 1992. "The Heartbeat of a West Indian Slave: 'A History of Mary Prince.'" *African American Review* 26: 131–145.

Patterson, Orlando. 1982. *Slavery and Social Death: A Comparative Study.* Cambridge: Harvard University Press.

Postma, Johannes Menne. 1990. *The Dutch in the Atlantic Slave Trade, 1660–1815.* Cambridge: Cambridge University Press.

Potkay, Adam, and Sandra Burr, eds. 1995. *Black Atlantic Writers of the Eighteenth Century: Living the New Exodus in England and the Americas.* New York: St. Martin's Press.

Prince, Mary. 1831. *The History of Mary Prince, a West Indian Slave, Related by Herself. With a Supplement by the Editor.* [Edited by Thomas Pringle.] London: Westley and Davis.

———. 1997. *The History of Mary Prince, a West Indian Slave, Related by Herself.* Rev. ed. Edited by Moira Ferguson. Ann Arbor: University of Michigan Press.

Reeve, Clara. 1974. *Plans of Education, With Remarks on the Systems of Other Writers.* Edited by Gina Luria. New York: Garland.

Richardson, Alan. 1993. "Romantic Voodoo: Obeah and British Culture, 1797–1807." *Studies in Romanticism* 32: 3–28.

Richardson, Alan, and Sonia Hofkosh, eds. 1996. *Romanticism, Race, and Imperial Culture, 1780–1834*. Bloomington: Indiana University Press.

Said, Edward W. 1994. *Culture and Imperialism*. New York: Vintage.

Sancho, Ignatius. 1994. *The Letters of Ignatius Sancho*. Edited by Paul Edwards and Polly Rewt. Edinburgh: Edinburgh University Press.

———. 1782. *Letters of the Late Ignatius Sancho, An African, to Which Are Prefixed, Memoirs of His Life*. 2 vols. London: J. Nichols.

———. 1995. *Letters of the Late Ignatius Sancho, An African*. Edited by Vincent Carretta. Harmondsworth, Eng.: Penguin.

Sandhu, Sukhdev, and David Dabydeen, eds. 1999. *Black Writers*. Vol. 1 of *Slavery, Abolition, and Emancipation: Writings in the British Romantic Period*. Edited by Peter J. Kitson and Debbie Lee. London: Pickering and Chatto.

Sandiford, Keith. 1988. *Measuring the Moment: Strategies of Protest in Eighteenth-Century Afro-English Writing*. Selinsgrove, Pa.: Susquehanna University Press.

Sayre, Gordon M., ed. 2000. *American Captivity Narratives: Selected Narratives with Introduction*. Boston: Houghton Mifflin.

Shyllon, F. O. 1974. *Black Slaves in Britain*. London: Oxford University Press.

Stepan, Nancy. 1982. *The Idea of Race in Science: Great Britain 1800–1960*. Hamden, Conn.: Archon.

Sterne, Laurence. 1983a. *The Life and Opinions of Tristram Shandy, Gentleman*. Edited by Ian Campbell Ross. Oxford: Clarendon Press.

———. 1983b. *A Sentimental Journey Through France and Italy, by Mr. Yorick*. Edited by Gardner D. Stout Jr. Berkeley: University of California Press.

Sypher, Wylie. 1942. *Guinea's Captive Kings: British Anti-Slavery Literature of the XVIII Century*. Chapel Hill: University of North Carolina Press.

Thomas, Helen. 2000. *Romanticism and Slave Narratives: Transatlantic Testimonies*. Cambridge: Cambridge University Press.

Viswanathan, Guari. 1989. *Masks of Conquest: Literary Study and British Rule in India*. New York: Columbia University Press.

Walvin, James. 1993. *Black Ivory: A History of British Slavery*. London: Fontana.

Wedderburn, Robert. 1817. *The Axe Laid to the Root, Or a Fatal Blow to Oppressors, Being an Address to the Planters and Negroes of the Island of Jamaica*. London: Wedderburn.

―――. 1824. *The Horrors of Slavery; Exemplified in the Life and History of the Rev. Robert Wedderburn, V.D.M*. London: Wedderburn.

―――. 1991. *The Horrors of Slavery and Other Writings*. Edited by Iain McCalman. New York: Markus Wiener.

Wheatley, Phillis. 1982. *The Poems of Phillis Wheatley*. Rev. ed. Edited by Julian D. Mason. Chapel Hill: University of North Carolina Press.

―――. 1773. *Poems on Various Subjects, Religious and Moral*. London: Bell.

Williams, Kenny J. 1986. "Phillis Wheatley." In *Dictionary of Literary Biography: Afro-American Writers Before the Harlem Renaissance*, vol. 50. Edited by Trudier Harris. Detroit: Gale Research.

FOR FURTHER READING

Anstey, Roger. *The Atlantic Slave Trade and British Abolition 1760–1810*. London: Macmillan, 1975.

Aravamudan, Srinivas. *Tropicopolitans: Colonialism and Agency, 1688–1804*. Durham: Duke University Press, 1999.

Baker, Houston A., Jr., Manthia Diawara, and Ruth H. Lindeborg. *Black British Cultural Studies: A Reader*. Chicago: University of Chicago Press, 1996.

Bayly, C. A. *Imperial Meridian: The British Empire and the World, 1780–1830*. London: Longman, 1989.

Bhabha, Homi K. *The Location of Culture*. New York: Routledge, 1994.

Boime, Albert. *The Art of Exclusion: Representing Blacks in the Nineteenth Century*. Washington, D.C.: Smithsonian, 1990.

Braidwood, Stephen J. *Black Poor and White Philanthropists: London's Blacks and the Foundation of the Sierra Leone Settlement 1786–91*. Liverpool: Liverpool University Press, 1994.

Burn, W. L. *Emancipation and Apprenticeship in the British West Indies*. London: Jonathan Cape, 1937. Reprint, Johnson Reprint Corp., 1970.

Bush, Barbara. *Slave Women in Caribbean Society, 1650–1832*. Bloomington: Indiana University Press, 1990.

Clifford, Mary Louise. *From Slavery to Freetown: Black Loyalists After the American Revolution*. London: McFarland, 1999.

Craton, Michael. *Empire, Enslavement, and Freedom in the Caribbean*. Oxford: James Currey, 1997.

———. *Sinews of Empire: A Short History of British Slavery*. New York: Anchor, 1974.

Craton, Michael, James Walvin, and David Wright. *Slavery, Abolition and Emancipation: Black Slaves and the British Empire, a Thematic Documentary.* London: Longman, 1976.

Curtin, Philip. *The Atlantic Slave Trade: A Census.* Madison: University of Wisconsin Press, 1969.

———. *The Image of Africa: British Ideas and Action, 1780–1850.* 1964. Reprint, 2 vols. in one. Madison: University of Wisconsin Press, 1973.

Dabydeen, David. *Hogarth's Blacks: Images of Blacks in Eighteenth Century English Art.* Manchester: Manchester University Press, 1987.

Davis, David Brion. *The Problem of Slavery in the Age of Revolution 1770–1823.* Ithaca: Cornell University Press, 1975.

Drescher, Seymour. *Capitalism and Antislavery.* New York: Oxford University Press, 1987.

Dunn, Richard S. *Sugar and Slaves: The Rise of the Planter Class in the English West Indies, 1624–1713.* Chapel Hill: University of North Carolina Press, 1972.

Edwards, Paul. *Unreconciled Strivings and Ironic Strategies: Three Afro-British Authors of the Georgian Era: Ignatius Sancho, Olaudah Equiano, Robert Wedderburn.* Occasional Papers 34. Edinburgh University: Center for African Studies, 1992.

Edwards, Paul, and James Walvin. *Black Personalities in the Era of the Slave Trade.* Baton Rouge: Louisiana University Press, 1983.

Falconbridge, Anna Maria. *Narrative of Two Voyages to the River Sierra Leone During the Years 1791–1792–1793.* Edited by Christopher Fyfe. Liverpool: Liverpool University Press, 2000.

Ferguson, Moira. *Subject to Others: British Women Writers and Colonial Slavery, 1760–1834.* New York: Routledge, 1992.

Fulford, Tim, and Peter J. Kitson, eds. *Romanticism and Colonialism: Writing and Empire, 1780–1830.* Cambridge: Cambridge University Press, 1998.

Gates, Henry Louis, Jr., ed. *Black Literature and Literary Theory.* New York: Methuen, 1984.

Glissant, Edouard. *Caribbean Discourse.* Translated by J. Michael Dash. Charlottesville: University of Virginia Press, 1992.

Honour, Hugh. *The Image of the Black in Western Art.* 5 vols. Cambridge: Harvard University Press, 1989.

Hulme, Peter. *Colonial Encounters: Europe and the Native Caribbean, 1492–1797*. London: Methuen, 1986.

James, C. L. R. *The Black Jacobins: Toussaint L'Ouverture and the San Domingo Revolution*. 2nd ed. New York: Vintage, 1963.

King, Reyahn [et al.]. *Ignatius Sancho: An African Man of Letters*. London: National Portrait Gallery, 1997.

Kitson, Peter J., and Debbie Lee, eds. *Slavery, Abolition, and Emancipation: Writings in the British Romantic Period*. 8 vols. London: Pickering and Chatto, 1999.

Lee, Debbie. *Slavery and the Romantic Imagination*. Philadelphia: University of Pennsylvania Press, 2002.

Lewis, Gordon K. *Main Currents in Caribbean Thought*. Baltimore: Johns Hopkins University Press, 1983.

Lively, Adam. *Masks: Blackness, Race, and the Imagination*. London: Chatto and Windus, 1999.

Makdisi, Saree. *Romantic Imperialism: Universal Empire and the Culture of Modernity*. Cambridge: Cambridge University Press, 1999.

Malchow, H. L. *Gothic Images of Race in Nineteenth-Century Britain*. Stanford: Stanford University Press, 1996.

Manzano, Juan Francisco. *The Autobiography of a Slave*. Translated by Evelyn Picon Garfield. Detroit: Wayne State University Press, 1996.

Marshall, P. J., and Glyndwr Williams. *The Great Map of Mankind: British Perceptions of the World in the Age of Enlightenment*. London: Dent, 1982.

Midgley, Clare. *Women Against Slavery: The British Campaigns, 1780–1870*. London: Routledge, 1992.

Paravisini-Gebert, Lizabeth, and Margarite Fernandez-Olmos, eds. *Sacred Possessions: Vodoun, Santeria, Obeah, and the Caribbean*. New Brunswick, N.J.: Rutgers University Press, 1997.

Pratt, Mary Louise. *Imperial Eyes: Travel Writing and Transculturation*. London: Routledge, 1992.

Robinson, William H. *Phillis Wheatley and Her Writings*. New York: Garland, 1984.

Sharpe, Jenny. "'Something Akin to Freedom': The Case of Mary Prince." *Differences* 8: 1 (1996): 31–54.

Shyllon, F. O. *Black People in Britain, 1555–1833*. London: Oxford University Press, 1977.

Thomas, Hugh. *The Slave Trade: The Story of the Atlantic Slave Trade. 1440–1870*. New York: Simon & Schuster, 1997.

Walvin, James, *England, Slaves and Freedom, 1776–1838*. Jackson: University Press of Mississippi, 1986.

Williams, Eric. *Capitalism and Slavery*. Chapel Hill: University of North Carolina Press, 1944.

Williams, Glyndwr. *The Expansion of Europe in the Eighteenth Century: Overseas Rivalry, Discovery, and Exploitation*. New York: Walker, 1966.

Wilson, Ellen Gibson. *John Clarkson and the African Adventure*. London: Macmillan, 1980.

Woodard, Helena. *African-British Writings in the Eighteenth Century: The Politics of Race and Reason*. Westport, Conn.: Greenwood Press, 1999.

Wright, Josephine, ed. *Ignatius Sancho (1729–80): An Early African Composer in England. The Collected Editions of His Music in Facsimile*. New York: Garland, 1981.